Systems and Software Engineering with Applications

Norman F. Schneidewind

Naval Postgraduate School

Published by
Standards Information Network
IEEE Press

To John Musa, a pioneer in software reliability engineering,
who inspired my work, and whom I valued as a friend and colleague.
I miss you a lot. Wherever you are, I hope the wine is great.

Acknowledgment

I am indebted to the reviewers whose many
thoughtful suggestions helped immensely to improve the book.

About the Author

Dr. Norman F. Schneidewind is Professor Emeritus of Information Sciences in the Department of Information Sciences and the Software Engineering Group at the Naval Postgraduate School. He is now doing research and publishing in software reliability and metrics with his consulting company, Computer Research. Dr. Schneidewind is a Fellow of the IEEE, elected in 1992 for "contributions to software measurement models in reliability and metrics, and for leadership in advancing the field of software maintenance."

Dr. Schneidewind was selected for an IEEE USA Congressional Fellowship for 2005 and worked with the Committee on Homeland Security and Government Affairs, United States Senate, focusing on homeland security and cyber security. In 2006, he received the IEEE Computer Society Outstanding Contribution Award: "For outstanding technical and leadership contributions as the Chair of the Working Group revising IEEE Standard 982.1." In 2001, he received the IEEE "Reliability Engineer of the Year" award from the IEEE Reliability Society. In 1993 and 1999, he received awards for Outstanding Research Achievement by the Naval Postgraduate School.

He is the developer of the Schneidewind software reliability model that is used by NASA to assist in the prediction of software reliability of the Space Shuttle, by the Naval Surface Warfare Center for Tomahawk cruise missile launch and Trident software reliability prediction, and by the Marine Corps Tactical Systems Support Activity for distributed system software reliability assessment and prediction. This model is one of the models recommended by the American National Standards Institute and the American Institute of Aeronautics and Astronautics (AIAA) Recommended Practice for Software Reliability.

Dr. Schneidewind has a B.S.E.E., University of California (Berkeley); a M.S.E.E. and a M.S.C.S., San Jose State University; a M.S.O.R. (Engineering) and a Doctorate with a major in O.R., University of Southern California.

He is a member of the Eta Kappa Nu (electrical engineering), Tau Beta Pi (all engineering), and Alpha Pi Mu (industrial engineering) honor societies and Sigma Xi research society and holds the Certificate in Data Processing (CDP) from the Institute for Certification of Computer Professionals. He is listed in *Who's Who in Science and Engineering* and *Who's Who in America*.

Contents

Chapter 6: Software Reliability Metrics   129

Recently new software reliability metrics have been developed and evaluated that are not included in the IEEE 982.1 *Standard Dictionary of Measures of the Software Aspects of Dependability*. (In plain English, this standard is about software reliability metrics!) In addition, modifications have been made to metrics in 982.1 to enhance their usability. The objective of this chapter is to describe, evaluate, and show how to apply these new and modified metrics, using failure data from several releases of the NASA Space Shuttle flight software. This chapter supports the use of tools in Chapter 7.

Recognizing that readers have other applications, the methodology, equations, and prediction plots are explained so that engineers can apply the metrics to their applications. The metrics are assessed from two standpoints: 1) identify metrics that support a specified purpose (e.g., demonstrate reliability growth) and 2) using the metrics, identify software releases that, based on reliability predictions, are ready to deploy and identify which software requires additional testing. Prediction accuracy is computed for all metrics and the metrics are compared based on the results.

Chapter 7: Software Reliability and Metrics Tools   153

First, learn how to measure the reliability of software using reliability and metrics prediction models. Then, learn about software reliability and metrics tools that will assist you in making predictions to improve the reliability of your software. You will be provided with background regarding the rationale for using tools and the knowledge required to use them effectively that includes, for example, reliability goals, risk of inadequate reliability, cost of prediction, and data requirements.

Chapter 8: Integrating Testing with Reliability   187

The activities of software testing and reliability are integrated for the purpose of demonstrating how the two activities interact in achieving testing efficiency and the reliability resulting from tests. "Integrating" means modeling the execution of a variety of tests on a directed graph representation of an example program. A complexity metric is used to construct the nodes, edges, and paths of the example program. Models are developed to represent the efficiency and achieved reliability of black-box and white-box tests. Evaluations are made of path, independent path, node, program construct, and random tests to ascertain which, if any, is superior with respect to efficiency and reliability. Overall, path testing has the edge in test efficiency. The results depend on the nature of the directed graph in relation to the type of test. While there is no dominant method, in most cases the tests that provide detailed coverage are better. For example, path testing discovers more faults than independent path testing. Predictions are made of the reliability and fault correction that result from implementing various test strategies. The methods can be used by researchers and practitioners to evaluate the efficiency and reliability of other programs.

Chapter 9: Architecture, Performance, Reliability, and Availability   211

The objectives of this chapter are: 1) evaluate the effects of configuration complexity, reliability, and availability on architecture performance, using real-world architectures as examples and 2) compare the architectures using evaluation criteria in 1). The reason for this chapter is the increasing reliance on the services provided by Web servers, which mandates that these services be offered with superior performance and reliability. The architecture of a Web server has a profound impact on its performance and reliability. The same statement could be made about any application.

In Chapter 1, some of the subjects covered were probability distributions—for example, the binomial, hardware reliability and failure analysis, and computer system availability. This chapter builds on those subjects to show how architecture influences computer performance, reliability, and availability. Also, recall the application of complexity metrics in Chapter 7 to analyze the complexity of a computer program. Now, in this chapter, you will see how these concepts are use to assess the complexity of computer architecture configurations.

Chapter 10: Internet Fault Tree Analysis for Reliability Estimation 227

Fault tree analysis, introduced in Chapter 1, is a popular analytical technique for reliability estimation. Fault trees are graphical models that represent logical relationships between events that lead to system failure. They also provide a systematic mathematical framework for analyzing potential causes of failure. From a design perspective, they allow the designer to understand the ways in which a system may fail. Fault trees comprise basic events connected by gates, in a logical path, to a top node that represents system or subsystem failure. You use this graphical model to conceptualize the reliability and safety of multiple Internet services accessed by an Internet user.

Chapter 11: Standard for Software Reliability 245

This chapter shows how a new standard—the IEEE Recommended Practice on Software Reliability—can be applied to predict the reliability of a software system and assess the risk of not meeting the reliability specification. It shows reliability basics that can be combined with the standard's reliability process and applied to the reliability assessment of a variety of applications. Because hardware and software have different characteristics, correspondingly, their models must differ.

This standard prescribes the methods for assessing and predicting the reliability of software, based on a life-cycle approach to software reliability engineering. It provides information necessary for the application of software reliability measurement to a project, lays a foundation for building consistent methods, and establishes the basic principle for collecting the data needed to assess and predict the reliability of software. The document prescribes how any user can participate in ongoing software reliability assessments and predictions.

Part 2: Applications of Systems and Software Engineering

Chapter 12: Simulation and Analytical Models: A Comparison 263

Queueing models have been applied to the software fault detection and correction process. In addition, analysis of the time spent by faults in a software testing system has led naturally to an increased interest in the dynamics of queuing networks, which are used to model such systems. Analytical as well as simulation models have been used to study the behavior of queues and fault correction stations in testing systems. Thus, you can employ both analytical and simulation models in relieving fault bottlenecks in fault correction systems. Simulation is the process of designing a model of a real system and conducting experiments to understand its behavior. The process involves evaluating strategies for operating the system. Simulation is used when, even if analytical results are available, a trace of the history of the process under study is desired. For example, analytical model results provide average values of the times that faults wait to be corrected, but you may be interested in the predicted wait time of each fault that can be obtained by simulation.

Chapter 13: Object-Oriented Methods for Modeling Software Reliability   289

Can object-oriented methods be applied to mathematical software? Apparently, the answer is yes, according to some researchers who say: It has been recognized in a number of different fields that object-oriented programming, in general, and software frameworks, in particular, provide a means to allow the efficient construction and maintenance of large-scale software systems. Since general-purpose numerical analysis codes certainly qualify as large-scale software, it makes sense for us to see how these methodologies can be applied to this field.

Chapter 14: Cyber Security Prediction Models   305

Predictive models for estimating the occurrence of cyber attacks are desperately needed to counteract the growing threat of cyber terrorism. Unfortunately, except to a limited degree, there is no genuine database of attacks, vulnerabilities, consequences, and risks to employ for model development and validation. However, it is still useful to provide definitions, equations, plots, and analyses to answer the "what if" questions concerning potential attacks. This is done by reasoning about the elements of predictive models and their relationships, which are needed to mirror objects and events in the real world of cyberspace. The application of these models is to provide the user with a vehicle for testing hypotheses about how to respond to a cyber attack before it occurs, using risk, vulnerabilities, time between attacks, and intrusion (number and duration) concepts.

Part 3: Systems and Software Engineering in the Workplace

Chapter 15: Ergonomics and Safety in the Workplace   333

In this chapter the engineer is provided with information about the following requirements for health and safety in the workplace.

Chapter 16: Facility Layout and Location Models   345

It is important to take a *systems approach* when engineering facility layouts and locations. While, for example, when designing a Web server application, it is obviously important to consider the content of the servers and the search strategy, we should not lose site of *system* factors such as layout and location. Thus, this chapter deals with methods and models for facilitating layout of manufacturing facilities. Interestingly, these facilities can be assets used in the manufacture of hardware items or for the production of software products and services such as Web systems. The problem is to assign departments to locations or to assign Web servers to locations based on several factors, including the need for interaction among the facilities. In addition, this chapter discusses the related problem of optimally locating facilities such that the cost of travel or transporting material among facilities is minimized.

Chapter 17: Inventory Control   375

Inventory control is a ubiquitous problem that challenges the engineer in a variety of systems. For example, in the manufacture of computer systems, various component parts must be available when needed to achieve smooth work flow. Controlling inventory is a challenge because unexpected demands for components, based on spurious demands by customers for finished products, can make complete control problematic. Some of the remedial measures are maintaining a safety stock, below which inventory must not fall, and using models to compute the quantity and time to produce or order to meet customer demand.

Part 4: Scheduling and Cost Control in Systems and Software

Chapter 18: Scheduling   389

This chapter deals with some of the models that can be used in sensibly assigning and scheduling resources so bottlenecks and idle time are minimized. Examples are drawn from the fields of software production and testing.

The CPM model's objective is to produce a schedule that will achieve the requirements of the project activities. For example, the software engineer may have to develop a schedule for predicting the reliability of Modules A and B, where A is predicted using A's failure data and B is predicted by using A's predictions and B's failure data on a computer that has multiple processes and processors that can run in parallel. Even for a small problem, it is not clear how to develop the schedule without using a structured approach, as provided by the CPM model. The reason is the presence of dependencies among activities.

Program Evaluation and Review Technique (PERT)   401
PERT is also a scheduling model that is used to schedule software reliability engineering activities. How does PERT differ from CPM? Whereas CPM requires only a single estimate of activity duration, PERT requires three. CPM is used on projects where there is a lot of experience (e.g., software testing); PERT is used on projects where there is a lot of uncertainty (e.g., software development).

Chapter 19: Forecasting Models   405

In many situations it is necessary to make forecasts of future events, such as the time to next failure of a software system. In this chapter you learn about the leading models for making such forecasts. These models—exponential smoothing, geometric exponential smoothing, moving average, regression, and autoregressive integrated moving average— in effect "average" past observations to make a fit to the forecasting function. In order to select the most accurate model for your forecasts, you should evaluate their accuracy using relative error and mean relative error metrics.

Chapter 20: Cost Analysis   415

A variety of cost analysis methods are presented, with the objective of considering benefits and costs in making decisions on the deployment of technology. Too often benefits and costs are ignored in decisions concerning the development of technological products and services. The aim of this chapter is to provide the engineer with the tools to put cost-benefit analysis on an equal footing with technical considerations in making investment decisions. Models are constructed and solved for weighing alternatives, taking into account a stream of benefits and costs over the lives of the assets being evaluated.

Preface

This book covers many aspects of systems and software engineering, but the most important is software reliability engineering (SRE). While hardware reliability is obviously important, the vast majority of problems reported about systems can be traced to unreliable software. Although maintaining high hardware reliability is not a trivial matter, it pales in significance to the challenge of keeping software reliable. If a hardware component fails, it can be replaced. With software, we do not have the luxury of replacement; the software must be fixed. Furthermore, software is a two-edged sword. On the one hand, the fact that it can be readily changed is a great benefit because this flexibility allows systems to evolve with changing requirements and technology. On the other hand, this flexibility leads to many bugs being introduced by these changes—new bugs on top of the ones already present in the initial version of the software. Thus, it is important for the reader to learn the principles of SRE in order to mitigate the risks of deploying software. This book provides numerous models and methods to accomplish this goal, accompanied by many real-world examples drawn from industry and government.

Rather than go into great detail about various software reliability models, this book focuses on important aspects of managing system and software engineering efforts and explaining how they are related to one another. For the reader who may be interested in the details of software reliability models, see *Handbook of Software Reliability Engineering,* edited by Michael R. Lyu, published by IEEE Computer Society Press and McGraw-Hill Book Company, 1996, Chapter 3.

Quantitative Methods to Ensure the Reliability, Maintainability, and Availability of Computer Hardware and Software

Objectives

This chapter provides the engineer with the quantitative methods that support computer hardware and software engineering. The important areas of software and computers are emphasized in the examples. One or more problems follow each method description. This chapter equips the reader with the basics of probability and statistics that are needed to understand other chapters that use these subjects. However, readers new to probability and statistics may wish to consult basic texts, such as David M. Levine, Patricia P. Ramsey, and Robert K. Smidt, *Applied Statistics for Engineers and Scientists* (Prentice Hall, 2001).

What You Will Learn From This Chapter

You will build your confidence in being able to handle the quantitative methods germane to systems and software engineering by seeing a structured approach, which includes definitions and model descriptions, followed by one or more solved problems, for each method.

Subjects

Probability and Statistics
Design of Experiments: ANOVA Randomized Block Model
Design of Experiments: One-way ANOVA
Chebyshev's Theorem: The Rarity of Outliers
Reliability and Failure Analysis
Multiple Component Reliability Analysis
Computer System Availability and Maintenance
Fault Tree Analysis
Confidence Intervals Model

Probability and Statistics

We start with some fundamentals of probability and statistics that will help you follow the material on hardware and software reliability.

A *probability distribution* describes the frequency of occurrence of a *random variable*. A random variable has values that depend on the probability of events—for example, the value obtained when dice are rolled (event). Probability distributions can be classified as *continuous* (e.g., normal) or *discrete* (e.g., Poisson). The random variable in a continuous distribution has non-integer values like the height of people, while a discrete distribution has integer values like the value obtained when rolling dice. The frequency of occurrence of a continuous random variable is called a *probability density function* (e.g., exponential), whereas the frequency of occurrence of a discrete random variable is called a *probability mass function* (e.g., Poisson). If the frequency of occurrence is cumulative, the probability distribution is called a *cumulative distribution function*. Lastly, the probability distribution of random variable values can be *symmetrical* about the mean (e.g., normal) or *skewed* (e.g., exponential)—more values on either side of the mean.

Now using the above characteristics, the properties of some important probability distributions are examined.

1. Normal Distribution (continuous)

The normal distribution has a complicated mathematical probability density function. It is better to understand it from a graphical perspective as in Figure 1.1, which shows the distribution of computer times to failure. The normal distribution is the so-called bell-shaped curve that is symmetrical about the mean. It is typically used in situations where there is approximately equal spread in values about the mean, such as in time to failure of a computer system that has approximately equal values above and below the mean.

To illustrate the construction of a normal curve, using time to failure data t, proceed as follows:

1. Compute the value of z that is known as the *standard normal score* [LEV01] in equation (1.1). Computing z involves using the difference between a random variable t and its mean $\bar{t}$, random sample size n, and standard deviation s.

FIGURE 1.1   Probability Density Function $p(t)$ of Computer System Time to Failure vs. Time to Failure t

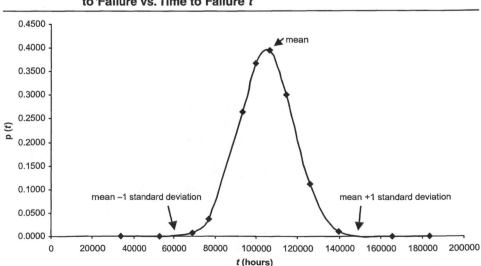

TABLE 1.1   Time to Failure Normal Curve Data and Computations

Time to Failure		Area Under Normal Curve	Reliability	Ordinate of Normal Curve		
t	z	$P(T \le t)$	$R(t, z)$	$p(t)$		
33480	−5.604	0.0000	1.0000	0.0000	$\bar{t}$	$+1\ s$
52920	−4.085	0.0000	1.0000	0.0001	**149553**	
69120	−2.819	0.0024	0.9976	0.0075		
77040	−2.201	0.0139	0.9861	0.0355	$\bar{t}$	$-1\ s$
93600	−0.907	0.1611	0.8389	0.2637	**60867**	
100080	−0.401	0.3446	0.6554	0.3668		
106920	0.134	0.5517	0.4483	0.3956		
114840	0.752	0.7734	0.2266	0.3011		
125640	1.596	0.9452	0.0548	0.1109		
139680	2.693	0.9964	0.0036	0.0107		
165600	4.718	1.0000	0.0000	0.0000		
183600	6.124	1.0000	0.0000	0.0000		
105210	$\bar{t}$		n	12		
44343	s					

2. Use the values of z in a table of normal distribution ordinate values that are available on the Web site: http://www.music.miami.edu/research/statistics/normalcurve/norm CurveAreas.html
3. Plot the ordinate values obtained in step 2 versus the values of t in Figure 1.1.
4. Compute the mean $\bar{t} \pm 1$ standard deviation (s) to show the spread of the distribution.
5. Tabulate the data and computations as shown in Table 1.1.

$$z = \frac{(t - \bar{t})\sqrt{n}}{s},$$ (1.1)

where $\bar{t}$ is the mean of t and n is the sample size.

Table 1.1 shows the probability $P(T \le t)$—the probability that a specified time to failure, T, is less than or equal to a given value of t. Also shown is the reliability $R(t, z)$ of the computer system, as computed in equation (1.2).

$$R(t, z) = 1 - P(T \le t)$$ (1.2)

2. Poisson Distribution (discrete)

The Poisson distribution is most often used in situations where the probability of the next state in a process is dependent only on the present state—the so-called "memoryless" systems. For example, this is the case when the probability of the next failure is dependent only on the current state of the software when a failure occurs. This distribution deals with events, such as failure counts and number of arrivals at a queue, and is shown in equation (1.3).

$$P(x) = \frac{e^{-m}(m)^x}{x!}$$ (1.3)

where x is number of events (e.g., number of software failures), and m is the mean of events (e.g., mean number of software failures). The parameters of the Poisson distribution are the following:

Mean: m,

Variance: m, and

Standard Deviation = $\sqrt{m}$

In order to provide a plot of the Poisson probability mass function, it is necessary to generate values of x corresponding to given values of $P(x)$ and m. This can be done by solving equation (1.3) for x. The solution is shown in equation (1.4).

$$x = \frac{\log P(x) + m + \log(x!)}{\log(m)} \qquad (1.4)$$

Random values of $P(x)$ can be generated by using the Excel RAND function. Random values of $P(x)$ are generated so that there is no bias in the computation of x. Because generating random values of $P(x)$ will cause the plot of $P(x)$ vs. x to be uneven, the data are smoothed by computing the frequency of each value of x and using these as the values of $P(x)$. This process is similar to creating a histogram. The data and computations used in computing equation (1.3) are shown in Table 1.2. The plot of $P(x)$ vs. x is shown in Figure 1.2, where you will note a useful property of the plot: identification of the number of failures x where the probability $P(x)$ is maximum.

The cumulative distribution function, corresponding to Figure 1.2, is computed in equation (1.3) by summing the probability mass function over the failure data x from 1 to n. The result is shown in Figure 1.3 on page 6.

The Cumulative Distribution Function (CDF) shown in equation (1.5) and plotted in Figure 1.3 is the probability that a specified number of failures X is less than or equal to a given number of failures x.

$$P(X \leq x) = \sum_{i=1}^{n} \frac{e^{-m}(m)^{x_i}}{x_i!} \qquad (1.5)$$

FIGURE 1.2   Poisson Probability Mass Function $P(x)$ vs. Number of Failures x

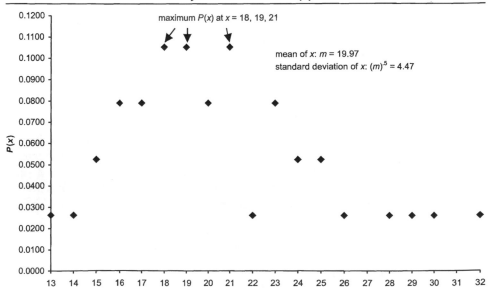

TABLE 1.2   Poisson Probability Mass Function

Number of Failures		RAND	Frequency	CDF
x	x	P(x)	P(x)	P (X ≤ x)
13	13	0.7734	0.0263	0.0263
14	14	0.5137	0.0263	0.0526
15	15	0.6781	0.0526	0.1053
15	16	0.0870	0.0789	0.1842
16	17	0.0601	0.0789	0.2632
16	18	0.0715	0.1053	0.3684
16	19	0.2812	0.1053	0.4737
17	20	0.4038	0.0789	0.5526
17	21	0.0723	0.1053	0.6579
17	22	0.0163	0.0263	0.6842
18	23	0.4526	0.0789	0.7632
18	24	0.4848	0.0526	0.8158
18	25	0.5858	0.0526	0.8684
18	26	0.3080	0.0263	0.8947
19	28	0.4595	0.0263	0.9211
19	29	0.8610	0.0263	0.9474
19	30	0.1308	0.0263	0.9737
19	32	0.2939	0.0263	1.0000
20		0.4525	1.0000	
20		0.1389	sum: P(x)	
20		0.2089		
21		0.4560		
21		0.4733		
21		0.4765		
21		0.1404		
22		0.8454		
23		0.3900		
23		0.5034		
23		0.5611		
24		0.8154		
24		0.8381		
25		0.0131		
25		0.3671		
26		0.4972		
28		0.9917		
29		0.4895		
30		0.0316		
32		0.3326		
mean	m	19.97		
std dev	$\sqrt{m}$	4.47		

FIGURE 1.3   Poisson Cumulative Distribution Function (CDF) $P(X \le x)$ vs. Number of Failures x

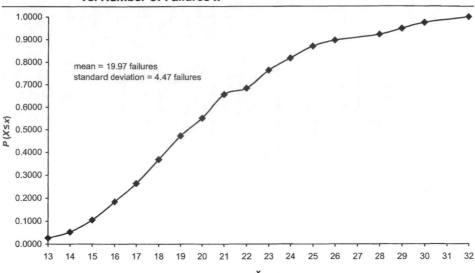

3. Exponential Distribution (continuous)

The exponential distribution is most often used when "time" is the random variable, such as the *time to failure* and the *time between arrivals* in a queue. This distribution is intimately related to the Poisson distribution by virtue of exponentially distributed time to or between events being associated with Poisson distributed event counts—for example, time to failures being associated with the failure counts. The probability density function, $P(t)$, of *time to events* is shown in equation (1.6), and is plotted in Figure 1.4.

$$P(t) = \lambda e^{-\lambda t}, \tag{1.6}$$

FIGURE 1.4   Exponential Probability Density Function $P(t)$ vs. Time to Failure t

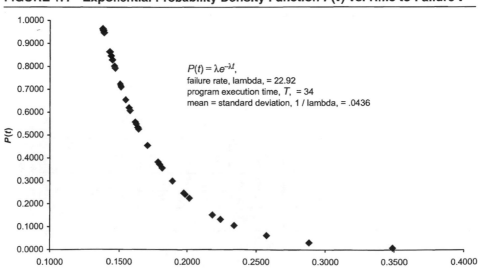

where t is time to an event (e.g., time from start of program to software failure), λ is the rate of events (e.g., software failures per unit time), for $t > 0$.

The parameters of the exponential distribution are:

Mean: $1/\lambda$,
Variance: $1/\lambda^2$, and
Standard Deviation $= 1/\lambda$

Since you are dealing with a continuous function, you would integrate the probability density function in equation (1.6) to produce the CDF in equation (1.7).

$$P\left(T \leq t\right) = \int_0^T \lambda e^{-\lambda t} dt = 1 - e^{-\lambda T}, \tag{1.7}$$

where T is a specified time to failure and t is a given time to failure. Equation (1.7) expresses the probability of T being less than or equal to t. In order to compute t for given values of $P(t)$, similar to what was done for the Poisson distribution, solve equation (1.6) for t in equation (1.8):

$$t = \frac{\log(\lambda / P(t))}{\lambda} \tag{1.8}$$

Now, the failure rate λ is needed to compute time to failure in equation (1.8). This is accomplished in equation (1.9), using the execution time T of the program. The data and computations are shown in Table 1.3 on page 8, where $T = 34$ was chosen to illustrate the procedure.

$$\lambda = \frac{\sum_{i=1}^{n} x_i}{T} \tag{1.9}$$

4. Binomial Distribution (discrete)

In general, the binomial distribution is used when you want to compute the probability $P(x)$ of x successes (failures) out of N trials or cases, with probability p of success (failure) on an individual trial or case. Thus, you have equation (1.10) where $\frac{N!}{x! \ (N-x)!}$ is the number of combinations of N events that can occur when taken x at a time.

$$P\left(x\right) = \frac{N!}{x! \ (N-x)!} p^x (1-p)^{N-x} \tag{1.10}$$

In terms of a reliability problem, $P(x)$ is the probability of x number of failures, x is an item from a random sample (e.g., number of computer failures), N is the sample size, and p is the probability of failures occurring in the population (e.g., population of computer parts from which the sample of size N is drawn). If the population p is unknown, the sample value $\hat{p}$ is used.

The parameters of the binomial distribution are given in equations (1.11) and (1.12):

$$\text{The mean} = Np \tag{1.11}$$

$$\text{and the standard deviation} = \sqrt{Np(1-p)} \tag{1.12}$$

TABLE 1.3 Exponential Probability Density Function

Number of Failures	RAND Exponential	Time to Failure
x	$P(t)$	t
13	0.1331	0.2246
14	0.7104	0.1516
15	0.6546	0.1551
15	0.4561	0.1709
16	0.8010	0.1463
16	0.8639	0.1430
16	0.9648	0.1382
17	0.3006	0.1891
17	0.9463	0.1390
17	0.3579	0.1815
18	0.5337	0.1640
18	0.9550	0.1386
18	0.5579	0.1621
18	0.1061	0.2345
19	0.5493	0.1628
19	0.9556	0.1386
19	0.0626	0.2575
19	0.7914	0.1468
20	0.8458	0.1439
20	0.2251	0.2017
20	0.6196	0.1575
21˙	0.8627	0.1431
21	0.2476	0.1975
21	0.7133	0.1514
21	0.8280	0.1449
22	0.0077	0.3489
23	0.3737	0.1796
23	0.7234	0.1508
23	0.9593	0.1384
24	0.2419	0.1985
24	0.0309	0.2884
25	0.1527	0.2186
25	0.8285	0.1448
26	0.7172	0.1511
28	0.3834	0.1785
29	0.6078	0.1584
30	0.7938	0.1467
32	0.5272	0.1646
779	λ	**22.92** failure rate
	T	**34** execution time

$$\sum_{i=1}^{n} x_i$$

FIGURE 1.5   Binomial Distribution Mass Function $P(x)$ [Probability of x Number of Failures] vs. Number of Failures x

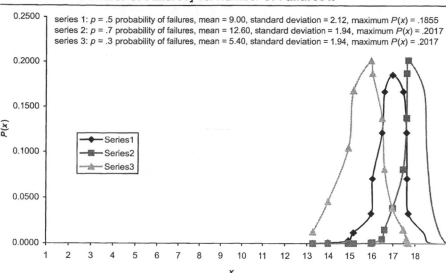

Figure 1.5 shows these relationships for an assumed number of failures in the range $x = 1, 18$. In addition, the figure annotates the maximum probability of number of failures, $P(x)$. Notice that for a high number of failures ($x = 16, 17, 18$), $P(x)$ is significant. Thus, this type of plot is useful in telling you at what number of failures their probability becomes critical.

Design of Experiments: ANOVA Randomized Block Model [LEV01]

Design of experiments involves measuring the variation of data in multiple dimensions (analysis of variation or ANOVA) (e.g., two-way analysis of variance). For example, you could take temperature readings on computers operating under different loads and would like to see whether there is a statistically significant difference in temperature depending on load. If the difference is significant, it could indicate that some of the computers could overheat. In this example, the computers and temperatures are the *block* or subject and the load is the *treatment*.

Definitions

Block: subject for which repeated observations are made

> *SSA*: sum of squares *across* treatments
> *SSB*: sum of squares *across blocks*
> *SSE*: sum of squares error
> *SST*: *total* sum of squares

> *MSB*: mean square across blocks
> *MSA*: mean square across treatments
> *MSE*: mean square error
> *MST*: mean square *total*

i: block (subject)
j: treatment
r: number of blocks (or subjects)
c: number of treatments
n: total number of observations $= rc$

X_{ij}: value in block i in treatment j
$\overline{X_i}$: mean for block i
$\overline{X_j}$: mean for treatment j
$\overline{\overline{X}}$: overall mean

$\sum_{j=1}^{c}\sum_{i=1}^{r} X_{ij}$: summation of values over all treatments and blocks

In plain English, "degrees of freedom" refers to sample size but taking into account the fact that if a statistic, like the mean (average) has been computed from the data, "1" is subtracted from the sample size. Degrees of freedom are used in ANOVA calculations, as you will see in the ANOVA model section that follows.

$c - 1$: degrees of freedom for *blocks*
$r - 1$: degrees of freedom for *treatments*
$n - 1$: degrees of freedom *total*
$(r - 1)(c - 1)$: degrees of freedom for *errors*
F Test Statistic: *variance of one sample divided by the variance of another sample*
α = significance level for F statistic test

In practical terms, the value of α refers to how confident you are that variations across treatments and blocks are significant, as given by the F test statistic.

ANOVA Model

Across Treatment Variation

The variation across treatments is computed with respect to the mean or average value—for example, the variation in load across computers.

Compute the mean value of the treatments:

$$\overline{X_j} = \frac{\sum_{i=1}^{c} X_{ij}}{c} \text{ for } j = 1, \ldots, r \tag{1.13}$$

Compute the sum of squares across treatments:

$$SSA = r\sum_{j=1}^{c}(\overline{X_j} - \overline{\overline{X}})^2 \tag{1.14}$$

The overall mean is computed using equation (1.15):

$$\overline{\overline{X}} = \frac{\sum_{i=1}^{c}\sum_{j=1}^{r} X_{ij}}{rc} \tag{1.15}$$

Compute the mean sum of squares across treatments:

$$MSA = SSA/(c-1) \qquad (1.16)$$

There are similar computations for variation across blocks—for example, the variation in temperature of computers.

Across Blocks Variation

$$\overline{X}_i \frac{\sum_{j=1}^{r} X_{ij}}{r} \text{ for } i-1, \ldots, c \qquad (1.17)$$

$$SSB = c \sum_{i=1}^{r} \left(\overline{X}_i - \overline{\overline{X}} \right)^2 \qquad (1.18)$$

$$MSB = SSB/(r-1) \qquad (1.19)$$

Total Variation

Total variation pertains to variations with respect to the total mean, computed across treatments and blocks.

$$SST = \sum_{j=1}^{c} \sum_{i=1}^{r} (X_{ij} - \overline{\overline{X}})^2 \qquad (1.20)$$

$$MST = SST / (n-1) \qquad (1.21)$$

Error Variation

In ANOVA, it is unlikely that the sum of squares across treatments SSA plus the sum of squares across blocks SSB will equal the total sum of squares SST because there are likely to be errors in measurement made by humans and errors due to limitations of measuring instruments. Therefore, the sum of squares error term SSE accounts for the difference in equation (1.22).

$$SSE = SST - SSA - SSB \qquad (1.22)$$

Then, the mean square error MSE is computed in equation (1.23).

$$MSE = SSE/[(r-1)(c-1)] \qquad (1.23)$$

The F test statistic for error variation across treatments is given by equation (1.24) and for error variation across blocks by equation (1.25). The computed values are compared with values of F tabulated in tables in statistics texts [LEV01] to determine whether the computed value of F is statistically significant.

$$\text{Across treatments: } FA = MSA/MSE \qquad (1.24)$$

$$\text{Across blocks: } FB = MSB/MSE \qquad (1.25)$$

Problem 1

Observations of temperature are made on four computer systems (i.e., blocks) under load conditions of 100, 200, and 300 transactions per second (i.e., treatments). The data and computations are recorded in Table 1.4. Determine whether there are statistically significant differences in temperature based on computer and load.

Specifications

i: computer (block)
j: computer load condition (treatment)
c: number of treatments (4 computers)
r: number of blocks (3 load conditions)
n: number of observations $= c\,r = 12$
X_{ij}:   temperature of computer i under load condition j
$\overline{X}_i$:   mean of temperature for computer i
$\overline{X}_j$:   mean of temperature for load condition j
$\overline{\overline{X}}$:   overall mean for computers and computer loads

Solution

Use the F Test Table on page 13 to obtain F values, according to the degrees of freedom (df) shown in Table 1.5; compare these values with the computed F values in Table 1.5.

TABLE 1.4   ANOVA: Computer Temperature Data

			Computer I					
			$\boxed{X_{ij}}$					
j	1	2	3	4	Load j	$\overline{X}_j$	$\boxed{(\overline{X}_j - \overline{\overline{X}})^2}$	
1	70	60	80	40	100	62.50	506.25	
2	90	100	60	70	200	80.00	25.00	
3	100	110	150	90	300	112.50	756.25	$\boxed{\sum_{j=1}^{c}(\overline{X}_j - \overline{\overline{X}})^2}$
							1287.5	
	86.67	90.00	96.67	66.67			5150.00	
c	3					85.00	SSA	
r	4							
	2.78	25.00	136.11	336.11	500.00	$\overline{\overline{X}}$	MSA	MSB
			$\boxed{(\overline{X}_i - \overline{\overline{X}})^2}$		SSB		2575.00	166.67

TABLE 1.5   ANOVA Computer Temperature Results

					F table			
SST	9100		$F - MSA$	4.4783	5.1433	$df = 3, 6$	$df = (c-1), (r-1)$ $(c-1)$	not significant across computer loads
	3450	575	$F - MSB$	0.2899	4.7571	$df = 2, 6$	$df = (r-1), (r-1)$ $(c-1)$	not significant across computers
	SSE	MSE						$\alpha = .05$

F TEST TABLE

df2/df1	1	2	3	4	5	6	7	8	9	10	12	15	20	24	30	40	60	120	INF
1	161.4476	199.5000	215.7073	224.5832	230.1619	233.9860	236.7684	238.8827	240.5433	241.8817	243.9060	245.9499	248.0131	249.0518	250.0951	251.1432	252.1957	253.2529	254.3144
2	18.5128	19.0000	19.1643	19.2468	19.2964	19.3295	19.3532	19.3710	19.3848	19.3959	19.4125	19.4291	19.4458	19.4541	19.4624	19.4707	19.4791	19.4874	19.4957
3	10.1280	9.5521	9.2766	9.1172	9.0135	8.9406	8.8867	8.8452	8.8123	8.7855	8.7446	8.7029	8.6602	8.6385	8.6166	8.5944	8.5720	8.5494	8.5264
4	7.7086	6.9443	6.5914	6.3882	6.2561	6.1631	6.0942	6.0410	5.9988	5.9644	5.9117	5.8578	5.8025	5.7744	5.7459	5.7170	5.6877	5.6581	5.6281
5	6.6079	5.7861	5.4095	5.1922	5.0503	4.9503	4.8759	4.8183	4.7725	4.7351	4.6777	4.6188	4.5581	4.5272	4.4957	4.4638	4.4314	4.3985	4.3650
6	5.9874	5.1433	4.7571	4.5337	4.3874	4.2839	4.2067	4.1468	4.0990	4.0600	3.9999	3.9381	3.8742	3.8415	3.8082	3.7743	3.7398	3.7047	3.6689
7	5.5914	4.7374	4.3468	4.1203	3.9715	3.8660	3.7870	3.7257	3.6767	3.6365	3.5747	3.5107	3.4445	3.4105	3.3758	3.3404	3.3043	3.2674	3.2298
8	5.3177	4.4590	4.0662	3.8379	3.6875	3.5806	3.5005	3.4381	3.3881	3.3472	3.2839	3.2184	3.1503	3.1152	3.0794	3.0428	3.0053	2.9669	2.9276
9	5.1174	4.2565	3.8625	3.6331	3.4817	3.3738	3.2927	3.2296	3.1789	3.1373	3.0729	3.0061	2.9365	2.9005	2.8637	2.8259	2.7872	2.7475	2.7067
10	4.9646	4.1028	3.7083	3.4780	3.3258	3.2172	3.1355	3.0717	3.0204	2.9782	2.9130	2.8450	2.7740	2.7372	2.6996	2.6609	2.6211	2.5801	2.5379
11	4.8443	3.9823	3.5874	3.3567	3.2039	3.0946	3.0123	2.9480	2.8962	2.8536	2.7876	2.7186	2.6464	2.6090	2.5705	2.5309	2.4901	2.4480	2.4045
12	4.7472	3.8853	3.4903	3.2592	3.1059	2.9961	2.9134	2.8486	2.7964	2.7534	2.6866	2.6169	2.5436	2.5055	2.4663	2.4259	2.3842	2.3410	2.2962
13	4.6672	3.8056	3.4105	3.1791	3.0254	2.9153	2.8321	2.7669	2.7144	2.6710	2.6037	2.5331	2.4589	2.4202	2.3803	2.3392	2.2966	2.2524	2.2064
14	4.6001	3.7389	3.3439	3.1122	2.9582	2.8477	2.7642	2.6987	2.6458	2.6022	2.5342	2.4630	2.3879	2.3487	2.3082	2.2664	2.2229	2.1778	2.1307
15	4.5431	3.6823	3.2874	3.0556	2.9013	2.7905	2.7066	2.6408	2.5876	2.5437	2.4753	2.4034	2.3275	2.2878	2.2468	2.2043	2.1601	2.1141	2.0658
16	4.4940	3.6337	3.2389	3.0069	2.8524	2.7413	2.6572	2.5911	2.5377	2.4935	2.4247	2.3522	2.2756	2.2354	2.1938	2.1507	2.1058	2.0589	2.0096
17	4.4513	3.5915	3.1968	2.9647	2.8100	2.6987	2.6143	2.5480	2.4943	2.4499	2.3807	2.3077	2.2304	2.1898	2.1477	2.1040	2.0584	2.0107	1.9604
18	4.4139	3.5546	3.1599	2.9277	2.7729	2.6613	2.5767	2.5102	2.4563	2.4117	2.3421	2.2686	2.1906	2.1497	2.1071	2.0629	2.0166	1.9681	1.9168
19	4.3807	3.5219	3.1274	2.8951	2.7401	2.6283	2.5435	2.4768	2.4227	2.3779	2.3080	2.2341	2.1555	2.1141	2.0712	2.0264	1.9795	1.9302	1.8780
20	4.3512	3.4928	3.0984	2.8661	2.7109	2.5990	2.5140	2.4471	2.3928	2.3479	2.2776	2.2033	2.1242	2.0825	2.0391	1.9938	1.9464	1.8963	1.8432
21	4.3248	3.4668	3.0725	2.8401	2.6848	2.5727	2.4876	2.4205	2.3660	2.3210	2.2504	2.1757	2.0960	2.0540	2.0102	1.9645	1.9165	1.8657	1.8117
22	4.3009	3.4434	3.0491	2.8167	2.6613	2.5491	2.4638	2.3965	2.3419	2.2967	2.2258	2.1508	2.0707	2.0283	1.9842	1.9380	1.8894	1.8380	1.7831
23	4.2793	3.4221	3.0280	2.7955	2.6400	2.5277	2.4422	2.3748	2.3201	2.2747	2.2036	2.1282	2.0476	2.0050	1.9605	1.9139	1.8648	1.8128	1.7570
24	4.2597	3.4028	3.0088	2.7763	2.6207	2.5082	2.4226	2.3551	2.3002	2.2547	2.1834	2.1077	2.0267	1.9838	1.9390	1.8920	1.8424	1.7896	1.7330
25	4.2417	3.3852	2.9912	2.7587	2.6030	2.4904	2.4047	2.3371	2.2821	2.2365	2.1649	2.0889	2.0075	1.9643	1.9192	1.8718	1.8217	1.7684	1.7110
26	4.2252	3.3690	2.9752	2.7426	2.5868	2.4741	2.3883	2.3205	2.2655	2.2197	2.1479	2.0716	1.9898	1.9464	1.9010	1.8533	1.8027	1.7488	1.6906
27	4.2100	3.3541	2.9604	2.7278	2.5719	2.4591	2.3732	2.3053	2.2501	2.2043	2.1323	2.0558	1.9736	1.9299	1.8842	1.8361	1.7851	1.7306	1.6717
28	4.1960	3.3404	2.9467	2.7141	2.5581	2.4453	2.3593	2.2913	2.2360	2.1900	2.1179	2.0411	1.9586	1.9147	1.8687	1.8203	1.7689	1.7138	1.6541
29	4.1830	3.3277	2.9340	2.7014	2.5454	2.4324	2.3463	2.2783	2.2229	2.1768	2.1045	2.0275	1.9446	1.9005	1.8543	1.8055	1.7537	1.6981	1.6376
30	4.1709	3.3158	2.9223	2.6896	2.5336	2.4205	2.3343	2.2662	2.2107	2.1646	2.0921	2.0148	1.9317	1.8874	1.8409	1.7918	1.7396	1.6835	1.6223
40	4.0847	3.2317	2.8387	2.6060	2.4495	2.3359	2.2490	2.1802	2.1240	2.0772	2.0035	1.9245	1.8389	1.7929	1.7444	1.6928	1.6373	1.5766	1.5089
60	4.0012	3.1504	2.7581	2.5252	2.3683	2.2541	2.1665	2.0970	2.0401	1.9926	1.9174	1.8364	1.7480	1.7001	1.6491	1.5943	1.5343	1.4673	1.3893
120	3.9201	3.0718	2.6802	2.4472	2.2899	2.1750	2.0868	2.0164	1.9588	1.9105	1.8337	1.7505	1.6587	1.6084	1.5543	1.4952	1.4290	1.3519	1.2539
inf	3.8415	2.9957	2.6049	2.3719	2.2141	2.0986	2.0096	1.9384	1.8799	1.8307	1.7522	1.6664	1.5705	1.5173	1.4591	1.3940	1.3180	1.2214	1.0000

$\alpha = .05$
Row (r): df1.
Column (d): df2.

$F_{(.05,df1,df2)}$

Table 1.5 shows that neither the variation in temperature across computer loads nor the variation in temperature across computers is statistically significant based on the results of the F test. Therefore, you would conclude that load condition does not affect computer temperature.

Problem 2

For the following *final temperature of computer parts* and *computer manufacturer supplier* data in Table 1.6, identify the statistically significant factors, if any (e.g., final temperature of computer parts, computer manufacturer suppliers). See whether you obtain the answer in the table.

Specifications

Factor FT: final temperature of computer parts
Factor S: computer manufacturer supplier
$a = 5$ values of FT (treatments): final temperature of computer parts
$b = 3$ values of Factor S (treatments): computer manufacturer supplier
$r = 5$ blocks or subjects (i.e., computers parts)
$\alpha = .05$ significance level

TABLE 1.6   ANOVA Table

Source of Variation	Sum of Squares (SS) (Treatments)	Degrees of freedom (df)	Mean Square (MS = SS/df)	F Ratio = MS/MSE	Degrees of freedom (df) for F test table
Factor FT: final temperature of computer parts	583.2	$a - 1 =$ $5 - 1 = 4$	145.8	145.8/8.67 = 16.81	$(a - 1) = 4$ $ab(r - 1) = 60$ $F = 2.53$ **significant**
Factor S: computer manufacturer supplier	61.7	$b - 1 =$ $3 - 1 = 2$	30.85	30.85/8.67 = 3.56	$(b - 1) = 2$ $ab(r - 1) = 60$ $F = 3.15$ **significant**
Interaction of FT and S	383.1	$(a - 1)(b - 1) =$ $4*2 = 8$	47.89	47.89/8.67 = 5.52	$(a - 1)(b - 1) = 8$ $ab(r - 1) = 60$ $F = 2.10$ **significant**
$SS_{Treatments}$	1028.0				
SS_{Error}	520.3	$ab(r - 1) =$ $5*3*4 = 60$	$MSE =$ $520.3/60 =$ 8.67		
$SS_{Total} =$ $SS_{Treatments} + SS_{Error}$	1548.3	$abr - 1 =$ $(5*3*5) - 1 = 74$	1548.3/74 = 20.92	20.92/8.67 = 2.41	$abr - 1 = (5*3*5)$ $- 1 = 74$ $ab(r - 1) = 5*3*4$ $= 60$ $F = 1.92$ (not in table. Closest is 60, 12) **significant**

$$\text{From Table 1.6, } SS_{\text{Treatments}} = 583.2 + 61.7 + 383.1 = 1028 \tag{1.26}$$

$$SS_{\text{Error}} = SS_{\text{Total}} - SS_{\text{Treatments}} = 1548.3 - 1028 = 520.3 \tag{1.27}$$

F Test for Significance: If (*F* Ratio) $\geq$ tabulated *F* for $\alpha = .05$, then the result is significant.

Result

Factor *FT*: final temperature of computer parts: significant
Factor *S*: computer manufacturer supplier: significant
Interaction of *FT* and *S*: significant
SS_{Total}: significant

Therefore, you would conclude that the computer manufacturer supplier has a significant effect on the final temperature of computer parts.

Design of Experiments: One-way ANOVA

Definitions

X_{ij}:   observation *i* in group *j*

$\overline{\overline{X}}$:   overall mean across and within groups

n_j: number of observations in group *j*

n: total number of observations

c: number of groups

$\overline{X}_j$:   sample mean of group *j*

SST: total variation sum of squares across and within groups

SSA: across group variation sum of squares

SSW: within group variation sum of squares

MSA: mean square across group variation

MSW: mean square within group variation

MST: mean square total variation across and within groups

F: *F* test statistic

df: degrees of freedom

ANOVA Model

$$df = c - 1 \text{ for across group variation} \tag{1.28}$$

$$df = n - c \text{ for within group variation} \tag{1.29}$$

$$df = n - 1 \text{ for total variation across and within groups} \tag{1.30}$$

Total Variation Across and Within Groups

$$SST = \sum_{j=1}^{c} \sum_{i=1}^{n_j} (X_{ij} - \overline{\overline{X}})^2 \tag{1.31}$$

$$\overline{\overline{X}} = \frac{\displaystyle\sum_{j=1}^{c} \sum_{i=1}^{n_j} X_{ij}}{n} \tag{1.32}$$

Across Group Variation

$$SSA = \sum_{j=1}^{c} (\overline{X_j} - \overline{\overline{X}})^2 \tag{1.33}$$

Within Group Variation

$$SSW = \sum_{i=1}^{c} \sum_{j=1}^{n_j} (X_{ij} - \overline{X_j})^2 \tag{1.34}$$

Mean Squares

$$\text{Across groups: } MSA = SSA/(c - 1) \tag{1.35}$$

$$\text{Within groups: } MSW = SSW/(n - c) \tag{1.36}$$

$$\text{Total: } MST = SST/(n - 1) \tag{1.37}$$

F test

$$F = MSA/MSW \tag{1.38}$$

One-way ANOVA involves the analysis of variation of a single variable across different groups, such as the cost of desktop, laptop, and notebook computers. The template for One-way ANOVA is shown in Table 1.7.

Problem 3

The source of variation of *computer vendor product quality* is given in Table 1.8 page 17. Is there a statistically significant difference in computer vendor product quality?

Specification

$c = 3$ groups of computer vendors
$n_j = 5$ observations of each computer vendor group j
$n = c * n_j = 3 * 5 = 15$ total observations

Solution

The solution, culminating in the F Test ($F = MSA/MSW$), equation (1.38):

At $\alpha = .05$, $F = MSA/MSW$ is **not** significant at F ratio $= .1660$, since the tabulated F ratio $= 3.8853$.

Note: In using the F table, enter with the horizontal df (e.g., 2) and the numerator df (e.g., 12). Thus, there is no significant difference in computer vendor product quality.

TABLE 1.7   One-way ANOVA Template

Source of Variation	Sum of Squares	Degrees of Freedom	Mean Square (*MSE*)	*F* ratio
Within Groups	SSW	$n - c$	$SSW/(n - c)$	$F = MSA/MSW$
Across Groups	SSA	$c - 1$	$SSA/(c - 1)$	
Total	SST	$n - 1$	$SST/(n - 1)$	

TABLE 1.8 Computer Vendor Quality

i (quality)	Computer Vendor j									
	X_{ij} 1	SSW	X_{ij} 2	SSW	X_{ij} 3	SSW	SST	MSA	F	F table (2, 12, α = .05)
1	70	220.03	60	560.11	80	0.25	39893.33	547.42	0.1660	3.8853 not significant
2	90	1213.36	100	266.78	60	420.25		MSW		df for MSA = c − 1 = 2
3	100	2010.03	110	693.44	150	4830.25		3296.83		df for MSW = n − c = 12
4	50	26.69	30	2880.11	170	8010.25		MST		df for MST = n − 1 = 14
5	20	1236.69	200	13533.44	20	3660.25		650		
$\overline{X}_j$	55.17		83.67		80.50					
Sum SSW		4706.80		17933.88		16921.25	Total SSW 39561.93	87.33		
$(\overline{X}_j - \overline{\overline{X}})^2$	1034.69		13.44		46.69	1094.833	Sum SSA	$\boxed{\overline{\overline{X}}}$		
c	3									
n_j	5									
n	15									

17

Chebyshev's Theorem: The Rarity of Outliers

Chebyshev's Theorem: The Rarity of Outliers:

$$(P|x-\mu| \geq k\sigma) \leq \frac{1}{k^2},$$
(1.39)

where P is probability, $k =$ is a positive number (preferably > 1), x is a random variable, and the probability distribution of x has population mean μ and standard deviation σ.

Or equivalently:

$$P\left(|x-\mu| \leq k\sigma\right) > 1 - \left(\frac{1}{k^2}\right)$$
(1.40)

That is, the probability that a random variable x will exceed k standard deviations σ from its mean μ is never greater than the reciprocal of k^2.

The theorem can be used to estimate the probability of an outlier (i.e., anomalous value) in a sample of values.

Problem 4

For the sample data below, what is the probability that there is a laptop measurement $R_i = 7.70$ in the *population*?

$R_i =$
  7.2
  6.8
  7.5
  7.2
  7.3
  6.9
  7.1

$$1.\ \text{Sample mean} = \overline{R}_i = \frac{1}{N}\sum_{i=1}^{N} R_i = 7.14$$
(1.41)

$$\text{Sample variance} = s^2 = \frac{1}{N-1}\sum_{i=1}^{N}(R_i - \overline{R}_i)^2 = 0.0562$$

$$s = \sqrt{.0562} = \mathbf{.2370} = \text{sample standard deviation}$$
(1.42)

From equation (1.40): $|x-\mu| \geq k\sigma$, where $R_i \equiv x$ and $\overline{R}_i \equiv \mu$, $k \leq |x-\mu|/\sigma$

$$|R_i - \overline{R}_i| - |7.70 - 7.14| = .56$$

$$k \leq .56/.2370 = \mathbf{2.3629}, \text{ assuming } s = \sigma$$

2. Using equation (1.40) and the assumptions that the sample mean $\overline{R}_i = \mu$ and standard

deviation $s = \sigma$, $(P|x-\mu| \geq k\sigma) \leq \frac{1}{k^2} \equiv (P|R_i - \overline{R}_i| = (P|R_i - 7.14| \geq .2370k \leq \frac{1}{k^2}$ (1.43)

Looking at Table 1.9 you see that the probability of the laptop case having a dimension of $R_i = 7.70$ is $\leq .1791$, which is 2.3629 standard deviations from the mean. Therefore, you would conclude that the probability of the laptop dimension $= 7.70$ is low, which you would also discern by examining the original data.

TABLE 1.9   Applying Chebyshev's Theorem to Laptop Cases

k	$ks = k * .2370$	$\left(P\left\| R_i - \overline{R_i} \right\| \right) \geq k\ .2370\ \leq \dfrac{1}{k^2}$
1	.2370	1.000
2	.4740	.2500
2.3629	.5600	.1791
3	.7110	.1111
4	.9480	.0625
5	1.1850	.0400
6	1.4220	.0278

FIGURE 1.6   Chebyshev's Theorem: Laptop Cases: Probability P of Laptop Case Dimension R_i and Number of Standard Deviations ks vs k

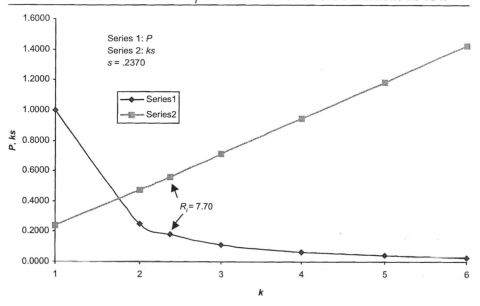

Figure 1.6 shows how the probability and the number of standard deviations from the mean vary with k.

Reliability and Failure Analysis

All engineers should be familiar with hardware and software reliability and failure analysis. Therefore, this section provides an introduction to reliability analysis so that engineers will understand how to analyze the hardware and software components of system reliability.

Definitions [LYU96]

First, some definitions are provided:

1. Reliability: letting T be the failure age of a hardware component, the reliability $R(t)$ or probability that a component survives to age $T > t = R(t) = 1 - F(t)$, where $F(t)$ is the

Cumulative Distribution Function (CDF) (probability that that a component survives to age $T \leq t$).

You see that reliability is related to the concept of survivability. That is, when hardware is tested or put into operation, its reliability will be based on the probability that it will survive for a time T under stated operating conditions (e.g., operated in a mission critical space application). $R(t)$ and $F(T)$ are given by equations (1.44) and (1.45), respectively:

$$R(t) = P(T > t) = 1 - F(t) = \int_{T}^{\infty} f(t)dt \tag{1.44}$$

$$F(t) = P(0 \leq T \leq t) = \int_{0}^{T} f(t)dt \tag{1.45}$$

2. Expected Value of Failure Age of a Component, $E(T)$ = Mean Time to Failure (MTTF).

MTTF refers to the summation of operating times from start to failure divided by the number of failures. It is a common metric for hardware reliability, but can be misleading because equipment will fail at specific times and not according to a mean value! Note: MTTF is used for items that are not repaired (i.e., discarded), whereas Mean Time Between Failures (MTBF) is used for items that are repaired.

The general form for MTTF, whether hardware or software, is derived from the reliability function $R(t)$, as follows:

$$\text{MTTF} = \int_{0}^{\infty} R(t)dt \tag{1.46}$$

3. Hazard Function: letting operating time t have the probability density function $p(t)$, the *instantaneous failure rate* at time t,

$$h(t) = p(t)/R(t) \tag{1.47}$$

The hazard function is frequently described in reliability literature, but a reliability metric that is more practical for calculations with empirical data is the failure rate $f(t)$. This is defined as the number of failures $n(t)$ at time t divided by t: $f(t) = n(t)/t$. The reason the hazard function may be impractical when dealing with empirical data is that the probability density function $p(t)$ may not be available.

4. Probability of Failure in the Interval $t, t + dt$: = $p(t)dt$.

For example, if the probability density function is available, such as the exponential $p(t) = \lambda e^{-\lambda t}$, the probability of failure in interval $dt = \lambda e^{-\lambda t} dt$.

5. Reliability for Exponential Failure Distribution:

$$R(t) = e^{-\lambda t}, \text{ where } \lambda \text{ is the failure rate} = 1/\text{MTTF} \tag{1.48}$$

The exponential distribution is the only failure distribution that has a constant failure rate λ and a constant hazard function $h(t)$ in the **operations phase** of the life cycle. This can be seen by using equations (1.47) and (1.48) as follows:

$$h(t) = p(t)/R(t) = \lambda e^{-\lambda t}/e^{-\lambda t} = \lambda.$$

6. Weibull Failure Distribution

One of the most widely used distributions for reliability is the Weibull Failure Distribution [LYU96]. It has the flexibility of allowing for constant, increasing, and decreasing hazard functions, as demonstrated by the following:

$$\text{Hazard Function: } h(t) = \alpha\lambda(t)^{(\alpha-1)} \qquad\qquad \text{[LLO62] (1.49)}$$

where α is a shape parameter and λ is a scale parameter of the hazard function $h(t)$. The parameter λ can also be considered to be the failure rate.

Using equation (1.49), you can generate equations (1.50) – (1.52):

$$\text{When } \alpha = 1, \ h(t) \text{ is constant (exponential)} = \lambda \qquad\qquad (1.50)$$

$$\text{When } \alpha = 2, \ h(t) \text{ is linear} = (2\lambda)(t) \text{ (increasing).} \qquad\qquad (1.51)$$

$$\text{When } \alpha = .5, \ h(t) \text{ is decreasing} = .5 \ \lambda/\sqrt{t} \qquad\qquad (1.52)$$

The Weibull probability density function (equation (1.53)) is flexible because it can represent software when the probability of time to failure t decreases or increases. The probability density function $p(t)$ of time to failure is given by equation (1.53).

$$p(t) = \alpha\lambda t^{(\alpha-1)} e^{-\lambda t^{\alpha}} \qquad\qquad \text{[LLO62] (1.53)}$$

Using equation (1.53), when $\alpha = 1$, $p(t)$ is the exponential distribution: $\lambda e^{-\lambda t}$ (1.54)

When you integrate equation (1.54), from 0 to t, you produce equation (1.55):

$$\text{Exponential Cumulative Distribution Function (CDF): } F(t) = 1 - e^{-\lambda t} \qquad (1.55)$$

Using the relationship that reliability = $R(t) = 1 - F(t)$, from equation (1.44), and applying equation (1.53), you obtain:

$$R(t) = P(T > t) = 1 = F(t) \int_{T}^{\infty} p(t)dt = \int_{T}^{\infty} \alpha\lambda t^{(\alpha-1)} e^{-\lambda t} dt \qquad\qquad (1.56)$$

The result of the integration process in equation (1.56) is the formula for reliability in equation (1.57).

$$R(t) = e^{-(\lambda t^{\alpha})} \qquad\qquad \text{[LLO62] (1.57)}$$

The parameters of the Weibull distribution are estimated according to reference [LL062] in equations (1.58) and (1.59):

$$\lambda = \frac{n}{\sum_{i=1}^{n} t_i^{\alpha}} \qquad\qquad (1.58)$$

$$\alpha = \frac{n}{\lambda \sum_{i=1}^{n} t_i^{\alpha} \log t_i - \sum_{i=1}^{n} \log t_i} \qquad\qquad (1.59)$$

However, trying to solve equations (1.58) and (1.59) is not practical because in order to solve for λ in equation (1.58), α is required, but to solve for α in equation (1.59), λ is required. A practical approach is to use the reliability function, equation (1.57) to solve for α, given values of λ and $R(t)$ for a specified value of t. The value of λ is computed by equation (1.60) and $R(t)$ is specified as a reliability goal to be achieved by time t.

$$\lambda = f/t, \qquad\qquad (1.60)$$

where f is the number of failures that occur during a test of duration t.

Now, solving equation (1.57) for α results in equation (1.61).

$$\alpha = \frac{\log[\dfrac{-\log(R(t))}{\lambda}]}{\log(t)}$$

(1.61)

However, notice the constraint on the maximum value of $R(t)$ that can be achieved to avoid trying to take the log of a negative quantity: $R(t) < e^{-\lambda}$. Therefore, after using equation (1.60) to compute λ, set the limit on $R(t)$ according to $R(t) < e^{-\lambda}$, substitute this value in equation (1.61), and solve for α.

Weibull Distribution Example

Using the above procedure, estimate λ for three situations. For example, suppose your software is tested three times, with each test duration of $t = 32$. Furthermore, suppose that there are $f = 10$, 6, and 2 failures on successive tests, producing an accelerated decreasing failure rate of $\lambda = f/t = 10/32$, 6/32, and 2/32 = .3125, .1875, and .0625, respectively. Next, use equations (1.49), (1.53), and (1.57) to solve for $h(t)$, $p(t)$, and $R(t)$, respectively, using the three paired values of λ and α. When these functions are plotted, you will be able to see how they vary across the three tests. The results will allow you to assess whether satisfactory progress has been made in meeting your reliability requirement of .9000, so that the software can be released for operational use.

Table 1.10 lists the results obtained by using the above procedure and Figures 1.7, 1.8, and 1.9 show the hazard function, probability density function, and reliability, respectively,

TABLE 1.10   Weibull Test Results

test	number of failures f	parameter λ	parameter α	reliability limit for $t = 32$ $R(t)$	sample size n
1	10	0.3125	0.000146	0.7315	32
2	6	0.1875	0.000240	0.8289	
3	2	0.0625	0.000555	0.9393	

FIGURE 1.7   Weibull Distribution: Hazard Function $h(t)$ vs. Time to Failure t

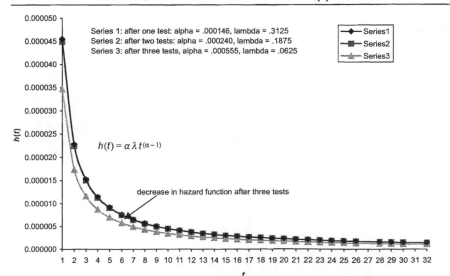

FIGURE 1.8   Weibull Probability Density Function $p(t)$ **(Probability of Time to Failure) vs. Time to Failure** t

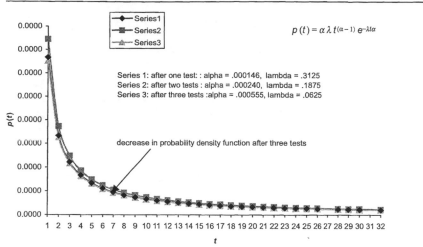

$$p(t) = \alpha \lambda\, t^{(\alpha-1)}\, e^{-\lambda t \alpha}$$

Series 1: after one test: : alpha = .000146, lambda = .3125
Series 2: after two tests : alpha = .000240, lambda = .1875
Series 3: after three tests :alpha = .000555, lambda = .0625

decrease in probability density function after three tests

FIGURE 1.9   Weibull Reliability $R(t)$ **vs. Test Time** t

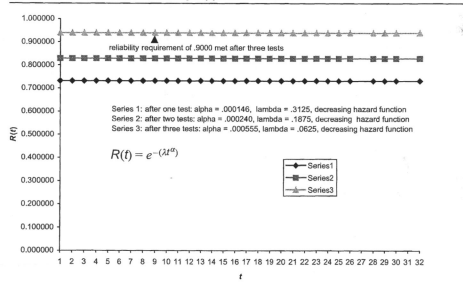

reliability requirement of .9000 met after three tests

Series 1: after one test: alpha = .000146, lambda = .3125, decreasing hazard function
Series 2: after two tests: alpha = .000240, lambda = .1875, decreasing hazard function
Series 3: after three tests: alpha = .000555, lambda = .0625, decreasing hazard function

$$R(t) = e^{-(\lambda t^{\alpha})}$$

for the three tests. The figure show that improvements are made in each of the three quantities across the three tests, and that after three tests, the reliability requirement is met for all values of test time.

Application of Weibull Distribution to the Analysis of NASA Space Shuttle Software

Now, an application of the Weibull distribution to the reliability analysis of the NASA Space Shuttle flight software is illustrated. For OI3 (Operational Increment 3—the name of the software release). Figures 1.10, 1.11, and 1.12 show, respectively, the hazard function, probability density function, and the reliability function. These figures show how the hazard function (i.e., instantaneous failure rate) is reduced, the probability of time to failure is reduced, and the reliability is improved, as the testing progresses. The data that were used in the Shuttle example are shown in Figure 1.12.

FIGURE 1.10   NASA Space Shuttle (OI3): Hazard Function $h(t)$ vs. Time to Failure t

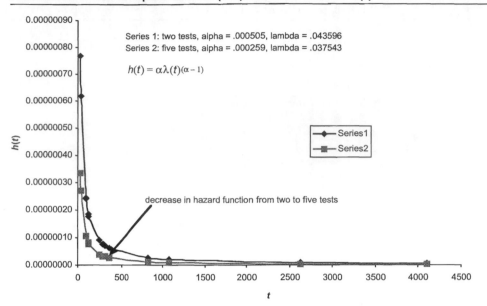

FIGURE 1.11   NASA Space Shuttle OI3: Probability Density Function $p(t)$
(Probability of Time to Failure) vs. Time to Failure t

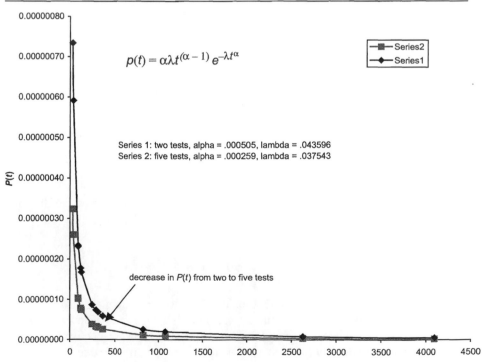

FIGURE 1.12   NASA Space Shuttle OI3: Reliability $R(t)$ vs. Test Time t

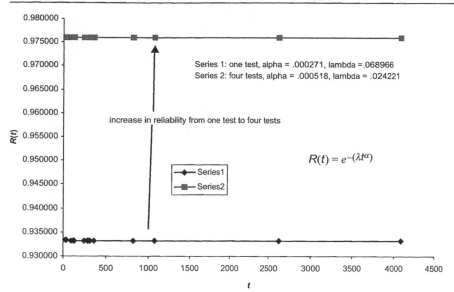

Normal Distribution

Definitions

s: standard deviation of operating time

t: operating time (hours)

$\overline{t}$:   mean (mean time to failure)

z: number of standard deviations from the mean $\overline{t}$

n: sample size

y: ordinate of normal curve

$P(T \le t)$:   probability that operating time is $T \le t$ (also known as cumulative distribution function (CDF))

Reliability Model

In order to predict reliability when the time to failure is assumed to be normally distributed, the quantity in equation (1.61), called the "normal deviate," must be computed, where t is the operating time and $\overline{t}$ is its mean value.

$$z = \frac{(t - \overline{t})\sqrt{n}}{s} \tag{1.62}$$

Now, the *probability of surviving for $T > t$* (i.e., reliability) $= R(t, z) =$ area under normal curve from t to ∞, corresponding to number of standard deviations from the mean z. Thus, the reliability at time t is predicted using equation (1.62):

$$R(t, z) = 1 - P(T \le t) \tag{1.63}$$

Problem 5

Hardware in a computer system has the following requirements: 1) an expected mean time to failure (MTTF) = $\overline{t} >$ **100000** hours and 2) $a \ge .85$ probability of surviving (i.e., reliability) for $t > 50000$ hours. Does the computer system meet these requirements?

FIGURE 1.13   Normal Probability Plot of Time to Failure _t_ (hours)

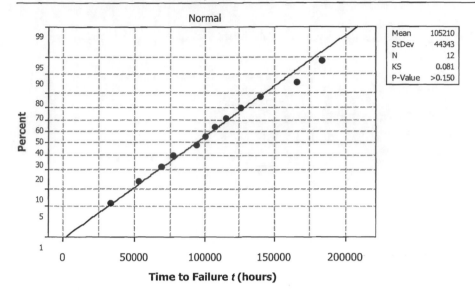

Time to Failure _t_ (hours)

Data Analysis

First, the data below must be subjected to a goodness of fit test to determine whether they fit a normal distribution in order for the appropriate reliability prediction equations to be employed. This is done in Figure 1.13, using Minitab, statistical software, or another statistical package. It can be seen that the data fit very closely to a normal distribution by virtue of the points falling on a straight line.

i	t (hours)
1	33480
2	52920
3	69120
4	77040
5	93600
6	100080
7	106920
8	114840
9	125640
10	139680
11	165600
12	183600

Solution

1. Requirement 1: mean time to failure > 100000 hours. The probability density function in Figure 1.14 shows that this requirement is satisfied. Also, you see that there is small variance because the standard deviation is much less than the mean. This is beneficial because, with small variance, you would have high confidence that the requirement can be met.
2. Requirement 2: .85 probability of surviving (i.e., reliability) for $t > 50000$ hours. Figure 1.15 shows that this requirement is satisfied only if the system is operated for $t < 77040$ hours.

FIGURE 1.14   Probability Density Function of Time to Failure $p(t)$ vs. Time to Failure t

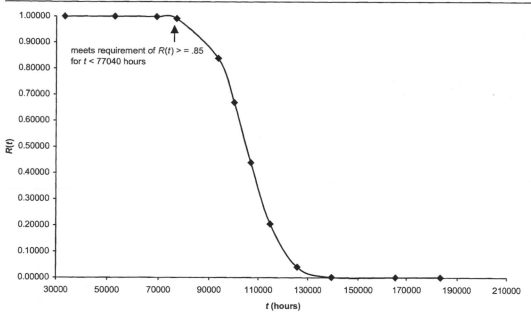

FIGURE 1.15   Reliability $R(t)$ vs. Time to Failure t

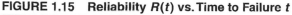

Multiple Component Reliability Analysis

Hardware (and software) components can be operated in serial or hardware configurations. In hardware, the differences are more obvious because of the physical connection between components. In software, the difference is not obvious because there are no physical

FIGURE 1.16   Parallel and Serial Reliability Configurations

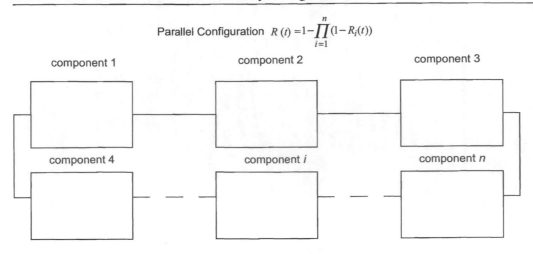

Parallel Configuration $R(t) = 1 - \prod_{i=1}^{n} (1 - R_i(t))$

component 1   component 2   component 3

component 4   component i component n

Parallel Hardware: Components Physically Connected in Parallel
Parallel Software: Components Execute Concurrently in Time

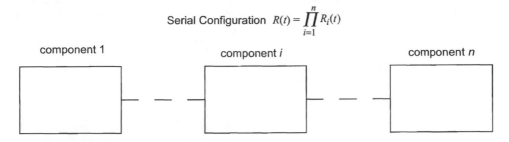

Serial Configuration $R(t) = \prod_{i=1}^{n} R_i(t)$

component 1   component i component n

Serial Hardware: Components Physically Connected in Series
Serial Software: Components Execute Serially in Time

connections. The difference is based on how the components execute, as explained in Figure 1.16.

Parallel and Series Reliability

Parallel System

For components with equal reliabilities, referring to Figure 1.16, the reliability of n components operating in parallel is given by equation (1.64):

$$R(t) = 1 - \prod_{i=1}^{n} (1 - R_i(t)) \qquad \text{[MUS87] (1.64)}$$

Using equation (1.65) and some algebraic manipulation, the reliability of two components operating in parallel is given by:

$$R(t) = [R_1(t) + R_2(t)] - [R_1(t)R_2(t)] = 1 - [(1 - R_1(t))(1 - R_2(t))] \qquad (1.65)$$

If both components have the same reliability, then in equation (1.66):

$$R(t) = 2R(t) - R^2(t) \qquad (1.66)$$

If the failures are exponentially distributed with failure rate λ, then using equation (1.48), obtain the expression for reliability in equation (1.67):

$$R(t) = 2\,e^{-\lambda t} - e^{-2\lambda t} \tag{1.67}$$

Using the definition of MTTF from equation (1.46), the mean time to failure for the parallel arrangement is given by equation (1.68):

$$MTTF = \int_0^\infty R(t)dt = \int_0^\infty (2e^{-\lambda t} - e^{-2\lambda t})dt = \left[\frac{-2e^{-\lambda t}}{\lambda}\right]_0^\infty - \left[\frac{-e^{-2\lambda t}}{2\lambda}\right]_0^\infty = \frac{1.5}{\lambda} \tag{1.68}$$

Series System

Referring to Figure 1.16, the reliability of n components operating in series is given by $R(t)$ in equation (1.69):

$$R(t)\prod_{i=1}^{n} R_i(t) \tag{1.69}$$

Using equation (1.69), the reliability of two components operating in series, with equal reliabilities, is given by equation (1.70), if the failures are exponentially distributed:

$$R(t) = R^2(t) = e^{-2\lambda t} \tag{1.70}$$

Then, the mean time to failure for the series arrangement is given in equation (1.71):

$$MTTF = \int_0^\infty R(t)dt = \int_0^\infty e^{-2\lambda t} = \frac{-\left[e^{2\lambda t}\right]_0^\infty}{2\lambda} = \frac{1}{2\lambda} \tag{1.71}$$

Now, using equations (1.67) and (1.70), the improvement of the parallel system reliability over a series system, for two components, can be shown as RI in equation (1.72):

$$RI = (2e^{-\lambda t} - e^{-2\lambda t}) - e^{-2\lambda t} = 2(e^{-\lambda t} - e^{-2\lambda t}) \tag{1.72}$$

In addition, using equations (1.68) and (1.71), the increase in *mean time to failure* is shown in equation (1.73):

$$\frac{1.5}{\lambda} - \frac{1}{2\lambda} = 1/\lambda \tag{1.73}$$

Differentiating RI equation (1.72) with respect to t, and setting it $= 0$, produces equation (1.74):

$$\frac{d(RI)}{d(t)} = 2(-\lambda)e^{-\lambda t} - 2(-2\lambda)e^{-2\lambda t} = 0 \tag{1.74}$$

If the derivative of equation (1.74) is negative (it depends on the values of t), you then know that RI in equation (1.72) would have a maximum value. To find this maximizing value of t, solve equation (1.74) for t, to yield equation (1.75):

$$t^* = -(1/\lambda)\,(\log(.5)) \tag{1.75}$$

Problem 6

For a computer system with failure rate of $\lambda = 0.001$ failures per hour and *time to failure* listed below, plot equations (1.67), (1.70), and (1.72), versus t, on the same graph and indicate the value of $t = t^*$ that maximizes the improvement in reliability, *RI*, assuming an exponential distribution of *time to failure t*.

t (hours)
100
200
300
400
500
600
700
800
900
1000
1100
1200
1300
1400
1500
1600
1700
1800
1900
2000

Solution

Figure 1.17 contrasts parallel reliability, serial reliability, and the improvement of parallel over serial reliability. The figure also identifies the operating time where the greatest improvement is achieved.

Problem 7

Two computers, A and B, operate in parallel. Each has a reliability of .95. What is the reliability of the parallel system?

Solution

$$R_A = R_B = .95$$

Using equation (1.65), the parallel reliability of computers A and B = $R_{AB}(t) = 1 - [(1 - R_A(t))(1 - R_B(t))] = 1 - [(1 - .95)(1 - .95)] = \mathbf{.9975}$ reliability of the parallel system.

Problem 8

Two computers, A and B, operate in series. Each has a reliability of .95. What is the reliability of the series system? What is the improvement in reliability of the parallel over the series system?

FIGURE 1.17   Reliability $R(t)$ vs. Operating Time t

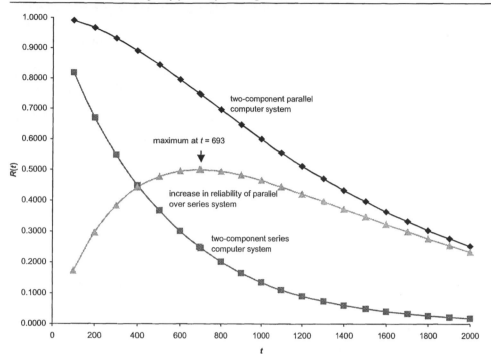

Solution

Using equation (1.69):

Series reliability of computers A and B = $R_{AB}(t) = R_A(t) R_B(t) = 95 \times 95 = .9025 =$ probability of being able to perform the intended operation.

The improvement in reliability of operating the parallel system compared with the serial system = .9975 – .9025 = **.0950.**

Problem 9

How many computers are needed to operate in parallel, if each computer has a reliability of $R(t) = .80$, and it is desired to achieve an overall reliability of $R_n(t) = .98$?

Solution

From equation (1.64), parallel reliability of n computers, each with a reliability of $R(t) =$

$$R_n(t) = 1 - (1 - R(t))^n \tag{1.76}$$

Solving equation (1.76) for n yields:

$$n = \ln (1 - R_n(t)) / \ln (1 - R(t)) =$$
$$n = (\ln (.02) / \ln.20) = -3.912 / -1.609 = 2.43 \text{ computers} = \mathbf{3} \tag{1.77}$$

Computer System Availability and Maintenance

Computer system availability models combine reliability and maintainability metrics into a unifying concept called *availability* that indicates the fraction of scheduled time a system—hardware or software—will be available for customer use, considering downtime due to preventive maintenance, failures, and the repair time necessary to restore the system to normal operation.

This is the definition of *preventive maintenance strategy:* Routine inspection and service activities designed to detect potential failure conditions and make adjustments and repairs that will help prevent major operating problems [MON96].

Two fundamental preventive strategies are differentiated, *time- and condition-based preventive maintenance.* In time-based preventive maintenance, after a fixed period of time, a component is serviced or overhauled, independent of the wear of the component at that moment. In condition-based preventive maintenance, one inspects a condition of a component, according to some schedule. If the condition exceeds a specified critical value, preventive maintenance is performed. With regard to the timing of the inspections, there are two variants, *constant* and *condition-based inspection interval.* If one applies a constant inspection interval, an inspection is performed after a fixed period of time, analogously to the time-based preventive maintenance. When deciding to perform a condition-based inspection interval, the time until the next inspection depends on the condition in the previous inspection. If the condition in the previous inspection was good, the time until the next inspection will be quite long. If the condition in the previous inspection was bad, the time until the next inspection will be quite short.

Predictive maintenance strategy: Predictive maintenance is a condition-based approach to maintenance. The approach is based on predicting equipment condition in order to assess whether equipment will fail during some future period, and then taking action to avoid the consequences of the failures.

A model that you can apply to achieve highly available systems is developed below.

Availability Model

Definitions

t_p: duration of preventive maintenance
t_o: duration of operation
t_f: duration of failure
t_r: duration of repair
f_p: frequency of preventive maintenance
f_o: frequency of operation
f_f: frequency of failure
f_r: frequency of repair
MTTF: mean time to failure
MTTR: mean time to repair

When frequencies are available, equation (1.78) is preferable for computing reliability because it provides greater accuracy than using *MTTF* and *MTTR*. When frequency data are not available, equation (1.79) is used.

$$A = \frac{f_o t_o}{f_o t_o + f_p t_p + f_f t_f + f_r t_r} \tag{1.78}$$

$$A = MTTF/(MTTF + MTTR) \tag{1.79}$$

The frequency approach is portrayed graphically in Figure 1.18.

FIGURE 1.18   Computer Maintenance Process

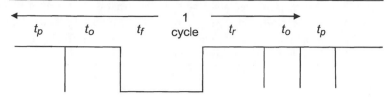

t_p : duration of preventive maintenance

t_o : duration of operation

t_f : duration of failure

t_r : duration of repair

Problem 10

For the following data, compute availability:

Duration of operation: $t_o = 10$
Duration of preventive maintenance: $t_p = 1$
Duration of failure: $t_f = .5$
Duration of repair: $t_r = 2$
Frequency of operation: $f_o = 20$
Frequency of preventive maintenance: $f_p = 20$ (for every operation there is preventive maintenance)
Frequency of failure: $f_f = 4$
Frequency of repair: $f_r = 4$ (for every failure there is a repair)

Solution

Using equation (1.78):

$$A = \frac{f_o t_o}{f_o t_o + f_p t_p + f_f t_f + f_r t_r}$$

$$A = \frac{(20)(10)}{(20)(10) + (20)(1) + (4)(.5) + (4)(2)} = .870$$

Software Availability

Software availability will be demonstrated by computing the *mean time to failure* of software by using the Schneidewind Single Parameter Model (SSPM) [SCH06].

To find the mean time to failure, you use the following equations:

The mean *number* of failures m_i in the interval time i is given in equation (1.80):

$$m_i = e^{-\beta i} \qquad \text{[SCH06] (1.80)}$$

Then solve for the interval i in equation (1.81):

$$i = -(\log (m_i))/\beta \qquad (1.81)$$

To solve for the mean value of i in equation (1.81), integrate it over time intervals, from i to j, and divide by the number of intervals. Using the fact that the integral of $\log(m_i) = m_i \log(m_i) - m_i$, the mean time to m_i failures, from interval i to interval j, is computed using equation (1.81), and recognizing that there are $(j - i + 1)$ time intervals involved in the transition from interval i to interval j, to produce equation (1.82):

$$\bar{i} = \frac{1}{\beta(j-i+1)} \int_i^j \log(m_i)di = \left(\frac{1}{\beta(j-i+1)}\right)[m_i \log(m_i) - m_i]_i^j \qquad (1.82)$$

$$= \left(\frac{1}{\beta(j-i+1)}\right)(m_j \log m_j - m_i \log m_i + (m_i - m_j))$$

Now, using equation (1.82), derive the *mean time to failure* from the first interval = 1 to interval i in equation (1.83):

$$\bar{i} = \left(\frac{1}{\beta i}\right)(m_i \log m_i - m_1 \log m_1 + (m_1 - m_i)) \qquad (1.83)$$

Then compute availability based on the definition: $A = MTTF/(MTTF + MTTR)$ in equation (1.79), producing equation (1.84):

$$A = \bar{i}/(\bar{i}+\bar{t}_r) \qquad (1.84)$$

The $\bar{i}$ for a given A is found from equation (1.84) to produce equation (1.85):

$$\bar{i} = A\,\bar{t}_r/(1-A) \qquad (1.85)$$

Problem 11

Assuming mean repair time $t_r = 2$, compute *MTTF* for given values of A and plot *MTTF* vs. A. Comment on the shape of the plot.

Solution

Figure 1.19 shows that extremely large values of *MTTF* (i.e., $\bar{i}$) would be necessary in order to satisfy high availability requirements.

Fault Tree Analysis

Highly related to reliability is the field of fault tree analysis. Fault tree analysis (FTA) provides a top-level view of reliability and safety, including hardware and software. A hazard to safety is postulated at the top level of the fault tree and the leaves are used to provide a progressive bottom-up trace to the root of the tree to identify those software and hardware faults that could lead to the hazard at the top level. This analysis is very useful for identifying problems at lower levels of the system hierarchy that could lead to a disastrous system fault at the top level.

FTA is a reliability and safety tool that allows the engineer to determine when a hazard exists (i.e., a condition in the software that could result in safety and reliability problems to the extent that personnel and equipment would be at risk). FTA can also be used to evaluate the safety and reliability characteristics of proposed system architectures. That is, if there

FIGURE 1.19   Mean Time to Failure (*MTTF*) Required for Given Availability (*A*) vs. *A*

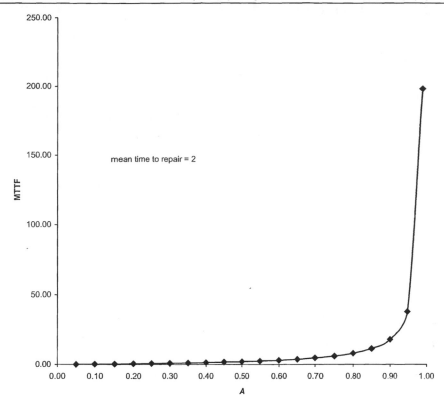

are safety and reliability flaws in the proposed architectures, they can be identified at an early stage in the system development process.

The characteristics, benefits, and capabilities of FTA are the following [SAN]:

Fault tree analysis is a logical, structured process that can help identify potential causes of system failure before the failures actually occur.

Benefits:

- Identify possible system reliability or safety problems at design time,
- Assess system reliability or safety during operation,
- Improve understanding of the system,
- Identify components that may need more testing and rigorous quality assurance scrutiny, and
- Identify root causes of equipment and software failures.

FTA is used at the system, hardware, and software levels to identify hazards by constructing a fault tree and analyzing from the bottom up whether a fault has been introduced at a leaf node and propagated all the way to the root.

Definitions

P_s: probability of *safe state* = probability at root of fault tree of combined n, m events, each with reliability $R \geq$ threshold probability:

$$P_s = [P(x)R^n, P(y)R^m] \geq P_t, \text{ where } P_t \text{ is a threshold probability}$$
that the probability of safe state must equal or exceed.

P_u: probability of *unsafe state* = probability at root of fault tree of combined events, with reliability R < threshold probability:

$$P_u = [P(x)R^n, P(y)R^n] < P_t$$

Fault Tree Model

Reliability

Serial reliability of n events (*assumed equal for all events; equally likely to have a fault associated with any of the events*) is computed in equation (1.86):

$$R_s = R^n \tag{1.86}$$

Using equation (1.86), the unreliability is computed in equation (1.87):

$$UR_s = 1 - (1 - R)^n \tag{1.87}$$

Probability of Events

Probability of events x *and* y:

$$P(x*y) = P(x)P(y) \tag{1.88}$$

Probability of event x *or* event y but not *both* x and y:

$$P(x + y) = P(x) + P(y) - P(x*y) \; (Exclusive\ OR) \tag{1.89}$$

Probability of event x *or* event y:

$$P(x + y) = [P(x) + P(y)] \; (Inclusive\ OR) \tag{1.90}$$

Probability of events x *and* y, each with equal serial reliability R:

$$P(x*y) = [(P(x))(P(y))]R^n \tag{1.91}$$

Probability of event x *o*r event y but not both x and y, each with equal serial reliability R of n events:

$$P(x + y) = [((P(x) + P(y))]R - [(P(x))(P(y))]R^n \; (Exclusive\ OR) \tag{1.92}$$

Probability of event x *o*r event y, each with equal serial reliability R of n events:

$$P(x + y) = [((P(x) + P(y))]R^n \; (Inclusive\ OR) \tag{1.93}$$

Problem 12

This is a problem in analyzing software reliability using FTA where several programs are executed concurrently. Word, Excel, and Minitab execute concurrently and Word and PowerPoint execute concurrently. Using the data below, construct the fault tree and determine whether it is possible to reach the safe state and with what probability. Compute all the quantities needed to make this determination. Assume a fault is introduced into the *Word* program.

Events

    w: Program *Word* executing
    p: Program *PowerPoint p* executing
    m: Program *Minitab* executing
    e: Program *Excel* executing

Probabilities

Probability of *Word* executing: $P(w) = .9$
Probability of *PowerPoint* executing: $P(p) = .8$
Probability of *Excel* executing: $P(e) = .5$
Probability of *Minitab* executing: $P(m) = .1$
The reliability of each of the four programs executing correctly $= R = .99$

$$P_t = \text{Threshold probability of safe state} = .90$$

Solution

Event Probabilities

$$P(w)R = .9 * .99 = \textbf{.8910} \quad \text{Probability of } \textit{Word} \text{ executing with reliability } .99 \qquad (1.94)$$

$$P(p)R = .8 * 99 = \textbf{.7920} \quad \text{Probability of } \textit{PowerPoint} \text{ executing with reliability } .99 \qquad (1.95)$$

$$P(m)R = .1 * .99 = \textbf{.0990} \quad \text{Probability of } \textit{Minitab} \text{ executing with reliability } .99 \qquad (1.96)$$

$$P(e)R = .5 * .99 = \textbf{.4950} \quad \text{Probability of } \textit{Excel} \text{ executing with reliability } .99 \qquad (1.97)$$

From equation (1.88): Probability of events x and y: $P(x*y) = P(x)P(y)$: $\qquad (1.98)$

$$P(w*m*e) = .9 * .1 * .5 = \textbf{.0450}:$$
Probability of *Word, Minitab,* and *Excel* executing concurrently $\qquad (1.99)$

$$P(w*p) = .9 * .8 = \textbf{.7200}:$$
Probability of *Word* and *PowerPoint* executing concurrently $\qquad (1.100)$

Using equations (1.99) and (1.100), compute probabilities of concurrent program operation in equations (1.101) and (1.102):

$$P(w*m*e)R^3 = .0450 * (.99)^3 = \textbf{.0437}:$$
Probability of *Word, Minitab,* and *Excel* executing concurrently,
each with reliability .99. $\qquad (1.101)$

$$P(w*p)R^2 = .7200 * (.99)^2 = \textbf{.7057}:$$
Probability of *Word* and *PowerPoint* executing concurrently,
each with reliability .99. $\qquad (1.102)$

Now compute the combined probability of concurrent program execution on the left side of Figure 1.20. From equations (1.99) and (1.100):

$$P(w*m*e) + P(w*p) = .0450 + .7200 = \textbf{.7650} \qquad (1.103)$$

Then, compute the combined probability of concurrent program execution, as shown in Figure 1.20, using equations (1.99) and (1.102):

$$P(w*m*e)R^3 + P(w*p)R^2 = .0437 + .7057 = \textbf{.7494} \qquad (1.104)$$

Equation (1.104) is probability at root of the fault tree of combined events. This probability is less than the threshold $P_t = .90$.

FIGURE 1.20   Fault Tree Analysis

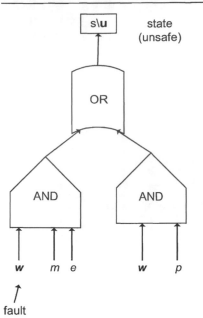

fault

Events: programs Word (*w*), PowerPoint (*p*), Minitab (*m*), and Excel (*e*) operating concurrently

Program events: $w*m*e + w*p$

Interpretation

The software system fails to meet the threshold of .90 for a safe state at the root. Therefore, you must have a higher R for each program and/or eliminate concurrent multitasking to make operation acceptable. The combination of concurrent multitasking and low reliability of combined events ($w*m*e + w*p$) dooms the process to wind up in the *unsafe* state (i.e., as Figure 1.20 shows, there is a fault in the operation of the *Word* program that propagates up the fault tree leading to an unsafe state).

Problem for Reader Solution: Solve the above problem to achieve the safe-state goal.

Confidence Intervals Model

Another tool to support reliability analysis is the *Confidence Intervals Model.* It is needed because the engineer should not depend on point estimates (e.g., mean values) to estimate reliability characteristics. Rather, the engineers should include confidence intervals in their models to account for the likelihood that the true values of their predictions will not equal the point values. Therefore, the engineer computes confidence intervals to represent the probability that the true value will fall within the intervals. Note that the use of confidence intervals assumes that reliabilities are normally distributed. This restriction can be relaxed if the sample size ≥ 30.

Definitions

R_i: reliability of computer part i

$\overline{R}$: mean reliability of computer parts

α: probability that R_i will lie outside confidence intervals

$Z_{1-\alpha/2}$: number of standard deviations at confidence level $1 - (\alpha/2)$

S: standard deviation

N: sample size

Equations

The confidence intervals for R_i are developed in equation (1.105):

$$\overline{R} - \left(Z_{1-\alpha/2} * S\right) \le R_i \le \overline{R} + \left(Z_{1-\alpha/2} * S\right) \tag{1.105}$$

and the standard deviation needed to compute (1.105) is computed in equation (1.106):

$$S = \sqrt{\sum_{i=1}^{N} \frac{(R_i - R_i)^2}{N-1}} \tag{1.106}$$

Problem 13

It is not necessary for reliability to be expressed as a probability; it can be expressed as time to failure. Computer laptop parts have *time to failure reliabilities* R_i, in hours, as follows:

$R_i =$
7.2
6.8
7.5
7.2
7.3
6.9
7.1

sample size $N = 7$.

What are the 97.5% and 2.50 confidence intervals of the reliability?

Solution

Mean reliability = $\overline{R}_i$ = (7.2 + 6.8 + 7.5 + 7.2 + 7.3 + 6.9 + 7.1) / 7 = 7.14 hours

$\alpha = .05$ = probability that R_i will lie outside confidence intervals

Obtain $Z_{1-\alpha/2}$ from the following normal distribution table.

	0.00	0.01	0.02	0.03	0.04	0.05	0.06	0.07	0.08	0.09
0.0	0.0000	0.0040	0.0080	0.0120	0.0160	0.0199	0.0239	0.0279	0.0319	0.0359
0.1	0.0398	0.0438	0.0478	0.0517	0.0557	0.0596	0.0636	0.0675	0.0714	0.0753
0.2	0.0793	0.0832	0.0871	0.0910	0.0948	0.0987	0.1026	0.1064	0.1103	0.1141
0.3	0.1179	0.1217	0.1255	0.1293	0.1331	0.1368	0.1406	0.1443	0.1480	0.1517
0.4	0.1554	0.1591	0.1628	0.1664	0.1700	0.1736	0.1772	0.1808	0.1844	0.1879
0.5	0.1915	0.1950	0.1985	0.2019	0.2054	0.2088	0.2123	0.2157	0.2190	0.2224
0.6	0.2257	0.2291	0.2324	0.2357	0.2389	0.2422	0.2454	0.2486	0.2517	0.2549
0.7	0.2580	0.2611	0.2642	0.2673	0.2704	0.2734	0.2764	0.2794	0.2823	0.2852
0.8	0.2881	0.2910	0.2939	0.2967	0.2995	0.3023	0.3051	0.3078	0.3106	0.3133
0.9	0.3159	0.3186	0.3212	0.3238	0.3264	0.3289	0.3315	0.3340	0.3365	0.3389
1.0	0.3413	0.3438	0.3461	0.3485	0.3508	0.3531	0.3554	0.3577	0.3599	0.3621
1.1	0.3643	0.3665	0.3686	0.3708	0.3729	0.3749	0.3770	0.3790	0.3810	0.3830
1.2	0.3849	0.3869	0.3888	0.3907	0.3925	0.3944	0.3962	0.3980	0.3997	0.4015
1.3	0.4032	0.4049	0.4066	0.4082	0.4099	0.4115	0.4131	0.4147	0.4162	0.4177
1.4	0.4192	0.4207	0.4222	0.4236	0.4251	0.4265	0.4279	0.4292	0.4306	0.4319
1.5	0.4332	0.4345	0.4357	0.4370	0.4382	0.4394	0.4406	0.4418	0.4429	0.4441
1.6	0.4452	0.4463	0.4474	0.4484	0.4495	0.4505	0.4515	0.4525	0.4535	0.4545
1.7	0.4554	0.4564	0.4573	0.4582	0.4591	0.4599	0.4608	0.4616	0.4625	0.4633
1.8	0.4641	0.4649	0.4656	0.4664	0.4671	0.4678	0.4686	0.4693	0.4699	0.4706
1.9	0.4713	0.4719	0.4726	0.4732	0.4738	0.4744	0.4750	0.4756	0.4761	0.4767
2.0	0.4772	0.4778	0.4783	0.4788	0.4793	0.4798	0.4803	0.4808	0.4812	0.4817
2.1	0.4821	0.4826	0.4830	0.4834	0.4838	0.4842	0.4846	0.4850	0.4854	0.4857
2.2	0.4861	0.4864	0.4868	0.4871	0.4875	0.4878	0.4881	0.4884	0.4887	0.4890
2.3	0.4893	0.4896	0.4898	0.4901	0.4904	0.4906	0.4909	0.4911	0.4913	0.4916
2.4	0.4918	0.4920	0.4922	0.4925	0.4927	0.4929	0.4931	0.4932	0.4934	0.4936
2.5	0.4938	0.4940	0.4941	0.4943	0.4945	0.4946	0.4948	0.4949	0.4951	0.4952
2.6	0.4953	0.4955	0.4956	0.4957	0.4959	0.4960	0.4961	0.4962	0.4963	0.4964
2.7	0.4965	0.4966	0.4967	0.4968	0.4969	0.4970	0.4971	0.4972	0.4973	0.4974
2.8	0.4974	0.4975	0.4976	0.4977	0.4977	0.4978	0.4979	0.4979	0.4980	0.4981
2.9	0.4981	0.4982	0.4982	0.4983	0.4984	0.4984	0.4985	0.4985	0.4986	0.4986
3.0	0.4987	0.4987	0.4987	0.4988	0.4988	0.4989	0.4989	0.4989	0.4990	0.4990

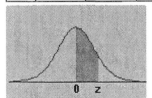

Z table: The table gives the area between 0 and Z. For the area between Z and ∞, use (1 − area between 0 and Z). For example, to compute $Z_{\alpha/2}$ for $\alpha/2 = .025$, find the value of Z for area = .5000 − .0250 = **.4750**, $Z_{1-\alpha/2} = 1.96 =$ at $\alpha/2$.

Using equation (1.106), compute the standard deviation S:

$$S = \sqrt{\sum_{i=1}^{7} \frac{(R_i - 7.1)^2}{6}}$$

$$= 0.2370$$

TABLE 1.11   Laptop Confidence Interval Calculations

i	R_i	$\left(R_i - \bar{R}_i\right)^2$	$\bar{R}_i - \left(Z_\alpha * S\right)$	$\bar{R}_i + \left(Z_{1-\alpha} * S\right)$
1	7.2	0.0033	6.68	7.61
2	6.8	0.1176	6.68	7.61
3	7.5	0.1276	6.68	7.61
4	7.2	0.0033	6.68	7.61
5	7.3	0.0247	6.68	7.61
6	6.9	0.0590	6.68	7.61
7	7.1	0.0018	6.68	7.61
	7.14	0.3371		
$\boxed{\bar{R}_i}$		sum		

$$Z_{1-\alpha} = Z_{.975} = 1.96$$

S	0.2370		$\alpha = .025$	$Z_\alpha = Z_{.025} = -1.96$

FIGURE 1.21   Probability Plot of R_i (time to failure in hours)

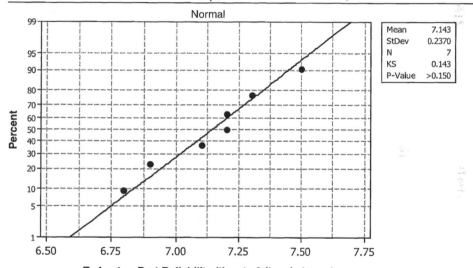

R_i: Laptop Part Reliability (time to failure in hours)

Using equation (1.105) compute the confidence intervals. The details of the calculations are shown in the Table 1.11. From the data in the table, determine whether the data are normally distributed by using Minitab to develop the normality test in Figure 1.21. Since the data lie on a straight line, you can conclude that they are normally distributed, and, hence, the confidence intervals computation is valid.

Interpretation

Looking at Figure 1.22, you can see that the laptop manufacturing system is in statistical control because the confidence intervals encompass the data. Note that the lower confidence interval is not meaningful *in this case* due to the negative values.

FIGURE 1.22   Confidence Intervals for Time to Failure R_i vs. Part Number i

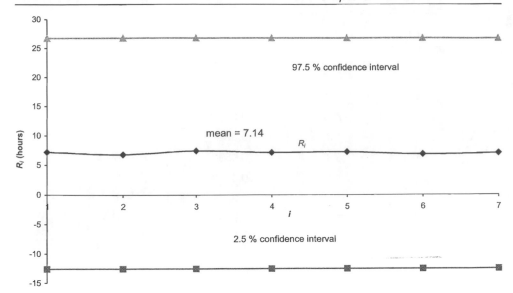

Summary

First, the fundamentals of probability and statistics were provided in order to equip the engineer with the quantitative tools necessary to support practical application of reliability analysis. Included in these tools are various probability distributions, such as the normal, Poisson, exponential, binomial, and Weibull. The normal distribution does not have much applicability to reliability processes because it is a symmetrical distribution, and few reliability phenomena are symmetrically distributed. However, an important exception is the case of a sufficiently large sample. The Poisson and exponential are intimately related in that while the former models failure counts in a time interval, the latter models *time to failure* or the *time between failures*. The binomial distribution is useful when the application involves estimating the probability of a given number of failures in a random sample drawn from a population of items, such as manufactured computer parts. You learned that the Weibull distribution is very flexible due to its property of two parameters—shape and scale—that allow it to be applied to a myriad of reliability problems—both hardware and software.

Additionally, you learned that probability distributions, such as the exponential, can be used to advantage to compute the reliability of parallel and serial hardware or software configurations, and how redundant (i.e., parallel) configurations can improve system reliability.

Probability distributions have wide applicability to reliability problems. However, used in isolation, they cannot readily portray a situation in which hardware and software components interact at various levels of a system. To address this problem, you learned that probability analysis integrated with fault tree modeling provides a powerful tool for solving multi-component, multi-level problems.

Finally, you saw that in many cases of reliability analysis it is important to compute the confidence intervals of reliability because a single estimate of reliability, such as the mean time to failure, may not be an accurate measure of reliability.

References

[LEV01] David M. Levine, Patricia P. Ramsey, and Robert K. Smidt, *Applied Statistics for Engineers and Scientists.* Prentice Hall, 2001.

[LLO62] David K. Lloyd, and Myron Lipow, *Reliability: Management, Methods, and Mathematics.* Prentice Hall, 1962.

[LYU96] Michael R. Lyu, editor, *Handbook of Software Reliability Engineering.* IEEE Computer Society Press and McGraw-Hill, 1996, page 93.

[MON96] Joseph G. Monks, *Operations Management,* Second Edition. McGraw-Hill, 1996.

[MUS87] John D. Musa, Anthony Iannino, and Kazuhira Okumoto, *Software Reliability: Measurement, Prediction, Application.* McGraw-Hill, 1987.

[SAN] Sandia National Laboratories, New Mexico, USA.

[SCH06] Norman F. Schneidewind, "A New Software Reliability Model." *The R & M Engineering Journal, American Society for Quality,* September 2006, Volume 26, Number 3, pp. 6–22.

2

Overview of Software Reliability Engineering

Objectives

The objectives of this chapter are to provide an introduction to Software Reliability Engineering (SRE) for the practitioner and researcher who are unfamiliar with this field. The purpose is to present a realistic appraisal of the state of the practice, giving both the advantages and limitations of this important field. The relationship between SRE and the application of computer-intensive standards is discussed. This chapter builds on the background provided in Chapter 1 on probability and statistics and reliability fundamentals.

What You Will Learn From This Chapter

The audience for this chapter is the technically literate practitioner, researcher, or student who is new to the field of software reliability. In this chapter, you will obtain a brief historical perspective of the development of the field of software reliability. This review is not intended to be exhaustive, but it will identify important issues in the field to provide you with the background for understanding why and how the field evolved from its origin to its present state. In addition, fundamentals of software reliability, modeling, and prediction will be covered. Finally, a case study of the application of Software Reliability Engineering to the NASA Space Shuttle is presented to show how the principles of SRE presented in this chapter are applied.

Subjects

Scope of Software Reliability Problem
What Is Software Reliability Engineering?
Principles of Software Reliability Engineering
Software Reliability Modeling
Software Reliability Applications
Software Reliability Data and Failure Scenarios
Interpreting Software Reliability Predictions
Failure Mode Effects Analysis
Bayesian Analysis

Scope of Software Reliability Problem

The size and complexity of computer-intensive systems have grown dramatically, and the trend will certainly continue in the future. Contemporary examples of highly complex hardware/software systems can be found in projects undertaken by **NASA,** the **Department of**

Defense, the Federal Aviation Administration, the telecommunications industry, and a variety of other private industries [LYU96]. For instance, the NASA Space Shuttle flies with approximately 500,000 lines of software code on board and approximately 3.5 million lines of code in ground control and processing. After being scaled down significantly from its original plan, the International Space Station Alpha has millions of lines of software to operate innumerable hardware pieces for its navigation, communication, and experimentation. In the telecommunications industry, operations for phone carriers are supported by hundreds of software systems, with hundreds of millions of lines of source code. In the avionics industry, almost all new payload instruments contain their own microprocessor system with extensive embedded software. A massive amount of hardware and complicated software also exists in the Federal Aviation Administration's Advanced Automation System, the new-generation air traffic control system. In our offices and homes, many personal computers cannot function without operating systems (e.g., Windows) ranging up to 28 million lines of code, and many other shrink-wrapped software packages of similar size provide our daily use of these computers in a variety of applications.

Within the computer revolution, achievement has been unbalanced: software continues to share a larger burden with less progress. It is the integrating potential of software that has allowed designers to contemplate more ambitious systems encompassing a broader and more multidisciplinary scope, and it is the growth in utilization of software components that is largely responsible for the high overall complexity of many system designs. However, in stark contrast with the rapid advancement of hardware technology, proper development of software technology has failed miserably to keep pace in all measures, including quality, productivity, cost, and performance. When we entered the last decade of the twentieth century, computer software had already become the major source of reported outages in many systems. Consequently, recent literature is replete with horror stories of projects gone awry, generally as a result of problems traced to software.

Software failures caught the media spotlight in several major programs. In the NASA Voyager project, the Uranus encounter was in jeopardy because of late software deliveries and reduced capability in the Deep Space Network. Several Space Shuttle missions have been delayed due to hardware/software interaction problems. In one DoD project, software problems caused the first flight of the AFTI/F-16 jet fighter to be delayed over a year, and none of the advanced modes originally planned could be used. Critical software failures have also affected numerous civil and scientific applications. The ozone hole over Antarctica would have received attention sooner from the scientific community if a data analysis program had not suppressed the anomalous data because it was "out of range." Software glitches in an automated baggage-handling system forced Denver International Airport to sit empty more than a year after airplanes were to fill its gates and runways. The Hong Kong Airport experienced a similar problem. A mysterious software fault in the new guidance computer of the Soyuz TMA-1 spacecraft was the cause of the high-anxiety off-course landing [NAS02].

Unfortunately, software can also kill people. The massive Therac-25 radiation therapy machine had enjoyed a perfect safety record until software errors in its sophisticated control systems malfunctioned and claimed several patients' lives in 1985 and 1986. On October 26, 1992, the Computer Aided Dispatch System of the London Ambulance Service broke down right after its installation, paralyzing the capability of the world's largest ambulance service to handle 5000 daily requests in carrying patients in emergency situations. In the recent aviation industry, although the real causes for several airliner crashes in the past few years remained mysteries, experts pointed out that software control could be the chief suspect in some of these incidents due to its inappropriate response to the pilots' desperate inquires during abnormal flight conditions.

Software Errors Cost Billions

Software glitches cost the U.S. economy $59.5 billion each year, according to a study by the U.S. Department of Commerce's National Institute of Standards and Technology [REU02]. The study, conducted by the Research Triangle Institute in North Carolina, found that software users are responsible for about 50 percent of the problems, and vendors and developers contribute the rest. However, the study also found that improved testing could reduce the bugs and remove $22.2 billion of the cost; and although nearly 80 percent of software development goes to locating and fixing defects, very few other products ship with these high error percentages of defects. The National Academy of Sciences issued a report describing how lawmakers must pass legislation to hold software vendors liable for security breaches. However, making vendors liable would dramatically raise the cost of their products. Europe had already begun addressing this issue when a Dutch judge convicted the Exact Holding organization of selling software with bugs, denying its claim that early versions of software are generally plagued with problems.

What Is Software Reliability Engineering?

Software Reliability Engineering (SRE) is an established discipline that can help organizations improve the reliability of their products and processes. The IEEE/AIAA Recommended Practice on Software Reliability [IEE08] defines SRE as "the application of statistical techniques to data collected during system development and operation to specify, predict, estimate, and assess the reliability of software-based systems." It is important for an organization to have a disciplined process if it is to produce high-reliability software. The life-cycle approach to SRE that takes into account the risk to reliability of requirements changes. A requirements change may induce ambiguity and uncertainty in the development process that cause errors in implementing the changes. Subsequently, these errors propagate through later phases of development and maintenance. These errors may result in significant risks associated with implementing the requirements. For example, reliability risk (i.e., risk of faults and failures induced by changes in requirements) may be incurred by deficiencies in the process (e.g., lack of precision in requirements). Figure 2.1 shows the overall SRE process.

Software is a complex intellectual product. Inevitably, some errors are made during requirements formulation as well as during designing, coding, and testing the product. The development process for high-quality software includes measures that are intended to discover and correct faults resulting from these errors, including reviews, audits, screening

FIGURE 2.1   Software Reliability Engineering Process

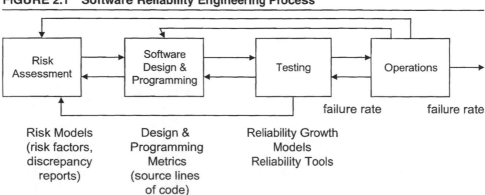

by language-dependent tools, and several levels of test. Managing these errors involves describing, classifying, and modeling the effects of the remaining faults in the delivered product, thereby helping to reduce their number and criticality.

Dealing with faults costs money. It also impacts development schedules and system performance (through increased use of computer resources such as memory, CPU time, and peripherals requirements). As is usually recognized, there can be too much as well as too little effort spent dealing with faults. Thus the engineer (along with management) can use reliability estimation and prediction to understand the current status of the system, forecast future reliability, and make cost-reliability tradeoff decisions.

History of Software Reliability Engineering

The origin of software reliability engineering can be traced to the early 1970s. Some early endeavors to quantify software reliability appeared in [FRE72]. At that time, Software Reliability Engineering (SRE) emerged in the form of proposed software reliability models that predicted the reliability of the software during test and operation. These models were discounted in many quarters because some software engineers declared that software could not fail. At that time, the concept of software reliability was met with derision in some quarters because some hardware engineers claimed that software does not fail like hardware—it does not wear out. As strange as it may seem today, with the common user experience of frequent personal computer crashes due to software defects, many engineers in the early 1970s assumed that the reliability of software was 100%! Another reason for ignoring the reliability of software was that some software developers, who knew their software could fail, did not want to admit it for fear this revelation would bring discredit to their products. Thus, the field of software reliability got underway in an aura of skepticism. This was unfortunate because there have been serious software reliability problems in a variety of applications [SHO83]. Fortunately, for the benefit of the software-using community, SRE is a discipline that is maturing as more organizations see the need to develop standard reliability practices. The IEEE/AIAA defines SRE as "the application of statistical techniques to data collected during system development and operation to specify, predict, estimate, and assess the reliability of software-based systems." The recommended practice is a composite of models, tools, and databases and describes the "what and how" of software reliability engineering (SRE) [IEE08].

An important benefit of using SRE is that it captures the *dynamic* behavior of software in *execution* during the test and operations phases, as opposed to *static* metrics of size and complexity of the software that can be obtained during the design and coding phases. However, an advantage of the static metrics, which are *surrogate* predictors of reliability, is that they can be obtained early in the life cycle when the cost of problem correction is low. Thus, there is a tradeoff between early but less accurate predictions, using static metrics models, and late but more accurate predictions, using reliability models [SCH02]. See *Chapter 6: Software Reliability Metrics* for the details of applying metrics as predictors of reliability.

Principles of Software Reliability Engineering

The following are some principles of SRE [SAN]:

> Reliability should be *designed and built into products* at the *earliest possible stages* of product development. As most of a product's life cycle cost has been locked in by the time its design is complete, designing for reliability is the most economically sound

FIGURE 2.2   Comparison of Predicted versus Observed MTBF

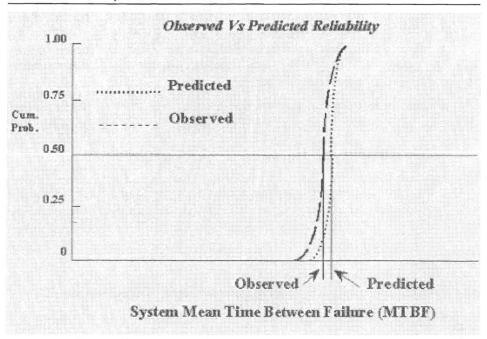

approach to take. Figure 2.2 compares observed with predicted Mean Time Between Failures (MTBF). The observed MTBF is achieved at a probability of .50, whereas the predicted MTBF is achieved at a probability of .90. This is a significant difference. This result indicates that the prediction is optimistic and should be investigated for the cause of the optimism (e.g., the prediction model does not provide sufficient accuracy).

Reliability Allocation

Reliability allocation is the process of specifying a level of reliability for each subsystem or module in a system in order to achieve the system reliability objective. This process should be performed early in the design cycle to guide engineers in choosing components, materials, and a design topology that will meet system objectives.

Software Reliability Modeling

The following are definitions [IEE90] applicable to software reliability modeling:

Failure—The inability of a system or system component to perform a required function within specified limits. A failure may be produced when a fault is encountered and a loss of the expected service to the user results.

Fault—A defect in the code that can be the cause of one or more failures.

Software Reliability—The probability that software will not cause the failure of a system for a specified time under specified conditions. The probability is a function of the inputs to and use of the system, as well as a function of the existence of faults in the software. The inputs to the system determine whether existing faults, if any, are encountered.

Software Reliability Estimation—The application of statistical techniques to observed failure data collected during system testing for the purpose of estimating reliability model parameters.

Software Reliability Model—A mathematical expression that specifies the general form of the software failure process as a function of factors such as fault introduction, fault removal, and the operational environment.

Software Reliability Prediction—A forecast of the reliability of the software based on parameters associated with the software product and its development environment.

Relationship with Hardware Reliability Models

Software reliability models are not based on hardware concepts. For example, hardware reliability models have a constant failure rate during operation (e.g., homogeneous Poisson process). In contrast, software reliability models have a decreasing failure rate trend (e.g., non-homogeneous process), indicating reliability growth (i.e., reliability improves over time). There can be exceptions to the trend when there are major changes in requirements or design.

Software Reliability Prediction Model Advantages and Limitations

The premise of most software reliability prediction models is that the failure rate is a direct function of the number of faults in the program and that the failure rate will be reduced (reliability will be increased) as faults are detected and eliminated during test or operations [IEE08]. This premise is reasonable for the typical test environment and it has been shown to give credible results when correctly applied. However, the results of prediction models will be adversely affected by:

- Change in failure criteria: the definition of what constitutes a failure changes
- Significant changes in the code under test: no longer dealing with the same software for modeling purposes
- Significant changes in the computing environment: changes in operating system, input load, output requirements, and user expectations

The problems posed by the above changes can be mitigated by applying Bayesian Analysis and the principles of conditional probability (see Problem 2 on page 61).

One solution is to reestimate reliability model parameters. Until this can be done, the effectiveness of the model will be impaired. Estimation of new parameters depends on the measurement of several execution time intervals between failures or failure counts in intervals. Another solution is to compute confidence intervals for the predictions rather than relying on the mean or expected value of the predictions that reliability models produce [FAR83]. Doing this protects the engineer from relying on a single point value, which could be way off the mark with respect to the actual reliability.

Major changes can occur with respect to several of the above factors when software becomes operational [IEE00]. In the operational environment, the failure rate is a function of the fault content of the program, of the variability of input and computer states, and of software maintenance policies. Software in the operational environment may not exhibit the reduction in failure rate with execution time that is an implicit assumption in most prediction models. Thus, the prediction of operational reliability from data obtained during test may not hold true during operations. To mitigate this problem, use an operational profile, for driving tests, that is representative of the operational environment. The operational profile characterizes in quantitative fashion how the software will be used. It lists all operations implemented by the software and the probability of occurrence and criticality of each operation [IEE08].

Another limitation of software reliability prediction models is their use for verifying ultra-high requirements [IEE08]. For example, if a program executes successfully for x hours, there is maybe a 0.5 probability that it will survive the next x hours without failing. Thus, to have the kind of confidence needed to verify a probability of failure of 10^{-9} requirement would require that the software execute failure-free for several billion hours. Clearly, even if the software could achieve such reliability, one could never assure that the requirement was met! The most reasonable verifiable requirement is in the 10^{-3} or 10^{-4} range. Although it is obviously infeasible to operate the software for a billion hours, the problem can be mitigated by running the software under a very heavy load for an extended period of time.

It is important to understand the nature of the program when discussing ultra-high requirements. Many ultra-reliable applications are implemented on relatively small, slow, inexpensive computers. Furthermore, the critical programs are small (less than 1000 source lines of code) and execute infrequently during an actual mission. With this knowledge, it may be feasible to test the critical program segment on several faster machines, running in parallel, considerably reducing the required test time.

Software Reliability Model Data Requirements

Software reliability models can both assess and predict reliability. The former deals with measuring past and current reliability. The latter provides forecasts of future reliability.

Both assessment and prediction need good data if they are to yield good forecasts. Good data imply accuracy (data are accurately recorded at the time the events occurred) and relevance (data relate to an environment that is equivalent to the environment for which the forecast is to be valid). However, you should not conclude that data have no value if they are incomplete. These reports may contain information about high severity faults. An example where the principle of relevance is violated is the use of data from early test runs, using an uncontrolled workload, to forecast the reliability of software during a later test, executed under a highly controlled workload.

Software Reliability Model Structure

This section describes the organization of software reliability models and important considerations in their application.

Classification

Software reliability models are classified as either failures per time interval or time between failures. This classification corresponds to the way failure data are input to the model. This classification can be misleading because both types of models provide failure count and time to failure predictions. The format of the input data is the only thing that differs between the two types of models. Time between failures is straightforward: just observe the sequence of time between failures. Failures per time interval can be ambiguous because a time interval for counting failures must be selected. However, experience indicates that prediction accuracy is not sensitive to interval length. In fact, using a variable length interval can provide good accuracy. A more important consideration is the quantity of data to use for assessing prediction validity. That is, you use a subset of the data to estimate model parameters and then use the model to predict in the range of the remaining data. Predictions are compared with the actual failure data to assess prediction accuracy. Experience suggests that a subset of two-thirds of the failure data is sufficient.

Components

Typically, models consist of two components: parameter estimation and prediction. Parameter estimation takes as input either failure counts in time intervals or time between failures and produces estimates of parameters related to failure rate or failure intensity, where failure rate is defined as the ratio of the number of failures of a given category to a given unit of measure [IEE90] and failure intensity is defined as the rate of change of the mean value of failures per unit time [MUS04]. Once the model has been fitted with its parameters, predictions can be made of the future reliability of the software. Although achieving a good model fit is important, you should note that it does not guarantee accurate predictions. A model's accuracy can be validated only by comparing its predictions with the actual *future* reliability of the software. However, it is important to obtain a good fit with historical data in order to obtain accurate model parameter estimates (e.g., accurate estimates of failure rate parameters).

Assumptions

Typical assumptions of models are the following [IEE08]:

- The number of failures detected in one interval is independent of the failure count in another.
- Only "new" failures are counted (i.e., failures that are repeated as a consequence of not correcting a fault are not counted).
- The fault correction rate is proportional to the number of faults to be corrected.
- The mean number of detected failures decreases from one interval to the next.
- The rate of failure detection is proportional to the number of faults in the program at the time of test.

Although these assumptions may appear to limit the applicability of the models, experience has shown the models provide sufficient prediction accuracy.

Limitations

Typical limitations of software reliability models are the following [IEE08]:

- They do not account for the possibility that the failures in different intervals may be related.
- They do not account for repetition of failures (i.e., failures that are repeated as a consequence of not correcting a fault).
- They do not account for the possibility that failures can increase over time as the result of software modifications.

These limitations can be ameliorated by configuring the software for reliability prediction purposes into the original version and succeeding versions that consist of carryovers from previous versions and new software. Reliability predictions are made for the original version and the new software in each succeeding version [KEL97].

Model Outputs

Typical model prediction equations are the following, where the number of intervals *t* can be test or operational time, and *time* can be measured as *CPU time, elapsed time,* or *calendar time* (see the next section, "Variables," for an elaboration of the variable *time*):

1. Cumulative Failures: *failure count in the range* $[1, t]$
2. Failures in an Interval Range: *failure count in the range* $[t_1, t_2]$
3. Maximum Failure (over the life of the software): *failure count in the range* $[1, \infty]$
4. Remaining Failures: *number of failures remaining in the range* $[t, \infty]$
5. Fraction Remaining Failures: *Remaining Failures / Maximum Failures*
6. Total Test Time to Achieve Specified Remaining Failures: *total time from the start of test required to achieve a specified number of remaining failures*
7. Time(s) to Next Failure(s): *time for the next n (one or more) failures to occur, when the current time is t*
8. Number of Faults Corrected: *number of faults corrected at the end of the fault correction activity*
9. Fault Correction Time: *time required to correct number of faults*
10. Remaining Faults: *number of faults remaining at the end of the fault correction activity*
11. Reliability Risk: *risk associated with not attaining the required remaining failures and time to next failure goals*

Variables

The most important variable in reliability models is *time*. The reason for this is that software reliability models are probability models that are based on the probability of the occurrence of failures after the passage of time from a given instant in time—usually the time when the last observed failure occurred. *Time* can assume one of several forms, depending on the reliability objectives and the data that are available. In decreasing order of preference, *time* can be CPU time, elapsed time (i.e., wall clock time), or calendar time. CPU time provides the most resolution, but in many applications, only calendar time is available. However, too much resolution can be a problem in some applications because the volume of data generated could be unmanageable and difficult to interpret (e.g., hundreds of failures recorded with one second resolution). *Time* is related to the other important variable—failure count—as either time between failures or failure count per time interval.

Parameters

Model parameters are the constants of reliability prediction equations that are estimated by maximum likelihood estimation (MLE): a form of parameter estimation that maximizes the probability that the estimated parameters occur in the population. The second parameter estimation method is least squares. Least-square parameter estimates can be obtained using linear or non-linear regression [IEE08]. Although computationally more difficult, MLE produces parameter estimates that are at least as good as any other method (e.g., least squares) and oftentimes better. MLE also has the advantage of producing minimum variance parameter estimates.

Model Validation

Obtaining a good fit of a model with historical failure data does not prove that a model will predict future reliability with high accuracy. This would be demonstrated only by comparing the actual *future* reliability with the predicted reliability. However, it is important to obtain a good fit with historical data in order to obtain accurate model parameter estimates (e.g., accurate estimates of failure rate parameters). Two of the validation methods are Mean Relative Error (MRE) and Mean Square Error (MSE). The method of MRE computes the mean of (actual values − predicted values) / actual values. The method of MSE computes the mean of (actual values − predicted values)^2. Another goodness-of-fit method is Kolmogorov-Smirnov, which measures the maximum vertical distance between the predicted and actual plots, and consults a table to determine the probability of obtaining the distance (a large distance and high probability indicate poor prediction accuracy) [LYU96].

Software Reliability Applications

The major software reliability model applications are described below. These are separate but related applications that, in total, comprise an integrated reliability program.

Prediction: Predicting future failures, fault corrections, time to next failure, remaining failures, reliability risk, and test stopping rules. The purpose of prediction is to provide software managers with a forecast of the reliability of the software and to flag components for detailed inspection whose predicted reliability falls outside pre-determined norms.

Reliability prediction involves estimating the reliability of equipment and software prior to their production or modification [SAN]. Successful reliability prediction generally requires developing a reliability model of the system. The level of detail of the model will depend on the level of design detail available at the time. Data required to quantify the model is obtained from sources such as fault and failure data records, company warranty records, customer maintenance records, component suppliers, or expert elicitation from design or field service engineers. Reliability prediction combines rigorous analysis procedures with expert judgment to develop a realistic forecast of product performance.

The following benefits are provided by prediction [SAN]:

- Provides an early indication whether a design is likely to meet reliability goals,
- Points to potential reliability problem areas in a new design or design modifications,
- Identifies areas where additional data are needed, and
- Identifies components needing further testing.

Control: Comparing prediction results with pre-defined goals and flagging software that fails to meet goals. The purpose of control is to allow software managers to identify software that has unacceptable reliability sufficiently early in the development process to take corrective action. Control also involves the tracking of the reliability of a component over its future life and to indicate possible degradation in reliability.

Assessment: This activity is distinguished from prediction by the fact that, in assessment, we are concerned with analyzing past and current reliability, whereas prediction concerns forecasting future reliability. Assessment also involves collecting and evaluating historical failure data and determining what action to take for software that fails to meet reliability goals (e.g., intensify inspection, intensify testing, redesign software, revise process). The purpose of assessment is to provide software managers with a rational basis for assigning priorities for quality improvement and for allocating personnel and computer resources to quality assurance functions. The formulation of test strategies is also a part of assessment. It involves the determination of priority, duration, and completion date of testing and allocation of personnel and computer resources to testing. Assessment also involves the evaluation of the relative reliability of software components. "Relative quality" is the quality of a given component compared with the quality of other components in the set.

Software Reliability Data and Failure Scenarios

In addition to reliability models, another important aspect of SRE is a variety of data that are necessary to support modeling and reliability prediction. These data are also used in making empirical assessments of reliability.

Failure Scenario

There are three types of software reliability data that are defined as follows [IEE90]:

> Error: A human action that produces an incorrect result. For example, an incorrect action on the part of a programmer or operator.
> Fault: An incorrect step, process, or data definition in a computer program.
> Failure: The inability of a system or component to perform its required functions within specified performance requirements.

The three types are related in the following chronological sequence:

> Error → Fault → Failure

FIGURE 2.3   Failure Detection Process

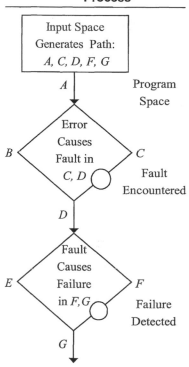

The above sequence is illustrated in Figure 2.3, which shows that the input space of a program generates path A, C, D, F, G. Unfortunately, there is a fault caused by a programmer error in branch C, D of the program space. This fault causes a failure to occur and to be detected in branch F, G. For example, a programmer could have specified incorrect navigational coordinates of an aircraft in branch C, D of the program. When these coordinates are read in branch F, G to set the course of the aircraft, the aircraft flies off course. In a large program, with many inputs, the number of possible input sequences is huge. This, combined with the large number of possible program paths (in some cases, infinite), generates a significant number of execution sequences in the program. Although individual execution sequences can be considered to be completely determined by input-program path combinations, in the aggregate, the detection of failures can be considered a random process under the condition of system testing and field operation. Thus, probability models can be employed for reliability prediction. It is important to make the distinction between the deterministic input-program path execution sequence executed by a programmer in the debug mode and the probabilistic execution sequences generated by a large and diverse number of inputs characteristic of system test and field operations.

Uses of Software Reliability Data

Failure data are obtained dynamically from the execution of programs. The following are some examples of the use of these data. This is not intended to be an exhaustive description.

- Empirically assess software reliability during test and operation against pre-determined reliability objectives.
- Estimate parameters for reliability models.
- Empirically analyze trends for reliability growth or decrease.
- Decide where and how much to inspect and test software.
- Make goodness-of-fit tests *retrospectively* to see how well model predictions compare with the actual data.

Optimal Selection of Failure Data

Optimally select failure data for improved parameter estimation and prediction accuracy [SCH92]. In the use of software reliability models, it is not necessarily the case that all the failure data should be used to estimate model parameters and to predict failures. The reason for this is that old data may not be as representative of the current and future failure process as recent data. Therefore, it may be possible to obtain more accurate predictions of future failures by excluding or giving lower weight to the earlier failure counts. In order to use the concept of data aging, there must be a criterion for determining the optimal value of the starting failure count interval. The mean square error criterion can be used to determine how much historical failure data to use in reliability predictions [SCH92]. The mean square error criterion minimizes the mean of the square of the difference between the predicted reliability (e.g., time to next failure) and the actual values in the range of the historical failure data. The time interval at which the minimum error occurs is used to either eliminate the preceding failure data or to give these data less weight in estimating the failure rate parameters, using the method of MLE. Research has shown that significantly improved reliability predictions can be obtained by using a subset of the failure data, based on applying this criterion for the Space Shuttle [SCH02] and other software.

Regression Testing

Use failure data in regression testing. Regression testing is performed after making a functional improvement or repair to the program. Its purpose is to determine if the change has adversely affected other aspects of the program. It is performed by rerunning the subset of the program's test cases—determined by the operational profile [MUS89]—that pertains to the change. Regression testing is important because changes and error corrections tend to be much more error-prone that the original code in the program (in much the same way that most typographical errors in newspapers are the result of last-minute editorial changes, rather than errors in the original copy). A plan for regression testing should include what to test, who will test, how to test, and when to test [MYE79].

A key factor in the Space Shuttle software development process achieving Software Engineering Institute Capability Maturity Model Level 5 is the use of regression testing when failures occur. First, the fault that caused the failure is corrected. Second, a determination is made as to whether the same fault exists in other parts of the code. Third, the root cause of the fault is determined. Fourth, regression tests, comprised of new tests related to the root cause of the fault, and all previous tests and data pertaining to this part of the code, are executed. This step is repeated until no additional failures and faults are detected, or until an appropriate tradeoff is achieved between increases in levels of reliability with increases in testing (i.e., cost of testing). Fifth, and most important, the deficient process steps are identified (e.g., inspections, tests) that allowed the faults to occur in the code. Sixth, the deficient process steps are corrected, thus integrating product and process quality [SCH01]. Unfortunately, failure data are often incomplete, lack definitions of the data elements, and are collected in a variety of inconsistent formats. This fact must be recognized when using reliability models and making predictions.

Interpreting Software Reliability Predictions

An important way to interpret reliability predictions is the risk to deploying the software that the predictions imply. For example, if the predicted *time to next failure* were less than the mission duration, this would be cause for alarm, and would suggest the need for additional inspections and testing to bring the predictions in line with the requirements.

FIGURE 2.4   OIO Failure Rate

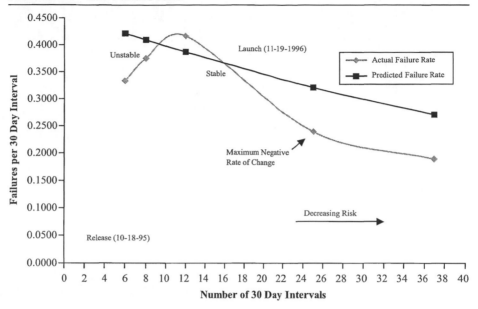

Another example is to plot actual and predicted failure rates as shown in Figure 2.4. These plots provide the following valuable information:

- See whether short-term process stability [SCH99] is achieved (e.g., failure rate asymptotically approaches zero with increasing test time).
- Ideally, in the short term (i.e., within a release), the failure rate of the release should decrease over test time, indicating increasing reliability. Practically, we would look for a decreasing trend, after an initial period of instability (i.e., increasing rate as personnel learn how to maintain new software).
- See how quickly reliability growth (i.e., decreasing failure rate) is achieved with respect to test time expended.
- Failure rate is an indicator of the risk involved in using the maintained software (i.e., an increasing failure rate indicates an increasing probability of failure with increasing use of the software).
- The actual failure rate plot, which uses historical failure data, shows the test time when the Space Shuttle Operational Increment OIO (i.e., release) transitions from an increasing failure rate (process instability) to a decreasing one (process stability) [SCH99].

In Figure 2.4, the maximum rate of change of the actual failure rate occurs at 25 intervals. This is a key point in achieving reliability growth of the product and maturity of the process because at this time, reliability is improving at the maximum rate. Of course, the Space Shuttle would not be launched until stability has been achieved (e.g., tested for 25 intervals), as shown in Figure 2.4.

Confidence Intervals

Rather than have a prediction based on only the expected value of a variable, it is appropriate to provide confidence intervals within which the variable is likely to lie (see Chapter 1 for an elaboration of confidence intervals). See the confidence interval plot in Figure 2.5, which shows the 95% and 5% confidence intervals of reliability $R(t)$ [SME83]. The

FIGURE 2.5   95% and 5% Confidence Limits of Reliability *R*(*t*) vs. Operating Time *t*

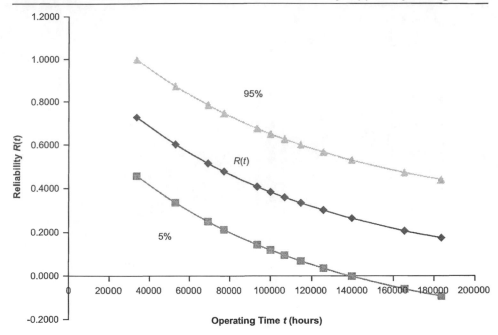

plot indicates that the 5% confidence interval is satisfactory for operating time *t* > 14,000 hours; however, for *t* > 14,000 hours, the lower interval goes negative. Since *R*(*t*) < 0 has no meaning, the lower limit is invalid for *t* > 14,000 hours. The 95% confidence interval is valid for all values of *t*.

Failure Mode Effects Analysis

This is an analytical technique that explores the effects of failures or malfunctions of individual components in a system, such as software (e.g., "If this software operates in this manner, what will be the result?)" [IEE]. The essential questions in determining failure mode effects are:

1. How can each component fail?
2. What might cause these modes of failure?
3. What would be the effects if the failures did occur?
4. How serious are these failure modes?
5. How is each failure mode detected?

The level of risk is determined by: Risk = probability of failure × severity category where severity is categorized in Table 2.1 on page 59. And probability of failure mode is categorized in Table 2.2.

Applications

A practical application of the FMEA technique involves the completion of a worksheet in which the failure modes of individual components, such as software, relays, and switches, are identified, evaluated, and risk priority codes identified, as in Table 2.1. A summary sheet can then be prepared in which failure modes are listed in declining order of risk

TABLE 2.1   Failure Categories

Category	Degree	Description
I	Minor	Failure of component—no potential for injury
II	Critical	Failure will probably occur without major damage to system or serious injury
III	Major	Major damage to system and potential serious injury to personnel
IV	Catastrophic	Failure causes complete system loss and potential for fatal injury

TABLE 2.2   Failure Modes

Level	Probability	Description	Failure Mode
A	10^{-1}	Frequent	Likely to occur frequently
B	10^{-2}	Probable	Likely to occur several times in the life of a component
C	10^{-3}	Occasional	Likely to occur sometime in the life of a component
D	10^{-4}	Remote	Unlikely to occur but possible
E	10^{-5}	Improbable	So unlikely that occurrence may not be experienced

Corrective action: changes in design, procedures, and organization; addition of redundant components; improved fault detection methods; and a change in maintenance policy.

priority codes. The summary should also list the corrective measures required to reduce the frequency of failure or to mitigate the consequences, as in Table 2.2. FMEA and fault tree analysis are related in the sense that Table 2.1 identifies the category of failure and Table 2.2 identifies the failure mode (i.e., the consequences of failures in various categories). This information can then be used to build the fault for determining the risk of catastrophic failures in a system.

FMEA can be used for single-point failure modes (e.g., single location in software) and can be extended to cover concurrent failure modes. It can be a costly and time-consuming process but once completed and documented, it is valuable for future reviews and as a basis for other risk assessment techniques such as Fault Tree Analysis (see Chapter 1). Other applications are the following:

Software Risk Assessment: Provide a warning to software managers of impending reliability problems early in the development cycle—during requirements analysis—by using risk factors to predict cumulative failures and the values of the risk factor thresholds where reliability would degrade significantly. Thus, software managers would be able to anticipate problems rather than react to them. In addition, more efficient software management would be possible because with advance warning of reliability problems, management would be able to better schedule and prioritize development process activities (e.g., inspections, tests). Some examples of software risk factors follow:

Risk Factor: attribute of a requirements change that can induce reliability risk, such as *memory space* and *requirements issues* [SCH99]:

Memory Space Issues: amount of memory space required to implement a requirements change (i.e., a requirements change uses memory to the extent that other functions do not have sufficient memory to operate effectively, and failures occur). This is an important risk factor for the NASA Space Shuttle flight software, where memory capacity is severely limited.

Requirements Issues: number of conflicting requirements (i.e., a requirements change conflicts with another requirements change, such as requirements to increase the search criteria of a Web site and simultaneously decrease its search time, with the added software complexity causing failures).

Bayesian Analysis

Bayesian techniques are sometimes used to analyze the reliability of software. The method is based on using prior knowledge of the condition of software and its reliability to predict future reliability. Note that while Bayesian techniques are cast in terms of probabilities, reliabilities are probabilities of survival.

Definitions

Probability of event $A = P(A)$.
Probability of *not* event $A = 1 - P(A)$.
Probability of event $B = P(B)$.
Probability of *not* event $B = 1 - P(B)$.
Conditional Probability of A given B: $P(B/A)$
Conditional Probability of B given A: $P(A/B)$

Bayesian rules are the following in equations (2.1) and (2.2):

$$\text{Probability of event } A \text{ given event } B = P(A/B) = \frac{P(B/A)P(A)}{P(B)} \tag{2.1}$$

$$\text{Probability of event } B \text{ given event } A = P(B/A) = \frac{P(A/B)P(B)}{P(A)} \tag{2.2}$$

Problem 1

A software system consists of two components, 1 and 2.

Reliability = .95 when component 1 is tested on computer A.
Reliability = .92 when component 2 is tested on computer B.

Reliability of the software system = .90 when component 2 is tested on B and receives input from component 1 being tested on A.

Predict the reliability of software system when component 1 is tested on A and receives input from component 2 being tested on B.

Solution

Define events:

Event A: software test of component 1 on computer A.
Event B: software test of component 2 on computer B.

Define reliabilities:

$P(A)$: reliability of software test of component 1 on computer A.
$P(B)$: reliability of software test of component 2 on computer B
$P(B/A)$: reliability of software system when component 2 is tested on B and receives input from component 1 being tested on A.

Applying the Bayesian rule in equation (2.2):

$$P(A/B) = \frac{P(B/A)P(A)}{P(B)} = (.90)(.95)/(.92) = \mathbf{0.93}$$

Problem 2

Suppose the system fails $x = 3$ times out of $n = 5$ tests when component 1 is tested on A and receives input from component 2 being tested on B. What is the reliability now?

Solution

Use the binomial distribution (refer to Chapter 1 for discussion of binomial distribution) and solve for reliability $= P = \dfrac{n!}{x!(n-x)!} p^x (1-p)^{n-x} = \left(5!/\left(3!2!\right)\right)\left(.93^3\right)\left(.07^2\right) = \mathbf{0.039}$

Interpretation

The very low reliability indicates a severe problem with the product and process that should be investigated.

Summary

This chapter has provided an overview of software reliability engineering, describing the history, rationale, and applications. In addition, the properties of software reliability models and their data requirements were illustrated with example problems. It was shown that Failure Mode Effects Analysis can be employed to prioritize the risk due to not satisfying reliability requirements.

References

[FRE72] Walter Freiberger, editor, *Statistical Computer Performance Evaluation.* Academic Press, New York, 1972.

[IEE] British Institute of Electrical Engineers.

[IEE08] IEEE/AIAA, 1633A, Recommended Practice on Software Reliability, July 2008.

[IEE90] *IEEE Standard Glossary of Software Engineering Terminology,* IEEE Std 610.12.1990. The Institute of Electrical and Electronics Engineers, New York, New York, March 30, 1990.

[FAR83] Dr. William H. Farr, *A Survey of Software Reliability Modeling and Estimating.* Naval Surface Weapons Center, NSWC TR 82-171, September 1983, pp. 4–88.

[KAR99] Zaven A. Karian and Edward J. Dudewicz, *Modern Statistical Systems, and GPSS Simulations,* Second Edition. CRC Press, 1999.

[KEL97] Ted Keller and Norman F. Schneidewind, "A Successful Application of Software Reliability Engineering for the NASA Space Shuttle." *Software Reliability Engineering Case Studies,* International Symposium on Software Reliability Engineering, November 3. Albuquerque, New Mexico, November 4, 1997, pp. 71–82.

[LYU96] Michael R. Lyu (editor-in-chief), *Handbook of Software Reliability Engineering.* Computer Society Press, Los Alamitos, CA and McGraw-Hill, New York, NY, 1996.

[MUS04] John D. Musa, *Software Reliability Engineering: More Reliable Software, Faster and Cheaper,* 2nd edition. Authorhouse, 2004.

[MUS89] John D. Musa and A. Frank Ackerman, "Quantifying Software Validation: When to Stop Testing?" *IEEE Software,* Vol. 6, No. 3, May 1989, pp. 19–27.

[MYE79] Glenford J. Myers, *The Art of Software Testing.* John Wiley and Sons, New York, 1979.

[NAS02] NASA, Houston, TX, May 5, 2002.

[REU02] Reuters News Agency, June 28, 2002.

[SAN] Sandia National Laboratories, New Mexico, USA.

[SCH01] Norman F. Schneidewind, Tutorial Notes, "Introduction to Software Reliability with Space Shuttle Example." 2001 Reliability and Maintainability Symposium, IEEE Reliability Society, Philadelphia, PA, January 23, 2001, 29 pages.

[SCH02] Norman F. Schneidewind, "Body of Knowledge for Software Quality Measurement." *IEEE Computer.* Computer Society Press, Los Alamitos, CA, February 2002, pp. 77–83.

[SCH75] Norman F. Schneidewind, "Analysis of Error Processes in Computer Software." Proceedings of the International Conference on Reliable Software, IEEE Computer Society, April 21–23, 1975, pp. 337–346.

[SCH92] Norman F. Schneidewind and T. W. Keller, "Application of Reliability Models to the Space Shuttle." *IEEE Software,* Vol. 9, No. 4, July 1992, pp. 28–33.

[SCH93] Norman F. Schneidewind, "Software Reliability Model with Optimal Selection of Failure Data." *IEEE Transactions on Software Engineering,* Vol. 19, No. 11, November 1993, pp. 1095–1104.

[SCH99] Norman F. Schneidewind, "Measuring and Evaluating Maintenance Process Using Reliability, Risk, and Test Metrics." *IEEE Transactions on Software Engineering,* Vol. 25, No. 6, November/December 1999, pp. 768–781.

[SHO83] Martin L. Shooman, *Software Engineering: Design, Reliability, and Management.* McGraw-Hill, New York, 1993.

[WAL04] Dolores R. Wallace, *Practical Software Reliability Modeling.* SRS Information Services, Software Assurance Technology Center, NASA Goddard Space Flight Center, Greenbelt, MD 20771.

3

Statistical Quality Control

Objectives

It is important to control the quality of software. Therefore, in this chapter control chart techniques and acceptance sampling are applied to controlling the quality of software, using numerous examples that are representative of quality control issues facing engineers and management in industry and government.

What You Will Learn From This Chapter

You will learn a variety of control chart techniques that can effectively detect anomalous software behavior and prevent catastrophic results if the software were put into operation. These techniques are composed of control charts that use the standard deviation and range as control limits. You will also be introduced to consumer and producer risk analysis and acceptance sampling that allow both the consumer and producer of software to reduce their risks of accepting low-quality software to acceptable limits.

Subjects

Stastical Quality Control
Acceptance Sampling
Single Sampling Plans for Consumer and Producer
Double Sampling Plans for Consumer and Producer

Statistical Quality Control

To set the stage for quality control analysis, some definitions are in order:

- Value of item subject to quality control, such as the *number of failures in a software module: x*
- Mean value of x: $\bar{x}$
- Sample size: n (number of software modules)
- Population standard deviation of failures per software module: σ
- Sample standard deviation of failures per software module: $s = \sigma / \sqrt{n}$
- Upper Control Limit (UCL) of quality (e.g., number of software failures): k standard deviations σ above $\bar{x}$ (Usually $k = 3$ for normal distribution.) See Chapter 9 for review of normal distribution properties.
- Lower Control Limit (LCL): k standard deviations σ below $\bar{x}$

Statistical Quality Control Methodology

As opposed to the mean, range is a non-parametric statistic. This means that it does not depend on the assumption of a distribution as in the case of the mean in the normal distribution.

The range is a good measure of variability in control charts. Both the range and the mean should be used in the control chart analysis.

The mean $\bar{x}$ of the normal distribution is computed in equation (3.1):

$$\bar{x} = \frac{\sum_{i=1}^{N} x_i}{N}, \text{ where } x_i \text{ is the } i^{\text{th}} \text{ data value and } n \text{ is the sample size.} \tag{3.1}$$

The mean value of the range R is computed in equation (3.2):

$$\bar{R} = \frac{\sum_{i=1}^{n} R_i}{N}, \text{ where } R_i = x_{\text{max}} - x_{\text{min}}, \text{ and where } x_{\text{max}} \text{ is the highest value}$$

$$\text{and } x_{\text{min}} \text{ is the lowest value in the } i^{\text{th}} \text{ sample} \tag{3.2}$$

Upper Control Limit (UCL) and Lower Control Limit (LCL), using the mean $\bar{x}$ and standard deviation s, are computed in equations (3.3) and (3.4), respectively:

$$\text{Upper Control Limit (UCL)} = \bar{x} + 3s \tag{3.3}$$

$$\text{Lower Control Limit (LCL)} = \bar{x} - 3s \tag{3.4}$$

UCL and LCL for the range using the mean $\bar{R}$ and standard deviation equation s_r, are computed in equations (3.5) and (3.6), respectively:

$$\text{Upper Control Limit (UCL)} = \bar{R} + 3s_r \tag{3.5}$$

$$\text{Lower Control Limit (LCL)} = \bar{R} - 3s_r \tag{3.6}$$

Control Conditions

LCL and UCL computations *assume the software failure data are normally distributed* (this may not be the case). A goodness-of-fit test for normality must be conducted on the data. Two of the validation methods are Mean Relative Error (MRE) and Mean Square Error (MSE). The method of MRE computes the mean of (actual values − predicted values)/ actual values. The method of MSE computes the mean of (actual values − predicted values)^2. Another goodness-of-fit method is Kolmogorov-Smirnov, which measures the maximum vertical distance between the predicted and actual plots, and consults a table to determine the probability of obtaining the distance (a large distance and high probability indicates poor prediction accuracy). (See Chapter 2.)

Out-of-control conditions of quality [LEV01], using software as an example:

1. one value of x (number of failures on software module) $> \bar{x} + 3s$ or one value of x $< \bar{x} - 3s$;
2. three successive values of x (number of failures on software module) $> \bar{x} + 2s$ or three successive values of x (number of failures on software module) $< \bar{x} - 2s$;
3. four values of x (number of failures on software module) $> \bar{x} + 1s$ or four values of $x < \bar{x} - 1s$, out of five successive values of x.

Problem 1

In a software quality function, the number of failures on software module x, is recorded as the test of the software proceeds. The number of failures on $n = 39$ software modules is recorded in Table 3.1. Is the software quality function process out of control?

TABLE 3.1   Control Chart Data and Calculations for Software Modules

Failures per Software Module		Mean		Module Number
x	UCL	LCL	$\bar{x}$	
5	15.95	−3.33	6.31	1
8	15.95	−3.33	6.31	2
6	15.95	−3.33	6.31	3
6	15.95	−3.33	6.31	4
3	15.95	−3.33	6.31	5
5	15.95	−3.33	6.31	6
1	15.95	−3.33	6.31	7
4	15.95	−3.33	6.31	8
7	15.95	−3.33	6.31	9
3	15.95	−3.33	6.31	10
2	15.95	−3.33	6.31	11
5	15.95	−3.33	6.31	12
6	15.95	−3.33	6.31	13
5	15.95	−3.33	6.31	14
9	15.95	−3.33	6.31	15
8	15.95	−3.33	6.31	16
4	15.95	−3.33	6.31	17
2	15.95	−3.33	6.31	18
5	15.95	−3.33	6.31	19
6	15.95	−3.33	6.31	20
4	15.95	−3.33	6.31	21
7	15.95	−3.33	6.31	22
3	15.95	−3.33	6.31	23
8	15.95	−3.33	6.31	24
11	15.95	−3.33	6.31	25
10	15.95	−3.33	6.31	26
3	15.95	−3.33	6.31	27
13	15.95	−3.33	6.31	28
9	15.95	−3.33	6.31	29
11	15.95	−3.33	6.31	30
8	15.95	−3.33	6.31	31
6	15.95	−3.33	6.31	32
5	15.95	−3.33	6.31	33
8	15.95	−3.33	6.31	34
1	15.95	−3.33	6.31	35
10	15.95	−3.33	6.31	36
14	15.95	−3.33	6.31	37
9	15.95	−3.33	6.31	38
6	15.95	−3.33	6.31	39
6.31	mean			
3.21	std dev			
15.95	UCL			
−3.33	LCL			

Solution

First, conduct a normality test on the data in Table 3.1 using Minitab or an equivalent statistical program. Since the failure data lie on a straight line in Figure 3.1 (page 66), conclude that the data are normally distributed so that the mean with

FIGURE 3.1   Normality Test for Software Module Failure Data

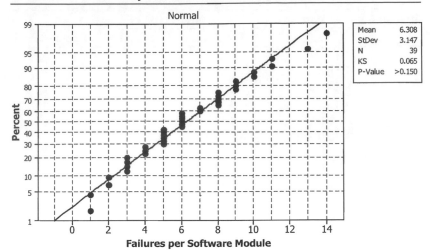

**FIGURE 3.2   Software Defects Per Module (x) Control Chart vs. Module Number
(mean = .0596 defects per Module)**

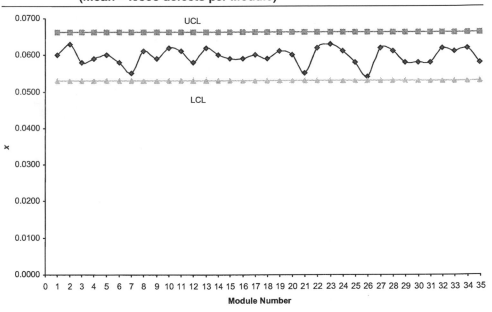

standard deviation control limits can be used to control quality. Based on the control chart in Figure 3.2, which is constructed from the data in Table 3.2, the software quality process is obviously in control because none of the data points are outside the control limits.

Problem 2

Given the data for x (defects per module) in Table 3.2, find the UCL, LCL, and the range of the defects per module). Is software quality in statistical control?

Solution

Again, the first thing to do is to test for normality. From Figure 3.3 (page 68), we can see that the data are normally distributed based on the data points falling mostly on a straight

TABLE 3.2   Control Limits for Defects per Module

Measurement	x	$\bar{x} + 3s$	$\bar{x} - 3s$
1	0.06	0.0663	0.0530
2	0.063	0.0663	0.0530
3	0.058	0.0663	0.0530
4	0.059	0.0663	0.0530
5	0.06	0.0663	0.0530
6	0.058	0.0663	0.0530
7	0.055	0.0663	0.0530
8	0.061	0.0663	0.0530
9	0.059	0.0663	0.0530
10	0.062	0.0663	0.0530
11	0.061	0.0663	0.0530
12	0.058	0.0663	0.0530
13	0.062	0.0663	0.0530
14	0.06	0.0663	0.0530
15	0.059	0.0663	0.0530
16	0.059	0.0663	0.0530
17	0.06	0.0663	0.0530
18	0.059	0.0663	0.0530
19	0.061	0.0663	0.0530
20	0.06	0.0663	0.0530
21	0.055	0.0663	0.0530
22	0.062	0.0663	0.0530
23	0.063	0.0663	0.0530
24	0.061	0.0663	0.0530
25	0.058	0.0663	0.0530
26	0.054	0.0663	0.0530
27	0.062	0.0663	0.0530
28	0.061	0.0663	0.0530
29	0.058	0.0663	0.0530
30	0.058	0.0663	0.0530
31	0.058	0.0663	0.0530
32	0.062	0.0663	0.0530
33	0.061	0.0663	0.0530
34	0.062	0.0663	0.0530
35	0.058	0.0663	0.0530
$\bar{x}$	**0.0596**		
s	**0.0022**		
max	**0.063**		
min	**0.054**		
range	**0.0090**	max-min	

line. It can be seen that x (defects per module) is in statistical control in Figure 3.4 (page 68). Also, in Table 3.3 (page 69), the range of the data (.0090 defects per module) is small relative to the mean and standard deviation, indicating small variation in the software defect measurements; this contributes to software quality being in control.

FIGURE 3.3   Normality Test for Defects per Module

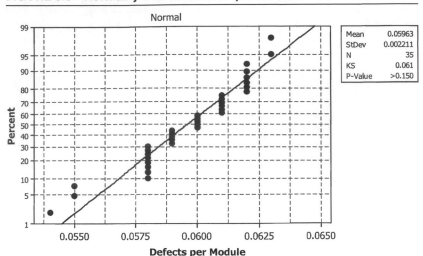

FIGURE 3.4   Upper and Lower Control Limits for Failures per Software Module x, Sample Size = n = 35 Modules

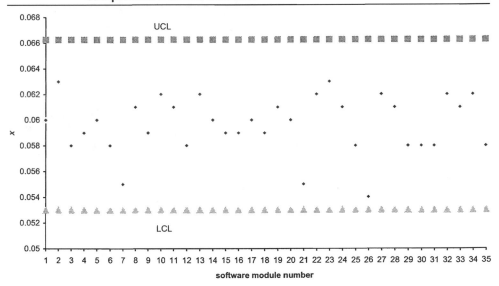

Problem 3

A company is developing software modules. The number of failures is sometimes excessive. The company wishes to use quality control charts to determine when the failure rate causes the software to become unacceptable. The data for 25 modules are shown in Table 3.3. It is suspected that at module 21, an out-of-control condition occurs. To make sure that they have exercised good quality control, the company uses both raw data x_i and range data R_i control charts. The company assumes the data are normally distributed.

Is the assumption of normality justified? Do the failures per module stay in control? Which is a better control procedure: raw data or range?

TABLE 3.3   Software Module Standard Deviation and Range Quality Control Data

module i	failures per module x_i	range R_i	$\dfrac{\sum_{i=1}^{N} x_i}{N}$	$\bar{x} + 3s$	$\bar{x} - 3s$	$\bar{R}$	$\bar{R} + 3s_r$	$\bar{R} - 3s_r$
1	117.2	25.2	117.56	138.03	97.09	26.76	34.63	18.90
2	107.5	30	117.56	138.03	97.09	26.76	34.63	18.90
3	114.7	27.9	117.56	138.03	97.09	26.76	34.63	18.90
4	116.1	25.4	117.56	138.03	97.09	26.76	34.63	18.90
5	120.6	28.8	117.56	138.03	97.09	26.76	34.63	18.90
6	106.1	26.3	117.56	138.03	97.09	26.76	34.63	18.90
7	108.8	30.4	117.56	138.03	97.09	26.76	34.63	18.90
8	120.2	28	117.56	138.03	97.09	26.76	34.63	18.90
9	114.9	20.1	117.56	138.03	97.09	26.76	34.63	18.90
10	113.4	28.2	117.56	138.03	97.09	26.76	34.63	18.90
11	116.6	26.9	117.56	138.03	97.09	26.76	34.63	18.90
12	112.5	22.8	117.56	138.03	97.09	26.76	34.63	18.90
13	122.1	23.5	117.56	138.03	97.09	26.76	34.63	18.90
14	126.2	25	117.56	138.03	97.09	26.76	34.63	18.90
15	115.3	27.7	117.56	138.03	97.09	26.76	34.63	18.90
16	117.1	29.7	117.56	138.03	97.09	26.76	34.63	18.90
17	113.7	25.9	117.56	138.03	97.09	26.76	34.63	18.90
18	119.4	25.3	117.56	138.03	97.09	26.76	34.63	18.90
19	114.4	29.1	117.56	138.03	97.09	26.76	34.63	18.90
20	112.2	28.9	117.56	138.03	97.09	26.76	34.63	18.90
21	116.6	25.8	117.56	138.03	97.09	26.76	34.63	18.90
22	121.8	29	117.56	138.03	97.09	26.76	34.63	18.90
23	126.5	22.9	117.56	138.03	97.09	26.76	34.63	18.90
24	129	30	117.56	138.03	97.09	26.76	34.63	18.90
25	136.1	26.3	117.56	138.03	97.09	26.76	34.63	18.90
mean	**117.56**	**26.76**						
standard deviation	**6.82**	**2.62**						

in control: $i = 1,\dots20$?

out of control: $i = 21,\dots25$?

Solution

Based on Figure 3.5 (p. 70), the company is justified in assuming normality—barely—because the data are marginally normally distributed. The software is under control as evidenced by the fact that no failure data are outside the limits in Figures 3.6 and 3.7. While both control charts based on raw data and range are useful, and both could be used to be on the safe side when controlling for quality, the raw data chart is more conservative and should be used if resources are not available for producing more than one chart. "More conservative" means that Figure 3.7 shows that indeed the software is starting to go out of control at module 21, whereas Figure 3.6 indicates that the process is stable at module 21.

FIGURE 3.5 Normality Test for Failures per Module

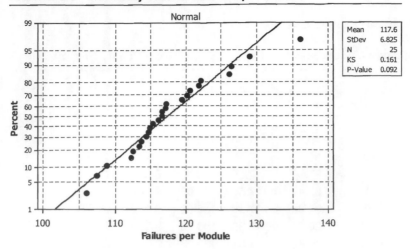

FIGURE 3.6 Failures per Software Module vs. Module Number *i* Using
$R_i \pm 3$ Standard Deviations

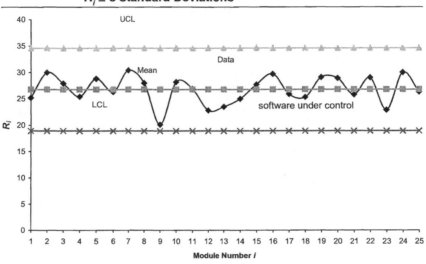

FIGURE 3.7 Failures per Software Module x_i vs. Module Number *i* Using
$x_i \pm 3$ Standard Deviations

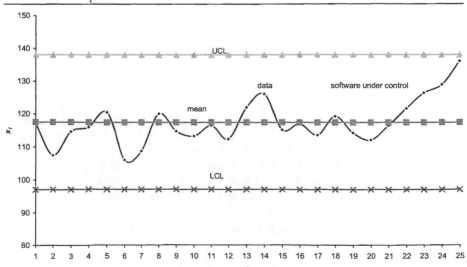

Acceptance Sampling

Introduction

Acceptance sampling is an important field of statistical quality control that was popularized by Dodge and Romig and originally applied by the U.S. military to the testing of bullets during World War II [NIS]. If every bullet was tested in advance, no bullets would be left to ship. If, on the other hand, none were tested, malfunctions might occur in the field of battle, with potentially disastrous results. Dodge reasoned that a sample should be picked at random from the lot, and on the basis of information that was yielded by the sample, a decision should be made regarding the disposition of the lot. In general, the decision is either to accept or reject the lot. This process is called *Lot Acceptance Sampling* or just *Acceptance Sampling*. Acceptance sampling is "the middle of the road" approach between no inspection and 100% inspection. Acceptance sampling is employed when one or several of the following hold:

- Testing is destructive
- The cost of 100% inspection is very high
- 100% inspection takes too long

The last two of these scenarios apply to software.

Basically, the acceptance quality control system encompasses the concept of protecting the *consumer* from getting unacceptable defective products by performing quality inspections of the goods provided by producers, and encouraging the *producer* to use process quality control by varying the quantity and severity of acceptance inspections in direct relation to the importance of the characteristics inspected [NIS]. While it might be assumed that the producer should produce only the minimally acceptable quality because of the cost involved in producing high-quality software, this is not the case because such a policy could result in a significant amount of business and good will.

Consumer and Producer Risk Analysis

The above concepts are fleshed out in the following software quality control examples: The analysis and data used in the following product risk analysis examples are typical of NASA Space Shuttle and NASA Goddard Space Flight Facility reliability processes.

For the Schneidewind Software Reliability Model (SSRM) [SCH97] the reliability at test time T_c is given by equation (3.7):

$$R(T_c) = e^{-[\alpha(e-\beta(T_c-s+1))]}, \text{ where } \alpha, \beta, \text{ and } s \text{ are model parameters} \qquad (3.7)$$

Then, use equation (3.7) to obtain equation (3.8): *consumer risk* CR, based on the idea of equating risk with unreliability, where unreliability is the complement of reliability in equation (3.7):

$$\text{CR unreliability} = 1 - e^{-[\alpha(e-\beta(T_c-s+1))]} \qquad (3.8)$$

Next, the *producer's risk* PR occurring at test time T_p, where $T_p < T_c$, can be computed in an analogous fashion by equation (3.9):

$$PR = 1 - e^{-[\alpha(e-\beta(T_p-s+1))]} \qquad (3.9)$$

The reason for the relationship between T_p and T_c is that the consumer tests the software only after the producer tests it and delivers it to the consumer. Consumer test time is greater than producer test time because, whereas the producer tests only "just enough" to meet specifications and keep cost within reason, the NASA consumer is responsible for the safety of the mission.

FIGURE 3.8   **Consumer Risk CR (T_c) vs. Test Time T_c (using SSRM, with alpha = 3.329, beta = .532, and s = 15)**

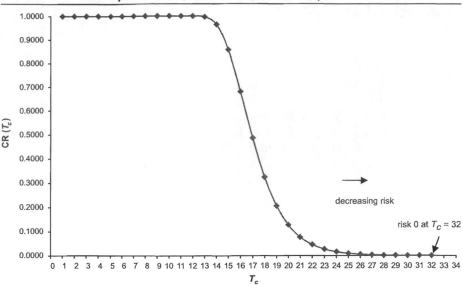

Now, Figure 3.8 shows how risk varies for the consumer as a function of the test time. You can see that the risk $R\,(T_c)$ *decreases* with increasing T_c. The reason for this is that SSRM, along with other reliability growth models, exhibits *increasing* reliability (i.e., *decreasing* unreliability) with increasing test time. Thus, you can see that the risk becomes 0 at $T_c = 32$.

Next, examine the risk the producer incurs, as a result of attempting to meet the customer's reliability expectations. The producer's risk, occurring before the consumer experiences risk, (i.e., $T_p < T_c$) is shown in Figure 3.9. This type of analysis is very practical for estimating and comparing the relative testing efforts between the consumer and software in order to achieve acceptable risk for both parties.

FIGURE 3.9   **Producer's Risk PR (T_p) vs. Test Time T_p (using SSRM with alpha = 3.329, beta = .532, and s = 15)**

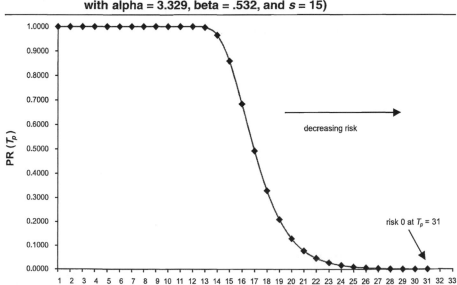

Binomial Distribution Method for Acceptance Sampling

Use the binomial distribution, equation (3.10), for acceptance sampling when it is necessary to accept, or reject, x defectives out of sample of N items in a lot of size n.

$$P(x) = \frac{N!}{x!\,(N-x)!}\,p^x(1-p)^{N-x}, \tag{3.10}$$

where $P(x)$ is the probability of x occurring in the sample of size N and the probability p is: $p = \bar{x}/n$, where $\bar{x}$ is the mean value of x.

Problem 4

Using a sample size of $N = 20$, a lot of computer circuit boards will be accepted if the number of defects $= x \le 1$. What is the probability of *rejecting* the lot if the probability of defects $(x > 1)\, p = .05$?

Solution

In this case, it is appropriate to use the binomial distribution because this is an "x out of N" problem.

Solve equation (3.11) for $P\,(x > 1) = 1 - [(P\,(x = 0) + P\,(x = 1)]$, the probability of rejecting the lot if there is a probability $p = .05$ of 1 or more defects:

$$P(x=0) = (1-p)^N = .95^{20} = .3585 \tag{3.11}$$

$$P(x=1) = Np(1-p)^{N-1} = 20(.05)(.95)^{19} = .3774 \tag{3.12}$$

Use equations (3.11) and (3.12) to obtain the solution in equation (3.13):

$$\mathbf{P(x>1)} = 1 - \left((.95)^{20} + \left(20*.05*(.95)^{19}\right) \right) = 1 - .3585 - .3774 = \mathbf{.2641} \tag{3.13}$$

Problem 5

If the number of defective circuit boards in a sample of $N = 20$, from a lot of size $n = 1000$, has an *assumed* binomial distribution with mean number of defective boards $= \bar{x} = 60$, what is the probability of having $x = 20$ or fewer defective boards (i.e., $p\,(x \le 20)$)?

Solution

First, find the value of p in the binomial distribution:

$$p = \bar{x}/N = 60/1000 = .06 \tag{3.14}$$

Then, using equation (3.14), evaluate it for $x = 1, \ldots, 20$ in equation (3.15) and tabulate the results in Table 3.4.

$$1 - P(x) = 1 - \sum_{x=1}^{20} \frac{N!}{x!\,(N-x)!}\,p^x(1-p)^{N-x}$$

$$= 1 - \sum_{x=1}^{20} \frac{20!}{x!\,(20-x)!}(.06)^x(1-.06)^{20-x} \tag{3.15}$$

Thus, the solution is $1 - \sum P(x) = 0.290106241$.

TABLE 3.4   Binomial Distribution Results

x	
1	0.370348393
2	0.224572962
3	0.086006666
4	0.023331596
5	0.004765603
6	0.000760468
7	0.000097081
8	0.000010070
9	0.000000857
10	0.000000060
11	0.000000003
12	0.000000000
13	0.000000000
14	0.000000000
15	0.000000000
16	0.000000000
17	0.000000000
18	0.000000000
19	0.000000000
20	0.000000000
sum ($P(x)$)	0.709893759
$1 -$ sum ($P(x)$)	**0.290106241**

$$P(X) = \boxed{\frac{N!}{x!\,(N-x)!} p^x (1-p)^{N-x}}$$

N	20
p	0.06

Single Sampling Plans for Consumer and Producer

In single sampling, a random sample of N items is selected from a lot. If the number c of defective items found in the sample is less than or equal to an acceptance number c_c for the consumer or c_p for the producer, the lot is accepted. Otherwise, the lot is rejected. The advantages of single sampling plans are: 1) they are easy to design and administer, and 2) for lots of medium quality, sample sizes are smaller than for double sampling. *A disadvantage is that when lot quality is either low or high, the sample sizes are larger than for double sampling.*

Definitions

N: sample size
c: number of defective items in a sample
c_c: consumer allowable number of defects
c_p: producer allowable number of defects

Lot Decision Rules

1. For the producer, accept the lot if the number of defects c in a sample of size N is $\leq (\alpha N)$; otherwise, reject the lot.
2. For the consumer, accept the lot if the number of defects c in a sample of size N is $\leq \beta (N)$; otherwise, reject the lot.

Problem 6

A producer has a risk of $\alpha = .0100$ of rejecting a good lot. A consumer has a risk of $\beta = .0200$ of accepting a bad lot. The sample size $N = 100$ and the allowable number of defects for the producer is $c_p = 1$ and $c_c = 2$ for the consumer. If the allowable number of defects c in the sample = 2, should the lot be accepted or rejected?

Solution

For the producer, apply Rule 1: risk $\alpha = .0100$: $c > (c_p = \alpha N)$. $(2 > (.0100 * 100 = 1))$. Therefore, reject the lot.

For the consumer, apply Rule 2: risk $\beta = .0200$: $c \leq (c_c = \beta N)$. $(2 \leq (.0200 * 100 = 2))$. Therefore, accept the lot.

Double Sampling Plans for Consumer and Producer

Definitions

c_c: consumer number of defects acceptance number
c_p: producer number of defects acceptance number
r_c: consumer number of defects rejection number
r_p: producer number of defects rejection number
N_1:   first sample size
N_2:   second sample size
d_1:   number of defectives in first sample
d_2:   number of defectives in second sample
D_2:   number of defectives in first and second samples

Double and multiple sampling plans were invented to give a questionable lot another chance. For example, if in double sampling the results of the first sample are not conclusive with regard to accepting or rejecting, a second sample is taken. Application of double sampling requires that a first sample of size N_1 is taken at random from a large lot. The number of defectives d_1 is then counted and compared to the first sample's acceptance numbers c_c and c_p and rejection numbers r_c and r_p.

Lot Decision Rules

If $d_1 \leq c_c$, the lot is accepted by consumer.
If $d_1 \leq c_p$, the lot is accepted by producer.
If $d_1 \geq r_c$, the lot is rejected by consumer.
If $d_1 \geq r_p$, the lot is rejected by producer.
If $c_c < d_1 < r_c$, or $c_p < d_1 < r_p$, a second sample is taken.

If a second sample of size N_2 is taken, the number of defectives, d_2, is counted. The total number of defectives is $D_2 = d_1 + d_2$. Now, this is compared to the acceptance numbers c_c and c_p and the rejection numbers r_c and r_p of sample 2. In double sampling, $r_c = c_c + 1$ and $r_p = c_p + 1$ to ensure a decision on the sample.

If $D_2 \leq c_c$ or c_p, the lot is accepted.
If $D_2 \geq r_c$ or r_p, the lot is rejected.

Problem 7

Sample size $N_1 = 100$, $N_2 = 200$, $c_c = 2$ for consumer, and $c_p = 1$ for producer, $d_1 = 2$, and $d_2 = 3$. Should the lot be accepted or rejected?

Solution

$r_c = c_c + 1 = 2 + 1 = 3$
$r_p = c_p + 1 = 1 + 1 = 2$
$D_2 = d_1 + d_2 = 2 + 3 = 5$

If $d_1 \leq c_c$, the lot is accepted by consumer: $2 \leq 2$, **consumer accepts.**
If $d_1 \leq c_p$, the lot is accepted by producer: 2 not $\leq$ 1, **producer does not accept.**
If $d_1 \geq r_c$, the lot is rejected by consumer: 2 not $\geq$ 3, **consumer does not reject.**
If $d_1 \geq r_p$, the lot is rejected by producer: $2 \geq 2$, **producer rejects.**

If $c_c < d_1 < r_c$: (2 not < 2 < 3), do not take second sample,
or $c_p < d_1 < r_p$: (1 < 2 not < 2), do not take a second sample.

Net result: lot is accepted by the consumer and rejected by the producer.

Summary

You have learned that it is very important to control the quality of products, particularly software, which has a history of reliability mishaps, as demonstrated by the anecdotal evidence that was reported. The key tool for monitoring and assessing quality is the control chart that provides confidence intervals for determining whether a product operates within acceptable quality limits. There are two types of quality control chart based on raw data and the range. By example, you learned that the former is more conservative and more likely to provide a true picture of product quality. Acceptance sampling was introduced as a process for assessing the risk to the consumer of accepting low-quality products and of the risk incurred by the producer in producing products of unacceptable quality that could drive the producer out of business.

References

[LEV01] David M. Levine, Patricia P. Ramsey, and Robert K. Smidt, *Applied Statistics for Engineers and Scientists*. Prentice Hall, 2001.
[NIS] "What is Acceptance Sampling?" *NIST/SEMATECH e-Handbook of Statistical Methods*, http://www.itl.nist.gov/div898/handbook/.
[SCH97] Norman F. Schneidewind, "Reliability Modeling for Safety Critical Software." *IEEE Transactions on Reliability*, Vol. 46, No. 1, March 1997, pp. 88–98.

4

Risk, Reliability,
and Testing Case Study

Objectives

This chapter provides the engineer with a case study that illustrates how software risk and reliability analysis can be used to reduce the risk of software failure and improve the overall reliability of the software product.

What You Will Learn From This Chapter

You will learn how sequential testing is used as a process to achieve risk and reliability goals.

Subjects

Overview of the Principles of Risk-Driven Reliability Model and Test Process
Model and Process Basics
Safety Critical Software Considerations
Risk Analysis
Reliability Analysis
Predictions and Prediction Accuracy
Tradeoff Between Consumer's Risk and Producer's Risk
Example Poisson Process Problem: First and Second Tests
NASA Space Shuttle Application

Overview of the Principles of Risk-Driven Reliability Model and Test Process

The risk-driven reliability model and testing process borrows concepts from classical sequential testing methodology that is used for hardware, with adaptation to software. Both consumer and producer risk are considered, reflecting the fact the consumer (e.g., customer) and producer (e.g., contractor) have different perspectives concerning what they consider to be tolerable risks of software failure. Similarly, there is also a differentiation based on what the consumer and producer consider to be acceptable reliability. Using the consumer-producer framework, a model and process are developed for executing sequential tests, based on software risk and reliability and model risk and reliability prediction accuracy. Rules are specified for determining at each decision point in testing whether the software and the model prediction accuracy are acceptable. In addition, the test rules serve as stopping criteria for testing (i.e., when it is cost-effective to stop testing). Both empirical and predicted quantities are assessed. The test rules are integrated with several levels of criticality of software (i.e., the higher the criticality, the more stringent the tests). Based on lessons learned, the model and process are improved for future applications. The analysis is started by developing a model and process template based on the Poisson distribution of failures that you learned in Chapter 1: *Quantitative Methods*. This hypothetical example allows the model and process to be debugged before it is applied to a real application involving the NASA Space Shuttle flight software.

Model and Process Basics

This case study is about the development and evaluation of a model and process that uses the risk of software failure to drive test scenarios and reliability predictions. Scenarios involve the comparison of the software's actual outputs, resulting from test scenario execution, with its expected outputs, as documented by a specification [WHI00]. Software actual outputs are empirical values of risk and reliability and the expected outputs are represented by specified threshold values of risk and reliability.

In addition, risk and reliability predictions provide stopping rules for testing. The foundation for these concepts of software testing is based on classical methods addressed to hardware [LLO62], but with significant modifications to tailor the models to software testing and reliability. On the one hand, the classical methods of sequential testing, involving the concepts of consumer and producer risks [LLO62], are very useful for structuring a testing and reliability model. On the other hand, these concepts are lacking in the literature on software testing [HOR96]. Software testing emphasizes techniques such as statement coverage, decision coverage, branch coverage, and data flow coverage [HOR96]. The classical methods are not entirely satisfactory for software because they are based on testing large quantities of homogeneous hardware items. This is not the situation with software because, in many cases, one-of-a kind of software is developed and tested. Thus, the classical methods require modification to be applicable to software.

Another important facet of the risk and reliability process is to evaluate not only the software but the *model* that predicts software risk and reliability, as well. If the model cannot predict accurately, the predictions cannot be used and you must try to validate another model (e.g., Weibull distribution, which was covered in Chapter 1: *Quantitative Methods*). Thus, in this approach, there is an intimate relationship between software testing and models that provide the predictions for evaluating the outputs of the tests.

One way to analyze the software testing process is to consider the mechanism that drives the number, type, criticality, sequence, and timing of tests. The operational profile—frequency of application functions, weighted by their criticality—is one way [MUS99]. However, the focus of this case study is consumer and producer risk in testing and models for quantifying the risk, with reasonable tradeoffs to balance competing consumer and producer objectives. To achieve this balance is important because on the one hand, the consumer desires highly reliable software at a low cost. On the other hand, the producer desires to deliver software that meets "reasonable" reliability requirements and results in high profit. To make this tradeoff, a balancing act is performed among risk, reliability, test time, acceptance and rejection criteria, and test sequence.

Safety Critical Software Considerations

To assist in making informed acceptance decisions, software risk analysis and reliability prediction are integrated to provide a comprehensive approach to implementing test rules designed to reduce risk and increase reliability. This approach is applicable to all software, and in particular, it is critical for certifying safety critical software because achieving improvements in the reliability of software, contributes to system safety [KEL97]. In addition, for this type of software, it is critical to have a feedback mechanism during testing to indicate when to continue to test and when to stop testing. Important feedback criteria are level of risk, reliability, and reliability growth. The inspiration for using this feedback mechanism comes from the concept expressed in [CAN01] of using a test manager to monitor the difference between observed reliability and reliability predicted by a model. The difference is fed back into the test process to control the next step in testing. In this case study, the differences between observed and required risk and reliability are used to control the test process.

Case Study Approach

The case study approach is to investigate the feasibility of applying the consumer risk-producer risk model of testing to software. This classical method for testing hardware has been used for decades—long before the advent of software. There is no reason why the principles of this approach cannot be applied to software with suitable modifications. The effectiveness of the consumer-producer model, as applied to software, is assessed by documenting the advantages and disadvantages, and the lessons learned.

The analysis begins by developing a risk and reliability model test template that addresses the major issues in consumer and producer risk and reliability. The test template is analogous to the concept described in [STO93]: A test template framework is a useful concept in specification-based testing (i.e., specification of risk and reliability requirements). The framework can be defined using any model-based specification notation and used to derive tests from model-based specifications (i.e., test sequence and acceptance criteria derived from risk and reliability specifications).

An example from the Poisson probability distribution (see Chapter 1: *Quantitative Methods*) is used to build the model template. The example is not entirely realistic because the reliability function that is a by-product of this process may not demonstrate reliability growth. In software reliability growth models, growth is possible because faults are removed as they are discovered; and assuming fewer new faults are introduced as old faults are removed, reliability will increase over test time. However, it is better to use a simple probability distribution at the outset to illustrate the model before delving into the analysis of real systems. Later, the NASA Space Shuttle flight software is used to provide a real-world example of applying the model, where reliability growth is part of the modeling process.

The model must be developed carefully and must include risk and reliability objectives. It is important that the model properly maps to the software under test. The method of model construction, when building testing scenarios, is to first build a template for guiding the construction of test sequences. Then in conducting the tests, iterate based on the test results at each stage until either the software is accepted or rejected.

Other Reliability Testing Methods

Reliability testing can be conducted at a macro or micro level. The former is used in sequential test scenarios in which the concern is about the big picture of risk, failure occurrence, and reliability, and how to mitigate risk and increase reliability. But in the micro view of testing, the focus is on methods that deal with the specifications, code, and data flow to produce effective fault removal in a cost-efficient manner. Specification-based testing produces test cases based on inputs, outputs, and program states. Code-based testing addresses computation results, predicate coverage, and control flow coverage. In data flow-based testing, test cases are produced to cover the execution space between where variables are declared and where they are used. Yet another method is mutation testing, in which mutants of the original code are produced by introducing faults into program statements and observing the resulting execution behavior [JUR06].

Lyu provides a brief description of some of the important white-box testing methods. White-box testing uses the structure of the software to measure the quality of testing. This type of testing includes statement and decision coverage. Statement coverage testing constructs test cases that force each statement or a basic block of code to be executed at least once. Decision coverage constructs test cases that force each decision in the program to be covered at least once. A decision is covered if, during some execution, it evaluates to true and in the same or another execution it evaluates to false [LYU98]. In [DAL99] the authors use data-driven testing combined with risk-driven testing.

None of these methods is superior to the others in all cases, and their effectiveness and efficiency are application-dependent. Selected tests at the micro level should be combined with a macro-level approach to provide a comprehensive attack on the software risk and reliability problem. In fact, the approach is to do model testing at the micro level (i.e., white-box testing) to provide failure count input to the macro-level model (i.e., black-box testing based on top-level specifications). The process does not have to stop there. You can use the two approaches synergistically by feeding black-box testing risk and reliability predictions to white-box testing so that the latter will provide an assessment of likely operational risk and reliability. Then, the white-box strategy would be adjusted to focus testing on the highest risk and lowest reliability software.

Definitions

Risk:　According to [NAS97], "risk is a function of: the possible frequency of occurrence of an undesired event, the potential severity of resulting consequences, and the uncertainties associated with the frequency and severity." This sounds good but would be difficult to implement because all of the risk factors would not be available in practice. Therefore, you should use a definition to account for not only the probability of an undesirable event but, in addition, the "severity of resulting consequences," as represented by failure count. Putting these two factors together, we define risk as the expected number of failures (i.e., probability * failure count).

L_m: risk limit (threshold that risk should not exceed)

Mission critical: an application in which high risk and low reliability would jeopardize the organization's survival

Safety critical: an application in which high risk and low reliability would jeopardize the safety of the crew and mission

t_m: Mission duration: length of computer operation, space flight, etc.

"actual" refers to reliability and risk that are computed by using historical data; there is no prediction of the future

"predicted" refers to reliability and risk that are computed by using historical data in order to make forecasts of the future

Risk Analysis

Actual Risk

In order to have a baseline against which to compute risk prediction errors, start by finding the actual probability of failure for the consumer and producer in equations (4.1) and (4.2), respectively:

$$P_{ac}(t, r_c): \text{ actual consumer probability of } r_c \text{ failures in time } t = \frac{r_c(t)}{\sum\limits_{t=1}^{N_c} r_c(t)}, \qquad (4.1)$$

where N_c is number of failures that occur on consumer software.

$$P_{ap}(t, r_p): \text{ actual producer probability of } r_p \text{ failures in time } t = \frac{r_p(t)}{\sum\limits_{t=1}^{N_p} r_p(t)}, \qquad (4.2)$$

where N_p is number of failures that occur on producer software.

Then applying the definition of risk, compute the actual consumer and producer risk in equations (4.3) and (4.4), respectively

$$\mu_c(t, r_c) = \left[P_{ac}(t, r_c) \right] * r_c \qquad (4.3)$$

$$\mu_p(t, r_p) = \left[P_{ap}(t, r_p) \right] * r_p \qquad (4.4)$$

Mean Time to Failure

Unlike hardware during its operations phase when the time to failure (MTTF) is assumed constant, software has a variable MTTF that is a function of the length of time the software has been operating or tested t and the number of failures r that have occurred during this time. Based on these consideration, you can compute the *consumer* MTTF in equation (4.5):

$$m_c(t, r_c) = \left(\frac{t}{\sum\limits_{t=1}^{t} r_c} \right) \qquad (4.5)$$

Then, it follows that you can compute the *producer* MTTF in equation (4.6):

$$m_p(t, r_p) = \left(\frac{t}{\sum\limits_{t=1}^{t} r_p} \right) \qquad (4.6)$$

If a Poisson distribution of failure counts is assumed for consumer failures r_c during time t, with mean time to failure $m_c(t, r_c)$, *predict* the probability of failure occurrence in equation (4.7):

$$P_c(t, r_c) = \left(\frac{t}{m_c} \right)^{r_c} \frac{e^{-\left(\frac{t}{m_c} \right)}}{r_c!} \qquad (4.7)$$

Predicted Risk

Again applying the definition of risk, *predict* the consumer risk in equation (4.8):

$$\alpha_c(t, r_c) = \left[P_c(t, r_c) \right] * r_c \qquad (4.8)$$

The consumer's risk is not the whole story about risk because you must consider the producer's risk in the sequential tests model. As you will recall, the producer wants to minimize the risk of rejecting good software. The producer wants to produce the minimum acceptable software for the consumer, but no more. To do otherwise would result in needless cost for the producer.

Similar to equation (4.7), if you assume a Poisson distribution of failure counts r_p for the producer, during time t, with mean time to failure $m_p(t, r_p)$, estimated in equation (4.6), you can *predict* the probability of failure occurrence in equation (4.9):

$$P_p\left(t, r_p\right) = \left(\frac{t}{m_p}\right)^{r_p} \frac{e^{-\left(\frac{t}{m_p}\right)}}{r_p!}$$ (4.9)

Then again applying the definition of risk, you can compute the producer risk in equation (4.10):

$$\beta_p\left(t, r_p\right) = \left[P_p\left(t, r_p\right)\right] * r_p$$ (4.10)

Reliability Analysis

Actual Reliabilities

The actual consumer reliability $R_{ac}(r, t_c)$ is computed during time t, using the Poisson distribution of failures r_c, as given by equation (4.11):

$$R_{ac}\left(t, r_c\right) = 1 - \left(\frac{\frac{r_c}{N_c}}{\sum_{t=1} r_c}\right)$$ (4.11)

Similarly, the actual producer reliability $R_{ap}(t, r_p)$ is computed in equation (4.12), using the Poisson distribution of failures r_p:

$$R_{ap}\left(t, r_p\right) = 1 - \left(\frac{\frac{r_p}{N}}{\sum_{t=1} r_p}\right)$$ (4.12)

Predicted Reliabilities

Formulate the consumer and producer *predicted* reliabilities by first considering the relationship between the reliability $R(t)$, the probability of survival in the interval t, and the cumulative distribution function $P(t)$ in the interval t. Once you have determined $P(t)$, you can compute $R(t)$ from equation (4.13).

$$R(t) = P\left(T > t\right) = 1 - P\left(t\right)$$ (4.13)

Now obtaining $P_c(t, r_c)$ from equation (4.7), use it in equation (4.14) to predict consumer reliability:

$$R_c\left(t\right) = 1 - P_c\left(t, r_c\right) = 1 - \left(\frac{t}{m_c}\right)^{r_c} \frac{e^{-\left(\frac{t}{m_c}\right)}}{r_c!}$$ (4.14)

Similarly obtaining $P_p(t, r)$ from equation (4.9), use it in equation (4.15) to predict producer reliability:

$$R_p\left(t\right)=1-P_p\left(t,r_p\right)=1-\left(\frac{t}{m_p}\right)^{r_p}\frac{e^{-\left(\frac{t}{m_p}\right)}}{r_p!} \tag{4.15}$$

Because predictions deal with the highly volatile future, they are subject to potentially large prediction errors. Therefore, it is prudent for both consumer and producer *predicted* reliabilities to exceed the actual reliabilities in order to allow for possible error. Therefore, this is a caveat that you should first investigate the prediction error before drawing conclusions about the validity of the prediction results. This is done in the next section.

Predictions and Prediction Accuracy

Risk Prediction

The method of assessing consumer and producer risk prediction accuracy is to see: 1) whether the *mandatory* criteria are satisfied: predicted consumer risk, predicted producer risk, and actual risk are less than the allowable limit; and 2) whether the *desirable* criteria are satisfied: predicted consumer risk and predicted producer risk are less than the actual risk. 1) is given in equations (4.16) and (4.17) and 2) is given in equations (4.18) and (4.19).

Mandatory Criteria

$$\alpha\left(t,\,r_c\right),\mu_c(t,\,r_c)<L_m \quad \text{(predicted and actual consumer risk} < \text{risk limit)} \tag{4.16}$$

$$\beta\left(t,\,r_p\right),\mu_p(t,\,r_p)<L_m \quad \text{(predicted and actual producer risk} < \text{risk limit)} \tag{4.17}$$

Desirable Criteria

$$\alpha\left(t,\,r_c\right)<\mu_c(t,\,r_c) \quad \text{(predicted consumer risk} < \text{actual consumer risk)} \tag{4.18}$$

$$\beta\left(t,\,r_p\right)<\mu_p(t,\,r_p) \quad \text{(predicted producer risk} < \text{actual producer risk)} \tag{4.19}$$

The rationale for the mandatory criteria is that if the risks exceed the limit, the safety of the software system would be jeopardized, whereas the desirable criteria reflect the aforementioned caveat of allowing for possible large prediction error.

Risk Prediction Accuracy

Now, equations (4.16), (4.17), (4.18), and (4.19) are insufficient because, since $\alpha(t,\,r_c)$ and $\beta(t,\,r_p)$ are predicted quantities, we need to see whether there is acceptable prediction accuracy with respect to actual consumer risk $\mu_c(t,\,r_c)$ and actual producer risk $\mu_p(t,\,r_p)$. You compute the mean square error in equations (4.20) and (4.21) for consumer risk and producer risk, respectively:

$$E_{Rc}=\sum_{t=1}^{T}\frac{[\mu_c(t,r_c)-\alpha(t,r_c)]^2}{T} \tag{4.20}$$

$$E_{Rp} = \sum_{t=1}^{T} \frac{[\mu_p(t,r_p) - \beta(t,r_p)]^2}{T},$$ (4.21)

where T is the last test time.

Next, you test whether the values in equations (4.20) and (4.21) satisfy the error thresholds in conditions (4.22) and (4.23), respectively, using the mean plus three standard deviations criterion:

$$S_{Rc} = [\mu_c(t,r_c) - \alpha(t,r_c)]^2 < \left(E_{Rc} + 3\sigma\right)$$ (4.22)

$$S_{Rp} = [\mu_p(t,r_p) - \beta(t,r_p)]^2 < \left(E_{Rp} + 3\sigma\right)$$ (4.23)

Reliability Prediction Accuracy

The reliability accuracy test is performed to compute the mean square error of the difference between 1) actual consumer reliability $R_{ac}(t,\ r_c)$ and predicted consumer reliability $R_c(t,\ r_c)$ and 2) between actual producer reliability $R_{ap}(t,\ r_p)$ and predicted producer reliability $R_p(t,\ r_p)$. E_{rc} and E_{rp} are the error quantities in equations (4.24) and (4.25), respectively:

$$E_{rc} = \sum_{t=1}^{T} \frac{\left[R_{ac}(t,r_c) - R_c(t,r_c)\right]^2}{T}$$ (4.24)

$$E_{rp} = \sum_{t=1}^{T} \frac{\left[R_{ap}(t,r_p) - R_p(t,r_p)\right]^2}{T}$$ (4.25)

Now, you can test whether the values in equations (4.24) and (4.25) satisfy the error threshold conditions (4.26) and (4.27), based on the mean plus three standard deviations criterion, respectively:

$$S_{rc} = \left[R_{ac}(t,r_c) - R_c(t,r_c)\right]^2 < \left(E_{rc} + 3\sigma\right)$$ (4.26)

$$S_{rp} = \left[R_{ap}(t,r_p) - R_p(t,r_p)\right]^2 < \left(E_{rp} + 3\sigma\right)$$ (4.27)

Tradeoff between Consumer's Risk and Producer's Risk

As mentioned in the Overview, it is desirable to balance the conflicting objectives of minimizing both consumer's risk and producer's risk. To do this, use the difference $[\alpha(t,\ r_c) - \beta(t,\ r_p)]$ between predicted consumer and producer risks to analyze whether balance has been achieved (i.e., you examine the minimum of this quantity, noting when it occurs in test time, and the failure counts at this test time).

Test Rules

One of the most difficult aspects of testing is to answer the question: "when to stop testing?" Myers suggests to stop testing when a given number of faults have been discovered and corrected [MYE79]. While this approach is *indirectly* related to reliability, and is certainly better than stopping when we run out of money and time, it is better to use criteria that are *directly* related to risk and reliability. With this approach, you can key the stopping

FIGURE 4.1   Risk-Driven Testing and Reliability Process (Part 1)

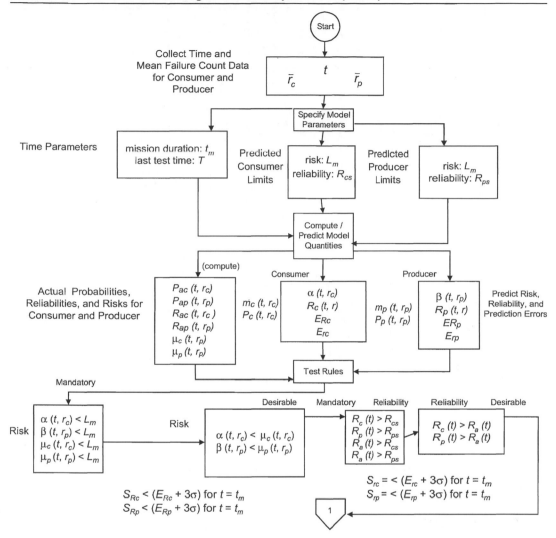

rules to achieving acceptable levels of risk and reliability. This concept is embodied in the test rules that follow.

Test rules should also include the criticality of the software being tested (see Figure 4.1, Part 2, on page 86). This factor is mentioned in [MAT00], where the authors state: "Many commercial products are not fully prepared for use in high assurance situations. In spite of the criticality of these applications, there currently exists a dearth of software assurance techniques to asses the robustness of both the application and the operating system under strenuous conditions. The testing practices that ordinary commercial products undergo are not thorough enough to guarantee reliability. High assurance applications require software components that can function correctly even when faced with improper usage or stressful environmental conditions." The aim is to guarantee reliability by using a model and test schema that require the software to pass several reliability and risk checks before it can be certified. "Improper usage" is reflected in the failure incidence and "stressful environmental conditions" is included by imposing the most stringent test conditions in acceptance tests for mission critical and safety critical software.

FIGURE 4.1   Risk-Driven Testing and Reliability Process (Part 2)

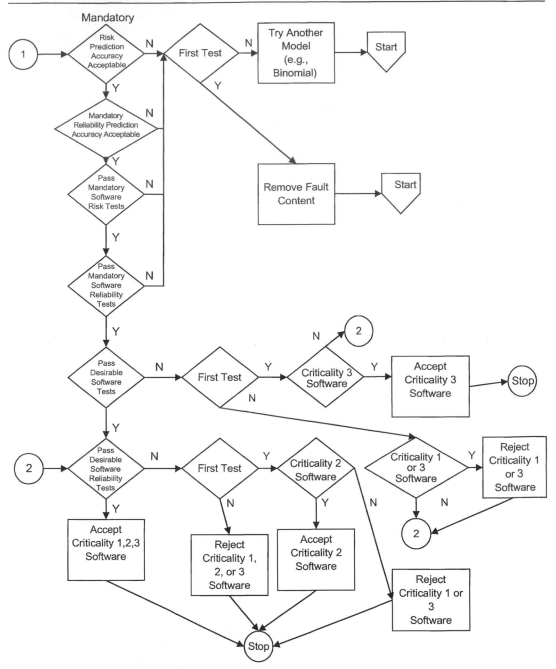

Based on the roadmap in Figure 4.1, and the three criticality levels of software (see the following discussion), you specify the rules for the *software* and *model* accept-reject decisions that follow. Accept *software* if the following *software* rules evaluate to "true." Accept *model* if the following *model* rules evaluate to "true." Mandatory rules are designed to ensure that there are no unacceptable risks in the operation of the software, whereas desirable rules are designed to ensure reasonable prediction accuracy. To be certified as safe to deploy, consumer and producer software must pass all parts of two sequential tests. If there is a failure to pass any part of the first test, the software is given a second chance to pass the two tests, after faults are removed.

1) Risk

Mandatory for Software

Risks of failure of consumer and producer software must be less than risk limit.

a. $\alpha(t, r_c) < L_m$ (predicted consumer risk < risk limit)
b. $\beta(t, r_p) < L_m$ (predicted producer risk < risk limit)
c. $\mu_c(t, r_c) < L_m$, $\mu_p(t, r_p) < L_m$ (actual consumer and producer risk < risk limit)

Mandatory for Prediction Model

Consumer and producer risk prediction model errors must be less than error limits.

d. $[\mu_c(t, r_c) - \alpha(t, r_c)]^2 < (E_{Rc} + 3\sigma)$ (consumer error < consumer error limit)
e. $[\mu_p(t, r_p) - \beta(t, r_p)]^2 < (E_{Rp} + 3\sigma)$ (producer error < producer error limit)

Desirable for Software

Desire predicted risks to be less than actual risks.

f. $\alpha(t, r_c) < \mu(t, r_c)$ (predicted consumer risk < actual consumer risk)
g. $\beta(t, r_p) < \mu(t, r_p)$ (predicted producer risk < actual producer risk)

Desire consumer to have lower risk than producer.

h. $\alpha(t, r_c) = \beta(t, r_p)$ (predicted consumer risk < predicted producer risk)

2) Reliability

Mandatory for Software

Predicted and actual reliabilities must be greater than specified reliabilities.

a. $R_c(t) > R_{cs}$ (predicted consumer reliability > specified consumer reliability)
b. $R_p(t) > R_{ps}$ (predicted producer reliability > specified producer reliability)
c. $R_a(t) > R_{cs}$ (actual reliability > specified consumer reliability)
d. $R_a(t) > R_{ps}$ (actual reliability > specified producer reliability)

Mandatory for Prediction Model

Consumer and producer reliability prediction errors must be less than error limits.

e. $[R_{ac}(t, r_c) - R_c(t, r_c)]^2 < (E_{rc} + 3\sigma)$ (consumer prediction error must be less than error limit)
f. $[R_{ap}(t, r_p) - R_p(t, r_p)]^2 < (E_{rp} + 3\sigma)$ (producer prediction error must be less than error limit)

Desirable for Prediction Model

Desire predicted reliabilities of the future to be greater than present actual reliabilities.

g. $R_c(t) > R_a(t)$ (consumer predicted reliability greater than actual reliability)
h. $R_p(t) > R_a(t)$ (producer predicted reliability greater than actual reliability)

The test rules and definitions are put in context by Figure 4.1, Part 1 and Part 2. These figures comprise a roadmap to the sequential testing and reliability process. In this scenario, two complete software tests, comprising the use of risk and reliability acceptance tests, are specified. In addition, acceptance criteria for three levels of criticality are used in the accept/reject decision process, from the most to the least critical: Criticality 1 (e.g., mission critical—Shuttle flight software), Criticality 2 (e.g., operating system), and Criticality 3 (e.g., spreadsheet). In the scenario, any one of the three types of software could be tested. The relationships between test rules and criticality are the following:

Criticality 1: must pass *all* tests to be accepted

Criticality 2: must pass *all* mandatory tests and *all desirable* reliability tests to be accepted

Criticality 3: must pass *all* mandatory tests and *all desirable risk* tests to be accepted

Note that according to Figure 4.1, Part 2, the testing process cannot proceed to the *desirable* risk and reliability tests until all *mandatory* tests are satisfied, both prediction accuracy and software. In addition, in Part 2, passing desirable reliability tests is considered more important that passing desirable risk tests. This is based on the logic that compared to risk, reliability can be easily quantified, understood, and applied. Thus, passing *desirable reliability tests* is associated with Criticality 2 software and passing *desirable risk tests* is associated with Criticality 3 software. Note also that if the software fails the first test, another model could be considered, such as the Binomial (see Chapter 1: *Quantitative Methods*).

Example Poisson Process Problem: First and Second Tests

Although according to Figure 4.1, tests take place in sequence, the results of the two tests are presented together in order to make a comparison. The outcomes of the two tests are presented in plots, using Figure 4.1 as a guide. In the two tests, use the Poisson distribution, which you learned in Chapter 1: *Quantitative Methods,* to predict consumer and producer risk and reliability. Using this distribution produces increasing reliability with test and operational time. This means that the software is run, faults that cause failures are removed, and reliability improves, as a consequence. A typical example is that a personal computer runs for a while, and then multiple failures occur and are cleared with a reboot. Some researchers call this time "soak time" [MUS99]. The reboot allows errant application code to be cleansed (i.e., faults are removed) such that the software can operate until the next incident occurs. In contrast, the second example, involving safety critical software like the Shuttle flight software, could not tolerate such a scenario. This point will be elaborated when the second example is introduced.

The following parameters are specified in the example problem (note that for illustrative purposes, the units of the quantities are immaterial):

$$t: \text{time} = \text{test plus operational time} (1, \ldots , t_N) = 1, \ldots ,28$$

Note: to make the plots easy to read, risk and reliability quantities are plotted against "test time" in the figures. This "test time" includes test time and operational time.

t_m: = *desired* mission duration = 8
N: number of failure count intervals = 28
L_m: risk limit = .500000

It is reasonable to ask on what basis the risk limit is chosen. Admittedly, it is somewhat subjective, but it is based on the following consideration: Risk is the (probability of *r* failures) × (*r* failure count). For this illustrative software, the assumption is made that the probability is .5 for $r = 1$ failure, or $L_m = .5$. The reason for six decimal places in the risk limit is that risks can be so close to zero that they must be computed to six places to be compared with the limit.

R_{cs}: specified *minimum* consumer reliability = .9000
R_{ps}: specified *minimum* producer reliability, where $R_{ps} < R_{cs} = .8500$

The choice of reliability thresholds is, again, a bit subjective but the important point is that the relationship must be $R_{ps} \le R_{cs}$, reflecting the desire to force greater reliability from the consumer's perspective than from the producer's.

For the Second Test, in order to illustrate the benefit of fault reduction and consequent failure reduction, mean failure count is reduced by approximately 50%. This action results in reducing consumer and producer risk and increasing consumer and producer reliability: Thus, the mean of Poisson distributed failure counts $\bar{r}_c$ for the consumer was reduced from 1.11 to .57. In addition, the mean of Poisson distributed failure counts $\bar{r}_p$ for the producer was reduced from 1.39 to .61.

Error Analysis

Risk Predictions

As seen in Figure 4.2, consumer risk passes its mandatory risk prediction accuracy test for the Second Test, but fails the First Test *during the mission*. In addition, as Figure 4.3 shows, producer risk passes its mandatory risk accuracy test for both the First Test and the Second Test *during the mission*. This result would not be comforting for the consumer. Thus, despite the good results achieved by the producer, faults would have to be removed from the consumer software before it is acceptable.

FIGURE 4.2   First Test & Second Test: Consumer Risk Prediction Error: $(\mu - \alpha)^2$ vs. Test Time t

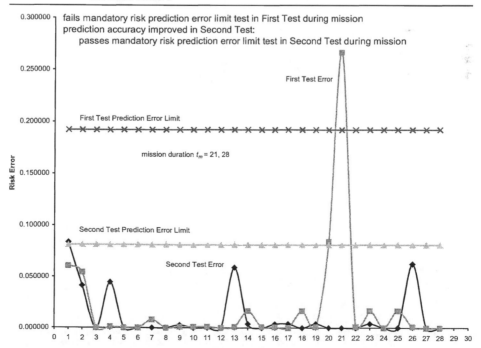

FIGURE 4.3   **First Test & Second Test: Producer Risk Prediction Error:**
                        $(\mu - \beta)^2$ vs. Test Time t

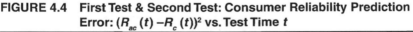

Reliability Predictions

Figures 4.4 and 4.5 tell us that both consumer and producer reliability prediction error pass their mandatory tests for First and Second Tests *during the mission*. At this point, considering the combination of risk prediction and reliability error results, you should conclude that it is too risky to release the software, and that more testing is necessary to remove faults.

Risk Analysis

Note that the risk functions can have variations that obscure the underlying patterns [NEL73]. The impact of this situation is that you can expect some variation in the prediction of risk over test time.

FIGURE 4.4   **First Test & Second Test: Consumer Reliability Prediction**
                         Error: $(R_{ac}(t) - R_c(t))^2$ vs. Test Time t

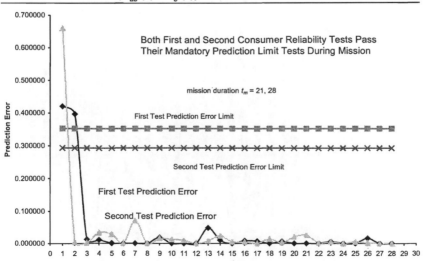

FIGURE 4.5   First Test & Second Test: Producer Reliability Prediction Error:
$(R_{ap}(t) - R_p(t))^2$ **vs. Test Time** t

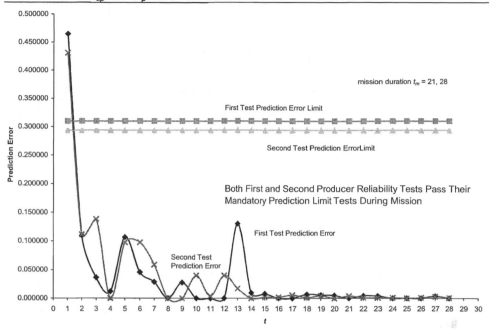

Figures 4.6 and 4.7 address consumer risk and producer risk, respectively. You see that, unfortunately, just one case of not meeting the criterion causes the mandatory risk test to fail: actual consumer risk $\mu_c(t, r_c)$ for the First Test exceeds the risk limit in Figure 4.6. All tests are passed in Figure 4.7. A consistent pattern is beginning to emerge: Producer software passes tests, but consumer software does not pass all tests. This is not an unusual situation because, as implied previously, the producer does not conduct tests with the same rigor as the consumer.

FIGURE 4.6   First & Second Test: Predicted Consumer Risk (α)
and Actual Consumer Risk (μ) vs. Test Time t

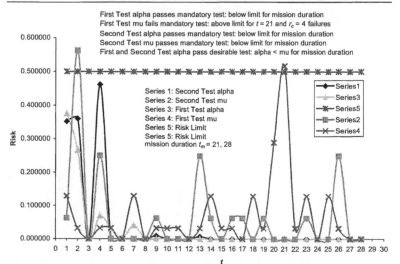

FIGURE 4.7   First & Second Test: Predicted Producer Risk (β) and Actual Producer Risk (μ) vs. Test Time *t*

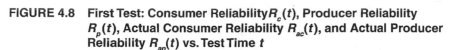

Reliability Analysis

Figure 4.8 tells us that the actual consumer reliability fails the mandatory test, although the predicted reliability passes it. Note that it is more important for actual reliability to pass because it is based on actual failure data, as opposed to predictions, which may or may not be accurate. Thus, consumer software continues to have problems. Figure 4.9 is more encouraging because all reliabilities pass the Second Test. The scenario of this outcome per Figure 4.1 (Part 2) would be remove fault from the consumer software, repeat and pass the First Test, and pass the Second Test.

FIGURE 4.8   First Test: Consumer Reliability $R_c(t)$, Producer Reliability $R_p(t)$, Actual Consumer Reliability $R_{ac}(t)$, and Actual Producer Reliability $R_{ap}(t)$ vs. Test Time *t*

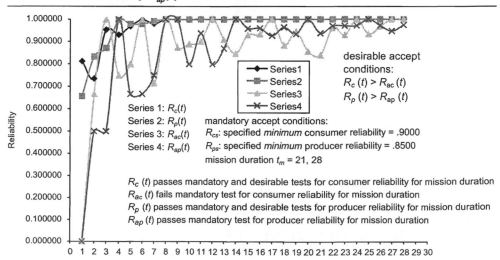

FIGURE 4.9   **Second Test: Predicted Consumer Reliability ($R_c(t)$), Predicted Producer Reliability ($R_p(t)$), Actual Consumer Reliability ($R_{ac}(t)$), and Actual Producer Reliability ($R_{ap}(t)$) vs. Test Time t**

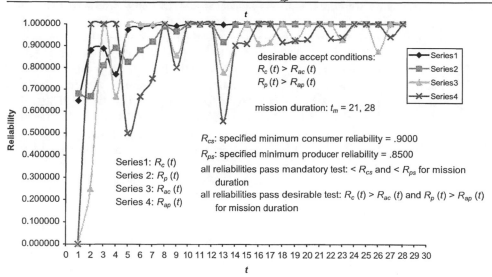

Risk Tradeoff Analysis

Risk tradeoff analysis is also a part of the model roadmap. It provides additional insight for making the accept/reject decision based on the relationship between consumer and producer risk. The idea behind Figure 4.10 is to determine the amount of test time required for consumer risk to equal producer risk—this is a good balance point. For example, while equality is obtained during the Second Test at $t = 8$, with zero failures, it is not obtained until $t = 21$ during the First Test, with zero failures. In other words, the requirement is not completed during the test phase ($t = 1, 20$); it is not completed until the beginning of the mission at $t = 21$. Thus, the decision would be to reject this software until it can satisfy this test.

FIGURE 4.10   **First & Second Tests: (Predicted Consumer Risk – Predicted Producer Risk) ($\alpha - \beta$) vs. Test Time t**

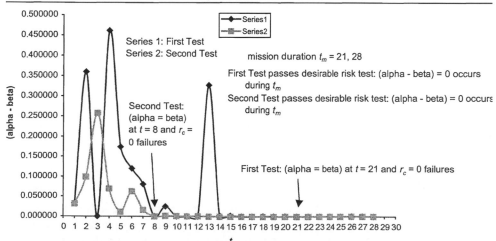

NASA Space Shuttle Application

Now use the roadmap in Figure 4.1 and apply it to the Shuttle flight software, using the Schneidewind Software Reliability Model (SSRM) [SCH97]. You were exposed to the concepts of software reliability models in Chapter 2: *Overview of Software Reliability Engineering*. Any software reliability growth model (srgm) would suffice for this purpose. You can expect to make some adjustments to the roadmap. For one thing, a srgm typically uses failure count time intervals or time to failure as the input to the models, whereas the Poisson model uses failure count at a given time. An assumption of srgm's is that reliability will increase with time, as faults are removed as they are discovered. Thus, a sufficiently long test time is required to: 1) collect sufficient failure data in order to estimate model parameters and 2) allow reliability growth to take place (e.g., reliability reaches an acceptable level). Once 1) and 2) have been accomplished, you can *predict* the reliability of the software for the specified mission duration t_m.

The first step is to provide definitions of model quantities.

Definitions and Assumption

Only the definitions that are particular to the Shuttle are given here. Previous definitions are not repeated.

t_{cp}: test time or operating time when $R_c(t, r_c) = R_p(t, r_p)$

s_c: SSRM parameter: Consumer starting interval for using observed failure data in parameter estimation

s_p: SSRM parameter: Producer starting interval for using observed failure data in parameter estimation

a_c: SSRM parameter: Consumer failure rate at the beginning of time interval s_c

a_p: SSRM parameter: Producer failure rate at the beginning of time interval s_p

b_c: SSRM parameter: Consumer negative of derivative of failure rate divided by failure rate (i.e., relative failure rate)

b_p: SSRM parameter: Producer negative of derivative of failure rate divided by failure rate (i.e., relative failure rate)

$r_c(t)$: The number of consumer software failures whose faults have been removed in time interval t

$r_p(t)$: The number of producer software failures whose faults have been removed in time interval t

$m_c(t)$: predicted mean number of failures occurring on consumer software during time interval t

$m_p(t)$: predicted mean number of failures occurring on producer software during time interval t

N_c: Total number of failures that occur in consumer software over all time intervals

N_p: Total number of failures that occur in producer software over all time intervals

Typically, in Shuttle software, there is a one-to-one relationship between faults and failures. Thus, this assumption is made in the analysis.

Test Rules

Since the Shuttle uses a reliability growth model, a modified set of test rules is called for to capture this important characteristic. To compute reliability growth quantitatively, Jeff Tian suggests that reliability growth measure *purification level,* the ratio between the number of faults (failures) removed during testing over the total faults (failures) at the beginning of testing. In this analysis it is convenient to define the purification level equal to actual reliability in equations (4.28) and (4.29). Tian states that the purification level captures overall reliability growth and testing effectiveness [TIA95]. The objective of using purification level is to produce tests that have high testability (i.e., use tests that will cause failures to be detected and faults to be exposed and removed).

Reliability growth is related to the principle of *testability*, as described by Voas and Kassab [VOA99]: "Software testability is a characteristic that either suggests how easy software is to test, how well the tests are able to interact with the code to detect defects, or some combination of the two." The authors suggest it is useful to employ the perspective that software testability is a measure of how good test cases will be at making defects detectable. In addition, Voas states [VOA91]: "A program is said to have high testability if it tends to expose faults during random black-box testing, producing failures for most of the inputs that execute a fault. A program has low testability if it tends to protect faults from detection during random black-box testing, producing correct output for most inputs that execute a fault." We embody these concepts in the following test rules, which are designed to expose faults and failures (testability) that will result in reliability growth.

Purification Levels

The actual purification level (i.e., actual reliability) for consumer and producer, using failure counts, is computed in equations (4.28) and (4.29), respectively:

$$\rho_c = 1 - \left(\frac{r_c(t)}{\sum_{t=1}^{N_c} r_c(t)} \right) \tag{4.28}$$

$$\rho_p = 1 - \left(\frac{r_p(t)}{\sum_{t=1}^{N_p} r_p(t)} \right) \tag{4.29}$$

Since it is important to assess the validity of the prediction system, by comparing the predictions with the actual purification levels, predict the purification levels. You do this by using equations (4.30) and (4.31) for the consumer and producer, respectively:

$$\rho_{cp} = 1 - \left(\frac{m_c(t)}{\sum_{t=1}^{N_c} m_c(t)} \right) \tag{4.30}$$

$$\rho_{pp} = 1 - \left(\frac{m_p(t)}{\sum_{t=1}^{N_p} m_p(t)} \right) \tag{4.31}$$

The reason equations (4.30) and (4.31) are predicted quantities, as opposed to equations (4.28) and (4.29), is that the former include predicted mean failures $m_c(t)$ and $m_p(t)$, whereas the latter include observed failure counts $r_c(t)$ and $r_p(t)$.

Test Rules

For the Shuttle, all previous test rules apply, with the following additions dealing with reliability growth and purification level:

Mandatory for Software Reliability Growth Model

Consumer reliability, predicted during times t_i and t_{i+1}: $R_c(t_{i+1}) > R_c(t_i)$ for all i

Producer reliability, predicted during times t_i and t_{i+1}: $R_p(t_{i+1}) > R_p(t_i)$ for all i

Desirable for Purity Level

Predicted consumer purity level > Actual consumer purity level: $\rho_{cp} > \rho_c$

Predicted producer purity level > Actual producer purity level: $\rho_{pp} > \rho_p$

Reliability growth and purity level tests have been added because, for safety critical systems like the Shuttle, it is important to demonstrate reliability growth, as contributing to the safety of the crew and mission. As pointed out by [MUS87], it may be necessary for an organization to demonstrate the reliability of its product "as delivered." For example, there could be a test where the consumer "buys off" the product from the producer. If this is the case for safety critical software, the test model and schema must enforce a high standard of reliability (and risk) before the product is accepted.

The Shuttle test rules, based on modifying the original roadmap with reliability growth and purity level criteria, are shown in Figure 4.11, Parts 1 and 2.

FIGURE 4.11   Shuttle Risk-Driven Testing and Reliability Process (Part 1)

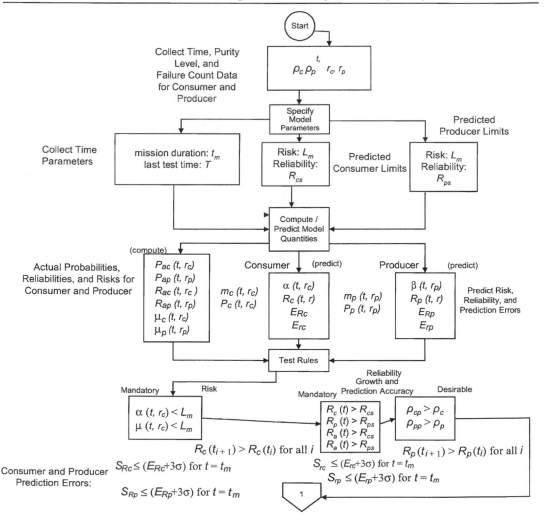

FIGURE 4.11   Shuttle Risk-Driven Testing and Reliability Process (Part 2)

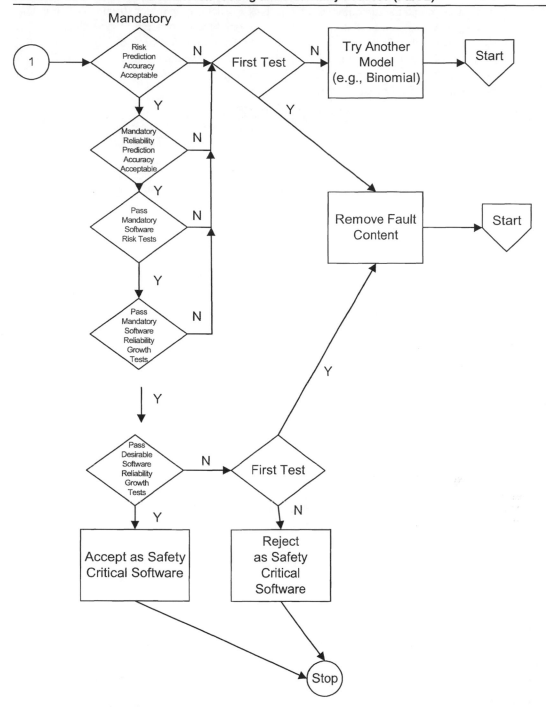

Risk Analysis

In the case of the Shuttle, the consumer and producer risk equations are developed, giving effect to the way that failure data are generated. There are several streams of failure data available for a given software release (i.e., operational increment (OI)): one from the producer (contractor), another from the customer (NASA), and another from the Shuttle simulator. One failure stream is used for the consumer and another for the producer. The logic of this is that the producer tests the software generating one stream, provides the software to the customer, and the customer tests the software generating another stream. The consumer attempts to increase the reliability over that delivered by the producer by continuing to test and remove faults. Thus, the next step is to formulate the probability of failures, assuming a Poisson distribution of failures, occurring at time t, using equations (4.32) and (4.33) for the consumer and producer, respectively. These equations will be used in the formulation of consumer and producer risk:

$$P_c(r_c) = \left(m(t)_c^r \, e^{-m(t)} \right) / r_c! \tag{4.32}$$

$$P_p(r_p) = \left(m(t)_p^r \, e^{-m(t)} \right) / r_p! \tag{4.33}$$

In order to estimate the *mean number of failures* $m(t)$ in equations (4.32) and (4.33), use equation (4.34):

$$\text{From SSRM [SCH97]: } m(t) = \frac{a}{b} \left(e^{-b(t-s)} - e^{-b(t-s+1)} \right) \tag{4.34}$$

Recalling that risk is the (probability of an undesirable event times the consequences of the event), use equations (4.32) and (4.33) to develop the following equivalences, based on the Poisson distribution:

$$\text{Consumer risk} = \alpha(t, r_c) = P_c(r_c) * r_c = \left[\left(m_c(t)^r \, e^{-m_c(t)} \right) / r_c! \right] * r_c \tag{4.35}$$

$$\text{Producer risk} = \beta(t, r_p) = P_p(r_p) * r_p = \left[\left(m_p(t)^r \, e^{-m_p(t)} \right) / r_p! \right] * r_p \tag{4.36}$$

With respect to actual risk, since it is based on empirical failure counts, use equations (4.37) and (4.38), respectively, for actual consumer probability, $P_{ac}(t, r_c)$, and actual producer probability $P_{ap}(t, r_p)$:

$$P_{ac}(t, r_c): \text{ actual consumer probablity of } r_c \text{ failures in test time } t = \frac{r_c(t)}{\sum_{t=1}^{N_c} r_c(t)} \tag{4.37}$$

$$P_{ap}(t, r_p): \text{ actual producer probablity of } r_p \text{ failures in test time } t = \frac{r_p(t)}{\sum_{t=1}^{N_p} r_p(t)} \tag{4.38}$$

This then leads to the equations for actual consumer risk and actual producer risk in equations (4.39) and (4.40), respectively.

$$\mu_c(t, r_c) = P_{ac}(t, r_c) * r_c \tag{4.39}$$

$$\mu_p(t, r_p) = P_{ap}(t, r_p) * r_p \tag{4.40}$$

Reliability Analysis

Using SSRM [SCH97], the general form of consumer and producer reliability at time t is given by equation (4.41):

$$R(t) = e^{-\left[a\left(e^{-b(t-s+1)}\right)\right]}$$

(4.41)

The reliability at time t_{cp} when consumer reliability is equal to producer reliability can be found by equating $R_c(t)$ to $R_p(t)$, using equation (4.41), and solving for $t = t_{cp}$. This is of interest because when $t > t_{cp}$, it is desirable for $R_c(t) > R_p(t)$, meaning that at this value of test time, the consumer has achieved a reliability greater than that delivered by the producer. The solution is found in equation (4.42):

$$t_{cp} = \frac{\left[\dfrac{\log(a_p)}{\log(a_c)} - b_c(s_c - 1) + b_p(s_p - 1)\right]}{(b_p - b_c)}$$

(4.42)

For the purpose of comparing predicted with actual values, the actual reliability is computed as follows for the consumer and producer reliability, in equations (4.43) and (4.44), respectively:

$$R_{ac}(t, r_c) = 1 - \left(\frac{r_c}{\dfrac{N_C}{\sum_{t=1}^{} r_c}}\right)$$

(4.43)

$$R_{ap}(t, r_p) = 1 - \left(\frac{r_p}{\dfrac{N_P}{\sum_{t=1}^{} r_p}}\right)$$

(4.44)

NASA Space Shuttle Application

The following parameters are specified, understanding that the failure data observed during tests are used for estimating model parameters. Then the fitted model is used to make forecasts for the prediction range.

> t: consumer test time = 1, . . . , 25; consumer prediction range = 26, . . . , 45
> t: producer test time = 1, . . . , 36; producer prediction range = 37, . . . , 45
> t_m: = *desired* mission duration = 8 (45 − 37)

Test time can be different for consumer and producer because each chooses to test a different amount of time, dependent on their risk and reliability objectives. For example, the producer may have more resources than the consumer to do testing and, therefore, test for a longer time, and, in addition, is getting paid by the consumer to do testing. This difference leads to different prediction times, given the end of the mission: $t = 45$. Of course, the mission duration must be the same for consumer and producer. A mission duration of 8 days is typical for the Shuttle.

> $\bar{r}_c$:   mean of consumer failure distribution = .2400 failures
> $\bar{r}_p$:   mean of producer failure distribution = .1818 failures

Since r_c is needed in the computation of consumer risk for the prediction range $t = 26, . . . , 45$, and there are no historical values available for this range, equation (4.34) is used to predict these quantities. Likewise, this equation is used to predict r_p for producer risk in the prediction range $t = 37, . . . , 45$.

L_m: risk limit = .500000
R_{cs}:   specified *minimum* consumer reliability = .9500
R_{ps}:   specified *minimum* producer reliability, where $R_{ps} < R_{cs} = .9000$

The choice of reliability thresholds is based on the criticality of the mission to the safety of the crew and Shuttle.

Results from Shuttle Tests

Figure 4.12 indicates that mandatory *risk* tests have been passed and that reliability growth has occurred. Figure 4.13 indicates that mandatory *reliability* tests have been passed. Fig-

FIGURE 4.12   Shuttle Test: Consumer Risk (α), Producer Risk (β) and Actual Risk (μ) vs. Time *t*

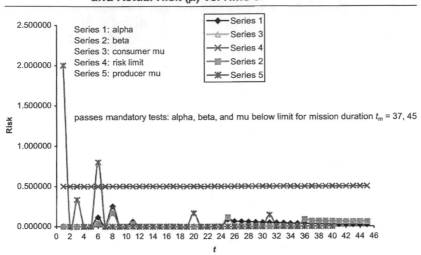

FIGURE 4.13   Shuttle First Test: Consumer Reliability $R_c(t)$, Producer Relibaility $R_p(t)$, Actual Consumer Reliability $R_{ac}(t)$, and Actual Producer Reliability R_{ap} vs. Time *t*

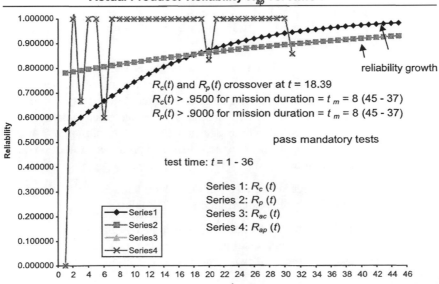

FIGURE 4.14   Shuttle First Test: Consumer Purity level (ρ) vs. Time *t*

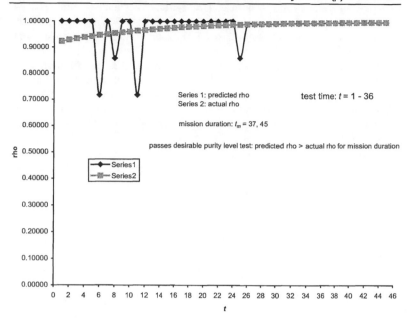

ure 4.14 demonstrates that the purity level test for the consumer has been passed. The producer test was also passed, but its plot is not shown because the result is almost identical to the consumer test. The final outcome is that this *safety critical* software would be accepted.

Summary

1. The test rule specifying consumer and producer predicted risks being less than their actual counterparts is a good idea. The rationale is that *future predicted* risks should be *less* than the actual historical risks. Furthermore, it is also a good idea to require consumer and producer reliability to exceed their actual counterparts. The rationale is to ensure that *future predicted* reliabilities would be *greater* than the actual historical reliabilities. Also the risk and reliability prediction accuracy rules should be adequate for ensuring model predictive validity.
2. For safety critical systems like the Shuttle, it is important to demonstrate reliability growth and growth in purity level. Thus, these tests were added for the Shuttle.
3. The detailed analysis required by the model test process provides a great deal of insight into the complex interrelationships among consumer and producer risk and reliability.

References

[CAN01] J. W. Cangussu, A. P. Mathur, and R. A. DeCarlo, "Feedback Control of the Software Test Process Through Measurements of Software Reliability." Proceedings of the 12th International Symposium on Software Reliability Engineering, 2001. ISSRE 2001, Nov. 27–30 2001, pp. 232–241.

[DAL99] S. R. Dalal, A. Jain, N. Karunanithi, J. M. Leaton, C. M. Lott, G. C. Patton, and B. M. Horowitz, "Model-Based Testing in Practice." Proceedings of 21st International Conference on Software Engineering (ICSE-99), May 16–22, 1999, Los Angeles, California, pp. 285–294.

[HOR96] Joseph R. Horgan and Aditya P. Mathur, "Software Testing and Reliability." *Handbook of Software Reliability Engineering,* Michael M. Lyu, editor. Computer Society Press, 1966.

[JUR06] Natalia Jursto, Ana M. Moreno, Sira Vegas, and Martin Solari, "In Search of What We Experimentally Know about Unit Testing." *IEEE Software,* Volume 23, Number 6, November / December 2006, pp. 72–79.

[KEL97] Ted Keller and Norman F. Schneidewind, "A Successful Application of Software Reliability Engineering for the NASA Space Shuttle." Software Reliability Engineering Case Studies, International Symposium on Software Reliability Engineering, November 3, Albuquerque, New Mexico, November 4, 1997, pp. 71–82.

[LLO62] David K. Lloyd and Myron Lipow, *Reliability: Management, Methods, and Mathematics.* Prentice Hall, 1962.

[LYU 98] M. R. Lyu. "An Integrated Approach to Achieving High Software Reliability." Proceedings of the Aerospace Conference, Volume: 4, pp. 123–136, 03/21/1998 - 03/28/1998, Snowmass at Aspen, CO.

[MAT00] Matthew Schmid, Anup Ghosh, and Frank Hill, "Techniques for Evaluating the Robustness of Windows NT Software." DARPA Information Survivability Conference and Exposition, January 2000, Hilton Head, SC.

[MUS87] John D. Musa, Anthony Iannino, and Kazuhira Okumoto, *Software Reliability: Measurement, Prediction, Application.* McGraw-Hill, 1987.

[MUS99] John D. Musa, *Software Reliability Engineering: More Reliable Software, Faster and Cheaper,* 2nd ed. Authorhouse, 1999.

[MYE79] Glenford J. Myers, *The Art of Software Testing.* John Wiley & Sons, New York: NY, 1979.

[NEL73] Charles R. Nelson, *Applied Time Series Analysis for Managerial Forecasting.* Holden-Day, 1973.

[NAS97] Software Safety, NASA Technical Standard, NASA-STD-8719.13A, September 15,1997.

[SCH97] Norman F. Schneidewind, "Reliability Modeling for Safety Critical Software." *IEEE Transactions on Reliability,* Vol. 46, No. 1, March 1997, pp. 88–98.

[STO93] P. A. Stocks and D. A. Carrington, "Test Templates: A Specification-Based Testing Framework." Proceedings of the 15th International Conference on Software Engineering, May 17–21, 1993, Baltimore, MD, pp. 405–414.

[TIA95] Jeff Tian, "Integrating Time Domain and Input Domain Analyses of Software Reliability Using Tree-Based Models." *IEEE Transactions On Software Engineering,* Vol. 21, No. 12, December 1995, pp. 945–958.

[VOA91] J. Voas, "Factors that Affect Software Testability." Proceedings of the 9th Pacific Northwest Software. Quality Conf., p. 235–247, October, 1991, Portland, OR. Publisher: Pacific Northwest Software Quality Conference, Inc.

[VOA99] J. Voas and Lora Kassab, "Using Assertions to Make Untestable Software More Testable." *Software Quality Professional Journal,* Vol. 1, No. 4, September 1999.

[WHI00] J. A. Whittaker. "What Is Software Testing? And Why Is It So Hard?" *IEEE Software,* January–February, 2000, Volume: 17, Issue: 1, pp. 70–79.

5

Models for Systems
and Software Engineering

Objectives

People and organizations learn at different rates. Since the rate of learning affects productivity in performing a variety of tasks, such as developing software, it behooves us to quantify the variables that influence learning. Thus, this chapter is aimed at fortifying the engineer with the knowledge and models necessary for this assessment. Another technology of great importance is the analysis of queuing systems. These systems occur in a myriad of production environments, such as software modules waiting to be tested. Thus, an additional objective is to apply queuing analysis to systems and software problems where queue build-ups cause loss of efficiency. Closely related to the problem caused by queues is the question of how to manage queue inputs so that queue size and wait times are minimized.

What You Will Learn From This Chapter

You will learn the following: 1) generic production time function and exponential function learning models; 2) software production learning models that incorporate defects and complexity variables; 3) application of single-server and multiple-server queuing models to solving software production problems; and 4) simulation of software fault correction systems as an adjunct to analytical queuing models.

Subjects

Learning curve models
    Production time learning function
    Exponential learning function
    Software production learning function
Queuing models
    Single server
    Multiple server
    Software production waiting time analysis
Software fault correction queuing systems
    Simulation of queue behavior under a variety of input loads
    Measures of fault correction effectiveness

Learning Curve Models

Learning in the context of operations management refers to the improved efficiency obtained from repetition of a production operation. Workers learn and improve by repeating operations. Learning is time-dependent and externally controllable. Several research studies have confirmed that human performance improves with reinforcement or frequent repetitions. Reductions in operation processing times achieved through learning curve effects can directly translate to cost savings for manufacturers and improved morale for employees [BAD92]. One interpretation of the learning curve is that initial projects are relatively more expensive than later projects and are even likely to be more expensive than projects produced under the old technology [KEM92].

Learning effects are the reductions in time per unit of output to perform specified activities. As the number of repetitions of doing a task increases, improvement occurs at an exponential rate because methods improve. Learning curve information is useful for planning and scheduling work [MON96].

This model provides functions for measuring the rate at which software organizations and personnel can learn a software process, such as a software test operation. By applying this model, the software engineer can, for example, determine when a contractor is justified in its charges for providing software test services.

Definitions

T_i: historical ith task time (e.g., installation time for ith computer)
T_j: predicted jth task time (e.g., installation time for jth computer)
T_{ave}:   predicted average task time (e.g., average computer installation time)
N: number of tasks (e.g., number of computers)
T_N: total task time (e.g., total time to install N computers)
LR_{ij}:   learning ratio of predicted jth task relative to historical ith task

This ratio is expected to decrease over the values of i because task time is expected to decrease as learning takes place (e.g., computer installation time).

s_{ij}:   exponent in learning curve function

Model

The predicted time to do the ith task is given by equation (5.1). This is the learning curve function.

$$T_j = T_i i_{ij}^s \tag{5.1}$$

The learning ratio is defined in equation (5.2):

$$LR_{ij} = T_j / T_i \tag{5.2}$$

Using equations (5.1) and (5.2), the learning curve function exponent is computed as:

$$i^{s_{ij}} = \log\left(LR_{ij}\right) / \log(i) \tag{5.3}$$

Now, the average of N predicted task times can be computed:

$$T_{ave} = \left(\sum_{j=1}^{n} T_j i^{s_{ij}}\right) / N \tag{5.4}$$

And the total task predicted time is computed as:

$$T_N = \left(\sum_{i=1}^{n} T_i i^{s_{ij}}\right) \tag{5.5}$$

It may be of interest to find the predicted rate of change of installation time with respect to the *i*th installation. This learning rate is obtained by differentiating equation (5.1) with respect to *i*:

$$\frac{d(T_j)}{d(i)} = (T_i s_{ij})(i^{(s_{ij}-1)}) \tag{5.6}$$

Problem 1

There are $N = 25$ computers. You estimate that the $n = 5$th computer will take 48 hours to install. The installation crew has experienced a learning ratio $LR_{ij} = .90$. What is the estimate of the total time T_N to install all $N = 25$ computers? Also identify the installation when there would be insignificant reduction in installation time.

Solution

The fifth predicted computer installation time is: T_j $(j = 5) = 48$ hours
    Using equation (5.2), the first computer historical installation time is estimated:

$$T_i = (i = 1) \ T_j / LR_{ij} = 48/.90 = 53.33 \text{ hours}$$

Then using these computations and equation (5.3), the learning curve function exponent is computed as:

$$s_{ij} = \log (LR_{ij})/\log (n) = \log (.90)/\log (5) = -.1054/1.6094 = -.0655$$

The average and total installation times are computed in Table 5.1 (p. 106, using equations (5.4) and (5.5), respectively. The individual installation times are plotted in Figure 5.1 with annotations of average and maximum installation times. In addition, the rate of change of installation time with respect to the *i*th installation is shown in Figure 5.2, which shows that about the fifteenth computer, there would be little reduction in installation time, as found by using equation (5.6).

FIGURE 5.1   Computer Installation Time T_j vs. Computer j

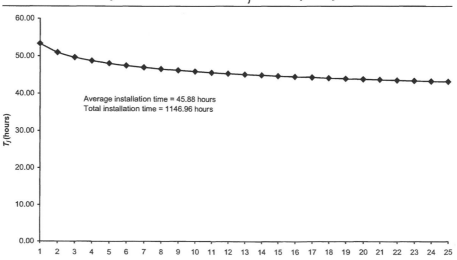

TABLE 5.1   Computer Installation Times

i	T_j
1	53.33
2	50.96
3	49.63
4	48.70
5	47.99
6	47.42
7	46.95
8	46.54
9	46.18
10	45.86
11	45.58
12	45.32
13	45.08
14	44.86
15	44.66
16	44.47
17	44.30
18	44.13
19	43.98
20	43.83
21	43.69
22	43.56
23	43.43
24	43.31
25	43.19
computer	**45.88** hours
T_{ave}	
T_N	**1146.96** hours

FIGURE 5.2   Rate of Change Computer Installation Time $d(T_j)\ /\ d(i)$ vs. Computer i

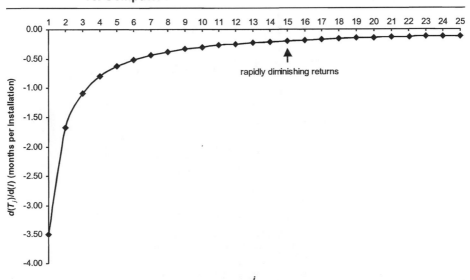

TABLE 5.2   History of Computer Installation Times

Computer i	Computer Installation Time T_i (hours)
10	120
20	108
30	102
40	97
50	94
60	90

Problem 2

The history of computer installation times is tabulated in Table 5.2. Using these times, predict the installation time for the 85th computer. In addition, compute the learning ratios and the values of the learning curve function exponent. Plot the results. Furthermore, tabulate the rate of change of predicted installation time. Based on this analysis, would there be much reduction in installation time if you continue installations beyond the 85th computer?

Solution

The solution must be obtained by successive computations. That is, once the first learning ratio is computed using the first historical and predicted installation times, the first exponent can be computed. Once the first exponent is computed, the next installation time is predicted. This process is continued for all the computers, and ends with the prediction of the 85th computer installation time. This process is shown in Table 5.3, with the succession of historical computer installation times T_i followed by predicted computer installation T_j. The predicted times become progressively smaller because the learning curve exponent becomes progressively smaller. This finding is reinforced by the fact that in Table 5.3 the rate of change of predicted installation times diminishes rapidly with the 60th computer. You would not expect significant reduction in installation time beyond this point.

TABLE 5.3   Computer Installation Times

Computer i	Historical Installation Time T_i (hours)	Predicted Installation Time T_j (hours)	Learning Ratio LR_{ij}	Learning Curve Exponent s_{ij}	Predicted Rate of Change $\dfrac{d(T_j)}{d(i)}$
10	120.00				
20	108.00	80.86	0.6738	−0.0966	−0.3906
30	102.00	99.82	0.9242	−0.0232	−0.0728
40	97.00	98.17	0.9624	−0.0104	−0.0242
50	94.00	93.60	0.9650	−0.0091	−0.0165
60	90.00	92.19	0.9807	−0.0048	−0.0070
85		87.04	0.9672	−0.0075	

hours

FIGURE 5.3   Computer Installation Time T_i, T_j vs. Computer i

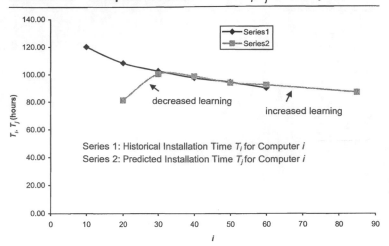

The historical and predicted installation times are plotted in Figure 5.3, where the predicted times become progressively less, once the installation crew overcomes its initial decreased learning, as it becomes accustomed to the problems of installation.

Learning Curve Exponential Model

Definitions

Production period: i
Number of units produced in period i: x_i
Labor time required to produce x_i units: y_i
a: estimated value of y_i when $x_i = 0$ (this can be considered production start-up time)
b: learning rate when $y_i = 1$

Model

The following learning curve model assumes that labor time y_i varies with number of units produced, x_i, according to the following exponential equation:

$$y_i = ae^{bx_i} \tag{5.7}$$

The learning rate LR can be obtained by differentiating equation (5.7) with respect to x_i as follows:

$$LR = \frac{d(y_i)}{d(x_i)} = bae^{bx_i} = by_i \tag{5.8}$$

Problem 3

Given the actual labor time involved in producing computers in Table 5.4, what is the forecast for the labor time required for producing 30 computers? What is the learning rate?

TABLE 5.4   Computer Production

Actual y_i	x_i	Predicted y_i
13000	1	10370
9600	2	9606
8200	3	8898
7500	4	8243
6800	5	7636
6700	6	7074
6200	7	6553
6100	8	6070
6000	9	5623
5800	10	5209
	30	1128
labor time hours	number of units	labor time hours

Indicate where learning is high and where it is low. Produce plots for both plots for the forecast and the learning rate.

Solution

Using Excel, the actual data are plotted and then an exponential curve is fitted. The result is Figure 5.4, with a forecast of 1128 hours to produce 30 computers. In Figure 5.5, we can see that the learning rate decreases rapidly with number of computers produced. This result tells the engineer that only minor gains in learning and, hence, productivity would be achieved as production quantities increase.

FIGURE 5.4   Labor Time y_i vs. Number of Computers x_i Produced in Period i

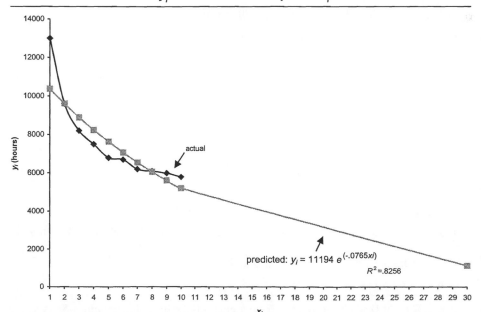

FIGURE 5.5   Learning Rate $d(y_i)/d(x_i)$ of Computer Production x_i vs. Number of Computers Produced in Period i

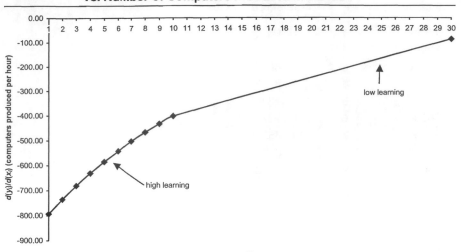

Problem 4

A team is revising computer manuals. The team can produce 10 manuals in 5 hours and 20 manuals in 8 hours. How many manuals can they produce in 100 hours? What are the values of the coefficients a and b? What are the interpretations of a and b?

Solution

Use equation (5.7) to express the two production conditions.

$$5 = ae^{10b} \qquad (5.9)$$

$$8 = ae^{20b} \qquad (5.10)$$

Divide equation (5.9) by equation (5.10) in order to solve for b:

$$.625 = e^{-10b} \qquad (5.11)$$

Use equation (5.11) to solve for b.

$$b = \text{Log}\,(.625)/(-10) = .0470$$

Now, use equation (5.9) to solve for a.

$$a = 5/e^{.0470} = 4.7704$$

Use equation (5.7) to solve x_i (i.e., production in 100 hours):

$$y_i = ae^{bx_i},\ y_i = 100,\ a = 4.7704,\ b = .0470$$
$$\text{Log}\,(100) = \text{Log}\,(4.7704) + (.0470 * x_i)$$

Estimated production for 100 hours: $x_i = (\text{Log}\,(100/4.7704))/.0470 = 64.74$ manuals

Interpretation of Parameters a *and* b

From equation (5.7), $y_i = ae^{bx_i}$

a $= y_0$ for $x_i = 0 = 4.7704$ hours $=$ estimated start-up time of production process.

From equation (5.8), $LR = \dfrac{d(y_i)}{d(x_i)} = bae^{bx_i} = by_i$

$b = .0470$ manuals per hour per hour = estimated learning rate when learning time $y_1 = 1$.

Software Production Time Model

The following is a software production model that includes only production time in the learning function. Later, this model will be expanded to include additional factors. Because of the great variability in software production data, cumulative production times are used in order to smooth the data. In this model, modules are developed in batches, as defined below. A batch is equivalent to a set of software modules in a release.

Definitions

t_i:	production time for module batch i
T_i:	cumulative production time for module batch i
T_{i-1}:	cumulative production time for module batch $i-1$
n:	number of module batches
$LR_{i, i+1}$:	learning rate of module batch $i+1$ relative to learning rate of module batch i
s_i:	exponent in learning curve function for module batch i
S_i:	source lines of code (sloc) for module batch i
d_i:	defect count on module batch i
dw_i:	defect count weight for module batch i
c_i:	software complexity count on module batch i (cyclomatic complexity)
cw_i:	complexity count weight for module batch i

Model

The actual cumulative failures Ta_i is computed in equation (5.12). Then the model for the predicted cumulative time to produce module batches 1 through n, Te_i, is given by equation (5.13) [GHA05]. This is the exponential learning curve function based on the idea that learning must reflect the fact that T_{i+1} will *decrease* relative to T_i by the exponent s_i, assuming negative values.

$$Ta_i = \left(\sum_{i=1}^{n} t_i \right) \tag{5.12}$$

$$Te_i = Ta_i i^{s_i} = \left(\sum_{i=1}^{n} t_i \right) i^{s_i} \tag{5.13}$$

Using the definition of the learning rate and the actual production data, Ta_i, the learning rate is computed in equation (5.14):

$$LR_{i, i+1} = Ta_{i+1}/Ta_i \tag{5.14}$$

Next, compute s_i, the learning curve function exponent, using equations (5.13) and (5.14). However, since equation (5.13) contains the predicted production time T_{ie}, which we will predict once we have solved for s_i, we use Ta_{i+1} to approximate T_{ie} in equation (5.13); equation (5.15) is the result.

$$s_i = \log (LR_{i, i+1})/\log (i) \tag{5.15}$$

In addition to production time, software organizations are interested in productivity. One metric of productivity, P_i, based on source lines of code (sloc), is computed in equation (5.16). This metric is the inverse of the typical software engineering productivity metric of source lines of code per unit time.

$$P_i = T_{ie} / S_i \qquad (5.16)$$

It is also of interest to find the rate of change of module batch development time with respect to the ith module batch. This rate is obtained by differentiating equation (5.13) with respect to i:

$$\frac{d(Te_i)}{d(i)} = (Ta_i s)(i^{(s_i^{-1})}) \qquad (5.17)$$

Software management has an interest in assessing whether productivity P_i exceeds a threshold value P_L. Modules that fail to meet this test are subject to detailed examination to determine the cause of deficient productivity (e.g., excessive complexity). Thus, we want $P_i \leq P_L$.

Software Production Regression Model

An alternative to the first software production model is to use classical regression analysis to derive the learning curve function.

Definitions

Software module production period: i
Number of modules produced in period i: x_i
Predicted cumulative time required to produce x_i units: T_i
Model parameters: a, b obtained by regression analysis

Model

The learning curve production regression model assumes that time T_i varies with number of modules produced, x_i, according to the following exponential equation [GHA05]:

$$T_i = ae^{bx_i} \qquad (5.18)$$

Obtain the solution to equation (5.18) by doing a log transformation and estimating the parameters a and b by regression analysis, in equations (5.19), . . . , (5.22):

$$\log (T_i) = \log (a) + b \log (x_i) \qquad (5.19)$$

$$Y_i = A + bX_i , \qquad (5.20)$$

$$\text{where } Y_i = \log (T_i), A = \log (a) \text{ and } X_i = \log (x_i) \qquad (5.21)$$

$$\text{Thus, } T_i = e^{Y_i}, a = e^{A}, \text{ and } x_i = e^{x_i} \qquad (5.22)$$

Then, using equations (5.20), . . . , (5.22), T_i can also be written as:

$$T_i = e^{(\log(a)+b\log(x_i))} \qquad (5.23)$$

Define the learning rate of this model as:

$$LR_{i,\, i+1} = Y_{i+1} / Y_i = \log(T_{i+1}) / \log(T_i) \qquad (5.24)$$

TABLE 5.5   NASA Project MC1 Data

Module Batch i	Day t_i	Day Ta_i Cumulative	d_i Defect Count	c_i Cyclomatic Complexity	x_i Modules Produced
1	0	0	10	19	1
2	112	112	3	33	2
3	1	113	15	404	3
4	13	126	11	127	4
5	28	154	14	263	5
6	6	160	10	94	6
7	8	168	26	470	7
8	18	186	13	207	8
9	22	208	7	42	9
10	13	221	10	24	10
11	18	239	0	94	11
12	28	267	9	34	12
13	15	282	20	128	13
14	13	295	10	286	14
15	55	350	8	82	15
16	20	370	12	104	16
17	0	370	7	20	17
18	2	372	0	2	18
19	47	419	9	173	19
20	56	475	14	268	20

NASA Satellite Application

Now, the learning curve equations are used to predict the learning curve function and productivity for a NASA satellite software project. To make the predictions, use software module batch size in thousands of source language statements (sloc), defects recorded against module batches, and module batch complexity. For complexity, use cyclomatic complexity developed by Tom McCabe [MCC76]. Use this complexity metric because it models the decision constructs in a program that are related to the time and effort required to debug software (i.e., learning rate). The NASA data used in the learning models are shown in Table 5.5.

Accounting for Defects and Complexity

Now account for the effects of software defects and complexity on learning rate and, hence, the ability of a software developer to produce software in a timely matter. Give effect to these factors by modifying equation (5.13), applying defect count and complexity weighting factors dw_i and cw_i, respectively.

First, the defect count weighting factor is shown in equation (5.25) and then applied to the unmodified predicted module batch production time Te_i to produce the modified time Td_i in equation (5.26). Note that increasing values of dw_i will lead to increasing values of Td_i.

$$dw_i = \frac{d_i}{\sum_{i=1}^{n} d_i} \qquad (5.25)$$

$$Td_i = Te_i / (1 - dw_i) \qquad (5.26)$$

Continuing in this vein, compute the complexity weighting factor in equation (5.27) and apply it to equation (5.26) to produce equation (5.28), the production time modified by *both* defect count and complexity count.

$$cw_i = \frac{c_i}{\sum\limits_{i=1}^{n} c_i} \tag{5.27}$$

$$Tdc_i = Td_i / (1 - cw_i) \tag{5.28}$$

Now assess *only* the influence of complexity on learning because defects may be highly correlated with complexity. Therefore, in equation (5.29) modify the *original* learning function Te_i by the complexity weights:

$$Tc_i = Te_i / (1 - cw_i) \tag{5.29}$$

Software Production Time Model Predictions

In the figures to be discussed, the module batch range $i = 1 - 20$ contains actual software production time data; data in the range $i = 1 - 15$ are used for estimating model parameters; and $i = 16 - 20$ is the prediction range (i.e., predictions are made for this range).

Figure 5.6 shows that there is a slight advantage of using the learning model from equation (5.13), as opposed to the straight-line regression function obtained by fitting a curve to the actual data, as computed by mean relative error (MRE) in the prediction range $i = 16 - 20$ module batches. This advantage would increase with the production of additional modules.

Figure 5.7 identifies those module batches whose productivity is less than the example limit, necessitating process improvement, perhaps more rigorous inspection to remove defects. Figure 5.8 tracks the rate of change of the predicted module batch production time in order to identify the trend in learning. As this rate of change moves in the positive direction,

**FIGURE 5.6   NASA Satellite Project MC1 Cumulative Module
Development Time T_i vs. Module Batch i**

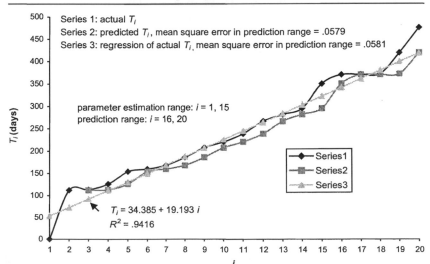

FIGURE 5.7   NASA Satellite Project MC1 Productivity P_i vs. Module Batch i

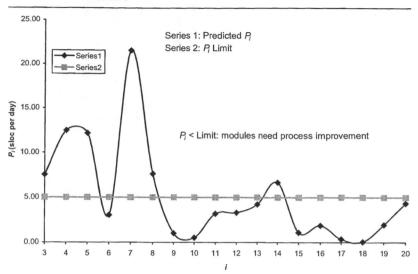

the learning rate diminishes with increasing modules to produce. This is to be expected because diminishing returns in learning will occur as more modules are produced.

Model Comparisons

In Figure 5.9, compare the production time learning model from equation (5.13) with the production regression model from equation (5.18), also showing the actual production time. Based on the MSE in the prediction range, the production time learning model is more accurate.

Figure 5.10 reinforces the result found in Figure 5.9—again, the production time learning model is superior because of its consistently higher learning rate, as modules are produced.

FIGURE 5.8   NASA Satellite Project MC1 Rate of Change Module Production Time $d(Te_i) / d(i)$ vs. Module Batch i

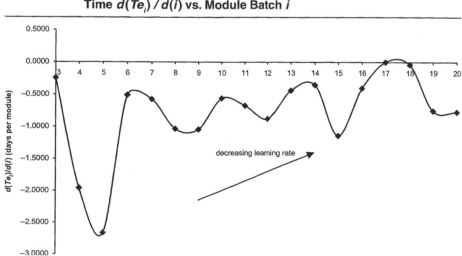

**FIGURE 5.9   NASA Satellite Project MC1 Module Production Time T_i
vs. Number of Modules Produced x_i**

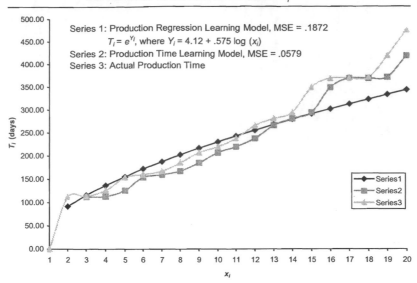

FIGURE 5.10   NASA Satellite Project MC1 Learning Rate LR vs. Module Batch i

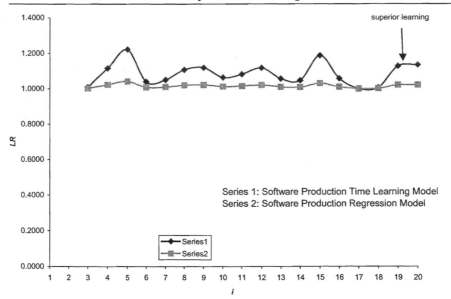

Assessing the Effect of Defects and Complexity on Learning

At this stage in the analysis, defect count and cyclomatic complexity count have not been included in the software production time model to see what influence these variables might have on software developer learning. While complexity may affect learning rate, it is not necessarily the case that defects would have a *direct* effect. The reason is that defects may be primarily caused by complexity, so that including both variables would be inappropriate. To assess the possible influence of complexity count on defect count, compute

FIGURE 5.11   NASA Satellite Project MC1 Production Time Increase
vs. Module Batch *i*

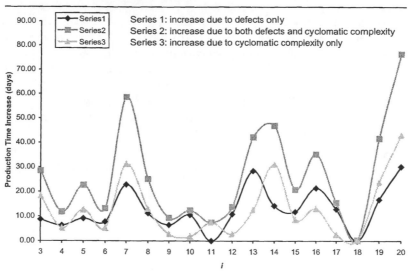

the square of the correlation coefficient between defect count and cyclomatic complexity count, using the data in Table 5.5. $R^2 = 0.5113$, which indicates that 51% of the variation in defect count can be attributed to variation in complexity count. This result is not insignificant. Therefore, in Figure 5.11, the best predictor of the increase in production time is the *cyclomatic complexity only* curve.

Summary

The software production time learning model works better than the regression model because it explicitly includes the learning rate, which better captures progress in learning than a regression function, which is limited to finding the best fit to empirical data. In other words, the software production time learning model is based on a theory of how learning varies over time with increasing production of software products, while the regression function has no theoretical base and depends on mimicking historical data. Also one has to be careful about including variables in models (i.e., defects and complexity) because the variables may not be independent predictors of software learning and productivity.

Queuing Analysis

Queuing analysis has wide applicability to problems in systems and software engineering. Queuing systems are important because many systems, such as supermarkets, gasoline stations, and software testing systems, may involve waiting for service because input exceeds system capacity. It would be economically and technically infeasible to provide systems that guarantee immediate service. Therefore, queuing models have been developed that are designed to analyze the properties of existing systems and to design new systems, such as the number of supermarket checkout stations required to serve the anticipated customer input. First, definitions are provided that apply to all queuing disciplines. In applying the definitions, it is important to note that all of the models you will study are assumed to operate in the steady state (i.e., mean values in the definitions below). Good references on queuing analysis are [KLE75, KLE76]. See these references for further details.

Generic Definitions (independent of specific application)

- Queue: a facility in which immediate service cannot be guaranteed, such as a supermarket checkout stand
- Customer: an object, such as a person or software module that enters a queue
- Mean arrival rate: λ, average rate that customers arrive in the queue
- Mean time between arrivals: t_a, average time between customer arrivals in the queue
- Mean service rate: μ, average rate that customers are served
- Mean service time: t_s, average time required to serve a customer
- Number of servers: c, number of stations that serve customers, such as number of pumps in a gasoline station
- Maximum number of customers, or system capacity: M, maximum number of stations, such as the number of supermarket checkout stands that are open to customers
- Utilization: ρ, probability that a station is busy serving customers
- Mean number of customers waiting to be served: n_w, average number of customers waiting in a queue
- Mean number of customers being served: n_s, average number of customers receiving service at stations
- Mean number of customers in system: n, average number of customers waiting and being served
- Probability of i customers in the system: p_i, chance that i number of customers are waiting for service and being served
- Mean wait time: t_w, average time that a customer waits to be served
- Mean service time: t_s, average time that is required to serve a customer
- Mean time in system: t, average time that a customer waits for service and is being served

Generic Queuing Model (independent of specific application)

Queue Times

The mean time between customers arriving in the system is given by the reciprocal of the mean arrival rate in equation (5.30).

$$t_a = 1/\lambda \tag{5.30}$$

The mean time that customers wait for service is equal to the mean number of customers waiting divided by the mean customer arrival rate in equation (5.31).

$$t_w = n_w/\lambda \tag{5.31}$$

The mean service time is equal to the reciprocal of the mean service rate in equation (5.32).

$$t_s = 1/\mu \tag{5.32}$$

The total mean time a customer spends in the system is the sum of mean waiting time from equation (5.31), plus mean service time from equation (5.32), computed in equation (5.33).

$$t = t_w + t_s \tag{5.33}$$

Queue Counts

The mean number of customers waiting for service is equal to the mean customer arrival rate times the mean customer wait time, from equation (5.31), computed in equation (5.34):

$$n_w = \lambda t_w \tag{5.34}$$

The mean number of customers being served is equal to the mean arrival rate divided by the mean service rate in equation (5.35).

$$n_s = \lambda/\mu \tag{5.35}$$

The total mean number of customers in the system is equal to the sum of mean number waiting plus mean number being serviced in equation (5.36).

$$n = n_w + n_s \tag{5.36}$$

Queue utilization is a critical parameter that relates mean input rate to mean service rate. It is the probability of the queue being busy. You can see this by observing that for a given mean input rate λ, the probability of the queue being busy will *decrease* as the mean service rate μ *increases*. Of course, this probability will decrease as the number of servers c is increased in equation (5.37).

$$\rho = \lambda/c\mu \tag{5.37}$$

Single-Server Fault Detection and Correction Model with Exponentially Distributed Time between Arrivals and Service Times

We all know about people queuing up to check out at a grocery store. Perhaps less obvious is the concept of faults that have been detected during software testing queuing up to be corrected. Testing is an important software development function. However, it may not be possible to test, detect faults, and correct faults immediately, because there could be a queue of faults that are being corrected; therefore, the faults must be queued and wait their turn for service. Therefore, queuing models are employed to estimate quantities such as wait time, service time, and number of faults waiting for service.

The following model is used when there is no information available about how customer arrivals and service times are distributed. There may be no information available about *individual* times between arrivals and service times; there may be only information about mean values. In this case, the best you can do is assume that arrivals and service time occur randomly, which corresponds to times between arrivals and service times being exponentially distributed. If you do have individual values available, you can perform statistical tests to identify the probability distribution. See Chapter 1 for a review of probability distributions.

It is convenient to segment the queuing problem according to questions that an engineer could pose about the software fault detection and correction system in Figure 5.12, using the model from [HIL01], as follows:

How many faults are in the system?

Mean number in system (waiting and being corrected) $n = \lambda/(\mu - \lambda)$ (5.38)

How many faults are waiting to be corrected?

Mean number waiting $= n_w = \lambda^2/\mu(\mu - \lambda)$ (5.39)

How long do faults have to wait to be corrected?

Mean waiting time $= t_w = \lambda/\mu(\mu - \lambda)$ (5.40)

FIGURE 5.12   Fault Detection and Correction Process

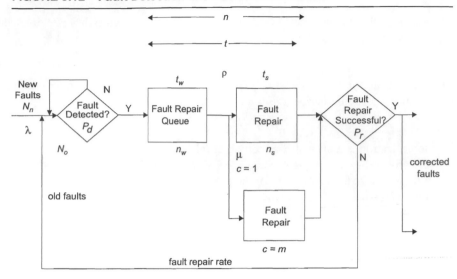

ρ : fault correction utilization

c : number of fault correction stations λ : fault input rate

N_n : number of new faults μ : fault repair rate

N_o : number of old faults

n : total number of faults in fault correction system

n_s : number of faults being corrected

n_w : number of faults waiting for correction

P_d : probability of fault detection

P_r : probability of correcting fault

t : total time in fault correction system

t_s : fault correction time

t_w : fault wait time

How long does it take to correct faults?

$$\text{Mean time being served} = t_s = (1 - \rho)/(\mu - \lambda) \tag{5.41}$$

How long do faults have to spend in the system?

$$\text{Mean time in the system (waiting and being served)} = t = 1/(\mu - \lambda) \tag{5.42}$$

What is the probability of i faults in the system?

Probability of i faults in the system is equal to the probability of the queue being busy for i faults (ρ^i) times the probability that the queue is busy for 0 faults (i.e., not busy $= 1 - \rho$):

$$p_i = \rho^i(1 - \rho) \tag{5.43}$$

What is the probability of 0 faults in the system?

Setting $i = 0$ in equation (5.43), solve for the probability of 0 faults in the system in equation (5.44).

Probability of 0 faults in the system (probability of queue not busy):

$$p_0 = \rho^0 (1 - \rho) = (1 - \rho), \tag{5.44}$$

as was found in equation (5.43).

What is the probability of n faults arriving during time t?

When the time between customer arrivals is exponentially distributed, the number of customers arriving is governed by the Poisson distribution in equation (5.45).

$$\text{Probability of } n \text{ arrivals during time } t = p(n,t) = \frac{(\lambda t)^n e^{-\lambda t}}{n!} \qquad (5.45)$$

What is the fault arrival rate?

The mean fault arrival rate into the system is given by the reciprocal of the mean time between arrivals:

$$\lambda = 1/t_a \qquad (5.46)$$

What is the rate at which faults are corrected?

The mean service rate for correcting faults is given by the reciprocal of the mean service time:

$$\mu = 1/t_s \qquad (5.47)$$

Problem 5

A fault detection and correction system is operating according to the queue discipline in Figure 5.12, with a single fault correction station. Measurements of the system have been taken, as follows:

t_a = mean time between fault arrivals into fault correction system = 240 minutes
t_s = mean fault correction time = 200 minutes

Answer the following questions:

1. What is the arrival rate of faults into the fault correction system?
   Use equation (5.46): $\lambda = 1/t_a = (1/240) = $ **.0042** *fault arrival rate* per minute
2. What is the rate at which faults are corrected in the fault correction system?
   Use equation (5.47): $\mu = 1/t_s = $ **.0050** *fault correction rate* (faults per minute)
3. What is the utilization of the fault correction system?
   Use equation (5.37), with $c = 1$ server; $\rho: = \lambda/\mu = 0042/.0050 = $ **.8400**
4. What is the probability of zero faults in the fault correction system?
   Use equation (5.44): $p_0 = \rho^0 (1 - \rho) = (1 - \rho) = 1 - .8400 = $ **.1600**
5. What is the probability of n faults, p_n, in the fault correction system, where $n = 0, \ldots, 10$?
   One way to do this is to plot p_n as a function of n in order to observe the trend, using equation (5.43). The plot is in Figure 5.13 on page 122, where you can see that the probability decreases rapidly with n.
6. What is the mean number of faults waiting to be corrected in the fault correction system?
   Use $n_w = \lambda^2/\mu(\mu - \lambda) = [(.0042)^2]/[.0050(.0050 - .0042)] = $ **4.41**
7. What is the mean number of faults in system (waiting and being served)?
   Use $n = \lambda/(\mu - \lambda) = [(.0042]/[(.0050 - .0042)] = $ **5.25**
8. What is the mean wait time in the fault correction system?
   Use $t_w = \lambda/\mu(\mu - \lambda) = [.0042]/[(.0050) (.0050 - .0042)] = $ **1,050** minutes per fault
9. What is the mean service time in the fault correction system?

FIGURE 5.13   Fault Correction Station Utilization (ρ) and Mean Number of Faults Waiting for Correction (n_w) vs. Number of Fault Correction Stations c

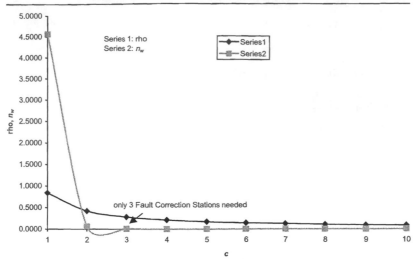

Use $t_s = (1 - \rho)/(\mu - \lambda) = (1 - .84) / (.0050 - .4200) = \mathbf{200}$ minutes per fault
This result confirms the value given in the problem.

10. What is the mean time in system in the fault correction system?
    Use $t = t_w + t_s = 1,050 + 200 = \mathbf{1,250}$ minutes per fault

The excessive times reported as answers to 8, 9, and 10 dramatize the need for multiple fault correction stations.

Multiple-Server Fault Detection and Correction Model with Exponentially Distributed Time between Arrivals and Service Times, and Finite Server Capacity [HIL01]

The relatively simple single-server queuing system was presented first to give the reader a sense of how queuing problems are modeled before delving into the complexities of multiple-server systems. You saw in Problem 5 that a single-fault correction system is unlikely to provide acceptable performance, hence the need for multiple-server models. The definitions and equations that follow are given in the context of a fault correction system, as shown in Figure 5.12.

Definitions of Basic Fault Correction Quantities

N_n: number of new faults
N_o: number of old faults
n: number of faults in system
N_c: number of faults corrected
N_u: number of faults uncorrected
P_d: probability of fault detection
P_r: probability of fault correction
c: number of fault correction stations

Model

Probability of zero faults in the fault correction system $= p_0 = 1/D$, where

$$D_i = \sum_{n_i=0}^{c} \left(\frac{(c\rho)^{n_i}}{n_i!} \right) + \left(\frac{(c\rho)^c}{(c!(1-\rho))^2} \right) \tag{5.48}$$

Mean number of faults waiting to be corrected:

$$n_w = \frac{(\lambda/\mu)^c \rho p_0}{c!(1-\rho)^2} \tag{5.49}$$

The mean number of faults being corrected is equal to the probability that multiple fault correction stations are busy, ρ, computed in equation (5.50):

$$n_s = (\lambda/\mu) \tag{5.50}$$

The expected number of corrected faults, N_c, is equal to the number of new faults times the probability of detection times the probability of correction in equation (5.51).

Equation (5.51) also shows that the expected number of old faults, N_o (i.e., new faults that are not corrected) is equal to the number of new faults that are detected times the probability that the detected faults are *not* corrected. See Figure 5.12.

$$N_c = N_n P_d P_r, \qquad N_o = (N_n P_d)(1 - P_r) \tag{5.51}$$

Thus, the *expected* number of faults in the fault correction system, in equation (5.52), must be equal to the sum of new faults and old faults (equation (5.51)) . See Figure 5.12.

$$n = N_n + N_o = N_n + (N_n P_d)(1 - P_r) = N_n(1 + P_d(1 - P_r)) \tag{5.52}$$

The utilization of the fault correction system is an important performance parameter and is given in equation (5.53):

$$\rho = \lambda/c\mu = t_s/(ct_a) \tag{5.53}$$

The utilization is the probability of each fault correction station being busy. You can see that the utilization will increase with increasing fault correction time t_s, decreasing number of stations c, and decreasing time between fault arrivals t_a.

Mean fault wait time t_w is computed by considering the number of faults waiting to be corrected and the rate of fault arrivals:

$$t_w = \frac{n_w}{\lambda} \tag{5.54}$$

Then, the mean time faults spend waiting for correction and being corrected t is computed in equation (5.55) by adding equation (5.54) to t_s, the mean fault correction time:

$$t = t_w + t_s \tag{5.55}$$

In order to compute the effectiveness of the fault correction process, that is the fault correction rate, the expected number of faults corrected (number of new faults times probability of detection times probability of correction) is divided by the time required to correct them, where this time is wait time plus correction time from equation (5.55). Thus, effectiveness, $E(t)$, is computed as follows:

$$E(t) = (N_n * P_d * P_r)/t \qquad (5.56)$$

Recalling from equation (5.48) that p_0 is the probability of 0 faults in the system, the probability of one or more faults in the system is given in equation (5.57):

$$P_{n>0} = 1 - p_0 \qquad (5.57)$$

A measure of *non-effectiveness* is the expected number of faults that have *not* been corrected N_u, computed by multiplying the expected number of faults detected by the probability of non-correction in equation (5.58):

$$N_u = (N_n * P_d) * (1 - P_r) \qquad (5.58)$$

Then, effectiveness of fault correction E_c is defined in equation (5.59), as $1 - $ (the proportion of faults that are uncorrected) using equations (5.52) and (5.58):

$$E_c = 1 - (N_u/n) = 1 - [(N_n * P_d) * (1 - P_r) / N_n(1 + P_d(1 - P_r))]$$

$$E_c = 1/(1 + P_d(1 - P_r)) \qquad (5.59)$$

Note that the larger the value of the fault correction rate P_r, the higher the value of E_c. In fact, when $P_r = 1.0$, $E_c = 1.0$.

Problem 6

A software testing organization wants to find out how many fault correction stations they should use in Figure 5.12 when the number of new faults that can enter the system is $N_n = 1, 2, 3, 4, 5, 6, 7, 8, 9$. Measurements of the system have been taken, as follows:

t_a = mean time between fault arrivals into fault correction system = 240 minutes
t_s = mean fault correction time = 200 minutes

Based on historical data compiled by the organization, P_d: probability of fault detection = .80 and P_r: probability of fault correction = .50.

The number of stations will be deemed sufficient when diminishing returns are reached as demonstrated by expected fault wait time no longer decreasing significantly.

Solution

The mean fault input rate and mean fault correction rate can be computed, as follows:

$\lambda = 1/t_a = 1/240 = .0042$ faults per minute
$\mu = 1/t_s = 1/200 = .0050$ fault corrections per minute

Note: when solving for the single-server case ($c = 1$), use the single-server equations; in the multiple-server case ($c > 1$), use the multiple-server equations.

Using the equations for mean number of faults waiting for correction (equation (5.50)) and fault correction station utilization (equation (5.53)), compute these quantities and plot them versus number of fault correction stations in Figure 5.13 to determine how many stations are needed. The solution is that only three stations are needed. Beyond that there is only a miniscule reduction in wait time. Also note that the station utilization is relatively low at three stations, indicating that additional fault input traffic could be easily accommodated.

Table 5.6 shows the data and calculations necessary to produce Figures 5.13 and 5.14.

Using the equation for fault correction effectiveness (equation (5.56)), make the plot shown in Figure 5.14. The purpose of the plot is to ascertain how quickly effectiveness increases with number of fault correction stations. You can see that there is a rapid increase

TABLE 5.6   Fault Correction Station Analysis and Effectiveness

c	ρ	P_0	N_n	n	$\dfrac{(c\rho)^n}{n!}$	$\dfrac{(c\rho)^c}{(c!(1-\rho))}$	D	n_w	t_w	t	E(t)
1	0.8400	0.1657	1	1.40	0.7834	5.2500	6.0334	4.57	1087.69	1287.69	0.0186
2	0.4200	0.1439	2	2.80	0.3069	0.6083	6.9486	0.06	15.09	215.09	0.2232
3	0.2800	0.1407	3	4.20	0.0200	0.1372	7.1058	0.01	1.79	201.79	0.3568
4	0.2100	0.1402	4	5.60	0.0031	0.0263	7.1352	0.00	0.23	200.23	0.4794
5	0.1680	0.1401	5	7.00	0.0001	0.0042	7.1394	0.00	0.03	200.03	0.5999
6	0.1400	0.1401	6	8.40	0.0000	0.0006	7.1400	0.00	0.00	200.00	0.7200
7	0.1200	0.1401	7	9.80	0.0000	0.0001	7.1401	0.00	0.00	200.00	0.8400
8	0.1050	0.1401	8	11.20	0.0000	0.0000	7.1401	0.00	0.00	200.00	0.9600
9	0.0933	0.1401	9	12.60	0.0000	0.0000	7.1401	0.00	0.00	200.00	1.0800
10	0.0840	0.1401	10	14.00	0.0000	0.0000	7.1401	0.00	0.00	200.00	1.2000
λ	0.0042	μ	0.0042	P_d	0.80	P_r	0.50	t_s	200.00		

FIGURE 5.14   Fault Correction Effectiveness *E(t)* vs. Number of Fault Correction Stations *c*

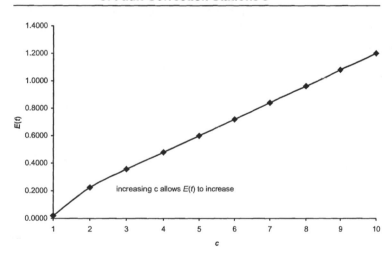

increasing c allows E(t) to increase

in effectiveness as number of fault correction stations increases. However, as determined in Figure 5.13, only three stations are necessary.

Problem 7

Assigning Faults to Fault Correction Stations

Up to this point, the focus has been on finding the optimal number of fault correction stations with respect to fault correction effectiveness. But this is not the whole story. We know that in the supermarket we usually choose the counter with the minimum number of customers waiting. It is no different with the fault correction system. Faults would "like" to be processed at a station with the shortest line. Therefore, by simulating the arrival of faults into the system, we can identify stations that are busy and ones that are not busy. Assuming equal probabilities of stations being busy, we can determine whether a station is busy or not busy by using uniformly distributed random numbers (e.g., Excel RAND function). Since

TABLE 5.7   Computation of Fault Counts

c	ρ	N_n	N_o	n
1	0.8400	1	0.40	1.40
2	0.4200	2	0.80	2.80
3	0.2800	3	1.20	4.20
4	0.2100	4	1.60	5.60
5	0.1680	5	2.00	7.00
6	0.1400	6	2.40	8.40
7	0.1200	7	2.80	9.80
8	0.1050	8	3.20	11.20
9	0.0933	9	3.60	12.60
10	0.0840	10	4.00	14.00

it was determined in Problem 6 that 3 fault correction stations were adequate, 3 stations are used for fault assignments. We will compare this solution with the steady-state solution in Table 5.7. The steady-state solution does not "know" whether a station is busy. It only "knows" the *probability* of a station being busy. Therefore, it will be interesting to compare the queue characteristics of the two solutions.

Solution

You can see that the steady-state solution for number of faults in the system, n, in Table 5.7, is approximately equal to the stated use of $c = 3$ stations and $n = 9$ faults: the fault count, n, for $c = 1, 2, 3, = (1.40 + 2.80 + 4.20) = 8.40$. Therefore, when the random number RN is generated, the assignments were made for 9 faults as follows:

$.000 \leq RN \leq .333$, assign fault to station 1
$.334 \leq RN \leq .666$, assign fault to station 2
$.667 \leq RN \leq 1.000$, assign fault to station 3

Other Problem Specifications

fault input rate $\lambda = .0042$ faults per minute
fault service rate $= .0050$ faults per minute
fault correction rate $P_r = .50$

N_o, the number of old faults in Table 5.7, is computed from $N_o = (N_n P_d)(1 - P_r)$, equation (5.51).

ρ, fault correction station utilization, is computed in Table 5.7 from $\rho = \lambda/(c\mu)$, equation (5.53).

n, the number of faults in the fault correction system is computed in Table 5.7 from $n = N_n(1 + P_d(1 - P_r))$, equation (5.52).

The assignment results are shown in Table 5.8, where the bolded quantities represent the assignment of faults to stations. These assignments are based on the values of random numbers, RN, as described above.

Table 5.9 shows "before" and "after" representing the original steady-state results and results of assigning faults to stations, respectively. The result that emerges from examining Table 5.9 is that it is worthwhile to conduct a simulation of individual fault assignments because results may differ from the steady-state solution. Interestingly, the assignment of faults on the basis of stations not being busy does not produce a consistently better result.

TABLE 5.8   Assigning Faults to Correction Stations

Random Number RN	Fault Number f_i	Fault Correction Station		
		c_1	c_2	c_3
0.3641	1	0	1	0
0.9475	2	0	0	1
0.9742	3	0	0	1
0.7326	4	0	0	1
0.6352	5	0	1	0
0.6994	6	0	0	1
0.6504	7	0	1	0
0.7708	8	0	0	1
0.0583	9	1	0	0
	n total	1	3	5

TABLE 5.9   Results of Assigning Faults to Correction Stations

c_i	n	Before n_w	After n_w	Before t_w	After t_w	Before t	After t	Before $E(t)$	After $E(t)$
1	1	4.5683	4.5259	1087.69	1077.59	1287.69	1277.59	0.000311	0.000313
2	3	0.0634	0.0648	15.09	15.43	215.09	215.43	0.003719	0.003714
3	5	0.0075	0.0077	1.79	1.83	201.79	201.83	0.005947	0.005946
station identification	number of faults	number waiting		wait time		total time		effectiveness	

This is due to the fact that the assignments are unbalanced in Table 5.8. A comprehensive simulation would involve doing the experiment 100 times and averaging the results.

Assessing Effectiveness of Fault Correction

Figure 5.15 shows both the expected number of faults corrected and fault correction effectiveness, as a function of probability of fault correction, for a given number of new faults that are input to the system. This plot can be used by a software developer to identify the improvement in fault correction that could be achieved by increasing the probability of fault correction. Fault correction effectiveness can be improved by combining testing with rigorous software inspections.

Summary

Queuing models have wide application in systems and software engineering. Prominent examples involving software fault correction processes were illustrated. Of primary concern is the number of servers or fault correction stations that is adequate to handle the fault input load. Computations for making this assessment were presented. You learned that it is not sufficient to rely only on mean value, or steady-state solutions, because it is also important to simulate individual fault inputs in order to highlight the weak and strong spots in the fault correction system.

**FIGURE 5.15   Expected Number of Faults Corrected N_c and Fault
Correction Effectiveness E_c vs. Probability of Fault
Correction P_r**

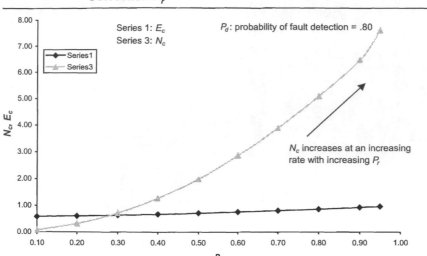

References

[BAD92] A.B. Badiru. "Computational Survey of Univariate and Multivariate Learning Curve Models." *IEEE Transactions on Engineering Management,* Volume 39, Issue 2, May 1992, pp. 176–188.

[GHA05] Ghaffari Abu, João W. Cangussu, and Janos Turi, "A Quantitative Learning Model for Software Test Process." Proceedings of the 38th Annual Hawaii International Conference on System Sciences (HICSS '05)—Track 3, 2005, p. 78b.

[HIL01] Fredrick S. Hillier and Gerald J. Lieberman, *Introduction to Operations Research,* Seventh Edition. McGraw-Hill, 2001.

[KEM92] Chris F. Kemerer, "How the Learning Curve Affects CASE Tool Adoption." *IEEE Software,* Vol. 09, No. 3, May/June 1992, pp. 23–28.

[KLE75] L. Kleinrock. *Queuing Systems, Vol. 1: Theory.* John Wiley & Sons, New York, 1975.

[KLE76] L. Kleinrock. *Queuing Systems, Vol. 2: Computer Applications.* John Wiley & Sons, New York, 1976.

[MCC76] Thomas J. McCabe, IEEE Transactions on Software Engineering, Vol. Se-2, No. 4, December 1976, pp. 308–320.

[MON96] Joseph G. Monks, *Operations Management,* Second Edition. McGraw-Hill, 1996.

6

Software Reliability Metrics

Objectives

Recently new software reliability metrics have been developed and evaluated that are not included in the IEEE 982.1 *Standard Dictionary of Measures of the Software Aspects of Dependability* [IEE06]. (In plain English, this standard is about software reliability metrics!) In addition, modifications have been made to metrics in 982.1 to enhance their usability. The objective of this chapter is to describe, evaluate, and show how to apply these new and modified metrics, using failure data from several releases of the NASA Space Shuttle flight software. The data are shown in Table 6.1, Parts 1 and 2 below.

Recognizing that readers have other applications, the methodology, equations, and prediction plots are explained so that engineers can apply the metrics to their applications. The metrics are assessed from two standpoints: 1) identify metrics that support a specified purpose (e.g., demonstrate reliability growth) and 2) using the metrics, identify soft-

TABLE 6.1   Part 1: Software Release Failure Data

Redesign of Main Engine Controller			Payload Re-manifest Capabilities			Crew Enhancements		
OI3			OI4			OI5		
Test Time 30-Day Intervals T_i	Severity Code s_i	Failures in Interval i x_i	Test Time 30-Day Intervals T_i	Severity Code s_i	Failures in Interval i x_i	Test Time 30-Day Intervals T_i	Severity Code s_i	Failures in Interval i x_i
0.97	3	2	0.67	3	1	0.97	2	2
1.20		0	4.33		0	1.20		0
3.03	3	2	4.90		0	3.03	3	1
3.07	2	2	5.27	3	1	4.00	3	2
4.00		0	6.00	3	2	4.33		0
4.23		0	7.00	3	1	7.43		0
8.20		0	7.43	3	2	9.77	3	1
9.63	3	1	13.63		0	12.73		0
9.70		0	16.93		0	17.50		0
9.77	2	4	27.07		0	23.70	2	1
10.37		0	43.80		0	45.17		0
12.13	3	1	135.33		0	58.27		0
27.67		0	178.43		0	65.03	3	1
35.93		0	KLOC	11.40		76.90		0
87.53		0				KLOC	5.90	

(continued)

TABLE 6.1   Part 2: Software Release Failure Data

Western Test Range			Centaur Development		
Enhance Propellant Dumps					
OI6			OI8		
Test Time 30-Day Intervals T_i	Severity Code s_i	Failures in Interval i x_i	Test Time 30-Day Intervals T_i	Severity Code s_i	Failures in Interval i x_i
1.87		0	3.57		0
2.37	2	2	4.03		0
3.47	2	1	6.07		0
3.50	2	2	7.03	3	2
3.97		0	7.47		0
9.77		0	9.17	3	1
12.73		0	9.23	3	2
17.50		0	12.70		0
23.70		0	12.87	3	2
45.17	3	1	13.20		0
58.27		0	17.17		0
65.03		0	29.53		0
76.90	3	1	44.57	1	3
181.27		0	49.70		0
KLOC	**8.80**		96.90		0
			KLOC	**6.60**	

ware releases that, based on reliability predictions, are ready to deploy and identify which software requires additional testing. Prediction accuracy is computed for all metrics and the metrics are compared based on the results.

The justification of assumptions that support the validity of the metrics are examined. Also, in addition to the metrics themselves, there are the trends in metrics, indicating whether reliability growth is being achieved, that are included in the engineer's metrics toolkit. In order to assess the validity of predictive metrics, the mean relative error (MRE) between predicted and actual values is computed.

Where predictive reliability metrics are introduced or modified, the Schneidewind Software Reliability Model (SSRM) [SCH97] is used. Other models recommended in the IEEE/AIAA Recommended Practice on Software Reliability [IEE08] could be used. In software reliability analysis, there are various time values: failure time, time *when* a prediction is made, time for which a prediction is *made,* etc. All of these are designated as T_i, where i identifies an event (e.g., failure i) or an interval of test or operational time of the software.

To validate the metric computations, C++ program results are compared with Excel computation results for the Shuttle releases (operational increments: OIs). The computations were not considered validated until the C++ program and Excel computations matched. Note that other programming languages or mathematical packages could be used, but it is important to use more than one computational method in order to validate the results.

What You Will Learn From This Chapter

You will learn the following: 1) how to identify reliability metrics that can be used to assess the quality of your software, 2) how to identify software releases that based, on their reliability assessments, are ready to deploy, 3) how to identify releases that require more testing and fault removal before they are ready to deploy, and 4) how to compute reliability metric prediction error. If necessary, you can refresh your knowledge of statistics and probability in Chapter 1 and software reliability engineering in Chapter 2.

Subjects

> Reliability Metric Assumptions
> New Software Reliability Metrics
> Modified Software Reliability Metrics
> Reliability Metrics Prediction Results
> Summary of Reliability Metric Results

Reliability Metric Assumptions

Independence of Successive Failures

Some researchers [GOS99] claim that the assumption of independence of successive software failures in applying software reliability models is inappropriate. Whether this is true depends on the kind of testing that is conducted. Sometimes different test scenarios are grouped according to high-level functionalities and a series of related test runs are conducted. In addition, input data may be chosen in order to increase the testing effectiveness, that is, to detect as many faults as possible. As a result, once a failure is observed, a series of related test runs are conducted to help isolate the cause of failure. This would also be the case during debugging when successive failures could be dependent because debugging is a fine-grained search for specific faults that may be violating the specification. On the other hand, the failure data that drive software reliability models are obtained during system test of program functions. Given the enormity of the input and program space, it is unlikely that two faults could cause two successive failures to be related [MUS87]. This is particularly the case if random selection of inputs is used in system testing. Rather than make an assumption that may turn out to be erroneous, the data should be subjected to an autocorrelation test, using a statistical package. For example, in order to test the assumption of independence of successive failures, autocorrelation functions are computed and plotted for several NASA space systems, using time to next failure T_i. The autocorrelation function is defined as follows [LYU96]:

$$\text{Autocorrelation } (T_i, \Delta t) = \text{Correlation } (T_i, T_i + \Delta t), \tag{6.1}$$

where Δt represents the lag between values of T_i. For example, $\Delta t = 1$ represents the series T_i, T_{i+1}, T_{i+2}, etc., $\Delta t = 2$ represents the series T_i, T_{i+3}, T_{i+5}, etc. When computing the autocorrelation function, confidence intervals of the function are produced in order to see when the function, plotted for various lags, falls outside the intervals. When this is the case, a high degree of correlation is indicated. In Figures 6.A1 . . . A4 in the Appendix to this chapter, for the NASA Space Shuttle flight software, there is no significant correlation, indicating that the independence assumption is justified for these data. However, in the case of the NASA satellite project JM1 in Figure 6.A5, there is significant autocorrelation for $\Delta t = 1$. Therefore, it would not be appropriate to use a model to predict the series T_i, T_{i+1}, T_{i+2}, etc.

Since there is no significant correlation at other values of Δt, predictions could be made, for example, of series T_i, T_{i+5}, T_{i+9}, etc.

A word about accounting for the passage of time: In some cases, time is measured at an instance in time, for example, a prediction of time to next failure. In other cases, time is measured in intervals, for example, failures occurring in the interval $(T_{i+1} - T_i)$.

New Software Reliability Metrics

Time Between Failures Trend

If the trend of a series of time between failures increases, it is suggestive of reliability growth, as expressed in equation (6.2):

$$M_{i+1} = (T_{i+2} - T_{i+1}) > M_i = (T_{i+1} - T_i) \tag{6.2}$$

Trend Analysis

A method is needed to ascertain whether the trend in a series like equation (6.2) indicates reliability growth. One such method by Bates [BAT55] is the following:

$$U_i = \frac{\sum_{i=1}^{N_i} M_i - ((N_i / 2)(T_i))}{T_i \left(\sqrt{\dfrac{N_i}{12}} \right)} \tag{6.3}$$

where N_i is actual cumulative number of failures at interval i, T_i is the time during which the N_i failures occur, and M_i is the series being examined. With $M_i = (T_{i+1} - T_i)$, increasing positive values of U_i indicate reliability growth [MUS87]. A similar trend test is the Laplace test [LYU96].

Predicted Software Reliability

Strangely, software reliability was not included in 982.1. Using SSRM, reliability is predicted in equation (6.4):

$$R(T_i) = e^{-\left[\frac{\alpha}{\beta} \left[e^{-\beta(T_i - s + 1)} - e^{-\beta(T_i - s + 2)} \right] \right]}, \tag{6.4}$$

where $R(T_i)$ uses the following definitions:

   α: initial failure rate
   β: rate of change of failure rate
   T_i: time for which the prediction is made
   s: first time interval when failure data are used in estimation of parameters α and β

Actual Software Reliability

In addition to predicted reliability, you can compute the actual reliability $R_a(T_i)$, based on failures observed in interval i, x_i, in relation to the total cumulative number of failures observed at interval t, X_t, in equation (6.5):

$$R_a(T_i) = 1 - \left(\frac{x_i}{X_t}\right) \tag{6.5}$$

Reliability Required to Meet Mission Duration Requirement

The original 982.1 does provide metrics for meeting the mission duration requirement by predicting the time to next failure and seeing whether the prediction *exceeds* the mission duration. Another approach is to predict the reliability at the mission duration t_m plus mission start, or launch time t_s (nominally the last test time), and see whether the result meets the required reliability *during* the mission. This is accomplished by reformulating equation (6.4) in equation (6.6):

$$R(t_s + t_m) = e^{-\left[\frac{\alpha}{\beta}\left[e^{-\beta\left((t_s+t_m)-s+1\right)} - e^{-\beta\left((t_s+t_m)-s+2\right)}\right]\right]} \tag{6.6}$$

Rate of Change of Software Reliability

In addition to predicted software reliability, its rate of change is also important to identify the amount of test or operational time where the rate of change is a maximum. Beyond this time, increases in reliability yield diminishing returns, although additional reliability may be warranted to meet reliability requirements. The rate of change is formulated by differentiating equation (6.4) and is given in equation (6.7):

$$\frac{d(R(T_i))}{d(T_i)} = \alpha R(T_i)\left[e^{-\beta(T_i-s+1)} - e^{-\beta(T_i-s+2)}\right] \tag{6.7}$$

Parameter Ratio

In [IEE08] it has been demonstrated that the parameter ratio $PR = \beta/\alpha$ from SSRM can accurately rank the reliability of a set of software modules or releases, *before* extended effort is involved in making reliability predictions, by just using the result of parameter estimates. That is, increasing values of PR are associated with increasing values of reliability. The reason is—referring to the definitions above—high values of β mean that the failure rate decreases rapidly and small values of α mean that the failure rate will decrease from a low starting value. The two parameters in concert, computed in PR, lead to increasing reliability, as can be seen by examining equation (6.4).

Software Restoration Time

When software fails and the fault that was the culprit is corrected, the question is: How long will it take to restore the system to the specified reliability? This metric was suggested by Harold Williams, editor of *The R & M Engineering Journal,* American Society for Quality. This metric can be obtained by solving equation (6.4) for T_i—the restoration time—specifying $R(T_i)$ as the required reliability when the system has been restored. The result is equation (6.8):

$$T_i = (-\frac{1}{\beta})\log\left[\frac{-\log(R(T_i)\beta)}{\alpha(1-e^{-\beta})}\right] + (s-1) \tag{6.8}$$

Predicted Cumulative Failures

There is no prediction of cumulative failures in 982.1, which is a fundamental reliability growth measure (i.e., $F(T_i)$ will increase at a decreasing rate if reliability growth is present). Therefore, cumulative failures are predicted using SSRM [SCH97] in equation (6.9):

$$F(T_i) = (\alpha / \beta)\left[1 - e^{-\beta(T_i - s + 1)}\right] + X_{s-1},\tag{6.9}$$

where $F(T_i)$ uses the following definitions:

T_i: time when $F(T_i)$ failures are predicted to occur.
X_{s-1}: observed failure count in the range $[s - 1, T_i]$.

Fault Correction Rate and Delay

An approach to fault correction prediction is to relate it to failure prediction, introducing a delay dT, between failure detection and the completion of fault correction (i.e., fault correction time) [SCH01]. Assume that the rate of fault correction is proportional to the rate of failure detection. In other words, assume that fault correction keeps up with failure detection, except for the delay $d(T_i)$ in correcting fault i. If this assumption is not met in practice, the model will underestimate the remaining faults in the code. Thus, the model provides a lower bound on remaining faults (i.e., the remaining faults would be no less than the prediction). Using this assumption, the cumulative number of faults corrected by time T_i, N_{ci}, would have the same form as the cumulative number of failures $F(T_i)$ that have been detected by time T_i, but delayed by the interval $d(T_i)$. The fault correction rate for fault i is modeled in equation (6.10), where x_i is the number of faults corrected in interval i:

$$c_i = \frac{x_i}{(T_{i+1} - T_i)}\tag{6.10}$$

Use a random variable to model the delay $d(T_i)$. For the Space Shuttle, $d(T_i)$ was found to be exponentially distributed with mean fault correction time $1/m_i$, where m_i is the mean fault correction rate in interval i in equation (6.11):

$$m_i = \sum_{i=1}^{i} \left(\left(\frac{x_i}{(T_{i+1} - T_i)}\right)/N_{ci}\right)\tag{6.11}$$

This distribution was confirmed for the Shuttle, using a sample of 85 fault correction times and a goodness of fit test. In addition, Musa found that failure correction times were exponentially distributed for 178 failure corrections [MUS87].

Due to the great variability in fault correction time that has been found in both the NASA Shuttle and NASA satellite project JM1 data, predicting limits is emphasized instead of expected values. For a given mean fault correction rate m_i, the cumulative probability distribution $F(dT_i)$ of the fault correction delay dT_i is used to specify an upper limit of $d(T_i)$. The concept is to bound the delay time, for example at $F(dT_i) = .99$, and to use this limit in the fault correction delay prediction. Thus, when making predictions, there would be high confidence that the actual delay is within the limit (e.g., probability of .01). The equation for $F(dT_i)$ for the cumulative exponential distribution is given by equation (6.12), when using m_i, computed in equation (6.11):

$$F(dT_i) = 1 - \exp\left(-(m_i)(dT_i)\right)\tag{6.12}$$

Equation (6.12) is manipulated to produce equation (6.13), which is used to compute the limit of $d(T_i)$, using the specified limit $F(dT_i)$:

$$d(T_i) = (-\log (1 - F (dT_i)))/m_i \qquad (6.13)$$

Cumulative Number of Faults Corrected

Knowing the correction rate for fault i from equation (6.10) and the time between failures from equation (6.2), assuming these times are equal to the times between faults, predict the cumulative number of faults corrected, N_{ci}, at interval i in equation (6.14) [SCH01]:

$$N_{ci} = \sum_{i=1}^{N_{ci-1}} \left(c*\left(T_{i+1} - T_i\right) \right) \qquad (6.14)$$

Proportion of Faults Corrected

Now having predicted the number of cumulative faults corrected in equation (6.14) and using the cumulative number of actual failures N_i, observed at interval i, and assuming number of faults equal number of failures, compute proportion of faults corrected at interval i in equation (6.15) [SCH01]:

$$P_{ci} = N_{ci}/N_i \qquad (6.15)$$

Predicted Failure Rate

It is important to have a prediction of failure rate that can take into account *future* test or operational time—for example, mission duration. The predicted failure rate is the derivative of the predicted cumulative failures in equation (6.9). The result is equation (6.16) [SCH97]:

$$f\left(T_i\right) = \frac{d(F(T_i))}{d(T_i)} = \alpha\, e^{\left[e^{-\beta(T_i - s + 1)}\right]} \qquad (6.16)$$

Predicted Number of Failures in Interval i

In addition to predicting cumulative failures, which aggregates failure count, a fine-grain prediction can be applied to the interval i. With this prediction, failures can be tracked from interval to interval to see whether any anomalies occur. Using SSRM [SCH97], the prediction is made in equation (6.17):

$$m\left(T_i\right) = \left(\frac{\alpha}{\beta}\right)\left[e^{-\beta(T_i - s + 1)} - e^{-\beta(T_{i+1} - s + 1)}\right] \qquad (6.17)$$

Predicted Normalized Number of Failures in Interval i

While equation (6.17) is very useful as a predictor of software quality, large values of $m(T_i)$ could simply be the result of large programs producing large numbers of failures! Therefore, you can normalize $m(T_i)$ by the size of the program S, in thousand lines of code (KLOC), as shown in equation (6.18). (See Table 6.1 for Shuttle program size.)

$$M(T_i) = m(T_i)/S \qquad (6.18)$$

Predicted Maximum Number of Failures (at $T_i = \infty$)

It is important to predict the number of failures over the life of the software. Because software is crucial to the economy and infrastructure of a nation, it is seldom discarded. Rather, it is maintained and upgraded. Thus, the prediction of total number of failures over the life of the software is highly relevant. To ensure that you have a conservative prediction of this metric, use infinity as its life in equation (6.9) that results in equation (6.19).

$$F(\infty) = \frac{\alpha}{\beta} + X_{s-1} \qquad (6.19)$$

Predicted Maximum Number of Remaining Failures

Additionally, the predicted maximum number of remaining failures is an excellent indicator of residual faults and failures that remain after testing is complete. This metric is computed by subtracting the cumulative number of failures X_t observed at the last test time t, from equation (6.19). This is done in equation (6.20):

$$RF(t) = \frac{\alpha}{\beta} + X_{s-1} - X_t \qquad (6.20)$$

Predicted Operational Quality

According to the former manager of the Shuttle flight software development, predicted operational reliability (1 − fraction of remaining failures) is an excellent managerial tool for assessing the overall quality of the software because it indicates—on a fractional (percentage) basis—the extent of fault and failure removal [KEL95]. This metric is computed by using equations (6.19) and (6.20). Equation (6.21) is the result:

$$Q(t) = 1 - \left(\frac{RF(t)}{F(\infty)} \right) \qquad (6.21)$$

Probability of x_i Failures

It is time now to address the probability that failures will occur because this metric provides the software developer with a measure of risk of operating the software. Most failure processes during test fit the Poisson process [MUS87]. Thus, the probability of x_i failures occurring during interval i is formulated as follows:

$$P(x_i) = ((m_i)^{x_i} e(- m_i))/x_i!, \qquad (6.22)$$

where m_i is the mean number of failures in interval i, computed as a cumulative value as follows:

$$m_i = \frac{x_i}{\displaystyle\sum_{i=1}^{i} x_i} \qquad (6.23)$$

The reason for computing equation (6.23), as shown, rather that summing to the total number of failures, is that the latter quantity would not be known at the time of making the computation. Thus, sum to the last known interval i.

Predicted Number of Faults Remaining

Once the *maximum number of failures over the life of the software* and the *cumulative number of faults corrected* have been predicted, the *number of faults remaining to be corrected at interval i* can be predicted in equation (6.24), assuming one-to-one correspondence between faults and failures. To make the prediction, use equation (6.14) (cumulative number of faults corrected, N_{ci}) and equation (6.19) (maximum number of failures, $F(\infty)$).

$$R_{ci} = F(\infty) - N_{ci} \tag{6.24}$$

Predicted Fault Correction Quality

Then, having predicted the *number of faults remaining to be corrected* in equation (6.24), the *fault correction quality* at interval *i* can be predicted in equation (6.25), where higher values correspond to higher fault correction quality:

$$Q_{ci} = 1 - (R_{ci}/F(\infty)) \tag{6.25}$$

Weighted Failure Severity

Up to this point nothing has been said about failure severity. Failures have been treated as if they were equal in severity. Of course, they are not. In the following formulation, develop a weighted severity metric for a software release. Designating s_i as the severity of fault *i*, s_m as the maximum *value* of s_i (*minimum* severity), w_r as the severity weight of software release *r*, x_i as the number of failures of severity s_i, and *N* as the number of failures that have occurred on release *r*, w_r is computed in equation (6.26).

For example, $s_i = 1, 2, 3, 4$, and 5, where $s_i = 1$ is the most severe, and $s_i = 5 = s_m$ is the least severe. The higher the value of w_r, the lower the quality of the software release. Table 6.2 shows the definition of the failure code used in the computation of weighted failure severity.

$$w_r = \sum_{i=1}^{N}\left(x_i * \left(1 - \left(\frac{(s_i - 1)}{s_m} \right) \right) \right) / N \tag{6.26}$$

Table 6.3 (p. 138) is a compilation of the definitions of new metrics, which have been expressed in the preceding equations.

Modified Software Reliability Metrics

Actual Mean Time to Failure

Whereas 982.1 computes the mean value of $(T_{i+1} - T_i)$ over the total $(T_{i+1} - T_i)$ and cumulative failure count, you can obtain a refined assessment by computing a value for each failure *i*, as follows:

TABLE 6.2   Definition of Failure Severity Code

s_1	Loss of life or system
s_2	Affects ability to complete mission objectives
s_3	Workaround available, therefore minimal effects on procedures—mission objectives met
s_4	Insignificant violation of requirements or recommended practices, not visible to user in operational use
s_5	Cosmetic issue which should be addressed or tracked for future action, but not necessarily a present problem

TABLE 6.3   Definition of New Software Reliability Metrics

Metric	Purpose	Data Requirement	Parameter Estimates
Time Between Failures Trend, M_i	Demonstrate Reliability Growth	Failure Time, T_i	
Trend Analysis, U_i	Demonstrate Reliability Growth	M_i, T_i; Actual Cumulative Failures, N_i	
Software Reliability, $R(T_i)$	Predict Reliability	Prediction Time, T_i	Failure Rate Parameters, α, β, s
Required Reliability, $R(t_s+t_m)$	Demonstrate Required Reliability	Mission Start Time, t_s; Mission Duration, t_m	α, β, s
Actual Reliability, $R_a(T_i)$	Assess Empirical (i.e., Historical) Reliability	Number of Failures in Interval i, x_i; Total Number of Failures at Interval t, X_t	
Rate of Change of Reliability, $\dfrac{d\left(R(T_i)\right)}{d(T_i)}$	Identify T_i where Gain in $R(T_i)$ is Maximum	$R(T_i)$, T_i	α, β, s
Parameter Ratio	Rank Reliability of Releases		α, β
Software Restoration Time, T_i	Predict Time When Software Will Achieve Its Specified Reliability $R(T_i)$	$R(T_i)$	α, β, s
Predicted Cumulative Failures, $F(T_i)$	Demonstrate Reliability Growth	T_i	α, β, s; Observed Failures in the Range 1, $s-1$, X_{s-1}
Fault Correction Rate, c_i	Predict Rate of Fault Correction	T_i, T_i+1; x_i	
Fault Correction Delay, $d(T_i)$	Predict Delay in Correcting Faults	Specified Limit, $F(dTi)$; Mean Fault Correction Rate, m_i	
Cumulative Number of Faults Corrected, N_{ci}	Assess Progress in Fault Correction	c_i; T_i, T_i+1	
Proportion of Faults Corrected, P_{ci}	Identify Variation in Fault Correction by Fault i	N_{ci}, Cumulative Number of Failures, N_i	
Predicted Failure Rate, $f(T_i)$	Predict *Future* Failure Rate	T_i	α, β, s
Predicted Number of Failures in Interval i, $m(T_i)$	Predict Failures on Fine-grained Basis	T_i, T_i+1	α, β, s
Predicted Normalized Number of Failures in Interval i, $M(T_i)$	Include Program Size in Failure Predictions	$m(T_i)$; Program Size, S	
Predicted Maximum Number of Failures, $F(\infty)$	Predict Failures Over the Life of the Software		α, β, X_{s-1}
Predicted Maximum Number of Remaining Failures, $RF(t)$	Predict Residual Failures Over the Life of the Software		α, β, X_{s-1}; Number of Observed Failures, X_t
Predicted Operational Quality, $Q(t)$	Predict Overall Quality of Software	$RF(t)$, $F(\infty)$	
Probability of x_i Failures, $P(x_i)$	Assess Risk of Operating Software	Mean Number of Failures in Interval i, m_i; x_i	
Predicted Number of Faults Remaining, R_{ci}	Determine Whether the Software is Ready to Deploy	$F(\infty)$, N_{ci}	
Predicted Fault Correction Quality, Q_{ci}	Assess Fault Correction Process	R_{ci}, $F(\infty)$	

$$M_a(T_i) = \frac{\sum_{i=1}^{N_i}(T_{i+1} - T_i)}{N_i} \tag{6.27}$$

where N_i is the number of cumulative failures at failure i.

Predicted Mean Time to Failure

The original 982.1 used SSRM to make this prediction. However, it has been found that equation (6.28) will result in less error (MRE) than the original model.

$$M_p(T_i) = \sum_{i=1}^{N_i}(T_{i+1} - T_i)/F(T_i), \tag{6.28}$$

where $F(T_i)$ is the predicted cumulative failures from equation (6.9).

Reliability growth would be demonstrated by an increasing $M_a(T_i)$ and $M_p(T_i)$, as a function of test time T_i.

Actual Failure Rate

Although 982.1 includes an incremental failure rate computed by dividing incremental failures by incremental test or operational time, you can compute an actual failure rate designed to demonstrate reliability growth, if it exists:

$$f(x_i, T_i) = \frac{\sum_{i=1}^{i} x_i}{T_i}, \tag{6.29}$$

where x_i is the failure count in time interval i and T_i is the time when x_i failures have been observed. Thus, it can be seen that equation (6.29) computes the failure rate on a *cumulative* basis.

Table 6.4 is a compilation of modified software reliability metrics, based on the preceding equations.

TABLE 6.4   Definition of Modified Software Reliability Metrics

Metric	Purpose	Data Requirement	Parameter Estimates
Actual Mean Time to Failure, $M_a(T_i)$	Assess Empirical (i.e., Historical) Reliability and Demonstrate Reliability Growth	T_i, T_{i+1}; Actual Cumulative Failures, N_i	Does not apply
Predicted Mean Time to Failure, $M_p(T_i)$	Predict *Future* Reliability and Demonstrate Reliability Growth	T_i, T_{i+1}; Predicted Cumulative Failures, $F(T_i)$	Does not apply
Actual Failure Rate, $f(x_i, T_i)$	Estimate Empirical (i.e., Historical) Failure Rate	T_i; Number of Failures in Interval i, x_i	Does not apply

Reliability Metrics Prediction Results

In this section are shown results from predictions, using the equations that have been presented and selected operational increments (OIs) of the Shuttle. Each subsection is dedicated to the purpose of the metrics, as identified in Tables 6.3 and 6.4. You should confirm these results with your own computations.

Demonstrate Reliability Growth

Trend Analysis, U_i

Figure 6.1 demonstrates reliability growth by virtue of the trend metric U_i increasing in the positive direction. A reliability engineer can use this kind of plot to test for reliability growth, for various reliability data, such as failure count—the technique is not limited to time to next failure trend.

> Cumulative Failures, $F(T_i)$
> Mean Time to Failure, MTTF

Figure 6.2 shows reliability growth from another perspective: $F(T_i)$ asymptotically approaches a maximum value as a function of test time T_i and MTTF increases monotonically as a function of T_i. You can also see that, based on MRE, $F(T_i)$ is a more accurate predictor of reliability than MTTF for *these* data. The practical application of these plots is see whether $F(T_i)$ and MTTF behave as shown in Figure 6.2. If they do not, the software development process should be investigated to determine the cause of excessive faults.

Predict Reliability, Demonstrate Required Reliability, and Predict Reliability Restoration Time

> Reliability, $R(T_i)$
> Reliability to Meet Mission Duration, $R(t_s + t_m)$

FIGURE 6.1   Time to Next Failure Trend U_i vs. Test Time T_i

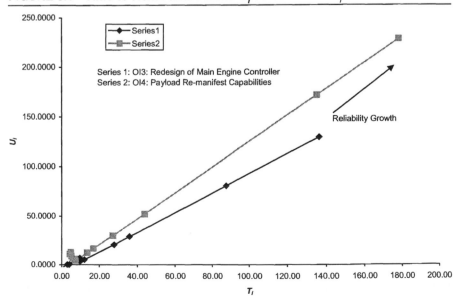

FIGURE 6.2   Shuttle OI3: Cumulative Failures and MTTF vs. Test Time T_i

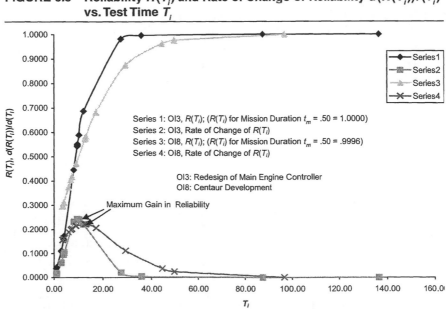

Rate of Change of Reliability, $\dfrac{d(R(T_i))}{d(T_i)}$

Reliability Restoration Time, T_i

It is important to predict reliability and to predict the reliability that would be achieved for the duration of the mission. For this purpose, the mission duration relevant for a given application should be used. In Figure 6.3, $t_m = .50$ (.50 months or 15 days for a typical Shuttle

FIGURE 6.3   Reliability $R(T_i)$ and Rate of Change of Reliability $d(R(T_i))/(T_i)$
vs. Test Time T_i

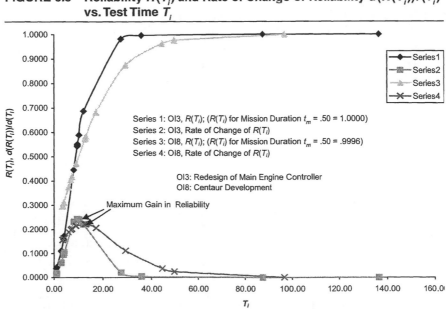

FIGURE 6.4   Restoration Time T_i vs. Reliability $R(T_i)$

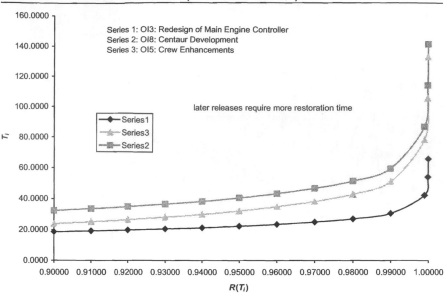

mission is used). Furthermore, it is of interest to identify the test time where maximum reliability is achieved. In Figure 6.3, this is accomplished by plotting the rate of change of reliability. This test time corresponds to the point of maximum payoff of reliability versus test time (i.e., cost). Of course, additional test time may be required to achieve the required reliability, but at diminishing returns to the investment in testing. If the required reliability for the mission duration is not achieved, the software should be subjected to additional testing to eliminate more faults.

If the specified reliability has been temporarily violated due to software failure, the restoration time—the operational time necessary to restore software reliability to its required value—can be predicted. In Figure 6.4, restoration time is shown as a function of specified reliability for several OIs. As Figure 6.4 shows, latter releases require more restoration time. This is probably due to the increasing functional complexity of the software across releases, reflecting the fact that each Shuttle release contains all the functionality of previous releases plus the added functionality of the current release. This plot would be used to predict whether the restoration time is acceptable for recovering from a failure, based on the specified reliability.

Predict and Assess Progress in Fault Correction

Fault Correction Rate, c_i
Fault Correction Delay, $d(T_i)$
Proportion of Faults Corrected, P_{ci}

Figure 6.5 demonstrates that at the maximum fault correction rate, the fault correction delay and the proportion of faults corrected stabilize (i.e., assume constant values), as a function of test time. This is a valuable relationship because a reliability engineer can make these plots and identify the test time where maximum progress is being made in correcting faults.

FIGURE 6.5   OI4: Fault Correction Rate c_i, Fault Correction Delay $d(T_i)$ and Proportion of Faults Corrected P_{ci} vs. Test Time T_i

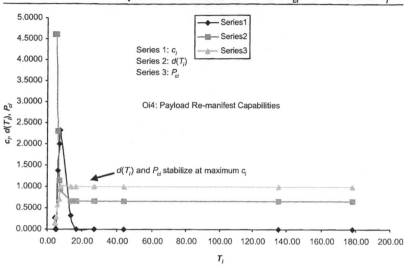

FIGURE 6.6   Number of Faults Remaining to be Corrected R_{ci} vs. Test Time T_i

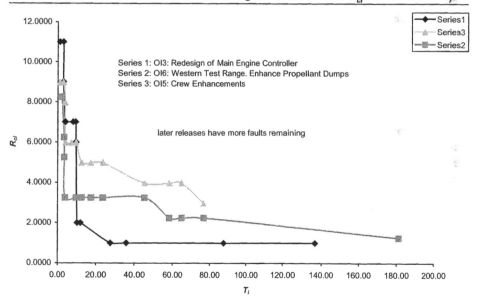

Predicted Number of Faults Remaining, R_{ci}

Figure 6.6 indicates that due to the greater functional complexity of later releases, the predicted number of remaining faults is higher. This plot is useful for indicating whether the software should be deployed on a mission. If the remaining faults are too high, as in the case of OI5, additional testing should be conducted until the remaining faults are predicted to be acceptable (e.g., $R_{ci} = 1$)

Predicted Fault Correction Quality, Q_{ci}

In Figure 6.7, the predicted fault correction quality provides an overall assessment of the fault correction process. This metric increases as the number of faults remaining to be corrected decreases. If this plot did not asymptotically approach a maximum with increasing test time, it would be indicative of an unstable correction process. In this case, the cause of the problem would be identified and corrected, such as inadequate test cases. Observe that correction quality becomes worse in a later release due to the aforementioned increase in functional complexity.

Perform Fine-grained Reliability Analysis

Predicted Number of Failures in Interval i, $m(T_i)$
Predicted Normalized Number of Failures in Interval i, $m(T_i)$

While reliability metrics based on cumulative values, such as cumulative failures, are useful for demonstrating reliability growth, they do not provide a focused prediction of reliability in each test time interval i. For this purpose, use $m(T_i)$. Now, while useful, $m(T_i)$ does not account for the size of the software. Therefore, a companion prediction is the normalized failures in the interval i, $M(T_i)$.

Figure 6.8 demonstrates that normalized predicted failures in interval i can vary considerably as a function of test time. The main point of the variation from a reliability standpoint is the test time when $M(T_i)$ begins to stabilize (i.e., decreases towards zero). Due to the increased functionality of OI8 versus OI3, OI8 stabilizes later in test time. This plot is a tool in the arsenal of the reliability engineer for identifying the test time when it is no longer cost-effective to continue testing. These times are $T_i = 30$ and 45 for OI3 and OI8, respectively.

Actual Failure Rate, $f(x_i, T_i)$
Predicted Failure Rate, $f(T_i)$

FIGURE 6.7   Fault Correction Quality Q_{ci} vs. Test Time T_i

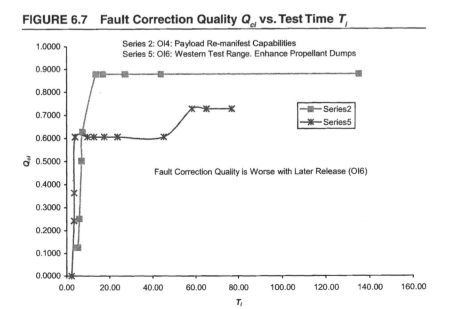

FIGURE 6.8   Normalized Predicted Failures in Interval i $M(T_i)$ vs. Test Time T_i

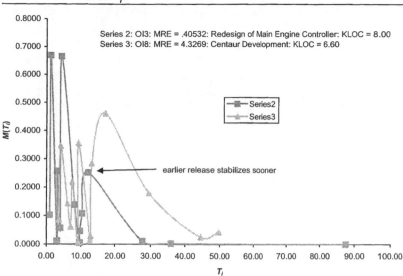

Other metrics that allow us to focus on fine-grained analysis are actual and predicted failure rate, with the distinction that the former estimates failure rate based on empirical (i.e., historical) failure data and the latter predicts *future* failure rate based on estimating model parameters, using empirical data. Because you do not have the "future" available for comparing the results produced by the two metrics, necessarily, you would compute MRE over the empirical failure data range. These values of MRE are shown on Figure 6.9,

FIGURE 6.9   Predicted Failure Rate $f(T_i)$ and Actual Failure Rate $f(x_i, T_i)$ vs. Test Time T_i

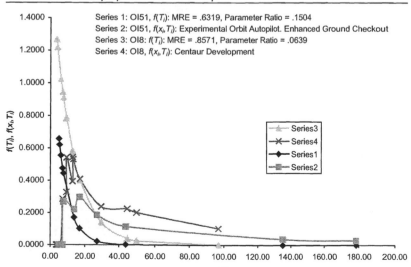

indicating that OI51 has better prediction accuracy than OI8. Also shown is the Parameter Ratio (PR). Recall that higher values of PR are associated with higher values of reliability (i.e., lower failure rate). This is the case in Figure 6.9 where OI51 has both lower predicted and actual failure rates than OI8.

An important application of these plots is to note that, for both OIs, the predictions monotonically decrease, but this is not the case for the actual rates. In the latter case, the failure rate can temporarily increase and then decrease, reflecting changes to the software that are made over test time. Interestingly, this phenomenon is accounted for in the Yamada S-shaped model, which allows for an increase in failure rate [XIE91]. If the reliability engineer has an application with this failure data characteristic, the Yamada model could be used, which is described in [IEE08].

Assess Reliability Risk

Probability of x_i Failures in Interval i, $P(x_i)$

In order to assess the risk to reliability of the incidence of failures, predict the probability of failures occurring in test time interval i. Of course, the threat to reliability would occur in *operational time* and not in test time. However, the idea of testing is to emulate, to the extent feasible, operational conditions. Therefore, with respect to realistic operational testing in Figure 6.10, the software could be released for operational use at test time $T_i = 17$ when the risk = .1 is reasonably low.

Track Number of Faults Corrected

Cumulative Number of Faults Corrected, N_{ci}

By tracking the cumulative number of faults corrected over test time you can determine whether this function reaches a maximum asymptotic value early or late in test time. The former is preferable because it is indicative of an accelerated fault correction process. This

FIGURE 6.10   OI4: Probability of x_i Failures in Interval i $P(x_i)$ vs. Test Time T_i

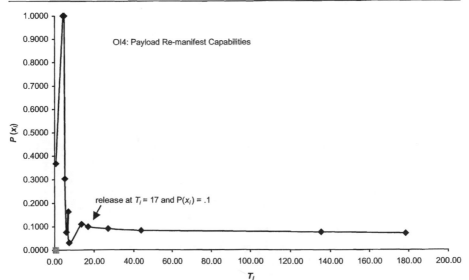

principle is illustrated in Figure 6.11, where OI3 produces the knee of the plot earlier than OI8. In other words, this is a method for evaluating test effectiveness.

Summary of Reliability Metric Results

Because a myriad of reliability metrics have been defined and analyzed, it is necessary to document the major results in Table 6.5 in order to identify: 1) the metrics that have the least variability across test time, as measured by the standard deviation, 2) the metrics that have the greatest predictive validity, as measured by MRE, and 3) the releases (OIs) that have the smallest predictive error, as measured by MRE. In some cases it is appropriate to use other measures, such as maximum fault correction rate. Some metrics do not appear in Table 6.5. These are metrics that are evaluated better by using a plot. In these cases, the reader is referred to the relevant figure. The best values per OI are bolded and the best values per metric italicized.

Although there is not a great deal of consistency in the results, you would conclude the following: 1) OI51 is the release with the most consistent "best" metrics (e.g., low standard deviation for reliability) and 2) for metrics where MRE can be computed, predicted cumulative failures has the lowest prediction error. This is due to the fact that cumulative functions smooth irregularities in the data. A reliability engineer could use this approach to: 1) identify software that is ready to deploy (OI51) and software that is not ready to deploy (OI8) and 2) rank reliability metrics by their predictive validity, using MRE.

Conclusions

Many metrics have been described and evaluated. There were no dominant metrics in the set with respect to producing the most desirable prediction (i.e., maximum fault correction

FIGURE 6.11   Predicted Number of Faults Corrected N_{ci} vs. Test Time T_i

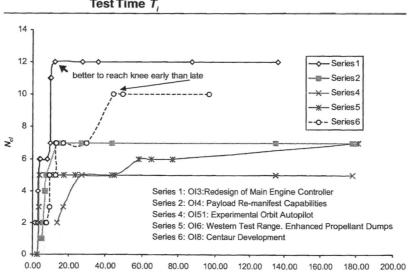

TABLE 6.5 Summary of Software Reliability Metrics Attributes

Metric	Operational Increment					
	OI3	OI4	OI5	OI51	OI6	OI8
	Value and MRE (Relative to Actual Value)					
Weighted Failure Severity, w_r	0.7000	0.6000	0.6750	0.6000	0.7429	0.7200
Reliability, $R(T)$, Standard Deviation	0.3634 MRE = 4.4606	0.2219 MRE = 0.3329	0.2012 MRE = 0.3380	0.1930 MRE = 0.3054	0.2302 MRE = 0.3268	0.2461 MRE = 0.8852
Reliability to Meet Mission Duration, $R(t_s + t_m)$, $t_m = .50$	1.0000	1.0000	.9989	1.0000	1.0000	.9996
Maximum Rate of Change of Reliability, $\dfrac{d(R(T_i))}{d(T_i)}$	0.2433	0.2216	0.1699	0.2092	0.2124	0.2228
Parameter Ratio	0.1430	0.1437	0.1115	0.1504	0.1213	0.0639
Software Restoration Time, T_r Standard Deviation	19.7805	17.7343	39.7789	8.7628	25.0460	43.1555
Predicted Cumulative Failures, $F(T)$, Standard Deviation	6.3457 MRE = 0.3269	2.1980 MRE = 0.6938	3.4076 MRE = 0.2719	1.7592 MRE = 0.5519	2.5764 MRE = 0.2831	5.0151 MRE = 0.5125
Fault Correction Rate, c_i, Maximum	50.0000	2.3256	8.6957	0.3226	33.3333	16.6667
Fault Correction Delay, $d(T_p)$, Standard Deviation	0.4965	1.7283	0.5969	0.5696	0.4564	0.6765
Cumulative Number of Faults Corrected, N_{cl}			See Figure 6.11			
Proportion of Faults Corrected, P_{cl}			See Figure 6.5			
Predicted Failure Rate, $f(T)$, Maximum	3.6376 MRE = 0.5874	1.2129 MRE = 0.8608	0.7645 MRE = 0.6139	0.6573 MRE = 0.7721	0.8648 MRE = 0.6566	1.2665 MRE = 0.8571
Predicted Number of Failures in Interval i, $m(T_i)$, Maximum	5.3530 MRE = 4.0532	3.3322 MRE = 1.4593	1.5659 MRE = 5.1715	0.5206 MRE = 1.1251	2.6196 MRE = 310.5204	3.0495 MRE = 4.3269
Predicted Normalized Number of Failures in Interval i, $M(T_i)$, Maximum	0.6691	0.2923	0.2654	0.1450	0.2977	0.4621
Predicted Maximum Number of Failures, $F(\infty)$	12.9952	7.9611	10.9714	6.6475	8.2457	15.6395
Predicted Maximum Number of Remaining Failures, $RF(t)$	0.9952	0.9611	2.9714	1.6475	1.2457	5.6395
Predicted Operational Quality, $Q(t)$	0.9234	0.8793	0.7292	0.7522	0.8489	0.6394
Probability of x_i Failures, $P(x)$, Minimum	0.0398	0.0712	0.0536	0.2388	0.0536	0.0067
Predicted Number of Faults Remaining, R_{cl}			See Figure 6.6			
Predicted Fault Correction Quality, Q_{cl}			See Figure 6.7			

rate). Nor were there dominant metrics with respect to minimum prediction error, although metrics based on aggregated failure values, such as cumulative failure, provided marginally more accurate predictions. In contrast, it was possible to identify a software release that generally yielded better predictions and less error than other releases. Based on these results, you would conclude that the reliability engineer should evaluate several, if not many, metrics to ensure that metrics can be identified that would be appropriate for a given application. Furthermore, the evaluated metrics should be used to predict reliability for the various software releases in order to determine which software is ready to be deployed and which software requires further testing.

Appendix

FIGURE 6.A1   Shuttle OI3: T_i, 5% Confidence Intervals Autocorrelation

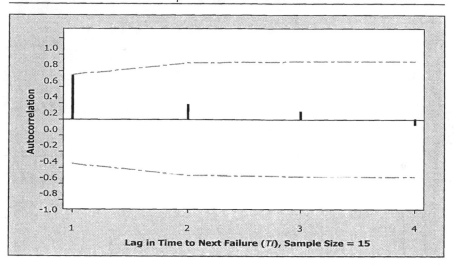

FIGURE 6.A2   Shuttle OI4: T_i, 5% Confidence Intervals Autocorrelation

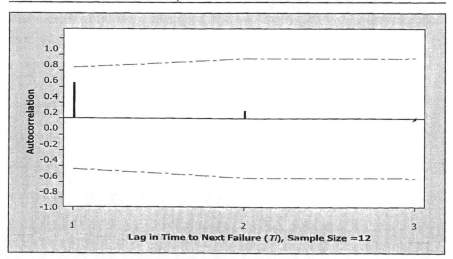

FIGURE 6.A3   Shuttle OI5: T_i, 5% Confidence Intervals Autocorrelation

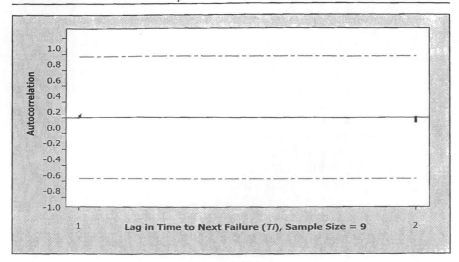

FIGURE 6.A4   Shuttle OI6: T_i, 5% Confidence Intervals Autocorrelation

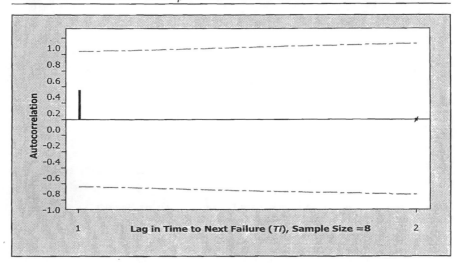

FIGURE 6.A5   Sattelite J M1, T_i, 5% Confidence Intervals Autocorrelation

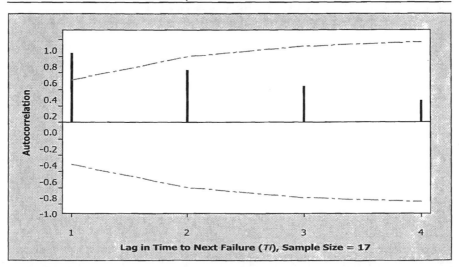

References

[BAT55] G. E. Bates, "Joint Distribution of Time Intervals for the Occurrence of Successive Accidents in a Generalized Polya Scheme," *Annals of Mathematical Statistics*, 26, pp. 705–720.

[GOS99] Katerina Goseva-Popstojanova and Kishor Trivedi, "Failure Correlation in Software Reliability Models." 10th International Symposium on Software Reliability Engineering, 1999, p. 232.

[IEE06] *Standard Dictionary of Measures of the Software Aspects of Dependability,* May 8, 2006.

[IEE08] IEEE/AIAA P1633™, *Recommended Practice on Software Reliability,* June 2008.

[LYU96] Michael R. Lyu, Editor, *Handbook of Software Reliability Engineering,* IEEE Computer Society Press and McGraw Hill, 1996.

[KEL95] Ted Keller, Norman F. Schneidewind, and Patti A. Thornton, "Predictions for Increasing Confidence in the Reliability of the Space Shuttle Flight Software." Proceedings of the AIAA Computing in Aerospace 10, San Antonio, TX, March 28, 1995, pp. 1–8.

[MUS87] John D. Musa, Anthony Iannino, and Kazuhira Okumoto, *Software Reliability: Measurement, Prediction, Application.* McGraw Hill, 1987.

[SCH01] Norman F. Schneidewind; "Modeling the Fault Correction Process." Proceedings of The Twelfth International Symposium on Software Reliability Engineering, Hong Kong, November 27–30, 2001, pp. 185–190.

[SCH97] Norman F. Schneidewind, "Reliability Modeling for Safety Critical Software." *IEEE Transactions on Reliability,* Vol. 46, No.1, March 1997, pp. 88–98.

[XIE91] Min Xie, *Software Reliability Modeling.* World Scientific, 1991.

7

Software Reliability
and Metrics Tools

Objectives

First, learn how to measure the reliability of software using reliability and metrics prediction models. Then, learn about software reliability and metrics tools that will assist you in making predictions to improve the reliability of your software.

What You Will Learn From This Chapter

You will be provided with background regarding the rationale for using tools and the knowledge required to use them effectively that includes, for example, reliability goals, risk of inadequate reliability, cost of prediction, and data requirements.

Subjects

Background that Supports the Use of Tools
Descriptions of Measurement Functions and Knowledge Requirements
Software Reliability Tools
Software Reliability Prediction Results
Software Metrics and Metrics Tools

Background that Supports the Use of Tools [SCH03]

Before you apply tools you should understand the rationale for using tools and the knowledge required to use them effectively. Therefore the linkage is made between the need for the measurement of reliability, using tools, in the software development life cycle and the body of knowledge that is required to satisfy this need.

Identifying the applicable body of reliability knowledge required is the first step in equipping engineers with the essential skill set.

Because tool-based measurement is the key to achieving high reliability software, it is important for engineers to be knowledgeable in this area. The engineer applies the body of knowledge to improve the reliability of software throughout the life cycle. In addition, the body of knowledge may be used as guidelines for practitioners, licensing of software professionals, and training in software reliability measurement. Without measurement, software engineers would not be able to achieve high reliability software. Thus, measurement and the tools to make measurements are the keys to developing reliable software. The focus is on reliability because the lack of it could result in significant costs to the supplier of software in terms of dissatisfied customers, loss of market share, rework caused by rejected and returned systems, and the costs to customers of faulty systems that fail to meet their mission goals. The benefit of this approach is that engineers can identify the knowledge and skills that are required to advance the measurement component of software engineering from a craft to a profession. Rather than focus on the coding phase of the development process, as has been the case historically, it is important to identify how measurement can be applied throughout the process and to key the requisite knowledge to the process phases. This approach is important for three reasons. First, early detection and resolution of reliability problems can save considerable time and money in software development. Second, product and process measurements must be integrated so that the interaction between the two can be assessed throughout the life cycle. Third, engineers must have comprehensive knowledge of the role of measurement in contributing to the development of high reliability products and the processes that produce them.

Descriptions of Measurement Functions and Knowledge Requirements

The following are brief examples of the functions and knowledge requirements listed in Table 7.1. The purpose is to explain to the engineer the functions and the knowledge requirements that address the issues in Table 7.1. In addition, techniques that can be employed to implement each of the functions are explained.

Issue 1: Goals

What reliability goals are specified for the system?

A quality requirement is defined as "a requirement that a software attribute (i.e., *reliability*) be present in software to satisfy a contract, standard, specification, or other formally imposed document" [IEE98]. You would interview key personnel and examine documentation in carrying out the function of "analyzing reliability goals and specifying reliability requirements." For example, a goal in a safety critical system could be that there would be no fault and failure that would jeopardize the mission and cause loss of life.

Reliability Engineering

Metrics are identified and data collection plans are developed for satisfying reliability goals. Criteria are identified for measuring and interpreting conformance with reliability requirements during inspection and testing. A complete methodology for implementing a software quality (e.g., reliability) metrics plan in an organization can be found in IEEE Standard 1061 [IEE98].

Requirements Engineering

One of the factors in specifying requirements is to assess the risk of introducing a new requirement into the system or changing an existing requirement. Risk is present because the introduction of a change may decrease the reliability and maintainability of the software. For example, the NASA Space Shuttle Flight Software organization performs a risk analysis on all requirements changes. To assess the risk of change, the software development contractor uses a number of risk factors, such as the size and location of the change, criticality of the change, number of change modifications, resources required to make the change, including personnel and tools, etc. No requirements change is approved by the change control board without an accompanying risk assessment. During risk assessment, the development contractor will attempt to answer such questions as: "Is this change highly complex relative to other software changes that have been made on the Shuttle?" If this were the case, a high-risk

TABLE 7.1   Knowledge Requirements in Software Reliability Measurement

Issue	Function	Knowledge
1. **Goals:** What reliability goals are specified for the system?	**Analyze** reliability goals and **specify** reliability requirements.	Reliability Engineering (Chapter 2)
2. **Cost and risk:** What is the cost of achieving reliability goals and the risk of not doing so?	**Evaluate** economics and risk of reliability goals.	Economic Analysis (Chapter 20), Risk Analysis (Chapter 4)
3. **Context:** What application and organizational structure is the system and software to support?	**Analyze** the application environment.	Systems Analysis Software Design ([DAV93])
4. **Operational profile:** What are the criticality and frequency of use of the software components?	**Analyze** the software environment.	Probability and Statistical Analysis (Chapter 1)
5. **Models:** What is the feasibility of creating or using an existing reliability model for assessment and prediction, and how can the model be validated?	**Model** reliability and **validate** the model.	Probability and Statistical Models (Chapters 1 and 2)
6. **Data requirements:** What data are needed to support reliability goals?	**Define** data type, phase, time, and frequency of collection.	Data Analysis [LYU96]
7. **Types and granularity of measurements:** What measurement scales should be used, what level of detail is appropriate to meet a given goal, and what can be measured quantitatively, qualitatively, or judgmentally?	**Define** the statistical properties of the data.	Measurement Theory [FEN97]
8. **Product and process test and evaluation:** How can product reliability measurements be fed back to improve process quality?	**Analyze** the relationship between product reliability and process stability.	Inspection and Test Methods (Chapter 4), Rates of Learning of Personnel in Test Organizations (Chapter 5), Identify Software Releases That, Based on Reliability Predictions, are Ready to Deploy and Identify Which Software Requires Additional Testing. (Chapter 6)
9. **Product Reliability and Process Quality Prediction:** What types of predictions should be made?	**Assess** and **predict** product reliability and process quality.	Measurement Tools (Chapter 3), Identify Software Releases That, Based on Reliability Predictions, are Ready to Deploy (Chapter 6)

value would be assigned for the complexity criterion. A useful book on software requirements analysis and specifications is by Davis [DAV93]. Another approach to getting requirements right is to use rapid prototyping. The rationale is that a quick development and implementation of a sample of the software system will uncover flaws in the requirements prior to investing large amounts of time and money in the development of the system [DAV93].

Issue 2: Cost and Risk

What is the cost of achieving reliability goals and the risk of not doing so?

For example, you would evaluate the tradeoff between increases in levels of reliability with increases in testing, which increase the cost of testing.

Economic Analysis

A common error in economic analysis of software systems is to limit the evaluation to total cost. An important criterion is marginal cost in relation to the marginal benefit that accrues by adding an increment of reliability to the software. For example, continuing with the reliability example, this involves comparing the marginal increase in reliability that is obtained through increased testing with the marginal increase in the cost of testing. Theoretically, testing can stop when the two quantities are equal. However, because it is difficult to convert increases in reliability into dollars, you would use the concept of the maximum Reliability/Cost Ratio (RCR), which is the ratio of relative increase in reliability to relative increase in cost, as given by the following equation:

$$RCR = \max [(\Delta R/R_t)/(\Delta C/C_t)], \tag{7.1}$$

where ΔR is the change in reliability from test time t to $t + \Delta t$, R_t is the reliability at time t, ΔC is the change in cost of testing from t to $t + \Delta t$, and C_t is the cost of testing at t, for increasing values of t [SCH97]. Testing continues until the criterion of equation (7.1) is achieved.

Risk Analysis

In a safety critical system, for example, it is necessary to achieve high reliability. In this case, relevant risk criteria would be used. For example, if you define your reliability goal as the reduction of failures that would cause loss of life, loss of mission, or abort of mission to an acceptable level of risk, then for software to be ready to deploy, after having been tested for total time t, the software must satisfy the following criteria [SCH97]:

1) predicted remaining failures $r(t) < r_c$,
   where r_c is a specified critical value , and   (7.2)
2) predicted time to next failure $T_F(t) > t_m$,
   where t_m is mission duration.   (7.3)

For systems that are tested and operated continuously, t, $T_F(t)$, and t_m are measured in computer execution time. If the criteria (7.2) and (7.3) are not met after testing for time t, you should continue to test until the criteria are met or until it is no longer economically feasible to continue to test.

Issue 3: Context

What application and organizational structure are the system and software to support?

This function involves analyzing, identifying and classifying the application domain (e.g., safety critical system, COTS product). The application domain has implications for reliability requirements. Reliability and safety would be major considerations for a safety critical system whereas time to market could be the major consideration for a COTS products, with reliability having a lesser role.

Systems Analysis

A system is defined as "an interdependent group of people, objects, and procedures constituted to achieve defined objectives or some operational role or performing specified functions. A complete system includes all of the associated equipment, facilities, material, computer programs, firmware, technical documentation, services, and personnel required for operations and support to the degree necessary for self-sufficient use in its intended environment." Thus, a system is composed of more than software. In order to specify reliability requirements intelligently, you must understand the *context* in which the software will function. Although it is not necessary to know how to perform system analysis, it is important to appreciate the influence of different hardware configurations—standalone, network, distributed, fault-tolerant—on software reliability requirements. For example, a network would have higher reliability and availability requirements than a standalone system because unreliable operations in a network could affect thousands of users simultaneously, whereas it would affect only a single user at a time in a standalone operation. In addition, engineers must be sensitive to the quality of service needs of the user organization.

Software Design

Increasingly, software designs (and analysis) are being expressed as object-oriented paradigms. In these situations, it would be important for engineers to learn the Unified Modeling Language [MUL97] and its various design diagrams (e.g., use case, scenario, sequence, state-chart), not only as a design tool but also as a means of identifying where critical reliability requirements exist in the system. For example, describing user interactions with the objects of a system with use-case scenarios and identifying the states and state transitions with state-charts can assist in identifying the operational profile (see the following discussion).

Issue 4: Operational Profile

What are the criticality and frequency of use of the software components?

The operational profile is defined as "the set of operations that the software can execute along with the probabilities of their occurrence" [LYU96]. The operational profile is a useful concept to employ for establishing reliability goals and for measuring whether they have been met in operation. The operational profile allows engineers to identify operations, their criticality, and the relative frequency of occurrence. For example, in an automatic pump system in a gas station, the display of the message "start pumping" is an operation. If this operation occurs 10 out of the 100 times that all operations occur in a given time interval (e.g., 15 minutes), the operation has a probability of occurrence of .10. In addition, this operation might have a criticality rank of 5 on a scale of 1 to 10, with "1" being the most critical, whereas the operation "print receipt" might have a criticality of 7. With this knowledge, you could assign the reliability and availability goals for the software, develop a test plan to reflect the operational profile, and ascertain whether the reliability goals have been achieved when the system is tested.

Probability and Statistical Analysis

First, you would examine the software design of the system in order to understand its operational modes. Then, elementary probability and statistical analysis may be applied to estimate the probability of occurrence of various operations. The latter estimate of probability is obtained by the relative frequency of occurrence (i.e., number of occurrences/ total occurrences). In addition, rather than limit the computation to a point estimate, you could apply statistical confidence intervals (see Chapter 1) to the probability of occurrence of a given operation (i.e., the limits within which the actual probability of occurrence is expected to fall). The fundamentals of probability theory can be found in the book by Ash [ASH93].

Issue 5: Models

What is the feasibility of creating or using an existing reliability model for assessment and prediction, and how can the model be validated?

A model is defined as *a representation of a real-world process, device, or concept*. Model validation involves retrospectively demonstrating that it consistently predicts actual values with acceptable accuracy [SCH97]. As an example of developing and validating a reliability model, consider a reliability control and prediction model that is used to identify modules that require priority attention during development and maintenance. This is accomplished in two activities: *validation* and *application*. Both activities occur during software development. During *validation,* you identify metrics that would be used to judge the reliability of the produced software. During *application,* if at least one of the module's metrics has a value that exceeds its critical value (e.g., threshold value of size or complexity), the module is identified as "high priority" (i.e., low reliability); otherwise, it is identified as "low priority" (i.e., high reliability). The objective is to identify and correct reliability problems during development so that a high reliability product can be delivered to maintenance, as opposed to waiting until maintenance when the cost of correction would be high [SCH971].

Probability and Statistical Models

Models for software measurement fall into two major categories: probability models for reliability prediction and statistical models that use software quality metrics as predictors of quality. The former use historical failure data to estimate model parameters that are related to the initial failure rate and the rate of change of failure rate. Once the model has been fitted, it is used to predict future reliability quantities, such as remaining failures and time to next failure [SCH97], as illustrated in the Software Reliability Tools section that begins on page 161. The latter uses software characteristics, such as the size and structure of the code, to predict quality factors, such as the number of defects. There is a tradeoff between early but less accurate predictions using statistical models, and late but more accurate predictions using reliability models.

You must be careful to avoid some common mistakes in software measurement. Among these is the problem of multi-co-linearity and the problem of performing arithmetic operations on non-commensurate quantities. The former problem occurs when several "independent variables" are used as predictor variables—for example, program size, program operator count, and program operand count. Since the latter two are themselves measures of size, these three metrics in combination may be poor predictors of number of defects. The latter problem occurs when quantities to be added or subtracted are not commensurate (e.g., number of modules is added to number of records in a data file to create "a count of items in a program").These are areas where it is advisable to seek the assistance of experts because of the detailed knowledge of probability and statistics that is required. However, it is important to be able to identify situations in which these models can be used to advantage. The book by LYU [LYU96] and the *IEEE/AIAA Recommended Practice on Software*

Reliability [IEE08] provide comprehensive treatment of software reliability theory and practice and the book by Zuse [ZUS98] does the same for software metrics.

Issue 6: Data Requirements

What data are needed to support reliability goals?

For each metric that supports reliability goals, data are collected by data type; life cycle phase; time of collection; frequency of collection; and assumptions that are made about the data (e.g., random sample, subjective measure, objective measure). In addition, the flow of data from point of collection to evaluation of metrics is shown; tools and their usage are described; data storage procedures are specified; data sources are identified; and the organizational entities that will participate in data collection are identified [IEE98].

Data Analysis

In planning for data collection and interpretation of the data, skills are needed in descriptive statistics (i.e., calculating the mean, standard deviation, median, range, etc.) and in analysis of distributions (i.e., are the data exponentially distributed, log-normally distributed, etc.?) (See Chapter 1.) These analyses characterize the data. For example, a large standard deviation relative to the mean and a large range of the data may indicate that the great variation in the data may make it difficult to accurately predict software reliability.

Issue 7: Types and Granularity of Measurements

What measurement scales should be used, what level of detail is appropriate to meet a given goal, and what can be measured quantitatively, qualitatively, or judgmentally?

In making assessments of software data, the concept of measurement scales is important [FEN97, ZUS98]. For example, software modules might be evaluated on the following scales—*nominal:* high or low reliability; *ordinal:* "module A" has higher reliability than "module B"; *interval:* the difference between the reliability of modules A and B is one fault per KLOC; *ratio:* the reliability of "module A" is twice that of "module B." Experience has shown that most software measurements are appropriate only for the nominal and ordinal scales. The reason for this is that software measurement data are frequently sparse, discrete, have large variability, and lack definitions and details of the environment and applications in which the data were collected. In general, the data do not exist on a continuous scale. Thus, in many cases, the best you can do is place the data in categories (i.e., nominal scale) or rank them (i.e., ordinal scale) [SCH971].

It is also important to understand the concept of granularity of measurement. For example, although it is desirable to record failure data in terms of computer execution time, organizations do not always collect data with this fine a granularity; the data might be collected in terms of calendar time. If this is the case, you must make adjustments in reliability predictions, for example, to cast the data in terms of failures per day.

Issue 8: Product and Process Test and Evaluation

How can product reliability measurements be fed back to improve process quality?

Measuring and evaluating the stability of software processes is important because of the recognized relationship between process quality and product reliability. A process can quickly become unstable because the very act of installing software changes the environment: Pressures operate to modify the environment, the problem, and the technological solutions. Changes generated by users and the environment and the consequent need for adapting the software to the changes are unpredictable and cannot be accommodated without iteration. Programs must be adaptable to change and the resultant change process must be planned and controlled. This situation has led to the development of trend, shape (e.g., shape of a failure rate curve), and change metrics that are used across releases and within a release for the dual purpose of assessing product reliability and process stability [SCH99].

Inspection and Test Methods

Experience has shown that rigorous inspection of various development artifacts, such as requirements, design, and code documents, has uncovered the majority of software faults prior to testing. However, testing must still be performed because inspections cannot evaluate the behavior of the software in execution. Testing also provides the data for making the metric calculations mentioned above. Furthermore, testing has a synergistic relationship with reliability modeling and prediction in that test results provide the failure data for fitting a reliability model, and the reliability predictions, in turn, indicate which parts of the software to emphasize in testing.

An example of a rigorous inspection method is the Fagan inspection, which is a group review method used to evaluate output of a given process. Fagan inspections define a process as an activity with pre-specified entry and exit criteria. In every activity for which entry and exit criteria are specified, Fagan inspections can be used to validate that the output of the process complies with the exit criteria specified for the process. The software development process is a typical application of Fagan inspections. The software development process is a series of operations that will deliver an end product and consists of operations such as requirements definition, design, coding, testing, and maintenance. As the costs to remedy defects are up to 10–100 times less in early phases compared to fixing a defect in the maintenance phase, it is essential to find defects as close to the point of insertion as possible. This is done by inspecting the output of each operation and comparing it to the output requirements or exit criteria for that operation [FAG76, FAG86].

Another approach to improving inspection effectiveness is to make the reading of documents (e.g., requirements specifications) during inspection meetings a disciplined process by assigning a focus for each inspector (e.g., ambiguous requirements) and by assigning inspectors to look for particular defects (e.g., no test is specified for a function specified in the requirements) [SHU].

Issue 9: Product Reliability and Process Quality Prediction

What types of predictions should be made?

You would assess historical failure data and predict future reliability in order to evaluate the risk of not meeting remaining failure and time to failure requirements, according to equations (7.2) and (7.3), respectively. If these predictions are unfavorable, they are indicative of both a high-risk product and a process that is in need of correction [SCH971].

Measurement Tools

There are measurement tools, such as the Statistical Modeling and Estimation of Reliability Functions for Software (SMERFS), for minimizing the burden of making reliability predictions [STA91]. Tools like SMERFS that implement a number of reliability models can increase productivity, but they are also much abused because some users plug numbers into them and use the results without understanding the capabilities and limitations behind the numbers. Software reliability tools are covered in the next section. SMERFS may be downloaded from: http://www.slingcode.com/smerfs/downloads/

Software Reliability Tools

SMERFS[3]

The Statistical Modeling and Estimation of Reliability Functions for Software (SMERFS[3]) [STA91] is a menu-driven tool that estimates reliability of software systems using a black-box approach. It provides a range of reliability models. SMERFS[3] is the latest version of the tool and is available for the Windows operating system.

After examining a project's characteristics, the engineer uses SMERFS[3] to select appropriate models for use in software reliability prediction. SMERFS[3] provides other services that free the engineer to be concerned only about the quality of the failure data and the interpretation of the results. The tool estimates the parameters needed for the various models and checks results for validity and accuracy of each model. It provides confidence intervals for reliability predictions. SMERFS[3] is only a tool. It does not interpret results; that is, it will not replace judgment of the engineer. The engineer must use knowledge about the project and judgment to understand meaning of the results. The tool performs curve fitting on the input data and will refuse to exercise the data on inappropriate models. Of the models it does execute, results may vary. Selected model predictions will now be illustrated and compared. An important application of all prediction quantities is for tradeoff analyses to determine optimal release time of the software or to determine when a given operational program is a prime candidate for a rewrite.

Musa's Logarithmic Poisson Execution Time Model

John Musa's Logarithmic Poisson Execution Time model may be executed only under a *Maximum Likelihood Method of Estimation*. It is suggested that the *Model Assumptions* and *Data Requirements* be reviewed before the model results are accepted.

Maximum Likelihood Estimation is a form of *parameter* estimation in which selected parameters maximize the probability that observed data could have occurred. A *parameter* is a variable or arbitrary constant appearing in a mathematical expression, each value of which restricts or determines the specific form of the expression.

Model Assumptions

The software is operated in a similar manner as the anticipated operational usage.
All faults are equally likely to occur and are independent of one another.
The expected number of faults is a logarithmic function of time.
The failure intensity decreases exponentially with the expected failures experienced.
The software will experience an infinite number of failures.

Data Requirements

The Time-Between-Failures as measured in computer CPU time.

Estimations

In addition to the estimates of the parameters defining the model, the output includes estimates for initial intensity function and current intensity function.

Predictions

Reliability over a specified time period
Mean time before next failure for the next K failures
Mean time before next failure

Time and number of failures to reach a desired intensity function
Number of failures expected in a specified time

Non-homogeneous Poisson for Execution Time Model

The Non-homogeneous Poisson model for execution time data may be executed only using the Maximum Likelihood Method of Estimation. As was the case with the Musa model, it is suggested that the *Model Assumptions* and *Data Requirements* be reviewed before the model results are accepted.

Estimations

In addition to the estimates of the parameters defining the model, the output includes estimates for Initial Intensity Function and Current Intensity Function.

Predictions

Total number of faults and total number of faults remaining
Expected reliability over a specified time period
Time to reach a specified reliability for a specified operational time
Time to reach a desired intensity function
Number of failures expected in a specified time

Schneidewind's Software Reliability Model (SSRM) [SCH97]

For this model, prediction equations are shown so that the reader can see, mathematically, what is involved in making predictions. Also, a C++ program shown in the Appendix to this chapter was developed to make predictions, using this model. A C++ compiler must be used to compile and execute the program. The program provides greater accuracy than can be achieved with SMERFS[3]. Therefore, in the examples the C++ program is used. The program will be used for this model's predictions, whereas SMERFS[3] will be used for the other models.

Definitions

α: initial failure rate parameter estimated from failure data
β: rate of change of failure rate parameter estimated from failure data
s: first failure count interval that is used in estimating α and β
t, t_1, t_2:   failure count intervals
X_{s-1}:   observed cumulative failure count in the range 1, $s-1$
$X(t)$:   observed cumulative failure count in the range 1, t, where t is the last failure count interval

Among the SSRM predictions is the number of failures in the interval t_1, t_2, as shown in equation (7.4):

$$m(t_1, t_2) = \left(\frac{\alpha}{\beta}\right)\left[e^{-\beta(t_1-s+1)} - e^{-\beta(t_2-s+1)}\right]$$ (7.4)

The cumulative number of failures at time t is given in equation (7.5):

$$F(t) = (\alpha/\beta)\left[1 - e^{-\beta(t-s+1)}\right] + X_{s-1}$$ (7.5)

In addition, reliability is computed in equation (7.6):

$$R(t) = e^{-\left[\frac{\alpha}{\beta}\left[e^{-\beta(t-s+1)}-e^{-\beta(t-s+2)}\right]\right]} \tag{7.6}$$

The maximum number of failures $F(\infty)$ is obtained in equation (7.7) by letting t go to infinity in equation (7.6):

$$F(\infty) = \frac{\alpha}{\beta} + X_{s-1} \tag{7.7}$$

The number of remaining failures $F(\infty)$, predicted at time t, after $X(t)$ failures have been observed is computed in equation (7.8). Note that $RF(t)$ is obtained by subtracting $X(t)$ from equation (7.7), the maximum number of failures:

$$RF(t) = \frac{\alpha}{\beta} + X_{s-1} - X(t) \tag{7.8}$$

Designating T as the predicted time to achieve specified reliability $R(T)$, and solving equation (7.6) for $t \equiv T$, this time is computed in equation (7.9):

$$T = -(1/\beta)\log\left[-\log\left(R(T) * (\beta/\alpha)\right]/([1 - \exp(-\beta)] + (s-1)\right. \tag{7.9}$$

Software Reliability Prediction Results

The results of predictions using several models are shown in this section. In order to evaluate prediction accuracy, the mean relative error is used defined as [FEN97]:

MRE = |(actual value – predicted value)/actual value|

For example, the MRE of reliability is computed in equation (7.10), where $R_a(t)$ is actual (empirical reliability) at time t. A second example is the MRE for cumulative failures, expressed in equation (7.11), where $f(t)$ is the actual cumulative failure count at time t. In both examples, N is the number of relative error computations.

$$MRE = \sum_{i=1}^{N}\left[\frac{|(R_a(t) - R(t))/R_a(t)|}{N}\right] \tag{7.10}$$

$$MRE = \sum_{i=1}^{N}\left[\frac{|(f(t) - F(t))/f(t)|}{N}\right] \tag{7.11}$$

Data

The NASA Space Shuttle data used in the predictions are shown in Table 7.2. See the preceding definitions for explanation of quantities used in the table. The data are based on two tests, as indicated in the table. In the second test, two faults and failures are removed. The effect of the test results is used in the prediction examples that follow.

Reliability Predictions

Figure 7.1 shows actual reliability, Musa Logarithmic Model predictions (SMERFS³), and Schneidewind (SSRM) (C++ program) predictions for the First and Second Tests. Two faults, and the failures they cause, are removed during the Second Test. You can see that

TABLE 7.2   NASA Space Shuttle: Software Release OI6

t_1 Time of Failure	t_2 Time of Failure	First Test $f(t)$ Failure Count	First Test Cumulative Failure Count	Second Test $f(t)$ Failure Count	Second Test Cumulative Failure Count	$R(T)$ Specified Reliability	$R_a(t)$ Actual Reliability
1.87	2.37	0	0	0	0	0.90000	1.0000
2.37	3.47	2	2	0	0	0.91000	0.7143
3.47	3.50	1	3	1	1	0.92000	0.8571
3.50	3.97	2	5	2	3	0.93000	0.7143
3.97	9.77	0	5	0	3	0.94000	1.0000
9.77	12.73	0	5	0	3	0.95000	1.0000
12.73	17.50	0	5	0	3	0.96000	1.0000
17.50	23.70	0	5	0	3	0.97000	1.0000
23.70	45.17	0	5	0	3	0.98000	1.0000
45.17	58.27	1	6	1	4	0.99000	0.8571
58.27	65.03	0	6	0	4	0.99900	1.0000
65.03	76.90	0	6	0	4	0.99990	1.0000
76.90	181.27	1	7	1	5	0.99999	0.8571
181.27		0	7	0	5	0.99999	1.0000

(30-day intervals)

	SSRM First Test	Second Test
s	1	2
α	1.1132	0.6355
β	0.1350	0.0850
X_{s-1}	0	0
$X(t)$	7	5

SSRM approximates the actual reliability for the Second Test better. Hence, SSRM has greater predictive accuracy for both tests for *these data*. (Note that the results could be different for other data.) It is important to use more than one model when making predictions to see which one would be most appropriate for your data. You do this by making the predictions and computing the MRE according to equation (7.11).The actual reliability at time t, $R_a(t)$, (Series 1) is computed in equation (7.12), where $f(t)$ is the failure count at time t and tf is the total number of failures.

$$R_a(t) = 1 - (f(t)/tf) \tag{7.12}$$

Cumulative Failure Predictions

The NHHP model and SSRM predictions of cumulative failures are compared in Figure 7.2 with the actual cumulative failures, again using the MRE to contrast prediction accuracy. You can see that there are different perspectives on reliability. In Figure 7.1, there is the probability of survival for a time greater than t. While this is important, it is not the whole story because the predicted cumulative failures over time tell you how bad failure occurrence is likely to be. SSRM does better in predicting because for both tests this model's

FIGURE 7.1 NASA Space Shuttle OI6: Reliability $R(t)$ vs. Time of Failure t

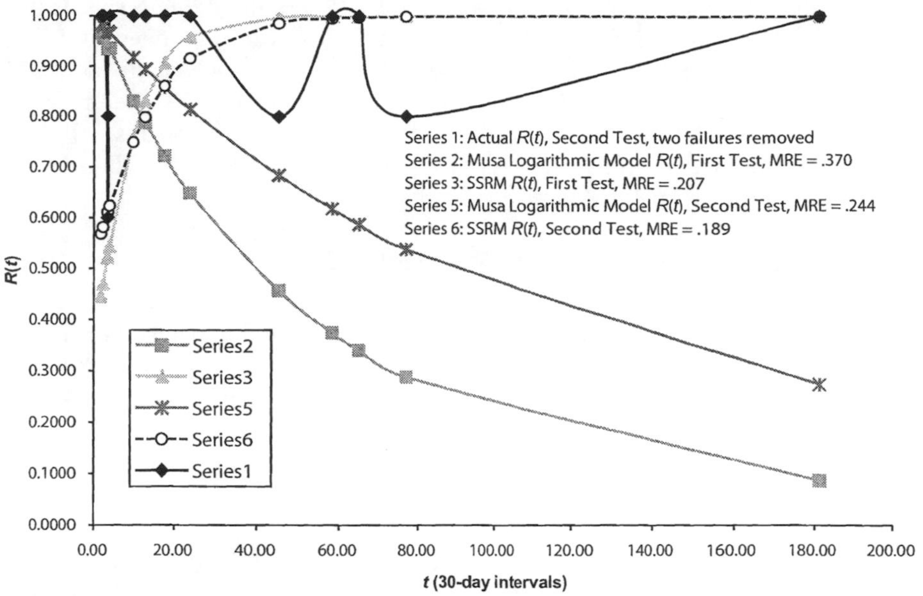

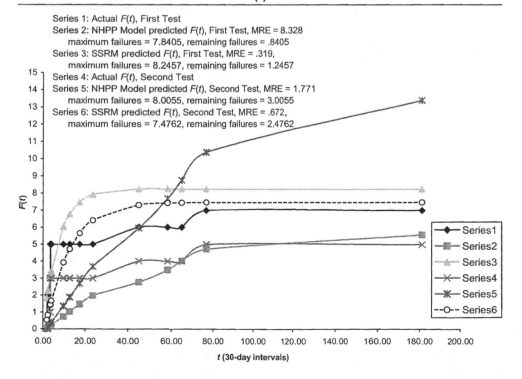

Series 1: Actual R(t), Second Test, two failures removed
Series 2: Musa Logarithmic Model R(t), First Test, MRE = .370
Series 3: SSRM R(t), First Test, MRE = .207
Series 5: Musa Logarithmic Model R(t), Second Test, MRE = .244
Series 6: SSRM R(t), Second Test, MRE = .189
Series2
Series3
Series5
Series6
Series1
R(t)
t (30-day intervals)

predictions approach an asymptotic value as time of failure increases. Thus, SSRM has better prediction accuracy because the model's behavior mimics the actual values, whereas the NHPP model predictions continue to rise for both tests.

FIGURE 7.2 Cumulative Failure Count $F(t)$ vs. Time of Failure t

Series 1: Actual F(t), First Test
Series 2: NHPP Model predicted F(t), First Test, MRE = 8.328
maximum failures = 7.8405, remaining failures = .8405
Series 3: SSRM predicted F(t), First Test, MRE = .319,
maximum failures = 8.2457, remaining failures = 1.2457
Series 4: Actual F(t), Second Test
Series 5: NHPP Model predicted F(t), Second Test, MRE = 1.771
maximum failures = 8.0055, remaining failures = 3.0055
Series 6: SSRM predicted F(t), Second Test, MRE = .672,
maximum failures = 7.4762, remaining failures = 2.4762
Series1
Series2
Series3
Series4
Series5
Series6
F(t)
t (30-day intervals)

Failures in Interval Predictions

The value of Figure 7.3, which shows predicted failures in time intervals, is that the two models—NHPP and SSRM—provide predicted failures in time intervals for both tests. Thus, you can see that this is another reason for using more than one model. Using this approach, you would have confidence that the actual failures lie between the two plots for each of the two tests. In particular, the NHPP plot for the Second Test tells you that the number of failures in an interval is not likely to exceed 3. With this information in hand, you could wisely plan future tests.

Time Required to Achieve Specified Reliability

Figure 7.4 shows one of the most important software reliability predictions because organizations have reliability goals and the amount of test or operational time required to meet those goals could be prohibitive if the reliability requirement is too high. You can see that time increases dramatically as specified reliability continues to increase. Therefore, there must be a reasonable tradeoff between time (i.e., cost) and reliability. A second factor to notice in Figure 7.4 is that time increases, for a given value of reliability, as the quality of the software increases by virtue of conducting additional tests that result in the removal of failures.

CASRE (Computer Aided Software Reliability Estimation) was developed as a software reliability measurement tool that is easier for non-specialists in software reliability engineering to use than many other currently available tools. CASRE incorporates the mathematical modeling capabilities of the public domain tool SMERFS (Statistical Modeling and Estimation of Reliability Functions for Software), and runs in a Microsoft Windows environment. CASRE may be downloaded from: http://www.openchannelfoundation .org/projects/CASRE_3.0.

FIGURE 7.3   NASA Space Shuttle OI6: Failures in Time Interval (t_1, t_2), $m(t_1, t_2)$ vs. Time of Failure t

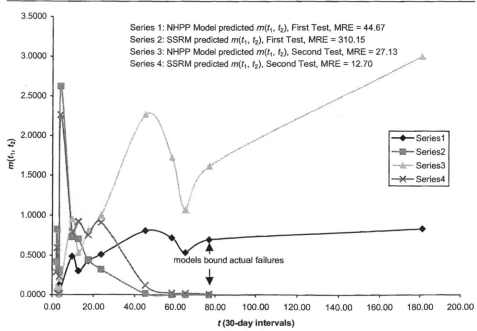

FIGURE 7.4   NASA Space Shuttle OI6: Time Required _T_ to Achieve Specified Reliability _R_(_T_) vs. _R_(_T_)

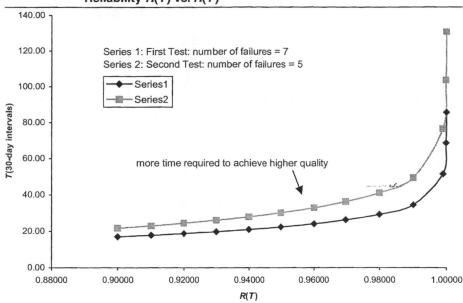

The command interface is menu driven; enabling and disabling of menu options guides users through the selection of a set of failure data, execution of a model, and analysis of model results. Input to the models is simultaneously displayed as text and as a high-resolution display that can be controlled to let users view the data in several different ways (e.g., time between successive failures, cumulative number of failures). Model predictions and statistical evaluations of a model's applicability (e.g., prequential likelihood ratio, model bias, bias trend) may be superimposed on the plot of the data used as input to the model. CASRE also incorporates earlier findings—that prediction accuracy may be increased by combining the results of several models in a linear fashion. Users can define their own model combinations, store them as part of the tool's configuration, and execute them in the same way as any other model.

New Features in Version 3.0

Version 3.0 also has a simpler input format than previous versions—for input data entered as the number of failures in a test interval of a specified length. However, version 3.0 will still read input data formatted for previous versions. Finally, version 3.0 simplifies model selection to a certain extent. Several models have different variants—for instance, the Schneidewind model has three variants that treat the failure data in different ways. Previous versions of CASRE would let users select the model, and then force them to select one of the variants—for example, if a user wanted to run the Schneidewind model, he or she would first select that model, and then select one of the three variants. This made the selection mechanism more complicated, and allowed users to run only one model variant at a time. Version 3.0 treats each model variant as a separate model—users now simply select all of a model's variants they want to run. This makes the selection mechanism somewhat simpler and more consistent, and users are now able to simultaneously run all variants of a model.

This tool should be useful to software development organizations searching for ways to more effectively manage their development resources. Since CASRE has been designed with the non-specialist in mind, it may be easier for managers and developers to use than those tools requiring detailed knowledge of the models.

Software Metrics and Metrics Tools

This section provides the engineer with descriptions of metrics and the tools to measure the metrics from the IEEE Std 982.1–2005, *IEEE Standard Dictionary of Measures of the Software Aspects of Dependability.*

Risk Factor Regression Model [SCH01]

Risk factor is the attribute of a requirements change that can induce reliability risk, such as memory space and requirements issues. The form of the regression equations (e.g., exponential, power) for the following metrics were obtained by fitting the actual data values in Excel, using R^2 (fraction of explained variation between dependent and independent variables) as the criterion for the best fit.

Memory space issues is the amount of memory space required to implement a requirements change (i.e., a requirements change uses memory to the extent that other functions do not have sufficient memory to operate effectively, and failures occur).

$$CF = ae^{CS}, \tag{7.13}$$

where CF is cumulative software failures, CS is cumulative memory space (over a set of requirements changes), and a is a coefficient of the exponential regression equation (7.13).

In Figure 7.5 the coefficient of the prediction equation was obtained by using Excel to plot CF vs. CS and fitting an exponential curve to the data. In addition to the plot, the value of R^2 gives the fraction of variation in CF accounted for by CS. Once the prediction function is available, it can be used to predict CF for values of CS beyond the actual CS data.

Requirements issues is the number of conflicting requirements (i.e., a requirements change conflicts with another requirements change, such as requirements to increase the search criteria of a Website and simultaneously decrease its search time, with the added software complexity causing failures).

$$CF = ae^{CI}, \tag{7.14}$$

where CF is cumulative software failures and CI is cumulative software issues (over a set of requirements changes) in the exponential regression equation (7.14).

Similar to the case of cumulative memory space requirement as a predictor of cumulative failures in Figure 7.5, cumulative requirements issues is shown as a predictor of cumulative failures in Figure 7.6, achieving about the same accuracy (i.e., R^2). However R^2 does not tell the whole story about goodness of fit because the mean residual, shown in Figures 7.5 and 7.6, must also be considered. The mean residual is defined as the average of the differences between the actual and predicted values. It is desirable to minimize this quantity [FEN97]. Thus, you can see that even though Figures 7.5 and 7.6 have approximately equal values of R^2, cumulative number of issues is a better predictor of cumulative failures in Figure 7.6. Using this process, you can identify the best predictor equation for your data.

Defect Density [FEN97] and Nikora et al. [NIK98]

Defect density (DD) is defined as cumulative failures divided by cumulative number of source lines of code, assuming a one-to-one relationship between defects and failures. The number of source lines of code includes executable code and non-executable data declarations per software release. The application of *DD* is to track software quality across a

FIGURE 7.5   NASA Space Shuttle: Cumulative Failures *CF* vs. Cumulative Memory Space *CS*

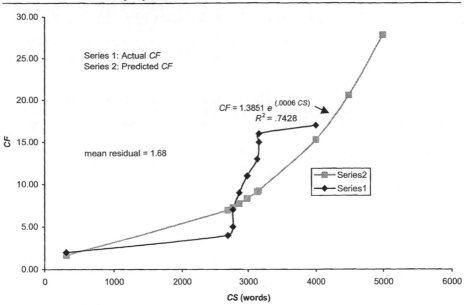

series of releases. The defect density, with respect to cumulative memory space *CS*, has the exponential form in equation (7.15).

$$DD = ae^{-.001CS} \tag{7.15}$$

FIGURE 7.6   NASA Space Shuttle: Cumulative Failures *CF* vs. Cumulative Number of Issues *CI*

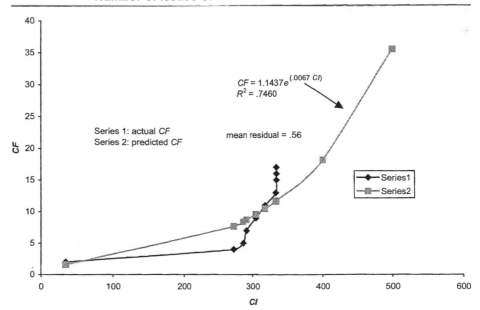

In contrast, the form of equation (7.16), with respect to cumulative number of issues, is a power function:

$$DD = .000001 \; CI^2 - 0.0005 \; CI + 0.08 \qquad (7.16)$$

Figures 7.7 and 7.8 provide a vivid demonstration of the case where one plot may have a higher R^2 (Figure 7.8) than another (Figure 7.7), but may have a higher mean residual

FIGURE 7.7   NASA Space Shuttle: Cumulative Defect Density *DD* vs. Cumulative Memory Space *CS*

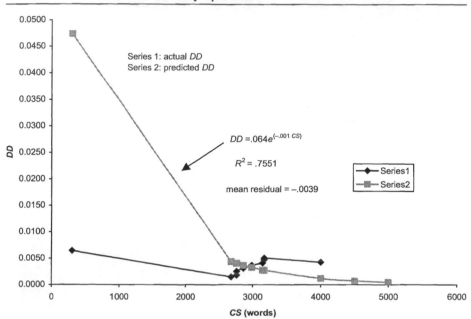

FIGURE 7.8   NASA Space Shuttle: Cumulative Defect Density *DD* vs. Cumulative Number of Requirements Issues *CI*

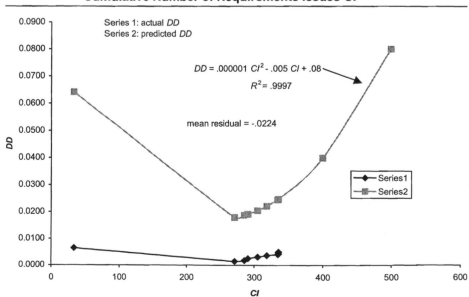

value, and hence, would not be a good predictor of cumulative defect density. Thus, you would use cumulative memory space requirements as the better predictor of cumulative defect density.

Summary

Software reliability metrics and tools have been described, analyzed, and discussed in order to provide the engineer with the background required to improve the quality of software in their organizations. Several reliability model predictions were made and compared to: 1) show how to evaluate and select models and 2) illustrate the use of the SMERFS[3] software reliability tool. In addition, a C++ program used to make software reliability predictions has been provided to show the reader an alternative to using packaged tools. Also, using the IEEE 982.1 standard, several reliability meters were computed, plotted, and evaluated. In particular, the reader was shown ways of evaluating prediction accuracy, using R^2 and mean residual value.

References

[ASH93] Carol Ash, *The Probability Tutoring Book.* IEEE Press, New York, 1993.

[DAV93] Alan M. Davis, *Software Requirements: Objects, Functions, and States.* Prentice Hall, 1993.

[FAG76] M. E. Fagan, "Design and Code Inspections to Reduce Errors in Program Development." *IBM Systems Journal,* Vol. 15, No. 3, 1976, pages 182–211.

[FAG86] M. E. Fagan, "Advances in Software Inspections." *IEEE Transactions on Software Engineering,* Vol. SE-12, No. 7, July 1986, pp. 744–751.

[IEE98] *Standard for a Software Quality Metrics Methodology,* IEEE Std 1061–1998, Revised in 2004.

[IEE08] IEEE/AIAA P1633™, *Recommended Practice on Software Reliability,* June 2008.

[FEN97] Norman F. Fenton and Shari Lawrence Pfleeger, *Software Metrics: A Rigorous & Practical Approach,* Second Edition. PWS Publishing Company, 1997.

[LYU96] Michael R. Lyu, editor, *Handbook of Software Reliability Engineering.* IEEE Computer Society Press and McGraw-Hill, 1996.

[MUL97] Pierre-Alain Muller, *Instant UML.* Wrox Press Ltd., Birmingham, UK, 1997.

[NIK98] A. Nikora, N. Schneidewind, and J. Munson, "IV&V Issues in Achieving High Reliability and Safety in Critical Control Software." Final Report, Volume 1—Measuring and Evaluating the Software Maintenance Process and Metrics-Based Software Quality Control; Volume 2—Measuring Defect Insertion Rates and Risk of Exposure to Residual Defects in Evolving Software Systems; and Volume 3—Appendices. Jet Propulsion Laboratory, National Aeronautics and Space Administration, Pasadena, CA, January 19, 1998.

[SCH01] Norman F. Schneidewind, "Investigation of the Risk to Software Reliability and Maintainability of Requirements Changes." Proceedings of the International Conference on Software Maintenance, Florence, Italy, Nov. 7–9, 2001, pp. 127–136.

[SCH03] Norman F. Schneidewind, "Life Cycle Core Knowledge Requirements for Software Reliability Measurement." *Reliability Review, The R & M Engineering Journal,* American Society for Quality, June 2003, Vol. 23, No. 2, pp. 18–29.

[SCH97] Norman F. Schneidewind, "Reliability Modeling for Safety Critical Software." *IEEE Transactions on Reliability,* Vol. 46, No.1, March 1997, pp. 88–98.

[SCH971] Norman F. Schneidewind, "Software Metrics Model for Integrating Quality Control and Prediction." Proceedings of the International Symposium on Software Reliability Engineering, Albuquerque, New Mexico, November 4, 1997, pp. 402–415.

[SCH99] Norman F. Schneidewind, "Measuring and Evaluating Maintenance Processing Using Reliability, Risk, and Test Metrics." *IEEE Transactions on Software Engineering,* Vol. 25, No. 6, November/December 1999, pp. 768–781.

[SHU] Forrest Shull, Jeffrey Carver, Guilherme H. Travassos, José Carlos Maldonado, Reidar Conradi, and Victor R. Basili, "Replicated Studies: Building a Body of Knowledge about Software Reading Techniques." *Software Engineering Empirical Methods.*

[STA91] G. E. Stark, "A Survey of Software Reliability Measurement Tools." IEEE International Symposium on Software Reliability, May 1991, pp. 90–97.

[ZUS98] Horst Zuse, *A Framework of Software Measurement.* Walter de Gruyter, Berlin, 1998.

Appendix

C++ program for making software reliability predictions using the Schneidewind Software Reliability Model:

//Schneidewind Software Reliability Model with keyboard and file input and file output

//program uses failure count data in the range [s, t] for $Xst > 0$ and in the range [1, t] $Xst = 0$ (i.e., $Xs\text{-}1 = Xt$)

//s: first failure count interval, t: last failure count interval, T: time when $F(T)$ to occur

//Xst: failure count in range [s,t], $Xs\text{-}1$: failure count in range [1, $(s-1)$]

//cumulative number of failures: $F(T) = (alpha/beta) * (1 - exp (1 - beta * (T - s + 1) + Xs\text{-}1))$

//beta maximum likelihood equation: $bn = (1/exp\ (beta\ n) - 1) - ((t - s + 1)/(exp\ (beta\ n\ (t - s + 1) - 1)))$

//beta maximum likelihood equation: $bn + 1 = (1/exp\ (beta\ n + 1) - 1) - ((t - s + 1)/(exp\ (beta\ n + 1\ (t - s + 1) - 1)))$

//mean of $bn + 1 = bn + ((mean\ beta - beta\ n)/(beta\ n + 1 - beta\ n)) * (bn + 1 - bn)$

//a = optimal beta factor = sum $[(k = 0), k = (t - s)]\ [k * x\ (k + s)/Xst]$

//linear interpolation likelihood function $L = (bn + 1 - a)$, using beta data input array

//parameter alpha equation: alpha = $(beta * Xst)/(1 - exp\ (- beta * (t - s + 1)))$

//choose parameters alpha and beta based on minimum L not = 0

//relative prediction error for cumulative failures: $RE = |(A(t) - P\ (t))/A(t)|$, where $A(t) =$ actual and $P(t)$ = predicted

//predicted reliability: $R(T) = exp\ [- (alpha/beta)\ [exp\ beta\ (T - s + 1) - exp - beta\ (T - s + 2)]$

//$R\ (tsm) = exp\ [- (alpha\ /\ beta)\ [exp\ beta\ ((ts + tm) - s + 1) - exp - beta\ ((ts + tm) - s + 2)]$:

//predicted reliability for start or launch time + mission duration

//actual failure rate: $f\ (xi, Ti) = sum\ xi/Ti$

//rate of change of predicted reliability: $d(R(T)/d(T) = R(T) * beta * (exp - beta * (T - s + 1)) * (1 + exp\ (beta))$

//number of failures in interval $Ti, Ti + 1$: $m(Ti) = (alpha/beta) * [exp\ (- beta * (Ti - s + 1) - exp\ (- beta * (Ti + 1 - s + 1)]$

//fault correction rate for fault $i = xi/delta\ Ti$

//mean fault correction rate: $M = sum\ (xi/delta\ Ti\ )/(t - 1)$

//fault correction delay: $dT = (-log\ (1 - F\ (dT)))/m$

//time to next failure: $T(t) = log\ (alpha/(alpha - beta * (Ft + Xst))/beta) - (t - s + 1)$

//Ft: number of specified failures to use in time to next failure predictions

//$Mp(Ti) = (\text{sum } (Ti + 1 - Ti))/FT$), predicted mean time to failure

//$Ma(Ti) = (\text{sum } (Ti + 1 - Ti))/Ni$, actual mean time to failure

//Ti: predicted time to achieve specified reliability $Ti = -(1/beta) \log [-\log (R (Ti) * (beta/alpha))]/(1 - \exp(-beta))] + (s - 1)$

//cumulative number of faults corrected at the interval i: $Nci = \text{sum } [(i = 1 \text{ to } Ni) ci * delta Ti]$

//proportion faults corrected: $Pci = Nci/Xt$

//predicted failure rate: $f(Ti) = alpha * \exp(-beta (Ti - s + 1))$

//probability of xi failures: $Pxi = (((mi)^{xi}) * (e^{(-mi)})) / xi!$

//predicted maximum number of failures at $Ti = $ infinity: $F(\text{infinity}) = (alpha/beta) + Xs1$

//predicted maximum number of remaining failures: $RF(t) = (alpha/beta) + (Xs - Xt)$

//predicted operational quality: $Q(t) = 1 - (RF(t)/F(\text{infinity}))$

//predicted number of faults remaining to be corrected: $Rci = FTi—Nci$

//predicted normalized number of cumulative failures in interval $(Ti, Ti + 1)$: MT / S

//predicted number of faults remaining: $Rci = F(\text{infinity})—NCi$

//predicted g fault correction quality: $Qci = 1 - (Rci/F(\text{infinity}))$

//compute actual reliability: $RaT = 1 - (\text{sum } xk/Xt)$

```
# include <iostream>//specify input output library
# include <math.h>//specify math library
#include <stdio.h>
#include <string.h>
#include <assert.h>
#include <fstream>
using namespace std;
using std::cout; //specify standard screen output
using std::cin; //specify standard screen input
using std::endl; //specify standard end of line
main()//beginning of main program
{
FILE *fp;//pointer to type FILE
fp = fopen("c:/models/numbers5.txt", "w"); //file for writing xk data output
FILE *fp1;//pointer to type FILE
fp1 = fopen("c:/models/numbers.txt", "w"); //file for writing beta data output
const char* format_string; //pointer to type char
double array RTi [40], Ti, Nci [40], Pci, sum Nci [40], tsm, tm, FTi, RFt, Qt, Rci, Qci;
```

//array of specified reliability values, predicted time to achieve reliability RTi

//predicted number of faults corrected at interval i, proportion of faults corrected at interval i

//predicted cumulative number of faults predicted at interval i

//start or launch time + mission duration, mission duration, predicted number of failures at $Ti = $ infinity

//predicted maximum number of remaining failures, predicted operational quality

//predicted number of faults remaining to be corrected at interval i

//predicted fault correction quality at interval i

double RT, $RT1$, Mt, $RTts$, $RT1ts$, RaT [40], $RTRE$, sumRT, $MRERT$; //declare predicted and part 1 of reliability, number of failures in interval t,

//predicted ana part 1 of reliability for start or launch time + mission duration,

//actual reliability, reliability relative error, sum of reliability relative error, reliability mean relative error

double dRT; //declare rate of change of reliability

double alpha, beta, mean beta [40], array bn [40], mean bn [40]; //declare parameters alpha, beta, mean value of beta array,

//beta maximum likelihood equation array, mean beta maximum likelihood equation array

double array beta [40], sum ks; //declare beta data input array, optimal beta factor

double Xst array [40], a [40], L [40], L min; //declare failure count in range $[s,t]$ array,

//linear interpolation likelihood function array, minimum value of L

double array T [40], FT [40]; //declare T data array, cumulative failure prediction

double RE, A [40];//declare relative prediction errors and actual cumulative failures array

double sumRE, MRE; //declare sum relative prediction error, mean relative prediction error

double RMt, sumRMt, $MREMt$; //declare mean number of failures in interval t relative error, sum, mean

double PR; //declare parameter ratio = beta/alpha

double $Xs1$; //declare failure count in range $[1, s]$

int Tcount; //declare number of T data entries

double alphas [40], mean betas [40]; //declare alpha and beta save arrays

double array Xst [40], Xs [40]; //declare failure count in range $[s,t]$ array, failure count in range $[1, s]$ range

double Xt ; //declare total failure count

double array xk [40]; //declare xk input array

double deltat array [40], M, sum$M$, MREM, Mtcount, Mcount; //actual $(Ti + 1) - Ti$, declare fault correction rate variables

//counter for computing mean Mt RE, correction rate count for fault i

double dTU, dTL, FTU, FTL; //fault correction delay, upper and lower, upper and lower values of CDF

double Tt [40], $MTTF$, Ma, sum array T [40], f, fTi; //prediction of next time to failure when current time is t

//predicted mean time to failure, actual mean time to failure, sum $(Ti + 1 - Ti)$, actual failure rate, predicted failure rate

int Ft; //number of specified failures to use in time to next failure predictions

double sum xk, fact [40], Pxi, mi [40], dTi [40], MT, S; //declare total number of failures, xi factorial, probability of xi failures,

//actual mean number of failures in interval i, predicted fault correction delay in interval i,

//predicted normalized number of cumulative failures, program size in KLOC int $i, j, s, mses, k, t, m, b, c, r, d$ [40]; //declare input array indices, first failure count interval, first failure count interval index,

//last failure count interval for linear interpolation and MSE, Xst array index, "a" sum control index, optimal beta array index

//relative prediction error array index

$i = 0$; //initialize xk array index

$j = 0$; //initialize beta data array index

$m = 0$; //initialize Xst array index

$r = 0$; //initialize relative prediction error and actual cumulative failures array indices

$Lmin = 0$; //initialize minimum value of L

$s = 1$; //initialize first failure count interval

$k = 1$; //initialize parameter "a" sum control index

$Xs1 = 0$, sum $xk = 0$, sum $ks = 0$; //initialize variables for summing failure counts

cout << "input upper limit of fault correction delay CDF"; //tell user to input upper value of dTi CDF

cin >> FTU; //upper limit of dT CDF inputted

cout << "input Ft"; //tell user to input number of failures to use in time to next failure prediction

cin >> Ft; //Ft inputted

cout << "input mission duration"; //tell user to input mission duration

cin >> tm; //tm inputted

cout << "input program size in KLOC"; //tell user to input program size

cin >> S; //program size inputted

ifstream infile ; //define xk file input

infile.open("c:/models/modelfailuredata.txt");

ifstream infile1 ; //define beta data file input

infile1.open("c:/models/betadata.txt");

ifstream infile2 ; //define T data file file input

infile2.open("c:/models/Tdata.txt");

ifstream infile3 ; //define cumulative failures file input

infile3.open("c:/models/cumfailures.txt");

ifstream infile4 ; //define specified reliability file input

infile4.open("c:/models/RTi.txt");

while(!infile3.eof())

//while eof not reached for cumulative failures file, store data in array

{

infile3 >> A [i]; //while eof not reached for cumulative failures file, store data in array

if(!infile3.eof()) //if eof not reached for cumulative failures file, increment culmulative failures array index

{

$i = i + 1$; //increment cumulative failures array index

}

```
}
i = 0;
while (!infile.eof())
//while eof not reached for xk file, store data in array
{
infile >> arrayxk [i];
if(!infile.eof()) //if eof not reached for xk file, increment xk array index
{
i = i + 1; //increment xt array index
}
}
t = array xk [0]; //store first (xk = t) file quantity in t
i = 1, k = 0;
while (k < = (t − 1)) //compute factorial for use in probability of xi failures (Pxi)
{
{
if (array xk [i] <= 1)
{
fact [i] = 1; //if xk = 0 or 1, set factorial to 1
}
else
{
fact [i] = array xk [i]; //otherwise, set factorial to xk
fact [i + 1] = fact [i] * (array xk [i] − 1); //compute xk factorial
}
i = i + 1;
}
k = k + 1;
}
i = 0;
while (!infile2.eof())
//while eof not reached for T data file, store data in array
{
infile2 >> array T [i];
if(!infile2.eof()) //if eof not reached for T data file, increment T data array index
{
i = i + 1; //increment T data array index
}
}
T count = array T [0]; //store number of T data entries
tsm = array T [T count] + tm; //compute last test time + mission duration
```

```
i = 0;
while(!infile4.eof())
//while eof not reached for RTi data file, store data in array
{
infile4 >> array RTi [i];
if(!infile4.eof()) //if eof not reached for RTi data file, increment RTi data array index
{
i = i + 1; //increment RTi data array index
}
}
i = 1, sum M = 0, sum Nci [0] = 0, M count = 0;
sum array T [i] = 0; //initialize sum (Ti + 1 – Ti)
while (i < = (T count – 1))
{
Deltat array [i] = array T [i + 1] – array T [i]; //compute Ti + 1 – Ti
sum array T [i + 1] = sum array T [i] + deltat array [i]; //sum (Ti + 1 – Ti)
if (deltat array [i] > 0)
{
M = array xk [i]/deltat array [i]; //compute fault correction rate for fault i
Nci [i] = M * deltat array [i]; //predict number of faults corrected at interval i
sum Nci [i] = sum Nci [i – 1] + Nci [i]; //predict cumulative number of faults corrected at
interval i
sum M = sum M + M; //sum fault correction rates
M count = M count + 1; //increment count for correction rate for fault i
}
if (sum Nci [i] > 0) //if cumulative number of faults corrected at interval i > 0,
//predict fault correction delay in interval i and output results
{
dTi [i] = (– log (1 – FTU))/sum Nci [i]; //predict fault correction delay in interval i
fprintf (fp1, "%s%\n", "Fault i", (char) 20);
fprintf (fp1,"%i%c%\n", i, (char) 6);
fprintf (fp1, "%s%\n", "Correction Rate for Fault i", (char) 20);
fprintf (fp1,"%f%c%\n", M, (char) 6);
fprintf (fp1, "%s%\n", "Cumulative Number of Faults Corrected at Interval i", (char) 20);
fprintf (fp1,"%f%c%\n", sum Nci [i], (char) 6);
fprintf (fp1, "%s%\n", "Predicted Fault Correction Delay in Interval i", (char) 20);
fprintf (fp1,"%f%c%\n", dTi [i], (char) 6);
}
i = i + 1;
}
MREM = sum M/(M count); //compute mean fault correction rate
```

```
fprintf (fp1, "%s%\n", "Mean Fault Correction Rate", (char) 20);
fprintf (fp1,"%f%c%\n", MREM, (char) 6);
k = 1;
s = 1;
while (s < = t)
{
while (k < s) //this ensures that summation of Xs – 1 only goes to s – 1
{
Xs1 = Xs1 + array xk [k]; //compute Xs – 1
k = k + 1;
}
array Xst [s] = Xs1; //store Xs-1 in Xst array
Xs [s]= Xs1; //save Xs – 1 in array
s = s + 1;
k = 1;
Xs1 = 0;
}
sum xk = 0; //initialize failure count sum
k = 0;
while (k < = T count – 1)
{
sum xk = sum xk + array xk [k + 1]; //sum xk failure count
f = sum xk/array T [k + 1]; //compute actual failure rate
mi [k] = array xk [k + 1] / sum xk; //compute mean number of failures in interval i for use
in computing probability of failures
Ma = sum array T [k + 1] / sum xk; //compute actual mean time to failure
fprintf (fp1, "%s%\n", "failure time", (char) 20);
fprintf (fp1,"%f%c%\n", array T [k + 1], (char) 6);
fprintf (fp1, "%s%\n", "actual failure rate", (char) 20);
fprintf (fp1,"%f%c%\n", f, (char) 6);
fprintf (fp1, "%s%\n", "actual mean time to failure", (char) 20);
fprintf (fp1,"%f%c%\n", Ma, (char) 6);
k =k + 1; //increment failure number count
}
Xt = sum xk; //store failure count sum in Xt
k = 0;
while (k <= t – 1)
{
RaT [k] = 1 – (array xk [k + 1] /Xt); //compute actual reliability
fprintf (fp1, "%s%\n", "actual reliability", (char) 20);
fprintf (fp1,"%f%c%\n", RaT [k], (char) 6);
```

```
k = k + 1;
}
s = 1;
while (s < = t)
{
Xst array [s] = Xt – array Xst [s]; //compute failure count in range [s,t]
if (Xst array [s] < = 0.0) //if Xst = 0, make Xs1 = Xt
{
Array Xst [s] = Xt;
}
//output s, Xst to numbers file
if (s < = 1) //if s = 0, Xs–1 = 0 and Xst = Xt
{
array Xst [s] = 0;
Xst array [s] = Xt;
}
fprintf (fp1, "%s%\n", "s", (char) 20);
fprintf (fp1,"%i%c%\n", s, (char) 6);
fprintf (fp1, "%s%\n", "Xst", (char) 20);
fprintf (fp1,"%f%c%\n", Xst array [s], (char) 6);
//output Xs-1 to numbers file
fprintf (fp1, "%s%\n", "Xs-1", (char) 20);
fprintf (fp1,"%f%c%\n", array Xst [s], (char) 6);
s = s + 1; //increment first failure count interval
//output Xt to numbers file
fprintf (fp1, "%s%\n", "Xt", (char) 20);
fprintf (fp1,"%f%c%\n", Xt, (char) 6);
}
s = 1;
b = 0;
sum ks = 0;
while (s <= t)
//"a" sum for new s and variable b
{
while (b < = (t – s))
{
if (Xst array [s] <= 0.0) //if Xst = 0, compute "parameter a" sum
{
Sum ks = sum ks + ((b * (array xk [b + s]))/Xt);
}
else//if Xst not = 0, compute parameter "a" sum
```

```
{
sum ks = sum ks + ((b * (array xk [b + s]))/(Xst array [s]));
}
b = b + 1; //increment for next array values
a [s] = sum ks; //store "parameter a" in an array for estimating parameters later
}//end of b control while
//output s and a to numbers5 file
fprintf (fp, "%s%\n", "s", (char) 20);
fprintf (fp, "%i%c%\n", s, (char) 6);
fprintf (fp, "%s%\n", "a", (char) 20);
fprintf (fp, "%f%c%\n", sum ks, (char) 6);
b = 0; //reinitialize variable b
s = s + 1; //increment first failure count interval
sum ks = 0; //reinitialize "a" sum variable
}//end of s control while
while (!infile1.eof())
//while eof not reached for beta data file, store data in array
{
infile1 >> array beta [j];
if(!infile1.eof())//if eof not reached for beta data file, output data to numbers.txt file
{
j = j + 1; //increment beta data array index
}
}
infile.close(); //close modelfailuredata.txt file
infile1.close(); //betadata.txt file
s = 1; //reinitialize first failure count interval
j = 0; //reinitialize beta data array index
i = 1; //initialize T data array index
while (j < = (t–1))
{
mean beta [j] = (array beta [j] + array beta [j + 1])/2; //compute mean value of beta
j = j + 1; //increment beta data array index
}
s = 1, j = 0, i = 0; //reinitialize s, j, i
while (s < = t)
//compute mean bn for all values of s
{
j = 0;
while (j < = (t − 1))
//while there is more beta data for given s, compute mean bn
```

```
{
array bn [j] = (1/(exp (array beta [j]) – 1)) – (t – s + 1)/(((exp (array beta [j]* (t—s + 1))))
– 1);
//estimate beta in interval n
array bn [j + 1] = (1/(exp (array beta [j + 1]) – 1))– (t – s + 1)/(((exp (array beta [j + 1]*
(t – s + 1)))) – 1);
//estimate beta in interval n + 1
mean bn [j + 1] = array bn [j] + (((mean beta [j] – array beta [j])/(array beta [j + 1] – array
beta [j])) *(array bn [j + 1] – array bn [j]));
//compute mean bn + 1
L [j] = fabs (mean bn [j] – a [s]) ; //compute linear interpolation function for L [j]
L [j + 1] = fabs (mean bn [j + 1] – a [s]) ; //compute linear interpolation function for L
[j+1]
if (L [j + 1] < = L [j])//if last L < = previous L, compute L
{
c = j + 1; //store index of mean beta = t, where L is a minimum
Lmin = L [c]; //if last L <= previous L, make it the minimum L
}
//end of if statement
j = j + 1; //increment mean beta array index
} //end of second while statement
//output mean bn and minimum L to numbers 5 file
fprintf (fp, "%s%\n", "s", (char) 20);
fprintf (fp, "%i%c%\n", s, (char) 6);
fprintf (fp, "%s%\n", "mean bn", (char) 20);
fprintf (fp, "%f%c%\n", mean bn [c], (char) 6);
fprintf (fp, "%s%\n", "minimum L", (char) 20);
fprintf (fp, "%f%c%\n", L min, (char) 6);
//estimate alpha
if (Xst array [s] < = 0.0)//if Xst = 0, estimate alpha
{
alpha = (mean beta [c-1] * Xt)/(1 – exp (– mean beta [c-1]* (t)));
}
else//if Xst not = 0, estimate alpha
{
alpha = (mean beta [c-1] * Xst array [s] )/(1 – exp (– mean beta [c-1]* (t – s + 1)));
}
alphas [s] = alpha; //save alpha for use in F(T)
mean betas [s] = mean beta [c – 1]; //save beta for use in F(T)
PR = mean beta [c-1]/alpha ; //compute parameter ratio
//predict time required to meet specified reliability
```

```
fprintf (fp, "%s%\n", "s", (char) 20);
fprintf (fp, "%i%c%\n", s, (char) 6);
fprintf (fp, "%s%\n", "alpha", (char) 20);
fprintf (fp, "%f%c%\n", alpha, (char) 6);
fprintf (fp, "%s%\n", "beta", (char) 20);
fprintf (fp, "%f%c%\n", mean beta [c-1], (char) 6);
fprintf (fp, "%s%\n", "parameter ratio", (char) 20);
fprintf (fp, "%f%c%\n", PR, (char) 6);
```

$s = s + 1;$ //increment first failure count interval

$i = 0;$ //initialize specified reliability array index

} //end of s control loop

$i = 0;$ //initialize specified reliability array index

$s = 1;$ //initialize first failure count interval

while $(s < = t)$

{

while $(i < = (T \text{ count} - 1))$

{

$Ti = ((- 1/\text{mean betas } [s]) * (\log ((- \log (\text{array } RTi [i]) * ((\text{mean betas } [s]/\text{alphas } [s])/(1 - \exp (- \text{mean betas } [s])))))))) + (s - 1);$

//predict time to achieve specified reliability

```
fprintf (fp, "%s%\n", "s", (char) 20);
fprintf (fp, "%i%c%\n", s, (char) 6);
fprintf (fp, "%s%\n", "time to achieve specified reliability", (char) 20);
fprintf (fp, "%f%c%\n", Ti, (char) 6);
```

$i = i + 1;$ //increment specified reliability array index

}

$s = s + 1;$ //increment first failure count interval

$i = 0;$ //reinitialize specified reliability array index

}

$s = 1;$ //reinitialize first failure count interval

$i = 1;$ //initialize T data array index

sum $RE = 0;$ //initialize cumulative failures relative prediction error sum

sum $RMt = 0;$ //initialize number of failures in interval t error sum

while $(s < = t)$ //output time to next failure and Ft for all values of s

{

while $(i < = T \text{ count})$ //output time to next failure and Ft for number of Ft values

{

//predict time to next failure

$Tt [i] = (\log ((\text{alphas } [s]/((\text{alphas } [s] - (\text{mean betas } [s] * (Ft + Xst \text{ array } [s])))))/\text{mean betas } [s])) - (\text{array } T [i] - s + 1);$

//output Ft and Tt to numbers 5 file

```
fprintf (fp, "%s%\n", "s", (char) 20);
fprintf (fp, "%i%c%\n", s, (char) 6);
fprintf (fp, "%s%\n", "Ft: number of specified failures", (char) 50);
fprintf (fp, "%i%c%\n", Ft, (char) 6);
fprintf (fp, "%s%\n", "Failure Time", (char) 50);
fprintf (fp, "%f%c%\n", array T[i], (char) 6);
fprintf (fp, "%s%\n", "Predicted Time to Next Failure", (char) 50);
fprintf (fp, "%f%c%\n", Tt[i], (char) 6);
i = i + 1;
}
s = s + 1;
i = 1;
}
s = 1;
i = 1;
```

sum $RMt = 0$; //initialize sum of number of failures in interval $Ti, Ti + 1$

sum array $T[0] = 0$; //initialize summation of $(Ti + 1 - Ti)$

Mt count $= 0$; //initialize Mt counter

sum $RT = 0$; //initialize reliability sum of relative error

while $(s < = t)$ //compute alpha, beta, T, and $F(T)$ for all values of s

{

while $(i < = T$ count)//compute reliability metrics and prediction errors while there is still T data input

{

$FT[i] = ($alphas $[s]/($mean betas $[s]) * (1 - $exp $(-$ mean betas $[s]*($array $T[i] - s + 1)))) + Xs[s]$;

//predict cumulative failures to occur at time T

sum array $T[i] = $ sum array $T[i - 1] + $ deltat array $[i]$; //sum $(Ti + 1 - Ti)$

$MTTF = $ sum array $T[i]/FT[i]$; //predict mean time to failure

$RT1 = ($exp $(-$ mean betas $[s] * ($array $T[i] - s + 1))) - ($exp $(-$ mean betas $[s] *($array $T[i] - s + 2)))$;

//compute part 1 of predicted reliability

$RT = $ exp $(- ($alphas $[s]/$mean betas $[s]) * RT1)$; //predict reliability

$RT1ts = ($exp $(-$ mean betas $[s] * (tsm - s + 1))) - ($exp $(-$ mean betas $[s] *(tsm - s + 2)))$;

//compute part 1 of predicted reliability for start or launch time + mission duration

$RTts = $ exp $(- ($alphas $[s]/$mean betas $[s]) * RT1ts)$; //predict reliability for start or launch time + mission duration

$RTRE = $ fabs $((RT - RaT[i - 1])/RT)$; //compute reliability relative error

sum $RT = $ sum $RT + RTRE$; //sum reliability relative error

$dRT = ($alphas $[s] * RT) * ($exp $(-$ mean betas $[s] * ($array $T[i] - s + 1) - ($exp $(-$ mean betas $[s] * ($array $T[i] - s + 2)))))$;

//predict rate of change of reliability

RE = fabs $((((A\,[i-1] - FT\,[i])) / FT\,[i]);$ //compute relative prediction error for cumulative failures

sum RE = sum $RE + RE$; //sum relative prediction error for cumulative failures

Pxi = ((pow ($mi\,[i-1]$, array $xk\,[i]$)) * (exp ($-\,mi\,[i-1]$))) / fact $[i]$; //compute probability of xi failures in interval i

fTi = alphas $[s]$ * (exp($-$ mean betas $[s]$ * (array $T\,[i] - s + 1$))); //predict failure rate

FTi = (alphas $[s]$/mean betas $[s]$) + $Xs\,[s]$; //predict maximum number of failures at Ti = infinity

Rci = FTi − sum $Nci\,[i]$; //predict number of faults remaining to be corrected at interval i

Qci = $1 - (Rci/FTi)$; //predict fault correction quality at interval i

RFt = (alphas $[s]$/mean betas $[s]$) + $Xs\,[s] - Xt$; //predict maximum number of remaining failures

Qt = $1 - (RFt/FTi)$; //predict operational quality

//output predictions and relative errors to numbers 2 file

fprintf (fp, "%s%\n", "s", (char) 20);

fprintf (fp, "%i%c%\n", s, (char) 6);

fprintf (fp, "%s%\n", "Failure Time", (char) 20);

fprintf (fp, "%f%c%\n", array $T[i]$, (char) 6);

fprintf (fp, "%s%\n", "Actual Cumulative Failures", (char) 50);

fprintf (fp, "%f%c%\n", $A[i-1]$, (char) 6);

fprintf (fp, "%s%\n", "Predicted Cumulative Failures", (char) 50);

fprintf (fp, "%f%c%\n", FT[i], (char) 6);

fprintf (fp, "%s%\n", "Cumulative Failures Relative Prediction Error", (char) 50);

fprintf (fp, "%f%c%\n", RE, (char) 6);

fprintf (fp, "%s%\n", "Predicted Reliability", (char) 20);

fprintf (fp, "%f%c%\n", RT, (char) 6);

fprintf (fp, "%s%\n", "Reliability Relative Error", (char) 20);

fprintf (fp, "%f%c%\n", $RTRE$, (char) 6);

fprintf (fp, "%s%\n", "Predicted Reliability for Mission Duration", (char) 20);

fprintf (fp, "%f%c%\n", $RTts$, (char) 6);

fprintf (fp, "%s%\n", "Predicted Rate of Change of Reliability", (char) 50);

fprintf (fp, "%f%c%\n", dRT, (char) 6);

fprintf (fp, "%s%\n", "Predicted Failure Rate", (char) 100);

fprintf (fp, "%f%c%\n", fTi, (char) 6);

fprintf (fp, "%s%\n", "Probability of xi Failures in Interval i", (char) 100);

fprintf (fp, "%f%c%\n", Pxi, (char) 6);

if ($i <$ = (T count − 1))//if not reached the last failure time, output predictions

{

fprintf (fp, "%s%\n", "Failure Time", (char) 20);

fprintf (fp, "%f%c%\n", array $T\,[i+1]$, (char) 6);

fprintf (fp, "%s%\n", "Predicted MTTF", (char) 50);

fprintf (fp, "%f%c%\n", MTTF, (char) 6);

fprintf (fp, "%s%\n", "Predicted Maximum Number of Failures at Ti = Infinity", (char) 100);

fprintf (fp, "%f%c%\n", FTi, (char) 6);

fprintf (fp, "%s%\n", "Predicted Maximum Number of Remaining Failures", (char) 100);

fprintf (fp, "%f%c%\n", RFt , (char) 6);

fprintf (fp, "%s%\n", "Predicted Operational Quality", (char) 100);

fprintf (fp, "%f%c%\n", Qt , (char) 6);

fprintf (fp, "%s%\n", "Predict Number of Faults Remaining to be Corrected at Interval i", (char) 100);

fprintf (fp, "%f%c%\n", $Rci,$ (char) 6);

fprintf (fp, "%s%\n", "Predict Fault Correction Quality at Interval i", (char) 100);

fprintf (fp, "%f%c%\n", $Qci,$ (char) 6);

//predict mean number of failures in interval $Ti, Ti + 1$

Mt = (alphas [s]/mean betas [s]) * ((exp (– mean betas [s] * (array T [i] – s + 1))) – (exp (– mean betas [s] * (array $T[i + 1]$ – s + 1))));

$MT = Mt/S$; //predict normalized number of failures in interval $Ti, Ti + 1$

if (Mt > .0) //do not compute relative error if $Mt < = 0$

{

fprintf (fp, "%s%\n", "Failure Time", (char) 20);

fprintf (fp, "%f%c%\n", array $T[i]$, (char) 6);

RMt = fabs ((Mt – array xk [i])/Mt); //compute relative error for number of failures in interval T

Mt count = Mt count + 1; //increment Mt counter for computing mean Mt RE

fprintf (fp, "%s%\n", "Number of Failures in Interval T Relative Prediction Error", (char) 100);

fprintf (fp, "%f%c%\n", RMt, (char) 6);

sum RMt = sum RMt + RMt; //sum relative error for mt

}

fprintf (fp, "%s%\n", "Failure Time", (char) 20);

fprintf (fp, "%f%c%\n", array T [i], (char) 6);

fprintf (fp, "%s%\n", "Predicted Number of Failures in Interval T", (char) 50);

fprintf (fp, "%f%c%\n", Mt, (char) 6);

fprintf (fp, "%s%\n", "Predict Normalized Number of Failures in Interval T", (char) 100);

fprintf (fp, "%f%c%\n", MT, (char) 6);

}

$i = i + 1$; //increment T data array index

}//end of T data loop

$MRERT$ = sum RT/t; //compute mean relative error for reliability

MRE = sum RE/T count; //compute mean relative prediction error for cumulative failures

$MREMt$ = sum RMt/Mt count; //compute mean relative prediction error for mean number of failures in interval t

```
//output error statistics to numbers2 file
fprintf (fp, "%s%\n", "s", (char) 20);
fprintf (fp, "%i%c%\n", s, (char) 6);
fprintf (fp, "%s%\n", "Mean Relative Error for Cumulative Failures", (char) 50);
fprintf (fp, "%f%c%\n", MRE, (char) 6);
fprintf (fp, "%s%\n", "Mean Relative Error for Number of Failures in Interval i", (char)
50);
fprintf (fp, "%f%c%\n", MREMt, (char) 6);
fprintf (fp, "%s%\n", "Mean Relative Error for Reliability", (char) 50);
fprintf (fp, "%f%c%\n", MRERT, (char) 6);
sum RE = 0, sum RMt = 0, sum RT = 0; //reinitialize relative prediction error sums
Mtcount = 0; //reinitialize counter for computing Mt MRE
s = s + 1; //increment first failure count
i = 1; //reinitialize T data array index
} //end of s loop
i = 1;
while (i < = T count)
{
fprintf (fp, "%s%\n", "interval i", (char) 20);
fprintf (fp, "%i%c%\n", i, (char) 6);
Pci = sum Nci [i]/Xt; //compute proportion of faults corrected at interval i
fprintf (fp, "%s%\n", "Proportion of Faults Corrected at Interval i", (char) 50);
fprintf (fp, "%f%c%\n", Pci, (char) 6);
i = i + 1;
}
return 0; //return to the operating system
} //executable code ends here
```

8

Integrating Testing with Reliability

Objectives

The objectives of this chapter are to show how the activities of software testing and reliability are integrated and to demonstrate how the two activities interact in achieving testing efficiency and the reliability resulting from tests. "Integrated" means modeling the execution of a variety of tests on a directed graph representation of an example program. A complexity metric is used to construct the nodes, edges, and paths of the example program. Models are developed to represent the efficiency and achieved reliability of black-box and white-box tests. Evaluations are made of path, independent path, node, program construct, and random tests to ascertain which, if any, is superior with respect to efficiency and reliability. Predictions are made of the reliability and fault correction that results from implementing various test strategies.

What You Will Learn From This Chapter

You will learn that, overall, path testing has the edge in test efficiency. The results depend on the nature of the directed graph in relation to the type of test. You will also learn that while there is no dominant method, in most cases the tests that provide detailed coverage are better. For example, path testing discovers more faults than independent path testing. Practitioners can use the methods to evaluate the efficiency and reliability of other programs.

Subjects

Challenges to Efficient Testing
Test Strategies (White-Box Testing, Black-Box Testing)
Testing Process (White-Box Tests, Path Testing, Random Path Testing, Node Testing, Random Node Testing, Black-Box Testing, and Test Assumptions)
Integrated Testing and Reliability Model
Constructing the Directed Graphs of Example Programs
Test Strategy Evaluation
Test Effectiveness
Results of Test Strategies Evaluation
Dynamic Testing Analysis
Black-Box Testing Analysis
Reliability Models that Combine Fault Correction with Testing
Empirical Approaches to Testing

Introduction

Software is a complex intellectual product. Inevitably, some errors are made during requirements formulation as well as during designing, coding, and testing the product. State-of-the-practice software development processes to achieve high-quality software include measures that are intended to discover and correct faults resulting from these errors, including reviews, audits, screening by language-dependent tools, and several levels of test. Managing these errors involves describing, classifying, and modeling the effects of the remaining faults in the delivered product and thereby helping to reduce their number and criticality [IEE08].

One approach to achieving high-quality software is to investigate the relationship between testing and reliability. Thus, this chapter addresses the comprehensive integration of testing and reliability methodologies. This is a new approach to integrate testing efficiency; the reliability resulting from tests; modeling the execution of tests with directed graphs; using complexity metrics to represent the graphs; and evaluations of path, independent path, node, random node, white-box, and black-box tests.

One of the reasons for integrating testing with reliability is that, as recommended by Hamlet [HAM94], the risk of using software can be assessed based on reliability information. He states that the primary goal of testing should be to measure the reliability of tested software. Therefore, it is undesirable to consider testing and reliability prediction as disjoint activities.

When integrating testing and reliability, it is important to know when there has been enough testing to achieve reliability goals. Thus determining when to stop a test is an important management decision. Several stopping criteria have been proposed, including the probability that the software has a desired reliability, and the expected cost of remaining faults [PRO04]. You can use the probabilities associated with path and node testing in a directed graph to estimate the closeness to the desired reliability of 1.0 that can be achieved. To address the cost issue, explicitly estimate the cost of remaining faults in monetary units and estimate it implicitly by the number of remaining faults compared with the total number of faults in the directed graph of a program.

Given that it cannot be shown that there are no more errors in the program, use heuristic arguments based on thoroughness and sophistication of testing effort and *trends in the resulting discovery of faults* to argue the plausibility of the lower risk of remaining faults [HAI02]. The progress in fault discovery and removal is used as a heuristic metric when testing is "complete." At each stage of testing, reliability is estimated to note the efficiency of various testing methods: path, independent path, random path, node, and random node.

Challenges to Efficient Testing

A pessimistic but realistic view of testing is offered by Beizer [BEI90]: An interesting analogy parallels the difficulty in software testing with pesticides, known as the Pesticide Paradox. Every method that is used to prevent or find bugs leaves a residue of subtler bugs against which those methods are ineffectual. This problem is compounded because the Complexity Barrier principle states [BEI90]: Software complexity and presence of bugs grow to the limit of the ability to manage complexity and bug presence. By eliminating the previously easily detected bugs, another escalation of features and complexity has arisen. But this time there are subtler bugs to face, just to retain the previous reliability. Society seems to be unwilling to limit complexity because many users want extra features. Thus, users usually push the software to the complexity barrier. How close to approach that barrier is largely determined by the strength of the techniques that can be wielded against ever more complex and subtle bugs. Even in developing the relatively simple example program this paradox was found to be true: As early-detected bugs (i.e., faults) were easily removed and complexity and features were increased, a residue of subtle bugs remained and was compounded by major bugs attributed to increased complexity. Perhaps as the fields of testing and reliability continue to mature, the fields will learn how to model these effects.

A further complication involves the dynamic nature of programs. If a failure occurs during preliminary testing and the code is changed, the software may now work for a test case that did not work previously. But the code's behavior on preliminary testing can no longer be guaranteed. To account for this possibility, testing should be restarted. The expense of doing this is often prohibitive [REL]. It would be possible to model this effect but at the cost of unmanageable model complexity engendered by restarting the testing. It appears that this effect could have been modeled by simulation.

Notations and Definitions

The analysis starts with the notations and definitions that are used in the integrated testing and reliability approach to achieving high-quality software. Please refer to these notations when reading the equations and analyses:

Notations

edge:	arc emanating from node
node:	connection point of edges
i:	identification of edge
n:	identification of node
c:	identification of program construct
k:	test number
empirical:	reliability metrics based on historical fault data

Independent Variables (i.e., not computed; generated by random process)

$f(n)$:	fault count in node n
n_f:	number of faults in program
e_n:	number of edges at node n
n_e:	number of edges in program (generated by random process in random path testing)
$n(c, k)$:	number of faults encountered and removed by testing construct c on test k

Dependent Variables i.e., computed or obtained by inspection)

Number of Program Elements

n_{nj}:	number of nodes on path j
n_n:	number of nodes in a program
n_j:	number of paths in a program

Probabilities

$p(j)$:	probability of traversing path j
$p(n)$:	probability of traversing node n

Expected Values

$E(n)$:	expected number of faults at node n during testing
$E(j)$:	expected number of faults on path j during testing

E_p: expected number of faults encountered in a program based on path testing

Reliabilities

R_n: empirical reliability at node n prior to fault removal
R_p: empirical reliability of program prior to fault removal
U_n: empirical unreliability at node n prior to fault removal
$U(j)$: empirical unreliability on path j prior to fault removal
$R(j)$: empirical reliability of path j prior to fault removal
$R(c, k)$: empirical reliability achieved by testing construct c during test k, after fault removal
$r_e(n)$: empirical number of remaining faults, at node n, prior to fault removal

Test Efficiencies

$e(j)$: efficiency of path testing
$e(n)$: efficiency of node testing
$e(c, k)$: efficiency of program construct c testing for test k
Mc: McCabe Cyclomatic Complexity metric (i.e., number of independent paths)
t: test or operational time

Test Strategies

There are two major types of tests, each with its own type of test case—white-box testing and black-box testing [CHE96]:

White-Box Testing

White-box testing is based on the knowledge about the internal structure of the software under test (e.g., knowledge of the structure of decision statements). The adequacy of test cases is assessed in terms of the level of coverage of the structure they reach (e.g., comprehensiveness of covering nodes, edges, and paths in a directed graph) [TON04].

Definition of White-Box Test Case: A set of test inputs, execution conditions, and expected results developed for a particular objective such as exercising a particular program path or to verify compliance with a specific requirement. For example, exercise particular program paths with the objective of achieving high reliability by discovering multiple faults on these paths.

Black-Box Testing

In black-box testing, it may be easier to derive tests at higher levels of abstraction. More information about the final implementation is introduced in stages, so that additional tests due to increased knowledge of structure are required in small manageable amounts, which greatly simplifies structural, or white-box, testing. However, it is not clear whether black-box testing (e.g., testing If Then Else statements) preceding or following white-box testing (e.g., identifying If Then Else paths) affects test effectiveness.

Definition of Black-Box Test Case: Specifications of inputs, predicted results, and a set of execution conditions for a test item. In addition, because only the functionality of the software is of concern in black-box testing, this testing method emphasizes executing functions and examining their input and output data [HOW87]. For example, specify functions to force the execution of program constructs (e.g., While Do) that are expected to result in an entire set of faults to be encountered and removed. There are no inputs and outputs specified because the C++ example program executes paths independently of inputs, but is dependent on function probabilities. The inputs specify parameters and variables used in program computations, and not path execution probabilities. The program produces a standard ouput dependent only on function probabilities.

A variant of black-box testing captures the values of and changes in variables during a test. In regression testing, for example, this approach can be used to determine whether a program, modified by removing faults, is behaving correctly [XIE05]. However, in this chapter, rather than observing variable changes, black-box testing is conducted by observing the results of executing decision statements and determining whether the correct decision is made.

Testing Process

White-Box Tests

Four types of testing are used, as described below. Path testing involves visiting both nodes and paths in testing a program, whereas node testing involves only testing nodes. For example, in testing an If Then Else construct, the *If Then* and *Else* components are visited in path testing, whereas in node testing, only the *If* component is visited. Recognize the limitations of using a directed graph for the purpose of achieving complete test coverage. For example, while it is possible to represent initial conditions and boundary conditions [MYE79] in a directed graph, the amount of detail involved could make its use unwieldy. Therefore, it is better to represent only the *decision* and *sequence constructs* in the graph. However, this is not a significant limitation because the decision constructs account for the majority of complexity in most programs and high complexity leads to low reliability. For illustrative purposes, a *short* program is used in Figure 8.1. This program may appear to be simple. Actually, it is complex because of the iterative decision constructs. Of course, only short programs are amenable to manual analysis. However, McCabe and Associates developed tools for converting program language representations to directed graphs for large programs [MCC].

The following is an outline of the characteristics of the various testing schemes that were considered. First, identify program constructs: If Then, If Then Else, While Do, and Sequence in the program to be tested. Then perform the following white box tests:

Path Testing

In path testing, it is desired to distinguish the independent paths from the non-independent ones. Therefore, since the McCabe Complexity Metric [MCC76] represents the number of independent paths, it is used to implement a test strategy. Using a random number generator, faults are randomly planted at nodes of a directed graph that is constructed with edges and nodes based on the McCabe metric, as shown in Figure 8.2. This process provides a random number of faults that are encountered as each path is traversed. Note that in path testing the selection of paths is pre-determined.

Random Path Testing

As opposed to path testing, which uses pre-determined paths, random path testing produces a random selection of paths. Thus, using the directed graph based on the McCabe metric, a random selection of path execution sequences, and the same random distribution of faults

FIGURE 8.1   Directed Graph Illustrating McCabe Complexity

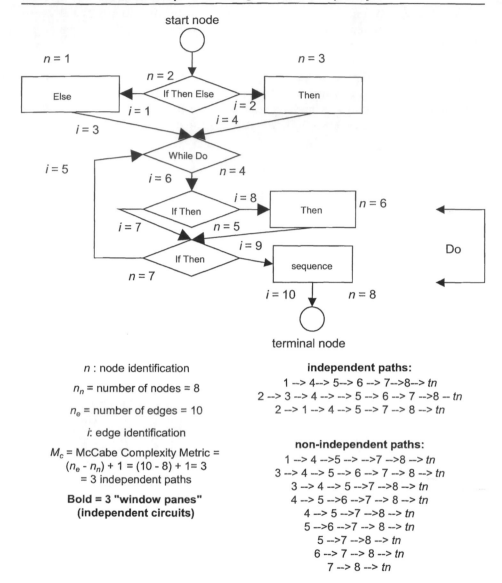

n : node identification

n_n = number of nodes = 8

n_e = number of edges = 10

i: edge identification

M_c = McCabe Complexity Metric =
$(n_e - n_n) + 1 = (10 - 8) + 1 = 3$
= 3 independent paths

**Bold = 3 "window panes"
(independent circuits)**

independent paths:

1 --> 4--> 5--> 6 --> 7-->8--> tn

2 --> 3 --> 4 --> --> 5 --> 6 --> 7 -->8 -- tn

2 --> 1 --> 4 --> 5 --> 7 --> 8 --> tn

non-independent paths:

1 --> 4 -->5 --> -->7 -->8 --> tn

3 --> 4 --> 5 --> 6 --> 7 --> 8 --> tn

3 --> 4 --> 5 -->7 -->8 --> tn

4 --> 5 -->6 -->7 --> 8 --> tn

4 --> 5 -->7 -->8 --> tn

5 -->6 -->7 --> 8 --> tn

5 -->7 -->8 --> tn

6 --> 7 --> 8 --> tn

7 --> 8 --> tn

at nodes as in path testing, a different sequence of fault encounters at the nodes will occur, compared with path testing.

Node Testing

Using the directed graph based on the McCabe metric and the same distribution of faults as before, node testing randomly encounters faults as *only the nodes* are visited.

Random Node Testing

Using the directed graph based on the McCabe metric and a different random distribution of faults than is used in the other tests, random node testing encounters a different set of faults, compared with node testing. A different random distribution of faults is used because otherwise the same result would be achieved as in node testing.

FIGURE 8.2   Planting Faults in Directed Graph

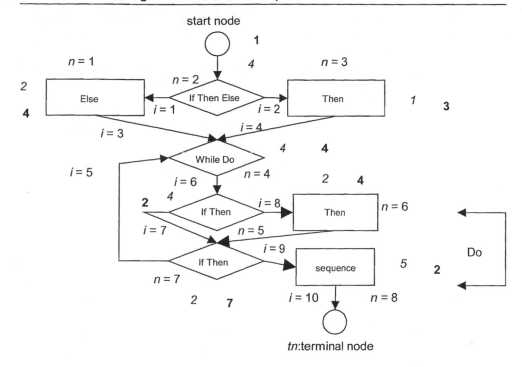

n : node identification

n_n = number of nodes = 8

n_e = number of edges = 10

i: edge identification

M_c = McCabe Complexity Metric = $(n_e - n_n) + 1 = (10 - 8) + 1 = 3$
= Number of Independent Paths

Bold = Number of Faults planted for path testing (24 faults total).

Italics = Number of Faults planted for random node testing (27 faults total).

Bold = minimum reliability path: 5 --> 6 --> 7 --> 8, reliability = .7292

Black-Box Testing

After the four types of white-box tests have been conducted, perform the following steps:

- Conduct black-box testing: Force function execution and observe resulting fault encounters and removals [MYE79].
- Conduct white-box testing: Observe response of program to path and node testing [HOW87].
- Make reliability predictions, using Schneidewind Single Parameter Model (SSPM) [SCH06], with randomly generated fault data. Faults are generated randomly so that there will be no bias in the fault distribution. Therefore the fault distribution is not intended to be representative of a particular environment. Rather, it is designed to be generic.
- Predict number of remaining faults and reliability with SSPM and compare with the empirical test values.
- Compare reliability predictions with results of black-box and white-box testing.

Test Assumptions

Recognize that the following assumptions impose limitations on the integrated testing and reliability approach. However, all models are abstractions of reality. Therefore the assumptions do not significantly detract from addressing the practical questions that follow.

When faults are discovered and removed, no new faults are introduced. This assumption overstates the reliability resulting from the various testing methods, but this effect will be experienced by all the testing methods.

Probability of traversing a node is independent of probability of traversing other nodes. This is the case in the directed graph that is used in the example program. It would not be the case in all programs.

No faults are removed until a given test is complete. Therefore, since path testing visits some of the same nodes on different tests, the expected number of faults encountered can exceed the actual number of faults.

Practical Questions

The following questions are important in evaluating the efficiency of test methods and their integration with reliability:

1. Does an independent path testing strategy lead to higher efficiency and reliability than path and random path testing?
2. Does a nodes testing strategy lead to higher reliability and efficiency than random node testing?
3. Does the McCabe Complexity Metric [MCC76] assist in organizing software tests?
4. Which of the testing strategies yields the highest reliability prior to or after fault removal?
5. Do reliability metrics, using SSPM, produce more accurate reliability assessments than node and random node testing?
6. Which testing method, white box or black box, provides more efficient testing and higher reliability?

Integrated Testing and Reliability Model

The following equations are used to implement the testing strategies and reliability predictions:

Fault Discovery Evaluation

Expected number of faults at node n:

$$E(n) = p(n)f(n), \tag{8.1}$$

where $p(n)$ is determined by the branch probabilities in Figure 8.1 and $f(n)$ is determined by randomly generating number of faults at each node.

The probability of traversing path j is given by equation (8.2):

$$p(j) = \prod_{n=1}^{n_{nj}} p(n) \tag{8.2}$$

Then, using equations (8.1) and (8.2) produces equation (8.3) for the expected number of faults *encountered* on path j:

$$E(j) = \left(\sum_{n=1}^{n_{nj}} p(n)f(n) \right) p(j) \qquad (8.3)$$

Furthermore, summing equation (8.3) over the number of paths in a program yields the expected number of faults in a program, *based on path testing,* in equation (8.4):

$$E_p = \sum_{j=1}^{n_j} E(j) \qquad (8.4)$$

Reliability Evaluation

Based on equation (8.1), the empirical reliability at node n prior to fault removal is shown in equation (8.5):

$$R_n = 1 - \frac{p(n)f(n)}{\displaystyle\sum_{n=1}^{n_n} p(n)f(n)} \qquad (8.5)$$

Now, the empirical unreliability at node n, based on equation (8.5), is given by equation (8.6):

$$U_n = 1 - R_n \qquad (8.6)$$

Then, using equations (8.5) and (8.6) the unreliability on path j prior to fault removal is given by equation (8.7):

$$U(j) = \sum_{n=1}^{n_n} [p(j)][U_n] = \sum_{n=1}^{n_n} [p(j)] \left[\frac{p(n)f(n)}{\displaystyle\sum_{n=1}^{n_n} p(n)f(n)} \right] \qquad (8.7)$$

Then, based on equation (8.6) the reliability of path j prior to fault removal is given by equation (8.8):

$$R(j) = 1 - U(j) \qquad (8.8)$$

Finally, the reliability of the program R_p is limited by the minimum of the path reliabilities computed in equation (8.8). Thus equation (8.9) is produced:

$$R_p = \min R(j) \qquad (8.9)$$

Continuing the analysis, find the empirical number of remaining faults at node n, prior to fault removal, according to equation (8.10):

$$r_e(n) = n_f - \sum_{n=1}^{n_n} p(n)f(n) \qquad (8.10)$$

Constructing the Directed Graphs of Example Programs

To obtain an operational profile of how program space was used, Horgan and colleagues [WON97] identified the possible functions of their program and generated a graph capturing the connectivity of these functions. Each node in the graph represented a function. Two nodes, A and B, were connected if control could flow from function A to function B. There was a unique start and end node representing functions at which execution began and terminated, respectively. A path through the graph from the start node to the end node represents one possible program execution. In 1976, Thomas McCabe proposed a complexity metric based on the idea of the directed graph as a representation of the complexity of a program. The directed graph can be based on functions, as in the case of Horgan's approach, or program statements that are used in this chapter. McCabe proposed that his metric be a basis for developing a testing strategy [MCC76]. The McCabe Complexity metric is used as the basis of constructing the example directed graph that is used to illustrate the integration of testing and reliability [FEN97]. There are various definitions of this metric. The one that is used is given in equation (8.11) [FEN97]:

$$M_c = (n_e - n_n) + 1 \tag{8.11}$$

And $n_n = -M_c + (n_e + 1)$ for $n_n < n_e$ and $n_n > -M_c + (n_e + 1)$, where n_n—number of nodes—represents program statements (e.g., If Then Else) and conditions (e.g., Then, Else); and n_e—number of edges—represents program control flow transition, as depicted in Figure 8.1.

This definition is convenient to use for the testing strategy because it corresponds to the number of independent paths and number of independent circuits ("window panes") in a directed graph. See Figures 8.1 and 8.2. "Strategy" means that paths are emphasized in the test plan.

The approach is used of specifying M_c and n_e and computing n_e from equation (8.11). Then knowing the number edges and nodes in a directed graph, for a given complexity, the information is in hand to represent a program. In the case of the While Do construct, only count one iteration in computing M_c.

The directed graph of the program shown in Figure 8.1 is based on a C++ program that was written for a software reliability model [SCH97]. The program has 420 C++ statements. The program computes cumulative number of failures, actual reliability, predicted reliability, rate of change of predicted reliability, mean number of failures, fault correction rate, mean fault correction rate, fault correction delay, prediction errors, and maximum likelihood parameter estimation. The directed graph represents the decision logic of the model.

Test Strategy Evaluation

As pointed out by Voas and McGraw, some people erroneously think that testing involves only software. In fact, according to them, testing also involves specifications [VOA98]. These results in Figure 8.1 support their view; in fact, the While Do loop in Figure 8.1 represents the condition for being able to make reliability predictions if the specified boundary condition on the equations is satisfied in the C++ program. Therefore, in all of the following testing strategies that are implemented in the example program, it is implicit that testing encompasses both specifications and software.

In black-box testing, the tester is unconcerned with the internals of the program being tested. The tester is interested in how the program behaves according to its specifications. Test data are derived from its specifications [HOW87]. In contrast, in white-box testing the tester is interested in how the program will behave according to its internal logic. Test data are derived based on the internal workings of the program [HOW87]. Some authors propose that black- and white-box testing be integrated in order to improve test efficiency and reduce test cost [BEY01].

In white-box testing, based on the test data, a program can be forced to follow certain paths. Research indicates that applying one or more white-box testing methods in conjunction with functional testing can increase program reliability when the following two-step procedure is used:

1. Evaluate the adequacy of test data constructed using functional testing.

2. Enhance these test data to satisfy one or more criteria provided by white-box testing methods [HOR92].

The approach is to adapt #2 to generate test data to satisfy path coverage criteria to find additional faults.

In black-box testing the program is forced to execute constructs (e.g., While Do) that are associated with the functional specifications. For example, continue to compute functions while there are input data. In white-box testing, test nodes and paths that are associated with the detailed logic and functions of the program. For example, a path would involve computing the error in predicting reliability metrics.

Related to black-box testing is the concept of the operational profile wherein the functions of the program, the occurrence rates of the functions, and the occurrence probabilities are listed [MUS04]. For a program, the functions in the operational profile are the program constructs (e.g., If Then Else), as shown in Figure 8.1. In the example program, occurrence rates of all constructs are 100%. Thus, rather than use occurrence rates, the importance of the constructs is more relevant (e.g., While Do more important than If Then).

In their study [CHE96] regarding system functionality, Chen and Yu began with the assumption that coding errors tend to be regional. Analysis of the results of the testing of the 53 system tasks within the six functional categories supported this assumption. The data indicate that tasks and categories that were executed frequently had more field deficiencies. These tasks and categories were more complex, containing a broader range of functions made possible through additional lines of code. Due to this complexity, these areas were more susceptible to errors.

These results suggest that there should be a focus in the testing effort on complex, high-payoff areas of a program like the While Do construct and associated constructs (see Figure 8.2), where there is a concentration of faults. These constructs experience high probabilities of path execution (i.e., "execution quantities").

According to AT&T [AT&T], the earlier a problem is discovered, the easier and less expensive it is to fix, making software development more cost-effective. AT&T uses a "break it early" strategy. The use of independent path testing attempts to implement this approach because it is comparatively easy and quick to expose the faults to these tests, with the expectation of revealing a large number of faults early in the testing process.

As stated by [MOG03], one of the principles of testing is the following: Define test completion criteria. The test effort has specific, quantifiable goals. Testing is completed only when the goals have been reached (e.g., testing is complete when the tests that address 100 percent functional coverage of the system have all executed successfully). While this is a noble goal, and is achieved in the small program, it infeasible to achieve 100 percent coverage in a large program with multiple iterations. Such an approach would be unwise due to the high cost of achieving fault removal at the margin.

Another principle stated in [MOG03] is to verify test coverage: Track the amount of functional coverage achieved by the successful execution of each test. Implement this principle as part of the black-box testing approach, where the discovery and removal of faults is executed as each construct is tracked (e.g., If Then Else) (see Table 8.2, page 205).

Test Effectiveness

One metric of test effectiveness is the ratio of number of paths traversed to the total number of paths in the program [SCH]. This is a good beginning, but it is only one characteristic of an effective metric. In addition, it is important to consider the presence of faults on the paths. This is the approach described below.

In order to evaluate the effectiveness of testing strategies, compute the fault coverage by two means: path coverage and edge coverage. Recall that the number of faults encountered during path testing can exceed the actual number of faults. Therefore, path testing must take this factor into account. Path testing efficiency is implemented by using equation (8.12), which imposes the constraint that the sum of faults found on paths must not exceed the number of faults in the program.

$$e(j) = \left(\sum_{j=1}^{n_j} E(j) \right) / n_f = \left(\sum_{j=1}^{n_j} \sum_{n=1}^{n_{nj}} p(n) f(n) p(j) \right) / n_f$$

$$\text{for } \left(\sum_{j=1}^{n_j} E(j) \right) \leq n_f \tag{8.12}$$

As long as the constraint is satisfied, path testing is efficient because no more testing is done than necessary to find all of the faults. However, for $\left(\sum_{j=1}^{n_j} E(j) \right) > n_f$, path testing is inefficient because more testing is done than is necessary to find all of the faults.

For independent path testing, use equation (8.12) just for the independent paths and compare the result with that obtained using all paths.

Another metric of efficiency is $\left(\sum_{j=1}^{n_j} E(j) \right)$, compared with n_f. This metric is computed using only independent paths. Then the computations are compared to see which testing method produces the greater fault coverage in relation to the number of faults in the program.

The final metric of testing efficiency is node testing efficiency, given in equation (8.13):

$$e(n) = \sum_{n=1}^{n_n} p(n) f(n) / n_f \tag{8.13}$$

An important point about test strategy evaluation is the effects on testing efficiency of the order of path testing because the number of faults encountered could vary with sequence. Take the approach in Figures 8.1 and 8.2 that path sequence is top down, testing the constructs like If Then Else in order.

Results of Test Strategies Evaluation

First, note that these are limited experiments in terms of the number of examples it is feasible to use. Therefore, there is no claim that these results can be extrapolated to the universe of the integration of testing with reliability strategies. However, it is suggested that researchers and practitioners can use these *methods* as a template for this type of research. In addition, the directed graph in the program example is small. However, this is not a limitation of the approach because large programs are modular (or should be). Thus a large program can be represented by a set of directed graphs for modules and the methods could be applied to each one.

Table 8.1 shows the results from developing the path and node connection matrix corresponding to the directed graph in Figure 8.1, which shows the independent circuits and

TABLE 8.1   Path and Node Connection Matrix

Path Number j	Nodes n								
	1	2	3	4	5	6	7	8	t_n
1	*1*	*0*	*0*	*1*	*1*	*1*	*1*	*1*	*1*
2	1	0	0	1	1	0	1	1	1
3	*1*	*1*	*0*	*1*	*1*	*1*	*1*	*1*	*1*
4	*1*	*1*	*0*	*1*	*1*	*0*	*1*	*1*	*1*
5	0	0	1	1	1	1	1	1	1
6	0	0	1	1	1	0	1	1	1
7	0	0	0	1	0	1	1	1	1
8	0	0	0	1	1	0	0	1	1
9	0	0	0	0	1	1	1	1	1
10	0	0	0	0	1	0	1	1	1
11	0	0	0	0	0	1	1	1	1
12	0	0	0	0	0	0	1	1	1

lists the paths: independent and non-independent. In this table a "1" indicates connectivity and a "0" indicates no connectivity. "Path number" identifies paths that are used in the plots on the following pages. A path is defined as the sequence of nodes that are connected as indicated by a "1" in the table. This table allows us to identify the independent paths that provide a key feature of the white-box testing strategy. These paths are italicized in Table 8.1: paths 1, 3, and 4. The definition of an independent path is that it cannot be formed by a combination of other paths in the directed graph [MCC76].

Figure 8.2 shows how faults are randomly seeded in the nodes of the directed graph in order to evaluate the various tests. This figure also shows the minimum reliability path

FIGURE 8.3   Path Testing Efficiency $e(j)$ vs. Test Number j

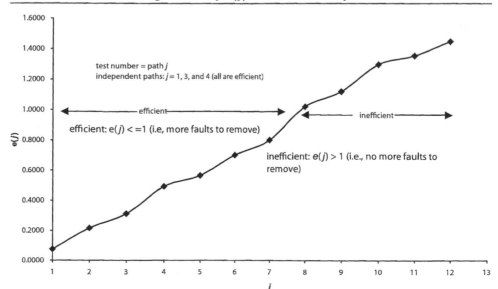

that is the reliability of the program because the reliability of the program can be no greater than the reliability of the weakest path. The minimum reliability path is also noted in the white-box testing of Figure 8.7 on page 202, where $R(j) = .7292$.

Noting that in Figure 8.3 paths are equivalent to number of tests, this figure indicates that path testing is efficient only for the first seven paths; after that there is more testing than necessary to achieve efficiency because tests $1, \ldots, 7$ have removed all the faults. All independent paths are efficient based on the fact that these paths were identified in Table 8.1. However, Figure 8.4 tells another story: Here the expected number of faults that is found in both path and independent path testing is compared with the number of actual faults. While independent path testing is efficient, it accounts for only 35.42% of the faults in the program. This result dramatically shows that it is unwise to rely on independent path testing alone to achieve high reliability.

In Figure 8.5, recognizing that number of nodes is equivalent to number of tests, it is seen that, with node testing, the tests do not cover all the faults in the program (i.e., efficiency = .7917). Of the three testing strategies, path testing provides the best coverage. It finds all of the faults but at the highest cost. The best method depends on the application, with path testing advisable for mission critical applications, and independent path and node testing appropriate for commercial applications because of their lower cost.

Dynamic Testing Analysis

Up to this point, the testing strategies have been static. That is, path testing, independent path testing, and node testing have been conducted, considering the number of tests, but without considering test time. Of course, time does not stand still in testing. With each node and edge traversal, there is an elapsed time. Now bring time into the analysis so that a software reliability model can be used to predict the reliability of the program in the example directed graph.

FIGURE 8.4   Expected Number of Cumulative Faults Encountered (and removed) sum $E(j)$ vs. Test Number j

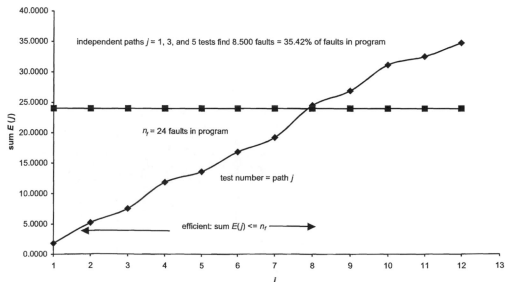

**FIGURE 8.5   Node Testing Cumulative Expected Number of Faults Found
sum [$p(n) * f(n)$] vs. Number of nodes n**

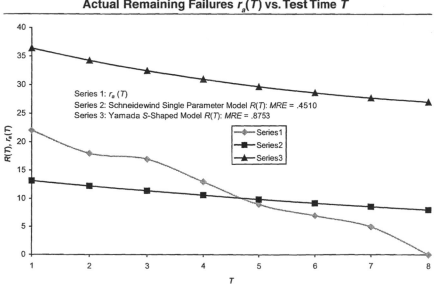

There are a number of predictions of reliability that can be made to answer the question "when to stop testing?" Among these are *remaining failures* and *reliability* [HOR92], which are predicted below using the Schneidewind Single Parameter Model SSPM [SCH06]. In order to consider more than one model for the analysis, remaining failures were predicted using the Yamada S-Shaped model [XIE91] and its mean relative prediction error was compared with SSPM. The result was that SSPM has lower error MRE = .4510 versus MRE = .8753 for Yamada, as shown in Figure 8.6, which compares actual remaining failures with the predicted values for SSPM and Yamada.

**FIGURE 8.6   Predicted Remaining Failures to Occur at Test Time T and
Actual Remaining Failures $r_a(T)$ vs. Test Time T**

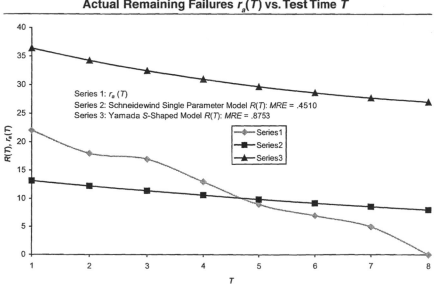

FIGURE 8.7   White-Box Testing: Reliability Obtained Prior to Fault Removal by Path Testing $R(j)$, Node Testing R_n, and Random Node Testing r_n vs. Test Number (j, n)

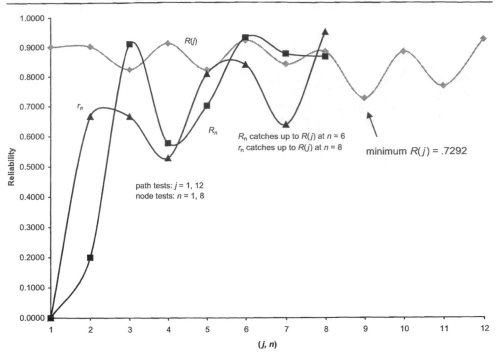

In addition, the mean number of failures in the test intervals was predicted for both models and their MREs were compared. For SSPM the value was .3865 and for Yamada, .4572. Thus, because of better prediction accuracy, SSPM predictions are compared with the results obtained with node and random node testing.

The first step in applying SSPM is to estimate the single parameter β from the randomly generated faults present at the directed graph nodes. (Parameter β is defined as the rate of change of failure rate and t is program test time.) Then faults are randomly seeded in the directed graph using the Excel random number generator.

Now, in preparing to develop the equation for predicting remaining failures, the cumulative number of failures predicted to occur at test interval T, is computed as follows [SCH06]:

$$F(T) = \int_0^T e^{-\beta t}\,dt = (1/\beta)\left[1 - e^{-\beta T}\right] \tag{8.14}$$

Then, using equation (8.14) the number of remaining failures is developed:

It can be seen that as $T \rightarrow \infty$ in equation (8.14) $F(T)$ becomes $(1/\beta)$ the total failures over the life of the software. Then subtracting $(1/\beta)[1 - e^{-\beta T}]$, the cumulative failures at time interval T, from $(1/\beta)$, the remaining failures are produced in equation (8.15):

$$R(T) = (1/\beta)e^{-\beta T} \tag{8.15}$$

Next compute the mean relative errors (MRE) [FEN97] for $R(T)$ and the remaining faults produced by node and random node testing. The error statistics are computed by comparing the remaining fault metrics with the remaining faults *after fault removal*. The results are shown in Figure 8.8, where random node testing yields the minimum MRE. One conclusion to be drawn from *this example* is that testing produced more accurate reliability assessments than reliability prediction.

Next, based on the assumption of fault occurrence being governed by a Non-Homogeneous Poisson Process (i.e., the mean m_t is *not* constant) in SSPM [SCH06], the reliability prediction is shown in equation (8.16):

$$R(t) = 1 - \sum_{t=1}^{n} \frac{m_t^{x_t} e^{-m_t}}{x_t!} \qquad (8.16)$$

where m_t is the predicted mean number of failures in interval t and x_t is number of failures in interval t.

In addition, the empirical number of failures in interval t is needed so that $R(t)$ and node and random node reliability assessments can be compared with the actual values given by equation (8.17).

$$ER(t) = 1 - \left(\frac{x_t}{\sum_{t}^{n} x_t} \right) \qquad (8.17)$$

Since reliability predictions are being compared, using SSPM, with node testing reliability assessments, it of interest whether specific or random test samples produce more accurate reliability assessments. According to one author [CHE96], random sampling may be used to reduce the test suite, but it leads to a reduction in fault-detection capability. This may be true in some programs, but, as Figure 8.8 shows, random node testing had the least error for remaining failures assessment.

FIGURE 8.8   Remaining Failures vs. Time Interval *t*

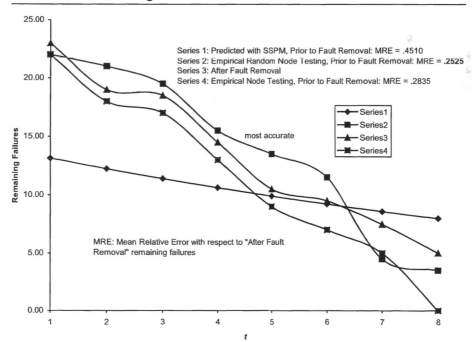

Black-Box Testing Analysis

For the purpose of the testing model, consider black-box testing to be composed of successive tests, each one exercising a program construct, encountering faults in the construct, and removing them. Thus formulate the reliability based on test k of construct c, as follows:

$$R(c,k) = \frac{\sum_k n(c,k)}{n_f} \tag{8.18}$$

where $n(c, k)$ is the number of faults removed on test k and n_f is the number of faults in the program in equation (8.17). Thus, fault removals are accumulated with each test, until as many faults as possible have been removed. The number of faults removed is limited by the number of faults associated with the constructs in the program.

In addition to reliability, the efficiency of black-box testing is evaluated in equation (8.19):

$$e(c,k) = \frac{\sum_k n(c,k)}{k} \tag{8.19}$$

The meaning of equation (8.19) is that $e(c, k)$ computes the cumulative faults removed divided by test number k, which is equal to the number of tests.

Answers to Practical Questions

1. Does an independent path testing strategy lead to higher efficiency and reliability than path and random path testing? Independent path testing alone will not uncover nearly the number of faults in a program. In the experiments, the results were even worse when paths were selected randomly because it is possible that random paths could be duplicated, rendering random path testing inefficient. This fact made it difficult to compare random testing efficiency with path testing because not every path was tested with random testing. Instead of comparing individual path efficiencies, the coefficients of variation for random path and path testing efficiency were computed to gain a sense of the variation in this metric. The values are 0.5544 and 0.5680 for random path and path testing, respectively. Thus, there is little to choose in terms of variability of efficiency.

Note that because *path testing* traverses all nodes and edges, theoretically path testing would yield a reliability of 1.0 *after fault removal;* this high reliability cannot be obtained with independent path and random path testing.

2. Does a nodes testing strategy lead to higher reliability and efficiency than random node testing? As Figure 8.9 shows, nodes testing provides higher prediction accuracy.
3. Does the McCabe Complexity Metric [MCC76] assist in organizing software tests? Yes, even though, as has been shown, independent path testing is lacking in complete fault coverage. Nevertheless, the metric is useful in identifying major components of a program to test.
4. Which testing strategy yields the highest reliability prior to fault removal? This question is addressed in Figure 8.7, which shows the superiority of white-box testing: path testing in early tests, with node testing and random node testing catching up in later tests. Thus, overall, path testing is superior. This is to be expected because path testing exercises both nodes and edges.

FIGURE 8.9   Reliability vs. Time Interval *t*

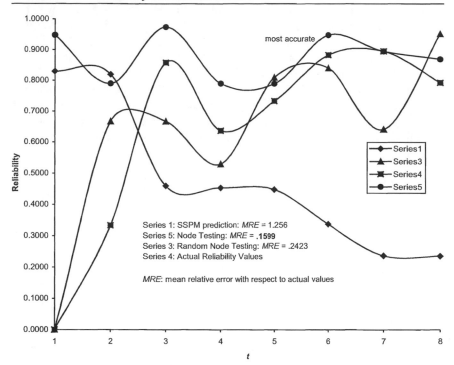

5. Do reliability metrics, using SSPM, produce more accurate reliability assessments than node and random node testing? The answer for remaining failure predictions is "no," as Figure 8.8 demonstrates. The answer for reliability predictions is also "no," as shown in Figure 8.9, where node testing produces minimum error. These results reinforce the idea that testing can produce reliability assessment accuracy that a reliability model may not be able to achieve.

TABLE 8.2   Black-Box Testing Strategy

Test Number k	Construct c	Cumulative Faults Removed $\sum\limits_{k} n(c,k)$	Testing Efficiency $e(c, k)$	Reliability $R(c, k)$
1	If Then Else	4	4.0	.1667
2	While Do	8	4.0	.3333
3	First If Then	12	4.0	.5000
4	Second If Then	14	3.5	.5833

Testing Efficiency: $e(c,k) = \dfrac{\sum\limits_{k} n(c,k)}{k}$

Reliability: $R(c,k) = \dfrac{\sum\limits_{k} n(c,k)}{n_f}$, n_f = number of faults = 24

6. Which testing method, white box or black box, provides more efficient testing and higher reliability? This question is addressed in Table 8.2, which shows the results of the black-box testing strategy. See Figure 8.2 to understand the fault removal process by noting how many faults are planted at each construct. Because black-box (equation (8.19)) and white-box testing (equation (8.13)) efficiency are computed differently, it is necessary to compare them on the basis of cumulative faults removed, as a function of test number. When black box in Table 8.2 is compared with path testing (i.e., white-box testing) in Figure 8.4, it is seen that for the same number of tests, black box is superior (removes more faults). The reason is that this particular type of black-box testing exercises complete program constructs, finding and removing a large number of faults during each test.

Now, comparing the black-box testing of Table 8.2 with the white-box testing of Figure 8.7, it is seen that white box yields the higher reliability. This is to be expected because white-box testing provides more detailed coverage of a program's faults.

Reliability Models that Combine Fault Correction with Testing

Thus far there has been the assumption that faults encountered in traversing a directed graph representation of a program have been removed (i.e., corrected). In reality, this may not be the case unless fault correction is explicitly considered. There are several software reliability models that include fault correction in addition to reliability prediction. These models are advantageous because the results of tests, based on fault correction, are used in reliability prediction to improve the accuracy of prediction. One such model [SCH04, SCH03] is used to make predictions based on fault correction. It would not make sense to compare test efficiency of the fault correction model with, for example, the path testing model because, as explained, the former includes fault correction but the latter does not. However, insight into the effectiveness of fault correction can be obtained by evaluating, for example, fault correction delay time over a series of test time intervals.

It was shown in [SCH04, SCH03], using Shuttle flight software failure data, that the cumulative number of faults corrected by test time T, $C(T)$, is related to the cumulative number of failures $F(T)$ detected by time T. In addition, in the case of the Shuttle data, the number of faults is equal to the number of failures. This is assumed to be the case in the hypothetical fault data of Figure 8.2 that is used in the predictions that follow. $C(T)$ and $F(T)$ are related by the delay time dT—the time between fault detection and completion of fault correction. Recalling that for SSPM, $F(T)$ is given in equation (8.20), then $C(T)$ can be written in equation (8.21):

$$F(T) = (1/\beta)[1 - e^{-\beta(T)}], \tag{8.20}$$

where $(1/\beta)$ is the total number of failures predicted over the life of the software.

$$C(T) = (1/\beta)[1 - e^{-\beta(T-dT)}] \tag{8.21}$$

A reasonable assumption is that dT is proportional to $[F(T)/(1/\beta)]$ (i.e., the larger number of failures detected, relative to the total, the longer the correction delay). Thus dT becomes:

$$dT = T * [F(T)/(1/\beta)] \tag{8.22}$$

Then the fault correction rate $CR(T)$ can be computed as:

$$CR(T) = C(T)/(1/\beta) \tag{8.23}$$

Also, the remaining faults resulting from fault correction is computed in equation (8.24):

$$R(T) = (1/\beta) - C(T) \tag{8.24}$$

The equations are implemented in Figure 8.10 using the fault data of Figure 8.2. The utility of these plots is that a software developer—usually having little information about its fault correction process—could at least obtain a rough idea of the likely outcome of tests by making the predictions shown in Figure 8.10. For example, the fact that correction delay is increasing could be a concern.

Another concern is the high number of remaining faults because in quality assurance programs, the number of faults that are found $F(T)$ during testing is often the basis for indicating software correctness. However, there is a paradox in this approach, since the remaining faults $R(T)$ is what impacts negatively on software correctness, not the faults that are found [ZAG03]. On the other hand, a beneficial trend is the increasing correction rate.

Empirical Approaches to Testing

Important aspects of fault correction and testing that are not covered by models, such as the preceding, are the fault correction efficiency in the various phases of software development that must be provided by empirical evidence. In a Hewlett-Packard division application, 31% of the requirements faults were eliminated in the requirements phase, 30% of requirements faults were eliminated in preliminary design, 15% during detailed design, and 24% removed during testing. Additionally, 51% of the detailed design faults slipped into the testing phase. The other important aspect of efficiency is the effort required to remove the faults. This investigation confirms that it is costly to wait. The total effort expended to remove 236 intra-phase faults was 250.5 hours while it took 1964.8 hours to remove the 248 faults that were corrected in later phases. Faults undetected within the originating phase took approximately eight times more effort to correct. In fact, the problem does not get better as time passes. Faults found in the field are at least an order of magnitude more

FIGURE 8.10   SSPM Predicted Cumulative Failures F(T), Correction Delay dT, Cumulative Faults Corrected C(T), and Remaining Faults R(T) vs. Test Time Interval t

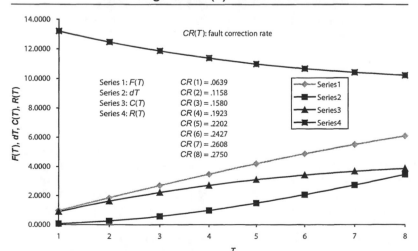

expensive to fix than those found while testing. Faults that propagate to later phases of development produce a nearly exponential increase in the effort, and thus in the cost, of fixing those faults [RUN04].

A confirming example is provided by Praxis Critical Systems development of the Certification Authority for the Multos smart card scheme on behalf of Mondex International. The authors claim that correctness by construction is possible and practical. It demands a development process that builds correctness into every step. It demands rigorous requirements definition, precise system-behavior specification, solid and verifiable design, and code whose behavior is precisely understood. It demands defect removal and prevention at every step. The number of system faults is low compared with systems developed using less formal approaches. The distribution of effort shows clearly that fault fixing constituted a relatively small part of the effort (6%) [HAL02]; this contrasts with many critical projects where fixing of late-discovered faults takes a large proportion of project resources, as in the Hewlett-Packard example.

Experiences like these should lead the software engineering community to adopt: 1) phase-dependent predictions in reliability and testing models and 2) defect removal and fault correction in all phases of the development process.

Conclusions

For white-box testing, path testing was the most efficient overall. This is not surprising because path testing exercises all components of a program—statements and transitions among statements. While not surprising, it was comforting to find that the law of diminishing returns has not been overturned by the black-box testing result in Table 8.2, where both testing efficiency and reliability increase at a decreasing rate. Results such as these can be used as a stopping rule to prevent an organization's testing budget from being exceeded.

An interesting result, based on Table 8.2 and Figure 8.3, is the superiority of black-box testing over white-box testing in finding and removing faults, due to its coverage of complete program constructs. On the other hand, the application of white-box testing yields higher reliability than black-box testing because the former, using path testing, for example, mirrors a program's state transitions that are related to complexity, and complexity is highly related to reliability [KHO90].

Because it is clear that models are insufficient for capturing pertinent details of the reliability and testing process, it is important to include empirical evidence in evaluating testing strategies. Therefore, a promising area for further analysis would be to incorporate empirical data, such as the data in the previous section, in integrated and reliability models to see whether testing efficiency is improved.

References

[AT&T] General Accounting Office, "Best Practices: A More Constructive Test Approach Is Key to Better Weapon System Outcomes." Washington: GAO, July 2000.

[BEI90] Boris Beizer, *Software Testing Techniques,* second edition. Van Nostrand Reinhold, 1990.

[BEY01] Sami Beydeda, Volker Gruhn, and Michael Stachorski, "A Graphical Class Representation for Integrated Black- and White-Box Testing." 17th IEEE International Conference on Software Maintenance (ICSM '01), 2001, p. 706.

[CHE96] T.Y Chen and Y.T. Yu, "On the Expected Number of Failures Detected by Subdomain Testing and Random Testing." *IEEE Transactions on Software Eng.*, Vol. 22, No. 2, February 1996, pp. 109–119.

[FEN97] Norman F. Fenton and Shari Lawrence Pfleeger, *Software Metrics: A Rigorous & Practical Approach,* second edition. PWS Publishing Company, Boston, 1997.

[HAI02] B. Hailpern and P. Santhanam, "Software Debugging, Testing, and Verification." *IBM Systems Journal,* Vol. 41, No. 1, 2002.

[HAL02] Anthony Hall and Roderick Chapman, "Correctness by Construction: Developing a Commercial Secure System." *IEEE Software,* Vol. 19, No. 1, Jan/Feb, 2002, pp. 18–25.

[HAM94] D. Hamlet, "Foundations of Software Testing: Dependability Theory." Proceedings, Second ACM SIGSOFT Symposium. Foundations of Software Engineering, 1994, pp. 128–139.

[HOR92] J.R. Horgan, and A.P. Mathur, "Assessing Testing Tools in Research and Education." *IEEE Software,* Volume 9, Issue 3, May 1992, pp. 61–69.

[HOW87] William E. Howden, *Functional Program Testing and Analysis.* McGraw-Hill, 1987.

[IEE08] IEEE/AIAA P1633™, *Recommended Practice on Software Reliability,* June 2008.

[KHO90] T. M. Khoshgoftaar and J.C. Munson, "Predicting Software Development Errors Using Software Complexity Metrics." *IEEE Journal on Selected Areas in Communications,* Vol. 8, No. 2, February 1990, pp. 253–261.

[MCC] http://www.mccabe.com/

[MCC76] Thomas J. McCabe, *IEEE Transactions on Software Engineering,* Vol. Se-2, No.4, December 1976, pp. 308–320.

[MOG03] Gary E. Mogyorodi, Bloodworth Integrated Technology, Inc., "What Is Requirements-Based Testing?" *Cross Talk,* March 2003.

[MYE79] Glenford Myers, *The Art of Software Testing.* John Wiley & Sons, 1979.

[MUS04] John D. Musa, *Software Reliability Engineering: More Reliable Software, Faster and Cheaper,* 2nd edition. Authorhouse, 2004.

[PRO04] S. J. Prowell, "A Cost-Benefit Stopping Criterion for Statistical Testing." Proceedings of the 37th Annual Hawaii International Conference on System Sciences (HICSS'04)—Track 9, 2004, p. 90304b.

[REL] Reliable Software Technologies Corporation, http://www.cigital.com/.

[RUN04] Per Runeson, Måns Holmstedt Jönsson, and Fredrik Scheja, "Are Found Defects an Indicator of Software Correctness? An Investigation in a Controlled Case Study." 15th International Symposium on Software Reliability Engineering (ISSRE '04), 2004, pp. 91–100.

[SCH] G. J. Schick and R. W. Wolverton, *A History of Software Reliability Modeling.* University of Southern California and Thompson Ramo Woodridge Corporation, undated.

[SCH03] Norman F. Schneidewind, "Modeling the Fault Correction Processes." *The R & M Engineering Journal,* American Society for Quality, December 2003, Vol. 23, No. 4, Part 1, pp. 6–15.

[SCH04] Norman F. Schneidewind, "Modeling the Fault Correction Processes." *The R & M Engineering Journal,* American Society for Quality, March 2004, Vol. 24, No. 1, Part 2, pp. 6–14.

[SCH06] Norman F. Schneidewind, "A New Software Reliability Model." *The R & M Engineering Journal,* American Society for Quality, September 2006, Vol. 26, Number 3, pp. 6–22.

[SCH97] Norman F. Schneidewind, "Reliability Modeling for Safety Critical Software." *IEEE Transactions on Reliability,* Vol. 46, No.1, March 1997, pp. 88–98.

[TON04] Paolo Tonella, Filippo Ricca, "A 2-Layer Model for the White-Box Testing of Web Applications," and Sixth IEEE International Workshop on Web Site Evolution (WSE'04), 2004, pp. 11–19.

[VOA98] Jeffrey M. Voas and Gary McGraw, *Software Fault Injection: Inoculating Programs Against Errors.* John Wiley & Sons, Inc., 1998.

[WON97] W. Eric Wong, Joseph R. Horgan, Aditya P. Mathur, and Alberto Pasquini, "Test Set Size Minimization and Fault Detection Effectiveness: A Case Study in a Space Application." COMPSAC '97 - 21st International Computer Software and Applications Conference, 1997, p. 522.

[XIE91] Min Xie, *Software Reliability Modeling,* World Scientific, 1991.

[XIE05] T. Xie and D. Notkin, "Checking Inside the Black Box: Regression Testing by Comparing Value Spectra." *IEEE Transactions on Software Engineering,* Volume 31, Issue 10, Oct. 2005, pp. 869–883.

[ZAG03] Dolores Zage and Wayne Zage, "An Analysis of the Fault Correction Process in a Large-Scale SDL Production Model," 25th International Conference on Software Engineering (ICSE '03), 2003, p. 570.

9

Architecture, Performance, Reliability, and Availability

Objectives

The objectives of this chapter are to: 1) evaluate the effects of configuration complexity, reliability, and availability on architecture performance, using real-world architectures as examples and 2) compare the architectures using evaluation criteria in 1). The reason for this chapter is provided by [GOK06]: Increasing reliance on the services provided by Web servers mandates that these services be offered with superior performance and reliability. The architecture of a Web server has a profound impact on its performance and reliability. The same statement could be made about any application.

What You Will Learn From This Chapter

Recall that in Chapter 1, some of the subjects covered were probability distributions—for example, the binomial, hardware reliability and failure analysis, and computer system availability. This chapter builds on those subjects to show how architecture influences computer performance, reliability, and availability. Also, recall the application of complexity metrics in Chapter 7 to analyze the complexity of a computer program. Now, in this chapter, you will see how these concepts are used to assess the complexity of computer architecture configurations.

Subjects

Non-Parallel Computer Availability Model
Parallel Computer Architectural Model
Architectural Characteristics
Integrating Reliability, Availability, and Performance
Processor Performance Specifications and Architectural Data Values
Comparing Computer Architectures
Comparing Hardware and Software Reliability and Analyzing Incremental Performance

Introduction

Architecture is the configuration of components in a system and their relationships and interactions [SAG00]. Software architecture reliability evaluation is a low-cost and high-profit method that can reduce the probability of disastrous system failures [YAC02]. You will see how performance, reliability, and availability are related to architecture. The theoretical performance of an architecture is reduced by: 1) the complexity of its configuration (i.e., the placement and interconnection of its parts), 2) its hardware and software reliability (i.e., the probabilities that the hardware and software will survive for a specified operating time), and 3) its availability (i.e., the probability that the system will be ready when needed).

Background

Several examples of research in architectural modeling from the literature that are related to this chapter are briefly described with comments about their relevance.

One of the early architectural models that included reliability is reported in [WAN99]. While making a significant advance, the model did not consider the reliability of component interconnections. A later model reported in [WAN07] improved the earlier model by including inter-component reliability. The approach of this chapter includes the complexity of architectural configurations, as it affects reliability. This complexity is based, in part, on the complexity of interconnection of components (e.g., the interconnections linking the Execution Core and Instruction Branch Target Cache in Figure 9.1 on page 215). The complexity of an architecture is also a function of algorithmic complexity, which in turn is a function of time and space complexity. If a computer architecture requires an excessive time to make a computation or requires an excessive amount of space to store programs and data, due to inefficient utilization of storage, the architecture is said to be complex [SHO83].

Semiconductor transient faults have become an increasingly important threat to microprocessor reliability. These faults occur in Simultaneous Multi Threaded (SMT) architectures that exploit thread-level parallelism to improve overall processor throughput. By considering *both performance and reliability,* SMT outperforms other architectures. The SMT reliability and its tradeoff with performance vary with the degree of parallelism [ZHA07]. While this chapter does not consider multithreading, it is interesting that the authors found that architecture influences reliability, as will be demonstrated in later sections.

Performance and fault tolerance are two major issues that need to be addressed when designing highly available and reliable systems. The network topology and connectedness among the network nodes defines the system communication architecture and is an important design consideration for fault tolerant systems [SAH06]. Yes, fault tolerance is a consideration in evaluating architectures because it is directly related to the number of computers that operate in parallel (i.e., the greater the number of computers connected in parallel, the greater the fault tolerance).

The importance of mobile and electronic commerce results in much attention given to credit-control systems. There are high non-functional requirements for such systems (e.g., high availability and reliability). These requirements can be met by changing the architecture of the credit-control system. Quantifying availability, reliability, performance, and cost enables designers to make better tradeoff decisions. In a similar vein, it will be shown how architecture influences reliability and availability.

Non-Parallel Computer Availability Model

First, the model for evaluating how architecture influences availability, performance, and reliability when parallelism is *not* employed, is developed, starting by defining quantities used in the equations.

Definitions

t: scheduled operating time

$A_j(t)$:   availability of architecture j during time t

$UA_j(t)$: unavailability of architecture j during time t

$U_j(t)$:   uptime of architecture j during time t
$D_j(t)$:   downtime of architecture j during time t
$F_j(t)$:   failure rate of architecture j during time t
$TF_j(t)$:   time to failure of architecture j during time t
$r_j(t)$:   recovery rate from failures of architecture j during time t
$N_{Rj}(t)$:   number of recoveries from failure of architecture j during time t
$TR_j(t)$:   time to recover from failure of architecture j during time t
$P_j(t)$:   performance of architecture j during time t (e.g., clock rate)
$R_j(t)$:   hardware reliability of architecture j during time t
$EP_j(t)$:   expected performance of architecture j during time t

The uptime of architecture j during time t is computed in equation (9.1) [SAN63, TRI82].

$$U_j(t) = A_j(t) * t \qquad (9.1)$$

Then, unavailability is computed in equation (9.2).

$$UA_j(t) = 1 - A_j(t) \qquad (9.2)$$

Downtime is computed by subtracting uptime from operational time in equation (9.3).

$$D_j(t) = t - U_j(t) \qquad (9.3)$$

The number of recoveries from failure of architecture j during time t is estimated by the recovery rate (due to maintenance actions) that occurs during time t, in relation to the scheduled operational time t, as shown in equation (9.4).

$$N_{Rj}(t) = r_j(t) * t \qquad (9.4)$$

The time to failure of architecture j during time t is computed by the reciprocal of the failure rate in equation (9.5).

$$TF_j(t) = 1/F_j(t) \qquad (9.5)$$

The recovery rate of architecture j during time t is computed by the reciprocal of the recovery time in equation (9.6).

$$r_j(t) = 1/TR_j(t) \qquad (9.6)$$

Availability, $A_j(t)$, as defined in [SHO83], is expressed in equation (9.7).

$$A_j(t) = TF_j(t)/((TF_j(t) + TR_j(t)) \qquad (9.7)$$

Then using unavailability $U_j(t)$ from equation (9.2) and solving equation (9.7) for recovery time $TR_j(t)$, produces equation (9.8).

$$TR_j(t) = (TF_j(t) * UA_j(t))/A_j(t) \qquad (9.8)$$

Parallel Computer Architectural Model

Next, the model that includes computers operating in parallel is developed by first defining additional quantities related to parallelism.

Definitions

$A_{jp}(t)$:   availability of parallel computer architecture j during time t

$P_{jp}(t)$:   performance of parallel computer architecture j during time t
$R_{jp}(t)$:   hardware reliability of parallel computer architecture j during time t
$EP_{jp}(t)$:   expected performance of parallel computer architecture during time t

Since availability, $A_j(t)$, is the probability of the system being ready for use, the expected *hardware* performance of architecture j during time t, is computed in equation (9.9). This equation takes into account the possibility of recovery from failures because, as can be seen in equation (9.7), availability is a function of recovery time.

$$EP_{jp}(t) = (A_{jp}(t)\, P_{jp}(t)) \tag{9.9}$$

The expected *hardware* performance of architecture j during time t, *not* taking into account the possibility of recovery from failures, is computed as shown in equation (9.10), where the reliability $R_{jp}(t)$ is the probability that a system has survived for a time $> t$. This is the case because unlike availability, reliability does not involve recovery from failures—only the ability of a system to survive a specified time.

$$EP_{jp}(t) = R_{jp}(t)\, P_{jp}(t) \tag{9.10}$$

There are many examples of performance, such as number of instructions executed per time period and number of transactions processed per time period. The performance metric that is used is in this chapter is clock rate.

Architectural Characteristics

Few techniques consider failure propagation in system architectures for system reliability assessment. One study that considered failure propagation analyzed failure propagation based on architectural service routes (ASRs). An ASR is a sequence of components that are connected through interfaces [MOH08]. In this chapter, failure propagation is generated by data flow paths, similar to components connected by interfaces. Architectural characteristics, such as data flow paths, influence the availability and reliability that can be achieved in a system. A data flow path that is a sequence of nodes and edges is shaded in Figure 9.1. This is an example of where failures could occur. In addition to the many avenues for failure that are exposed by an architecture with many data flow paths, this condition makes it difficult to recover from failures and to repair the faults responsible for failures. Another consideration is making a division in the architecture between computation and memory that isolates errors in processing from storage [GOL05]. This concept is illustrated in Figure 9.1, where instruction execution in the Execution Core is separated from storage functions; the latter is managed by the Memory Management Unit.

Integrating Reliability, Availability, and Performance

Because hardware reliability, availability, and performance are not independent, it is important to integrate them when modeling architectures. For example, one technique lets designers apply redundancy to the architecture in order to increase reliability and availability [SRI05]. Another technique is the following: Web service redundancy is an approach to improving the reliability and availability of Web services. In this approach, a Web service that requires high reliability and availability will be hosted by multiple servers [JIA05].

An important aspect of redundancy is the possibility of parallel operations, using redundant computers in standby mode. It can be seen that reliability and availability are increased at the expense of greater hardware and operating system complexity, and, hence, cost. To illustrate the concept, consider n computers operating in parallel. Assume in equa-

FIGURE 9.1   Processor Architecture (Based on Intel XScale Technology Block Diagram)

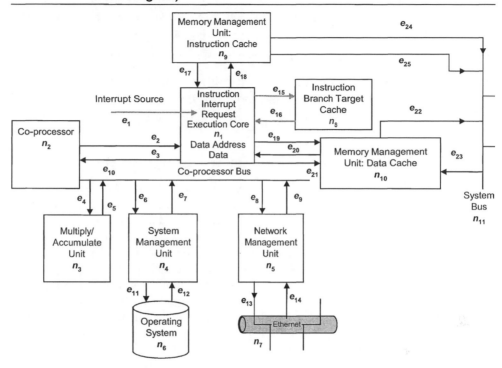

Number of Nodes: $N_n = 11$
Number of Edges: $N_e = 25$
Cyclomatic Complexity: $CC = N_e - N_n + 1 = 15$

tion (9.11) that the hardware reliability, $R_j(t)$, of each of n computers is equal, in the common case of identical processors. Also, assume that failure occurrences are independent because a computer in standby mode does not affect an active computer.

$$R_{jp}(t) = 1 - \prod_{j=1}^{n} (1 - R_j(t))$$ (9.11)

Then rewriting equation (9.11) as equation (9.12), yields:

$$R_{jp}(t) = 1 - (1 - R_j(t))^n$$ (9.12)

Solving equation (9.12) for $R_j(t)$ results in equation (9.13):

$$R_j(t) = (1 - R_{j_p}(t))^{\frac{1}{n}}$$ (9.13)

To illustrate how small values of reliability, $R_j(t)$, can satisfy a large specified reliability requirement, $R_{jp}(t)$, when parallel processing is used, assume $R_{jp}(t)$ is required to be .9900 and $n = 10$. Then, solving equation (9.13) results in $R_j(t) = .3690$.

Since availability is significantly related to reliability [LYU96], equation (9.13) is used as a template for computing availability $A_j(t)$, in equation (9.14), as a function of $A_{jp}(t)$, the availability considering parallel processing.

$$A_j(t) = 1 - (1 - A_{jp}(t))^{\frac{1}{n}} \tag{9.14}$$

Using equations (9.10) and (9.12), the *expected hardware* performance in period during time t, *not* taking into account recovery from failure, is computed in equation (9.15).

$$EP_{jp}(t) = R_{jp}(t) P_{jp}(t) = 1 - (1 - R_j(t))^n) P_{jp}(t) \tag{9.15}$$

Similarly using equations (9.9) and (9.14), the *expected hardware* performance during time t, taking into account recovery from failure, is computed in equation (9.16).

$$EP_{jp}(t) = A_{jp}(t) P_{jp}(t) = (1 - (1 - A_j(t))^n) P_{jp}(t) \tag{9.16}$$

Reliability Related to Processor Configuration

Some characteristics of processor architecture are related to system configuration rather than to periods in time. An example is shown in Figure 9.1, which shows a processor architecture based on the Intel XScale Technology [INT]. Complexity is an intuitive notion based on the relationship of nodes and edges in a directed graph of a system. Figure 9.1 is an example. The concept is that the greater the number of interconnections among the nodes and edges, the more difficult it will be to understand, design, and manufacture a processor architecture. The complexity of the configuration will influence the reliability and availability of the system. You account for this complexity by enumerating the nodes and edges in the configuration, and then computing the cyclomatic complexity (CC) [FEN97] from these elements, as shown in Figure 9.1. Cyclomatic complexity is used as a weighting factor and applied to reliability and availability to account for the complexity of the architecture.

The cyclomatic complexity for architecture j is computed in equation (9.17), where N_{je} is number of edges and N_{jn} is number of nodes.

$$CC_j = (N_{je} - N_{jn}) + 1 \tag{9.17}$$

To compute a weighting factor, a maximum value CC_m of CC_j is needed to normalize the complexity in equation (9.16). CC_m is obtained by recognizing that the most complex architecture is one that has a single node composed of CPU, I/O, RAM, etc., each with edges communicating over a common bus. In other words, $N_{jn} = 1$ in equation (9.17), so that maximum cyclomatic complexity is expressed in equation (9.18).

$$CC_m = N_{je} \tag{9.18}$$

Using equations (9.17) and (9.18), the weighting factor for architecture j is expressed in equation (9.19).

$$w_j = CC_j/CC_m = (N_{jn} - 1)/N_{je} \tag{9.19}$$

Now, applying the weighting factor in equation (9.19) to the equation for expected *hardware* performance of n computers in equation (9.15), produce equation (9.20).

$$EP_{jp}(t) = [(1 - (1 - R_j(t))^n] [P_{jp}(t) (N_{jn} - 1)/N_{je}] \tag{9.20}$$

Using equation (9.16), the possibility of recovery is considered, which leads to including availability in performance. Thus, the weighted expected *hardware* performance of n computers is computed in equation (9.21).

$$EP_{jp}(t) = [(1 - (1 - A_j)(t))^n] [P_{jp}(t)(N_{jn} - 1)/N_{je}] \tag{9.21}$$

Integrating Software Reliability

Up to this point, software reliability has not been addressed. Now, include software reliability in the architectural model. To do this, use the binomial distribution to represent the probability $P(x)$, of x number of instructions in a program that fail, each with a probability of failure p, in a program of size N, in equation (9.22). Define a reliable program as one that has $x = 0$ instructions that fail. Therefore, equation (9.22) is compressed to equation (9.23), which is the software reliability of a program with N instructions.

$$P(x) = \left(\frac{N!}{(x!)(N-x)!} \right)(p^x)(1-p)^{(N-x)} \tag{9.22}$$

$$R_s(N) = P(0) = (1-p)^N \tag{9.23}$$

Then the expected *hardware-software* performance of n computers operating in parallel, with a program of N instructions, is computed in equation (9.24), using equations (9.20) and (9.23).

$$EP_{jp}(t) = [(1 - (1-R_j)(t))^n] \, [P_{jp}(t) \, (N_{jn} - 1)/N_{je}] \, (1-p)^N \tag{9.24}$$

As noted in [SES07], you should not include redundancy in the formulation of software reliability, as was the case for hardware reliability, because identical programs in the n computers will not increase reliability, if failures occur.

TABLE 9.1   Architecture Data Values

Operational Time t	Number of Computers n	Intel Processor		Intel Chip Set	
		Clock Speed MHz	Probability of 0 Instructions Failing p	Clock Speed MHz	Probability of 0 Instructions Failing p
1	1	100		**100**	
2	2	200		200	
3	3	**266**	0.000100	**266**	0.000200
4	4	300	0.000090	**333**	0.000180
5	5	**400**	0.000080	400	0.000160
6	6	500	0.000070	**533**	0.000140
7	7	**533**	0.000060	600	0.000120
8	8	600	0.000050	800	0.000100
9	9	700	0.000040	1000	0.000080
10	10	800	0.000030	**1066**	0.000060
11	11	900	0.000020	1200	0.000040
12	12	1000	0.000010	**1333**	0.000020
baseline reliability:R_{jp0}		0.9990	0.000009	0.9870	0.000018
baseline availability:A_{jp0}		0.9980	0.000008	0.9860	0.000016
N_{je}		25		50 number of edges	
N_{jn}		11		19 number of nodes	
N		10,000		10,000 number of instructions	

Similarly, there will be a reduction in availability caused by failed software. Thus, equation (9.21) is combined with equation (9.23) to compute expected *hardware-software* performance that includes availability in equation (9.25).

$$EP_{jp}(t) = [(1 - (1 - Aj(t))^n] [P_{jp}(t) (N_{jn} - 1)/N_{je}] (1 - p)^N \tag{9.25}$$

Processor Performance Specifications and Architectural Data Values

Selected processor specifications are listed below that will be used in evaluating and comparing computer architecture performance. In addition, Table 9.1 lists the data (i.e., non-computed values) used in the computations, where the bolded quantities are the clock rates listed below.

Intel XScale Processor

Clock rates:

- 266 MHz
- 400 MHz
- 533 MHz

Intel Chip Set Architecture

Clock rates:

- 266 MHz
- 333 MHz
- 533 MHz
- 1066 MHz
- 1333 MHz

Accounting for Outages and Maintainability

Now, account for outages and maintainability that, in turn, are a function of failure rate. As shown in [SEI02], microprocessor failure rate increases exponentially with clock rate. Therefore, the failure rate of architecture j during time t is computed in equation (9.26), where P_m is the maximum performance (e.g., maximum clock rate). In this formulation, the ratio of failure rate of $j = 2$ to $j = 1$, for example, is computed in equation (9.27).

$$F_j(t) = e^{\left(P_j(t)/P_m\right)} \tag{9.26}$$

$$e^{\left(P_2(t)/P_m\right)}/e^{\left(P_1(t)/P_m\right)} = e^{\left(\frac{P_2(t) - P_1(t)}{P_m}\right)} \tag{9.27}$$

Figure 9.2 shows a plot of equation (9.26) demonstrating how failure rate increases rapidly with performance (i.e., clock speed), for the Intel XScale Processor Architecture. Figure 9.3 demonstrates how hardware reliability alone and hardware reliability combined with software reliability affects performance. The important point about this plot is that it identifies the optimal number of computers to use in a redundant configuration—the number of computers that results in maximum performance. Additionally and fortunately, for the Intel Processor Architecture the gap between the two performance curves decreases with increasing operating time.

FIGURE 9.2   Failure Rate of Architecture j During Time t, $F_j(t)$ vs. Performance of Architecture j During Time t, $P_j(t)$

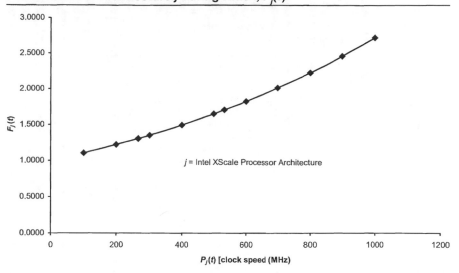

FIGURE 9.3   Expected Performance of Architecture j, During Time t, $EP_j(t)$ vs. Operating Time t and Number of Computers n

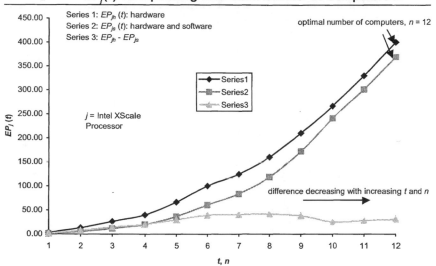

Figure 9.4 is useful for indicating when uptime exceeds downtime. For the Intel XScale Processor Architecture this does not occur until maximum operational time. The plot is also useful for comparing the recovery times of different architectures. Figure 9.4 shows that the Intel Chip Set Architecture has slightly higher recovery times than the XScale Processor. Referring to equation (9.8), you can see the reason: The Chip Set Architecture has higher time to failure and unavailability, which results in higher recovery time.

Comparing Computer Architectures

Previously, the Intel XScale Processor architecture was introduced and evaluated. Now, a second architecture—Intel Chip Set architecture—shown in Figure 9.5, is compared with

FIGURE 9.4 Uptime $U_j(t)$, Downtime $D_j(t)$, and Time to Recover $TR_j(t)$ vs. Operational Time t

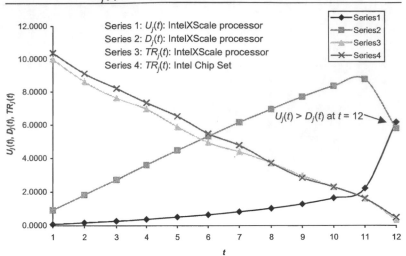

FIGURE 9.5 Chip Set Architecture

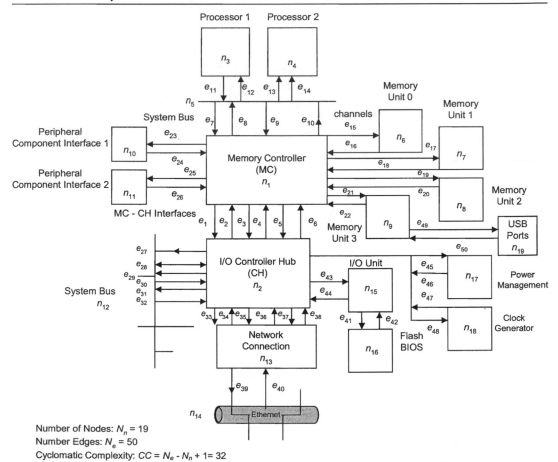

Number of Nodes: $N_n = 19$
Number Edges: $N_e = 50$
Cyclomatic Complexity: $CC = N_e - N_n + 1 = 32$

the Intel XScale Processor architecture in order assess how different configurations and complexities relate to reliability, availability, and performance. The hardware reliability of parallel architecture j, $R_{jp}(t)$ and the availability of parallel architecture j, $A_{jp}(t)$, are specified by typical values in order to illustrate the comparison. The specified reliability is computed in equation (9.27), where R_{pj0} is the baseline reliability—the reliability for number of computers $n = 1$ and maximum operational time $t = t_m$. The concept is that reliability increases with number of computers in parallel, according to $R_{jp0}^{1/n}$, and this increase is modified by operational time according to (t/t_m). Similarly, specified availability increases according to equation (9.28), using the baseline availability A_{jp0}. Exploiting increased parallelism yields high susceptibility to transient faults [FU08]. This is the reason the factor (t/t_m) is used in equations (9.27) and (9.28) to account for increased fault occurrence, as it affects reliability and availability, with the passage of time t. This factor reduces the effect of increasing parallelism as n increases.

Lower baseline values, listed in Table 9.1, are specified for the Chip Set architecture due to its greater complexity, as can be seen by comparing Figures 9.1 and 9.5.

$$R_{jp} = \left(\left(R_{jp0} \right)^{\frac{1}{n}} \right) \left(\frac{t}{t_m} \right) \tag{9.28}$$

$$A_{jp} = \left(\left(A_{jp0} \right)^{\frac{1}{n}} \right) \left(\frac{t}{t_m} \right) \tag{9.29}$$

Interestingly, Figure 9.6 shows that the two architectures have the same failures rates, but the Chip Set Architecture experiences them at higher performance than the Processor Architecture because Table 9.1 indicates that the former has higher clock rate performance.

Figure 9.7 shows that the Chip Set Architecture has higher *expected* hardware performance and higher *expected* hardware-software performance than the XScale Processor Architecture for all values of t and n. This is the case despite its greater complexity, as documented in Figure 9.5. The explanation is its higher clock rate. Thus, even if an architecture has greater configuration complexity, this attribute would not necessarily lead to poor *expected* performance if a basic performance feature, such as clock rate, is high.

FIGURE 9.6   Failure Rate of Architecture *j* Comparison During Time *t*, $F_j(t)$, vs. Performance of Architecture *j*, During Time *t*, $P_j(t)$

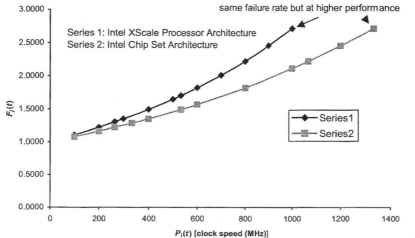

FIGURE 9.7   **Expected Performance of Architecture j, $E_{jp}(t)$, During Time t, vs. Operating Time t and Number of Computers n**

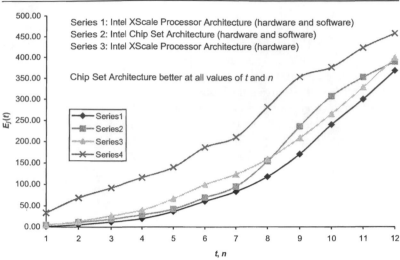

There were no significant differences observed between the two architectures with respect to other quantities, such as time to failure, uptime, downtime, recovery rate, and number of recoveries. The reason for this is that these quantities do not depend on configuration complexity. Rather, they depend on specified reliability and availability, which are not significantly different.

Comparing Hardware and Software Reliability and Analyzing Incremental Performance

High reliability is insufficient if performance is low. Conversely, if performance is high and reliability is low, there is no benefit to be gained by high performance. Therefore, let us see how reliabilities compare over operational time and number of computers. This is done by comparing hardware reliability $R_j(t)$ with software reliability $R_s(N)$ in equations (9.30) and (9.31), respectively. These reliabilities were computed previously but are listed again for convenience. In Figure 9.8, $R_j(t)$ is dependent on specified reliability $R_{jp}(t)$ and number of computers operating in parallel n, whereas $R_s(N)$ is dependent on specified probability p of zero instructions failing and number of instructions $N = 10,000$. Figure 9.8 reveals that, *with the specified data,* software reliability is much higher than hardware reliability. Since the number of computers n is already large, you would attempt to increase hardware reliability by increasing the specified baseline reliability $R_{jp0}(t)$. To see whether the baseline could be achieved, the architecture would be tested using one computer for the maximum planned operational time (see equation (9.28)).

$$R_j(t) = 1 - (1 - R_{j_p}(t))^{\frac{1}{n}} \qquad (9.30)$$

$$R_s(N) = (1 - p)^N \qquad (9.31)$$

Now, analyzing incremental performance, there are three variants: 1) includes hardware reliability only, 2) includes hardware reliability and configuration complexity, and

FIGURE 9.8   **Hardware Reliability of Architecture _j_, _R_ⱼ(_t_), and Software Reliability _R_ₛ (_N_) vs. Operational Time _t_ and Number of Computers _t, n_**

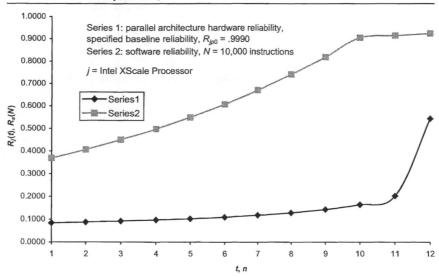

3) includes 2) and software reliability. These performances were presented previously but are listed again for convenience in equations (9.32), (9.33), and (9.34), respectively. Figure 9.9 demonstrates that the contribution of configuration complexity to reducing performance is much greater than the contribution of software reliability. Unfortunately, configuration complexity cannot be reduced and still satisfy application requirements (i.e., all the functionality of Figure 9.1 must be retained). A possible solution is to increase the baseline reliability in equation (9.28).

$$EP_{jp}(t) = (1 - (1 - R_j(t))^n)\, P_{jp}(t) \tag{9.32}$$

FIGURE 9.9   **Performance of Parallel Architecture _EP_ⱼₚ(_t_) vs. Operational Time _t_ and Number of Computers _n_**

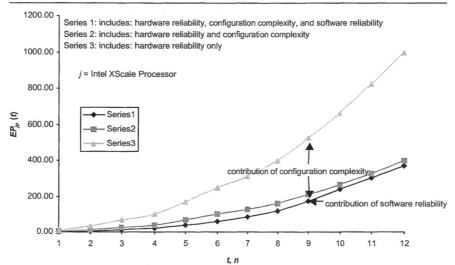

$$EP_{jp}(t) = [(1 - (1 - R_j(t))^n)] \; [P_{jp}(t) \, (N_{jn} - 1)/N_{je}] \tag{9.33}$$

$$EP_{jp}(t) = [(1 - (1 - R_j(t))^n)] \; [P_{jp}(t) \, (N_{jn} - 1)/N_{je}] \, (1 - p)^N \tag{9.34}$$

Summary

Rather than considering architecture as an isolated characteristic of computer systems, this chapter has shown how architectural characteristics, such as configuration complexity, influence the performance, availability, and reliability that can be achieved in a system. Two architectures from industry were evaluated and compared. Both non-parallel and parallel architecture were included in the models in order to assess the effect of using multiple computers. The benefit of the models is to identify architectural characteristics that have major effects on performance, availability, and reliability so that the architecture can be changed, if necessary, to meet performance, availability, and reliability goals.

References

[FEN97] Norman F. Fenton and Shari Lawrence Pfleeger, *Software Metrics: A Rigorous & Practical Approach,* second edition. PWS Publishing Company, 1997.

[FU08] Xin Fu, Wangyuan Zhang, Tao Li, and Joe Fortes, "Optimizing Issue Queue Reliability to Soft Errors on Simultaneous Multithreaded Architectures." 37th International Conference on Parallel Processing, 2008, pp. 190–197.

[GOL05] Brian T. Gold, Jangwoo Kim, Jared C. Smolens, Eric S. Chung, Vasileios Liaskovitis, Eriko Nurvitadhi, Babak Falsafi, James C. Hoe, and Andreas G. Nowatzyk, "TR USS: A Reliable, Scalable Server Architecture." *IEEE Micro,* Vol. 25, No. 6, November/December, 2005, pp. 51–59.

[GOK06] Swapna S. Gokhale, Paul J. Vandal, and Jijun Lu, "Performance and Reliability Analysis of Web Server Software Architectures." 12th Pacific Rim International Symposium on Dependable Computing (PRDC '06), 2006, pp. 351–358.

[INT] http://download.intel.com/design/network/datashts/25247907.pdf

[JIA05] M. Jiang and A. Willey, "Service-Oriented Architecture for Deploying and Integrating Enterprise Applications." 5th Working IEEE/IFIP Conference on Software Architecture, WICSA 2005, pp. 272–273.

[LYU96] Michael R. Lyu, editor, *Handbook of Software Reliability Engineering.* IEEE Computer Society Press and McGraw-Hill, 1996.

[MOH08] Atef Mohamed and Mohammad Zulkernine, "On Failure Propagation in Component-Based Software Systems." The Eighth International Conference on Quality Software, 2008, pp. 402–411.

[SAG00] Andrew P. Sage and James E. Armstrong, Jr., *Introduction to Systems Engineering.* John Wiley & Sons, Inc., 2000.

[SAH06] Indranil Saha, Debapriyay Mukhopadhyay, and Satyajit Banerjee, "Designing Reliable Architecture for Stateful Fault Tolerance." Seventh International Conference on Parallel and Distributed Computing, Applications and Technologies (PDCAT '06), 2006, pp. 545–551.

[SAN63] G. H. Sandler, *Systems Reliability Engineering.* Prentice Hall, Englewood Cliffs, New Jersey, 1963.

[SEI02] Norbert Seifert, Xiaowei Zhu, and Lloyd W. Massengill, "Impact of Scaling on Soft-Error Rates in Commercial Microprocessors." *IEEE Transactions on Nuclear Science,* Vol. 49, No. 6, December 2002.

[SES07] S. Seshadri, Ling Liu, B. F Cooper, L. Chiu, K. Gupta, and P. Muench. "A Fault-Tolerant Middleware Architecture for High-Availability Storage Services." IEEE International Conference on Services Computing, July 9–13, 2007, pp. 286–293.

[SHO83] M. L. Shooman, *Software Engineering.* McGraw-Hill, New York, 1983.

[SRI05] Jayanth Srinivasan, Pradip Adve, S. V Bose, and J. A. Rivers, "Lifetime Reliability: Toward an Architectural Solution." *IEEE Micro,* Volume 25, Issue 3, May-June 2005, pp. 70–80.

[TRI82] K. S. Trivedi, *Probability and Statistics with Reliability, Queuing, and Computer Science Applications.* Prentice Hall, Englewood Cliffs, New Jersey, 1982.

[WAN07] Jun Wang, Weiru Chen, and Jun Liu, "A Modeling of Software Architecture Reliability." IFIP International Conference on Network and Parallel Computing Workshops, September 18–21, 2007, pp. 983–986.

[WAN99] W. L. Wang, Y. Wu, and M. H. Chen, "An Architecture-Based Software Reliability Model." *Dependable Computing,* Dec. 1999, pp. 143–150.

[YAC02] S. M. Yacoub and H. H. Ammar, "A Methodology for Architecture-Level Reliability Risk Analysis." *IEEE Transactions on Software Engineering,* June 2002, pp. 529–547.

[ZHA07] Wangyuan Zhang, Xin Fu, Tao Li, and J. Fortes, "An Analysis of Microarchitecture Vulnerability to Soft Errors on Simultaneous Multithreaded Architectures." IEEE International Symposium on Performance Analysis of Systems & Software, 2007, pp. 169–178.

10

Internet Fault Tree Analysis for Reliability Estimation

Objectives

Building on the introduction to fault tree analysis in Chapter 1, you will learn how to apply fault tree analysis to achieving reliability and safety goals in information systems, using Internet services as an application example.

In addition, you will learn how to assess the applicability of fault tree analysis to the evaluation of the risk incurred by Internet users of multiple services. This assessment is made by estimating the probabilities of unsafe events at various points in the fault tree, supported by real-world Internet event and vulnerability data.

What You Will Learn From This Chapter

You will learn that fault tree analysis (FTA) is as a way of modeling multiple Internet services composed of local network, Internet, and network services. Probabilities of branch and path transitions on the tree, and associated unreliabilities of the Internet services, are used to identify whether a safe state can be achieved at the root node of a fault tree. Internet services are used to illustrate FTA because of the importance of the Internet and the pervasiveness of its services. Fault correction and consequent failure reduction, combined with a modest amount of component redundancy, is superior in achieving safety as opposed to using massive amounts of component redundancy, absent fault correction. You will learn both empirical and predictive fault correction approaches to evaluate improvements in Internet services safety.

Subjects

Fault Tree Analysis
Model of FTA for Internet Services
Event Failure Analysis
Fault Tree for Analyzing Internet Service Failures
Predicting Failure Rates with Fault Correction

Introduction

Fault tree analysis is a popular analytical technique for reliability estimation. Fault trees are graphical models that represent logical relationships among events that lead to system failure. They also provide a systematic mathematical framework for analyzing potential causes of failure. From a design perspective, they allow the designer to understand the ways in which a system may fail. Fault trees comprise basic events connected by gates, in a logical path, to a top node that represents system or subsystem failure [PAI02]. You can use this graphical model to conceptualize the reliability and safety of multiple Internet services accessed by Internet users.

Fault tree analysis (FTA) has become standardized on an international scale [IEC06]. One approach used by this standard is largely quantitative, where FTA models an entire product, process, or system, and the events and failures have a probability of occurrence determined by analysis or test. The final result is the probability of occurrence of a top event representing probability of fault or a failure. In this chapter, a model is developed to represent a system of Internet services that have vulnerabilities, faults, and failures that can lead to an unsafe user state.

Analysis of software fault trees exposes hardware and software failure events that lead to unsafe system states, and provides insight on improving safety throughout each phase of the software life cycle [NEE06]. Thus, FTA can be applied to address the urgent need to resolve reliability problems in the Internet, as they affect the user at the local level.

Today, much of software development involves the use of components. Thus, components are used as our basic fault tree building blocks. In addition, components support parallel and serial reliability analysis [SHO90].

Fault Tree Analysis

Fault tree analysis provides a top-level view of reliability and safety, including hardware and software. A hazard to safety is postulated at the top level of the fault tree and the leaves are used to provide a progressive bottom-up trace to the root of the tree to identify those software and hardware faults that could lead to the hazard at the top level. This analysis is very useful for identifying problems at lower levels of the system hierarchy that could lead to a disastrous system hazard at the top level. In using FTA to model the reliability and safety of Internet users, their Internet Service Providers (ISPs), and network nodes and links, the focus is on the hazards at the user computer root, as affected by unreliable and unsafe operations at lower levels of the tree. It is important to point out that it is not necessary to *directly* prevent the root cause failure from happening. It is merely necessary to break the chain of events at any node in the tree so that the root cause failure cannot occur [DOW]. In other words, you do not need to make a user's computer highly reliable and fault tolerant. Instead, you can focus on correcting the chain of Internet unreliabilities that lead to failures in the user's operation.

Applicability of FTA

As suggested by Musa [MUS87], FTA is not applicable to specific faults in software. He says that if you know there is a fault, you would fix it. True, but we are also interested in the effects of faults on other parts of the system and in using FTA as a system design tool. For these purposes, FTA is useful. Musa does grant that FTA is useful at the module level to identify the modules most critical for successful system operation. This is highly applicable in Internet systems because there are many interconnected hardware and software modules where faults can occur. Dugan says that given the great size and complexity of software systems (e.g., the Internet), failures are bound to occur in the systems' lifetime [DUG96]. She explains that fault trees can expose vulnerabilities in a system and aid in determining where to focus tests.

Pfleeger [PFL01] points out that FTA should put the emphasis on failures instead of faults because it is the former that we want to eliminate. Yes, but it is important to note that faults cause failures, and that vulnerabilities to faults and failures are also important. In this chapter, fault and failure are used interchangeably. Pfleeger also suggests that the analysis begin by identifying possible failures. Failures and vulnerability to failures can be identified in Internet services, in their connected nodes and links, and in user local networks.

Scope of FTA Application

Figure 10.1—a diagram inspired by [VES81]—shows the scope of the Internet entities that are used in modeling the effects on the computer user of vulnerabilities and failures in the Internet. As the diagram suggests, there are several ways to account for vulnerabilities and failures and only one way to account for success. The reason for only one route to success is that all functions in Figure 10.1 must operate without failure for services to be delivered reliably to the computer user.

Advantages and Limitations of FTA

One of the advantages of FTA is that you can focus on a specific hazardous state and identify each of the preconditions that need to be satisfied in order to reach such a state. Of course, this could also become a disadvantage if FTA is the only technique used to identify hazardous states. This is due to the possibility of overlooking other specific hazardous states [TOW03]. You can avoid this pitfall by exhaustively examining all the events and states that could lead to a hazard.

A general weakness of FTA, and other catastrophic event prevention methods, is that the top event must be recognized prior to performing the analysis. In general, FTA cannot be used to discover previously unidentified catastrophic events [KEY00]. While this may be true in general, it is not true in the Internet services case because you would know in advance that if a request for Internet service (e.g., query to a search engine) is not answered, this is reflected as a top-level hazard at the user computer.

If an event can occur only based on the occurrence of another event (i.e., event dependency), FTA is not a good choice and another approach like common cause analysis has to be used [ORT04]. Furthermore, the Boolean logic used in FTA assumes that failure events

FIGURE 10.1   Internet Failure-Success Meter

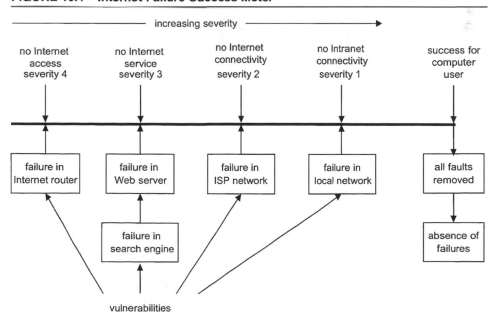

occur independently of one another. In real systems, this is not always true [KEY00]. However, events are not always dependent. For example, considering Figure 10.1, failures in a Web server and ISP network are unrelated. Thus, you could assume that events, such as the vulnerabilities and failures in a Web server, are independent from those in an ISP network, resulting in a series configuration for computing reliability. Even if this assumption does not always hold, computing reliability on a series basis provides a conservative assessment (i.e., a single failure in the chain in Figure 10.1 causes a system failure).

Fault tree analysis frequently produces large and complex diagrams of the conditions (or events) required to model a catastrophic accident or other undesired event. These diagrams can be so complex that it becomes difficult to extract essential information. The concept of cut sets was developed to simplify the results of fault tree analysis so that one can focus on preventing the events that must be satisfied for the hazard to occur [KEY00]. For example, to do a proper FTA assessment of Figure 10.1, you do not have to analyze every possible hardware and software fault in the Internet in order to assess the impact on the user computer. Thus, it is sufficient to know that *any* of these faults would cause failure in a Web server module, and thus negatively impact the user's operation.

Some authors claim that identifying a hazard is driven by intuition and that afterward the events leading to the hazard are formalized by gates in the fault tree [XIA04]. Other authors disagree with this notion because the structure of FTA forces the engineer to think in detail about both the top-level and lower-level events and states of a system.

Model of FTA for Internet Services

Definitions

Failure, as defined by [IEE08], has several interpretations:

1. The inability of a system or system component to perform a required function within specified limits.
2. The termination of the ability of a functional unit to perform its required function.
3. A departure of program operation from program requirements. A failure may be produced when a fault is encountered and a loss of the expected service to the user results.

Fault, as defined by [IEE08], also has more than one interpretation:

1. A defect in the code that can be the cause of one or more failures.
2. An accidental condition that causes a functional unit to fail to perform its required function.

A fault is synonymous with a bug. A fault is an error that should be fixed with a software design change.

Vulnerability: risk to a system's operation when a fault and failure occur
Catastrophic event: a fault and failure that renders a system inoperable
Failure events in the Internet: $x_1, \ldots, x_i, \ldots, x_n$
  Px_i: probability of event x_i
   n: number of events (e.g., number of service failures across the Internet)
Failure or vulnerability rate of event x_i: λx_i
  P_s: probability of *safe state* = probability that n events, each with reliability Rx_i, will produce a *safe* state
  P_{us}: probability of *unsafe state* = probability that n events, each with unreliability $(1 - Rx_i)$, will produce an *unsafe* state

Safe State *s*:   reach a specified level of fault tree with a probability P_s greater than or equal to a specified threshold

Unsafe State *u*:   reach a specified level of fault tree with a probability P_{us} greater than a specified threshold

P_t: allowable probability of reaching an unsafe state (i.e., threshold)

t: time that user accesses Internet services in a session (i.e., operational time)

T: total time that user accesses Internet services across multiple sessions

$V(t)$:   predicted vulnerability rate at time *t* that is assumed equal to fault and failure count rates

$C(t)$:   predicted fault correction rate at time *t*

$R(t)$:   predicted rate at which faults and failures *remain* in the code at time *t*

Model Development

It is reasonable that the higher the fraction of time $(f = t/T)$ that a user accesses Internet services in a *given session,* the higher the probability that Internet events occur. Therefore, the factor *f* appears in the probability formulations that follow.

When failure events are independent, equation (10.1) uses the AND function to express the probability of series events (e.g., faults occur in two components in a computer system that are connected in series). However, when the events occur in parallel (e.g., faults occur in two components that are connected in parallel), equation (10.2) uses the OR function on the left side and the AND function on the right side to subtract probabilities of events occurring simultaneously (e.g., simultaneous occurrence of faults in components connected in parallel).

$$P((x_1, \ldots, x_i, \ldots, x_n), f) = (P(x_1) * \ldots, P(x_i), * \ldots, P(x_n)) * f \tag{10.1}$$

$$\left(\sum_{i=1}^{n} Px_i - \prod_{i=1}^{n} Px_i \right) * f \text{ , for } x_i \text{ events, taken 1, 2, } \ldots, n \text{ at a time} \tag{10.2}$$

Series Unreliability

The *series* unreliability of *n* events, each with reliability Rx_i is as follows:

$$Urx_i = \left(1 - \prod_{i=1}^{n} Rx_i \right) \tag{10.3}$$

(See Chapter 1 for a review of how to compute the unreliability of *n* events.)

Then using equations (10.2) and (10.3), the criterion for reaching an *unsafe* state, with *series* unreliability is:

$$P_{us} = \left(P(x_1) * \ldots, P(x_i), * \ldots, P(x_n) * f \right) \left(1 - \left(\prod_{i=1}^{n} Rx_i \right) \right) < P_t , \tag{10.4}$$

where the probability of unsafe state must be less than the threshold P_t, and the criterion for reaching the *safe* state is:

$$P_s = \left(P(x_1) * \ldots, P(x_i), * \ldots, P(x_n) * f \right) \left(1 - \left(\prod_{i=1}^{n} Rx_i \right) \right) \geq P_t \tag{10.5}$$

Since we have no data on the probability distribution of failures rates in the Internet, we assume that they are exponentially distributed (i.e., higher probability of low failure rate and lower probability of high failure rate). Thus, we use equation (10.4) to expand the criterion for reaching the *unsafe* state, as follows:

$$P_{us} = \left(P(x_1) * \ldots, P(x_i), * \ldots, P(x_n) * f\right)\left(1 - \left(\prod_{i=1}^{n} e^{-\lambda x_i t}\right) < P_t\right) \tag{10.6}$$

A similar formulation is used for the safe state, using equation (10.5).

Parallel Unreliability

Now, if redundant components become necessary due to unreliable operation of one or more Internet services, we will recast the unreliabilities as follows:

The unreliability of *n* components operating in parallel is given by equation (10.7):

$$URx_i = \prod_{i=1}^{n}(1 - Rx_i) \quad [\text{MUS87}] \tag{10.7}$$

And using the assumption of exponentially distributed times between failures, we have:

$$URx_i = \prod_{i=1}^{n}\left(1 - e^{-\lambda x_i t}\right) \tag{10.8}$$

Probability of Unsafe State

We must be concerned with the probability of reaching the root of the fault tree in the unsafe state (i.e., with a hazard present propagated from the leaves of the tree). This probability P_{us} is computed in equation (10.9) by generating the *Exclusive OR* function of the event probabilities Px_i:

$$P_{us} = \left(\sum_{i=1}^{n} Px_i - \prod_{i=1}^{n} Px_i\right) * f, \text{ for } x_i \text{ events, taken } 1, 2, \ldots, n \text{ at a time} \tag{10.9}$$

Recognizing that the root of the fault tree can be reached by either a *series* of unreliability events (AND functions) or by *parallel* unreliability events (OR functions), equations (10.3) and (10.9) are combined for the *series* case to produce equation (10.10) and equations (10.7) and (10.9) are combined for the *parallel* case to produce equation (10.11).

$$\text{Series case: } P_{us} = \left(\left[\left(\sum_{i=1}^{n} Px_i * f\right) - \left(\prod_{i=1}^{n} Px_i * f\right)\right]\left(1 - \prod_{i=1}^{n} Rx_i\right)\right) * f, \tag{10.10}$$

for x_i events, taken $1, 2, \ldots, n$ at a time

$$\text{Parallel case: } P_{us} = \left(\left[\left(\sum_{i=1}^{n} Px_i * f\right) - \left(\prod_{i=1}^{n} Px_i * f\right)\right]\left(\prod_{i=1}^{n}(1 - Rx_i)\right)\right) * f, \tag{10.11}$$

for x_i events, taken $1, 2, \ldots, n$ at a time

where equations (10.10) and (10.11) must obey the threshold criterion $<P_t$.

Data Used in FTA Model

It is important in FTA to identify the major services that can lead to an unsafe state [TOW03]. These critical services are shown in Table 10.1 on page 234 with the vulnerability rates, λx_i, and the remaining vulnerability rates after fault correction, $R(t)$. Based on the failure data in the Internet attributed to vulnerabilities, as reported by [OPP] and [GAN], the probability of failures is shown in Table 10.1. The vulnerability rate functions $V(t)$ were developed by regression analysis from data in the NIST/DHS National Vulnerability Database [NVD]. The database classifies vulnerabilities by *Local Network, Internet Services,* and *Network.* Examples of vulnerabilities are lack of buffer limits checks, failure to authenticate users,

FIGURE 10.2   Network Vulnerability Rate $V(t)$ (vulnerabilities per month) vs. Year t

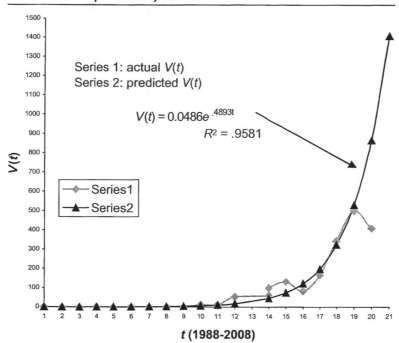

FIGURE 10.3   Local Network Vulnerability Rate $V(t)$ (vulnerabilities per month) vs. Year t

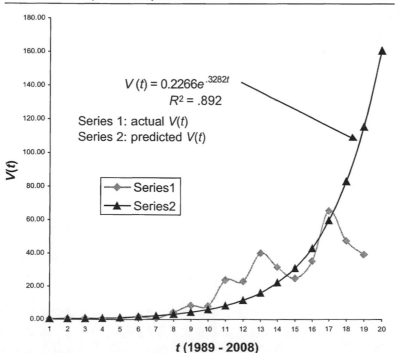

TABLE 10.1   Vulnerability Rate Distribution

Source:	Local Network	Internet Services	Network
Example:	*Ethernet Network*	*Web Server*	*ISP Network*
	Probability of Failure Attributed to Vulnerability (fraction of total failures)		
	$P(x_1) = .4120$	$P(x_2) = .1694$	$P(x_3) = .4186$
	Vulnerability Rates (per month)		
Source:	Local Network	Internet Services	Network
Predicted Vulnerability Rate Function	$V(t) = 0.2266e^{-.3282t}$	$V(t) = 0.0868e^{-.35t}$	$V(t) = 0.0486e^{-.4893t}$
2008 Predicted Vulnerability Rates	$\lambda x_1 = 160.70$	$\lambda x_2 = 16.54$	$\lambda x_3 = 1409.80$
2008 Predicted Remaining Vulnerability Rates	$R(t) = 4.34$	$R(t) = 1.32$	$R(t) = 112.72$

and lack of validity checks for access to programs and files. We equate faults, which lead to failures, with vulnerabilities.

The actual vulnerability rates and predictor functions for Network and Local Network vulnerabilities are plotted in Figures 10.2 and 10.3, respectively; the predictor functions are also shown in Table 10.1. Of course no prediction is perfect. Therefore, there are differences between the predicted and actual functions in Figures 10.2 and 10.3. The discrepancies are caused by the assumption of exponential functions for the predictors that is not entirely true over the range of time. However, the R^2 values of .9581 and .892 for Figures 10.2 and 10.3, respectively, indicate respectable prediction accuracy.

In order to provide a prediction for the Internet Services category, we used the vulnerability rate from a major ISP recorded in [NVD]. The actual Internet services vulnerability rate and predictor function are shown in Figure 10.4; the predictor functions are also shown in Table 10.1. Having predictor functions allows us to predict the vulnerability rates for 2008. These are shown in Table 10.1.

Event Failure Analysis

The event failures discussed in points 1 and 2 below refer to failure events occurring at nodes below the root node in the fault tree (see Figure 10.5).

To assist the reader in understanding the Internet fault tree in Figure 10.5, Table 10.2 (page 236, Parts 1 and 2) is provided to show the sequence of calculations necessary to build the fault tree. You can see that there are many values in the table. There is insufficient room in Figure 10.5 to show all the values. Therefore, only the maximum values, corresponding to the maximum values of t and f, are shown. The process is the following:

1. Use equation (10.1) to compute the probabilities of AND functions AND1, AND2, AND3, and AND4 in Figure 10.5.
2. Use equation (10.2) to compute the probability of the Exclusive OR function in Figure 10.5.

FIGURE 10.4 Internet Services Vulnerability Rate $V(t)$
(vulnerabilities per month) vs. Year t

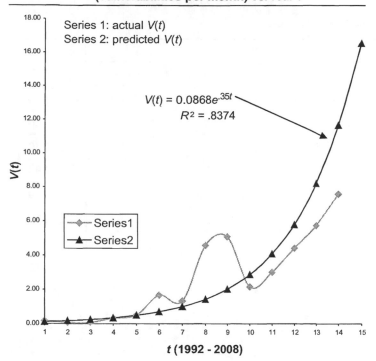

Series 1: actual $V(t)$
Series 2: predicted $V(t)$

$V(t) = 0.0868e^{.35t}$
$R^2 = .8374$

Series1
Series2

t (1992 - 2008)

FIGURE 10.5   Internet Fault Tree

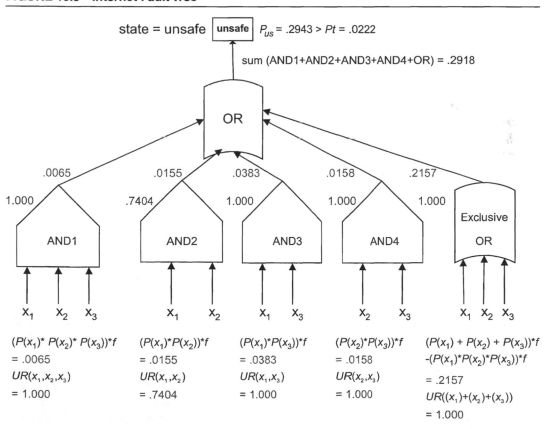

state = unsafe   unsafe P_{us} = .2943 > Pt = .0222

sum (AND1+AND2+AND3+AND4+OR) = .2918

OR

.0065   .0155   .0383   .0158   .2157

1.000   .7404   1.000   1.000   1.000

Exclusive
OR

AND1   AND2   AND3   AND4

x_1 x_2 x_3 x_1 x_2 x_1 x_3 x_2 x_3 x_1 x_2 x_3

$(P(x_1)* P(x_2)* P(x_3))*f$ $(P(x_1)*P(x_2))*f$ $(P(x_1)*P(x_3))*f$ $(P(x_2)*P(x_3))*f$ $(P(x_1) + P(x_2) + P(x_3))*f$
= .0065   = .0155   = .0383   = .0158 $-(P(x_1)*P(x_2)*P(x_3))*f$
$UR(x_1,x_2,x_3)$ $UR(x_1,x_2)$ $UR(x_1,x_3)$ $UR(x_2,x_3)$ = .2157
= 1.000   = .7404   = 1.000   = 1.000 $UR((x_1)+(x_2)+(x_3))$
= 1.000

TABLE 10.2 (Part 1) Internet Fault Tree Example

Session Time t	Fraction of Time f	Probability of Events x_i					Root Node
		$P(x_1) * P(x_2)$ $* P(x_3) * f$	$P(x_1) *$ $P(x_2) * f$	$P(x_1) *$ $P(x_3) * f$	$P(x_2) *$ $P(x_3) * f$	$(P(x_1) + P(x_2) +$ $P(x_3)) * f - (P(x_1) *$ $P(x_2) * P(x_3)) * f$	Sum of Probabilities
0.0014	0.0278	0.0008	0.0019	0.0048	0.0020	0.0270	0.0365
0.0028	0.0556	0.0016	0.0039	0.0096	0.0039	0.0539	0.0730
0.0042	0.0833	0.0024	0.0058	0.0144	0.0059	0.0809	0.1094
0.0056	0.1111	0.0032	0.0078	0.0192	0.0079	0.1079	0.1459
0.0069	0.1389	0.0041	0.0097	0.0240	0.0098	0.1348	0.1824
0.0083	0.1667	0.0049	0.0116	0.0287	0.0118	0.1618	0.2189
0.0097	0.1944	0.0057	0.0136	0.0335	0.0138	0.1888	0.2553
0.0111	0.2222	**0.0065**	**0.0155**	**0.0383**	**0.0158**	**0.2157**	**0.2918**
0.0500		Probability of Event x_i			Failure Rates		
$T =$ sum(t)	$f = t/T$	$P(x_1)$ 0.4120	$P(x_2)$ 0.1694	$P(x_3)$ 0.4186	$\lambda x_1 + \lambda x_2 + \lambda x_3$ 1587.04	$\lambda x_1 + \lambda x_2$	$\lambda x_1 + \lambda x_3$	$\lambda x_2 + \lambda x_3$
						177.24	1570.50	1426.34

TABLE 10.2 (Part 2) Internet Fault Tree Example

Session Time t	Fraction of Time f	Unreliabilities				Probability of Unsafe State at Root Node P_{us}
		URx_{123}	URx_{12}	URx_{13}	URx_{23}	
0.0014	0.0278	0.7042	0.0476	0.7869	0.7432	0.0255
0.0028	0.0556	0.9639	0.1512	0.9747	0.9623	0.0689
0.0042	0.0833	0.9960	0.2727	0.9971	0.9948	0.1072
0.0056	0.1111	0.9996	0.3924	0.9997	0.9993	0.1444
0.0069	0.1389	1.0000	0.5012	1.0000	0.9999	0.1816
0.0083	0.1667	1.0000	0.5955	1.0000	1.0000	0.2190
0.0097	0.1944	1.0000	0.6749	1.0000	1.0000	0.2566
0.0111	0.2222	**1.0000**	**0.7404**	**1.0000**	**1.0000**	**0.2943**

3. Sum the probabilities in steps 1 and 2. The result is the probability at the root node in Figure 10.5, where only the maximum is shown.

4. Use equation (10.8), failure rates in Table 10.2 (Part 1), and the session times to unreliabilities for each AND and OR function in Figure 10.5. The reason for the large unreliabilities is the large failure rates.

5. Use equation (10.11)—parallel case—to compute the probability of reaching the root node in the unsafe state. The parallel computation is used because the AND and OR functions at the leaves of the tree culminate at the OR function at the root of the tree. Although, as stated, only the maximum values are shown in Figure 10.5, the result is

FIGURE 10.6 Probability of Unsafe State P_{us} for Single Events vs. User Operational Time t

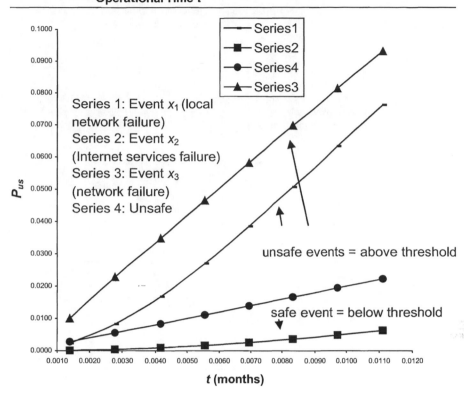

the same for all values of t: $P_{us} > P_t$ (arbitrarily selected threshold for unsafe state at root node).

1. Single Event Failures

Single event failures refer to the case where the user experiences a failure in only one of the Internet services. Figure 10.6 shows the probability of an unsafe state as a function of user operational time. The probability or risk increases with time, with the local network and network services posing the greatest risk. A solution would be to use redundant Ethernets for the local network and redundant routers in the network. There is no risk associated with the Internet services category because this event is well under the threshold.

2. Combined Event Failures

Combined event failures occur when the user experiences failures in two or more services concurrently. These are represented as AND functions in Figure 10.5. Figure 10.7 shows that multiple event failures pose less risk due to the lower probability of concurrent failures. In addition, again, we see that local network and network services are more likely to put the user's operation in an unsafe state.

3. Failures Propagated to the Root of the Fault Tree

The failure analysis culminates with the propagation of events, their probabilities, and associated unreliabilities, from lower levels to the root of the fault tree. Figure 10.8 captures this

FIGURE 10.7 **Probability of Unsafe State for Combined Events P_{us} vs. Operational Time t**

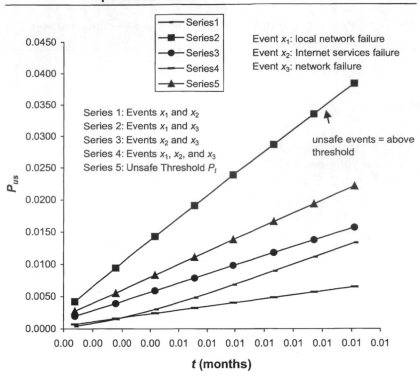

FIGURE 10.8 **Internet Fault Tree**

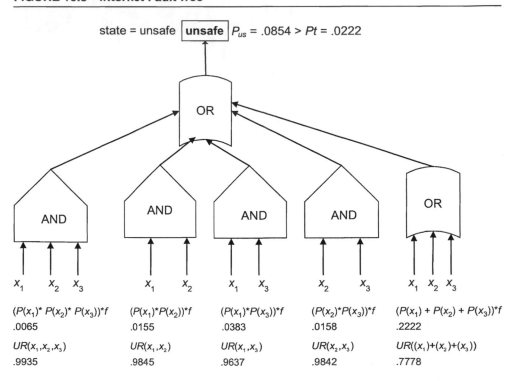

result. Now, even though the probability of reaching the unsafe state is decreasing with time, the probability, taking into account unreliabilities, is a different story. In the latter case, the lower probabilities are overwhelmed by the increasing unreliabilities over time. The unfortunate result is that the risk of reaching the unsafe state is significant for all values of the user's operational time. Again, it appears that the remedy is to employ redundant components in the local network and network services, incurring higher cost as the price of safety.

Fault Tree for Analyzing Internet Service Failures

Next, we revisit the Internet services fault tree in Figure 10.5. The root cause of an unsafe state is defined as the chronologically top event in a sequence of events that leads to a service failure. The immediate trigger is the event or events preceding the service failure [GAN]. In FTA, it is conventional to start at the root of the tree, defining the hazard, and work down the tree to identify the events that cause the hazard [DEH04]. We follow this structure by defining the root node hazard as reaching an unsafe state at the user's computer. The events in Figure 10.5 (x_1 and x_3) that trigger the unsafe state at the root are the local network and network functions, as identified in Figure 10.8. These functions are candidates for redundant components. With redundant components, we will see whether the safe state criterion can be met.

FIGURE 10.8.1   Probability of Reaching Unsafe State at Root of Fault Tree P_{us} vs. Operational Time t

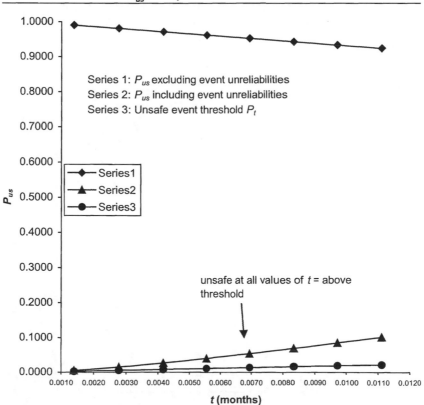

Using Redundant Components

A tradeoff analysis between number of components n and risk of reaching an unsafe state at the root node will be performed to see where there is a good balance between the cost of redundancy, as represented by n, and risk as represented by P_{us}. Referencing equation (10.7), we solve for n as follows:

$$n = \log\left[\frac{Rx_i}{(1 - Rx_i)}\right] \text{ for equal } Rx_i \tag{10.12}$$

Using equation (10.12), we will see whether any values of n satisfy the unsafe state criterion P_t at the root note.

Results of Applying Redundancy

As an example, we chose the Local Network service to make the redundancy analysis. We examined an odd number of redundant components in addition to two components. The reason is to provide for majority voting in resolving faults and failures [MCA96]. In Figure 10.9 we see that as n increases, the threshold is met at increasing operational times for local network services but at an increasingly high cost. An organization could use plots like Figure 10.9 to decide how much cost can be tolerated to achieve a safe operation. An attractive solution is available if the organization is running multiple Ethernets at different locations to meet different application requirements. Users could be connected to these multiple Ethernets and only incur the minor cost of additional links.

FIGURE 10.9   Tradeoff Between Probability of Unsafe State P_{us} for Local Network Services and Number of Redundant Components vs. Operational Time t

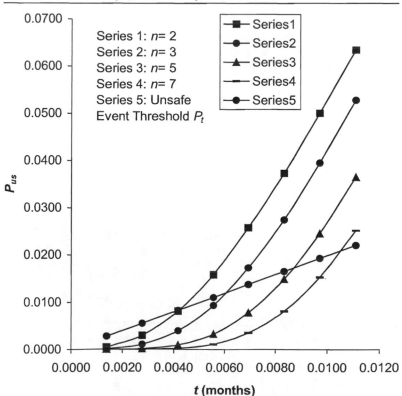

In Figure 10.10, it is now apparent that even with a high degree of redundancy (e.g., $n = 7$), it is impossible to satisfy the requirement for the probability of reaching the unsafe state at the root node. The reason is the relatively high failure rates generated by the local network and network services.

Predicting Failure Rates with Fault Correction

Up to this point, we have not considered the possibility of fault and failure reduction—the original number of faults and failures has remained unchanged throughout the analysis. In [SCH01] we modeled fault correction to be proportional to the number of failures with a random delay between failure occurrence and fault correction. In that paper, we had data from the Space Shuttle that allowed us to model the delay. In this chapter we have only aggregate failure data [OPP], but we will assume the delay t_r is inversely proportional to the probability of x_i number of failures. This is based on the idea that if there is a low probability of failure, the priority of correcting the fault is also low (i.e., fault correction delay is high). Conversely, if the probability of failure is high, the priority of fault correction is also high (i.e., fault correction delay is low). Therefore, the correction delay t_r is computed in equation (10.13).

$$t_r = t\,(1 - Px_i) \qquad (10.13)$$

Once the correction delay is computed, it can be used in the fault correction rate $C(t)$ that is assumed to have the same exponential form as the vulnerability rate $V(t)$ in Table 10.1. Thus,

$$C(t) - a\,e^{b(t - t_r)}, \qquad (10.14)$$

where a and b are the regression coefficients shown for $V(t)$ in Table 10.1.

**FIGURE 10.10   Probability of Reaching Unsafe State at Root
Node P_{us} vs. Operational Time t**

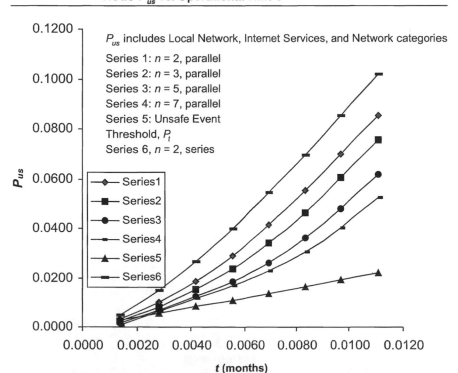

P_{us} includes Local Network, Internet Services, and Network categories

Series 1: $n = 2$, parallel
Series 2: $n = 3$, parallel
Series 3: $n = 5$, parallel
Series 4: $n = 7$, parallel
Series 5: Unsafe Event Threshold, P_t
Series 6, $n = 2$, series

t (months)

Next, having computed the correction delay in equation (10.13), which will be applied to the correction rate $C(t)$ in equation (10.14), the reduction in vulnerability *count* $r(t)$ can be computed as follows:

$$r(t) = R(t) * t = [V(t) - C(t)] * t, \tag{10.15}$$

where $R(t)$ is the *rate* of remaining vulnerabilities (equal to rate of remaining faults and failures). Then for Local Network, Internet, and Network services, compute t_r, $C(t)$, and $r(t)$, and note the *revised* value of vulnerability *count* $rV(t)$ in equation (10.16), which results from the reduction:

$$rV(t) = (V(t) * t) - r(t) \tag{10.16}$$

Prediction Results with Fault Correction

Prediction Based on Probability of Reaching an Unsafe State

Figure 10.11 shows the dramatic change in probability of reaching an unsafe state with just two parallel components, when faults are corrected by using the remaining vulnerability rates $R(t)$ shown in Table 10.1. It is now obvious that that we cannot rely on redundancy alone for systems like these to achieve acceptable risk. Even with a redundancy level of $n = 2$, and no fault correction, it was not possible to achieve safety, but with fault removal and low-cost redundancy, the goal can be easily achieved.

Prediction Based on Fault Correction Model

Figure 10.12 shows that by modeling the vulnerability, fault, and failure correction process, dramatic improvements are predicted for vulnerability, fault, and failure reduction. (For

FIGURE 10.11   Probability of Reaching Unsafe State at Root Node P_{us} vs. Operational Time t

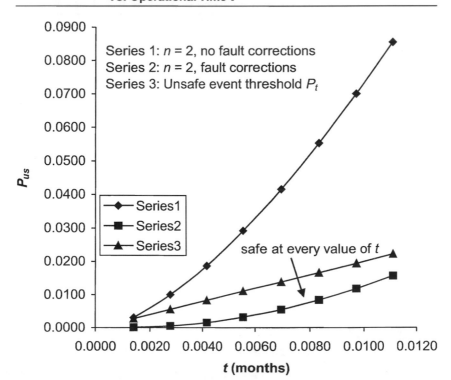

**FIGURE 10.12   Predicted Vulnerability Count (V)t * t and Remaining
Vulnerability Count $rV(t)$ vs. Operational Time t**

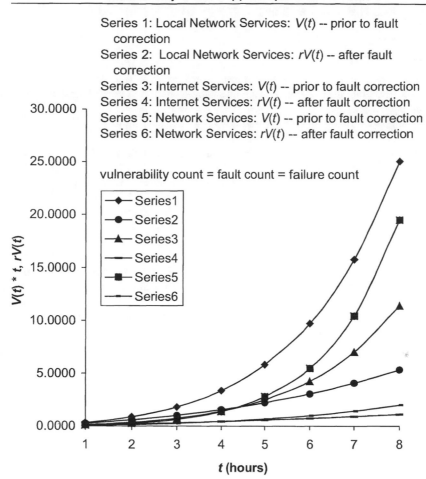

Series 1: Local Network Services: $V(t)$ -- prior to fault
        correction
Series 2: Local Network Services: $rV(t)$ -- after fault
        correction
Series 3: Internet Services: $V(t)$ -- prior to fault correction
Series 4: Internet Services: $rV(t)$ -- after fault correction
Series 5: Network Services: $V(t)$ -- prior to fault correction
Series 6: Network Services: $rV(t)$ -- after fault correction

vulnerability count = fault count = failure count

better clarity of presentation, operational time is shown in hours, equivalent to the months
that were shown previously.) A software development organization could use this model,
with parameters a and b estimated by regression analysis, using its own vulnerability data,
collected over user operating sessions.

Summary

Fault tree analysis is quite appropriate for modeling multiple Internet services for the purpose of determining whether a system is safe and reliable by first identifying probabilities
of failure and failure rates, and then using Boolean functions to compute the path probabilities from the leaves to the root of the fault tree. Then, the path probabilities are applied to
the unreliabilities of the Internet services. Next, these computations culminate in the computation of the probability of reaching an unsafe state at the root node. Last, this probability
is compared with the unsafe state threshold to see whether a safe state has been achieved.

Fault correction combined with a modest amount of component redundancy proved
to be the solution to achieving safety for these applications, based on their collected vulnerability data. Assessments of improvement in vulnerability can be made using two approaches: 1) observe the reduction in vulnerability rate generated by fault correction, then

compute the probability of reaching an unsafe state for various series and parallel network configurations; and 2) use a fault correction model to predict the reduction in vulnerability count produced by correcting faults.

References

[DEH04] Josh Dehlinger and Robyn R. Lutz, "Software Fault Tree Analysis for Product Lines." Eighth IEEE International Symposium on High Assurance Systems Engineering (HASE '04), 2004, pp. 12–21.

[DOW] http://www.downtimecentral.com/Root_Cause_Analysis.htm.

[DUG96] Joanne Betcha Dugan, " Software Systems Analysis Using Fault Trees." *Handbook of Software Reliability Engineering,* edited by Michael R. Lyu. Published by IEEE Computer Society Press and McGraw-Hill, 1996.

[GAN] Archana Ganapathi, "Failure Analysis of Internet Services." Computer Science Division, Department of Electrical Engineering and Computer Sciences, University of California, Berkeley, http://www.cs.berkeley.edu/~archanag/publications/csthesis.pdf.

[IEC06] IEC 61025 Ed. 2.0 (2006): Fault tree analysis (FTA).

[IEE08] IEEE/AIAA P1633™/Draft 14e, *Recommended Practice on Software Reliability,* May 2008.

[KEY00] W. Monroe Keyserling, IOE 539 Notes: Fault Trees and Cut Sets. Industrial and Operations Engineering, The University of Michigan, Ann Arbor, Michigan, http://ioe.engin.umich.edu/ioe539/fta.pdf.

[MCA96] D. F. McAllister and M. A. Vouk, "Fault Tolerant Software Reliability Engineering." *Handbook of Software Reliability Engineering,* Michael R. Lyu, editor. IEEE Computer Society Press and McGraw-Hill, 1996.

[MUS87] John D. Musa, Anthony Iannino, and Kazuhira Okumoto, *Software Reliability: Measurement, Prediction, Application.* McGraw-Hill, 1987.

[NEE06] D. Needham and S. Jones, "A Software Fault Tree Metric." ICSM, pp. 401–410, 22nd IEEE International Conference on Software Maintenance (ICSM '06), 2006.

[NVD] http://nvd.nist.gov/.

[OPP] David Oppenheimer and David A. Patterson, "Studying and Using Failure Data from Large-scale Internet Services." University of California at Berkeley, EECS Computer Science Division, http://roc.cs.berkeley.edu/papers/sigops-failures.pdf.

[ORT04] Frank Ortmeier and Wolfgang Reif, "Safety Optimization: A Combination of Fault Tree Analysis and Optimization Techniques." 2004 International Conference on Dependable Systems and Networks (DSN '04), 2004, p. 651.

[PAI02] G. J. Pai and J. B. Dugan, "Automatic Synthesis of Dynamic Fault Trees from UML System Models." *Software Reliability Engineering,* 2002. ISSRE 2002. Proceedings, 13th International Symposium on Nov. 12–15, 2002, pp. 243–254.

[PFL01] Shari Lawrence Pfleeger, *Software Engineering: Theory and Practice,* 2nd edition. Prentice Hall, 2001.

[SCH01] Norman F. Schneidewind; "Modeling the Fault Correction Process." Proceedings of The Twelfth International Symposium on Software Reliability Engineering, Hong Kong, November 27–30, 2001, pp. 185–190.

[SHO90] M.L. Shooman, *Probabilistic Reliability: An Engineering Approach.* McGraw Hill, New York, NY, 1968; 2nd edition, Krieger, Melbourne, FL, 1990.

[TOW03] Massood Towhidnejad, D.R.Wallace, and A.M. Gallo, Jr., "Validation of Object-Oriented Software Design with Fault Tree Analysis." Software Engineering Workshop, 2003. Proceedings, 28th Annual NASA Goddard, December 3–4, 2003, pp. 209–215.

[VES81] W.E. Vesely, F. F. Goldberg, N. H. Roberts, and D. F. Haasl, *Fault Tree Handbook.* U.S. Nuclear Regulatory Commission, NUREG-0492, January 1981.

[XIA04] Jianwen Xiang, Kokichi Futatsugi, and Yanxiang He, "Fault Tree and Formal Methods in System Safety Analysis." The Fourth International Conference on Computer and Information Technology (CIT '04), 2004, pp. 1108–1115.

Standard for Software Reliability

Objectives

Show how a new standard—the IEEE Recommended Practice on Software Reliability—can be applied to predict the reliability of a software system and assess the risk of not meeting the reliability specification.

What You Will Learn From This Chapter

You will learn reliability basics that can be combined with the standard's reliability process and applied to the reliability assessment of a variety of applications. You will find that because hardware and software have different characteristics, correspondingly, their models must differ.

Subjects

Reliability Basics
Hardware Reliability
Software Reliability Engineering Risk Analysis
Software Reliability Model Parameter Analysis
Overview of Recommended Software Reliability Models

Introduction

Computer systems, whether hardware or software, are subject to failure. Precisely, what is a failure? IEEE 100 has a sophisticated definition of a failure, but for reasons of simplicity, it is: the termination of the ability of an item to perform a required function [IEE08]. A failure may be produced in a system or product when a fault is encountered that results in the non-operation or disability of the required function and a loss of the expected service to the user. This brings us to the question, what is a fault? A fault is a defect in the computer hardware or computer software code that can be the cause of one or more failures [IEE07]. A fault, if encountered, may cause a failure [IEE08]. A fault may also be an accidental condition that causes a functional unit to fail to perform its required function [IEE08].

Software-based systems have become the dominant player in the computer systems world. Since it is imperative that computer systems operate reliably, considering the criticality of software, particularly in safety critical systems, the IEEE and AIAA commissioned the development of a new standard called the Recommended Practice on Software Reliability, IEEE P1633 [IEE07]. This chapter serves the purpose of elaborating on key software reliability process practices in more detail than can be specified in IEEE P1633. While the focus of the IEEE P1633 Standard is software reliability, software and hardware do not operate independently of each other; therefore, both software and hardware are addressed in an integrated fashion. The narrative of the chapter is augmented with illustrative problems and solutions.

The recommended practice [IEE07] is a composite of models and tools and describes the "what and how" of software reliability engineering. It is important for an organization to have a disciplined process if it is to produce highly reliable software. This process uses a life-cycle approach to software reliability that takes into account the risk to reliability due to software errors caused by requirements changes. Subsequently, these errors may propagate through later phases of development and maintenance [SCH01].

Reliability Basics

To set the stage for discussing software and hardware reliability models, the following definitions and concepts are provided. (See Chapter 1 if you need to refresh your knowledge of probability and statistics.)

Component:	any hardware or software entity, such as a module, sub-system, or system
t:	operating time
$P(T \leq t)$:	probability that operating time T of a component is $\leq t$ (also known as cumulative distribution function (CDF))
λ:	failure rate (software or hardware failure rate)
Reliability $R(t)$:	$P(T > t)$: probability of software or hardware surviving for $T > t = 1 - P(T \leq t)$ [LYU96]
Hazard Function:	letting operating time t have the probability density function $p(t)$, the *instantaneous failure rate* at time t is defined as

$$h(t) = p(t)/R(t) \text{ [LYU96]}, \tag{11.1}$$

where $p(t)$ is defined as the probability that a failure will occur in the interval $t, t + 1$.

The hazard function is frequently described in reliability literature, but a reliability metric that is more practical for calculations with empirical data is the failure rate $f(t)$. This is defined as the number of failures $n(t)$ in the interval t divided by t: $f(t) = n(t)/t$. The reason the hazard function may be impractical, when dealing with empirical data, is that the probability density function $p(t)$ may not be known because the distribution of the failure data is unknown.

Comparing Hardware and Software

A comparison of hardware and software attributes that pertain to reliability is shown in Table 11.1.

You could infer that based on Table 11.1, software reliability is difficult to predict. However, by continually refining predictions, using more failure data, and providing confidence intervals for predictions, it is practical to provide bounds on reliability [KEL97]. In addition, if the application does not require continuity of execution (e.g., personal computer), the software can be rejuvenated and reliability improved by restarting. According to Professor Trevidi of Duke University, "Software rejuvenation is a proactive fault management technique aimed at cleaning up the system internal state to prevent the occurrence of more severe crash failures in the future. It involves occasionally terminating an application or a system, cleaning its internal state and restarting it" [LI02].

TABLE 11.1   Hardware vs. Software

Hardware	Software
Subject to wear.	Interestingly, subject to "wear" under stressful or long-term operating conditions (e.g., buffer overflow). This also known as software aging [LI02]
Vibration, shock, and temperature affect reliability.	Does not apply.
Constant failure rate assumed in operational phase.	Variable failure rate assumed monotonically decreasing during testing and operation. However, during operation, some customers may be afraid to makes changes, so failure rate would be constant.
Accurate reliability predictions easy to make because components infrequently change.	Accurate reliability predictions are more difficult to make because of variety and frequency of changes.
Standard, mass-produced components.	Usually, one-of-a-kind components.
Reliability governed by laws of physics: minimum variability in reliability of components.	No physical laws. Significant variability in component reliability, both at release time and over operational time.
Highly automated production process using robots.	No robots! Development and quality processes are very important in developing high-reliability software, for example, CMMI and Six Sigma.
Reliability can be stated as a set of "nines."	Set of "nines" difficult to compute. Time to next failure and failure count more appropriate.

Hardware Reliability

The exponential failure distribution with constant failure rate is particularly applicable to hardware reliability because it is assumed that the failure rate remains constant after the initial burn-in period and before wearout occurs. More precisely, the exponential distribution is frequently used for probabilistic modeling of electronic components. However, reliability engineers widely use other classical time-to-failure distributions, such as the following: the Weibull distribution is a general-purpose distribution used to model time-to-failure phenomena (its hazard rate follows a general power-law); the Lognormal distribution is used in hardware reliability to model stress-strength fatigue phenomena; and the Extreme-value distribution is used in reliability models for environmental phenomena [WAS2003] .

Two of the most important distributions—exponential and Weibull—are elaborated below.

$$\textit{Exponential Failure Distribution: } \lambda e^{-\lambda t} \qquad (11.2)$$

This distribution has a constant failure rate λ. The exponential distribution is the only failure distribution that has a constant failure rate λ and a constant hazard function $h(t)$ in the *operations phase* of the life cycle. This failure rate is $\overline{t} = 1/\overline{t}$, where $\overline{t}$ is the mean time to failure (MTTF).

Thus reliability is

$$R(t) = e^{-\lambda t}, \tag{11.3}$$

obtained by integrating equation (11.2) from 0 to t, to obtain $P(T \leq t)$, and applying the definition of reliability $R(t) = 1 - P(T \leq t)$. Thus, computing λ from historical failure and time data, you can predict the reliability of your hardware, during the operational phase, for any value of operating time t.

Then using equations (11.1), (11.2), and (11.3), the hazard function for exponentially distributed failures is:

$$h(t) = p(t)/R(t) = \lambda e^{-\lambda t}/e^{-\lambda t} = \lambda \tag{11.4}$$

Now applying the definition of MTTF for the exponential distribution to equation (11.3), equation (11.5) is produced:

$$R(t) = e^{-(t/\overline{t})} \tag{11.5}$$

Equation (11.5) may be more convenient to use than equation (11.3) because you may have available the MTTF for your hardware based on lab tests.

To solve for t for a given value of $R(t)$, equation (11.5) is solved for t in equation (11.6):

$$t = -\ln (R(t))\overline{t} \tag{11.6}$$

Equation (11.6) is useful if you want to predict the time that your hardware will operate with no failures for a specified reliability $R(t)$.

Problem 1

Specifications

1. Hardware in a computer system should have an expected (**mean**) life $\overline{t} > \mathbf{100000}$ (MTTF) hours at a reliability of $R(t) = .85$. What is the minimum number of hours t the computer system would have to survive to meet these specifications?
2. If the hardware should have a .85 probability of surviving (i.e., reliability) for $t > 50000$ hours, what is the MTTF required to meet these specifications?

Solution

1. Use equation (11.5) to compute t:

    t = –ln (.85)(100000) = –(–.1625)(100000) = **16,250** hours

2. Solve equation (11.6) for $\overline{t}$:

    $\overline{t} = t/[-\ln (R(t)] = 50000/[-\ln (.85)] = \mathbf{307{,}656}$ hours

Software Reliability Engineering Risk Analysis

Software reliability engineering (SRE) is an established discipline that can help organizations improve the reliability of their products and processes. The IEEE/AIAA defines SRE as "the application of statistical techniques to data collected during system development and operation to specify, predict, estimate, and assess the reliability of software-based systems." The IEEE/AIAA recommended practice is a composite of models and tools and describes the "what and how" of software reliability engineering [IEE07]. It is important for

FIGURE 11.1   Software Reliability Engineering Risk Analysis

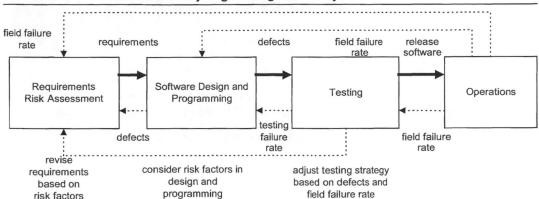

an organization to have a disciplined process if it is to produce software that is reliable. The process includes a life-cycle approach to SRE that takes into account the risk to reliability due to requirements changes. A requirements change may induce ambiguity and uncertainty in the development process that cause errors in implementing the changes. These errors may propagate through later phases of development and maintenance. These errors may result in significant risks associated with implementing the requirements. For example, reliability risk (i.e., risk of faults and failures induced by changes in requirements) may be incurred by deficiencies in the process (e.g., lack of precision in requirements). Figure 11.1 shows the overall SRE closed-loop holistic process.

In the figure, risk factors are metrics that indicate the degree of risk in introducing a new requirement or making a requirements change. For example, in the NASA Space Shuttle, program size and complexity, number of conflicting requirements, and memory requirements have been shown to be significantly related to reliability (i.e., increases in these risk factors are associated with decreases in reliability) [SCH07]. Organizations should conduct studies to determine what factors are contributing to reliability degradation. As shown in Figure 11.1, organizations could use feedback from operations, testing, design, and programming to determine which risk factors are associated with reliability, and revise requirements, if necessary. For example, if requirements risk assessment finds through risk-factor analysis that defects are occurring because of excessive program size, design and programming would receive revised requirements to modularize the software.

A reliability risk assessment should be based on the risk to reliability due to software defects or errors caused by requirements and requirements changes. The method to ascertain risk based on the number of requirements and the impact of changes to requirements is inexact, but nevertheless, it is necessary for early requirements assessments of large-scale systems.

Criteria for Safety

In safety critical systems, in particular, safety criteria are used, in conjunction with risk factors, to assess whether a system is safe to operate. Two criteria are used. One is based on predicted remaining failures in relation to a threshold and the second is based on predicted time to next failure in relation to mission duration [SCH97]. These criteria are computed as follows:

Compute predicted *remaining failures* $r(t_t) < r_c$, where r_c is a specified remaining failures critical value, and compute predicted *time to next failure* $T_F(t_t) > t_m$, where t_m is mission duration. Once $r(t_t)$ has been predicted, the risk criterion metric for *remaining failures* at total test time t_t is computed in equation (11.7):

$$\text{RCM}\, r(t_t) = \frac{r(t_t) - r_c}{r_c} = \frac{r(t_t)}{r_c} - 1 \tag{11.7}$$

In order to illustrate the remaining failure risk criterion in relation to the predicted maximum number of failures in the software $F(\infty)$, the following parameter is needed:

$p(t)$:   Fraction of remaining failures predicted at time t_t in equation (11.8):

$$p(t_t) = \frac{r(t_t)}{F(\infty)} \tag{11.8}$$

The risk criterion metric for *time to next failure* at total test time t_t is computed in equation (11.9) based on the predicted time to next failure in equation (11.10) [SCH07]:

$$\text{RCM}\, T_F(t_t) = \frac{t_m - T_F(t_t)}{t_m} = 1 - \frac{T_F(t_t)}{t_m} \tag{11.9}$$

$$T_F(t_t) = -\frac{1}{\beta} \log\left[1 - ((F(t_t) + X_{s-1})) \left(\frac{\beta}{\alpha}\right) \right] + (s-1) \tag{11.10}$$

$$for\ (F(t_t) + X_{s-1})\left(\frac{\beta}{\alpha}\right) < 1,$$

where β and α are parameters estimated from the failure data. β is the rate of change of the failure rate and α is the initial failure rate. The parameter s is the starting failure interval count that produces the most accurate reliability predictions, and X_{s-1} is the observed failure count in the range of the test data from $s - 1$ to t_t. Finally, $F(t_t)$ refers to the specified number of failures—usually one—that is used in the prediction.

In addition to the two safety criteria that have been described, safety also involves fault severity mitigation and containment. The following are some examples [KEE02]:

- Fault tree analysis
- Failure mode effects analysis
- Requirements for what the system "shall not do" as well as what it "shall do"
- Fault insertion to see whether a system can detect and recover from the fault
- Incorporating an independent safety monitor that can, for example, check on computations to see whether they fall within the allowable range
- Firewalls to isolate critical parts of the software
- Voting schemes to validate outputs

Problem 2

Part 1: Remaining Failures Risk

Using one of the models in [IEE08] recommended for initial use and either the software reliability tool SMERFS or CASRE, compute equations (11.7) and (11.8) to produce Figures 11.2 and 11.3 for the NASA Space Shuttle software release OI6. The failure counts for each value of test time t_t for OI6 is shown in Table 11.2. The data represent the failure counts for each interval, starting with the first time interval and ending with the last. Once

FIGURE 11.2   Predicted Remaining Failures $r(t_t)$ and Risk Criterion Metric RCM $r(t_t)$ vs. Test Time t_t for NASA Space Shuttle Release OI6

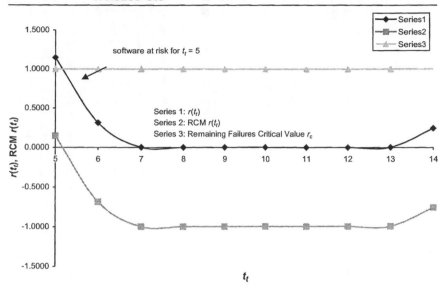

you have inputted a text file of these counts, one at a time, the software reliability tools will compute $r(t_t)$ and $F(\infty)$ for each of the ten cases. The tools can be downloaded at www. slingcode.com/smerfs/ for SMERFS and at www.openchannelfoundation.org/projects/ CASRE_3.0 for CASRE.

FIGURE 11.3   Cost of Testing t_t vs. Software Quality $p(t_t)$ for NASA Space Shuttle Release OI6

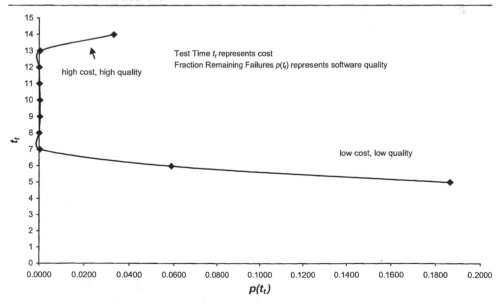

TABLE 11.2   Failure Counts for NASA Space Shuttle Software Release OI6

t_t	5	6	7	8	9	10	11	12	13	14
	0	0	0	0	0	0	0	0	0	0
	2	2	2	2	2	2	2	2	2	2
	1	1	1	1	1	1	1	1	1	1
	2	2	2	2	2	2	2	2	2	2
	0	0	0	0	0	0	0	0	0	0
		0	0	0	0	0	0	0	0	0
			0	0	0	0	0	0	0	0
				0	0	0	0	0	0	0
					0	0	0	0	0	0
						0	0	0	0	0
							0	0	0	0
								0	0	0
									1	1
										1

Part 2: Time to Next Failure Risk

In this part, a specific recommended model in [IEE08] is used [SCH97] in order to illustrate the use of this model's predicted time to next failure in equation (11.10) and the application of the prediction to evaluating the risk of not satisfying the mission duration requirement, as formulated in equation (11.9). Other recommended models in the standard could be used to perform the analysis.

After using one of the tools to estimate the parameters in equation (11.10), predict $T_F(t_t)$ for one more failure and plot it and the risk criterion metric, from equation (11.10), in Figure 11.4, as a function of the test time t_t in Table 11.2.

FIGURE 11.4   Predicted Time to Next Failure $T_F(t_t)$ and Risk Criterion Metric RCM $T_F(t_t)$ vs. Test Time t_t

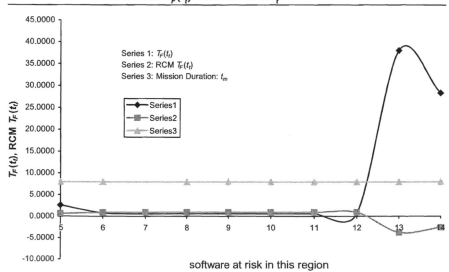

Solution to Part 1

Figure 11.2 delineates the test time = 5 where the risk of exceeding the critical value of remaining failures is unacceptable. Therefore, a test time of at least 6 is required. Figure 11.3 shows how the software reliability analyst can do a tradeoff of the cost of testing versus the quality of software produced by testing [KEL97]. The reason for the discontinuity is that for several values of test time, fraction of remaining failures is close to zero. Since test time is usually directly related to cost, the figure indicates that a very high cost would be incurred for attempting to achieve almost fault-free software. Therefore, tolerating a fraction remaining failures of about .0600 would be practical.

Solution to Part 2

Switching now to the evaluation of risk with respect to time to next failure, Figure 11.4 demonstrates that unless the test time is greater than 12, the time to failure will not exceed the mission duration. The engineer using such a plot would use a mission duration appropriate for the software being tested. The concept of Figure 11.4 is that the software should be tested sufficiently long such that the risk criterion metric goes negative.

Prediction Error Analysis

Figures 11.2, 11.3, 11.4, and 11.5 involve predictions of remaining failures or time to next failure. Therefore, it is appropriate to document predictions errors, as provided by the SMERFS software reliability tool [FAR] in Table 11.3. Mean square error (MSE) and Chi-Square goodness of fit are used. In addition, since test time presents a cost, you want to minimize the product of test time and MSE. As Table 11.3 shows, to achieve minimal (Test Time * MSE) for remaining failures, a significant amount of failure data are required that are accompanied by increasing test time (see Table 11.2). In contrast, time to failure predictions become less accurate with increasing test time, despite the fact that more failure data have been collected. The reason is that it becomes increasingly difficult to predict the future accurately as the future becomes more distant from the beginning of the test. This factor explains why time to next failure predictions are less accurate than remaining failure predictions.

Since the Chi-Square statistic relies on the assumption that the data can be approximated by a multinomial distribution [LYU, page 774], which is not the case for the data in Table 11.2, you would have less confidence in it than in MSE, which does not assume

TABLE 11.3   Prediction Errors for Space Shuttle Software Release OI6

Test Time (30-day intervals)	Mean Square Error (MSE) for Remaining Failures	Test Time * MSE	Mean Square Error (MSE) for Time to Next Failure	Test Time * MSE	Chi-Square for Remaining Failures	Chi-Square for Time to Next Failure
5	.152	.7600	.581	2.9050	2.0154	2.0154
6	.188	1.1280	1.369	8.2140	2.9115	5.4833
7	.113	.7910	12.26	8.5820	3.0998	7.6117
8	.091	.7280	21.64	170.08	3.1090	7.8573
9	.113	1.0170	12.26	110.34	3.0998	7.6117
10	.113	1.1130	12.26	122.60	3.0998	7.6117
11	.101	1.1110	16.62	182.82	3.1062	7.7606
12	.091	1.0920	21.64	259.68	3.1090	7.8573
13	**.046**	**.5980**	19.85	258.05	2.9650	17.689
14	.140	1.0900	1.618	22.6520	3.1074	11.002

a particular distribution of the data. Nevertheless, it is a good idea to use more than one method when computing prediction error statistics, so that one method can be a check on the other.

A comment about the long test times in Table 11.3 is in order. These times are long because the Shuttle is continuously tested by contractor personnel at their desks, in the Shuttle mockup simulator, in the Shuttle mission simulator for training astronauts, and during flight [KEL97].

Lastly, the reliability engineer could compute (Test Time * MSE) incrementally, as test time is increased, to serve as a guide to stop testing.

Software Reliability Model Parameter Analysis

It is possible to assess risk after the parameters α and β have been estimated by a tool, such as SMERFS and CASRE [IEE08], but *before* predictions are made. An example is provided in Figure 11.5, where remaining failures and its risk criterion are plotted against the parameter ratio β/α [SCH07]. The reason for this result is that a high value of β means that the failure rate decreases rapidly, coupled with a low value of α, which leads to high reliability. High reliability in turn means low risk of unsafe software. Furthermore, increasing values of PR are associated with increasing values of test time, thus decreasing risk. Thus, even *before* predictions are made, it is possible to know how much test time is required to yield predictions that the software is safe to deploy. In Figure 11.2, this time is 6. A cautionary note is that the foregoing analysis is an a priori assessment of likely risk results and does not mean, necessarily, that high values of β/α will lead to low risk.

FIGURE 11.5   Risk Criterion Metric: RCM $r(t_i)$ and Remaining Failures $r(t_i)$ vs. Parameter Ratio PR (β/α) for NASA Space Shuttle Release OI6

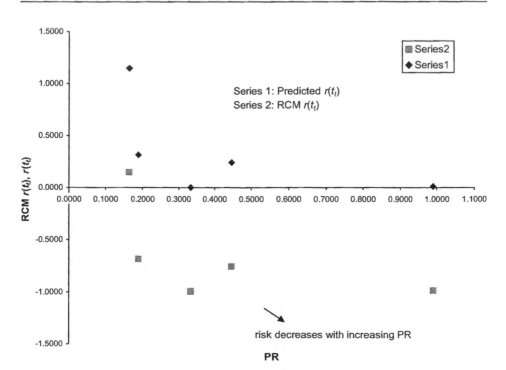

Problem 3

After obtaining estimates of β and α using one of the reliability tools, for each value of test time in Table 11.2, plot Figure 11.5 to show that risk decreases with increases in the parameter ratio.

Figure 11.5 is the solution.

Overview of Recommended Software Reliability Models

In [IEEE07] it is stated that there are "initial models" recommended for using on an application, but if these models do not satisfy the organization's need, other models that are described in the document could be used. Since this tutorial has included several practice problems, based in part on models, an overview is presented of two of the initially recommended models: Musa-Okumoto and Schneidewind. The third model—Generalized Exponential—involves a great amount of detail that cannot be presented here. For readers interested in more detail on these models or to learn about the other models, the recommended practice can be consulted.

Musa-Okumoto Logarithmic Poisson Execution Time Model

Objectives

The logarithmic Poisson model is applicable when the testing is done according to an operational profile that has variations in frequency of application functions and when early fault corrections have a greater effect on the failure rate than later ones. Thus, the failure rate has a decreasing slope. The operational profile is a set of functions and their probabilities of use [MUS04].

Assumptions

The assumptions for this model are:

* The software is operated in a similar manner as the anticipated operational usage.
* Failures are independent of one another.
* The failure rate decreases exponentially with execution time because faults are discovered and removed from the code.

Structure

From the model assumptions:

$\lambda(t)$ = failure rate after t amount of execution time has been expended $\lambda_0 e^{-\theta\mu(t)}$

The parameter λ_0 is the initial failure rate parameter and θ is the failure rate decay parameter with $\theta > 0$.

Using a re-parameterization of $\beta_0 = \theta^{-1}$ and $\beta_1 = \lambda_0\theta$, then the estimates of β_0 and β_1 are made, according to equations (11.11) and (11.12), respectively:

$$\hat{\beta}_0 = \frac{n}{\ln(1+\hat{\beta}_1)t_n} \tag{11.11}$$

$$\frac{1}{\hat{\beta}_1}\sum_{i=1}^{n}\frac{1}{1+\hat{\beta}_1 t_i} = \frac{nt_n}{(1+\hat{\beta}_1 t_i)\ln(1+\hat{\beta}_1 t_i)} \tag{11.12}$$

Here, t_n is the cumulative CPU time from the start of the program to the current time. During this period, n failures have been observed. Once estimates are made for β_0 and β_1, the estimates for θ and λ_0 are made in equations (11.13) and (11.14):

$$\hat{\theta} = \frac{1}{n}\ln\left(1+\hat{\beta}_1 t_n\right) \tag{11.13}$$

$$\hat{\lambda}_0 = \hat{\beta}_0\hat{\beta}_1 \tag{11.14}$$

Limitation

- The failure rate may rise as modifications are made to the software violating the assumption of decreasing failure rate.

Data Requirements

The required data are either:

- The time between failures, represented by X_i's

- The time of the failure n^{th} occurrences, given by $t_n = \sum_{i=1}^{n} X_i$

Applications

The major applications are described below. These are separate but related applications that, in total, comprise an integrated reliability program.

Prediction: Predicting future failure times and fault corrections.

Control: Comparing prediction results with pre-defined goals and flagging software that fails to meet goals.

Assessment: Determining what action to take for software that fails to meet goals (e.g., intensify inspection, intensify testing, redesign software, and revise process). The formulation of test strategies is also a part of assessment. It involves the determination of priority, duration and completion date of testing, and allocation of personnel and computer resources to testing.

Reliability Predictions

In [MUS87] it is shown that from the previous assumptions and the fact that the derivative of the mean value function of failure count is the failure rate function, equation (11.15) is obtained:

$\hat{\mu}(\tau) =$ mean number of failures experienced by the time τ has elapsed

$$= \frac{1}{\hat{\theta}}\ln\left(\hat{\lambda}_0\hat{\theta}\tau + 1\right) \tag{11.15}$$

Implementation and Application Status

The model has been implemented by the Naval Surface Warfare Center, Dahlgren, VA as part of SMERFS and in CASRE.

Schneidewind Model [SCH97]

Objectives

The objectives of this model are to predict the following software reliability metrics:

$F(t_1, t_2)$ Predicted failure count in the range $[t_1, t_2]$
$F(\infty)$ Predicted failure count in the range $[1, \infty]$; maximum failures over the life of the software
$F(t)$ Predicted failure count in the range $[1, t]$
$p(t)$ Fraction of remaining failures predicted at time t
$Q(t)$ Operational quality predicted at time t; the complement of $p(t)$; the degree to which software is free of remaining faults (failures)
$r(t_t)$ Remaining failures predicted at test time t_t
t_t Test time predicted for given $r(t_t)$
$T_F(t_t)$ Time to next failure predicted at test time t_t

Parameters Used in the Predictions

α Initial failure rate
β Rate of change of failure rate
r_c Critical value of remaining failures used in computing the Risk Criterion Metric for remaining failures: (RCM) $r(t_t)$
t_m Mission duration (end time-start time) used in computing the Risk Criterion Metric for time to next failure: RCM $T_F(t_t)$

The philosophy of this model is that as testing proceeds with time, the failure detection process changes. Furthermore, recent failure counts are usually more useful than earlier counts in predicting the future. Three approaches can be employed in utilizing the failure count data (i.e., number of failures detected per unit of time). Supposing there are t intervals of testing and f_i failures were detected in the ith interval, one of the following is done:

- Use all of the failures for the t intervals
- Ignore the failure counts completely from the first $s - 1$ time intervals ($1 \le s \le t$) and only use the data from intervals s through t.
- Use the cumulative failure count from intervals 1 through $s - 1$: $F_{s-1} = \sum_{i=1}^{s-1} f_i$

The first approach should be used when it is determined that the failure counts from all of the intervals are useful in predicting future counts. This would be the case with new software, where little is known about its failure count distribution. The second approach should be used when it is determined that a significant change in the failure detection process has occurred and thus only the last $t - s + 1$ intervals are useful in future failure forecasts. The last approach is an intermediate one between the other two. Here, the combined failure counts from the first $s - 1$ intervals and the individual counts from the remaining intervals are representative of the failure and detection behavior for future predictions. This approach is used when the first $s - 1$ interval failure counts are not as significant as in the first approach, but are sufficiently important not to be discarded, as in the second approach.

Assumptions

- The number of failures detected in one interval is independent of the failure count in another. Note: In practice, this assumption has not proved to be a factor in obtaining prediction accuracy.
- Only new failures are counted because it is reasonable to assume that the faults that caused old failures have been removed.
- The fault correction rate is proportional to the number of faults to be corrected.
- The software is tested in a manner similar to the anticipated operational usage.
- The mean number of detected failures decreases from one interval to the next.

- The mean number of detected failures is proportional to the number of failures within the program at the time of test. The failure detection process is assumed to be a non-homogeneous Poisson process with an exponentially decreasing failure detection rate [SCH07]. The rate is of the form $f(t) = \alpha e^{-\beta(t-s+1)}$ for the tth interval where $\alpha > 0$ and $\beta > 0$ are the parameters of the model.

Structure

The method of maximum likelihood (MLE) is used to estimate parameters. This method is based on the concept of maximizing the probability that the true values of the parameters are observed in the failure data [MUS04]. Two parameters are used in the model that were previously defined: α and β. In these estimates, t is the last observed failure count interval; s is the starting interval for using observed failure data in parameter estimation; X_k is the number of observed failures in interval k; X_{s-1} is the number of failures observed from 1 through $s - 1$ intervals; $X_{s,t}$ is the number of observed failures from interval s through t; and $X_t = X_{s-1} + X_{s,t}$. The likelihood function (based on MLE) is then developed as:

$$
\begin{aligned}
\log L = X_t &\left[\log X_t - 1 - \log\left(1 - e^{\beta t}\right)\right] \\
&+ X_{s-1}\left[\log\left(1 - e^{-\beta(s-1)}\right)\right] \\
&+ X_{s,t}\left[\log\left(1 - e^{-\beta}\right)\right] - \beta \sum_{k=0}^{t-s}(s + k - 1)X_{s+k}
\end{aligned}
\tag{11.16}
$$

Equation (11.16) is used to derive the equations for estimating α and β for each of the three approaches described earlier. The parameter estimates can be obtained by using the SMERFS or CASRE tools.

Approach 1

Use all of the failure counts from interval 1 through t (i.e., $s - 1$). Equations (11.17) and (11.18) are used to estimate β and α, respectively.

$$
\frac{1}{e^{\beta} - 1} - \frac{t}{e^{\beta t} - 1} = \sum_{k=0}^{t-1} k \frac{X_{k+1}}{X_t}
\tag{11.17}
$$

$$
\alpha = \frac{\beta X_t}{1 - e^{-\beta t}}
\tag{11.18}
$$

Approach 2

Use failure counts only in intervals s through t (i.e., $1 \leq s \leq t$). Equations (11.19) and (11.20) are used to estimate β and α, respectively. (Note that approach 2 is equivalent to approach 1 for $s = 1$.)

$$
\frac{1}{e^{\beta} - 1} - \frac{t - s + 1}{e^{\beta(t-s+1)} - 1} = \sum_{k=0}^{t-s} k \frac{X_{k+s}}{X_{s,t}}
\tag{11.19}
$$

$$
\alpha = \frac{\beta X_{s,t}}{1 - e^{-\beta(t-s+1)}}
\tag{11.20}
$$

Approach 3

Use cumulative failure counts in intervals 1 through $s - 1$ and individual failure counts in intervals s through t (i.e., $2 \leq s \leq t$). This approach is intermediate to approach 1, which uses all of the data, and approach 2, which discards "old" data. Equations (11.21) and (11.22) are used to estimate β and α, respectively. (Note that approach 3 is equivalent to approach 1 for $s = 2$.)

$$\frac{(s-1)X_{s-1}}{e^{\beta(s-1)} - 1} + \frac{X_{s,t}}{e^{\beta} - 1} - \frac{tX_t}{e^{\beta m} - 1} = \sum_{k=0}^{t-s}(s+k-1)X_{s+k} \tag{11.21}$$

$$\alpha = \frac{\beta X_t}{1 - e^{-\beta t}} \tag{11.22}$$

Limitations

- Model does not account for the possibility that failures in different intervals may be related.
- Model does not account for repetition of failures.
- Model does not account for the possibility that failures can increase over time as the result of software modifications.

These limitations should be ameliorated by configuring the software into versions that, starting with the second version, the next version represents the previous version plus modifications introduced by the next version. Each version represents a different module for reliability prediction purposes. The model is used to predict reliability for each module. Then, the software system reliability is predicted by considering the N modules to be connected in series (i.e., worst-case situation) and computing the MTTF for N modules in series [SCH92].

Data Requirements

The only data requirements are the number of failures, f_i, $i = 1, \ldots, t$, per testing interval. A reliability database should be created for several reasons: Input data sets will be rerun, if necessary, to produce multiple predictions rather than relying on a single prediction; reliability predictions and assessments could be made for various projects; and predicted reliability could be compared with actual reliability for these projects. This database will allow the model user to perform several useful analyses: to see how well the model is performing; to compare reliability across projects to see whether there are development factors that contribute to reliability; and to see whether reliability is improving over time for a given project or across projects.

Applications

The major model applications are described below. These are separate but related uses of the model that, in total, comprise an integrated reliability program.

- Prediction: Predicting future reliability metrics such as remaining failures and time to next failure.
- Control: Comparing prediction results with pre-defined reliability goals and flagging software that fails to meet those goals.
- Assessment: Determining what action to take for software that fails to meet goals (e.g., intensify inspection, intensify testing, redesign software, and revise process).

The formulation of test strategies is also part of assessment. Test strategy formulation involves the determination of priority, duration and completion date of testing, allocation of personnel, and allocation of computer resources to testing.
* Risk Analysis: Computing risk criterion metrics for remaining failures and time to next failure.

Predict *test time* required to achieve a specified *number of remaining failures* at t_r, $r(t_r)$ in equation (11.23):

$$t_r = [\log[\alpha/(\beta[r(t_r)])]]/\beta \qquad (11.23)$$

Implementation and Application Status

The model has been implemented in FORTRAN and C++ by the Naval Surface Warfare Center, Dahlgren, Virginia, as part of the Statistical Modeling and Estimation of Reliability Functions for Software (SMERFS). In addition, it has been implemented in CASRE. It can be run on IBM PCs under all Windows operating systems.

Known applications of this model are:

* IBM, Houston, Texas: Reliability prediction and assessment of the on-board NASA Space Shuttle software
* Naval Surface Warfare Center, Dahlgren, Virginia: Research in reliability prediction and analysis of the TRIDENT I and II Fire Control Software
* Marine Corps Tactical Systems Support Activity, Camp Pendleton, California: Development of distributed system reliability models
* NASA JPL, Pasadena, California: Experiments with multi-model software reliability approach
* NASA Goddard Space Flight Center, Greenbelt, Maryland: Development of fault correction prediction models
* Hughes Aircraft Co., Fullerton, California: Integrated, multi-model approach to reliability prediction

Summary

The purpose of this chapter has been twofold: 1) introduce the reader to the IEEE/AIAA Recommended Practice on Software Reliability, published in July, 2008 and 2) assist the engineer in understanding and applying the principles of hardware and software reliability, based on the principles in the standard. Due to the prevalence of software-based systems, the focus has been on learning how to produce high-reliability software. However, since hardware faults and failures can cause the highest-quality software to fail to meet user expectations, considerable coverage of hardware reliability was provided. Practice problems with solutions were included to provide the reader with real-world applications of the principles that were discussed.

References

[FAR] W. H. Farr and O. D. Smith, *Statistical Modeling and Estimation of Reliability Functions for Software (SMERFS) Users Guide.* NAVSWC TR-84–373, Revision 2, Naval Surface Warfare Center, Dahlgren, Virginia.
[IEE07] IEEE/AIAA P1633™/Draft 14, *Recommended Practice on Software Reliability.* 2007.
[IEE08] IEEE 100, *The Authorative Dictionary of IEEE Standard Terms.*

[KEE02] Samuel Keene and Gavin Watt, "Developing Trustworthy Software for Safety Critical Systems." *Reliability Review,* Vol. 22, Number 4, December 2002, pp. 14–22.

[KEL97] Ted Keller and Norman F. Schneidewind, "A Successful Application of Software Reliability Engineering for the NASA Space Shuttle." Software Reliability Engineering Case Studies, International Symposium on Software Reliability Engineering, Albuquerque, New Mexico, November 4, 1997, pp. 71–82.

[LI02] Lei Li, Kalyanaraman Vaidyanathan, and Kishor S. Trivedi, "An Approach for Estimation of Software Aging in a Web Server." International Symposium on Empirical Software Engineering (ISESE'02), 2002, p. 91.

[LYU96] Michael R. Lyu, editor, *Handbook of Software Reliability Engineering.* IEEE Computer Society Press and McGraw-Hill, 1996.

[MUS87] John D. Musa, Anthony Iannino, and Kazuhira Okumoto, *Software Reliability: Measurement, Prediction, Application.* McGraw-Hill, 1987.

[MUS04] John D. Musa, *Software Reliability Engineering: More Reliable Software, Faster and Cheaper*, 2nd edition. Authorhouse, 2004.

[SCH01] Norman F. Schneidewind, "Reliability and Maintainability of Requirements Changes." Proceedings of the International Conference on Software Maintenance, Florence, Italy, November 7–9, 2001, pp. 127–136.

[SCH07] Norman F. Schneidewind, "Risk-Driven Software Testing And Reliability." *International Journal of Reliability, Quality and Safety Engineering,* Vol. 14, No. 2 (2007). pp. 99–132.

[SCH92] N. F. Schneidewind and T. M. Keller, "Applying Reliability Models to the Space Shuttle." *IEEE Software,* July 1992, pp. 28–33.

[SCH97] Norman F. Schneidewind, "Reliability Modeling for Safety Critical Software." *IEEE Transactions on Reliability,* Vol. 46, No.1, March 1997, pp. 88–98.

[WAS2003] Gary S. Wasserman, *Reliability Verification, Testing, and Analysis in Engineering Design.* Taylor & Francis, 2003.

12

Simulation and Analytical Models: A Comparison

Objectives

Learn how simulation and analytical models can be used to evaluate the performance of queuing systems, such as software fault correction systems, by using various metrics related to software faults detection and correction. The NASA Space Shuttle fault correction process is used as the environment for illustrating modeling concepts. Refer to Chapter 5 to refresh your knowledge of queuing systems.

What You Will Learn From This Chapter

You will learn the following: 1) queuing models for software development, 2) analytical models for software fault detection and correction, 3) simulation models for software fault detection and correction, 4) strengths and weaknesses of the models, 5) interpretation of model results, and 6) C++ program for simulation modeling a fault correction system (see the program in the Appendix to this chapter). The source language must be compiled and executed with a C++ compiler.

Subjects

Queuing Models for Software Development
Model Results

Introduction

Queueing models have been applied to the software fault detection and correction process [MUS87, HUA08]. In addition, analysis of the time spent by faults in a software testing system has led naturally to an increased interest in the dynamics of queuing networks, which are used to model such systems. Analytical as well as simulation models have been used to study the behavior of queues and fault correction stations in testing systems [GOV99]. Thus, you can employ both analytical and simulation models in relieving fault bottlenecks in fault correction systems. Simulation is the process of designing a model of a real system and conducting experiments to understand its behavior. The process involves evaluating strategies for operating the system. Simulation is used when, even if analytical results are available, a trace of the history of the process under study is desired [SHA75]. For example, analytical model results provide average values of the times that faults wait to be corrected, but you may be interested in the predicted wait time of each fault that can be obtained by simulation.

We all know about people queuing up to check out at a grocery store. Perhaps less obvious is the concept of faults that have been detected during software testing and queuing up to be corrected. Testing is an important software development function. Interestingly, testing is essentially a queuing process. When a fault is in a queue, it attempts to move to a fault correction station (see Figure 12.1). If, at that moment, the station is full, the fault is forced to reside in the queue until a place becomes available in a station. The queue remains blocked during this period of time [AKY88]. Therefore, it may not be possible to test, detect faults, and correct faults immediately because there could be a queue of faults that are being corrected; therefore, the faults must be queued and wait their turn for service. Thus, queuing models are employed to estimate quantities such as wait time, service time, and number of faults waiting for service.

There are two ways that queues can be analyzed. One way is by analytical models that provide steady-state or mean-value solutions. These models also assume a single queue feeding multiple fault correction stations, as shown in Figure 12.1, because with a single queue, the faults can be assigned to correction stations on the basis of not busy status, fault priority, and fault severity. This is akin to banks in which a single queue feeds multiple teller stations. Another approach is simulation that is similar to discrete-event simulation [GOK98], which is used to analyze the reliability of component-based software. This approach relies on random generation of faults in components, using a procedure that computes the inter-failure arrival time of faults into queues [XIA07]. Simulation has the advantage of providing finer grain solutions of, for example, predicting the number of faults

FIGURE 12.1   Analytical Model Queuing Process

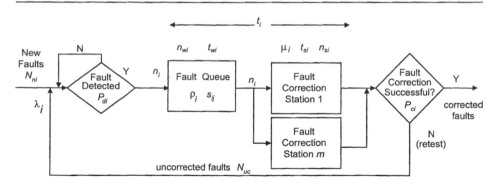

n_i : number of faults in queue when fault i occurs

λ_i : occurrence rate for fault i

ρ_i : utilization of queue when fault i occurs

N_{ni} : *potential* number of new faults when fault i occurs

N_{ui} : number of uncorrected faults from when fault i occurs

n_i : expected number of faults in queue when fault i occurs

n_{si} : number of faults being corrected when fault i occurs

n_{wi} : number of faults waiting for correction when fault i occurs

P_{di} : probability of detecting fault i

t_i : total time fault i spends in fault correction system

t_{si} : correction time for fault i

t_{wi} : time fault spends waiting for correction

μ_i : correction rate of fault i

s_{ij} : fault i severity level j

P_{ci} : probability of correcting fault i

in individual fault correction stations. In this approach, as shown in Figure 12.2, multiple queues feed multiple stations. This configuration is used because the NASA Shuttle software testing process involves multiple testers detecting faults that form multiple queues $1, \ldots i, \ldots n$ and, for efficiency purposes, streams of faults are fed from the queues into multiple correction stations $1, \ldots c, \ldots m$ (i.e., fault correction specialists and computers for executing the software to be tested). Both approaches are used and compared. The analytical approach uses the classical models [HIL01]. For the simulation approach, a C++ program was written. Results may differ because the simulation model uses tests based on random numbers to determine when an event, such as a fault entering a queue, would occur, whereas the analytical model does not deal in events. Rather, it computes expected values (i.e., mean), such as the expected number of faults in a queue.

Analyses Objectives

One objective is to identify the optimal number of fault correction stations, where "optimal" is defined as the number of stations where additional stations would yield diminishing returns in correcting faults. A second objective is to identify which faults may require excessive processing time. This is done in order to feed back this information to improve the quality of the output of the software development process. Another objective is to compare assignment of faults to correction stations in *order of occurrence* with assignment based on choosing the station with *minimum existing fault count*. The first plan corresponds to the situation where fault correction is attempted without delay. The second plan corresponds to batching the faults for the purpose of achieving fault correction efficiency. In order to implement this plan, the faults counts are sorted in ascending sequence and assigned to the first empty fault correction station. The process continues, filling empty stations.

FIGURE 12.2   Simulation Model Queuing Process

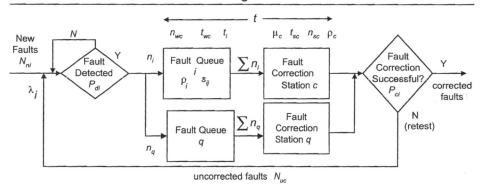

n_i : number of faults in queue when fault i occurs

λ_i : occurrence rate of fault i

ρ_i : utilization of queue when fault i occurs

N_{ni} : *potential* number of new faults when fault i occurs

N_{uc} : number of uncorrected faults from station c

n_i : expected number of faults in queue i

n_{sc} : number of faults being corrected at station c

n_{wc} : number of faults waiting to be corrected at station c

P_{di} : probability of detecting fault i

t : total time fault i spends in fault correction system

t_{sc} : fault correction time at station c

t_i : test time per fault

t_{wc} : time fault spends waiting for correction at station c

μ_c : fault correction rate at station c

s_{ij} : fault i severity level j

P_{ci} : probability of correcting fault i at station c

ρ_c : utilization of fault correction station c

Queuing Models for Software Development

As an example of a fault detection and correction system, multiple fault correction stations (i.e., servers) are modeled, using fault data from NASA Space Shuttle release OI4 (operational increment) in Table 12.1. As opposed to classical queuing models, which are restricted to using steady-state or mean values, queue characteristics are modeled as individual faults occur. In order to determine whether the faults occur according to an exponential distribution, a t-test [LEV01] was conducted of the actual times between fault occurrences versus an exponentially distributed set derived from its mean. The probability of the two sets coming from the same population is .9288. Therefore, this was justification to use the exponential distribution.

Analytical Model

Fault Generation

In Figure 12.1 there is a stream of new faults N_{ni} that attempt to enter the fault correction system. Whether they will be "admitted" depends on whether they will be detected. The probability of fault detection is generated by using the simulation program. The analytical model is supported by the simulation model to the extent that a stream of faults attempting to enter the system is subjected to a detection test by comparing the probability of fault detection, P_{di}, generated by random numbers, with test values, also generated by random numbers. If the test succeeds, N_{ni} is incremented by "1" (i.e., a fault is detected); otherwise, no incrementation takes place (i.e., no fault is detected).

Fault Severity

The most severe faults can preempt less severe faults because given the reasonable assumption that the most severe faults have the highest impact on reliability, reducing their correction time is given priority attention [SWA06]. Therefore, it is appropriate to consider the severity of faults when analyzing a fault correction system because the time to correct faults, and the number of faults at correction stations, is a function of their severity. Furthermore, increased correction times caused by high severity impact the time that faults

TABLE 12.1   NASA Space Shuttle Fault Data

OI4 Fault ID i	Fault Severity s_{ij}	Fault Occurrence Time T_i(days)	Probability of Fault Detection Pd_i	Probability of Fault Correction P_{ci}
1	3	20	0.66	0.07
2	3	130	0.03	0.42
3	3	147	0.55	0.71
4	3	158	0.32	0.86
5	3	180	0.60	0.01
6	3	210	0.73	0.38
7	2	223	0.89	0.47
8	3	409	0.82	0.32
9	3	508	0.61	0.55
10	3	812	0.75	0.61
11	3	1314	0.13	0.07
12	3	4060	0.59	1.00
13	2	5353	0.34	0.59

wait to be corrected. This is analogous to the supermarket when customers with complex purchases cause large processing times at the checkout counter that result in long lines and waiting times of other customers. To reflect this condition, compute a fault severity weighting factor w_{ij} in equation (12.1), corresponding to fault i and fault severity j, and apply it to *increase* the appropriate metrics below. Of course these metrics do not actually increase, but the weighting scheme is a method to more realistically represent the fault queue process. Note that for these severities, s_{i1} is the least severe and s_{im} is the most severe, but s_{i1} has the lowest numerical value and s_{im} has the highest value. Given these conditions, the weights in equation (12.1) sum to 1.0 over the m faults and n fault severity levels.

$$w_{ij} = f\left(1 - \left(\frac{s_{ij}}{s_{im}}\right)\right),$$
(12.1)

$$\text{where } f = \frac{1}{\sum\limits_{i=1,j=1}^{m,n}\left(1 - \frac{s_{ij}}{s_{im}}\right)}$$

Faults in Queue

Once the number of new faults N_{ni} has been generated, the weighted expected number of faults n_i in the queue, when fault i occurs in Figure 12.1, is determined by whether the new faults are detected, according to the probability of detection P_{di}, as shown in equation (12.2).

$$n_i = (N_{ni} * P_{di})(1 + w_{ij})$$
(12.2)

Fault Occurrence Rate

The occurrence rate of fault i is given by the reciprocal of the time, t_{ai}, between fault i and fault $i + 1$ occurring in equation (12.3).

$$\lambda_i = 1/t_{ai}$$
(12.3)

Uncorrected Faults

The expected number of uncorrected faults, after faults have been processed at stations, is computed by noting in Figure 12.1 that some of the n_i faults do not get corrected. Thus, accounting for probability of fault correction, P_{ci}, equation (12.4) is computed:

$$N_{ui} = (n_i) * (1 - P_{ci})$$
(12.4)

Queue Utilization

Now you can compute queue utilization in equation (12.5). This is a critical parameter that is the probability of the queue being busy, or the utilization of the queue when fault i occurs. Do this by dividing the number of faults in queue i by the cumulative number of faults in queue 1 to queue q. Note that the number of faults occurring, n_i, has already been increased by the fault severity weighting factor in equation (12.2).

$$\rho_i = \frac{n_i}{\sum\limits_{i=1}^{q} n_i}$$
(12.5)

Queue Dwell Times

The total time that fault i spends in a fault correction system is equal to the total number of faults in the queue divided by the fault input rate.

$$t_i = n_i/\lambda_i \tag{12.6}$$

The time that a fault spends being corrected increases with queue utilization ρ_i, for a given number of stations c and time between fault occurrences t_{ai}, and is computed in equation (12.7).

$$t_{si} = \rho_i(ct_{ai}) \tag{12.7}$$

The fault wait time is computed in equation (12.8) by subtracting the time that faults spend being corrected, computed in equation (12.7), from the total time that faults spend in the fault correction system, computed in equation (12.6):

$$t_{wi} = t_i - t_{si} \tag{12.8}$$

Queue Correction Counts

Using the fault occurrence rate from equation (12.3) and the time faults spend being corrected from equation (12.7), the number of faults being corrected is computed in equation (12.9).

$$n_{si} = \lambda_i t_{si} \tag{12.9}$$

Queue Correction Rates

Using equation (12.7), you can compute the rate of fault correction in equation (12.10):

$$\mu_i = 1/t_{si} \tag{12.10}$$

State of the System

If there are zero faults in the system, this is a good omen for fault i because it can be processed for correction without delay. Thus it is important to know the probability of the state of the system. The probability of zero faults in the fault correction system, when fault i occurs, is computed in equation (12.11) [HIL01]:

$$p_{0i} = 1/D_i, \text{ where} \tag{12.11}$$

$$D_i = \sum_{n_i=0}^{c}\left(\frac{(c\rho_i)^{n_i}}{n_i!} + \frac{(c\rho_i)^c}{(c!(1-\rho_i))} \right), \tag{12.12}$$

where ρ_i is the utilization of queue i, n_i is the number of faults in queue i, and c is the number of fault correction stations.

Then the probability of $n_i \geq 0$ faults in the fault correction system is given by equation (12.13):

$$p_{ni} = 1 - p_{0i} \tag{12.13}$$

An important concern in software testing is: What is the probability that a fault will end up being queued? [RAM00] Another way of phrasing this question is: What is the probability of n_i faults already in the queue when fault i is detected? If n_i is too large, faults are blocked [DAI07], and deferred for later processing. Using equation (12.11), compute this probability in equation (12.14) [HIL01].

$$P_{ni} = p_{0i}((\lambda_i / \mu_i)_i^n / n_i !) \tag{12.14}$$

Wait Queue Counts

Since, in general, faults cannot be corrected immediately, use equation (12.3), λ_i, and equation (12.8), t_{wi}, to compute the number waiting in the queue for correction:

$$n_{wi} = \lambda_i t_{wi} \tag{12.15}$$

Efficiency of Testing

The efficiency of testing fault i is computed as follows, where n_i is the number of faults, N_{ui} is the number of uncorrected faults, and t is the time spent in the fault correction system per fault:

$$E_i = (n_i - N_{ui})/t \tag{12.16}$$

Simulation Model

Simulation can be considered as a tightly coupled and iterative three-stage process composed of model design, model execution, and execution analysis [VAZ99]. Our model design is represented in Figure 12.2. Model execution is represented by Figure 12.3 and by the equations that follow. Execution analysis is the reporting of simulation results in the "Model Results" section of this chapter.

As in the case of the analytical model, it is necessary to account for the effect of fault severity by weighting the number of faults in queue i, n_i, and the number of faults in correction station c, n_c, by the factor $(1 + w_{ij})$. Thus, borrowing equation (12.12) from the analytical model, the number of faults in queue i, n_i, is weighted in equation (12.17). The weighting factors are computed by equation (12.1). Since the faults n_c are the summation of faults n_i, as shown in Figure 12.3, these faults will have been weighted.

$$n_i = (N_{ni} * P_{di})(1 + w_{ij}) \tag{12.17}$$

Test Time, Time of Fault Occurrence, and Fault Occurrence Rate

Through testing, NASA faults occur at times T_i (see Figure 12.2) [SCH97], where n_c represents the number of faults that are assigned to fault correction station c. Since n_c faults are in station c at time T_i, the test time per fault is computed as:

$$t_i = T_i / n_c \tag{12.18}$$

It is of interest to compute the occurrence rate of fault i, λ_i, and compare it with the fault correction rate μ_i to see whether the correction rate can keep up with the occurrence rate. If it cannot, this means that the fault correction system becomes unstable. First, you need the time between consecutive fault occurrences, t_{ai}, computed in equation (12.19):

$$t_{ai} = T_{i+1} - T_i \tag{12.19}$$

Then using equation (12.19), the fault occurrence rate is computed as follows:

$$\lambda_i = 1/t_{ai} \tag{12.20}$$

Queue Utilization

In the simulation model, the weighted utilization for each queue is computed. This approach gives a more realistic assessment of utilization than is the case with the analytical

FIGURE 12.3 Simulation Model Queing Computations

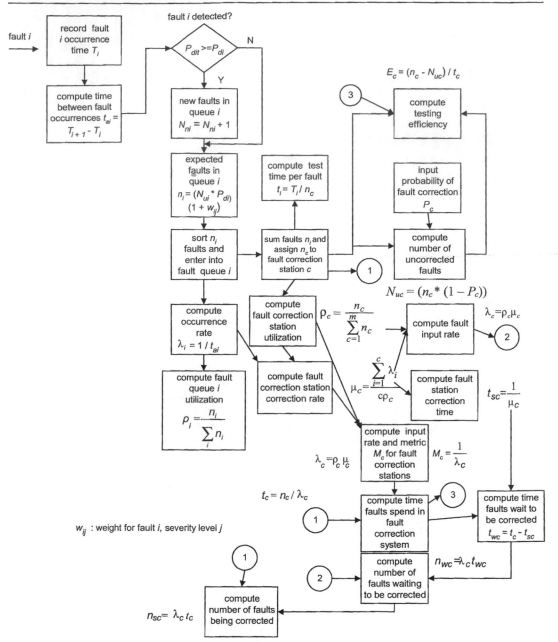

model that computes utilization for a single queue. The approach is initiated by detecting a fault in Figure 12.2, incrementing the number of new faults N_{ni}, computing the number of faults n_i in queue i, and assigning them to fault correction stations. This is accomplished in Figure 12.2 and in the C++ simulation program by sorting the n_i faults in ascending order, summing the faults in pairs of adjacent queues, and assigning the pairs sequentially from 1 to m, where m is the number of stations. Thus, utilization of each fault queue i is computed as follows:

$$\rho_i = \frac{n_i}{\displaystyle\sum_{i=1}^{q} n_i} \tag{12.21}$$

Fault Correction Station Utilization

In addition to queue utilization, it is important to compute the utilization of each fault correction station because, after all, this is where the primary action in software testing takes place. Therefore, the weighted utilization of fault correction station c is computed in equation (12.22), where n_c is the number of faults assigned to station c and m is the number of stations. Note that the denominator in equation (12.21) is equal to the denominator in equation (12.22) because all of the faults are assigned to the stations.

$$\rho_c = \frac{n_c}{\displaystyle\sum_{c=1}^{m} n_{sc}} \tag{12.22}$$

Fault Correction Rate and Time

In order to compute the station fault correction rate μ_c, you must sum the fault occurrence rates in the queues, λ_i, before dividing by the product of the number of stations and station utilization, to arrive at a fault occurrence rate for fault correction station c, as shown in equation (12.23). Note that increasing the number of stations and station utilization decreases the fault correction rate *per station*. In other words, the fault queue load is distributed more evenly across stations.

$$\mu_c = \left(\sum_{i=1}^{c} (\lambda_i) \right) / (c\rho_c) \tag{12.23}$$

Once the fault station correction rate has been computed in equation (12.23), you can compute the fault station correction time, t_{sc}, in equation (12.24).

$$t_{sc} = 1/\mu_c \tag{12.24}$$

Time Spent in System and Input Rate

Now you can compute the time faults spend in the fault correction system (waiting to be corrected and being corrected), t_c, by using the rate of fault input to fault correction stations, λ_c, and the number of faults, n_c, at the stations, in equation (12.25).

$$t_c = n_c / \lambda_c \tag{12.25}$$

Using equations (12.22) and (12.23), the input rate to fault correction stations is computed in equation (12.26).

$$\lambda_c = \rho_c \mu_c \tag{12.26}$$

Wait Time, Number Waiting, and Number Being Corrected

Then, once the fault correction time is computed in equation (12.24), the time that faults have to wait to be corrected, t_{wc}, is computed by equation (12.27):

$$t_{wc} = t_c - t_{sc} \tag{12.27}$$

Continuing, with t_{wc} in hand, you can compute the number of faults waiting to be corrected n_{wc}:

$$n_{wc} = \lambda_c t_{wc} \tag{12.28}$$

Using input rate to fault correction stations, λ_c, from equation (12.26), and the time that faults spend being corrected, t_{sc}, from equation (12.24), you can compute the number of faults being corrected in equation (12.29):

$$n_{sc} = \lambda_c t_{sc} \tag{12.29}$$

Uncorrected Faults

As noted in Figure 12.2, not all faults are corrected due to deficiencies in the test process (e.g., inadequate test cases). Therefore, you need to estimate the number of faults from station c that were not corrected, by multiplying the number of faults in station c by the probability of *not* correcting faults, as shown in equation (12.30), where P_c is the probability of correcting faults in station c:

$$N_{uc} = n_c * (1 - P_c) \tag{12.30}$$

Testing Efficiency

Testing efficiency at correction station c is computed as follows, where N_{uc} is the number of *uncorrected* faults and t_c is the time faults spend in station c. The objective is to identify the number of stations that maximizes the ratio of number of *corrected* faults, $(n_c - N_{uc})$, to time spent in the station:

$$E_c = (n_c - N_{uc})/t_c \tag{12.31}$$

Fault Correction Effectiveness Metric

Since waiting time, correction time, and total time spent in the fault correction system are metrics that correspond to faults waiting, being corrected, and total number in the system, respectively, it is important to normalize these quantities by their respective number of faults, where M_{wc} is normalized wait time, M_{sc} is normalized correction time, and M_c is normalized total time.

$$M_{wc} = t_{wc}/n_{wc}, M_{sc} = t_{sc}/n_{sc}, M_c = t_c/n_c$$

With some algebra, it can be shown that all three metrics reduce to:

$$M_c = 1/\lambda_c, \tag{12.32}$$

the reciprocal of the fault input rate to station c. At first blush, this result seems counterintuitive, but upon reflection, you can see that an increasing input rate leads to efficiency in fault correction because the station is kept busy. This result holds up as long as the station utilization does not become excessive (i.e., $\rho_c > .90$). The objective is to identify the number of stations that minimize equation (12.32).

A similar result holds for the analytical model in equation (12.33),

$$M_c = 1/\sum_i^c \lambda_i, \tag{12.33}$$

pertaining to the metric for station c. The fault occurrence rates are summed in equation (12.33) in order to provide a fair comparison with M_c in the simulation model that uses summed fault input rates at the stations.

Model Results

Test Time Tradeoffs

Of great concern to software testers is the tradeoff between test effort, represented by test time, and the number of faults removed by the test effort. Figure 12.4 shows that testing and queuing efficiencies increase with increasing number of fault correction stations. However, increasing the number of fault correction stations may not be feasible [PEN01] because doing so would require more test personnel and computer equipment. Therefore, a practical value of number of fault correction stations in Figure 12.4 is $c = 3$. Another lesson learned from Figure 12.4 is that sorting faults preliminary to assignment to fault correction stations does not increase efficiency. Thus, it would be better to assign faults to the first available station. The application of this plot would be to serve as a planning document for subsequent releases of the software for determining the number of stations, using unsorted fault assignment and assuming similar testing and fault occurrence characteristics, as is the case with the Shuttle. The reason for the large values of test time and time in the system is that the Shuttle software is tested continuously by the developer, in the simulation testbed, in the Shuttle simulator for astronaut training, at the launch site, and in flight [KEL97].

FIGURE 12.4   NASA Space Shuttle OI4: Test Time per Fault and Time in System per Fault vs. Number of Fault Correction Stations *c* (simulation model)

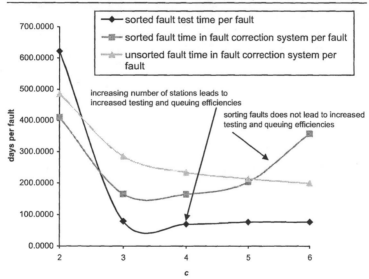

Optimal Number of Fault Correction Stations, Test Efficiency, and Fault Correction Effectiveness

As stated, one of the objectives is to identify the optimal number of fault correction stations to use in a software testing system, where "optimal" can have several interpretations. One interpretation is the number of fault correction stations where testing efficiency is a maximum. This occurs at $c = 4$ in Figure 12.5 for both the analytical and simulation models. Of course, each application would have a different solution, but the type of plot in Figure 12.5 serves as a roadmap for *any* application.

FIGURE 12.5   NASA Space Shuttle OI4: Test Efficiency E_c vs. Number of Fault Correction Stations c

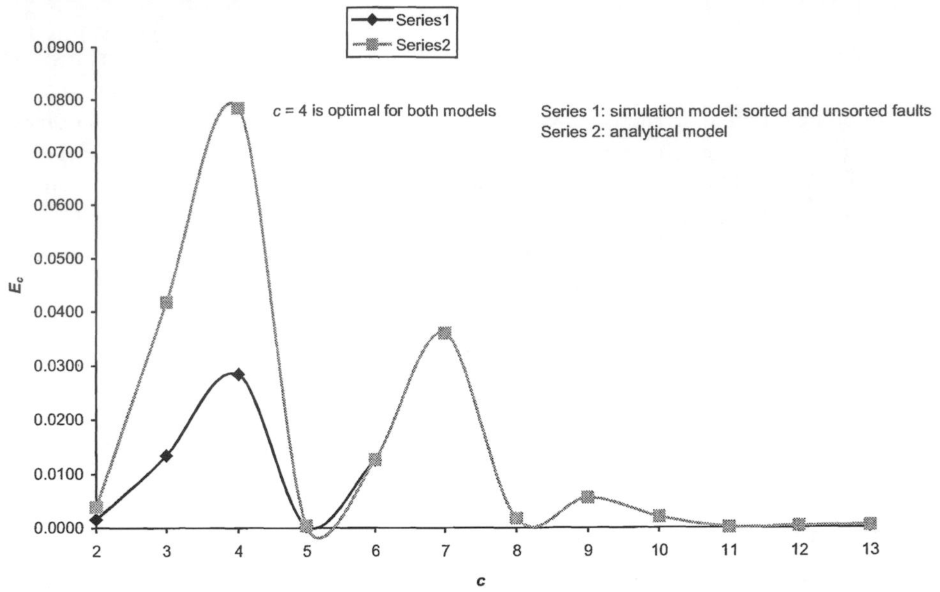

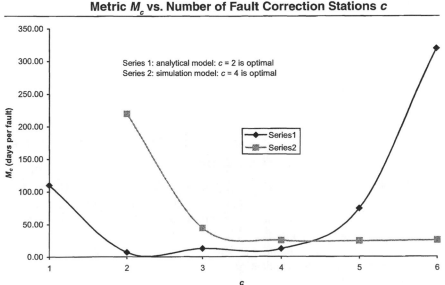

A second way of viewing station optimality is to employ fault correction effectiveness, as illustrated in Figure 12.6. Here, the solution is $c = 2$ using the analytical model; in contrast the solution was $c = 4$ in Figure 12.5. Now, in practice, what if the solutions differ, as in this case? The way to solve the dilemma is to choose the fault correction effectiveness criterion—Figure 12.6—if this is a safety critical application, as in the case of the Shuttle. Otherwise, opt for the testing efficiency solution—Figure 12.5.

FIGURE 12.6   NASA Space Shuttle OI4: Fault Correction Effectiveness Metric M_c vs. Number of Fault Correction Stations c

Worst-Case Number of Fault Correction Stations

Equally important with identifying the optimal number of fault correction stations is the identification of the "worst-case" situation. This criterion is based on the number of fault correction stations corresponding to the maximum number of uncorrected faults, as shown in Figure 12.7 for the two models. Again, you can see that sorting faults has no advantage and that the analytical model produces optimistic predictions while the simulation model generates pessimistic predictions. This fact can be used to bound the solution. In the figure, the correct solutions lies between $c = 5$ and $c = 8$. Other applications could yield other solutions, but this approach would be applicable to *any* application.

FIGURE 12.7   NASA Space Shuttle OI4: Number of Uncorrected Faults N_u vs. Test Efficiency E_c vs. Number of Fault Correction Stations c

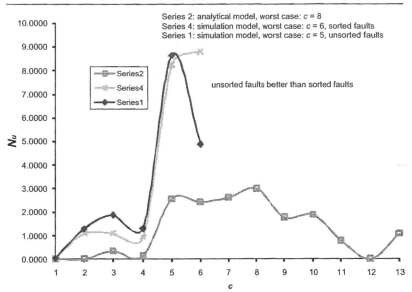

Order of Fault Occurrence Assignment versus Minimum Existing Fault Count Assignment

As described, you can use two methods of assigning faults to stations: 1) order in which faults are detected, and 2) examine the existing fault count in stations and assign where the count is minimum. To implement 2, sort the number of faults and assign them in ascending order. As mentioned, 1 is applicable to safety critical systems, where urgency of fault correction is paramount. On the other hand, 2 is applicable where time can be taken to batch the faults in an attempt to achieve test efficiency and fault correction effectiveness. A surprising result is shown in Figure 12.8 on page 276, where 1 is superior to 2 because the sorted faults plot continues to increase, whereas the unsorted faults plot reaches a maximum and then decreases. This is a fortuitous result since Shuttle data are used in the analysis.

Ability to Process Faults

You would expect that the ability to process faults—after they are detected—for correction in fault correction stations would decrease with increasing fault input into the system. You would have this expectation because, with increasing fault input, it becomes increasingly difficult

FIGURE 12.8 NASA Space Shuttle OI4: Fault Counts *n* vs. Number of Fault Correction Stations *c* (simulated model)

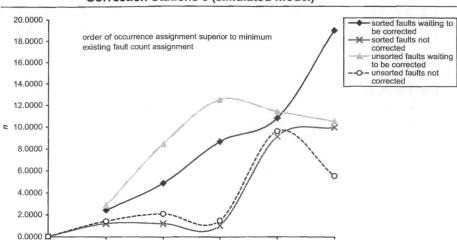

FIGURE 12.9 NASA Space Shuttle OI4: Probability of n_i Faults in Queue (P_{ni}) and Probability of One or More Faults in Queue ($p_{ni} > 0$) vs. Fault *i* (analytical model)

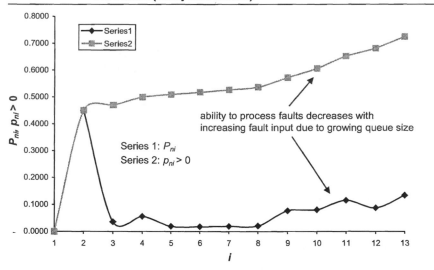

for testers to handle the load. Figure 12.9 attests to this result. In practice, this plot would be used to anticipate the load on the testers and stations, as a function of fault detection.

Track Number of Faults Waiting as a Function of Number of Fault Correction Stations

It is important to track a key queuing performance metric, such as the number of faults waiting to be corrected as a function of number of fault correction stations [CHE]. This is shown in Figure 12.10 where, again, you can see that: 1) it does not pay to sort faults prior to assigning them to fault correction stations and 2) the simulation model and analytical model provide upper and lower bounds, respectively, on the metric of interest.

FIGURE 12.10   NASA Space Shuttle OI4: Number of Faults Waiting to be Corrected n_{wi} vs. Number of Fault Correction Stations c

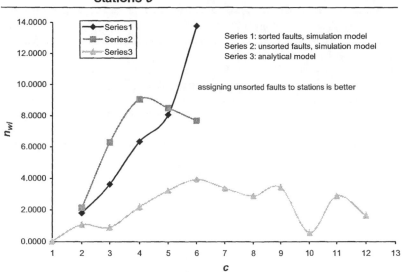

Summary

The objectives of the chapter were to: 1) identify the test time tradeoff function, showing how fault removal varies with test time; 2) identify the number of fault correction stations that produce the best values of testing efficiency and fault correction effectiveness; 3) identify the worst-case number of stations in terms of the number of uncorrected faults, since uncorrected faults are obviously detrimental to the reliability of the software; and 4) evaluate two methods for assigning faults to correction.

Analytical and simulation models were used to evaluate the testing efficiency and fault correction effectiveness of the fault detection and correction process. Two models—analytical and simulation—were used so that there could be a reasonableness check on the solutions. Recognize that the analytical model yields steady-state or mean-value results and the simulation model provides event-driven values. Thus, you would not expect the results to be identical. An exception is the result in Figure 12.5, which showed identical results for test efficiency.

The simulation model consistently produced a lower bound on metrics and the simulation model produced an upper bound. This is a valuable property because you would know that the actual value lie between these bounds.

More important than specific numerical results is the methodology that was demonstrated that can be applied to *all* applications.

References

[AKY88] I.F. Akyildiz, "On the Exact and Approximate Throughput Analysis of Closed Queuing Networks with Blocking." *IEEE Transactions on Software Engineering,* Vol. 14, No. 1, January, 1988, pp. 62–70.

[CHE] Naveen Cherukuri, Natarajan Gautam, Gokul Kandiraju, and Anand Sivasubramaniam, "Queueing Model for Performance Analysis of a Network Interface Card." ZD Net Australia.

[DAI07] Yuan-Shun Dai, Yi Pan, and Xukai Zou, "A Hierarchical Modeling and Analysis for Grid Service Reliability." *IEEE Transactions on Computers,* Vol. 56, No. 5, May, 2007, pp. 681–691.

[GOK06] Swapna S. Gokhale and Robert E. Mullen, "Queuing Models for Field Defect Resolution Process." 17th International Symposium on Software Reliability Engineering (ISSRE'06), 2006, pp. 353–362.

[GOV99] Manish K. Govil and Michael C. Fu, "Queueing Theory in Manufacturing: A Survey." *Journal of Manufacturing Systems,* 1999.

[HIL01] Fredrick S. Hillier and Gerald J. Lieberman, *Introduction to Operations Research,* seventh edition. McGraw-Hill, 2001.

[HUA08] Chin-Yu Huang and Wei-Chih Huang, "Software Reliability Analysis and Measurement Using Finite and Infinite Server Queueing Models." *IEEE Transactions On Reliability,* Vol. 57, No. 1, March 2008, pp. 192–203.

[KEL97] Ted Keller and Norman F. Schneidewind, "A Successful Application of Software Reliability Engineering for the NASA Space Shuttle." *Software Reliability Engineering Case Studies,* International Symposium on Software Reliability Engineering, Albuquerque, New Mexico, November 4, 1997, pp. 71–82.

[LEV01] David M. Levine, Patricia P. Ramsey, and Robert K. Smidt, *Applied Statistics for Engineers and Scientists.* Prentice Hall, 2001.

[MUS87] John D. Musa, Anthony Iannino, and Kazuhira Okumoto, *Software Reliability: Measurement, Prediction, Application.* McGraw-Hill, 1987.

[PEN01] M. Di Penta, G. Casazza, G. Antoniol, and E. Merlo, "Modeling Web Maintenance Centers Through Queue Models." Fifth European Conference on Software Maintenance and Reengineering, 2001, pp. 131–138.

[RAM00] Ramkumar Ramaswamy, "How to Staff Business-Critical Maintenance Projects." *IEEE Software,* Vol. 17, No. 3, May/June, 2000, pp. 90–94.

[VAZ99] Nunzio-Nicolo Savino-Vazquez and Ramon Puigjaner, "A UML-Based Method to Specify the Structural Component of Simulation-Based Queuing Network Performance Models." Thirty-Second Annual Simulation Symposium, 1999, p. 71.

[SCH97] Norman F. Schneidewind, "Reliability Modeling for Safety Critical Software." *IEEE Transactions on Reliability,* Vol. 46, No.1, March 1997, pp. 88–98.

[SHA75] Robert E. Shannon, *Systems Simulation: The Art and Science.* Prentice Hall, 1975.

[SWA98] S. Gokhale et al., "Reliability Simulation of Component-Based Software Systems." Proceedings of the 9th International Symposium, Software Reliability Engineering, 1998, pp. 192–201.

[XIA07] Wang Xia and Qu Huang, "Queuing Analysis and Performance Evaluation of Workflow Through WFQN." First Joint IEEE/IFIP Symposium on Theoretical Aspects of Software Engineering (TASE '07), 2007, pp. 178–187.

Appendix

C++ Program for Fault Detection and Correction

```
// expected weighted number of faults in queue i: ni = (Nni * Pdi) * (1 + wij)

//time between fault occurrences: tai = Ti+1 - Ti

//test time per fault: ti = Ti / nc

// fault occurrence rate: lambdai = 1 / tai

// utilization of fault queue i: rhoi = ni / sum ni

// number of faults assigned to fault correction station c: nc = sum ni

// utilization of fault correction station c: (rhoc = nc / sum nc) * (1 + wij)

// fault correction rate at station c: muc = lambdai / rhoc

// fault station correction time: tsc = 1 / muc

// rate of fault input to fault correction stations: lambdac = rhoc * muc

// time faults spend in the fault correction system: tc = (nc / lambdac )

// time that faults have to wait to be corrected: twc = twc = tc – tsc
```

```
// number of faults waiting to be corrected: nwc = lambdac * twc
// number of faults being corrected: nsc = lambdac * tsc
// number of uncorrected faults from station c: Nuc = nc * (1 - Pc)
// fault severity weight: wij = f * (1 - (sij / sim))
// f = 1 / (sum (i, j) (1 - (sij / sim)))
// efficiency of testing: Ec = (nc—Nuc) / tc
// metric Mc: Mc = 1 / lambdac
# include <iostream> // specify input output library
# include <math.h> // specify math library
#include <stdio.h>
#include <string.h>
#include <assert.h>
#include <fstream>
using namespace std;
using std::cout; // specify standard screen output
using std::cin; // specify standard screen input
using std::endl; // specify standard end of line
const char* format_string; // pointer to type char
main() // beginning of main program
{
FILE *fp;//pointer to type FILE
fp = fopen("c:/queuing/results.txt", "w"); // file for writing results
ifstream infile ; // define probability of detecting fault i
infile.open("c:/queuing/Pdi.txt");
ifstream infile1 ; // define probability of detecting fault i random numbers
infile1.open("c:/queuing/Pdi test random numbers.txt");
ifstream infile2 ; // define probability of correcting faults in station c
infile2.open("c:/queuing/Pc.txt");
ifstream infile3 ; // define fault occurrence times Ti
infile3.open("c:/queuing/Ti.txt");
ifstream infile4 ; // define fault severity
infile4.open("c:/queuing/fault severity.txt");
int i, c, j, n, q, sim, M ; // array index, number of fault correction stations, number of
faults
// minimum number of faults array index, fault correction station index, number of fault
queues,
// maximum value of fault severity
double arrayPdi [20], arrayPditest [20]; // probability of detecting fault i arrays
double arrayn [20], arraynwc [20], arraynsc [20], arrayNn [20]; // faults in queue, faults
waiting, faults being corrected,
// new faults
```

```
double arraynt [20], nmin, arrayrho [20], nitotal; // number of faults in fault correction ar-
ray, minimum number of faults.
// fault queue i utilization, summation of ni faults,
double arrayTi [20], arraylambdai [20], arraytai [20], arrayc [20]; // fault occurrence time,
//occurrence rate of fault i, time between fault occurrence times, number of faults in cor-
rection station
double csum, arrayti [20], arrayrhoc [20], arraymu [20] ; // summation of faults assigned
to
// fault correction stations, test time per fault,
// fault correction station utilization, fault correction station correction rate
double arraytsc [20], arraylambdac [20], arraytc [20], arraytwc [20]; // station fault correc-
tion time, station fault input rate,
// time faults spend in station c, time faults spend wauting to be corrected
double arrayPc [20], arrayNuc [20], arraywij [20], arraysij [20] ; // probability of correcting
fault in station c,
// number of uncorrected faults from station c, fault severity weight, fault severity array
double lambdaisum [20], arrayEc [20]; // for summing lambdai, efficiency of testing array
double arrayMc [20], sumTi, sumij, f; // metric Mc, sum fault occurrence times, sum of
(1 - (sij / sim))
// fault severity weighting factor
i = 0, arrayNn [0]= 0, arraylambdai [0] =0; // initialize array index, number of new faults
array,
//fault occurrence rate array
cout << "input number of fault queues";
cin >> q;
cout << "input number of fault correction stations";
cin >> c;
cout << "input maximum value of fault severity";
cin >> sim;
cout << "input number of faults";
cin >> M;
while(!infile.eof())
// while eof not reached for Pdi file, store data in array
{
infile >> arrayPdi [i];
if(!infile.eof()) // if eof not reached for Pdi file, increment Pdi array index
{
i = i + 1;
}
}
i = 0;
while(!infile1.eof())
```

```
// while eof not reached for Pdi test file, store data in array
{
infile1 >> arrayPditest [i];
if(!infile1.eof()) // if eof not reached for Pdi test file, increment Pdi test array index
{
i = i + 1;
}
}
i = 0;
while(!infile2.eof())
// while eof not reached for Pc file, store data in array
{
infile2 >> arrayPc [i];
if(!infile2.eof()) // if eof not reached for Pdi test file, increment Pdi test array index
{
i = i + 1;
}
}
i = 0;
while(!infile3.eof())
// while eof not reached for Ti file, store data in array
{
infile3 >> arrayTi [i];
if(!infile3.eof()) // if eof not reached for Ti file, increment Ti array index
{
i = i + 1;
}
}
i = 0;
sumij = 0; // initialize fault severity weighting factor sum
 while(!infile4.eof())
// while eof not reached for fault severity file, store data in array
{
infile4 >> arraysij [i];
if(!infile4.eof()) // if eof not reached for fault severity file, increment fault severity array
index
{
sumij = sumij + (1 - arraysij [i] / sim); // sum to compute fault severity weighting factor f
i = i + 1;
}
}
```

```
f = 1 / sumij; // compute fault severity weighting factor
i = 0;
while (i <= M - 1)
{
arraywij [i] = f * (1 - (arraysij [i] / sim )); // compute fault severity weight
fprintf (fp, "%s%\n", "fault i", (char) 20);
fprintf (fp,"%i%c%\n", i + 1, (char) 6);
fprintf (fp, "%s%\n", "fault severity weight", (char) 20);
fprintf (fp,"%f%c%\n", arraywij [i], (char) 6);
i = i + 1;
}
i = 0;
nitotal = 0; // initialize ni total fault count
arraytai [i] = 0, arraylambdai [i] = 0; // set time between fault occurrences and occurrence
rate to 0 for queue i
// because these values are undefined
lambdaisum [i] = 0; // initialize fault occurrence rate
while (i <= (q - 1 ))
{
if (arrayPditest [i] >= arrayPdi [i])
{
arrayNn [i + 1] = (arrayNn [i] + 1); // increment number of new faults in next array value
arrayn [i + 1] = (arrayNn [i] * arrayPdi [i])* (1 + arraywij [i]); // compute weighted number
of faults in queue i
}
else
{
arrayNn [i + 1] = (arrayNn [i]); // do not increment number of new faults
arrayn [i + 1] = (arrayNn [i] * arrayPdi [i])* (1 + arraywij [i]); // compute weighted number
of faults in queue i
}
arraytai [i + 1] = arrayTi [i + 1] - arrayTi [i]; // compute time between fault occurrences
arraylambdai [i + 1] = 1 / arraytai [i + 1]; // compute occurrence rate for fault i
lambdaisum [i + 1] = lambdaisum [i] + arraylambdai [i + 1]; // sum fault occurrence rate
arrayti [i] = arrayTi [i] / arrayn [i + 1]; // compute test time per fault
fprintf (fp, "%s%\n", "fault queue i", (char) 20);
fprintf (fp,"%i%c%\n", i + 1, (char) 6);
fprintf (fp, "%s%\n", "new faults", (char) 20);
fprintf (fp,"%f%c%\n", arrayNn [i], (char) 6);
fprintf (fp, "%s%\n", "number of unsorted faults in queue i", (char) 20);
```

```
fprintf (fp,"%f%c%\n", arrayn [i + 1], (char) 6);
fprintf (fp, "%s%\n", "time between fault occurences", (char) 20);
fprintf (fp,"%f%c%\n", arraytai [i], (char) 6);
fprintf (fp, "%s%\n", "fault occurrence rate", (char) 20);
fprintf (fp,"%f%c%\n", arraylambdai [i], (char) 6);
fprintf (fp, "%s%\n", "fault occurrence time", (char) 20);
fprintf (fp,"%f%c%\n", arrayTi [i], (char) 6);
fprintf (fp, "%s%\n", "test time per fault", (char) 20);
fprintf (fp,"%f%c%\n", arrayti [i], (char) 6);
nitotal = nitotal + arrayn [i + 1]; // sum weighted ni faults
i = i + 1;
}
fprintf (fp, "%s%\n", "total number of faults", (char) 20);
fprintf (fp,"%f%c%\n", nitotal, (char) 6);
j = 0;
n = 1;
while (j <= (c - 1)) // control loop for computing and assigning faults to stations randomly
(i.e., unsorted faults)
{
if (j <= (c - 2)) // if this is the first c - 1 stations, add two consecutive fault counts
{
arrayc [j + 1] = arrayn [n] + arrayn [n + 1];
}
else // if this is station c, add three consecutive fault counts
{
arrayc [j + 1] = arrayn [n] + arrayn [n + 1] + arrayn [n + 2];
}
arrayrhoc [j] = arrayc [j + 1] / nitotal; // compute utilization of fault correction stations
arraymu [j] = (lambdaisum [j]) / ((arrayrhoc [j])* (j + 1)); // compute unsorted correction
rate
arraytsc [j] = (1 / arraymu [j]); // compute station unsorted fault correction time
arraylambdac [j] = arrayrhoc [j] * arraymu [j]; // compute unsorted fault station input rate
arraytc [j] = arrayc [j + 1]/ arraylambdac [j]; // compute total time unsorted faults spend in
correction stations
arraytwc [j] = arraytc [j] - arraytsc [j]; // compute time unsorted faults wait to be corrected
arraynwc [j] = arraylambdac [j] * arraytwc [j]; // compute number of unsorted faults wait-
ing to be corrected
arraynsc [j] = (arraylambdac [j] * arraytsc [j]); // compute number of unsorted faults being
corrected
arrayNuc [j] = (arrayc [j + 1] * (1 - arrayPc [j])) ; // compute number of unsorted faults not
corrected
```

```
arrayEc [j] = (arrayc [j + 1] - arrayNuc [j]) / arraytc [j]; // compute efficiency of testing
arrayMc [j] = 1 / arraylambdac [j]; // compute metric Mc
fprintf (fp, "%s%\n", "fault correction station", (char) 20);
fprintf (fp,"%i%c%\n", j + 1, (char) 6);
fprintf (fp, "%s%\n", "number of unsorted faults in station", (char) 20);
fprintf (fp,"%f%c%\n", arrayc [j + 1], (char) 6);
fprintf (fp, "%s%\n", "utilization of station for unsorted faults", (char) 20);
fprintf (fp,"%f%c%\n", arrayrhoc [j], (char) 6);
fprintf (fp, "%s%\n", "unsorted fault correction rate", (char) 20);
fprintf (fp,"%f%c%\n", arraymu [j], (char) 6);
fprintf (fp, "%s%\n", "unsorted fault correction time", (char) 20);
fprintf (fp,"%f%c%\n", arraytsc [j], (char) 6);
fprintf (fp, "%s%\n", "unsorted fault station input rate", (char) 20);
fprintf (fp,"%f%c%\n", arraylambdac [j], (char) 6);
fprintf (fp, "%s%\n", "time unsorted faults spend in stations", (char) 20);
fprintf (fp,"%f%c%\n", arraytc [j], (char) 6);
fprintf (fp, "%s%\n", "time unsorted faults wait to be corrected", (char) 20);
fprintf (fp,"%f%c%\n", arraytwc [j], (char) 6);
fprintf (fp, "%s%\n", "number of unsorted faults waiting to be corrected", (char) 20);
fprintf (fp,"%f%c%\n", arraynwc [j], (char) 6);
fprintf (fp, "%s%\n", "number of unsorted faults being corrected", (char) 20);
fprintf (fp,"%f%c%\n", arraynsc [j], (char) 6);
fprintf (fp, "%s%\n", "number of unsorted faults not corrected", (char) 20);
fprintf (fp,"%f%c%\n", arrayNuc [j], (char) 6);
fprintf (fp, "%s%\n", "efficiency of testing unsorted faults", (char) 20);
fprintf (fp,"%f%c%\n", arrayEc [j], (char) 6);
fprintf (fp, "%s%\n", "metric Mc of unsorted faults", (char) 20);
fprintf (fp,"%f%c%\n", arrayMc [j], (char) 6);
n = n + 2;
j = j + 1;
}
i = 0; // initialize fault array index
n = 0; // initialize number of fault correction stations
j = i; // initialize minimum number of faults index
nmin = arrayn [i]; // store first fault value in minimum number of faults
while (n <= (q - 1))// control loop for fault queues
{
while (i <= (q - 1))// control loop for sorting faults
{
if (nmin <= (arrayn [i + 1]))// if number of faults in queue i is minimum, do nothing
{
```

```
}
else
{
nmin = arrayn [i + 1]; // store number of faults in queue i + 1 in minimum number of
faults
j = i + 1;// capture location of minimum number of faults
}
i = i + 1; // increment fault counter
}
arraynt [n] = nmin; // store minimum number of faults in fault correction station array
arrayn [j] = 100; // store large number in what was minimum number of faults
i = 0; // reset fault array index
nmin = arrayn [i + 1]; // set minimum number of faults to number of faults in next fault
array location
arrayrho [n] = arraynt [n] / nitotal; // compute queue i utilization
fprintf (fp, "%s%\n", "queue i", (char) 20);
fprintf (fp,"%i%c%\n", n + 1, (char) 6);
fprintf (fp, "%s%\n", "number of sorted faults in queue i", (char) 20);
fprintf (fp,"%f%c%\n", arraynt [n], (char) 6);
fprintf (fp, "%s%\n", "sorted faults queue utilization", (char) 20);
fprintf (fp,"%f%c%\n", arrayrho [n], (char) 6);
n = n + 1; // increment fault correction station number
}
n = 0; // initialize fault counter
i = 0; // initialize fault correction station counter
csum = 0; // initialize sum of faults in correction stations
sumTi = 0; // initialize fault occurrence time sum
while (i <= (c - 2)) // continue if there are more stations to assign
{
arrayc [i] = arraynt [n] + arraynt [n + 1] ; // assign sorted faults to first c - 1 correction
stations
arrayrhoc [i] = (arrayc [i] * (1 + arraywij [i])) / nitotal; // compute utilization of first c - 1
fault correction stations
arraymu [i] = (lambdaisum [i]) / ((arrayrhoc [i])* (i + 1)); // compute correction rate
// for first c - 1 fault correction stations
arraytsc [i] = 1 / arraymu [i]; // compute station fault correction time for first c - 1 fault
correction stations
arraylambdac [i] = arrayrhoc [i] * arraymu [i]; // compute fault station input rate
// for first c - 1 fault correction stations
arraytc [i] = arrayc [i] / arraylambdac [i]; // compute time faults spend in first c - 1 fault
correction stations
```

arraytwc [i] = arraytc [i] - arraytsc [i]; // compute time faults wait to be corrected for first c - 1 stations

arraynwc [i] = arraylambdac [i] * arraytwc [i]; // compute number of sorted faults waiting to be corrected for first c - 1 stations

arraynsc [i] = (arraylambdac [i] * arraytsc [i]); // compute number of sorted faults being corrected for first c - 1 stations

arrayNuc [i] = (arrayc [i] * (1 - arrayPc [i])) ; // compute number of sorted faults not corrected for first c - 1 stations

arrayEc [i] = (arrayc [i] - arrayNuc [i]) / arraytc [i]; // compute efficiency of testing for first c - 1 stations

arrayMc [i] = 1 / arraylambdac [i]; // compute metric Mc for first c - 1 stations

sumTi = sumTi + arrayTi [i]; // sum occurrence times for first c - 1 stations

arrayti [i] = sumTi / arrayc [i]; // compute test time per fault for first c - 1 stations

csum = csum + arrayc [i]; // sum number of sorted faults assigned to fault correction stations

if (csum <= nitotal) // if sum of sorted faults in correction stations < total number of faults, output faults in correction stations

{

fprintf (fp, "%s%\n", "fault correction station", (char) 20);

fprintf (fp,"%i%c%\n", i + 1, (char) 6);

fprintf (fp, "%s%\n", "number of sorted faults in station", (char) 20);

fprintf (fp,"%f%c%\n", arrayc [i], (char) 6);

fprintf (fp, "%s%\n", "correction station sorted faults utilization", (char) 20);

fprintf (fp,"%f%c%\n", arrayrhoc [i], (char) 6);

fprintf (fp, "%s%\n", "station sorted fault correction rate", (char) 20);

fprintf (fp,"%f%c%\n", arraymu [i], (char) 6);

fprintf (fp, "%s%\n", "station sorted fault correction time", (char) 20);

fprintf (fp,"%f%c%\n", arraytsc [i], (char) 6);

fprintf (fp, "%s%\n", "station sorted fault input rate", (char) 20);

fprintf (fp,"%f%c%\n", arraylambdac [i], (char) 6);

fprintf (fp, "%s%\n", "time sorted faults spend in fault correction stations", (char) 20);

fprintf (fp,"%f%c%\n", arraytc [i], (char) 6);

fprintf (fp, "%s%\n", "time sorted faults spend waiting to be corrected", (char) 20);

fprintf (fp,"%f%c%\n", arraytwc [i], (char) 6);

fprintf (fp, "%s%\n", "number of sorted faults waiting to be corrected", (char) 20);

fprintf (fp,"%f%c%\n", arraynwc [i], (char) 6);

fprintf (fp, "%s%\n", "number of sorted faults being corrected", (char) 20);

fprintf (fp,"%f%c%\n", arraynsc [i], (char) 6);

fprintf (fp, "%s%\n", "number of sorted faults not corrected", (char) 20);

fprintf (fp,"%f%c%\n", arrayNuc [i], (char) 6);

fprintf (fp, "%s%\n", "efficiency of testing sorted faults", (char) 20);

fprintf (fp,"%f%c%\n", arrayEc [i], (char) 6);

```
fprintf (fp, "%s%\n", "metric Mc of sorted faults", (char) 20);
fprintf (fp,"%f%c%\n", arrayMc [i], (char) 6);
fprintf (fp, "%s%\n", "test time per sorted faults", (char) 20);
fprintf (fp,"%f%c%\n", arrayti [i], (char) 6);
}
n = n + 2; // increment fault counter for next two assignments
i = i + 1; // increment fault correction station counter
}
arrayc [c] = (nitotal—csum);// assign remaining sorted faults to faults to the last fault cor-
rection station
arrayrhoc [c] = arrayc [c] / nitotal; // compute utilization of last fault correction station
arraymu [c] = (lambdaisum [c - 1])/ (arrayrhoc [c]* c); //compute correction rate of
// last fault correction station
arraytsc [c] = (1 / arraymu [c]); // compute station fault correction time of last station
arraylambdac [c] = arrayrhoc [c] * arraymu [c]; // compute fault input rate for last station
arraytc [c] = arrayc [c] / arraylambdac [c]; // compute time faults spend in last station
arraytwc [c] = arraytc [c] - arraytsc [c]; // compute time faults wait to be corrected for last
station
arraynwc [c] = arraylambdac [c] * arraytwc [c]; // compute number of sorted faults waiting
to be corrected for last station
arraynsc [c] = (arraylambdac [c] * arraytsc [c]);// compute number of sorted faults being
corrected for last station
arrayNuc [c] = (arrayc [c] * (1 - arrayPc [c - 1])) ; // compute number of sorted faults not
corrected for last station
arrayEc [c] = (arrayc [c] - arrayNuc [c]) / arraytc [c]; // compute efficiency of testing for
last station
arrayMc [c] = 1 / arraylambdac [c]; // compute metric Mc for last station
arrayti [c] = (sumTi + arrayTi [c - 1]) / arrayc [c]; // compute test time per fault for last
station
fprintf (fp, "%s%\n", "fault correction station number", (char) 20);
fprintf (fp,"%i%c%\n", c, (char) 6);
fprintf (fp, "%s%\n", "sorted faults in correction station", (char) 20);
fprintf (fp,"%f%c%\n", arrayc [c], (char) 6);
fprintf (fp, "%s%\n", "correction station sorted faults utilization", (char) 20);
fprintf (fp,"%f%c%\n", arrayrhoc [c], (char) 6);
fprintf (fp, "%s%\n", "station sorted faults correction rate", (char) 20);
fprintf (fp,"%f%c%\n", arraymu [c], (char) 6);
fprintf (fp, "%s%\n", "station sorted faults correction time", (char) 20);
fprintf (fp,"%f%c%\n", arraytsc [c], (char) 6);
fprintf (fp, "%s%\n", "sorted faults station input rate", (char) 20);
fprintf (fp,"%f%c%\n", arraylambdac [c], (char) 6);
fprintf (fp, "%s%\n", "time sorted faults spend in fault correction station", (char) 20);
```

```
fprintf (fp,"%f%c%\n", arraytc [c], (char) 6);
fprintf (fp, "%s%\n", "time sorted faults spend waiting to be corrected", (char) 20);
fprintf (fp,"%f%c%\n", arraytwc [c], (char) 6);
fprintf (fp, "%s%\n", "number of sorted faults waiting to be corrected", (char) 20);
fprintf (fp,"%f%c%\n", arraynwc [c], (char) 6);
fprintf (fp, "%s%\n", "number of sorted faults being corrected", (char) 20);
fprintf (fp,"%f%c%\n", arraynsc [c], (char) 6);
fprintf (fp, "%s%\n", "number of sorted faults not corrected", (char) 20);
fprintf (fp,"%f%c%\n", arrayNuc [c], (char) 6);
fprintf (fp, "%s%\n", "efficiency of testing sorted faults", (char) 20);
fprintf (fp,"%f%c%\n", arrayEc [c], (char) 6);
fprintf (fp, "%s%\n", "metric Mc of sorted faults", (char) 20);
fprintf (fp,"%f%c%\n", arrayMc [c], (char) 6);
fprintf (fp, "%s%\n", "test time per sorted fault", (char) 20);
fprintf (fp,"%f%c%\n", arrayti [c], (char) 6);
return 0; // return to the operating system
} // executable code ends here
```

13

Object-Oriented Methods for Modeling Software Reliability

Objectives

Become familiar with object-oriented (O-O) methods for developing software and be able to evaluate O-O methods in relation to other developmental methods, such as structured design.

What You Will Learn From This Chapter

You will learn the following: 1) how O-O methods can be applied to mathematical software, 2) object-oriented design, 3) how O-O methods provide software frameworks—in particular, provide a means to allow the efficient construction and maintenance of large-scale software systems, and 4) O-O methods applied to modeling software reliability.

Subjects

Background on Object-Oriented Design
O-O Concepts Applied to Software Reliability Model
What Do O-O Designers Say Is Good Practice?
Experience Using UML
O-O Analysis
Object-Oriented Design Process
Implementing O-O Methods
Conclusions About Applicability of O-O and UML to Mathematical Software

Background on Object-Oriented Design

Can object-oriented methods be applied to mathematical software? Apparently, according to Beall and Shepard [BEA94], who say: It has been recognized in a number of different fields that object-oriented programming, in general, and software frameworks, in particular, provide a means to allow the efficient construction and maintenance of large-scale software systems. Since general-purpose numerical analysis codes certainly qualify as large-scale software, it makes sense for us to see how these methodologies can be applied to this field.

First, we will provide some background on O-O design to set the stage for the analysis of the applicability of O-O methods to the development of software reliability. (For additional details about O-O methods, visit the Object Management Group Web site: http://www.omg.org/).

The development of computer science as a whole proceeded from an initial concern with programming alone, through increasing interest in design, and only later to concern with analysis methods [GRA]. It was only in the 1980s that object-oriented *design* methods emerged. Object-oriented *analysis* methods emerged during the 1990s. Until the 1980s, apart from a few fairly obscure AI applications, object orientation was largely associated with the development of graphical user interfaces (GUIs), and few other applications became widely known. Up to this period, not a word had been mentioned about analysis or design for object-oriented systems. In the 1980s, Grady Booch published a paper on how to design for Ada but gave it the prophetic title: "Object-Oriented Design." Booch was able to extend his ideas to a genuinely object-oriented design method by 1991 in his book with the same title, revised in 1993 [BOO94].

A primary concept of O-O is the object. Software objects are conceptually similar to physical objects: They too consist of state and related behavior. An object stores its state in fields (variables in some programming languages) and exposes its behavior through methods (functions in some programming languages). Methods operate on an object's internal state and serve as the primary mechanism for object-to-object communication. Hiding internal state and requiring all interaction to be performed through an object's methods is known as data encapsulation—a fundamental principle of object-oriented programming. Dividing code into individual software objects provides a number of benefits, including:

- Modularity: The source code for an object can be written and maintained independently of the source code for other objects. Once created, an object can be easily passed around inside the system.
- Information hiding: By interacting only with an object's methods, the details of its internal implementation remain hidden from the outside world.
- Code re-use: If an object already exists (perhaps written by another software developer), you can use that object in your program. This allows specialists to implement, test, and debug complex, task-specific objects, which you can then trust to run in your own code.
- Pluggability and debugging ease: If a particular object turns out to be problematic, you can simply remove it from your application and plug in a different object as its replacement. This is analogous to fixing mechanical problems in the physical word. If a bolt breaks, you replace it, not the entire machine.

Object-Oriented Reverse Engineering

Unfortunately, many software designs and codes—even O-O software—are lacking in documentation. Therefore, it may be necessary to reverse engineer this software to comprehend it, and therefore make it maintainable and extensible. Aiming to support object-oriented program comprehension, reverse engineering seeks to create representations of object-oriented systems, and the relationship between classes and objects. The biggest challenge for a reverse engineering tool is to capture a large amount of information using descriptive and understandable representations, while at the same time not overwhelming the users with too much detail. Large-scale object-oriented systems typically consist of hundreds of classes as well as a high degree of interdependence among them. However, humans have limited information storing and manipulating abilities [MIL56]. If the representation is too complex, maintainers may drown in the information overload. Moreover, too much information on one diagram may decrease tool performance significantly [MEL00].

A commonly used strategy to address this challenge is to synthesize representations at a coarse level of granularity. Many existing tools generate package diagrams by dividing classes into packages, which act as coarse-grained proxies for their contained classes [OMO, RIV02, TON05]. While grouping classes into packages provides better readability of classes and their interrelations, it harms the comprehensibility of objects as independent units. Because the static description of an object can end up being distributed across multiple packages due to inheritance, it can be difficult to capture the external properties of the software object at a coarse-grained level.

To address this problem, a hybrid approach has been developed. The hybrid model blends the use of model elements at different levels of granularity. Instead of grouping programming language classes, the complete static descriptions of software objects are aggregated, so that each coarse-grained entity of the hybrid model represents a set of objects. At a low level of abstraction, software objects can be understood as independent units, while at a higher level, each coarse-grained entity can be understood as a whole and be mapped to real world objects [GOD07]. While this approach is interesting, it is not necessary for mathematical software because: 1) packages are useful for modeling use cases in Figure 13.1, and 2) the ultimate tool for reverse engineering mathematical software is the equation!

O-O Concepts Applied to Software Reliability Model

In this section, you will learn how O-O methods can be applied to mathematical software by using an integrated set of software development process diagrams. First, let us see how key O-O attributes relate to the diagrams.

Use Cases [BOO94, DOU99, RUM91]

Scenarios of the relationship between the human participants (called actors) and the system, in this case the operation of mathematical software (see Figure 13.1).

FIGURE 13.1   Use Cases for Mathematical Software

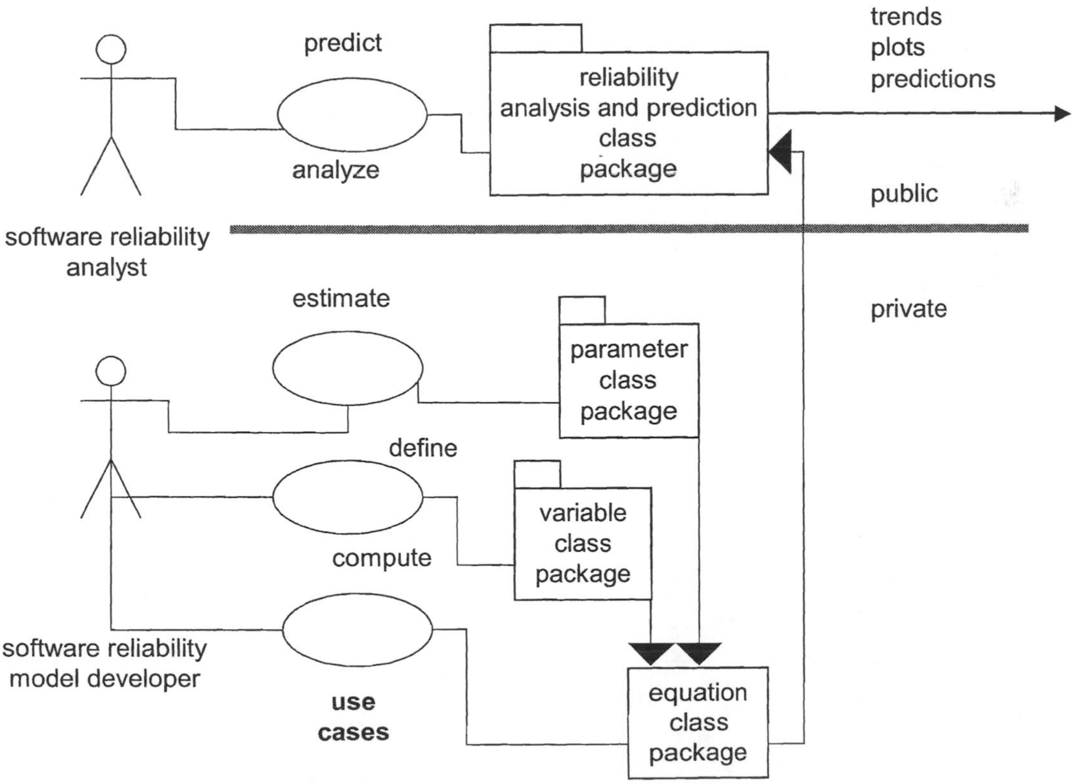

Activity Diagram

The purpose of the activity diagram is to model the procedural flow of actions that are part of a larger activity. In projects in which use cases are present, activity diagrams can model a specific use case at a more detailed level [RAT03]. For example, see Figure 13.2.

Association

Relationship between objects (e.g., interaction between equations and parameters). See Objects Hierarchy Chart, Figure 13.3.

FIGURE 13.2   Software Reliability Activity Chart

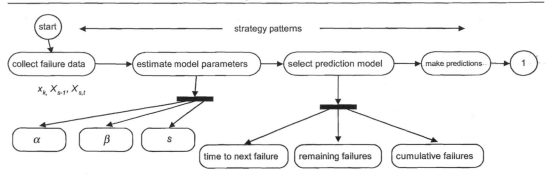

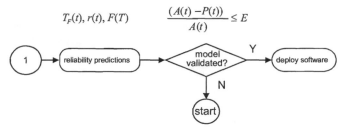

Definitions:

$T_F(t)$	Time to next failure(s) predicted at time t
$r(t)$	Remaining failures predicted at time t
$F(T)$	Cumulative number of failures after time T
α	Failure rate at the beginning of interval s
β	Negative of derivative of failure rate divided by failure rate
s	Starting interval for using observed failure data in parameter estimation
$A(t)$	actual value of a software reliability quantity
$P(t)$	predicted value of a software reliability quantity
E	prediction error limit
x_k	number of observed failures in interval k
X_{s-1}	observed failure count in the range $[1,s-1]$
$X_{s,t}$	observed failure count in the range $[s,t]$

FIGURE 13.3   Objects Hierarchy Chart

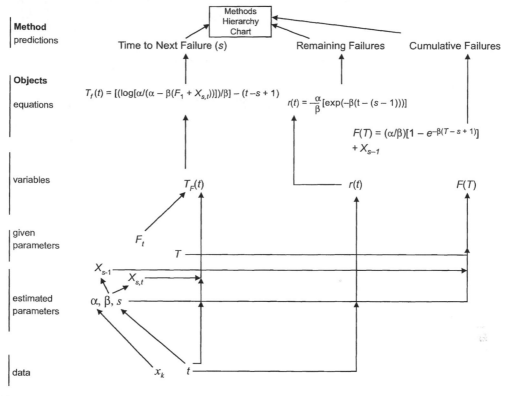

Definitions:

- $r(t)$ Remaining failures predicted at time t
- $T_F(t)$ Time to next failure(s) predicted at time t
- α Failure rate at the beginning of interval s
- β Negative of derivative of failure rate divided by failure rate
- s Starting interval for using observed failure data in parameter estimation
- t Last interval of observed failure data
- T Time of prediction
- x_k number of observed failures in interval k
- X_{s-1} observed failure count in the range $[1,s-1]$
- $X_{s,t}$ observed failure count in the range $[s,t]$
- $F(T)$ Cumulative number of failures after time T

«requirement»
$r(t)$, $T_F(t)$, and $F(T)$: floating point and 6 characters
alpha and beta: floating point and 6 characters
s, t, and T; floating point and 6 characters
x_k, X_{s-1}, and $X_{s,t}$: floating point and 6 characters

Polymorphism

The same operation (i.e., method) may act differently on different classes and objects [RUM91]. For example, a software reliability prediction method would predict differently for *time to next failure* versus *remaining failures* objects. See Objects Hierarchy Chart, Figure 13.3.

Methods

Operations that may be performed on an object [BOO94] (e.g., the object *equations* is executed by method *predict*). See Methods Hierarchy Chart, Figure 13.4, page 294.

FIGURE 13.4   Methods Hierarchy Chart

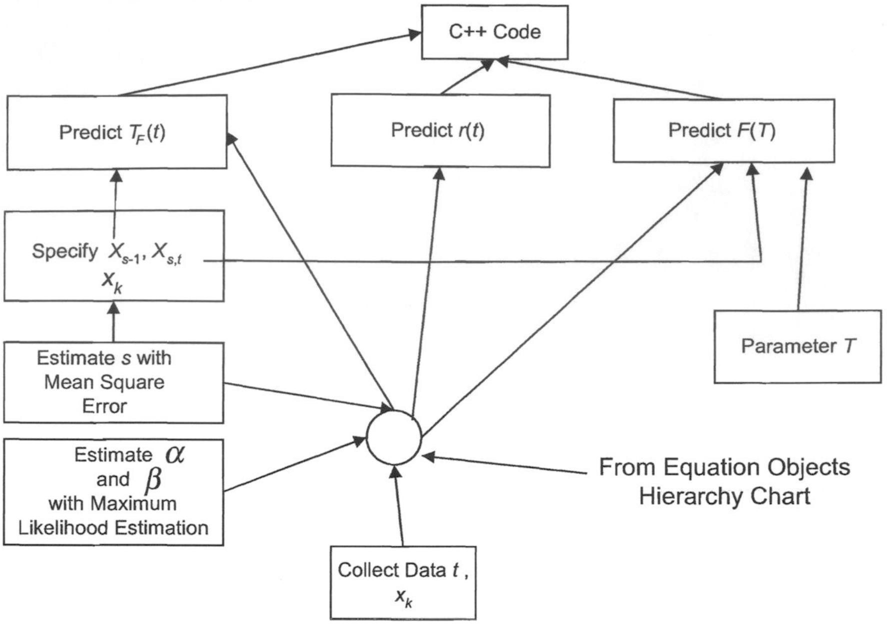

Definitions:

$T_F(t)$	Time to next failure(s) predicted at time t
$r(t)$	Remaining failures predicted at time t
$F(T)$	Cumulative number of failures after time T
X_{s-1}	observed failure count in the range $[1, s-1]$
$X_{s,t}$	observed failure count in the range $[s, t]$
s	Starting interval for using observed failure data in parameter estimation
α	Failure rate at the beginning of interval s
β	Negative of derivative of failure rate divided by failure rate
t	Cumulative time in the range $[1, t]$
T	Time of prediction
x_k	Number of observed failures in interval k

Objects

Real-world objects have two characteristics: *state* (e.g., data and variables initialized) and *behavior* (e.g., prediction accuracy) [BOO94]. See Structure Chart of Software Reliability Model, Figure 13.5.

Classes

In the object-oriented world, *class* is an abstraction of the common properties from a set containing many objects [DOU99]. In the real world, you often find many individual ob-

FIGURE 13.5   Structure Chart of Software Reliability Model

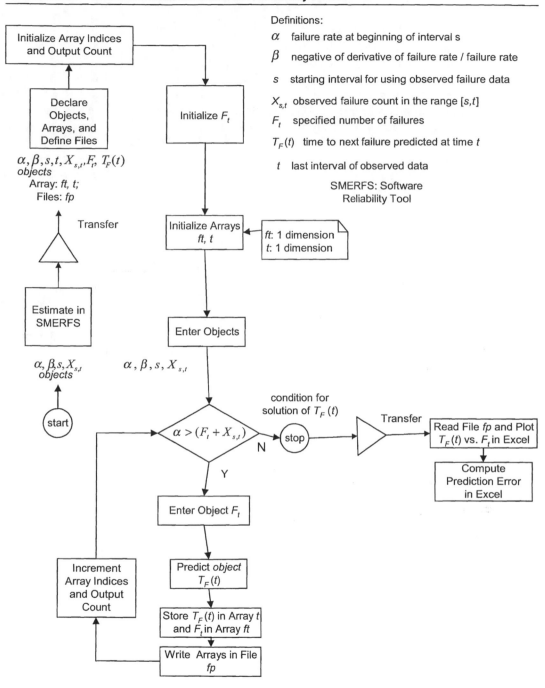

Definitions:

α failure rate at beginning of interval s

β negative of derivative of failure rate / failure rate

s starting interval for using observed failure data

$X_{s,t}$ observed failure count in the range [s,t]

F_t specified number of failures

$T_F(t)$ time to next failure predicted at time t

t last interval of observed data

SMERFS: Software
Reliability Tool

jects that are all of the same class. For example, there may be many reliability model equations in existence, but all are from the same model. Each equation was built from the same set of model concepts. In object-oriented terms, we say that the *time to next failure* equation is an instance of the class of objects called equation. See Structure Chart of Software Reliability Model, Figure 13.5.

What Do O-O Designers Say Is Good Practice?

Patterns

Larman [LAR] considers the following issues: How should objects interact? What classes should do what? These are critical questions in the design of a system. Certain tried-and-true solutions to design problems can be (and have been) expressed as best-practice principles, heuristics, or design patterns—named problem-solution formulas that codify exemplary design principles. O-O analysis and design are strongly related to the prerequisite activity of requirements analysis, which includes writing use cases. Use cases and design patterns are independent of any particular process and apply to many processes. While at first blush it seemed that use cases and patterns would be irrelevant to the design and coding of mathematical software, further reflection suggested that this is not the case, and both diagrams have been included in the design: use cases in Figure 13.1 and design patterns in the activity chart of Figure 13.2.

A pattern is the formalization of a common problem within a context [DOU99]. In this chapter, the common problem is predicting software reliability and the context is applying the predictions to the Space Shuttle. The *Strategy Pattern* is used when there are a number of implementations to achieve a specific goal [LIB98]. For example, there are many software reliability equations that can be programmed in C++ to predict Shuttle reliability. *Strategy Patterns* of failure data collection, parameter estimation, model selection, and prediction were used to code equations in Figure 13.2.

Design patterns can be put to good use in mathematical software development because many of the constituents can be reused: parameters, variables, equations, and data. As a simple example, C++ code from one reliability model could be reused in another by copying and pasting from one program to another! On a more serious note, Gamma and colleagues noticed that many problems yield a similar design [GAM95].

Object-oriented design patterns typically show relationships and interactions between classes or objects, without specifying the final application classes or objects that are involved. Design patterns can speed up the development process by providing tested, proven development paradigms. Effective software design requires considering issues that may not become visible until later in the implementation. Reusing design patterns helps to prevent subtle issues that can cause major problems and improves code readability for coders and architects familiar with the patterns (Wikipedia, the free encyclopedia.)

Structured Programming Versus O-O Programming

Ellis [ELL88] distinguishes between structured programming and O-O programming mindsets. He says the former consists of procedures and functions that define an algorithm to solve the problem at hand. The data to be manipulated are only of secondary interest. The main program is defined first, then the data that are needed to support the program are identified. In the case of the O-O mindset, data are defined first, then the programs that are needed to process the data are identified. This contrast is strange. The program and the data are equally important! The two are interdependent, certainly in mathematical software.

Importance of Standard Notation

Ambler [AMB05] states that standard notation is very important in communicating model development to members of a team. He has detailed instructions for creating UML diagrams, such as standard symbols to use in creating various UML diagrams. Following his guidelines will reduce costly miscommunications. In general one could agree, but there is a benefit and cost to everything. Ambler talks about benefit. The down side is that for a small project like this, which is not part of a team, the cost of complete standardization is very high. Efforts devoted to adhering to standards represents an opportunity cost. This time could be better spent on understanding the problem and using notation that is most advantageous for the *particular* problem at hand.

O-O Benefits

Proponents of O-O claim many benefits. Unfortunately, these claims *may not* be accompanied by a discussion of disadvantages. An obvious one is that O-O is highly abstract; instructors who have taught this model report that students find the abstractions difficult to grasp.

As claimed, the benefits of object-oriented analysis and design include (comments added) [GRA]:

- required changes are localized and unexpected interactions with other program modules are unlikely; (how is this different from information hiding and modular design?)
- inheritance makes O-O systems more extensible, contributing to more rapid development; (inheritance with respect to classes *does* clarify the relationships among software objects)
- object-based design is suitable for distributed, parallel, or sequential implementation; (like any development model, the O-O approach helps you understand the problem)
- objects correspond more closely to the entities in the conceptual worlds of the designer and user, leading to greater traceability; (agree, and this objective can be supported by effective software management, requiring traceability among software products and the process steps that produce them)
- shared data areas are encapsulated, reducing the possibility of unexpected modifications or other update anomalies. (agree)

Experience Using UML

Because the analysis involved the possibility of adapting UML to specify software reliability model process and product, some relevant experiences of other researchers are noted below.

According to [DOY05], using only the object-oriented representations in UML 1.2, he found it impossible to get started. Although the use case diagrams were good at showing what the system does, they provide no insight how it does it. People seemed to need a single view that explained approximately how the system worked in terms of a *few comprehensible chunks* (emphasis added). The ability to organize a system into comprehensible chunks was also important for project management. The decomposition (using a functional model) provided a basis for creating a team structure and managing the project. Because functions are named according to their purpose, there is no need to learn a new vocabulary when trying to understand the system in a process-oriented model. In object-oriented development, creating the architectural classes can be viewed as populating the model with a plethora of pseudo-natural objects in an artificial world. Early in the development, he experienced the phenomenon of the team being linguistically challenged as it struggled to adjust to the new vocabulary. Although the team eventually got past this, it presented difficulty early in the system design. Note that the author used an older version of UML. However, a review of UML 2.0 did not indicate an improvement in this regard.

Although prior research has compared modeling performance using different systems development methods, there has been little research examining the *comprehensibility* of models generated by those methods [AGA99]. The authors report the results of an empirical study comparing user comprehension of object-oriented (O-O) and process-oriented (P-O) models. The fundamental difference is that while O-O models tend to focus on structure, P-O models tend to emphasize behavior or processes. Proponents of the O-O modeling approach argue that it lends itself naturally to the way humans think. However, evidence from research in cognitive psychology and human factors suggests that human problem solving is innately procedural [CAN95].

Given these conflicting viewpoints, researchers investigated empirically whether O-O models are in fact easier to understand than P-O models [AGA99]. But, as suggested by the theory of cognitive fit, model comprehension may be influenced by task-specific characteristics. Therefore, the authors compared O-O and P-O models based on whether the comprehension activity involves: 1) only structural aspects, 2) only behavioral aspects, or 3) a combination of structural and behavioral aspects. They measured comprehension through subjects' responses to questions designed along these three dimensions. Two analyses were conducted, each with a different application and a different group of subjects. Each subject was first trained in both methods, and then participated in one of the two analyses, answering several questions relating to his or her comprehension of an O-O or a P-O model of a business application. The comprehension questions ranged in complexity from relatively simple (addressing either structural or behavioral aspects) to more complex ones (addressing both structural and behavioral aspects). Results show that for most of the simple questions, no significant difference was observed insofar as model comprehension is concerned. For most of the complex questions, however, the P-O model was found to be easier to understand than the O-O model.

O-O Analysis

A careful and detailed analysis was conducted to see whether object-oriented analysis, design, and language are applicable in general to mathematical models and, in particular, to software reliability models. Several "UML–like" diagrams are included that were used to model a software reliability model. The exact standard UML notation was not used because it was found that the modified diagrams expressed mathematical software characteristics better than the standard. Therefore, *modified* UML diagrams were developed for capturing the relationships among mathematical objects and methods. These are called "Objects Hierarchy Chart" (Figure 13.3), "Methods Hierarchy Chart" (Figure 13.4), and "Structure Chart of Software Reliability Model" (Figure 13.5). These diagrams are keyed to traditional O-O diagrams, such as the Activity Diagram.

While it is easy to see that the O-O approach is compatible with developing, let us say, a Web site, it is was not clear how this approach applies to developing mathematical functions. In the case of a Web site, there are activities (e.g., client access to a Web server) so that an activity diagram would apply. However, in the case of equations, would activity diagrams and state charts apply? Would it make sense to consider an equation as an object or as a class? According to Beall and Shephard [BEA94], the answer is "yes." They applied O-O to mathematical software. To be satisfied that what they say applies to this software, the O-O approach was applied to model many facets of both the software reliability product (i.e., the software reliability model) and the *process* that produces the product (e.g., collecting failure data in order to estimate model parameters). Given the fact that some O-O diagrams emphasize activity, this feature would apply to process scenarios.

It was also of interest to see whether the O-O representation of entities can be accurately mapped to the problem domain (e.g., do equations have "state and behavior"?) It is clear that they have functions, parameters, and variables. Actually, equations do have state and behavior. For example, an equation can be in a dormant state: embedded in C++ code or in the active state—executed. In addition, an equation can exhibit behavior (e.g., prediction accuracy). The mapping process is carried all the way down to producing a C++ code fragment in the Appendix to this chapter. The source language must be compiled and executed with a C++ compiler.

It appears that the closer one gets to code, the more applicable the O-O paradigm is to equations. However, there are some tools that can translate from UML to C++ (e.g., Rational Rose). A problem is that the mapping may not be completely compatible with a given compiler. (Some O-O tools are listed in the Appendix to this chapter.)

Object-Oriented Design Process

In the design approach, use the steps below suggested by Graham and Wills [GRA], with the domain examples in parentheses.

Object-oriented analysis and design methods use the following steps, although the details and the ordering of the steps vary quite a lot:

- identify objects and methods; (e.g., equations, failure data, parameters, and variables; estimate, predict)
- establish the relationships between objects; (e.g., equations use failure data)
- establish the interface(s) of each object and exception handling; (e.g., equation does not converge → no solution → program exit)
- implement and test the objects. (e.g., compare predictions with actual values)

Use Cases

According to Hassan Gomaa [GOM], in the analysis modeling phase, static and dynamic models of the system are developed. The static model defines the structural relationships among problem domain classes. Object structuring criteria are used to determine the objects to be considered for the analysis model. A dynamic model is then developed in which the use cases from the requirements model are refined to show the objects that participate in each use case and how they interact with one another. In Figure 13.1, it is shown how the *software reliability analyst* use case interacts with the *software reliability model developer* use cases. The figure also shows the separation of public and private domains: The analyst need not know anything about how the model is developed, but it would be helpful if the developer understands the analyst's application!

An example is the modeling of use case packages in Figure 13.1. Activity diagrams can also be used to model system-level functions, such as predicting software *time to next failure* in Figure 13.2. In addition, Figure 13.2 shows the time phase activities that are necessary to construct a software reliability model. The chart is elaborated with the following specifications.

Software Reliability Model Specifications

- Predict at time t for mission duration t_m, time to next failure $T_F(t)$ with accuracy A_t
- Predict at time t for mission duration t_m, remaining failures $r(t)$ with accuracy A_r
- Predict for mission duration t_m, cumulative failures $F(T)$, to occur at time T, with accuracy A_c

Next, the prediction activity specified in Figure 13.2 is implemented in Figure 13.3 in the form of the hierarchical relationship of objects and methods. It was found that this figure provided an excellent roadmap for writing the C++ code shown in the Appendix to this chapter.

The next step is to list the methods below, and to integrate the equation objects from Figure 13.3 with the methods that operate on them in Figure 13.4.

Methods (operations)

Collect software failure data
Estimate and specify software reliability model parameters
Predict software reliability

Now you can move the logic of the software reliability model close to the coding stage, such as inputting and outputting objects to and from the program, and initializing arrays. This is done in Figure 13.5.

Then the C++ code can be developed for the time to next failure(s) predictions, in accordance with the quasi-UML diagrams. One example is the code fragment in the Appendix to this chapter.

Implementing O-O Methods

Finally, you can use the C++ code in the Appendix to this chapter, derived from the O-O design, by plotting the time to next failure(s) predictions against the specified number of failures, F_t, and computing the mean prediction error in accordance with Figure 13.2. This is done in Figure 13.6 shows a mean prediction error of -13.8%, which is considered acceptable for reliability models, where experience indicates we should expect about a 20% error. The reason for the difference in the number of data points between the predicted and actual values

FIGURE 13.6   NASA Space Shuttle Time to Next Failure(s) $T_F(t)$ [days] vs. Failure Count F_t

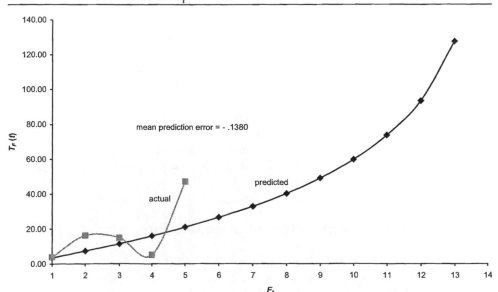

is that there are only five data points available for the latter. Naturally, as more actual time to failure data become available, there would be more data points on the plot.

Conclusions About Applicability of O-O and UML to Mathematical Software

As cited earlier, some authors believe models generated with O-O and UML lack comprehensibility [AGA99]. There is some disagreement about this because it was found that UML diagrams provided a good view of the *process of design* involving the relationship, for example, between objects and methods. However, it seems that the O-O paradigm may be too complex for mathematical software. For this software, there is probably no better model than the equation! On the positive side, it was found that the UML diagrams provided a convenient way to integrate all of the details of the software reliability model design. But you would wonder whether another approach like structured design would not have provided at least equal capability. One area where O-O code is definitely superior is the ability to make *public-* and *private-*type declarations, for example in the use case diagram in Figure 13.1. This is a valuable security feature.

In making conclusions about the applicability of O-O and UML to mathematical software, it is important calibrate conclusions against current UML developments. Therefore, it is instructive to review the UML 2.1.1 specifications [UML07]: UML is a language with a very broad scope that covers a large and diverse set of application domains. Not all of its modeling capabilities are necessarily useful in all domains or applications. The modeling concepts of UML are grouped into language units. A language unit consists of a collection of tightly coupled modeling concepts that provide users with the power to represent aspects of the system under study according to a particular paradigm or formalism. For example, the state machines language unit enables modelers to specify discrete event-driven behavior using a variant of the well-known state charts formalism, while the activities language unit provides for modeling behavior based on a workflow-like paradigm. From the users' perspective, this partitioning of UML means that they need only be concerned with those parts of the language that they consider necessary for their models.

Thus, as a user of UML, you would need only the diagrams that have been provided to represent software reliability models. For example, state charts could have been provided, but these were not needed to formulate the problem.

In the final analysis, O-O methods did not provide advantages for *mathematical software* that could have been obtained using *another paradigm,* such as structured design. The important point is to use a design approach that you are comfortable with and that provides faithful *representation* of *your* problem.

References

[AGA99] R. Agarwal, P. De, and A P. Sinha, "Comprehending Object and Process Models: An Empirical Study." *IEEE Transactions on Software Engineering,* July/August 1999, Vol. 25, No. 4, pp. 541–556.

[AMB05] Scott W. Ambler, *The Elements of UML 2.0 Style.* Cambridge University Press, 2005.

[BEA94] Mark W. Beall and Mark S. Shephard, *An Object-Oriented Framework for Reliable Numerical Simulations, Object-Oriented Software.* Addison-Wesley, 1994.

[BOO94] Grady Booch, *Object-Oriented Analysis and Design with Applications,* second edition. Benjamin/Cummings, 1994.

[CAN95] S. N. Cant, D. R. Jeffrey, and B. Henderson-Sellers, "A Conceptual Model of Cognitive Complexity of Elements of the Programming Process." *Information and Software Technology,* Vol. 37, No. 7, 1995, pp. 351–62.

[DOU99] Bruce Powel Douglass, *Real-Time UML: Developing Efficient Objects for Embedded Systems,* 2nd edition. Addison-Wesley, 1999.

[DOY05] Laurence Doyle and Michael Pennotti, "Systems Engineering Experience with UML on a Complex System." 2005 Stevens Institute of Technology, Proceedings CSER 2005, March 23–25, Hoboken, NJ.

[ELL88] John R. Ellis, *Objectifying Real-Time Systems.* Cambridge University Press, 1998.

[GAM95] Erich Gamma, Richard Helm, Ralph Johnson, and John Vlissides, *Design Patterns: Elements of Reusable Object-Oriented Software.* Addison-Wesley, 1995.

[GOD07] Michael W. Godfrey, "A Hybrid Program Model for Object-Oriented Reverse Engineering." 15th IEEE International Conference on Program Comprehension (ICPC '07), 2007, pp. 81–90.

[GOM] Hassan Gomaa, *Designing Concurrent, Distributed, and Real-Time Applications with UML.* Addison-Wesley, 2000.

[GRA] Ian Graham and Alan Wills, UML—a tutorial, TriReme International, Ltd.

[LAR] Craig Larman, *Applying UML and Patterns—An Introduction to OOA/D and the Unified Process.* Prentice Hall, 2004.

[LIB98] Jesse Liberty, *Beginning Object-Oriented Design with C++.* Wrox Press, 1988.

[MEL00] I. Herman, G. Melancon, and M. S. Marshall, "Graph Visualization and Navigation in Information Visualization: A Survey." *IEEE Transactions on Visualization and Computer Graphics,* 6(1):24–43, 2000.

[MIL56] G. A. Miller, "The Magical Number Seven, Plus or Minus Two: Some Limits on Our Capacity for Processing Information." *The Psychological Review,* 63:81–97, 1956.

[OMO] Omondo Eclipse UML. URL: http://www.omondo.com/.

[RAT03] The Rational Edge. URL: http://www.therationaledge.com/content/sep_03/f_umlbasics_db .jsp.

[RIV02] C. Riva and J. V. Rodriguez, "Combining Static and Dynamic Views for Architecture Reconstruction." In Proceedings of the 6th European Conference on Software Maintenance and Reengineering, IEEE, Washington, DC, 2002, pp. 47–56.

[RUM91] James Rumbaugh, et al., *Object-Oriented Modeling and Design.* Prentice Hall, 1991.

[TON05] P. Tonella and A. Potrich, *Reverse Engineering of Object Oriented Code.* Springer, 2005.

[UML07] Unified Modeling Language: Superstructure, Version 2.1.1, February 2007.

Appendix

The following is the C++ code fragment for the prediction of time to next failure(s):

//Software Reliability Model with keyboard input and file output

//*s*: first failure count interval, *t*: last failure count interval, ft: specified failure count,

//*xst*: failure count in range [*s*,*t*]

//The time to next failure: $T = [(\log[\text{alpha}/(\text{alpha-beta} * (Ft+Xst))]/\text{beta}] - (t-s+1))$

include <iostream> //specify input output library

include <math.h> //specify math library

include <stdio.h>

include <string.h>

using namespace std;

using std::cout; //specify standard screen output

using std::cin; //specify standard screen input

using std::endl; //specify standard end of line

```
main() //beginning of main program
//executable code begins here
FILE *fp;//pointer to type FILE
fp = fopen("c:/models/numbers2.txt", "w");
//"w" opens a text file for writing
const char* format_string; //pointer to type char
int i; //declare output count
i = 0; //initialize output count
double s,t,ft,xst; //declare parameters
double T, alpha, beta; //declare variable T, parameters alpha and beta
int j, k; //declare array indices
j =0, k = 0; //initialize array indices
ft =0; //initialize ft so that while command will work
double arrayft [20]; //declare failure count array
double arrayt [20]; //declare time to next failure array
cout << endl; // start output on a new line
cout << "input alpha =" ; //tell the user to input alpha
cin >> alpha; //inputted alpha
cout << "input beta =" ; //tell the user to input beta
cin >> beta; //inputted beta
cout << "input s =" ; //tell user to input s
cin >> s; //inputted s
cout << "input xst =" ; //tell the user to input xst
cin >> xst; // inputted xst
cout << "input t =" ; //tell the user to input t
cin >> t; //inputted t
while ((alpha > (beta * (ft + xst))) & (i <= 20))//predict T, if a solution can be obtained
{//start of while command
cout << "input ft =" ; //tell the user to input ft
cin >> ft; //inputted ft
T = ((log (alpha/(alpha-beta*(ft+xst)))/beta)-(t-s+1)); // predict T
arrayft [j]= ft; //store ft in array
arrayt [k]= T; //store T in array
fprintf (fp,"%f%c%f%c%\n", arrayft [j], (char) 6, arrayt [k], (char)6);
// output ft, T to numbers2.txt file
i = i + 1; //increment ft input count
j = j +1 ; //increment array index
k = k + 1; //increment array index
}// end of while command
```

fclose(fp); //close numbers2.txt file

return 0; //return to the operating system

} //executable code ends here

The following is a list of O-O and UML tools that may be of interest to readers:

Eclipse: Open Source Tool with many code generators available for investigation, such as for C++.   http://www.eclipse.org/

Objecteering: Commercial UML tool, containing a Fortran code generator, designed to be more culturally acceptable to the scientific community.   www.objecteering.com/

Lapack++: a version of Lapack adapted for C++, for linear algebra. Provides an example of how scientific libraries may be "objectified."   http://lapackpp.sourceforge.net/

Many other libraries are objectified: http://math.nist.gov/

14

Cyber Security Prediction Models

Objectives

This chapter provides the engineer with the knowledge necessary to predict cyber security attacks on information technology (IT) systems. The material prepares the engineer to identify vulnerabilities in IT systems and shows how to mitigate the consequences of cyber attacks. In addition, it shows how software risk analysis can be used to reduce the risk of software failure and improve the security of software products.

What You Will Learn From This Chapter

Predictive models for estimating the occurrence of cyber attacks are desperately needed to counteract the growing threat of cyber terrorism. Unfortunately, except to a limited degree, there is no genuine database of attacks, vulnerabilities, consequences, and risks to employ for model development and validation. However, it is still useful to provide definitions, equations, plots, and analyses to answer the "what if" questions concerning potential attacks. You will learn how this is accomplished by reasoning about the elements of predictive models and their relationships with the real world of cyberspace. The application of these models provides the user with a vehicle for testing hypotheses about how to respond to a cyber attack before it occurs, using risk, vulnerabilities, duration of attacks, and intrusion (number and duration) concepts.

Subjects

Cyber Security Strategies
Cyber Security Threat to the Internet
Internet Vulnerabilities
Cyber Security Threat to Critical Infrastructure
Cyber Security Issues
Cyber Security Theory
Importance of Cyber Security Models
Cyber Security Model Validation
Data Resources
Relationship of Availability and Security
Measurements in Cyber Security
Risk Model
Exponential Model #1
Exponential Model #2
Vulnerability Model

Application Example
Intrusion Model
Relative Measures of Effectiveness
Time Duration of Intrusions Model

Introduction

The Need for Cyber Security Protection

The nation's health, wealth, and security rely on the production and distribution of goods and services. The array of physical assets, processes, and organizations across which these goods and services move are called critical infrastructures (e.g., Internet, electricity, the power plants that generate it, and the electric grid upon which it is distributed). The national security community has been concerned for some time about the vulnerability of critical infrastructure to both physical and cyber attack. In May 1998, President Clinton released Presidential Decision Directive No. 63. The Directive set up groups within the federal government to develop and implement plans that would protect government-operated infrastructures and called for a dialogue between government and the private sector to develop a National Infrastructure Assurance Plan that would protect all of the nation's critical infrastructures by the year 2003. While the Directive called for both physical and cyber protection from both manmade and natural events, implementation focused on cyber protection against manmade cyber events (i.e., computer hackers). However, given the physical damage caused by the September 11 attacks, physical protection of critical infrastructures is receiving greater attention.

Following the events of September 11, the Bush Administration released two relevant Executive Orders (EOs). EO 13228, signed October 8, 2001, established the Office of Homeland Security. Among its duties, the Office shall "coordinate efforts to protect the United States and its *critical infrastructure* from the consequences of terrorist attacks." EO 13231, signed October 16, stated the Bush Administration's policy and objectives for protecting the nation's *information infrastructure* and established the President's Critical Infrastructure Protection Board chaired by a Special Advisor to the President for Cyber Security (both of which were later abolished by an amending executive order). More recently (December17, 2003), the Bush Administration released Homeland Security Presidential Directive 7, reiterating and expanding upon infrastructure protection policy and responsibilities that remain relatively unchanged through two Administrations.

Congress passed legislation in 2002 creating a Department of Homeland Security, consolidating into a single department a number of offices and agencies responsible for implementing various aspects of homeland security. However, infrastructure protection activities remain spread out among various directorates and agencies within the Department, including the *Information Analysis and Infrastructure Protection Directorate* and the *Transportation Security Administration*. Issues in critical infrastructure protection include how to integrate cyber and physical protection; mechanisms for *sharing information among the government, the private sector, and the public;* the need to set priorities; and whether or not the federal government will need to employ more direct incentives to achieve an adequate level of protection by the private sector and states.

Cyber Security Strategies

Conventional thinking about cyber security strategy is defense oriented because it seems to be infeasible to go on the offensive. Sometimes it is difficult to know the sources of attacks.

However, the characteristics of some attacks have been observed for a long time, such as the case of viruses and worms. Although it may not be possible to seek out and destroy the hacker's resources and capabilities, it would be desirable to proactively increase monitoring of high-incident targets and to increase the defenses in these areas, with the objective of reducing the attacks by virtue of enhanced defenses. Defense-oriented cyber security involves the following countermeasures:

Monitor Suspicious Activity

Identify objects that should be monitored:

- Web server interface
- Intranet—Internet interface
- Router interface
- Firewall interface

Identify Data To Be Monitored

- Flows at the above interfaces

Identify Data Flow Threshold

- Identify anomalies in data flow (e.g., buffer overflow caused by denial of service attacks)

Establish Criterion for Alert

- Data flow exceeds the threshold

Develop Monitoring Database

- Dump and analyze suspicious data

Invoke Countermeasures When an Alert Occurs

- Analyze suspicious data and, if a violation is found, reject future data flow of this type (e.g., attempts to connect to organization's network)

Cyber Security Threat to the Internet

Internet Protocol (IP) routing is dynamic. Dynamic routing calls for routes to be calculated automatically at regular intervals by software in routing devices. This contrasts with static routing, where routers are established by the network administrator and do not change until the network administrator changes them. IP routing specifies that IP datagrams (i.e., messages or parts of a message) travel through internetworks one hop at a time. The entire route is not known at the onset of the journey, however. Instead, at each stop, the next destination is calculated by matching the destination address within the datagram with an entry in the current node's routing table.

Traffic observed at Internet routers tends to exhibit a wide range of round-trip times, including relatively short round trip times (< 50 ms) [FLO]. The load on the network is not static. It is different at different times of the day and different days of the year, and hence the network must support all of the load distributions that occur. In order to guarantee a level of reliability, networks have alternate paths and sufficient additional capacity to carry the traffic even if a link or a node fails. Networks must also have sufficient spare capacity to support the future predicted traffic for at least the time it takes to install new facilities [FLO]. The characteristic of Internet routing that makes the Internet vulnerable to attack is the great variation in data flow that makes it difficult to distinguish between legitimate traffic and a cyber attack.

What is typically not considered in the design process is how well the network copes with unpredicted shifts in the traffic load. The ability of a network to support unexpected changes in load is becoming more important because of: 1) the way fibers are installed; 2) recent and expected advances in wavelength division multiplexing (WDM) and dense WDM (DWDM); and 3) the new Internet services that are being introduced. Because of the first two factors, installed network topologies now have adequate capacity for a longer time than in the past and will be able to cope with greater shifts in demand. The third factor is causing the shifts in demands to occur more frequently and more suddenly than they have in the past [MAX 05].

Internet queue oscillations are widely considered a serious potential problem in Internet queue management. Moderate changes in the traffic mix can strongly affect oscillation dynamics. In particular, adding short-lived flows, reverse-path traffic, and a range of round-trip times—characteristics ubiquitous on the Internet, as in the Transmission Control Protocol (TCP)—changes simple oscillations into more complex burst behavior. This dramatic change highlights the importance of traffic flow variations that can affect the ability to detect cyber attacks [FLO].

As reported in [YUA05], stealthy Denial of Services (DoS) attacks can have a devastating effect on router congestion, with congestion flooding the victim (e.g., ISP customer host). These attacks increase flow rate and variations in flow rate, making detection of attacks difficult. The DoS attacks overwhelm the receiving end of router network, such as customer hosts. Distinguishing between normal and attack data is difficult. As stated in [SUL05], malicious hackers can launch attacks against IP routers by flooding them with messages. ISP recovery components can isolate and respond to such denial-of-service attacks and dispose of excess messages. IP traceback methods provide the victim's network administrators with the ability to identify the address of the true source of the packets causing a DoS attack. IP traceback is vital for restoring normal network functionality as quickly as possible, preventing reoccurrences, and, ultimately, holding the attackers accountable [IEE03].

Internet Vulnerabilities

Among the various types of Internet vulnerabilities are routing attacks and packet forwarding attacks. Routing attacks can involve false advertising of routes among Internet routers, or intruding on an Internet Service Provider (ISP) network to the extent of changing the routing sequence among nodes. In the packet forwarding realm, attackers can divert traffic to routes that are undesired by the ISP. Furthermore, attackers can cause routing loops such that packets never reach their destinations.

Finally, the worst type of attack is the Denial of Services (DoS) attack that dumps junk into the ISP network and wastes valuable network resources [YAN04]. By misconfiguring the ISP routing topology, attackers can cause erroneous routes to be implemented. The cyber threat to the Internet can be mitigated by providing a capability to identify choke points in the Internet. A choke point is defined as a node or link in the Internet where information flow is impeded. The problem could be caused by information flow rates that exceed the capacities of the nodes and links, such as excessive data flow at the interface of the Intranet and Internet, as suggested by Figure 14.1 (attack A_1).

FIGURE 14.1   Cyber Security in the Critical Infrastructure

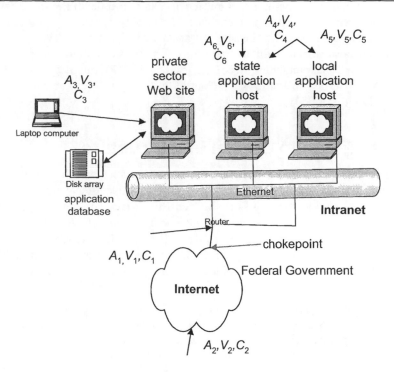

A_i : Attack, Risk Priority i (Order of Priority)   Vulnerability V_i

A_1 : Denial of Service: Flood Router V_1: Firewall

A_2 : Packet Sniffer: Capture Passwords V_2: No Password Capture Protection

A_3 : Probe: Obtain Web Server Account Information V_3: No Web Server Firewall

A_4 : Worm: Replicates Itself V_4: No Anti-Worm Software

A_5 : Virus: Corrupt Operating System V_5: No Anti-Virus Software

A_6 : Trojan Horse: Hide in Host and Corrupt V_6: No Software to Detect Trojan Horse
        Applications

Consequence C_i

C_1 : Loss of Connectivity Between Internet and Intranet

C_2 : Intranet Passwords Compromised

C_3 : Web Server Programs Hijacked

C_4 : Intranet Brought Down

C_5 : Operating System Rendered Inoperable

C_6 : Application Programs Corrupted

Bandwidth attacks are attempts to consume resources, such as network bandwidth or equipment throughput. High-data-volume attacks can consume all available bandwidth on the link between an ISP site and a customer. The link fills up, and legitimate traffic slows down. Timeouts may occur, causing retransmission, generating even more traffic. An attacker can consume bandwidth by transmitting any traffic at all nodes on the network connection. A flood attack might use User Data Protocol (UDP), Internet Control Message Protocol (ICMP) packets, or Transmission Control Protocol (TCP) packets to consume all available bandwidth [HOU01].

Cyber Security Threat to Critical Infrastructure

The U.S. electric power system has historically operated at such a high level of reliability that any major outage, caused by either sabotage, weather, or operational errors, makes news headlines. The transmission system is extensive, consisting mainly of transformers, switches, transmission towers and lines, control centers, and computer controls. A spectrum of threats exists to the electric system, ranging from weather-related incidents to terrorist attacks—including physical attacks as well as attacks on computer systems, or cyber attacks [CRS05].

The criticality of the cyber threat problem is expressed in excerpts from the following report:

> The Nation's information technology (IT) infrastructure, still evolving from U.S. technological innovations such as the personal computer and the Internet, today is a vast fabric of computers— from supercomputers to handheld devices—and interconnected networks enabling high-speed communications, information access, advanced computation, transactions, and automated processes relied upon in every sector of society. Because much of this infrastructure connects to the Internet, it embodies the Internet's original attributes of openness, inventiveness, and the assumption of good will [PIT05].

> These attributes have made the United States information technology infrastructure an irresistible target for vandals and criminals worldwide. The President's Information Technology Advisory Committee (PITAC) believes that terrorists will inevitably follow suit, taking advantage of vulnerabilities including some that the nation has not yet clearly recognized or addressed. The computers that manage critical United States facilities, infrastructures, and essential services can be targeted to set off system wide failures, and these computers frequently are accessible from virtually anywhere in the world via the Internet [PIT05].

> Computing systems control the management of power plants, dams, the North American power grid, air traffic control systems, food and energy distribution, and the financial system, to name only some. The reliance of these sensitive physical installations and processes on the IT infrastructure makes that infrastructure itself critical and in the national interest to safeguard [PIT05].

Further evidence of this problem is contained in the following excerpt from an article in the *Washington Post* [GRA05]:

> Web sites in China are being used heavily to target computer networks in the Defense Department and other U.S. agencies, successfully breaching hundreds of unclassified networks, according to several U.S. officials. Classified systems have not been compromised, the officials added. But U.S. authorities remain concerned because, as one official said, even seemingly innocuous information, when pulled together from various sources, can yield useful intelligence to an adversary.

It is evident that the potential for cyber attacks is not limited to sources in the United States. For example, William Yurcik and David Doss report in their paper "Internet Attacks: A Policy Framework for Rules of Engagement" [YUR01] that there is also concern about foreign sources as well, as articulated in the following testimony: "We are detecting, with increasing frequency, the appearance of doctrine and dedicated offensive cyber warfare programs in other countries. We have identified several [countries], based on all-source intelligence information, that are pursuing government-sponsored offensive cyber programs. Information warfare is becoming a strategic alternative for countries that realize that, in conventional military confrontation with the United States, they will not prevail."

In the commercial arena, Microsoft has instituted the following policy: "With the implementation of Trustworthy Computing, security has become the number one priority. Default installations aimed at ease of use are now not always sufficiently secure, but, going forward, security in Microsoft's products will take precedence over ease of use." Given Microsoft's influence in the software industry, it is interesting that they have endorsed the idea of cyber security modeling in that threat modeling is a key part of its Trustworthy Computing program [SCH05].

Cyber Security Issues

In response to the cyber security crisis, issues that are important to address are:

1. Can various representations and models of cyber security be developed that would provide a framework advancing the field?
2. Can theoretical prediction models be developed to assess the risk of various types of cyber attacks?
3. Can an empirical model, using Computer Emergency Response Team (CERT) data [MOO01], be developed to assess the risk of vulnerabilities to cyber attacks?

Cyber Security Theory

In the theory of cyber security there are various views of security. One is empirical, focusing on the contemporary scenario of attacks and vulnerabilities, as shown in Figure 14.1. This portrayal assists decision makers in identifying vulnerabilities and the means to respond to them. This representation allows cyber security officials to delineate the critical elements in the network infrastructure that require increased security. Cyber security theory is based on the following factors: the interaction of entities in the critical infrastructure, as shown in Figure 14.1, and the ability to predict various cyber security quantities, if only on an approximate basis.

Importance of Cyber Security Models

Models are important in developing and understanding the theory of cyber security. These models support the objective of predicting cyber security risks. One type of model, the *risk model*, predicts the risk of attack, given the vulnerabilities and consequences of a specified cyber security situation. The second model, the *exponential model,* is time-based and predicts the probability of attack as a function of duration of attacks. Duration of attacks is a surrogate measure of risk because the shorter the duration, the greater the risk for the user due to the higher probability of attack. The third model, the *vulnerability model,* uses vulnerability data from the CERT databases [MOO01]. First, the CERT data are used to make a regression model fit. Then, using the fit, a regression equation is identified that can be used for predicting future vulnerabilities, conditioned on confidence intervals, within which the vulnerabilities are expected to lie. Lastly, the fourth model, the *intrusion model,* relates characteristics of intrusion attacks to the risk of intrusions occurring.

Cyber Security Model Validation

It is important to note that these models cannot be validated against real-world attack events because the nature of future attacks is unknown. The best you can do is to *illustrate* for cyber security officials the important parameters and variables in the cyber security environment and the likely outcome of cyber security scenarios under specified "what if" conditions.

According to [NIC04], no methodology currently exists that can quantify the amount of security provided by a particular approach. Nevertheless, models can be applied to hypothetical but realistic data to provide a template for Internet decision makers to counteract the cyber threat. So far, most attempts at validation of security have been qualitative, focusing more on the process used to build a system that should be secure. Since it is impossible in practice to build a perfectly secure system, it is desirable to quantitatively validate models concerning attacker behavior, the effects of exploited vulnerabilities on attacker behavior, and the system's responses to attacks. The value of most quantitative security models is in gaining insight and making decisions about how best to make a system secure, rather than making a precise statement about a specific system's security [NIC04].

Data Resources

Ideally, the types of data to counteract cyber attacks are the following: Internet router and host node identification, along with data flow rates; congestion information; node reliability experience; and detailed cyber attack experience. Unfortunately, these data are not available from published sources. Thus, you are forced to resort to hypothetical but realistic data and probability distributions in the models. The model concepts, and example model results, provide insight for ISP managers to mitigate the threat of Internet cyber attacks on router networks. Using the models, these managers could use their proprietary threat data to develop countermeasures in their particular environment to reduce the risk to their customer resources.

Relationship of Availability and Security

Availability is a system attribute that is not ordinarily associated with security. The IEEE *Standard Glossary of Software Engineering Terminology* defines *availability* as follows: "The degree to which a system or component is operational and accessible when required for use, often expressed as a probability" [IEEE90]. However, in their paper, "End-to-End Availability Policies and Noninterference," Lantian Zheng and Andrew C. Myers relate *availability* to security [ZHE05]. Although this approach does not comport with the standard definition cited above, it is a valuable idea because if a system is attacked and compromised, its availability has been decreased. Thus, it would make sense to include *unavailability* as one of the consequences of a cyber attack. Unfortunately, this attribute is not included in cyber security databases.

Measurements in Cyber Security

Data are required to support model validation. In this regard, William Yurcik, David Loomis, and Alexander D. Korzyk, Sr., in their paper, "Predicting Internet Attacks: On Developing an Effective Measurement Methodology" [YUR00], one of the first articles to call for measurement in cyber security, state that "available metrics that could be collected to develop an Internet attack prediction methodology" include:

1. Type of Internet attack based on a common taxonomy
2. Number and percentage of Internet attack frequency growth
3. Number and percentage of detected Internet attacks
4. Number and percentage of successful Internet attacks
5. Number and percentage of reported Internet attacks
6. Number and percentage of automated Internet attacks
7. Types of automated Internet attacks—tools used and ports probed
8. Duration of Internet attacks (day/month/year)
9. Number of hosts involved in Internet attacks
10. Cost estimate of Internet attacks
11. Geographical location of Internet attacks
12. Targeted systems (location, organization, vendor, operating system)

While all these data would be useful to collect and analyze, the list does not include information about vulnerabilities, risks, and consequences, the pillars of cyber security analysis.

Now, cyber security prediction models are described and applied.

Risk Model

Definitions

R_i: risk of priority i
Risk priority is the consequences of a given type of attack (e.g., denial of service) relative to the consequences of other types of attacks (e.g., virus)

P_{ai}:   relative probability of attack of risk priority i

P_{vi}:   probability of vulnerability of risk priority i
Since little is known about organizations' vulnerabilities (they are not going to admit to any!), it is necessary to randomize this probability in the analysis so that there will be no bias in the computations.

C_i: consequence associated with risk priority i
Example: Destruction of cyber infrastructure
Example: Number of network objects affected (e.g., routers, ISPs, servers, hosts, Web sites, links)

$T_L(i)$:   subjective relative threat level of attack of risk priority i
n: total number of attacks
V_i: vulnerability associated with risk priority i

Model Structure

This model relates probability of attack, relative probability of vulnerability, and consequence of an attack, as shown in Figure 14.1. It is assumed that risk can be accurately computed using equation (14.1). The justification is that, intuitively, risk would increase as all three quantities comprising equation (14.1) increase.

Risk = Relative Probability of Attack * Probability of Vulnerability * Consequence (14.1)

$$R_i = P_{ai} * P_{vi} * C_i \qquad (14.2)$$

Examples of equation (14.2):

$$R_1 = P \text{ (Denial of Service)} * P \text{ (No Firewall)} * C_1 \text{ (Consequence of Risk Priority 1)} \quad (14.3)$$

$$R_2 = P \text{ (Virus)} * P \text{ (No Anti-Virus Software)} * C_2 \text{ (Consequence of Risk Priority 2)} \quad (14.4)$$

While it is not feasible to include probability of attack per se because the data that would allow us to estimate this quantity are not available, it is possible to use a surrogate measure—relative probability of attack—that is computed from evaluations of the relative threat level of various types of attacks, as shown in equation (14.5).

$$P_{ai} = \frac{T_L(i)}{\sum_{i=1}^{n} T_L(i)} \quad (14.5)$$

Example Calculations for Risk Model

Next are shown example calculations and plots that illustrate risk model outputs. The data in Table 14.1 were developed as follows:

The table shows eleven types of attacks, starting with *denial of service* (DoS)—the most severe—and ending with *corruption of database*—the least severe.

$T_L(i)$ represents a subjective assessment of the relative threat level of various types of attacks, starting with *denial of service* = 100 and ending with *corruption of database* = 3. Note that the purpose of the example is illustrative; a different assignment of relative threat levels to types of attack would lead to different results.

The relative probability of attack of threat i, P_{ai}, is computed from equation (14.5).

As stated previously, data are not available for the probability of vulnerability of risk priority i, P_{vi}. Thus it is necessary to randomize this quantity in the range: 0, . . . ,1.

C_i is assigned linearly to the types of attacks, assigning 11 to DoS, 10 to virus, etc.

The desired output risk = R_i is computed from equation (14.2). The bolded values in the table highlight the significant (i.e., high risk) results. Figure 14.2 shows how risk varies with probability of attack. The plot is annotated with the attack types associated with the

TABLE 14.1   Evaluation of Risks of Cyber Threats

Attack	Threat $T_L(i)$	P (attack) P_{ai}	P (vulner.) P_{vi}	Consequence C_i	Risk R_i
Denial of Service	100	**0.2288**	0.4384	11	**1.1034**
Virus	100	**0.2288**	0.1355	10	0.3101
Probe	71	**0.1625**	0.7639	9	**1.1170**
Scan	45	0.1030	0.7190	8	0.5923
Account Compromise	33	0.0755	0.1741	7	0.0921
Packet Sniffer	26	0.0595	0.4932	6	0.1761
Root Compromise	26	0.0595	0.0213	5	0.0064
Trojan Horse	13	0.0297	0.6479	4	0.0771
Worm	12	0.0275	0.2946	3	0.0243
Spyware	8	0.0183	0.8708	2	0.0319
Corruption of Database	3	0.0069	0.1832	1	0.0013

FIGURE 14.2   Risk R_i vs. Probability of Attack P_{ai}

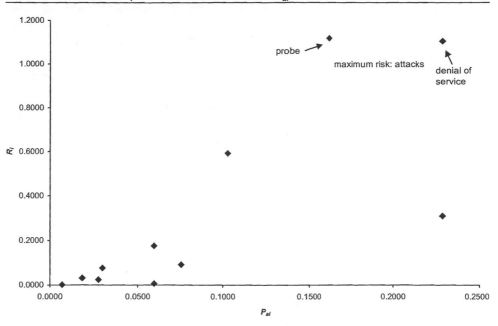

major risk vales. As a practical matter, the plot indicates that risk would rise rapidly at a value of $P_{ai} \cong .15$. This could be considered a significant risk and the user should prepare, in particular, against *DoS* and *Probe* attacks. However, note that R_i is significantly a function of *consequences* C_i. Thus, a sensitivity analysis of the assignment of C_i to the relative threat levels could be performed to see whether the pattern in Figure 14.2 would change.

Figure 14.3 shows that risk increases with consequences, as you would expect, and again the diagram is annotated with the major risk attacks of *DoS* and *Probe*. The reason

FIGURE 14.3   Risk R_i vs. Consequence C_i

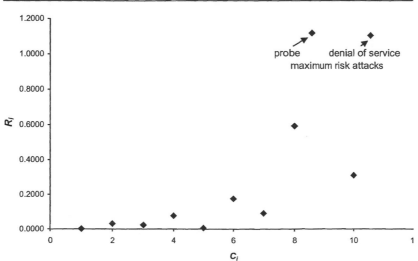

for using both Figures 14.2 and 14.3 is that the relationships among risk, probability of attack, and consequences are not obvious *a priori*. It is important to have more than one view of the relationships so that one view can confirm the other (i.e., Figure 14.3 confirms the Figure 14.2 result of *DoS* and *Probe* attacks being the major risks).

Using these results, you would prioritize risk R_i (i.e., order values of R_i). This would provide one of the inputs for allocating resources for employing countermeasures.

Exponential Model #1

Assume the *probability of attack* $P_a(t)$ is exponentially distributed, where the justification of this assumption is the skewed nature of the distribution of duration of attacks *t*. Thus, the key parameters and variables in this formulation follow.

λ: rate of attacks

λt = number of attacks in time interval *t* (duration of attacks)

$P_a(t) = \lambda e^{-\lambda t}$ = probability of an attack in time interval *t*   (14.6)

Note that this formulation does not account for priority of risk *i* nor does it differentiate types of attacks Thus, this model might be considered inferior to the risk model; however, it is easier to implement and does provide useful information, as Figure 14.4 attests. That is, the user could establish objectives of duration of attacks = 2 days and probability of attack = .184 and estimate the expected number of attacks = 10.96.

Table 14.2 shows an example of this model, wherein 11 values of time between attacks $t = 1, \ldots, 11$ days and a rate of attack ($\lambda = NT/T$ attacks per day) are the inputs to the model that produce two outputs: probability of attack $P_a(t)$ and expected number of attacks λt.

Exponential Model # 2

The concept of this model is that the duration of attacks t_a is a key variable in counteracting attacks. Since, as mentioned, data on probability of attack, P_{ai}, are not available, you are forced to use the surrogate measure, relative threat level, T_L, in order to estimate P_{ai}. Additionally, t_a can be interpreted as a surrogate measure of risk (i.e., the smaller the value of t_a, the higher the risk due to the higher probability of attack). Note that this model, as opposed to Exponential Model # 1, accounts for risk priority *i* and specific types of attacks.

FIGURE 14.4   Expected Number of Attacks vs. Probability of Attack, $P_a(t)$

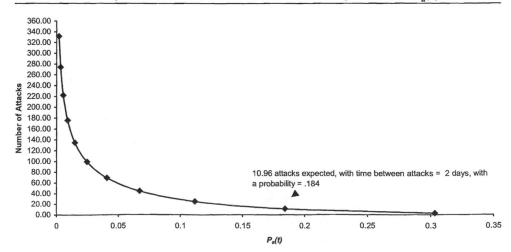

TABLE 14.2   Exponential Model #1

Type of Attack	N(T) Attacks per Year	λ Attacks per Day	t Duration of Attacks	λt Number of Attacks	$P_a(t) = \lambda e^{-\lambda t}$ Probability of Attack
Denial of Service	1000	2.74	1	2.74	0.303
Virus	2000	5.48	2	10.96	0.184
Probe	3000	8.22	3	24.66	0.112
Scan	4000	10.96	4	43.84	0.068
Account Compromise	5000	13.70	5	68.49	0.041
Packet Sniffer	6000	16.44	6	98.63	0.025
Root Compromise	7000	19.18	7	134.25	0.015
Trojan Horse	8000	21.92	8	175.34	0.009
Worm	9000	24.66	9	221.92	0.006
Spyware	10000	27.40	10	273.97	0.003
Corruption of Database	11000	30.14	11	331.51	0.002
T	365 days		days		

To develop the model, formulate probability of attack as a function of *relative threat level* in equation 14.7.

T_L = relative threat level
$P_{ai} = f(T_L)$ = relative probability of attack of risk priority i (14.7)
t_a = duration of attacks (e.g., days)
$N(T)$ = number of attacks in Time T
T = specified attack time (e.g., in 365 days)

$$\lambda = \frac{N(T)}{T} = \text{mean rate of attacks (e.g., attacks per day)} \quad (14.8)$$

Equation (14.9) is the probability density function for the exponentially distributed duration of attacks t_a and the relative probability of attack of risk priority i (equation (14.7)).

$$P_{ai} = \lambda e^{-\lambda t_a} \quad (14.9)$$

To solve for duration of attacks t_a, first take the logarithms of both sides of equation (14.9):

$$\log(P_{ai}) = \log \lambda - \lambda t_a \quad (14.10)$$

Then, rearrange terms in equation (14.10):

$$\lambda t_a = \log \lambda - \log(P_{ai}) \quad (14.11)$$

Solving equations (14.9), (14.10), and (14.11) for t_a, obtain equation (14.12):

$$t_a = \frac{1}{\lambda} \log\left(\frac{\lambda}{P_{ai}}\right) \quad (14.12)$$

Duration of Attacks Calculations

Table 14.3 shows sample calculations for duration of attacks. The first column, $N(T)$, is an assumed set of number of attacks per year; $T = 365$ days; $N(T)/T = \lambda$, the attack rate; P_{ai} is

TABLE 14.3   Duration of Attack Calculations

Type of Attack	$N(T)$ Attacks per Year	$\dfrac{N(T)}{T}$	P_{ai} Probability of Attack	$\dfrac{1}{\lambda}\log\left(\dfrac{\lambda}{P_{ai}}\right)$	$t_a * 24$ Duration of Attacks (hours)	Rate of change of P_{ai} $\dfrac{d(t_a)}{d(P_{ai})}$
Denial of Service	1000	2.74	0.0069	2.19	52.47	−19.4064
Virus	2000	5.48	0.0183	1.04	24.97	−1.8194
Probe	3000	8.22	0.0275	0.69	16.65	−0.5391
Scan	4000	10.96	0.0297	0.54	12.94	−0.2799
Account Compromise	5000	13.70	0.0595	0.40	9.53	−0.0896
Packet Sniffer	6000	16.44	0.0595	0.34	8.21	−0.0622
Root Compromise	7000	19.18	0.0755	0.29	6.93	−0.0360
Trojan Horse	8000	21.92	0.1030	0.24	5.87	−0.0202
Worm	9000	24.66	0.1625	0.20	4.89	−0.0101
Spyware	10000	27.40	0.2288	0.17	4.19	−0.0058
Corruption of Database	11000	30.14	0.2288	0.16	3.89	−0.0048
T	365 days	λ attacks per day		t_a duration of attacks		days per probability

obtained from equation (14.9); the fourth column computes the time between attacks t_a in days; and fifth column provides t_a in hours, which is plotted in Figure 14.5.

Using equation (14.12), the plot of duration of attacks t_a versus probability of attack P_{ai} is shown in Figure 14.5, where the region to the right of the assumed objective of $t_a > 24$ hours is noted as the region to avoid. This policy would allow *DoS* and virus attacks. This decision is illustrative; another user may find this policy unacceptable due to the severity of *DoS* and virus attacks. However, the significant effort and cost involved in implementing countermeasures against *DoS* and virus attacks should be considered. This plot shows

FIGURE 14.5   Duration of Attacks (t_a) vs. Probability of Attack of Risk Priority $I(Pa_i)$

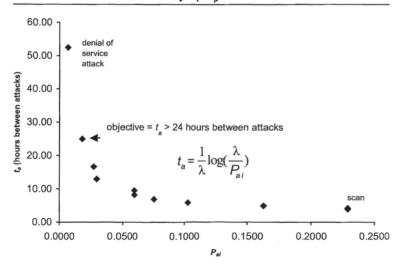

how tradeoffs can be made between threat level (P_{ai}) and risk (t_a). The 24-hour point corresponds to P_{ai} = .0183, whereas a policy to protect against *DoS* corresponds to the 52-hour point, with a P_{ai} =.0069 (see Table 14.3). The user would have to decide whether it is worth the effort and cost to employ increased countermeasures in the face of very low probabilities of attack.

Rate of Change of Duration of Attacks

Another criterion for prioritizing attacks is the rate of change of duration of attacks relative to the probability of attack, obtained by differentiating equation (14.12) and is given by equation (14.13).

$$\frac{d(t_a)}{d(P_{ai})} = -\frac{1}{\lambda}\left(\frac{1}{P_{ai}^2}\right)\left(\frac{P_{ai}}{\lambda}\right) = -\left(\frac{1}{\lambda^2}\right)\left(\frac{1}{P_{ai}}\right) \qquad (14.13)$$

This quantity is of interest because you can see when the rate of change of t_a—a surrogate for risk—becomes so small that the threat is virtually non-existent. This situation is tabulated in Figure 14.6 and Table 14.3, where P_{ai} = .0275 corresponds to a *probe* attack. At this point, the rate of change is miniscule, meaning that the rate of change of *risk* is very small. Using this criterion, probe attacks would not be given high priority even though the t_a > 24-hour policy is violated.

Correspondence between Probability of Attack and Risk of Attack

Figure 14.7 (page 320) demonstrates that probability of attack and risk of attack are related. Since probability of attack is a function of attack duration, you can conclude again that attack duration is a meaningful surrogate for risk.

FIGURE 14.6   Rate of Duration of Attacks, $d(t_a)/d(P_{ai})$ vs. Probability of Attack, P_{ai}

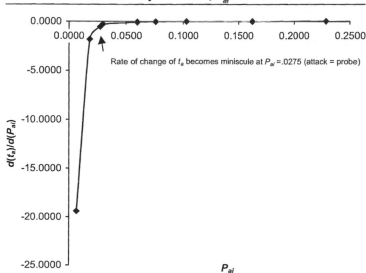

FIGURE 14.7 Risk R_i vs. Probability of Attack Pa_i

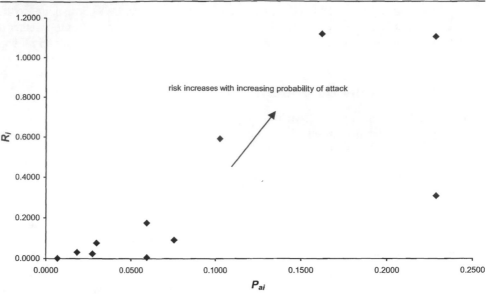

Vulnerability Model

Due to the availability of vulnerability count data, it is possible to develop a prediction model based on these data. This example includes both the actual data and predicted plot of CERT vulnerability data [MOO01] in Figure 14.8. The prediction is obtained from a fit to the actual data. Since there is a good fit (i.e., $R^2 = .8953$), the regression in equation (14.4) was obtained.

$$F(T) = 150.45 * e^{.3952T}, \tag{14.14}$$

where $F(T)$ = CERT Vulnerability Count and T = Years Since First Recording (1995). This model would be used to predict future vulnerability counts $F(T)$ for a specified Years Since

FIGURE 14.8 CERT Recorded Vulnerabilities

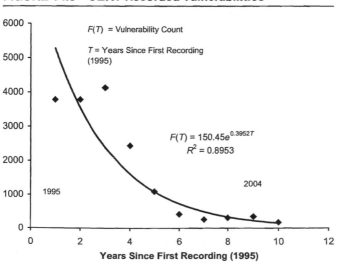

FIGURE 14.9   CERT Actual and Predicted Vulnerabilities Counts

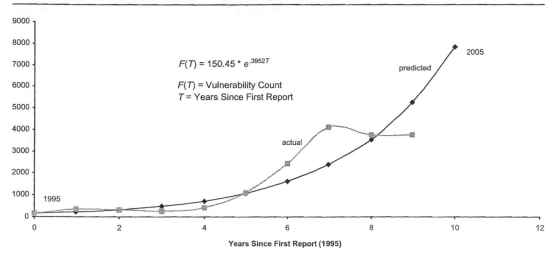

First Recording T. Notice that $F(T)$ can be considered a measure of risk (i.e., the longer the time from the baseline of 1995, the higher the count, and, hence, the higher the risk of increased vulnerabilities). Actually, equation (14.14) can only be used to predict vulner-abilities for one year into the future because, from Figure 14.9, you can see that the actual vulnerability count has flattened out, whereas equation (14.14) predicts a steep increase to the year 2005. Thus, confidence intervals are needed to bound the prediction. These inter-vals are developed in the next section.

Development of Confidence Intervals for CERT Vulnerability Count

The CERT confidence interval calculation is shown in equation (14.15):

$$F\left(\hat{T}\right)-\left(Z_{i-\alpha/2}*S\right)\le F(T)\le F\left(\hat{T}\right)+\left(Z_{i-\alpha/2}*S\right) \quad \text{[FAR83]}, \tag{14.15}$$

where S is the standard deviation, N is the sample size, $(Z_{\alpha/2} = -1.96$, and $Z_{1-\alpha/2} = 1.96$, standardized deviations from the mean for the normal distribution), and $\alpha = .05$.

$$S=\sqrt{\sum_{i=1}^{N}\frac{\left(F_i\left(\hat{T}\right)-F\left(\hat{T}\right)i\right)^2}{N-1}} \tag{14.16}$$

Using equations (14.15) and (14.16), the confidence intervals are plotted in Figure 14.10 on page 322. The meaning of the figure is that you would expect the vulnerability count to fall between these intervals for the years 1995–2005. Including more recent data in the calculations would allow you to update the confidence interval plots.

Application Example

Now, the three models are integrated to produce a scenario of how network managers might use them to assess the risk of a specified type of attack—using a *DoS* attack as an

FIGURE 14.10   CERT Vulnerability Count Confidence Limits vs. Years from First Report (1995)

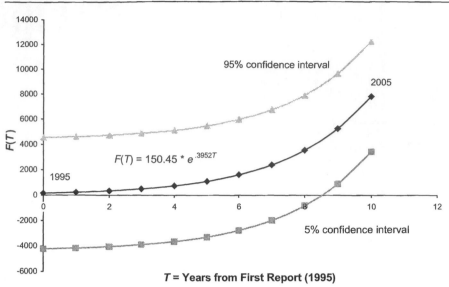

example. Using Figure 14.1 as the baseline for analysis, develop the scenario. Referring to this figure, a *DoS attack* (A$_1$) has occurred at the router between the Internet and Intranet, breaking the communication between Federal and non-Federal sectors. The attack has been

FIGURE 14.11   Cyber Security Feedback System

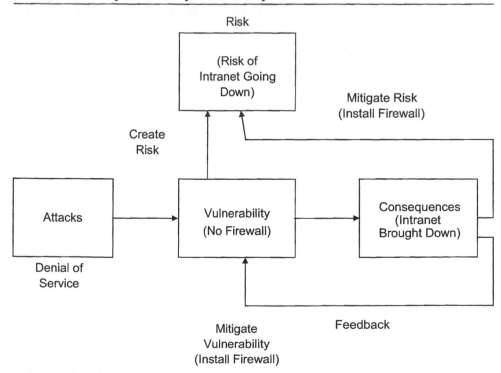

successful due to the *vulnerability* (V_1) of no firewall between the Internet and Intranet. The *consequence* (C_1) is loss of connectivity between Internet and Intranet—the Intranet is brought down. In response to these events, the network managers launch a *countermeasure* to deter future attacks. The countermeasure is depicted in Figure 14.11, where there is feedback from the consequences to mitigate the *vulnerability* and *risk* by installing a firewall.

Before the managers launch the countermeasure, they want to assess the risk of a future *DoS* attack in order to estimate whether the cost and effort to install the firewall are warranted based on the risk. The cost and effort of obtaining and installing a firewall are not significant; however, the labor involved in analyzing logged packet traffic for anomalous behavior and the cost of firewall hardware and software maintenance (e.g., establishing and upgrading filter rules) are not trivial. Therefore, the risk model and the accompanying Figures 14.2 and 14.3 are used to evaluate *probability* of attack, *consequences,* and *risk* of taking no action. These figures inform the managers that all three variables have significant values.

Intrusion Model [SCH04]

Overview of Intrusion Models

An overview of the intrusion models is shown in Figure 14.12, wherein the inputs x, m, and λ, operated on by the probabilities of the model, shown in the box, produce the relative effectiveness and intrusion metric outputs. The effectiveness metrics RE_x and RE_t can be used

FIGURE 14.12   Intrusion Model

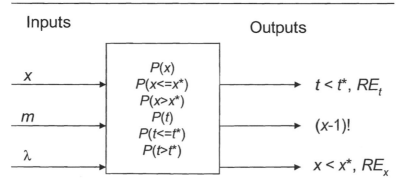

x: number of intrusions

m: mean number of intrusions

λ : mean intrusion rate

t: time duration of intrusion

$(x\text{-}1)!$: intrusion metric

t^*: limit on time duration of intrusions

x^*: limit on number of intrusions

RE_x: relative effectiveness of preventing x number of intrusions

RE_t: relative effectiveness of preventing intrusions of duration t

as risk metrics to adjust cyber security policy. Because "threat of intrusions" is a nebulous term, and number of intrusions x is easily understood, x is used as a surrogate.

In order to provide a baseline for understanding the intrusion model, the following definitions are provided:

Intrusion: an unauthorized incursion into a computer or network system

λ: mean intrusion rate (intrusions per hour)

t: duration of intrusion (hours)

t^*:   limit on duration of intrusion (hours)

$\overline{t}$:   mean of intrusion duration (hours)

T: given value of t (hours)

x: number of intrusions $= \lambda t$ intrusions in time t

m: mean number of intrusions

x^*:   limit on mean number of intrusions $= \lambda\ t^*$ in t_u hours

X: given value of x

n: sample size

$P(x)$:   probability of x intrusions

$P(x \leq X)$:   probability that there are equal to or less than X intrusions

$P(x > X)$:   probability that there are equal to or greater than X intrusions

$P(t)$:   probability that the duration of intrusions $= t$

$P(t \leq T)$:   probability that the duration of intrusion is equal to or less than time T

$P(t > T)$:   probability that the duration of intrusion is greater than time T

RE_x: relative effectiveness of intrusion prevention

RE_t: relative effectiveness of preventing intrusions of duration t

Poisson Intrusion Model

The Poisson intrusion model is based on the assumption that the number of intrusions can be modeled by the Poisson distribution. A property of the Poisson distribution is "the law of rare events"; it is assumed that the number of intrusions during a time t would be "rare," where "rare" must be defined in relation to the probability of x intrusions in time t. (See Chapter 1 for a review of the Poisson distribution.) To test this assumption, Figure 14.13 is provided, where $x = .9$ intrusions occur at probability $P(t) = .1220$, which may be considered a "rare" occurrence. Note that there are no empirical data to test this assumption; instead, data are derived from the theoretical distribution in equation (14.19).

The development of the model proceeds by first computing the mean number of intrusions m in equation (14.17), which is the product of the mean intrusion rate λ, and the mean time of intrusions $\overline{t}$, which in turn is computed using equation (14.18).

$$m:\ \text{mean number of intrusions} = \lambda\ \overline{t} \tag{14.17}$$

$$\overline{t} = \left(\sum_{i=1}^{n} t_i \right) / n \tag{14.18}$$

Then, the probability of x intrusions is computed from the Poisson distribution in equation (14.19).

$$P(x) = \frac{e^{-m}}{x!} m^x \tag{14.19}$$

Next, $P(x \leq X)$, the probability that there are equal to or less than X intrusions, which is a cumulative distribution function (CDF), is obtained from equation (14.20).

FIGURE 14.13   Number of Intrusions, $x = \lambda * t$, vs. Probability of Intrusion, $P(x)$

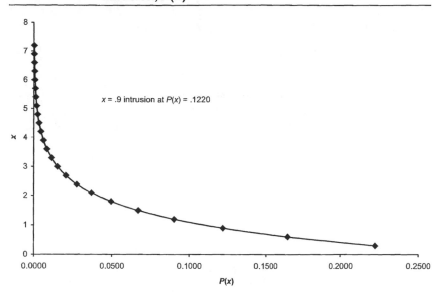

$x = .9$ intrusion at $P(x) = .1220$

Cumulative Distribution Function (CDF) $P\left(x \leq X\right) = \sum_{i=1}^{n} \dfrac{e^{-\lambda ti} \lambda t^{Xi}}{x_i!}$ \hfill (14.20)

$$P\left(x > X\right) = 1 - \sum_{i=1}^{n} \dfrac{e^{-\lambda ti} \lambda t^{Xi}}{x_i!}$$

Relative Measures of Effectiveness

It is necessary to put a limit x^* on the number of intrusions, x, in equation (14.21) in order to compute the relative effectiveness of preventing intrusions (to be shown in a later section).

$$x^* = \lambda\, t^* = \text{limit on mean number of intrusions} \tag{14.21}$$

In some cases it is desirable to solve for the number of intrusions x for given values of $P(x)$ and m. Since it is not feasible to solve for x directly in equation (14.19), it is solved iteratively by using equation (14.22), which is obtained by manipulating equation (14.19).

$$x = \frac{\log[P(x)x!] + m}{\log(m)} \tag{14.22}$$

Equation (14.22) is a metric to evaluate the effectiveness of controlling the number of intrusions. It is desirable to have small values of the metric at small values of the probability of x intrusions, $P(x)$. Equation (14.22) represents the "break-even" point ($x = 3.53$) between excessive and non-excessive intrusions in Figure 14.14.

Two types of intrusion measures of effectiveness are developed: one for number of intrusions x per time period t and the other the time duration of intrusions. In both cases, the concept is to relate the threshold measure x^* in the case of x and t^* in the case of t to the baseline measure x or t, respectively. These relationships are shown in Figure 14.12.

Number of Intrusions Relative Effectiveness

Equation (14.23) gives the *relative effectiveness* for number of intrusions RE_x. In this measure, for a given value of x^*, the ratio $\dfrac{x^*}{x}$ should be high; thus, this ratio is subtracted from 1 to create a decreasing number, preferably as negative as possible, where $x = x^*$ is the "break-even" value. This is illustrated in Figure 14.14, where $x^* = 3.53$ intrusions is the break-even value, and $x > 3.53$, $RE_x > 0$ is the region of risk. This is the region where it is necessary to tighten security.

$$RE_x: \text{relative effectiveness of preventing } x \text{ number of intrusions} = 1 - \frac{x^*}{x} \qquad (14.23)$$

Figure 14.15 reinforces the result obtained in Figure 14.14, wherein the maximum probability of intrusions $P(x) = .6359$ in Figure 14.15 corresponds to the region of $RE_x > 0$ in Figure 14.14. That is, the region where intrusions are excessive (i.e., $x > 3.53$ (break-even point)).

Time Duration of Intrusions Model

This intrusion model is based on the assumption that the time duration of intrusions is exponentially distributed (i.e., a skewed distribution with high frequency of low values of t and low frequency of high values of t, as shown in the frequency count diagram in Figure 14.16). Note that we do not have empirical data to test this assumption; we are using data derived from the theoretical distribution in equation (14.24).

FIGURE 14.14   Relative Effectiveness of Intrusion Prevention RE_x vs. Number of Intrusions x

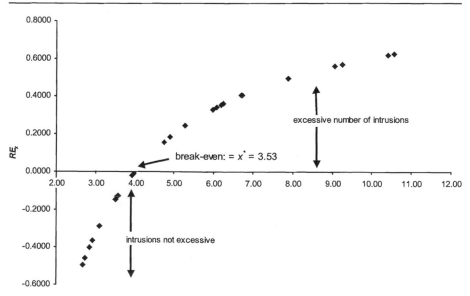

FIGURE 14.15   Probability of *x* Number of Intrusions *P(x)* vs. Number of Intrusions *x*

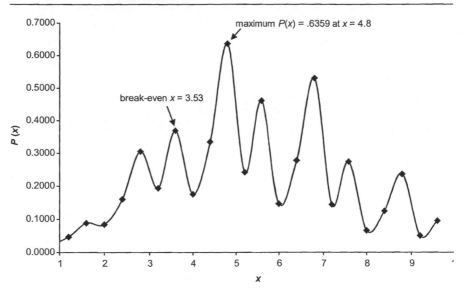

FIGURE 14.16   Frequency of Intrusion Duration *t*

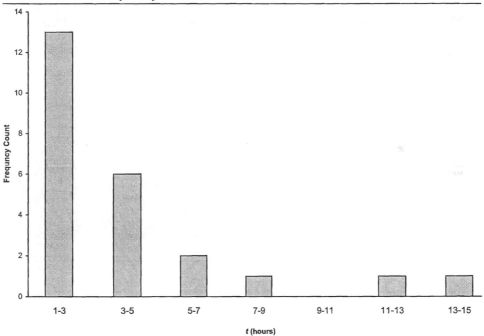

Exponential Model

The exponential model for estimating the duration of intrusions proceeds by first computing the probability of an intrusion lasting for *t* time and is given by equation (14.24).

$$P(t) = \lambda e^{-\lambda t} , \qquad (14.24)$$

where λ is the rate of intrusions.

FIGURE 14.17   Probability $P(t > T)$ of Duration Time of Intrusion $> T$

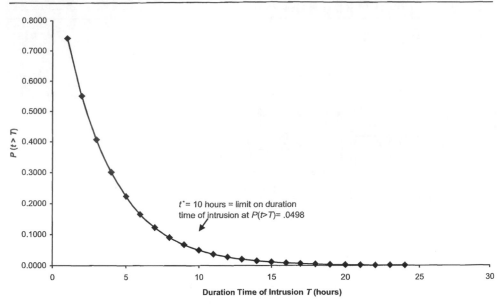

FIGURE 14.18   Relative Effectiveness of Preventing Intrusions of Duration t, RE_t, vs. Duration of Intrusion t

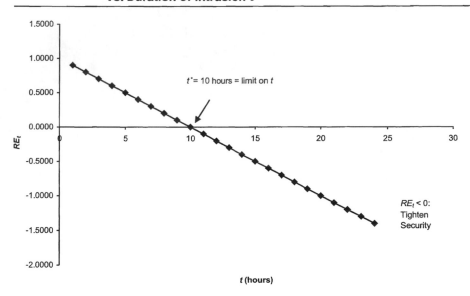

Equation (14.24) shows the probability of an intrusion lasting for at least time T (i.e., the cumulative distribution). The cumulative distribution is useful for estimating the probability that the duration of an intrusion *will not be greater* than a specified time T (e.g., 24 hours). Conversely, equation (14.25) estimates the probability that the duration of an intrusion *will be greater* than T. Obviously, this probability should have a low value.

$$P(t \leq T) = \int_0^T \lambda e^{-\lambda t} dt = 1 - e^{-\lambda T} \qquad (14.25)$$

TABLE 14.4   Intrusion Model Calculations

Duration of intrusion t	Number of Intrusions = λt x	Probability of Intrusion Computed P(x)	Specified by Random Variable P(x)	Computed from Specified P(x) x	Relative Effectiveness Preventing x RE_x	Relative Effectiveness Preventing t RE_t
1	0.40	0.0128	0.6625	2.85	−0.4031	0.9000
2	0.80	0.0244	0.9858	3.10	−0.2912	0.8000
3	1.20	0.0465	0.7519	2.93	−0.3654	0.7000
4	1.60	0.0885	0.5551	2.74	−0.4594	0.6000
5	2.00	0.0842	0.9208	3.49	−0.1474	0.5000
6	2.40	0.1603	0.2496	2.68	−0.4953	0.4000
7	2.80	0.3052	0.9988	3.54	−0.1310	0.3000
8	3.20	0.1937	0.6122	3.92	−0.0217	0.2000
9	**3.60**	**0.3687**	**0.3315**	**3.53**	−0.1319	0.1000
10	4.00	0.1755	0.7494	4.90	0.1840	0.0000
11	4.40	0.3340	0.1631	3.95	−0.0115	−0.1000
12	4.80	0.6359	0.5705	4.73	0.1548	−0.2000
13	5.20	0.2421	0.9790	6.07	0.3408	−0.3000
14	5.60	0.4609	0.8363	5.97	0.3300	−0.4000
15	6.00	0.1462	0.4647	6.72	0.4046	−0.5000
16	6.40	0.2784	0.2184	6.25	0.3599	−0.6000
17	6.80	0.5299	0.1969	6.18	0.3533	−0.7000
18	7.20	0.1441	0.4358	7.89	0.4929	−0.8000
19	7.60	0.2743	0.0678	6.73	0.4058	−0.9000
20	8.00	0.0653	0.4971	9.26	0.5681	−1.0000
21	8.40	0.1243	0.3572	9.06	0.5583	−1.1000
22	8.80	0.2366	0.0008	5.29	0.2435	−1.2000
23	9.20	0.0500	0.4601	10.58	0.6219	−1.3000
24	9.60	0.0953	0.3523	10.41	0.6159	−1.4000

$$P(t > T) = e^{-\lambda T} \tag{14.26}$$

Example Calculations for Time Duration of Intrusions Model

Figure 14.17 portrays the *illustrative* decision to limit the intrusion time to $t = 10.8$ hours at a probability of $P(t > T) = .0183$ (i.e., probability $= .0183$ that the duration of intrusion is greater than time $T = 10.8$ hours). Any intrusion time greater than 10.8 hours is considered unacceptable.

Intrusion Duration Relative Effectiveness

Equation (14.27) gives the *relative effectiveness* for duration of intrusions RE_t. Using this measure, for a given value of t^*, the ratio $\dfrac{t}{t^*}$ should be low; thus, this ratio is subtracted

from 1 to create an increasing number, preferably as positive as possible, where $t = t^*$ is the "break-even" value. This is illustrated in Figure 14.18, where $t^* = 10$ hours is the break-even value, and $t < 10$ and $RE_t < 0$ is the region of risk, where it is necessary to tighten security.

$$RE_t: \text{relative effectiveness of preventing intrusions of duration } t = 1 - \frac{t}{t^*} \qquad (14.27)$$

Summary

Table 14.4 summarizes the calculations that were made by using the intrusion model equations that were used in making the plots. In column 1, durations of intrusion are specified. Column 2 uses a specified mean intrusion rate $\lambda = .4$ intrusions per hour and the data in column 1 to produce the values of x in column 2. Then the probability of intrusions $P(x)$ is computed in column 3 using the values of x and the specified mean number of intrusions $m = 5$ intrusions per hour. Next, values of $P(x)$ are specified in column 4 by generating random numbers using the Excel RAND function. The purpose of this operation is to calculate x—the intrusion metric—in column 5, using equation (14.22). The bolded quantities correspond to the break-even solutions for number of intrusions. Finally, the relative effectiveness of preventing intrusions is computed in columns 6 and 7 for *number of intrusions* and *duration of intrusions,* respectively.

In the *Introduction,* the following questions were posed:

1. Can various representations and models of cyber security be developed that would provide a framework for advancing the field?
2. Can theoretical prediction models be developed to assess the risk of various types of cyber attacks?
3. Can an empirical model, using CERT data, be developed to assess the risk of vulnerabilities to cyber attacks?

In considering these questions, refer to pertinent plots, as shown in Table 14.5, which summarizes key characteristics. For example, the *Risk* model, Figure 14.2, identifies the maximum risk attacks, *probe* and *DoS,* and responds to issue 2. The researcher and practitioner can use Table 14.5 as a guide to determine which model, plot, variables, and key point would be applicable to analyzing a given cyber security issue.

References

[CRS05] *Report for Congress, Government Activities to Protect the Electric Grid.* Amy Abel, February 4, 2005.

[FAR83] William H. Farr, "A Survey of Software Reliability Modeling and Estimating." Naval Surface Weapons Center, NSWC TR 82–171, September 1983, p. 4–88.

[FLO] Sally Floyd and Eddie Kohler, "Internet Research Needs Better Models." ICSI Center for Internet Research, Berkeley, California.

[GRA05] Bradley Graham, "Hackers Attack Via Chinese Web Sites, U.S. Agencies' Networks Are Among Targets." *The Washington Post,* Thursday, August 25, 2005, Page A01.

[HOU01] Allen Householder, CERT/CC, Art Manion, CERT/CC, Linda Pesante, CERT/CC, George M. Weaver, CERT/CC, in collaboration with Rob Thomas, "Managing the Threat of Denial-of-Service Attacks." CERT® Coordination Center. V10.0, October 2001.

[IEE03] "IP Traceback: A New Denial-of-Service Deterrent?" *IEEE Security & Privacy,* May/June 2003, pp. 24–31.

[IEEE90] Standard 610.12–1990, *IEEE Standard Glossary of Software Engineering Terminology.*

[MAX 05] Nicholas F. Maxemchuk, Iradj Ouveysi, and Moshe Zukerman, "A Quantitative Measure for Telecommunications Networks Topology Design." *IEEE/ACM Transactions on Networking,* Vol. 13, No. 4, August 2005, pp. 731–742.

TABLE 14.5   Summary of Key Points

Model	Figure	Independent Variable	Dependent Variable	Key Point
Risk	14.2	Probability of Attack	Risk	Identifies Maximum risk attacks
	14.3	Consequence	Risk	Identifies Maximum risk attacks
Exponential #1	14.4	Probability of Attack	Expected Number of Attacks	Relationship among cyber security variables
Exponential #2	14.5	Probability of Attack	Duration of Attacks	Duration of Attacks threshold
	14.6	Probability of Attack	Rate of Change of Duration of Attacks	Rate of change threshold
	14.7	Duration of Attacks	Risk of Attack	Correspondence between Duration of Attacks and Risk of Attack
Vulnerability	14.8	Years Since First Recording	Vulnerability Count	Development of Prediction Equation
	14.9	Years Since First Recording	Actual and Predicted Vulnerabilities Count	Prediction vs. Actual Vulnerabilities Counts
Intrusion	14.12	Probability of Intrusion	Number of Intrusions	"The law of rare events"
	14.13	Probability of Intrusion	Intrusion Metric	Control of Number of Intrusions
	14.14	Number of Intrusions	Probability of Intrusion	Number of Intrusions Threshold
	14.16	Duration of Intrusions	Probability of Intrusion	Duration of Intrusions Threshold
	14.17	Number of Intrusions	Relative Effectiveness of Intrusion Prevention	Number of Intrusions Risk
	14.18	Relative Effectiveness of Preventing Intrusions of Duration *t*	Duration of Intrusion	Duration of Intrusion Limit

[MOO01] D. Moore, G. Voelker, and S. Savage, "Inferring Internet Denial of Service Activity." In Usenix Security Symposium, 2001.

[NIC04] David M. Nicol, William H. Sanders, and Kishor S. Trivedi, "Model-Based Evaluation: From Dependability to Security." *IEEE Transactions On Dependable And Secure Computing*, Vol. 1, No. 1, January-March 2004, pp. 48–65.

[PIT05] President's Information Technology Advisory Committee, "Cyber Security: A Crisis of Prioritization." February 2005.

[SCH04] Norman F. Schneidewind, "Developing Software for Safety Critical Systems—When Failure is not an Option." Tutorial, International Conference on Software Maintenance, November 2004.

[SCH05] Glenn Schoonover, CISSP MCSE, Microsoft Security Solutions Specialist, "Enhancing Customer Security: Built-in versus Bolt-on." *DoD Software Tech News, Secure Software Engineering,* Vol. 8. No. 2, July 2005

[SUL05] Florin Sultan, Aniruddha Bohra, Stephen Smaldone, Yufei Pan, Pascal Gallard, Ialiun Neamtiu, and Liviu Iftode, "Recovering Internet Service Sessions from Operating System Failures." *IEEE Internet Computing,* March, April 2005, pp. 17–26.

[YAN04] Hao Yang, et al., "Security in Mobile and Ad Hoc Networks: Challenges and Solutions." *IEEE Wireless Communications,* February 2004, pp. 38–47.

[YUA05] Jian Yuan and Kevin Mills, "Monitoring the Macroscopic Effect of DDoS Flooding Attacks." *IEEE Transactions on Dependable and Secure Computing,* Vol 2. No. 4, October–December 2005, pp. 324–335.

[YUR00] William Yurcik, David Loomis, and Alexander D. Korzyk, Sr., "Predicting Internet Attacks: On Developing an Effective Measurement Methodology," Proceedings of the 18th Annual International Communications Forecasting Conference (ICFC-2000), Seattle, WA, September 2000.

[YUR01] William Yurcik and David Doss, "Internet Attacks: A Policy Framework for Rules of Engagement." Department of Applied Computer Science, Illinois State University, 2001.

[ZHE05] Lantian Zheng and Andrew C. Myers, "End-to-End Availability Policies and Noninterference." Proceedings of the 18th IEEE Computer Security Foundation Workshop (CSFW '05), June 2005.

15

Ergonomics and Safety in the Workplace

Objectives

The objective is to understand that there is more to achieving success in an enterprise than return on investment and technological innovation. There are also the issues of worker safety and job satisfaction. These issues are as relevant in computer manufacturing as in any other industry. Information technology (IT) workers must be provided with a safe work place, and, of course, job satisfaction is very important in retaining skilled IT workers, who are in short supply. To address these issues, the field of ergonomics is applied to set reasonable limits on human performance requirements. In addition, worker safety criteria are applied to prevent accidents in the workplace. Furthermore, examples are provided of methods designed to support employee job satisfaction. In addition, the human-machine (computer) interface is obviously important in the IT work place.

What You Will Learn From This Chapter

In this chapter the engineer is provided with information about the following requirements for health and safety in the work place:

- Formulas for assessing the feasibility of lifting and moving heavy objects, such as large computers.
- Work model for computing the work done in moving objects from one location to another in order to evaluate the feasibility of humans performing these tasks.
- How to apply Permissible Noise Levels (PELS) criteria in the workplace.
- Various disorders that can affect worker performance.
- The importance of the human-machine interface.
- Site selection factors for maximizing worker job satisfaction.

Subjects

Application of the National Institute of Occupational Safety and Health (NIOSH) Formula
Work Model
Occupational Safety and Health Agency (OSHA) Permissible Noise Levels (PELS)
Cumulative Trauma Disorders of the Upper Extremities
Rapid Upper Limb Assessment (RULA)
Definition of Anthropometric
Human-Machine Interface
Site Selection Factors

Application of NIOSH Formula

The NIOSH lifting equation is a tool used to assess a lifting task and given the conditions, determine a **recommended weight limit (RWL)** for the task. The RWL is calculated using the equation that is constrained by a lifting constant $L = \textbf{51 pounds}$ and takes into account characteristics of the load and the lifting conditions, such as **horizontal (H)** and **vertical (V)** location of load, the **distance the load will be moved (D),** and **asymmetry (A).** See http://www.ergonomics.com.au/niosh.htm

Definitions

$$
\begin{aligned}
RWL &= \text{ weight limit} \\
H &= \text{ horizontal distance} \\
V &= \text{ vertical distance} \\
D &= \text{ vertical travel distance} \\
A &= \text{ angle between load origin and destination} \\
F &= \text{ frequency of the lift}
\end{aligned}
$$

NIOSH Formula

See Figure 15.1.

$$RWL = 51(10/H)(1 - .0075(|V - 30|))(.82 + 1.8/D)(1 - .0032A)$$

The NIOSH formula assumes that (1) lifting frequency is no greater than one lift every 5 minutes and (2) the person can get a good grip on the object being lifted.

FIGURE 15.1 Computer Lift Problem

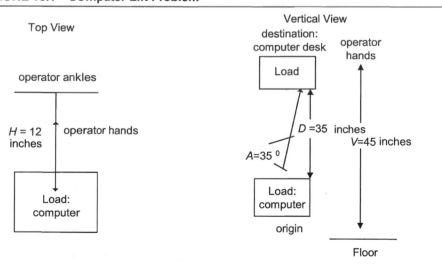

H = horizontal distance of the operator hands from the midpoint of the line joining the inner ankle bones to a point projected on the floor directly below the computer center

V = vertical distance of the operator hands from the floor

D = vertical travel distance between the computer and destination of the lift to the computer desk

A = angle between load origin and destination, in degrees

Problem 1

Referring to Figure 15.1 and the values of the parameters as follows, how much could a computer weigh for the operator to safely lift the computer from the floor to the table? Determine the recommended weight limit according to the *NIOSH Formula.*

$H =$ horizontal distance = 12 inches
$V =$ vertical distance = 45 inches
$D =$ vertical travel distance = 35 inches
$A =$ angle between load origin and destination = 35 degrees
$RWL =$ weight limit

Solution

$$
\begin{aligned}
RWL &= 51(10/H)(1 - .0075(|V - 30|))(.82 + 1.8/D)(1 - .0032A) \\
&= 51(10/12)(1 - .0075(|45 - 30|))(.82 + (1.8/35))(1 - .0032*35) \\
&= (42.5)(.8875)(.8714)(.8880) \\
&= \textbf{29.19 pounds}
\end{aligned}
$$

Problem 2

A computer lifting job has the following requirements:

$F =$ lifting frequency = 4 computer lifts per minute
8 hour shift
shift allowance = 15%

1. Compute number of computer lifts that can be performed per shift.
2. Is the specification in compliance with NIOSH standards?

Solution

1. ($F = 4$ computer lifts per minute) * (60 minutes per hour) * (8 hours per shift) * $(1 - .15$ shift allowance) = **1632 computer lifts per shift**
2. The specification is not in compliance with NIOSH standards. It far exceeds the limit of one lift every five minutes.

Problem 3

For the data in Problem 1, what is the vertical distance D for lifting $RWL = 6.8$ kg?

$RWL =$ 6.8 kg = 6.8 × 2.2 = 14.96 lb
$H =$ horizontal distance = 12 inches
$V =$ vertical distance = 45 inches
$D =$ vertical travel distance = 35 inches
$A =$ angle between load origin and destination = 35 degrees

Solution

$RWL = 51(10/H)(1 - .0075(|V - 30|))(.82 + 1.8/D)(1 - .0032A)$
Let $X = 51(10/H)(1 - .0075(|V - 30|))(1 - .0032A)$
$RWL = (.82 + 1.8/D)X$

Solving for D:

$D = (1.8\ X)/(RWL - .82X)$

$X = 51(10/35) \times (1 - .0075(45 - 30)) \times (1 - .0032 \times 35) = 14.5714 \times .8875 \times .8880 = 11.4837$

$D = (1.8)(11.4837)/[14.96 - (.82)(11.4837)] = 20.6707/[14.96 - 9.4167] = 20.6707/5.54533 = \textbf{3.7290 inches}$

Work Model

Work models express the work done in moving a load from its origin to its destination. Work involves velocity, load displacement, acceleration, mass, force, angle between force and displacement, and time. The work model is used to determine the feasibility of moving a load from one position to another. For example, is it feasible for a human to lift a computer from the floor to the desk or is a forklift required? See http://www.ergonomics.com.au/niosh.htm.

Definitions

$v(t)$:   velocity by time t
v_0:   initial velocity at time $t = 0$
a: horizontal acceleration
g: acceleration due to gravity
$d(t)$:   delta load displacement by time t
$D(t)$:   load displacement by time t
w: weight of load
m: mass of load
F: force required to reposition load
W: work required to reposition load
θ: angle between the force and the displacement

Model

(See http://www.ergonomics.com.au/niosh.htm.)

The delta load displacement by time t is given by equation (15.1).

$$d(t) = v(t)\, dt \tag{15.1}$$

The velocity of the load's movement by time t is given by equation (15.2).

$$v(t) = v_0 + at \tag{15.2}$$

Using equations (15.1) and (15.2), the load displacement by time t is computed in equation (15.3).

$$D(t) = \int v(t)dt = \int (v_0 + at)dt = v_0 t + \frac{at^2}{2} \tag{15.3}$$

If the load starts from rest ($v_0 = 0$), displacement is computed in equation (15.4).

$$D(t) = \frac{at^2}{2} \tag{15.4}$$

FIGURE 15.2   Work Model

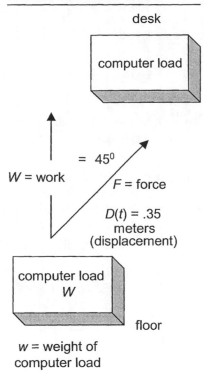

desk

computer load

$= 45^0$

W = work

F = force

$D(t) = .35$ meters (displacement)

computer load W

floor

w = weight of computer load

In order to compute the work required to move a load, the force required, F, is given in equation (15.5).

$$F = ma \qquad (15.5)$$

Since the weight, w, of the load will be given but not its mass, m, it is necessary to compute mass in equation (15.6).

$$m = w/g \qquad (15.6)$$

Thus, using equations (15.5) and (15.6), force is recomputed in equation (15.7).

$$F = (w/g)a \qquad (15.7)$$

See Figure 15.2 to understand that work, W, can be expressed by equation (15.8).

$$W = F * d * \text{Cos } \theta = (w/g)a * d * \text{Cos } \theta \qquad (15.8)$$

Problem 4

If $w = 6.8$ kg is the weight of the computer load that must be lifted a distance $d = .35$ meters, a lift requires $t = 2$ seconds, and $\theta = 45$ degrees (Cos $\theta = .7071$) is the angle between force F and displacement d, how much work, W, is done in kg – meters?

Solution

Referring to Figure 15.2: The acceleration due to gravity, denoted g, is defined as exactly 9.80665 m/s² (almost exactly 32.174 ft/s²), which is approximately equal to the acceleration due to gravity on the earth's surface at sea level.

Using equation (15.4), the horizontal acceleration $a = (2D(t))/t^2 = (2 * .35)/4 = .175$ meters/sec².

Perform a dimensional analysis to help ensure computational accuracy:

$$W = F * D(t) * \text{Cos } \theta = (w/g)a * D(t) * \text{Cos } \theta$$
$$W = (\text{kg}/(\text{meters/sec})^2)(\text{meters/sec})^2) * \text{meters} = \text{kg} - \text{meters}$$

Now, compute the work required to lift the computer:

$W = (6.8$ kg load$)/9.80665$ ((meters/sec^2))) * ($.175$ meters/sec² acceleration) * ($.35$ meters displacement) * (Cos $45° = .7071$) = **2.881 kg-meter**

OSHA Permissible Noise Levels (PELS)

OSHA requires that employers administer a continuing, effective hearing conservation program whenever employee noise exposure equals or exceeds a *time-weighted average sound level* of *85 decibels*. See http://bfa.sdsu.edu/ehs/pdf/HearingConservation.pdf. Table 15.1 contains examples of permissible levels (PELs) for occupational noise. OSHA assumes a 5 dB change in the sound level L_n equates to a factor of two in the duration of the noise level T_n. For example, in Table 15.1 when the noise level L_n *increases* from 85 to 90, T_n *decreases* from 16 to 8.

A dose, D, is defined in equation (15.9):

$$\text{Dose } D = \sum_1^n \frac{C_n}{T_n}, \qquad (15.9)$$

TABLE 15.1   OSHA Permissible Noise Exposure Levels

Duration of L_n hours T_n	Noise Level Decibels (PELS) L_n	Exposure Time Hours C_n	$\dfrac{C_n}{T_n}$	$L_{ni}T_{ni}$
16	85.00	15	0.9375	1359.99
10	88.39	9	0.9000	883.90
8	90.00	7	0.8750	720.00
6	92.08	5	0.8333	552.45
4	95.00	3	0.7500	380.00
3	97.08	2	0.6667	291.23
2	100.00	1	0.5000	200.00
1.5	102.08	0.75	0.5000	153.11
1	105.00	0.5	0.5000	105.00
0.5	110.00	0.25	0.5000	55.00
52			**6.9625**	4700.69
			D dose	$\sum_{i=1}^{N} L_{ni}T_{ni}$
$\sum_{i=1}^{N} T_{ni}$				**90.40**
N	10			$\overline{L_n}$

where C_n = permissible time of exposure at a specified noise level L_n and T_n is the duration of L_n.

L_n = measured sound level in decibels (PELS) in equation (15.10).

$$L_n = 90 + 5 \ (\log_2 \ (8/T_n))$$ (15.10)

Then, converting $\log_2 \ (8/T_n)$ to log base e:

$$\log_2 \ (8/T_n) = \log_e \ (8/T_n)/\log_e \ (2) = [\log_e \ (8/T_n)]/.6931$$ (15.11)

Equation (15.11) is substituted into equation (15.10) to produce equation (15.12).

$$L_n = 90 + [5 \ ([\log_e \ (8/T_n)]/.6931]$$ (15.12)

Time-weighted average of sound level L_n is computed in equation (15.13):

$$\bar{L}_n = \frac{\sum_{i=1}^{N} L_{ni} T_{ni}}{\sum_{i=1}^{N} T_{ni}},$$ (15.13)

where N is the number of recorded sound levels and durations.

Problem 5

1. Compute the values of L_n for the values of T_n in Table 15.1.
2. Plot L_n as a function of T_n.
3. Is the OSHA time-weighted average of sound level L_n exceeded?
4. Show the computation.

Solution

1. Using equation (15.12), the solution for L_n is shown in Table 15.1.
2. See Figure 15.3 on page 340, which shows that permissible exposure level (PELS) decreases as the duration of exposure increases.
3. The time-weighted exposure requirement is exceeded.
4. This value = 90.40 and is shown in Table 15.1 and Figure 15.3.

Cumulative Trauma Disorders of the Upper Extremities

Cumulative trauma disorders of the upper extremities (CTDUEs) is a term that describes a collection of painful impairments affecting any part of the body from the fingers to the base of the neck and having as a *contributing cause, repetitive manual work*. An example is the repetitive stress put on the fingers, wrists, and neck of an operator sitting at a computer for many hours. See http://www.ncbi.nlm.nih.gov/pubmed/9646740.

Rapid Upper Limb Assessment (RULA)

The Rapid Upper Limb Assessment (RULA) method is a postural targeting method for *estimating the risks of work-related upper limb disorders.* See http://www.rula.co.uk/. A RULA assessment gives a quick and systematic assessment of the postural risks to a worker. The analysis can be conducted before and after an intervention to demonstrate that the intervention has worked to lower the risk of injury. This ergonomic technique evaluates individuals'

FIGURE 15.3 **Permissible Noise Level L_n in decibels (PELS) vs. Duration of Exposure T_n**

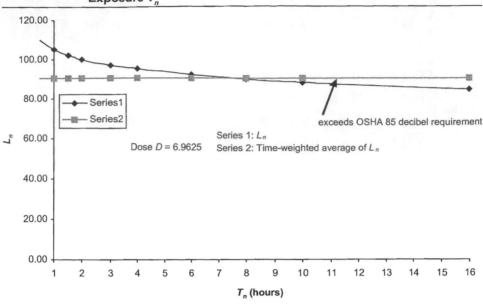

exposures to postures, forces, and muscle activities that have been shown to contribute to repetitive strain injuries (RSIs). Use of this ergonomic evaluation approach results in a *risk score between one and seven, where higher scores signify greater levels of apparent risk*. A low RULA score does not guarantee that the work place is free of ergonomic hazards and a high score does not assure that a severe problem exists. *It was developed to detect work postures or risk factors that deserve further attention*. For example, assessments are made of computer maintenance personnel in their tasks of lifting computer equipment from the floor to a workbench, involving rapid motion of arms and shoulders.

Definition of Anthropometric

"Anthropometric" refers to the study of the sizes of human bodies or their parts, especially the *comparison of sizes* at different ages, in different races, etc. These data can be used to adapt technology, such as computers, to the characteristics of human operators. For example, computer monitors could be designed with adjustable height so that users of various torso heights could be accommodated.

Human-Machine Interface (HMI)

Nowadays humans interact more with computer-based technology than with hammers and drills. Unlike tools, the visible shape and controls of a computer do not communicate its purpose. The task of an HMI is to *make the function of a technology self-evident*. Much like a well-designed hammer fits the user's hand and makes a physical task easy, a well-designed HMI must fit the user's mental map of the task he or she wishes to carry out. HMI effectiveness is measured by a number of criteria, such as ease of use and productivity. These criteria are sometimes brought together under the title of "usability," also known as *quality of use*.

ISO Definition of Quality of Use

The ISO 9241 standard (http://www.usabilitynet.org/tools/r_international.htm#9126–4) defines three criteria of quality of use applicable to the design of HMIs:

Effectiveness—Does the product do what the *users require*? *Does it do the right thing?* For example, does a computer operating system manage system resources in an effective way such that user requirements for access to and utilization of application software are satisfied?

Efficiency—Can users carry out their tasks with minimum expended effort, including a *minimum of errors*? Does it improve the productivity/effort ratio? *Does it do things right?* For example, does a personal computer refrain from issuing irrelevant and incessant messages (e.g., "updates are ready for your computer") that have nothing do with the task at hand and lower the user's productivity/effort ratio?

Satisfaction—Do users express satisfaction with the product? Does the new product reduce stress? *Do the end users now have a more satisfying job?* For example, are the desktop hardware and software supporting worker productivity to the extent that workers are promoted to more satisfying jobs?

Site Selection Factors

Several factors are involved in selecting a site that will best support an organization's needs. Among these are factors that will lead to employee satisfaction, and hence, improve the organization's competitiveness in the marketplace. A site is selected by identifying the site with the maximum weighted factor score.

Definitions

i = employee factor
j = site
n = number of employee factors
s_j = score for site j
w_i = weight for employee factor i
w_{ij} = weight for employee factor i and site j

Weights and Score

Sum of weights for employee factors i must sum to 1:

$$\sum_{i=1}^{n} w_{i=1} \tag{15.14}$$

Sum of employee factors i over sites j must sum to 1:

$$\sum_{i=1,j=1}^{n} w_{ij} = 1 \tag{15.15}$$

Using equations (15.14) and (15.15), the score for site j^* is computed in equation (15.16).

$$sj^* = \text{ score for location } j^* = \sum_{i=1,j=j^*}^{n} w_i w_{ij}{}^* \tag{15.16}$$

Problem 6

This is a computer company site selection problem involving evaluating employee preference factors. Based on the employee factors i and sites j, given in Tables 15.2 and 15.3, what is the score for site $j = 2$?

Solution

For example, $w_{ij}^* = w_{12}$, for $j^* = 2$, is the weight for site 2, and w_i is the weight for number of employees:

$$s_2 = \text{score for location } 2 = \sum_{i=1, j=2}^{4} w_1 w_{12} + w_2 w_{22} + w_3 w_{32} + w_4 w_{42}$$

$$= (.3333)(.2800) + (.2500)(.3200) + (.1667)(.1600) + (.2500)(.2400)$$

$$= .0933 + .0800 + .0267 + .0600 = \mathbf{.2600}$$

TABLE 15.2   Employee Factor Weights

Factor i	Number of Employees and Factor i Weights	Site $j = 1$ Weight	Site $j = 2$ Weight	Site $j = 3$ Weight	Number of Employees
Safety in the Workplace $i = 1$	200 $w_{11} = 200/600 = .3333$	80	70	50	200
Near Day Care Center $i = 2$	150 $w_{21} = 150/600 = .2500$	50	80	70	150
Access to Public Transportation $i = 3$	100 $w_{31} = 100/600 = .1667$	100	40	60	100
Employee Parking $i = 4$	150 $w_{41} = 150/600 = .2500$	90	60	50	150
Sum of site weights		320	250	230	600

TABLE 15.3   Computer Site Weights

Factor i	Computer Site $j = 1$	Computer Site $j = 2$	Computer Site $j = 3$
Safety in the Workplace $i = 1$	$w_{11} = 80/320$ $= .2500$	$w_{12} = 70/250$ $= .2800$	$w_{13} = 50/230$ $= .2174$
Near Day Care Center $i = 2$	$w_{21} = 50/320$ $= .1563$	$w_{22} = 80/250$ $= .3200$	$w_{23} = 70/230$ $= .3043$
Access to Public Transportation $i = 3$	$w_{31} = 100/320$ $= .3125$	$w_{32} = 40/250$ $= .1600$	$w_{33} = 60/230$ $= .2609$
Employee Parking $i = 4$	$w_{41} = 90/320$ $= .2813$	$w_{42} = 60/250$ $= .2400$	$w_{43} = 50/230$ $= .2174$
Sum	1.0000	1.0000	1.0000

The same procedure would be used to compute the scores for the other two sites, and the site with the largest score would be selected.

Summary

The application of ergonomics and safety to the workplace has been demonstrated. This material provides templates for the engineer to apply these principles in his or her organization, with the objective of maximizing worker satisfaction and productivity. Numerous problems were solved, applying the principles.

16

Facility Layout
and Location Models

Objectives

It is important to take a *systems approach* when engineering facility layouts and locations. When designing a Web server application, for example, it is obviously important to consider the content of the servers and the search strategy. In addition, you should not lose site of *system* factors such as layout and location. Thus, the objective of this chapter is to demonstrate methods and models for facilitating layout of manufacturing facilities. Interestingly, these facilities can be assets used in the manufacture of hardware items or for the production of software products and services such as Web systems. The problem is to assign departments to locations or to assign Web servers to locations based on several factors, including the need for interaction among the facilities. In addition, the related problem of optimally locating facilities such that the cost of travel or transporting material among facilities is minimized.

What You Will Learn From This Chapter

Several problems in facility layout, resource allocation and assignment, and facility location, routing, and connectivity are addressed. You will see how models and tools from the fields of systems engineering, industrial engineering, and operations research can be applied to these problems. Computer system applications are used, focusing on the Naval Postgraduate School network connectivity problem. Using this problem, the adaptation of manufacturing system models to the network system domain is illustrated. Example problem and solutions are provided for a variety of applications. The iterative use of heuristics—approximating an optimal solution—helps the engineer rationalize and improve model results. Complexity metrics from the field of software engineering are used to evaluate facility connectivity complexity. You will also learn that that the subject of materials handling can be applied to a wide variety of problems.

Subjects

Determinants of Facility Layout and Location
Facility Layout and Location Model Development
Heuristic for Achieving Closeness of Facilities
Complexity of Connectivity
Centroid Method for Facility Location Analysis
REL Chart for Layout and Location Design
From To Charts for Layout Design
Component Routing and Assignment Analysis

Introduction

The subject of IT facility layout and location model has not been reported in the manufacturing systems literature. However, given the importance of IT in contemporary society, it is appropriate to understand how manufacturing systems tools can be used to improve the cost-effectiveness of IT systems.

Material Handling

Today's market demands that manufacturing must be efficient. This requires the efficient operation of manufacturing plants and their ability to quickly respond to changes in service mix and demand, such as the combination of services and exploding demand of computer-based systems. In addition, studies show that material handling costs make up between 20 and 50 percent of the total operating cost. One of the objectives of facility design is to minimize material handling costs [LIU06] (note that material handling can involve the handling of data in computer networks). When efficiency and cost requirements exist, the problem is called the dynamic facility layout problem of *systems* [MCK06]. Thus, for example, when designing a Web server application, it is important to consider the efficiency of client-server connections within the cost constraint of the installation budget, Web search strategy, and *system* factors such as layout and location. This chapter deals with methods and models for facilitating the layout and location of service and manufacturing facilities, focusing on computer systems. Interestingly, manufacturing facility concepts can be applied to computer systems, realizing that these systems handle data, not physical resources.

Assignment Problem and Impact on Users

The assignment problem is to assign departments to locations or to assign clients to Web servers based on several factors, including the need for interaction among the facilities. In addition, there is the related problem of optimally locating facilities such that the cost of transporting material among facilities is minimized [DAS06]. In the case of computer networks, "the cost of transporting material among facilities" is the cost of transmitting data packets among the nodes. In addition, some models consider the need to reconfigure facility layouts and changing demand for facility services [MAH05]. When addressing the facilities layout and location problem—or any problem for that mater—it is important to assess the impact of the alternative solutions on the user community [SAG00]. Will the solution make a difference? For example, if you connect clients and Web servers in Figure 16.1 with a single Ethernet in order to save on network installation cost, what will be the impact on client performance?

Determinants of Facility Layout and Location

The design criterion routinely used in most layout design procedures—a measure of long-term material handling efficiency—fails to capture the priorities of the flexible factory. As a result, layout performance tends to deteriorate significantly with fluctuation in either product volumes, mix, or routings. Using a static measure of material handling efficiency also fails to capture the impact of layout configuration on operational performance, such as work-in-process accumulation, queue times at processing departments, and throughput rates. Consequently, layouts that improve material handling often result in inefficiencies elsewhere in the form of long lead times or large in-process inventories. Hence, there is a need for a new class of layouts that are more flexible and responsive [BEN00]. These problems are addressed by using of a *dynamic* flow model, as described in the following sections.

Facility layouts are determined by the following factors:

Type of product (e.g. automobile, software), type of process (e.g., assembly line, job shop), and volume of production (e.g., large quantity of a standard product, one-of-a-kind production). For example, an automobile product uses an assembly for high-volume production while software production uses a job-shop process producing one or few copies [MON96].

Assembly Line Process

An assembly line is a set of sequential workstations that are typically connected by a continuous material-handling system. The line is designed to handle component parts and related operations necessary to produce a finished product. The assembly activity is divided into phases, such as inserting an integrated circuit chip into a circuit card. The product is passed down the line, visiting each workstation. When the product exits the line, it is complete [ASK93]. The assembly-line process is not applicable to Figure 16.1 because access

FIGURE 16.1   Naval Postgraduate School Network Diagram

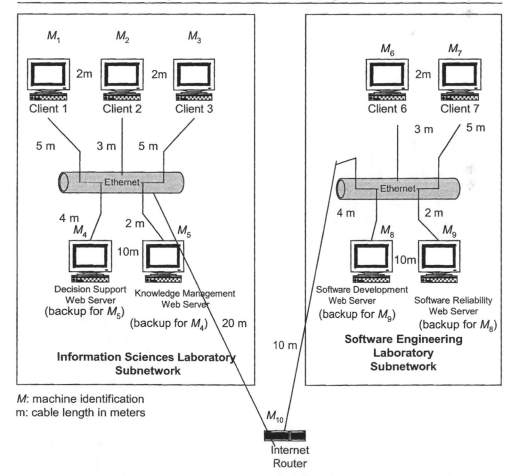

by clients to Web servers is not sequential. Access depends on the need for data that are essentially unpredictable.

Ford Motor Company is an example of an assembly-line process. The company is applying artificial intelligence (AI) and knowledge-based technologies within its manufacturing arena, including an AI-based approach for vehicle-assembly process planning and a system that uses machine translation to translate assembly-build instructions for assembly plants that do not use English as their primary language [RYC07]. It would be possible to build a knowledge database of experiences in connecting facilities, like those shown in Figure 16.1, such that future problems in connectivity could benefit from the experiential effectiveness and cost data recorded in the database, aided by an AI algorithm to optimize connections.

Job Shop Process

The job shop process is used when a *small volume* of many *different products* are to be produced. This is a manufacturing facility that groups similar equipment into departments or areas and organized by function. Production orders are moved to *successive departments* as required to complete all operations. Jobs pass through functional departments in lots, and each lot may have a different routing. The application in Figure 16.1 conforms to none of these attributes: For example, volume could be large and similar equipment is not necessarily grouped. Thus, computer networks require a new model that is called *semi random*. For example, while there are individual client-Web server access patterns, there is no overall access pattern when viewed across the network.

Some researchers have developed models for simultaneously locating facilities and designing their capacities [REN07]. For example, simultaneously it would be possible to model the location of clients and Web servers and compute their capacities in Figure 16.1.

Facility Layout and Location Model Development

Interestingly, the facility layout and location model can be applied to data flow in a network, as well as the traditional material flow in a physical system. This problem has traditionally been approached as a static one wherein material flow is ignored. Some researchers employ variants of genetic algorithms borrowed from the field of evolutionary biology to model dynamic layout problems in which material flow must be considered [CHA02]. A location criterion proposed by Lewis and Block [LEW80] based on dynamic flow dominance is developed as follows:

$$w_{ij} = [(f_{ij} * t) + (h_{ij} * d_{ij})]k \qquad (16.1)$$

where w_{ij} is the cost of moving material from location i to j, f_{ij} is the material flow volume (e.g., megabits per second), t is the time duration of flow, h_{ij} is the unit cost of connecting facilities—labor plus cable cost—(e.g., dollars per meter), d_{ij} is the distance moved or distance between facilities i and j, and $k = 1$ if i connected to j and $k = 0$ if i not connected to j. Then the total cost of moving material over all i, j is:

$$W_{ij} = \sum_{ij}^{M} w_{ij}, \qquad (16.2)$$

where M is the number of facilities.

A flow dominance measure f can be computed in equation (16.3) that is defined as the coefficient of variation of the flow [ASK93]:

$$f = \frac{\sqrt{\dfrac{\displaystyle\sum_{j=1}^{M}\left(w_{ij}k - \overline{w}\right)^2}{M-1}}}{\overline{w}} \quad \text{for } i = 1, \ldots, M, \text{ where } \overline{w} \text{ is the mean cost of data flow} \quad (16.3)$$

When applied to connecting computer facilities, the interpretation of w_{ij} is the cost of connecting facility i to facility j, where "connecting" means access among clients and Web servers *within* a subnetwork in Figure 16.1. Then f_{ij} is interpreted as data flow (e.g., megabits per second) and h_{ij} the unit cost of installing cable (e.g., dollars per meter).

$f = 0$ will be minimum for $w_{ij}k = \overline{w}$, for all i and j, for a given value of M (i.e., minimum dominance), and f will be maximum for $w_{ij}k \gg \overline{w}$ (maximum dominance). In other words, flow dominance is minimum when all connection costs equal the mean cost, and flow dominance is maximum when all connection costs greatly exceed the mean cost.

The interpretation of f for connecting computer facilities is that large values represent large variation in data flow resulting in potential performance problems. For example, in Figure 16.1, data flow variations can adversely affect the ability of the Internet router to accommodate transfer of data between subnetworks. Flow dominance is useful for identifying where cost reductions can be made in a computer network, as will be shown in the following example.

Computer Facility Connectivity Example

Figure 16.1 shows a computer connectivity diagram, using the Naval Postgraduate School as an example, illustrating the connectivity of client computers to laboratory Web servers, including an Internet router, with distances between machines annotated. A connectivity matrix can be constructed from this diagram in order to determine the values of k so that equations (16.1) and (16.2) can be computed.

The computer network distance matrix corresponding to Figure 16.1 is shown in Table 16.1. Tables 16.2 and 16.3 are the data flow and connection cost matrices, respectively, computed by using a random number generator in order to not introduce bias into the problem. Random numbers can be generated by using the RAND function in Excel. (Note that

TABLE 16.1 d_{ij}: Distance Matrix in Meters (Original Connectivity)

j i	1	2	3	4	5	6	7	8	9	10	Total per Node i
1	0	8	10	9	7	38	40	39	37	25	213
2	8	0	8	7	5	36	38	37	35	23	197
3	10	8	0	9	7	38	40	39	37	25	213
4	9	7	9	0	6	37	39	38	36	24	205
5	7	5	7	6	0	35	37	36	34	22	189
6	38	36	38	37	35	0	8	7	5	13	217
7	40	38	40	39	37	8	0	9	7	15	233
8	39	37	39	38	36	7	9	0	6	14	225
9	37	35	39	36	34	5	7	6	0	12	211
10	25	23	25	24	22	13	15	14	12	0	173
total per node j	213	197	215	205	189	217	233	225	209	173	2076 meters total cable

TABLE 16.2 f_{ij}: Data Flow in Megabits per Second (Original Connectivity)

j i	1	2	3	4	5	6	7	8	9	10	Sums
1	0.00	**0.64**	0.32	0.77	0.47	0.00	0.00	0.00	0.00	0.51	2.71
2	**0.97**	0.00	0.71	0.03	0.78	0.00	0.00	0.00	0.00	0.43	2.92
3	0.30	0.77	0.00	0.65	**0.83**	0.00	0.00	0.00	0.00	0.37	2.93
4	0.34	**0.76**	0.75	0.00	0.68	0.00	0.00	0.00	0.00	0.19	2.72
5	0.14	0.27	**0.30**	0.07	0.00	0.00	0.00	0.00	0.00	0.27	1.06
6	0.00	0.00	0.00	0.00	0.00	0.00	**0.67**	0.43	0.53	0.36	1.99
7	0.00	0.00	0.00	0.00	0.00	0.40	0.00	0.46	0.43	**0.96**	2.24
8	0.00	0.00	0.00	0.00	0.00	0.82	0.48	0.00	**0.88**	0.35	2.53
9	0.00	0.00	0.00	0.00	0.00	0.67	**0.77**	0.28	0.00	0.05	1.76
10	0.07	**0.84**	0.04	0.25	0.25	0.13	0.04	0.31	0.80	0.00	2.71
											23.58
											total flow rate

TABLE 16.3 h_{ij}: Connection Cost in Dollars per Meter (Original Connectivity)

j i	1	2	3	4	5	6	7	8	9	10
1	0.00	2.46	5.73	7.92	6.03	0.00	0.00	0.00	0.00	9.65
2	3.51	0.00	8.81	1.86	8.16	0.00	0.00	0.00	0.00	2.21
3	5.26	9.01	0.00	3.96	6.32	9.74	0.00	0.00	0.00	8.75
4	7.13	9.43	0.94	0.00	3.37	0.00	0.00	0.00	0.00	1.84
5	9.66	7.77	3.91	3.89	0.00	0.00	0.00	0.00	0.00	2.26
6	0.00	0.00	0.00	0.00	0.00	0.00	9.43	1.48	3.13	7.72
7	0.00	0.00	0.00	0.00	0.00	1.84	0.00	5.94	4.12	9.10
8	0.00	0.00	0.00	0.00	0.00	6.51	9.26	6.48	0.64	3.60
9	0.00	0.00	0.00	0.00	0.00	2.39	8.39	4.08	0.00	4.16
10	4.15	4.43	3.10	0.38	3.91	4.55	7.48	4.41	6.13	0.00

since h_{ij} (unit cost of connecting facilities) includes labor and cable costs, it is not constant due to variations in the difficulty of pulling cable.)

Then, using a flow time of $t = 60$ seconds, for illustrative purposes, the cost matrix is computed in Table 16.4 using equation (16.1). The flow time is expanded in a series of steps 60, . . . ,660, and the resultant flow dominance f is plotted as a function of t in Figure 16.2. Furthermore, to predict the flow dominance for $t > 660$, a power function was fitted to the actual data, yielding $R^2 = .8416$. With power function prediction, f will increase with increasing t. The implication for Figure 16.1 is that clients and servers that generate large data flows—maximum f_{ij} for a given node i (bolded in Table 16.2)—*might* overwhelm the network. Therefore, a load distribution scheme should be considered that would add more clients and servers so that the load could be more evenly distributed.

Another factor is cabling cost h_{ij}, which is a factor in the computation of flow dominance f in Table 16.5 on page 352. Note the bolded quantities in this table that identify the connections with relatively high cost. These are connections that should be made with shorter cable runs. These are the connections node i 1, 3, and 7 connected to node $j = 10$. Therefore,

TABLE 16.4 $w_{ij} * k$: Cost Matrix in Dollars (Original Connectivity)

j i	1	2	3	4	5	6	7	8	9	10
1	0	58	76	118	71	0	0	0	0	272
2	86	0	113	15	88	0	0	0	0	77
3	71	118	0	75	94	0	0	0	0	241
4	84	112	54	0	61	0	0	0	0	56
5	76	55	45	28	0	0	0	0	0	66
6	0	0	0	0	0	0	116	36	48	122
7	0	0	0	0	0	39	0	81	54	194
8	0	0	0	0	0	95	112	0	57	71
9	0	0	0	0	0	52	105	41	0	53
10	108	152	80	24	101	67	114	80	121	0

$\boxed{\bar{w}}$ **40**

Total Cost   **4387**

FIGURE 16.2   Flow Dominance f for 10 Computers vs. Flow Time t

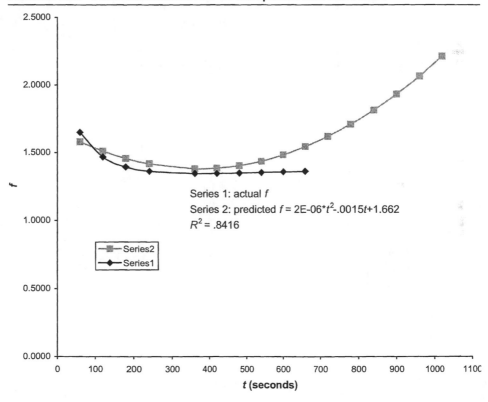

Series 1: actual f
Series 2: predicted $f = 2\text{E-}06*t^2-.0015t+1.662$
$R^2 = .8416$

— Series2
— Series1

t **(seconds)**

assuming that the placement of the Internet router can be changed as shown in Figure 16.3, this results in both a reduction in cable length, as shown in Table 16.6, and decreases in total and average costs, as shown in Table 16.7 (page 353). The cost reductions are confirmed in the revised flow dominance in Table 16.8 (page 354), where it can be seen that there is considerable reduction in costs, compared with Table 16.5, for rows $i = 1$, 3, and 7.

TABLE 16.5   Flow Dominance (Original Connectivity)

$$\left(w_{ij}k - \bar{w}\right)^2 / (M-1)$$

i \ j	1	2	3	4	5	6	7	8	9	10	Sum
1	177	37	147	672	105	177	177	177	177	**5966**	**7811**
2	237	177	596	71	253	177	177	177	177	152	2193
3	106	687	177	136	327	177	177	177	177	**4503**	**6643**
4	220	571	21	177	49	177	177	177	177	27	1772
5	146	26	3	16	177	177	177	177	177	76	1152
6	177	177	177	177	177	177	637	2	7	747	2452
7	177	177	177	177	177	0	177	187	24	**2647**	**3918**
8	177	177	177	177	177	334	581	177	31	111	2118
9	177	177	177	177	177	16	468	0	177	18	1564
10	512	1399	176	27	417	80	617	183	738	177	4325
											f **1.6490**

FIGURE 16.3   Naval Postgraduate School Computer Network Diagram (revised)

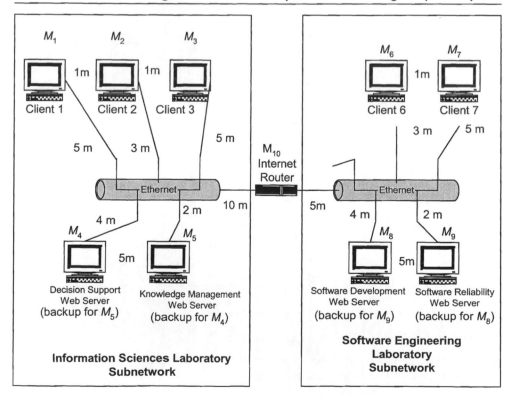

M: machine identification
m: cable length in meters

TABLE 16.6 d_{ij}: Distance Matrix in Meters (Revised Connectivity)

j i	1	2	3	4	5	6	7	8	9	10	
1	0	8	10	9	7	23	25	24	22	15	
2	8	0	8	7	5	21	23	22	20	13	
3	10	8	0	9	7	23	25	24	22	15	
4	9	7	9	0	6	22	24	23	21	14	
5	7	5	7	6	0	20	22	21	19	12	
6	23	21	23	22	20	0	8	7	5	8	
7	25	23	25	24	22	8	0	9	7	10	
8	24	22	24	23	21	7	9	0	6	9	
9	22	20	22	21	19	5	7	6	0	7	
10	15	13	15	14	12	8	10	9	7	0	
	143	127	143	135	119	137	153	145	129	103	1334
											meters total cable

TABLE 16.7 $w_{ij} * k$: Cost Matrix in Dollars (Revised Connectivity)

j i	1	2	3	4	5	6	7	8	9	10
1	0	58	76	118	71	0	0	0	0	175
2	86	0	113	15	88	0	0	0	0	55
3	71	118	0	75	94	0	0	0	0	154
4	84	112	54	0	61	0	0	0	0	37
5	76	55	45	28	0	0	0	0	0	44
6	0	0	0	0	0	0	116	36	48	83
7	0	0	0	0	0	39	0	81	54	149
8	0	0	0	0	0	95	112	0	57	53
9	0	0	0	0	0	52	105	41	0	32
10	66	108	49	21	62	44	77	58	91	0
									$\boxed{\overline{w}}$	37
									Total Cost	3689

With the revised connectivity, the flow dominance f is reduced from 1.6490 in Table 16.5 to 0.9216 in Table 16.8, for 60 seconds of Web service time, using equation (16.3).

Logical Connectivity

In addition to *physical* connectivity, *logical* connectivity is important. For example, placing sufficient intelligence in the router makes it possible to detect problems and offer solutions, such as re-routing around failed clients and Web servers, without facility disruption caused by manual intervention [CHA].

Most recently, IT organizations have relied on clusters of redundant servers to control systems like Web servers. The redundancy of these clusters helps reduce Web server downtime, thus reducing downtime to the user. Another approach to reducing downtime is

TABLE 16.8 Flow Dominance (Revised Connectivity)

$$\left(w_{ij}k - \bar{w}\right)^2 / (M - 1)$$

j *i*	1	2	3	4	5	6	7	8	9	10	Sum
1	177	37	147	672	105	177	177	177	177	2032	**3876**
2	237	177	596	71	253	177	177	177	177	25	2066
3	106	687	177	136	327	177	177	177	177	1439	**3578**
4	220	571	21	177	49	177	177	177	177	1	1746
5	146	26	3	16	177	177	177	177	177	1	1077
6	177	177	177	177	177	177	637	2	7	209	1914
7	177	177	177	177	177	0	177	187	24	1316	**2587**
8	177	177	177	177	177	334	581	177	31	21	2027
9	177	177	177	177	177	16	468	0	177	7	1552
10	77	512	9	42	54	2	153	38	287	177	1351
										f	**0.9216**

to use more reliable, fault tolerant (FT) servers. The total cost of ownership of FT servers is significantly lower than clusters or other options [NEC07]. A simple but cost-effective solution is to replicate the databases in Figure 16.1 to provide backups. If a server fails, a backup is available, albeit with reduced performance.

Heuristic for Achieving Closeness of Facilities

Sometimes it is important to have certain facilities close to one another [ASK93]. For example, it may be desirable to have certain Web servers that have the same circuit boards to be close or even adjacent so that hardware maintenance can be performed efficiently. On the other hand, this requirement may fly in the face of a requirement to have some servers close to the Internet router because these servers and router may be owned by an Internet Service Provider. Therefore, what is required is a balancing act to achieve a compromise between the competing demands. A function that is designed to achieve this balance is given in equation (16.4):

$$\text{Minimize } Z = \sum_{ij}^{M} S_{ij} d_{ij}, \tag{16.4}$$

where S_{ij} is a nominal score based on the desirability of facilities i and j being close or adjacent and d_{ij} is the distance between them. When it is desirable for facility i to be close or adjacent to facility j, $S_{ij} = 1$; $S_{ij} = 0$, otherwise. For example, in Figures 16.1 and 16.3, it is desirable for clients to be close, *within a laboratory subnetwork,* so that students and faculty can collaborate ($S_{ij} = 1$). In addition, it is desirable for Web servers to be close, *within a laboratory subnetwork,* for ease of maintenance ($S_{ij} = 1$). Contrariwise, it is not important for clients, Web servers, and the Internet router to be close ($S_{ij} = 0$).

Computer Facility Closeness Example

Table 16.9 shows closeness scores that were assigned to Figure 16.1 according to the above criteria in order to illustrate the process. For example, M_1 and M_2 are adjacent, so $S_{12} = 1$.

TABLE 16.9 S_{ij}: Closeness Scores (Original Connectivity)

j i	1	2	3	4	5	6	7	8	9	10
1	0	1	1	0	0	0	0	0	0	0
2	1	0	1	0	0	0	0	0	0	0
3	1	1	0	0	0	0	0	0	0	0
4	0	0	0	0	1	0	0	0	0	0
5	0	0	0	1	0	0	0	0	0	0
6	0	0	0	0	0	0	1	0	0	0
7	0	0	0	0	0	1	0	0	0	0
8	0	0	0	0	0	0	0	0	1	0
9	0	0	0	0	0	0	0	1	0	0
10	0	0	0	0	0	0	0	0	0	0

On the other hand, M_1 and M_4 are not adjacent; therefore, $S_{14} = 0$. Table 16.10 shows the closeness cost matrix computed using equation (16.4) that shows a total cost of 60. The next step is to revise the closeness of facilities in Figure 16.1 to those in Figure 16.3 by using one-half the distances, as an illustration. It is confirmed that, with this heuristic, the configuration in Figure 16.3 is superior because Table 16.11 indicates a total closeness cost reduction from 60 to 30.

Complexity of Connectivity

The model of a manufacturing system can be represented by a directed graph that shows both physical complexity (e.g., physical connectivity) and the data flow complexity (e.g., mean flow rate) of the system model. Such a model fits the connectivity of facilities in a manufacturing system [PRO97], such as connecting Web servers to "manufacture" Web services, for clients, as suggested in Figure 16.4 on page 356. Therefore, another consideration in connecting facilities is the resultant physical and data flow complexity. By physical

TABLE 16.10 $S_{ij}\, d_{ij}$ Closeness Cost Matrix (Original Connectivity)

j i	1	2	3	4	5	6	7	8	9	10	Sums
	0	2	4	0	0	0	0	0	0	0	6
1	2	0	2	0	0	0	0	0	0	0	4
2	4	2	0	0	0	0	0	0	0	0	6
3	0	0	0	0	10	0	0	0	0	0	10
4	0	0	0	10	0	0	0	0	0	0	10
5	0	0	0	0	0	0	2	0	0	0	2
6	0	0	0	0	0	2	0	0	0	0	2
7	0	0	0	0	0	0	0	0	10	0	10
8	0	0	0	0	0	0	0	10	0	0	10
9	0	0	0	0	0	0	0	0	0	0	0
10	0	0	0	0	0	0	0	0	0	0	0
											$Z = 60$

TABLE 16.11 $S_{ij}\, d_{ij}$ **Closeness Cost Matrix (Revised Connectivity)**

j											
i	1	2	3	4	5	6	7	8	9	10	Sums
1	0	1	2	0	0	0	0	0	0	0	3
2	1	0	1	0	0	0	0	0	0	0	2
3	2	1	0	0	0	0	0	0	0	0	3
4	0	0	0	0	5	0	0	0	0	0	5
5	0	0	0	5	0	0	0	0	0	0	5
6	0	0	0	0	0	0	1	0	0	0	1
7	0	0	0	0	0	1	0	0	0	0	1
8	0	0	0	0	0	0	0	0	5	0	5
9	0	0	0	0	0	0	0	5	0	0	5
10	0	0	0	0	0	0	0	0	0	0	0
											$Z = 30$

**FIGURE 16.4   Data Flow and Physical Complexity of Figure 16.1: Naval Postgraduate
School Laboratory Subnetworks**

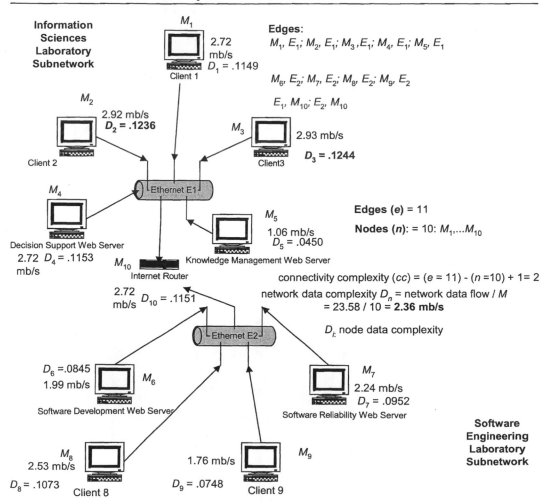

Information Sciences Laboratory Subnetwork

M_1
2.72 mb/s
$D_1 = .1149$
Client 1

Edges:
$M_1, E_1; M_2, E_1; M_3, E_1; M_4, E_1; M_5, E_1$

$M_6, E_2; M_7, E_2; M_8, E_2; M_9, E_2$

$E_1, M_{10}; E_2, M_{10}$

M_2
2.92 mb/s
$D_2 = .1236$
Client 2

M_3
2.93 mb/s
$D_3 = .1244$
Client3

M_4
Decision Support Web Server
2.72 $D_4 = .1153$ mb/s

Ethernet E1

M_5
1.06 mb/s
$D_5 = .0450$
Knowledge Management Web Server

Edges (e) = 11
Nodes (n): = 10: $M_1,...M_{10}$

M_{10}
Internet Router
2.72 $D_{10} = .1151$ mb/s

connectivity complexity (cc) = (e = 11) - (n =10) + 1= 2
network data complexity D_n = network data flow / M
= 23.58 / 10 = **2.36 mb/s**

D_i: node data complexity

Ethernet E2

$D_6 = .0845$
1.99 mb/s
M_6
Software Development Web Server

M_7
2.24 mb/s
$D_7 = .0952$
Software Reliability Web Server

Software Engineering Laboratory Subnetwork

M_8
2.53 mb/s
$D_8 = .1073$
Client 8

1.76 mb/s
$D_9 = .0748$
M_9
Client 9

complexity we mean the complexity of the directed graph representing the branches and paths of the interconnected facilities [ASK93]. McCabe introduced the notion of cyclomatic complexity as applied to testing software systems [MCC76]. He stated that the minimum number of paths to test in a program is given by the cyclomatic complexity number $cc = e - v + 1$, where e is the number of edges and v is the number of vertices in the program. This concept can be applied to networks, where cc is now connectivity complexity, e is the number of data flow edges, and v is the number of network nodes.

Network data flow complexity is represented by the mean value of data flow in a system in equation (16.5). That is, network data flow complexity D_n = network data flow/M network nodes:

$$D_n = \frac{\sum_{j=1}^{M} d_{ij} \, (\text{for } i = 1,...,M)}{M}, \tag{16.5}$$

where d_{ij} is the data flow from node i to node j.

Node data flow complexity is equal to: (node generated data flow/total data flow) in equation (16.6). That is, data flow complexity of node i is D_i:

$$D_i = \frac{\sum_{j=1}^{M} d_{ij}}{\sum_{j=1}^{M} d_{ij} \, (\text{for } i = 1,...,M)} \tag{16.6}$$

Equation (16.6) can be interpreted as the percentage data flow in the network generated and transmitted by node i. Also, equation (16.6) plays a dual role with respect to the data flow received by node j. This consideration leads to equation (16.7): the *received* data flow complexity:

$$d_j = \frac{\sum_{i=1}^{M} d_{ij}}{\sum_{j=1}^{M} d_{ij} \, (\text{for } i = 1,...,M)}, \tag{16.7}$$

where d_{ij} is the data flow received at node j from node i. Equation (16.7) is of interest when the focus is on identifying network congestion caused by *received* data flow. Similar to equation (16.6), equation (16.7) can be interpreted as the percentage of data flow in the network received at node j.

In general, when cyclomatic complexity increases, data flow complexity also increases, as you will see. An important point about data flow complexity is that the McCabe metric minimizes traffic congestion by providing the maximum amount of direct flow (i.e. avoidance of a rat's nest physical interconnection scheme) that researchers have suggested is highly desirable to promote facility efficiency [CHI02].

These ideas can be applied to problems like alternatives for connecting the Naval Postgraduate School networks. Figure 16.4 shows the data flow and physical complexity corresponding to the original connectivity in Figure 16.1. Using equation (16.5), the generated data flow complexity for each node i is computed and listed in Table 16.12 on page 358 and shown on Figure 16.4, where the large data flow complexities are bolded.

While the data flow is two-way in Figure 16.4, the edges point in only one direction in order to adhere to the convention of drawing a directed graph. Note that connectivity

TABLE 16.12 f_{ij}: Data Flow in Megabits per Second

i \ j	1	2	3	4	5	6	7	8	9	10	Sums	Node i	Data Flow Complexity
1	0.00	0.64	0.32	0.77	0.47	0.00	0.00	0.00	0.00	0.51	2.71	1	0.1149
2	0.97	0.00	0.71	0.03	0.78	0.00	0.00	0.00	0.00	0.43	2.92	2	0.1236
3	0.30	0.77	0.00	0.65	0.83	0.00	0.00	0.00	0.00	0.37	2.93	3	0.1244
4	0.34	0.76	0.75	0.00	0.68	0.00	0.00	0.00	0.00	0.19	2.72	4	0.1153
5	0.14	0.27	0.30	0.07	0.00	0.00	0.00	0.00	0.00	0.27	1.06	5	0.0450
6	0.00	0.00	0.00	0.00	0.00	0.00	0.67	0.43	0.53	0.36	1.99	6	0.0845
7	0.00	0.00	0.00	0.00	0.00	0.40	0.00	0.46	0.43	0.96	2.24	7	0.0952
8	0.00	0.00	0.00	0.00	0.00	0.82	0.48	0.00	0.88	0.35	2.53	8	0.1073
9	0.00	0.00	0.00	0.00	0.00	0.67	0.77	0.28	0.00	0.05	1.76	9	0.0748
10	0.07	0.84	0.04	0.25	0.25	0.13	0.04	0.31	0.80	0.00	2.71	10	0.1151
Sums	1.82	3.28	2.11	1.78	3.01	2.01	1.96	1.48	2.64	3.50	**23.58**	sum	1.0000
Data Flow Complexity	0.0770	0.1393	0.0896	0.0754	0.1278	0.0852	0.0829	0.0628	0.1118	**0.1482**			

D_n = network data flow complexity   2.36

complexity cc is small because the nodes are connected through two Ethernets. If the nodes were directly connected, cc would be much larger. The node data flow complexity is highest for Client 2 and 3. This result serves as an alert to monitor these traffic streams for increases in data flow that might create congestion in the Information Sciences Subnetwork.

As shown in Figure 16.5, cc for the revised network is 16, a large increase over $cc = 2$ for the original network! This change causes congestion at the Internet router in Figure 16.5, where it is shown that the router has the largest *received data flow complexity* of any of the nodes ($d_{10} = .1482$), which was computed in equation (16.7) and listed in Table 16.12. As suggested earlier, this result is due to the absence of the Ethernets, causing a data pile-up at the router.

Centroid Method for Facility Location Analysis

The centroid method provides the engineer with a method for approximating the optimal location of facilities that will minimize the cost of travel or distributing material among the facilities. The centroid method uses x-y coordinates to locate a distribution center such that the travel or distribution cost to customer locations will be minimized [MON96]. To continue with IT applications, the centroid method is used for locating a software distribution

FIGURE 16.5   Data Flow and Physical Complexity of Figure 16.4 (revised)

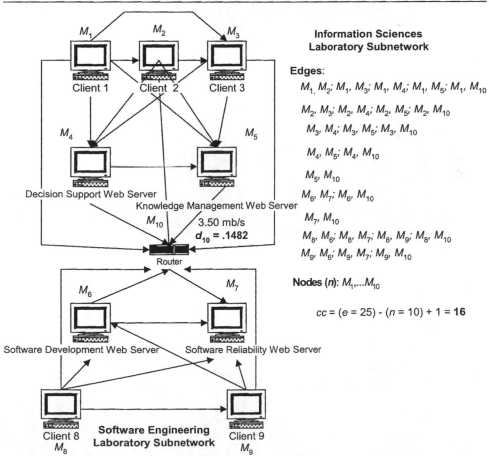

Information Sciences
Laboratory Subnetwork

Edges:

$M_1, M_2; M_1, M_3; M_1, M_4; M_1, M_5; M_1, M_{10}$

$M_2, M_3; M_2, M_4; M_2, M_5; M_2, M_{10}$

$M_3, M_4; M_3, M_5; M_3, M_{10}$

$M_4, M_5; M_4, M_{10}$

M_5, M_{10}

$M_6, M_7; M_6, M_{10}$

M_7, M_{10}

$M_8, M_6; M_8, M_7; M_8, M_9; M_8, M_{10}$

$M_9, M_6; M_9, M_7; M_9, M_{10}$

Nodes (n): $M_1,...M_{10}$

$cc = (e = 25) - (n = 10) + 1 = $ **16**

center such that the cost of distributing software to customer locations will be minimized. Two types of distance metrics are employed: rectangular and Euclidian.

Definitions

w_i: trips per time period from distribution center to customer location i
a_i: x coordinate of customer location i relative to $x = 0, y = 0$
b_i: y coordinate of customer location i relative to $x = 0, y = 0$
x: optimal x coordinate of distribution location
y: optimal y coordinate of distribution
M: total cost of making trips from distribution center to customer locations (trips per time period × distance)

$$\text{minimize } M = \sum_{i}^{m} w_i[|x - a_i| + |y - b_i|] \tag{16.8}$$

Note: M is an absolute value quantity.

The centroid values of x and y can be *approximated* by equations (16.9) and (16.10), which represent weighted averages of the x and y coordinates, respectively [MON96]. The coordinates are approximated because it is likely that one of the existing locations, with coordinates a_i and b_i, will yield the minimum value of M since one pair of coordinates in equation (16.8) will be zero.

$$x = \frac{\sum_{i}^{m} w_i a_i}{\sum_{i}^{m} w_i} \tag{16.9}$$

$$y = \frac{\sum_{i}^{m} w_i b_i}{\sum_{i}^{m} w_i} \tag{16.10}$$

Problem 1

A software distribution center in Figure 16.6 serves five customer locations: A, B, C, D, and E, with the x-y coordinates given below. The optimal values of x and y are to be found, using rectangular coordinates. In addition, a layout of the solution is to be provided, realizing that the values obtained, using equations (16.9) and (16.10), will not necessarily yield the minimum value of M. However, it is required that the distribution center be disjoint from any of the customer locations. Thus, the solution provided by equations (16.9) and (16.10) would be acceptable. In addition to the coordinates, the frequency of travel from the distribution center to customer locations is the following: $w_A = 90$, $w_B = 60$, $w_C = 80$, $w_D = 50$, and $w_E = 50$ (trips per day).

x coordinates	y coordinates
$a_A = -300$ (kilometers)	$b_A = 100$ (kilometers)
$a_B = -100$	$b_B = 0$
$a_C = -600$	$b_C = -200$
$a_D = -600$	$b_D = 100$
$a_E = -200$	$b_E = 0$

FIGURE 16.6   Software Distribution Location: Centroid Method

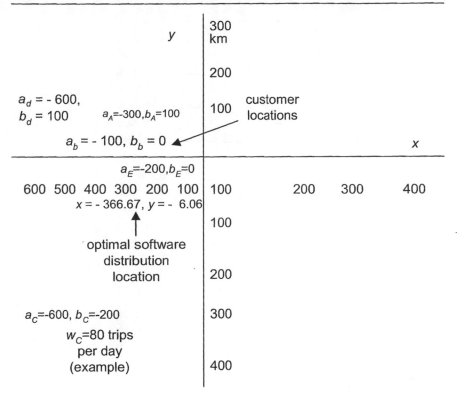

Solution

Rectangular Coordinates

Using equation (16.8):

$$\sum_{i}^{m} w_i a_i = \left[90x(-300) + 60x(-100) + 80x(-600) + 50x(-600) + 50(-200) \right]$$

$$= -121,000$$

$$\sum_{i}^{m} w_i = 90 + 60 + 80 + 50 + 50 = 330$$

Using equation (16.9), solve for *x:*

$$x = -120,000 / 330 = \textbf{-366.67} \text{ kilometers}$$

Using equation (16.8) again:

$$\sum_{i}^{m} w_i b_i = \left[90x(100) + 60x(-0) + 80x(-200) + 50x(100) + 50(0) \right] = -2,000$$

Using equation (16.10), solve for *y:*

$$y = -2,000/330 = -6.06 \text{ kilometers}$$

Substituting the values of x and y into equation (16.8) yields $M = 91697$. However, if you use $x = -300$ and $y = 100$, which is one of the customer location coordinate pairs, you

TABLE 16.13   Centroid Method Using Rectangular Coordinates

x	y	w_i	a_i	b_i	M
−300	100	90	−300	100	**91000**
−100	0	60	−100	0	118000
−600	−200	80	−600	−200	141000
−600	100	50	−600	100	112000
−200	0	50	−200	0	97000
−366.67	−6.06				91697
300	−100				267000
100	0				184000
600	200				387000
600	−100				366000
200	0				217000
0	0				151000

get $M = 91000$. However, since the software distribution center must be disjoint from any of the customer locations, you are forced to use the sub-optimal solution $x = -366.67$ and $y = -6.06$. Table 16.13 shows the small difference in M for the two solutions. In addition, there are several additional pairs of coordinates in Table 16.13 that are not of the original set, that are used to demonstrate: 1) $x = -300$ and $y = 100$ is still optimal and 2) $x = -366.67$ and $y = -6.06$ is still the best choice when the software distribution center must be disjoint from the customer locations (see Figure 16.6).

Euclidian Distance

Now, using Euclidian distance, the optimal solution of minimizing M is shown in equation (16.11).

$$\text{Minimize } M = \sum_{i=1}^{m} w_i \left[\sqrt{(x-a_i)^2 + (y-b_i)^2} \right] \tag{16.11}$$

The optimal values of x and y are computed using the same equations as in the case of rectangular coordinates:

$$x = \frac{\sum_{i}^{m} w_i a_i}{\sum_{i}^{m} w_i} \tag{16.12}$$

$$y = \frac{\sum_{i}^{m} w_i b_i}{\sum_{i}^{m} w_i} \tag{16.13}$$

The Euclidian distance between coordinate pairs x, y and a_i, b_i is given by:

$$d = \sqrt{(x - a_i)^2 + (y - b_i)^2}$$ (16.14)

Solution

Euclidian Distance

Table 16.14 shows that $x = -366.67$ and $y = -6.06$ yields the minimum value of M, as was the case using rectangular coordinates. The Euclidian distances are given in the last column of the table, using equation (16.14). For example, the straight-line distance between the optimal location of the software distribution center and the customer located at ($a_i = -300$, $b_i = 100$) is 125 kilometers. In addition, values of M are shown for various values of x and y, including the customer location coordinates that show, indeed, $x = -366.67$ and $y = -6.06$ yield the minimum value of M. Note that the Euclidian distance alternative is better than using rectangular coordinates because the former is based on the minimum straight-line distance between two sets of coordinates. This conclusion is supported by the fact that the $x = -366.67$ and $y = -6.06$ solution is better than $x = -300$, $y = 100$, as was the case using rectangular coordinates.

REL Chart for Layout and Location Design

The Activity Relationship Chart (REL Chart) is among the earliest and most popular tools for expressing *subjective, uncertain, and linguistic considerations in layout and location design*. Typically, activity relationships are translated into relative proximity requirements between facilities that are used in making location decisions. These proximity requirements are expressed in REL through an ordinal *closeness rating* such as: $1 > 2 > 3 > 4 > 5$. The REL is designed to facilitate consideration of qualitative factors such as political needs, or situations where precise data cannot be made available due to financial and other practical constraints. Ratings do not provide the means for *handling conflicting preferences* and may result in *inconsistent ratings*. Such factors contribute to the inflexibility and limitations of

TABLE 16.14   Centroid Method Using Euclidian Distance

x	y	w_i	a_i	b_i	M	Distance between Distribution Center and Customer Locations for Optimal M
-366.67	**-6.06**	90	-300	100	**8860606**	125
-300	100	60	-100	0	11450000	267
-100	0	80	-600	-200	20600000	303
-600	-200	50	-600	100	24050000	256
-600	100	50	-200	0	19700000	167
-200	0				13450000	
300	-100				83650000	
100	0				44800000	
600	200				170050000	
600	-100				164500000	
200	0				61850000	
0	0				31050000	

REL. However, several advantages of REL, such as *ease of use* and *ease of learning,* have contributed to wide acceptance of its various adaptations.

Applying the REL Chart to the problem in Table 16.14, Table 16.15 shows that requiring the distribution center to be co-located with one of the customer locations ($x = -300$, $y = 100$), say for political reasons, incurs an increase in M of $11{,}450{,}000 - 8{,}860{,}606 = 2{,}589{,}394$, compared with the optimal location of $x = -366.67$, $y = -6.06$. Thus, if, for example, political considerations outweigh cost, ($x = -300$, $y = 100$) would be the preferred solution.

From To Charts for Layout Design

The From To Chart (FTC), or Flow Matrix, is one of the earliest tools adopted for assisting layout designers in the facility development process [TUR93]. It contains numbers representing some measure of interactions between pairs of modules. For instance, it could contain information flow between two nodes in a computer network

Actually, FTC addresses the same problem as the data flow equation discussed earlier in equation (16.1):

$w_{ij} = [(f_{ij} * t) + (h_{ij} * d)]k$, if you confine your attention to the cabling cost, as expressed by equation (16.15).

$$c_{ij} = \sum_{i=1,j=1}^{M} d_{ij}h_{ij}k \, , \qquad (16.15)$$

where c_{ij} is the physical connection cost over M nodes; d_{ij} is the distance between nodes i and j; h_{ij} is the cabling cost between nodes i and j; and $k = 1$ if i and j are connected, and $k = 0$, if not connected.

Naval Postgraduate School Network Application

Equation (16.15) is applied to the original Naval Postgraduate School network in Figure 16.1. The result is shown in Table 16.16, which shows the cabling costs between nodes i and j; the costs of cabling from each node i; the cost of cabling to each node j; and the total cost. It is natural that the Internet router, node 10, has the largest costs because this node is directly connected to every other node in the network. When the connectivity is revised, as in Figure 16.3, and equation (16.15) is again applied, the resultant costs are shown in Table 16.17. While router and total costs have been reduced, node 10 is still the bottleneck from a data flow standpoint (see Figure 16.5). If these costs and congestion were of major concern to the Naval Postgraduate School, it could consider additional connectivity schemes to alleviate congestion and to further reduce costs.

TABLE 16.15   REL Chart for Locating Software Distribution Center (Euclidian Distance)

	Customer Locations				
Software Distribution center located at:	A (−330, 100)	B (−100, 0)	C (−600, −200)	D (−600, 100)	E (−200, 0)
Activity Rating	1	3	5	2	4
M from Table 16.14	**11,450,000**	20,600,000	24,050,000	19,700,000	13,450,000

TABLE 16.16   Cabling Cost of Figure 16.1

j i	1	2	3	4	5	6	7	8	9	10	Cost of Cabling from Node i Sums
1	0.00	19.69	57.35	71.26	42.19	0.00	0.00	0.00	0.00	241.28	431.76
2	28.06	0.00	70.45	13.01	40.82	0.00	0.00	0.00	0.00	50.83	203.18
3	52.62	72.11	0.00	35.65	44.25	0.00	0.00	0.00	0.00	218.79	423.41
4	64.15	65.98	8.46	0.00	20.20	0.00	0.00	0.00	0.00	44.16	202.95
5	67.65	38.83	27.38	23.31	0.00	0.00	0.00	0.00	0.00	49.64	206.82
6	0.00	0.00	0.00	0.00	0.00	0.00	75.41	10.35	15.67	100.31	201.73
7	0.00	0.00	0.00	0.00	0.00	14.69	0.00	53.42	28.84	136.56	233.51
8	0.00	0.00	0.00	0.00	0.00	45.56	83.37	0.00	3.86	50.46	183.25
9	0.00	0.00	0.00	0.00	0.00	11.96	58.71	24.47	0.00	49.88	145.03
10	103.66	101.97	77.49	9.09	86.06	59.18	112.20	61.79	73.57	0.00	**685.03**
sums	316.14	298.58	241.14	152.33	233.51	131.41	329.69	150.03	121.94	**941.92**	**2916.68**
				cost of cabling at node j							total cost

TABLE 16.17   Cabling Cost of Figure 16.3

j i	1	2	3	4	5	6	7	8	9	10	Cost of Cabling from Node i Sums
1	0	0	24.6	51.6	55.4	0	0	0	0	0	131.65
2	7.73	0	0	61.6	9.29	0	0	0	0	0	78.67
3	3.03	42.1	0	0	27.7	0	0	0	0	0	72.86
4	3.03	49.9	84.8	0	0	0	0	0	0	0	137.77
5	0.99	48.3	54.4	23.5	0	0	0	0	0	0	127.15
6	0	0	0	0	0	0	0	66	7.39	25.1	98.44
7	0	0	0	0	0	0	0	0	41.5	41.2	82.75
8	0	0	0	0	0	0	58.6	0	0	5.79	64.37
9	0	0	0	0	0	0	16.8	50.3	0	0	67.07
10	1.02	53.9	66.5	43.4	4.55	31.3	45.5	67.3	30.9	0	**344.40**
sums	15.8	194	230	180	97	31.3	121	184	79.8	**72.1**	**1205.12**
				cost of cabling at node j							total cost

Component Routing and Assignment Analysis

Component routing refers to the movement of components among machines [ASK93]—for example, routing data packets among network nodes in order to maximize the benefit-cost ratio (e.g., packet throughput/routing cost).

Definitions

B/C: benefit/cost ratio
f: network data flow rate
s: network data packet size

T: network data flow throughput

RC: network route cost

lc: network link cost

d_{ij}: network link distance, where the most direct link between two nodes has a distance of one (see Figure 16.7)

n: network route distance (see Figure 16.7)

Equations

$$T = f/s \tag{16.16}$$

$$n = \sum_{ij} d_{ij} \tag{16.17}$$

$$RC = n * lc \tag{16.18}$$

$$B/C = T/RC = (f/s)/RC \tag{16.19}$$

Network Routing Application

Data packets are routed on four computers A, B, C, and D. In order to get to their destination E, the packets can be routed among the four computers according to the routing sequences given in Figure 16.7. There are three routes: 1, 2, and 3. The objective is to identify the route that provides the maximum benefit cost ratio. The parameters of the network

FIGURE 16.7 Network Routing Diagram

Route 1 network node

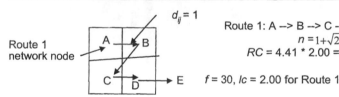

$d_{ij} = 1$

Route 1: A --> B --> C --> D --> E

$n = 1 + \sqrt{2} + 1 + 1 = 4.41$

$RC = 4.41 * 2.00 = 8.82$

$f = 30$, $lc = 2.00$ for Route 1

$B/C = 30 / (.001*8.82) = 3401.36$

Route 2

Route 2: A --> D --> B --> C --> E

$n = \sqrt{2} + 1 + \sqrt{2} + 2 = 5.82$

$f = 20$, $lc = 1.50$ for Route 2

$RC = 5.82 * 1.50 = 8.73$

$B/C = 20 / (.001*8.73) = 2290.95$

Route 3

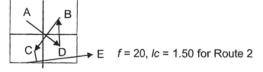

Route 3: A --> C --> D --> B --> E

$n = 1 + 1 + 1 + \sqrt{5} = 5.24$

$C = 5.24 * 1.00 = 5.24$

$f = 40$, $lc = 1.00$ for Route 3

$B/C = 40 / (.001* 5.24) = 7633.59$
(best route)

data flow = f (megabits per second)

data packet size s = 1000 bits per packet = .001 megabits per packet

throughput T (packets per second)

benefit cost ratio B/C (packets per second per dollar)

are given in Figure 16.7. The solution is Route 3—shown on Figure 16.7—obtained by using equations (16.16)–(16.19). This route has the maximum benefit-cost ratio.

Facility Location Analysis with Weighted Scoring

In some cases there is the need to determine facility location based on factors like user preference for a facility location. This is done by weighting the factors and locations and producing scores that reflect user preference. This approach is similar to the REL Charts covered earlier, but with more factors and more quantification of user preferences.

Definitions

i: factor (e.g., client node performance at location j)
j: facility location (e.g., computer network client location)
w_i: weight for factor i
n_i: number of users who users who favor factor i
n_{ij}:   number of users who favor factor i and location j
N_f: number of factors
N_l: number of locations
N_i: number of users expressing a factor preference for factor i (can be less than total number of users)
N_j: number of users expressing a factor preference for factor j (can be less than total number of users)
N_{ij}:   number of users expressing preference for factor i and location j (can be less than total number of users)
s_{ij}:   score for factor i and location j

Facility Location Model

$$\text{Weight for factor } i: w_i = n_i/N_i \tag{16.20}$$

Sum of weights for factor i must sum to 1:

$$\sum_{i=1}^{N_f} w_i = 1 \tag{16.21}$$

Score for factor i, location j:

$$s_{ij} = n_{ij}/N_{ij} \tag{16.22}$$

Sum of scores for factor i, location j must sum to 1:

$$\sum_{j=1}^{N_l} s_{ij} = 1 \tag{16.23}$$

Weighted score for specified location j^*:

$$s_j^* = \sum_{i=1}^{N_f} w_i s_{ij}^* \tag{16.24}$$

Network Client Location Application

Based on the factors i and locations j, given in Table 16.18, what is the score for client node location $j^* = 2$?

Complete Table 16.18 by using equations (16.20)–(16.24) to compute factor weights and location scores and ensure that weights and scores sum to 1.0.

After the table is completed, use Equation (16.24) to compute the weighted score for client node location 2:

$$s_2^* = \text{score for client location 2} = \sum_{i=1}^{4} w_1 s_{12} + w_2 s_{22} + w_3 s_{32} + w_4 s_{42}$$

$$= (.3333)(.3500) + (.2500)(.3478) + (.1667)(.2353) + (.2500)(.3000) = .3177$$

Interpretation

Since there are three plant locations, one would expect an average score = .3333. Thus, with a score of only .3177, this result does not constitute an endorsement for client node location 2!

Facility Capacity Analysis

Facilities have capacities and productivities. When manufacturing systems have flexible capacities (i.e., capacity for growth), productivity can be increased [MAT05]. It is important to compute the efficiencies of these facilities for both perfectly reliable system components—to serve as a baseline for comparison—and components that experience some unreliability [MON93]. Because facility capacity may be reduced by unreliable components, system capacity refers to the facility, in a series of facilities, that has the minimum—or limiting—productive capability. In addition, it is important to identify bottlenecks in the production process, as well as under-capacity and over-capacity facilities.

Definitions

S_c: System capacity is the *minimum* output of producing a product across n facilities; it does *not* account for defect rates of facilities

S_{ce}:   Effective system capacity is the *minimum effective* productivity across n facilities; it does account for defect rates of facilities

SE: System efficiency (mean productivity across n facilities/system capacity); it does *not* account for defect rates of facilities

SE_e: Effective system efficiency (mean productivity across n facilities/effective system capacity); it does account for defect rates of facilities

P_i: productivity of facility i

P_{ei}:   effective productivity of facility i

P_m: mean productivity across n facilities

P_{me}:   mean effective productivity across n facilities

D_i: defect rate of facility i

Facility Capacity Model

Define system efficiency as the fraction of system capacity that leads to productivity in equation (16.25):

TABLE 16.18   Network Client Factors and Locations

Factor i, Location j	Number of Users who Prefer Factor i: n_i, and Factor Weights w_i $w_i = n_i/N_i$	Number of Users Who Prefer Factor i and Location j: n_{ij}, and Scores s_{ij} $s_{ij} = n_{ij}/N_{ij}$			
		Location 1	Location 2	Location 3	Sums
Client Node Performance, Factor 1	$n_1 = 200$ $w_1 = 200/600$ $= .3333$	$n_{11} = 80$ $s_{11} = 80/200$ $= .4000$	$n_{12} = 70$ $s_{12} = 70/200$ $= .3500$	$n_{13} = 50$ $s_{13} = 50/200$ $= .2500$	$N_{1j} = 200$ $\sum_{j=1}^{N_i} s_{1j} = 1$
Client Node Near User, Factor 2	$n_2 = 150$ $w_2 = 150/600$ $= .2500$	$n_{22} = 50$ $s_{21} = 50/230$ $= .2174$	$n_{23} = 80$ $s_{22} = 80/230$ $= .3478$	$n_{24} = 100$ $s_{23} = 100/230$ $= .4348$	$N_{2j} = 230$ $\sum_{j=1}^{N_i} s_{2j} = 1$
Degree of Security Provided in Client Node, Factor 3	$n_3 = 100$ $w_3 = 100/600$ $= .1667$	$n_{31} = 70$ $s_{31} = 70/170$ $= .4118$	$n_{32} = 40$ $s_{32} = 40/170$ $= .2353$	$n_{33} = 60$ $s_{33} = 60/170$ $= .3529$	$N_{3j} = 170$ $\sum_{j=1}^{N_i} s_{3j} = 1$
Application Software Available at Client Node, Factor 4	$n_4 = 150$ $w_4 = 150/600$ $= .2500$	$n_{41} = 90$ $s_{41} = 90/200$ $= .4500$	$n_{42} = 60$ $s_{42} = 60/200$ $= .3000$	$n_{43} = 50$ $s_{43} = 50/200$ $= .2500$	$N_{4j} = 200$ $\sum_{j=1}^{N_i} s_{4j} = 1$
Sums	$N_i = 600$ $\sum_{i=1}^{N_i} w_i = 1$	320	250	230	$N_j = 800$

$$\text{System efficiency } SE = P_m/S_c = P_m/\text{Min}\,(P_i) \tag{16.25}$$

If $SE > 1$, productivity exceeds capacity, therefore there is under capacity in facility i, not taking into account defect rate D_i.

If $SE < 1$, capacity exceeds productivity, therefore there is over capacity in facility i, not taking into account defect rate D_i.

$$\text{Mean productivity for } n \text{ facilities: } P_m = \sum_i^n P_i/n \tag{16.26}$$

$$\text{Effective productivity of facility } i = P_{ei} = (1 - D_i) \times P_i \tag{16.27}$$
$$\text{(taking into account defect rate } D_i \text{ at facility } i)$$

$$\text{Based on the definition of effective system capacity, } S_{ce} = \text{Min}\,(P_{ei}) \tag{16.28}$$

$$\text{Mean effective productivity for } n \text{ facilities: } P_{me} = \sum_i^n ((1 - D_i) \times P_i)/n) \tag{16.29}$$

Using equations (16.28) and (16.29):

$$\text{Effective system efficiency} = SE_e = P_{me}/S_{ce} = \sum_i^n ((1 - D_i) \times P_i)/n) / \min\left(P_{ei}\right) \tag{16.30}$$

If $SE_e > 1$, productivity exceeds capacity, therefore there is under capacity in facility i, taking into account defect rate D_i.

If $SE_e < 1$, capacity exceeds productivity, therefore there is over capacity in facility i, taking into account defect rate D_i.

Software Production Capacity Analysis Application

For a software production process with the facilities shown in Figure 16.8, and the productivities P_i for each facility i, the quantities given by equations (16.25), . . . , (16.30) are computed and annotated on Figure 16.8. The key finding is that the development facility is the production bottleneck because, taking into account defect rate, it has the lowest effective system efficiency.

FIGURE 16.8 Capacity Analysis of Software Module Production

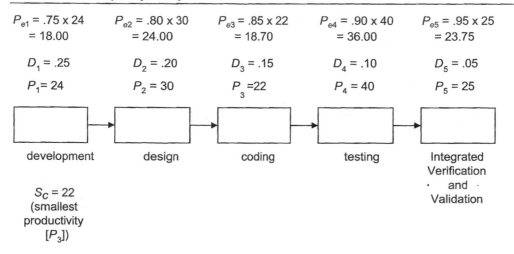

$$P_{e1} = .75 \times 24 \qquad P_{e2} = .80 \times 30 \qquad P_{e3} = .85 \times 22 \qquad P_{e4} = .90 \times 40 \qquad P_{e5} = .95 \times 25$$
$$= 18.00 \qquad\qquad = 24.00 \qquad\qquad = 18.70 \qquad\qquad = 36.00 \qquad\qquad = 23.75$$

$$D_1 = .25 \qquad\qquad D_2 = .20 \qquad\qquad D_3 = .15 \qquad\qquad D_4 = .10 \qquad\qquad D_5 = .05$$

$$P_1 = 24 \qquad\qquad P_2 = 30 \qquad\qquad P_3 = 22 \qquad\qquad P_4 = 40 \qquad\qquad P_5 = 25$$

| development | design | coding | testing | Integrated Verification ·   and · Validation |

$$S_C = 22$$
(smallest productivity $[P_3]$)

System capacity $= S_c = \text{Min}\,(P_i) = 22$ modules per day in coding facility

Mean productivity $P_m = \sum_i^n P_i \, / \, n = (24 + 30 + 22 + 40 + 25) / 5 = 28.2$ modules per day

System efficiency $SE = P_m \, / \, S_c = P_m \, / \, \text{Min}\,(P_i) = 28.2 \, / \, 22 = 1.2818$

SE: 28.18% under capacity

D_i: defect rate of facility i

Effective productivity of facility $i = P_{ei} = (1 - D_i) \times P_i$

Mean effective productivity $P_{me} = \sum_i^n ((1-D_i) \times P_i) / \, n = (18.00 + 24.00 + 18.70 + 36.00 + 23.75) / 5 = 120.45 / 5 = 24.09$ modules per day

Effective system capacity $= S_{ce} = \text{Min}\,(P_{ei}) = 18.00$ in development facility

Effective system efficiency $= SE_e = P_{me} / S_{ce} = (\sum_i^n ((1-D_i) \times P_i) / \, n) \, / \, \text{Min}\,(P_{ei}) = 24.09 \, / \, 18.00 = 1.3383$

SE_e: 33.83% under capacity

Least-Cost Assignment Methods

The least-cost assignment method involves finding the least-cost assignment of one resource to another resource—for example, assigning computers to plants so that manufacturing cost of computers is minimized.

Definitions

i: resource to be assigned
j: resource to receive the assignment
c_{ij}:   cost of manufacturing resource i when it is assigned to resource j
C_{ij}:   total cost of manufacturing resources i that are assigned to resources j, is given by equation (16.31):

$$C_{ij} = \sum_{i,j}^{n} c_{ij} ,$$ (16.31)

where n is the number of resources to be assigned.

Computer Manufacturing Application

For manufacturing purposes, four computers, 1, 2, 3, and 4 are to be assigned to four plant locations 1, 2, 3, and 4, in such a way that the sum of the manufacturing costs is minimized. The plants have variable costs with respect to the type of computer to be manufactured. We find the least-cost assignment as shown in Table 16.19 (pp. 372–373), using the Hungarian Method.

Hungarian Method [BRO97]:

The steps in this method are the following:

0. Show the original cost matrix.
1. Subtract the entries of each row by the row minimum.
2. Subtract the entries of each column by the column minimum based on the result in Step 1.
3. Select rows and columns and draw lines in such a way that all the zeros are covered and that the minimum number of lines has been drawn.
4. A test for optimality.
   (i) If the number of the lines = n, choose $i \rightarrow j$ assignments from the original cost matrix so that C_{ij} is minimized (i.e., for each row, with a line covering "0s", select $i > j$ for minimum cost).
   (ii) If the number of the lines is < n, go to Step 5.
5. Find the smallest element that is not covered by any of the lines. Then subtract it from each entry that is not covered by the lines and add it to each entry that is covered by a vertical and a horizontal line. Go back to Step 3.
4. A test for optimality.

   If the number of the lines is < $n = 4$, go to Step 5. If the number of lines = $3 < n = 4$, go to Step 5.

   The smallest element is at $i = 3, j = 3$ and $i = 4, j = 3$ (= 2).
4. A test for optimality.

   If the number of the lines = $n = 4$, choose $i \rightarrow j$ assignments from the original cost matrix so that C_{ij} is minimized (i.e., for each row, with a line covering "0s", select $i \rightarrow j$ for minimum cost). The number of lines = $n = 4$.

TABLE 16.19   Hungarian Method for Assigning Computers to Plants

	Step 0. Show the original cost matrix. j (plants)			
i (computers)	1	2	3	4
1	9	2	2	7
2	7	3	3	6
3	1	4	3	10
4	2	5	4	8

	Step 1. Subtract the entries of each row by the row minimum. j (plants)			
i (computers)	1	2	3	4
1	7	0	0	5
2	4	0	0	3
3	0	3	2	9
4	0	3	2	6

	Step 2. Subtract the entries of each column by the column minimum. j (plants)			
i (computers)	1	2	3	4
1	7	0	0	2
2	4	0	0	0
3	0	3	2	6
4	0	3	2	3

	Step 3. Select rows and columns and draw lines in such a way that all the zeros are covered and that the minimum number of lines has been drawn. j (plants)			
i (computers)	1	2	3	4
1	7	0	0	2
2	4	0	0	0
3	0	3	2	6
4	0	3	2	3

(continued)

Refer to the original cost matrix. Possible assignments, based on the bolded zeros, are:

1 → 2, 1 → 3; 2 → 2, **2 → 3,** 2 → 4; **3 → 1,** 3 → 3; **4 → 1,** 4 → 3.

Select 1 → 2: $c_{12} = 2$. Select 2 → 3: $c_{23} = 3$. Select 3 → 1: $c_{31} = 1$. Select 4 → 1: $c_{41} = 2$ $C_{ij} = 2 + 3 + 1 + 2 = 8$. **Interpretation:** Plant number 4 is not used due to its high cost.

Summary

You have learned that a system approach to analyzing resource assignment and allocation problems is important in order to develop appropriate models for rationally allocating resources. In general, the examples and problems that have been addressed are solved only by heuristic methods. Thus, you can never be sure that you have achieved the optimal solu-

TABLE 16.19 (continued)   Hungarian Method for Assigning Computers to Plants

Step 5. Find the smallest element that is not covered by any of the lines (bolded).

	j (plants)			
i (computers)	1	2	3	4
1	7	0	0	2
2	4	0	0	0
3	0	3	2	6
4	0	3	2	3

Continue Step 5. Subtract the smallest element from each entry that is *not* covered by the lines *and* add it to each entry that *is* covered by a vertical *and* a horizontal line (bolded). Go back to Step 3.

	j (plants)			
i (computers)	1	2	3	4
1	9	0	0	2
2	6	0	0	0
3	0	1	0	4
4	0	1	0	1

Step 3. Select rows and columns and draw lines in such a way that all the zeros are covered and that the minimum number of lines has been drawn.

	j (plants)			
i (computers)	1	2	3	4
1	9	0	0	2
2	6	0	0	0
3	0	1	0	4
4	0	1	0	1

tion, but you can be confident that your solution is close to the optimum. The problems that we have addressed involve connecting, assigning, locating, and routing computer-based facilities, such as computer networks. The tools that we have employed for solving these problems have a long history of application in the fields of systems engineering, industrial engineering, and operations research in manufacturing systems. These tools have been adapted to problems such as assigning clients to a Web server in computer networks. A number of tools have been illustrated because no one tool is best for solving all resource assignment problems. Rather, a tool should be selected that matches the problem's characteristics. Finally, an innovative approach was used to reduce computer system connectivity complexity by applying software complexity metrics.

References

[ASK93] Ronald G. Askin and Charles R. Standridge, *Modeling and Analysis of Manufacturing Systems.* John Wiley & Sons, 1993.

[BEN00] Saifallah Benjafaar, Sunderesh S. Heragu, and Shahrukh A. Irani, "Next Generation Factory Layouts: Research Challenges and Recent Progress." December, 2000, http://www.me.umn.edu/labs/ngfl/ngfl.pdf.

[BRO97] Richard Bronson and Govindasami Naadimuthu, *Operations Research,* second edition. McGraw-Hill, 1997.

[CHA] Christy Chatmon, Clement Allen, and Sara Stoecklin, "UML Based Design For An Intelligent Manufacturing Workcell Controller." Department of Computer Information Science, Florida Agricultural & Mechanical University, Tallahassee, Florida, www.cs.fsu.edu/~stoeckli/Publications Vitae/UMLWorkcellChristy.htm.

[CHA02] Ming Chang, K. Ohkura, K. Ueda, and M. Sugiyama, "A Symbiotic Evolutionary Algorithm for Dynamic Facility Layout Problem." *Evolutionary Computation,* 2002. CEC APOS; '02. Proceedings of the 2002 Congress, Volume 2, 2002, pp. 1745–1750.

[CHI02] Wen-Chyuan Chiang, Panagiotis Kouvelis, and Timothy L. Urban, "Incorporating Workflow Interference in Facility Layout Design: The Quartic Assignment Problem." *Management Science,* Vol. 48, No. 4 (Apr., 2002), pp. 584–590.

[DAS06] Anatoli I. Dashchenko, editor, *Reconfigurable Manufacturing Systems and Transformable Factories,* Springer, 2006.

[LEW80] W.P. Lewis and T. E. Block, "On the Application of Computer Aids to Plant Location." *International Journal of Production Research, 18* (1), 1980, pp. 11–20.

[LIU06] Xiaobing Liu and Xiufei Li, "An Improved Genetic Algorithms-based Approach on Supply Chain-oriented Facility Layout Scheduling System." Intelligent Control and Automation, 2006. WCICA 2006. The Sixth World Congress, Volume 1, 2006, pp. 3081–3084.

[MAH05] Maher Lahmar and Saif Benjaafar, "Design of Distributed Layouts." Institute of Industrial Engineers Transactions, April 1, 2005.

[MAT05] Andrea Matta (editor) and Quirico Semeraro (editor), *Design of Advanced Manufacturing Systems: Models for Capacity Planning in Advanced Manufacturing Systems.* Springer, 2005.

[MCC76] T. McCabe, "A Software Complexity Measure." *IEEE Transactions on Software Engineering,* SE-2(4), 1976, pp. 308–20.

[MCK06] Alan R. McKendall, Jr. and Jin Shang, "Hybrid Ant Systems for the Dynamic Facility Layout Problem." *Computers and Operations Research,* Volume 33, Issue 3, March 2006, pp. 790–803.

[MON96] Joseph G. Monks, *Operations Management,* second edition. McGraw-Hill, 1996.

[NEC07] NEC America, Inc., "The Always On Assembly Line—How Fault Tolerant Servers Boost Ouput and Reduce Costs for Manufacturing." Vendor white paper, November 2007, 9 pages.

[PRO97] J.M. Proth, "Petri Nets for Modeling and Evaluating Deterministic and Stochastic Manufacturing Systems." 6th International Workshop on Petri Nets and Performance Models (PNPM '97), 1997, p. 2.

[REN07] Ming Ren, Chao Yang, and Bo He, "An Integrated Model and Algorithm for Facility Location under Uncertainty." Third International Conference on Natural Computation (ICNC 2007), Vol I, 2007.

[RYC07] Nestor Rychtyckyj, "Intelligent Systems for Manufacturing at Ford Motor Company." *IEEE Intelligent Systems,* Vol. 22, No. 1, January/February, 2007, pp. 16–19.

[SAG00] Andrew P. Sage and James E. Armstrong, Jr., *Introduction to Systems Engineering.* John Wiley & Sons, 2000.

[TUR93] Wayne C. Turner, Joe H. Mize, and John W. Nazemetz, *Introduction to Industrial and Systems Engineering,* third edition. Prentice Hall, 1993.

Inventory Control

Objectives

Inventory control is a ubiquitous problem that challenges the engineer in a variety of systems. For example, in the manufacture of computer systems, various component parts must be available when needed to achieve smooth work flow. Controlling inventory is a challenge because unexpected demands for components, based on spurious demands by customers for finished products, can make complete control problematic. Some of the remedial measures are maintaining a safety stock below which inventory must not fall and using models to compute the quantity and time to produce or order to meet customer demand. The objectives are to show you how to evaluate inventory problems and to find solutions by modeling and controlling the demand and production factors that lead to inventory fluctuations.

What You Will Learn From This Chapter

You will learn how various inventory control models can be employed to meet the demands of customers in a timely manner and, at the same time, reduce the cost of holding inventory to meet customer demands.

Subjects

Basic Economic Order Quantity (EOQ) Model
Inventory with Demand and Production Runs But No Safety Stock (Case Study)
Inventory with Demand, Production Runs, and Safety Stock

Basic Economic Order Quantity (EOQ) Model

The basic model for portraying demand-production dynamics is the economic order quantity (EOQ) model. This model assumes a repetitive demand and replenishment cycle shown in Figure 17.1. As Figure 17.1 illustrates, there is no safety stock to protect against shortages, the assumption being that inventory will start to be replenished instantly as inventory is exhausted. Now, of course, this is an idealized view because inventory cannot be replenished instantaneously—there would be delays in restarting the process. However, the model is easy to visualize and implement. It should be used when approximate values are satisfactory and time is of the essence—for example, maintaining inventory in a computer store, where customer demand must be met quickly for a variety of components.

Definitions

t: time
a: demand rate = constant rate at which units are ordered or produced and withdrawn from inventory (units per time t):

FIGURE 17.1 EOQ Model

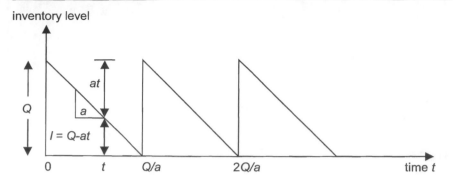

Q: order or production quantity (units)

a: demand: rate at which units are ordered or produced and withdrawn from inventory (units per time)

Q/a: cycle time = replenish time

Q - at: inventory level at time t

at: units withdrawn from inventory during time t

at: number of units withdrawn from inventory during time t

Q: [ordered or produced] (units)

$I = (Q - at)$: inventory level at time t (units)

Q^*: optimal value of Q (i.e., value of Q at which total inventory cost is minimized)

c: cost of purchasing or producing one unit (dollars per unit)

h: holding cost per unit per unit of time held in inventory (dollars per unit)

K: setup cost for ordering or producing one batch (dollars)

T: total inventory cost per cycle (dollars)

Assumption

No shortages can occur because when $I = 0$, a quantity Q is ordered or produced instantaneously.

Model

$$\text{Cycle time} = (\text{order or production quantity})/\text{demand rate} = Q/a \text{ (time)} \quad (17.1)$$

$$\text{Production or purchase cost} = (\text{unit cost for purchasing or producing one unit}) = c \times Q \text{ (dollars)} \quad (17.2)$$

$$\text{Average holding cost per unit time} = (hQ)/2 \text{ (dollars per time)} \quad (17.3)$$

From equations (17.1) and (17.3):

$$\text{Average holding cost per cycle} = (Q/a) * (hQ)/2 = (hQ^2)/2a \text{ (dollars)} \quad (17.4)$$

Note that the result in equation (17.4) is equal to $[h((Q^2)/2)a]$ = area of the triangle in Figure 17.1.

Adding the setup cost K, and using equations (17.2) and (17.4), the total cost per cycle is obtained in equation (17.5):

$$\text{Total inventory cost} = [K + cQ + (hQ^2)/2a] \text{ (dollars)} \tag{17.5}$$

From equations (17.1) and (17.5), compute total inventory cost per cycle:

$$T = [K + cQ + [(hQ^2)/2a]/(Q/a) = ((aK)/Q) + ac + ((hQ)/2) \text{ (dollars per time)} \tag{17.6}$$

To find the value of Q, Q^*, that minimizes equation (17.6), take the derivative of equation (17.6) with respect to Q and set it = 0 in equation (17.7).

$$\frac{dT}{dQ} = -\frac{aK}{Q^2} + \frac{h}{2} = 0 \tag{17.7}$$

$$\text{Thus, } Q^* = \sqrt{\frac{2aK}{h}} \tag{17.8}$$

Take the derivative of equation (17.7) to see whether it is positive:

$$\frac{d^2T}{dQ^2} = \frac{2aK}{Q^3} \rightarrow \text{positive} \rightarrow \text{minimum} \tag{17.9}$$

The quantity Q is ordered when the inventory level $I = Q - at = 0$; that is, at time:

$$t = Q/a, \text{ when } I = 0. \tag{17.10}$$

Problem 1

Table 17.1 on page 378 shows the data and the solution for T, the total inventory cost per cycle, using equation (17.6), and the solution for Q^*, the optimal order quantity, using equation (17.8). In addition, Figure 17.2 on page 379 shows T and Q^* in graphical form.

Inventory with Demand and Production Runs But No Safety Stock (Case Study)

Because a computer parts manufacturer BPC does not have the capability to produce computer parts in house, it must obtain them from the outside in order to meet customer demands. BPC must balance the cost of holding inventory—all of which may not be used—against the possibility of an insufficient inventory of computer parts and the consequence of losing customers. To do this tradeoff, BPC acquires the services of the Always Reliable (AR) consultant, to develop an inventory-control model to provide quantitative advice for its inventory-control problem. AR developed the following model, which allows the total cost of the inventory per time period F to be computed and *minimized*. Since AR wishes to provide BPC with an economical model because of its limited budget, AR does not provide a model with safety stock, which would add to the cost and complexity of the model.

Definitions

See Figure 17.3 on page 380 for elaboration of definitions.

- a: demand rate: computer parts needed by BPC per unit time (parts/day)
- k: production rate of supplier: computer parts per unit time (parts/day)
- h: holding cost per one computer part held in inventory by BPC per unit time (dollars per part per day)
- C: computer parts purchasing cost by BPC (dollars per part)
- TC: BPC total inventory cost (dollars)
- F: total cost of inventory *per inventory cycle* incurred by BPC (dollars per day)

TABLE 17.1   Economic Order Quantity Example

Q	T			
50	43000	**optimal order quantity**		
100	26500		*Q**	412 units per day
200	19000	**demand**		
300	17167		a	850 units per day
400	16750	**setup cost**		
412	**16746**		K	2000 dollars per batch
500	16900	**holding cost**		
600	17333		h	20 dollars per unit
700	17929	**purchasing cost**		
800	18625		c	10 dollars per unit
831	18856			
900	19389			
1000	20200			
1100	21045			
1200	21917			
1300	22808			
1400	23714			
1500	24633			
1600	25563			
1700	26500			
1800	27444			
1900	28395			
2000	29350			
units per day	dollars per day			

K: set-up cost: cost of setting up a production run of computer parts by supplier (dollars)

Q: number of computer parts produced per production run by supplier

t: cycle time = time interval between production runs by supplier (days)

t_1:   time during which inventory is both demanded by BPC and replenished by the supplier (days)

t_2:   time during which inventory is depleted by BPC (days)

t^*:   optimal inventory cycle time (days): time when F is a minimum

Assumptions

Production run sizes Q by the supplier are constant.

A new production run will be started whenever inventory at BPC reaches zero.

Inventory is replenished simultaneously as it is demanded (see Figure 17.3).

Model

Cycle time t = the sum of time during which inventory is demanded and replenished plus the time during which it is depleted, as in equation (17.11):

FIGURE 17.2   Total Cost of Inventory Cost per Cycle *T* vs. Order Quantity *Q*

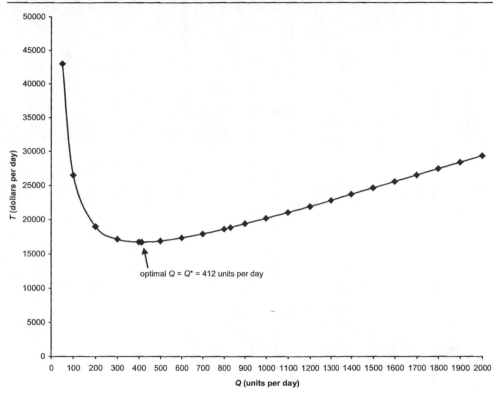

$$t = t_1 + t_2 \tag{17.11}$$

Level of inventory after a production run is completed $= Q - at_1$ (the height NC in Figure 17.3).

Notes: During time t_1, at_1 parts have been demanded (i.e., demand does not stop to wait for production to finish). This is why the slope of side ON in Figure 17.3 is $(k - a)$ instead of k.

Using Figure 17.3, the following relationships are obtained:

$$(\text{production rate} - \text{demand rate}) = (k - a)$$
$= (\text{net inventory level})/(\text{time during which inventory is demanded and replenished})$
$$= (Q - at_1)/t_1 \tag{17.12}$$

$$(\text{number of parts per production run})$$
$= (\text{production rate}) \times (\text{time during which inventory is demanded and replenished})$
$$= Q = kt_1 \tag{17.13}$$

Therefore, from equation (17.13) and Figure 17.3:

$$t_1 = Q/k \tag{17.14}$$

From Figure 17.3, the demand rate $a = NC/BC$, yielding equation (17.15):

$$\text{Demand rate}$$
$= (\text{net inventory level})/(\text{time during which inventory is depleted})$
$$= a = (Q - at_1)/t_2 \tag{17.15}$$

FIGURE 17.3   Inventory Model with Demand and Production Rates

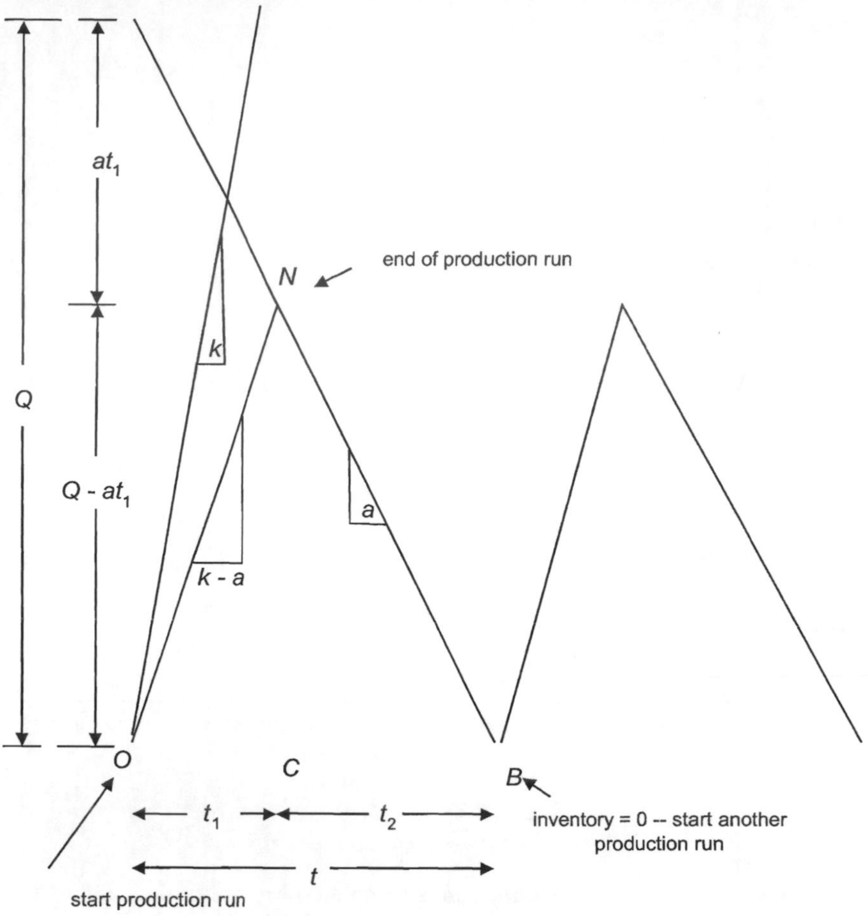

Q: number of computer parts produced per production run by supplier

a: demand rate: computer parts per unit time (parts/day)

t_1: time during which inventory is demanded and replenished (days)

t_2: time during which inventory is depleted (days)

t: cycle time = time interval between production runs (days)

k: production rate (parts per day)

$Q - at_1$ = net inventory level

Therefore, solving for t_2 in equation (17.15) and substituting for t_1 from equation (17.14) produces equation (17.16):

$$t_2 = (Q/a) - t_1 = (Q/a) - (Q/k) = Q/((1/a) - (1/k)) \qquad (17.16)$$

Then, using equation (17.14) again, combined with equation (17.16), arrive at equation (17.17) for the inventory cycle time in Figure 17.3:

$$t = t_1 + t_2 = (Q/k) + Q/((1/a) - (1/k)) = Q/a \qquad (17.17)$$

Now, compute the *total holding cost*:

The logic behind this computation is that: 1) the inventory is replenished and depleted, represented by the altitudes of the triangle *ONB* in Figure 17.3, and 2) the changes in inventory level occur during the cycle time *t* in Figure 17.3, represented by the base of triangle *ONB* = *OB*. Therefore, the area of *ONB* represents the quantity (parts * day) that is multiplied with *h* (dollars per part per day) to produce total holding cost (dollars).

Therefore, the area *A* of the triangle *ONB* = (1/2)(*CN*)(*OB*) in Figure 17.3, or:

$$A = (1/2)t(Q - at_1) \tag{17.18}$$

From equation (17.14), substituting $t_1 = Q/k$ in equation (17.18):

$$A = (1/2)t(Q(1 - a/k))(\text{days * computer parts per production run}) \tag{17.19}$$

$$\text{total holding cost} = (\text{holding cost})\ h[\text{dollars per part per day}]$$
$$\times A(\text{parts * day}) = (1/2h)t(Q(1 - a/k))\ [\text{dollars}] \tag{17.20}$$

Set-up cost = *K* = cost of setting up a production run (dollars)

Total purchase cost = (purchase cost) *C* [purchasing cost (dollars per part)] × *Q* (parts per production run) [dollars]

Total Cost *TC* in dollars = *set-up cost + total holding cost + total purchase cost* =

$$TC = K + (1/2h)t(Q(1 - a/k)) + CQ \tag{17.21}$$

Now, compute *F*, the total cost *per inventory cycle t*. Obtain this quantity in equation (17.22) by dividing equation (17.21) by the cycle time *t*.

$$F = TC/t = (K/t) + (h/2)(Q(1 - a/k)) + (CQ)/t \tag{17.22}$$

In order to put *F* in terms of *Q* and *a* by eliminating *t*, substitute equation (17.17) in equation (17.22) to arrive at:

$$F = ((Ka)/Q) + (h/2)(Q(1 - a/k)) + Ca \tag{17.23}$$

To find the optimal value of *Q*, *Q**, differentiate equation (17.23) with respect to *Q* and set it = 0:

$$\frac{dF}{dQ} = -\frac{Ka}{Q^2} + (h/2)\left(1 - \frac{a}{k}\right) = 0 \tag{17.24}$$

Using equation (17.24), compute equation (17.25):

$$Q^* = \sqrt{\frac{2Ka}{h\left(1 - \dfrac{a}{k}\right)}} \tag{17.25}$$

Using equation (17.17), the optimal cycle time is:

$$t^* = Q^*/a = \sqrt{\frac{2K}{ha\left(1 - \dfrac{a}{k}\right)}} \tag{17.26}$$

Problem 2

Specifications

Demand *a* = 6,000 computer parts per day

Set-up cost $K = 312,000$ dollars
Number of computer parts per production run by supplier $Q = 10,000$
Holding cost $h = 8$ dollars per day per part
Production rate $k = 10,000$ computer parts per day
Purchase cost $C = 100$ dollars per part

Solve

Total cost F per inventory cycle.

Solution

Using equation (17.23):

F = total cost per inventory cycle = set-up cost + holding cost per cycle + purchase cost per cycle:

$F = ((Ka)/Q) + (1/2h)(Q(1 - a/k)) + Ca = ((312,000 \times 6,000)/10,000) +$
$(4)(10,000 \times (1 - 6,000/10,000)) + 100(6,000) =$

Set-up cost $= ((312,000 \times 6,000)/10,000) = \textbf{187.2K}$
Holding cost $= (4) \times (10,000 \times (1 - 6,000/10,000)) = \textbf{16K}$
Purchase cost $= 100 \times 6,000 = \textbf{600K}$
Total cost $= \textbf{803.2K}$

Problem 3

Determine the optimal order quantity Q^* and optimal cycle time t^* for Problem 2.

Solution

Using equation (17.25), Q^* is computed as follows:

$$Q^* = \sqrt{\frac{2Ka}{h\left(1-\frac{a}{k}\right)}} = \sqrt{\frac{2*310,000*6,000}{8\left(1-\frac{6,000}{10,000}\right)}} = 34,096 \text{ computer parts}$$

Since only 10,000 computer parts were ordered and the optimal quantity is 34,096, there was a gross error in the ordering decision.

Using equation (17.26), optimal cycle time t^* is computed as follows:

$$t^* = \sqrt{\frac{2K}{ah\left(1-\frac{a}{k}\right)}} = \sqrt{\frac{2\times312,000}{6,000\times8\times\left(1-\frac{6,000}{10,000}\right)}} = 5.701 \text{ days}$$

Inventory with Demand, Production Runs, and Safety Stock

Some inventory situations involve the use of safety stock as a protection against running out of inventory. This model accounts for safety stock as a buffer to prevent the inventory level from dropping below the buffer size. In addition, the model discounts future costs by the rate of interest in order to make all costs equivalent, independent of when they occur. Refer to Chapter 20 to see the present value method of evaluating economic alternatives.

Definitions

Q:	order quantity [computer parts per order]
P:	production rate [computer parts per year]
D:	demand rate [computer parts per year]
S:	safety stock [computer parts]
$Q - S$:	inventory requirement [computer parts]
t_1:	time during which inventory is demanded and replenished [years]
t_2:	time during which inventory is depleted [years]
t:	cycle time = time interval between production runs [years]
n:	number of production runs
i :	annual rate of interest
C_p:	set-up cost per production run [dollars per production run]
C:	annual unit production cost [dollars per computer part per year]
$h =$	unit holding cost [dollars per computer part per year]
C_T:	annual total cost of inventory [dollars]
F:	annual total cost of inventory per inventory cycle [dollars per year]

Model

The area of the triangle ABC in Figure 17.4 = (production run size × cycle time) = (1/2) $[((Q - S) - Dt_1)]t$ (computer parts – years)

$$\text{Production rate } P = ((\text{inventory requirement})/t_1)$$
$$= (Q - S)/t_1 \text{ (computer parts per year)} \qquad (17.27)$$

Using triangle AEF in Figure 17.4 and equation (17.27), compute time of inventory demand and replenishment, in equation (17.28):

$$t_1 = (Q - S)/P \text{ (years)} \qquad (17.28)$$

Using triangle FBC in Figure 17.4, compute the demand rate:

$$\text{Demand rate } D = ((\text{production run size})/t_2) = [(Q - S) - Dt_1]/t_2$$
$$\text{(computer parts per year)} \qquad (17.29)$$

Using equation (17.29), compute the time during which inventory is depleted:

$$t_2 = [(Q - S) - Dt_1]/D \text{ (years)} \qquad (17.30)$$

Substituting t_1 from equation (17.28) in equation (17.30), produce equation (17.31):

$$t_2 = (Q - S)(1/D - 1/P) \qquad (17.31)$$

Then, using triangle ABC in Figure 17.4 and adding equations (17.28) and (17.31), generate equation (17.32), inventory cycle time:

$$t = t_1 + t_2 = (Q - S)/D \text{ (years)} \qquad (17.32)$$

Using equations (17.28) and (17.32) and the area of triangle ABC in Figure 17.4, recompute (production run size × cycle time) to produce equation (17.33).

$$(1/2) * t * ((Q - S) - Dt_1) =$$

$$= (1/2)((Q - S)/D) * ((Q - S) - Dt_1) = (1/2)((Q - S)/D)\left[(Q - S)\left(1 - \frac{D}{P}\right)\right] \qquad (17.33)$$

To compute the holding cost, first find the area of triangle ABC + area of rectangle $ACGH$ in Figure 17.4, using equations (17.32) and (17.33).

$$\frac{\left[(Q-S)\left(1-\frac{D}{P}\right)\right]\left(\frac{(Q-S)}{D}\right)}{2} + St$$

$$= \frac{\left[(Q-S)\left(1-\frac{D}{P}\right)\right]\left(\frac{(Q-S)}{D}\right)}{2} + S\left(\frac{(Q-S)}{D}\right)$$

$$= \frac{\left[(Q-S)^2\left(1-\frac{D}{P}\right)\right]}{2D} + S\left(\frac{(Q-S)}{D}\right) \qquad (17.34)$$

FIGURE 17.4 Inventory Model with Safety Stock

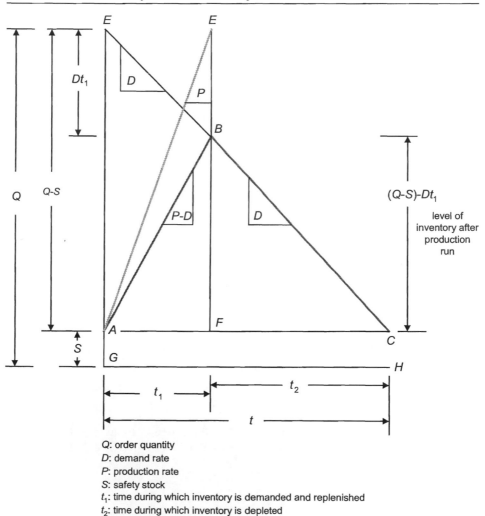

Q: order quantity
D: demand rate
P: production rate
S: safety stock
t_1: time during which inventory is demanded and replenished
t_2: time during which inventory is depleted
t: cycle time = time interval between production runs
Point A: start production run at rate P
Point C: start another production run when inventory = S
Inventory Requirement = Q - S

Using equation (17.34), and including the rate of interest i, compute the present value of the holding cost in equation (17.35).

$$\text{Total holding cost} = h \left[\frac{[(Q-S)^2 \left(1-\frac{D}{P}\right)]}{2D(1+i)} + S\left(\frac{(Q-S)}{D(1+i)}\right) \right] \text{ dollars} \qquad (17.35)$$

The present value of *annual production cost* = [unit annual production cost, C (dollars per computer part)] * [(production rate, P, – demand rate, D) = net production rate (computer parts per year)] is computed in equation (17.36).

$$\frac{C(P-D)}{(1+i)} \text{ dollars} \qquad (17.36)$$

Number of production runs = n = (inventory requirement/production run size)

$$n = (Q-S)/((Q-S) - Dt_1)$$

Substituting equation (17.28) for t_1, equation (17.37) is computed for n.

$$n = (Q-S)/[(Q-S) - D(Q-S)/P] = P/(P-D) \qquad (17.37)$$

Using equation (17.37), and realizing that there will be a set up cost per production run, C_p, each time a production run is made, the set-up cost is formulated in equation (17.38):

$$\text{Set-up cost} = \frac{C_p P}{(P-D)} \qquad (17.38)$$

The total cost of inventory (present value) = total holding cost (equation (17.35)) + annual production cost (equation (17.36)) + setup cost (equation (17.38)):

$$\text{Total cost of inventory} =$$

$$C_T = \frac{h(Q-S)^2 \left(1-\frac{D}{P}\right)}{2D(1+i)} + hS\left(\frac{(Q-S)}{D(1+i)}\right) + \frac{C(P-D)}{(1+i)} + \frac{C_p P}{(P-D)} \qquad (17.39)$$

Now use equation (17.32): $t = ((Q-S)/D)$ to compute F, total cost inventory per inventory cycle in equation (17.40).

$$F = C_T/t = \frac{h(Q-S)(1-\frac{D}{P})}{2(1+i)} + \left(\frac{hS}{(1+i)}\right) + \frac{CD(P-D)}{(Q-S)(1+i)} + \frac{C_p DP}{(Q-S)(P-D)} \qquad (17.40)$$

In order to compute the optimal order quantity Q^* that will minimize C_T, obtain the derivative of equation (17.40), with respect to $(Q - S)$ and set it equal to 0, in equation (17.41):

$$\frac{dC_T}{d(Q-S)} = \frac{h\left(1-\frac{D}{P}\right)}{2(1+i)} - \frac{CD(P-D)}{(Q-S)^2(1+i)} - \frac{C_p DP}{(Q-S)^2} = 0 \qquad (17.41)$$

Once equation (17.41) is obtained, Q^* can be obtained in equation (17.42) by solving equation (17.41) for Q.

$$Q^* = \sqrt{\frac{2[CD(P-D)+(1+i)C_p DP]}{h\left(1-\dfrac{D}{P}\right)}} + S \qquad (17.42)$$

Problem 4

Given the computer parts production data that follow, 1) compute and plot the total inventory cost per inventory cycle, F, as a function of order quantity, Q, and determine 2) the optimal reorder quantity Q^*, 3) number of production runs n, and 4) minimum inventory cost.

$P =$ production rate of 2400 computer parts per year
$C_p =$ set-up cost per production run of \$8,000
$C =$ annual production cost [dollars per computer part per year] = \$1200
$D =$ demand rate for computers parts per year = 400
$i =$ annual rate of interest of 15%
$h =$ holding cost = \$66.60 per computer part per year
$Q =$ order quantity in computer parts per production run
$S =$ safety stock = 12 computer parts

1. Applying equation (17.40), the total inventory cost per inventory cycle, F, is plotted in Figure 17.5.
2. Applying equation (17.42), the optimal reorder quantity $Q^* = 5897$ in Figure 17.5.
3. Applying equation (17.37), the number of production runs $n = P/(P-D) = 2400/(2400-400) = 1.2$.
4. The minimum value of F, corresponding to $Q^* = 5897$, is shown on Figure 17.5 and equals 285204.

FIGURE 17.5   Total Inventory Cost Per Cycle F vs. Order Quantity Q

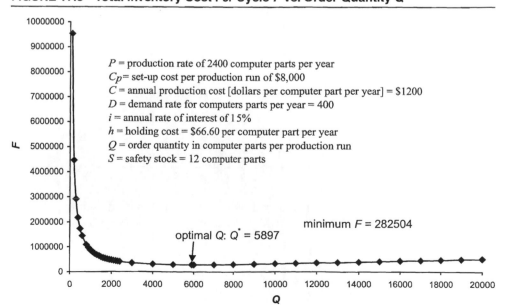

Summary

Three inventory-control models were presented:

- Basic economic order quantity (EOQ) model
- Inventory with demand and production runs but no safety stock (case study)
- Inventory with demand, production runs, and safety stock

The EOQ model is applicable when a low-cost and timely answer to the question of how much and when to order is required. This model does not explicitly account for the interdependency of demand and production runs. Therefore, it has minimal accuracy but is appropriate when approximate solutions are acceptable, such as maintaining inventory in a computer store.

The second model includes the interdependency of demand and production runs but excludes consideration of safety stock. Thus in using this model, it is possible to experience stock outs (i.e., zero inventory). This model is used in applications where stock outs are not a major problem, such as an automobile dealer being out of stock on an automobile that is no longer manufactured. Since the dealer cannot obtain the automobile from the manufacturer, the dealer persuades the customer to purchase the new model!

The third model is the most expensive and time-consuming to implement but provides protection against stock outs. For example, it would be unacceptable to run out of a vital rocket engine part for the space Shuttle, prior to launch, when the safety of the crew and the prestige of the nation are on the line.

18

Scheduling

Objectives

This chapter deals with some of the models that can be used to sensibly assign and schedule resources so that bottlenecks and idle time are minimized. Examples are drawn from the fields of software production and testing. This chapter covers cost of testing in the context of cost of scheduling test facilities. For readers interested in models for estimating the cost of testing as a function of many variables, see *Software Cost Estimation with Cocomo II,* by Barry W. Boehm, et al. (Prentice Hall, Upper Saddle River, New Jersey).

What You Will Learn From This Chapter

You will learn that bottlenecks in the flow of materials to produce products can be alleviated by applying models that can predict how long, and at what cost, it takes for materials to traverse alternate paths from station to station. Then the models identify the minimal time or cost path.

Subjects

Job Scheduling Model
Workflow Model
Critical-Path Method (CPM) of Scheduling
Program Evaluation and Review Technique (PERT)

Job Scheduling Model

Job scheduling models are used to determine the sequence of job processing that would achieve the job schedule (i.e., the last job completes at or before the scheduled time). For example, we could be interested in assigning software modules that have been designed and coded to computers for testing such that test time is minimized, assuming that test times are sufficient for achieving quality objectives.

Definitions

i: software module
j: computer
M_i: software module i
C_j: computer j
T_{ij}: time of software module M_i on computer C_j

Model

software module job sequence $\sum_{ij} T_{ij} \ (M_i \to C_j)$

makespan: minimize $\sum_{ij} T_{ij} \ (M_i \to C_j)$

Problem 1

A software module scheduling operation is shown in Figure 18.1. What software module job sequence should be used to minimize the makespan? (The makespan of a schedule is the latest software module finishing time.)

Find the software module job sequence such that $\sum_{ij} T_{ij} \ (M_i \to C_j)$ is minimized:

Solution

Step 0: Initial $i \to j$ matrix

FIGURE 18.1　Software Module Test Scheduling

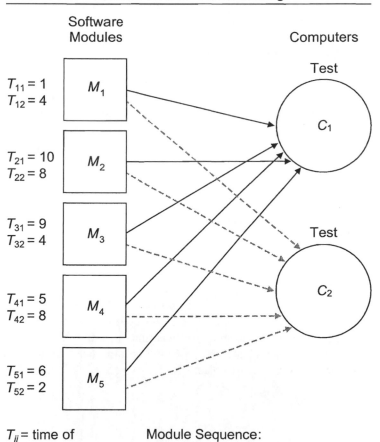

$T_{11} = 1$
$T_{12} = 4$

$T_{21} = 10$
$T_{22} = 8$

$T_{31} = 9$
$T_{32} = 4$

$T_{41} = 5$
$T_{42} = 8$

$T_{51} = 6$
$T_{52} = 2$

T_{ij} = time of
Module M_i on
Computer C_j

Module Sequence:
$M_i \to C_1, M_i \to C_2$

	To j	
From i	C_1	C_2
Software Module M_1	1	4
Software Module M_2	10	8
Software Module M_3	9	4
Software Module M_4	5	8
Software Module M_5	6	2

Step 1: Subtract minimum value from each row in matrix $i \rightarrow j$, and mark rows and columns that have zero values.

	To j	
From i	C_1	C_2
Software Module M_1	0	3
Software Module M_2	2	0
Software Module M_3	5	0
Software Module M_4	0	3
Software Module M_5	4	0

Solution: $M_1 \rightarrow C_1, M_2 \rightarrow C_2, M_3 \rightarrow C_2, M_4 \rightarrow C_1, M_5 \rightarrow C_2$

This is where horizontal and vertical lines intersect.

$$\sum_{ij} T_{ij}\ (M_i \rightarrow C_j) = T_{11} + T_{22} + T_{32} + T_{41} + T_{52} = 1 + 8 + 4 + 5 = 2 = \mathbf{20}$$

Problem 2

A software module scheduling operation is shown Figure 18.2 on page 392. What is the makespan for the software module sequence $M_1 \rightarrow M_2 \rightarrow M_3 \rightarrow M_4$?

Solution

Find the job sequence such that $\sum_{ij} T_{ij}\ (M_i \rightarrow C_j)$ is minimized:

Minimize makespan (i.e., minimize $\sum_{ij} T_{ij}\ (M_i \rightarrow C_j)$

Step 0: Initial $i \rightarrow j$ matrix

FIGURE 18.2   Module Scheduling on Computers

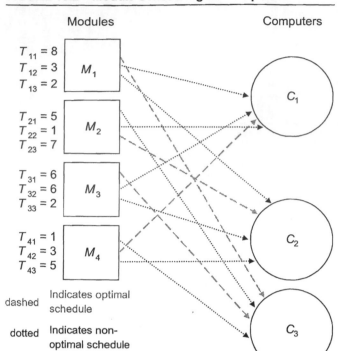

Modules   Computers

$T_{11} = 8$
$T_{12} = 3$ M_1
$T_{13} = 2$

$T_{21} = 5$
$T_{22} = 1$ M_2
$T_{23} = 7$

$T_{31} = 6$
$T_{32} = 6$ M_3
$T_{33} = 2$

$T_{41} = 1$
$T_{42} = 3$ M_4
$T_{43} = 5$

C_1

C_2

C_3

dashed   Indicates optimal schedule

dotted   Indicates non-optimal schedule

T_{ij} = Time of Module M_i on Computer C_j

Module Sequence: $M_i \rightarrow C_j$

		to j	
From i	C_1	C_2	C_3
M_1	8	3	2
M_2	5	1	7
M_3	6	6	2
M_4	1	3	5

Grayscale values turn out to be minimum costs in optimal solution.

Step 1: Subtract minimum value from each row in matrix $i \rightarrow j$, and mark rows and columns that have zero values.

		To j	
From i	C_1	C_2	C_3
M_1	6	1	0
M_2	4	0	6
M_3	4	4	0
M_4	0	2	4

Solution: $M_1 \rightarrow C_3$, $M_2 \rightarrow C_2$, $M_3 \rightarrow C_4$, $M_4 \rightarrow C_1$

This is where horizontal and vertical lines intersect.

Grayscale values turn out to be minimum costs in optimal solution.

Compute T_{ij} from the original matrix.

$$\sum_{ij} T_{ij} \; (M_i \rightarrow C_j) = T_{13} + T_{22} + T_{33} + T_{41} = 2 + 1 + 2 + 1 = \mathbf{6}$$

Workflow Model

The purpose of work flow models is to achieve minimum cost of transporting material (e.g., software modules) from origins (e.g., software development facilities) to destinations (e.g., software test facilities). In order to apply the model, capacities at origins and destinations, and material flow rates from origins to destinations, must be specified.

Problem 3

Software modules are received from a vendor at the development facilities, inspected, and routed via conveyors to test facilities, where they are tested, according to the flow diagram in Figure 18.3. Assume the conveyor travel distances are equal.

Definitions

> mph: modules per hour
> T_{ij}: cost of testing module i at test facility j
> C_i: capacity at origin i
> C_j: capacity at destination j

FIGURE 18.3   Software Module Flow Diagram

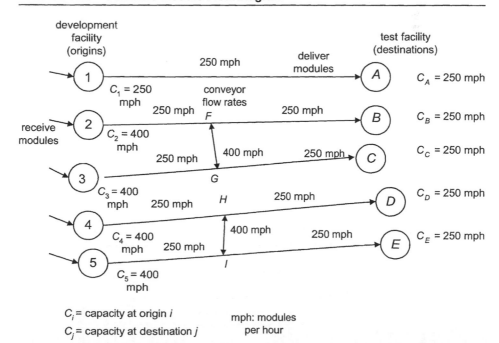

C_i = capacity at origin i

C_j = capacity at destination j

mph: modules per hour

Based on the assumption of equal conveyor link distances, the following are the average flow rates:

Average Flow Rates		
From i	**To j**	**Average Rate**
1	A	250
2	B	250
2, F, G	C	300
3, G, F	B	300
3	C	250
4	D	250
4, H, I	E	300
5	E	250

Capacities

Total capacity of development facilities at origins =

$$\sum_{i=1}^{5} C_i = (C_1 + C_2 + C_3 + C_4 + C_5) = 250 + 400 + 400 + 400 + 400 = 1850 \text{ mph}$$

Total capacity of test facilities at destinations =

$$\sum_{j=1}^{5} C_j = (C_A + C_B + C_C + C_D + C_E) = 250 + 250 + 250 + 250 + 250 = 1250 \text{ mph}$$

Solve

1. How many origins are necessary to fill destination A as fast as possible with modules?

   One at origin 1. $1 \rightarrow A$ is the only connection to A.

2. What is the *fastest routing* possible, individually to destinations, and in total?

   $(1 \rightarrow A = \mathbf{250}$ mph$) + (3 \rightarrow G \rightarrow F \rightarrow B = \mathbf{250}$ mph$) + (2 \rightarrow F \rightarrow G \rightarrow C = \mathbf{250}$ mph$)$
   $+ (5 \rightarrow I \rightarrow H \rightarrow D = \mathbf{250}$ mph$) + (4 \rightarrow H \rightarrow I \rightarrow E = \mathbf{250}) = \mathbf{1250}$ *mph.*

3. What is the lowest cost distribution, given the costs T_{ij} in the matrix that follows, when all test facilities must be served and all conveyors must be used?

Original Cost Matrix. Step 0: Initialize i, j matrix, where ∞ signifies that there is no connection between i and j.

Costs T_{ij}					
Test Facility j					
Development Facility i	A	B	C	D	E
1	9	∞	∞	∞	∞
2	∞	1	3	∞	∞
3	∞	6	7	∞	∞
4	∞	∞	∞	6	8
5	∞	∞	∞	4	9

Step 1: Subtract minimum value from each row in matrix $i \rightarrow j$, ignoring cells that have ∞.

Costs T_{ij}					
Test Facility j					
Development Facility i	A	B	C	D	E
1	7	∞	∞	∞	∞
2	∞	0	2	∞	∞
3	∞	0	1	∞	∞
4	∞	∞	∞	0	2
5	∞	∞	∞	0	5

Step 2: Subtract minimum value from each column, excluding columns that already have zeros, in matrix $i \rightarrow j$, ignoring cells that have ∞.

Costs T_{ij}					
Test Facility j					
Development Facility i	A	B	C	D	E
1	0	∞	∞	∞	∞
2	∞	0	1	∞	∞
3	∞	0	0	∞	∞
4	∞	∞	∞	0	0
5	∞	∞	∞	0	3

Step 3: Mark rows and columns that have zeros, in matrix $i \rightarrow j$. Draw the minimum number of lines that cover the zeros.

	Costs T_{ij}				
	Test Facility j				
Development Facility i	A	B	C	D	E
1	0	∞	∞	∞	∞
2	∞	0	1	∞	∞
3	∞	0	0	∞	∞
4	∞	∞	∞	0	0
5	∞	∞	∞	0	3

Step 4: The optimal solution is when there are no cells uncovered and there is a zero in a cell j for a given cell i.

Solution:

	Cost
$1 \rightarrow A$	9
$2 \rightarrow B$	1
$3 \rightarrow C$	7
$4 \rightarrow E$	8
$5 \rightarrow D$	4
Total	**29**

Note that there is a choice of test facility D or E for development facility 4. The lower cost alternative E is chosen.

4. What is the lowest cost distribution, given the costs in the matrix below, when all test facilities must be served and all conveyors must be used, and C_6 has been added, as shown in Figure 18.4?

FIGURE 18.4   Software Module Flow Diagram, with C_6 added

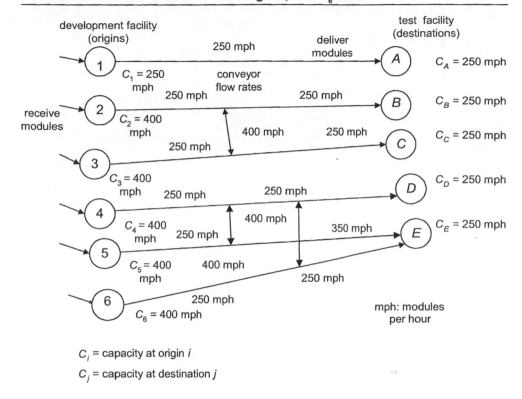

C$_i$ = capacity at origin *i*

C$_j$ = capacity at destination *j*

Original Cost Matrix.   Step 0: Initialize *i, j* matrix, where ∞ signifies that there is no connection between *i* and *j*.

Costs T_{ij}					
Test Facility *j*					
Development Facility *i*	A	B	C	D	E
1	9	∞	∞	∞	∞
2	∞	1	3	∞	∞
3	∞	6	7	∞	∞
4	∞	∞	∞	6	8
5	∞	∞	∞	4	9
6	∞	∞	∞	4	9

Step 1: Subtract minimum value from each row in matrix $i \rightarrow j$, ignoring cells that have ∞.

Costs T_{ij}					
Test Facility j					
Development Facility i	A	B	C	D	E
1	0	∞	∞	∞	∞
2	∞	0	2	∞	∞
3	∞	0	1	∞	∞
4	∞	∞	∞	0	2
5	∞	∞	∞	0	5
6	∞	∞	∞	0	5

Step 2: Subtract minimum value from each column, excluding columns that already have zeros, in matrix $i \rightarrow j$, ignoring cells that have ∞.

Costs T_{ij}					
Test Facility j					
Development Facility i	A	B	C	D	E
1	0	∞	∞	∞	∞
2	∞	0	1	∞	∞
3	∞	0	0	∞	∞
4	∞	∞	∞	0	0
5	∞	∞	∞	0	3
6	∞	∞	∞	0	3

Step 3: Mark rows and columns that have zeros in gray, in matrix $i \rightarrow j$, ignoring cells that have ∞. Draw the minimum number of lines that cover the zeros.

Costs T_{ij}					
Test Facility j					
Development Facility i	A	B	C	D	E
1	0	∞	∞	∞	∞
2	∞	0	1	∞	∞
3	∞	0	0	∞	∞
4	∞	∞	∞	0	0
5	∞	∞	∞	0	3
6	∞	∞	∞	0	3

Step 4: The optimal solution is when there are no cells uncovered and there is a zero in a cell j for a given cell i.

Solution:

	Cost
$1 \rightarrow A$	9
$2 \rightarrow B$	1
$3 \rightarrow C$	7
$4 \rightarrow E$	8
$5 \rightarrow D$	4
Total	**29**

Note: No assignment is made using C_6 because the other origins have sufficient capacity to supply all the destination demands. In other words, adding C_6 has no effect on total cost.

Critical-Path Method (CPM) of Scheduling

The CPM model's objective is to produce a schedule that will achieve the requirements of the project activities. For example, the software engineer may have to develop a schedule for predicting the reliability of Modules A and B, where A is predicted using A's failure data and B is predicted by using A's predictions and B's failure data on a computer that has multiple processes and processors that can run in parallel. Even for a small problem, it is not clear how to develop the schedule without using a structured approach, as provided by the CPM model. The reason is the presence of dependencies among activities.

Problem 4

In the **CPM diagram**—Figure 18.5—find the critical path for software development.

Definitions

Number of software development activities: N
Activity $i \rightarrow j$ with duration d_{ij}

Software Development Events

1. Early event time for event i, for **non-critical** events = TEN_i = **earliest time event i can start** (see Figure 18.5 and Table 18.1). This is computed by using the **minimum** sum of the task durations d_{ij} in the **forward** path that **precede** the given event (e.g., event **2**: $(1 \rightarrow 2) = 3$).
2. Early event time for event i, for **critical** events = TEC_i = **earliest time event i can start** (see Figure 18.5 and Table 18.1). This is computed by using the sum of the task durations d_{ij} in the **forward critical** path that **precede** the given event (e.g., event **4**: $6 \ (1 \rightarrow 5) + 2 \ (5 \rightarrow 4) = 8$).
3. Late event time for event i, for **non-critical** events = TLN_i = **latest time event i can start** (see Figure 18.5 and Table 18.1). This is computed by using the **minimum** quantity obtained by subtracting the sum of task durations d_{ij} in the **backward** path that **follow** the given event, from the allowable completion time for all activities = t_a (e.g., event **2**: $17 - 5 \ (6 \rightarrow 4) - 1 \ (4 \rightarrow 2) = 11$).
4. Late event time for event i, for **critical** events = TLC_i = **latest time event i can start** (see Figure 18.5 and Table 18.1). This is computed by using the quantity obtained by subtracting the sum of task durations d_{ij} in the **backward critical** path, that **follow**

FIGURE 18.5   Critical-Path Method (CPM) for Scheduling Software Development

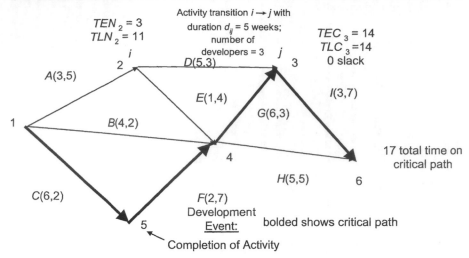

Non-critical Development Events	Examples:
TEN_i : earliest time Development Event i can start	$TEC_3 = 6 + 2 + 6 = 14$ (forward path)
TLN_i : latest time Development Event i can start	$TLC_3 = 17 - 3 = 14$ (backward path)
Critical Development Events	$TEN_2 = 3$ (forward path)
TEC_i : earliest time Development Event i can start	$TLN_2 = 17 - 5 - 1 = 11$
TLC_i : latest time Development Event i can start	$t_s = TLN_2 - TEN_2 = 11 - 3 = 8$
Slack	
$t_s = TLN_i - TEN_i$	

the given event, from the allowable completion time for all activities $= t_a$ (e.g., event 4: $17 - 3 (6 \rightarrow 3) - 6 (3 \rightarrow 4) = 8$).

Note that for critical events, $t_{ej} = t_i$ (i.e., 0 slack).

5. Slack $= t_s = TLN_i - TEN_i =$ Latest Time Non-Critical Event can Start – Earliest Time Non-Critical Event can Start on a non-critical path

6. Critical event: zero slack: $t_s = 0$

7. Non-critical event: slack $t_s \neq 0$

8. Critical path: path with slack $t_s = 0$ for all N events (i.e., have to start all activities at early event time to make schedule)

9. Forward path: trace through Figure 18.5 from left to right: determines early event times t_{ej}

10. Backward path: trace through Figure 18.5 from right to left: determines late event times t_{lj}

Note: Referring to Figure 18.5, the completion of a software development activity, such as A, is associated with the terminal point of the activity (i.e., Event 2).

Solution

Allowable completion time for all software development activities $= t_a = \sum_{ii}^{N} d_{ij}$ on **critical path** $= 1 \rightarrow 5, 5 \rightarrow 4, 4 \rightarrow 3, 3 \rightarrow 6 = 6 + 2 + 6 + 5 = \mathbf{19}$

Critical events ($t_s = 0$): **1, 5, 4, 3, 6**

Non-critical events: Event 2: slack time = $t_s = t_{lj} - t_{ej} = 11 - 3 = 8$

Result

In Table 18.1, the **bolded** software development events and activities are on the critical path (i.e., 0 slack). The table shows both an event orientation and an activity orientation.

Problem 5

If software development activity A in Figure 18.5 is delayed 3 weeks, what is the earliest time that the project can be completed?

TABLE 18.1   Software Development CPM Schedule

Event	Early Event Time	Path	Late Event Time	Slack Time = t_s
1	$TEC_i = 0$		$TLC_i = 17 - (3 + 6 + 2 + 6)$ $= 0$	$TLC_i - TEC_i = 0$
2	$TEN_i = 3$	$1 \to 2$	$TLN_i = 17 - (5 + 1) = 11$	$TLN_i - TEN_i = 8$
3	$TEC_i = 6 + 2 + 6$ $= 14$	$1 \to 5, 5 \to 4,$ $4 \to 3$	$TLC_i = 17 - 3 = 14$	$TLC_i - TEC_i = 0$
4	$TEC_i = 6 + 2 = 8$	$1 \to 5, 5 \to 4$	$TLC_i = 17 - (3 + 6) = 8$	$TLC_i - TEC_i = 0$
5	$TEC_i = 6$	$1 \to 5$	$TLC_i = 17 - (3 + 6 + 2) = 6$	$TLC_i - TEC_i = 0$
6	$TEC_i = 6 + 2 +$ $6 + 3 = 17$	$1 \to 5, 5 \to 4,$ $4 \to 3, 3 \to 6$	$TLC_i = 17 - 0 = 17$	$TLC_i - TEC_i = 0$
Activity	**Corresponding Events**	**Early Event Times for Activity**	**Late Event Times for Activity**	**Slack Time = t_s**
A	1,2	$TEN_i = 3$	$TLN_i = 17 - (5 + 1) = 11$	$TLN_i - TEN_i = 8$
B	1,4	$TEN_i = 4, 3 + 1 = 4$	$TLN_i = 17 - 5 = 12$	$TLN_i - TEN_i = 8$
C	1,5	$TEC_i = 6$	$TLC_i = 17 - (3 + 6 + 2) = 6$	$TLC_i - TEC_i = 0$
C	1,5	$TEC_i = 6$	$TLC_i = 17 - (3 + 6 + 2) = 6$	$TLC_i - TEC_i = 0$
D	2,3	$TEN_i = 3 + 5 = 8$	$TLN_i = 17 - 3 = 14$	$TLN_i - TEN_i = 6$
E	2,4	$TEN_i = 4, 3 + 1 = 4$	$TLN_i = 17 - 5 = 12$	$TLN_i - TEN_i = 8$
F	5,4	$TEC_i = 6 + 2 = 8$	$TLC_i = 17 - (3 + 6) = 8$	$TLC_i - TEC_i = 0$
G	4,3	$TEC_i = 6 + 2 + 6$ $= 14$	$TLC_i = 17 - 3 = 14$	$TLC_i - TEC_i = 0$
H	4,6	$TEN_i = 4 + 5,$ $3 + 1 + 5$ $= 9$	$TLN_i = 17 - 0 = 17$	$TLN_i - TEN_i = 8$
I	3,6	$TEC_i = 6 + 2 +$ $6 + 3$ $= 17$	$TLC_i = 17 - 0 = 17$	$TLC_i - TEC_i = 0$

Note: Referring to Figure 18.5, the completion of a software development activity, such as A, is associated with the terminal point of the activity (i.e., Event 2).

Solution

From Table 18.1 and Figure 18.5, it is seen that the earliest start time t_{ej} for software development activity A is 3 weeks. Thus, no time is lost from the project if Activity A is delayed 3 weeks. Also, it is important to note that Activity A is not on the critical path. Thus, the delay is irrelevant to meeting the project schedule. It can still be completed in 17 weeks.

Program Evaluation and Review Technique (PERT)

PERT is also a model that is used to schedule software reliability engineering activities. How does PERT differ from CPM? Whereas CPM requires only a single estimate of activity duration, PERT requires three (see the following discussion). CPM is used on projects where there is a lot of experience (e.g., software testing); PERT is used on projects where there is a lot of uncertainty (e.g., software development).

Definitions

d_{ij}: activity duration from $i \rightarrow j$
a: minimum estimated activity duration d_{ij} (e.g., .01 probability of $a < d_{ij}$)
b: maximum estimated activity duration d_{ij} (e.g., .99 probability of $b > d_{ij}$)
m: modal (most likely) activity duration d_{ij}
μ: mean of activity duration d_{ij}
σ^2: variance of activity duration d_{ij}

Model

Mean activity duration $d_{ij} = \mu = (a + 4m + b)/6$
Variance of activity duration $d_{ij} = \sigma^2 = (b - a)^2/36$

FIGURE 18.6 Computer Process PERT Chart

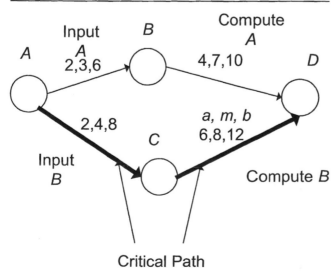

Critical Path

Problem 6

The PERT Chart in Figure 18.6 shows a computer processing schedule for process A and process B along with a, m, and b for each activity duration d_{ij}, and the critical path. Path $A \rightarrow C \rightarrow D$ is critical because it has the larger activity durations d_{ij}.
   Using Figure 18.6 and Table 18.2:

1. Provide sample calculations for activity **AB (Input A in Figure 18.6):**

   Compute mean activity duration $d_{ij} = \mu = (a + 4m + b)/6 = (2 + 4 * 3 + 6)/6 = 3.33$
   Compute variance of activity duration $d_{ij} = \sigma^2 = (b - a)^2/36 = (6 - 2)^2/36 = 0.444$

2. Provide sample calculations for activity **BD (Compute A in Figure 18.6):**
3. Compute mean activity duration (**Compute A**):

$$d_{ij} = \mu = (a + 4m + b)/6 = (4 + 4 * 7 + 10)/6 = 7$$

4. Compute variance of activity duration (**Compute A**):

$$d_{ij} = \sigma^2 = (10 - 4)^2/36 = 1$$

5. Critical Path AC (Input B) $\rightarrow$ CD (Compute B), total $\mu = 4.33 + 8.33 = 12.66$; $\sigma^2 = 1 + 1 = 2$

TABLE 18.2   PERT Computer Process

Activity	Predecessors	a	m	b	μ	σ^2
AB	none	2	3	6	3.33	0.444
AC	none	2	4	8	**4.33**	1
BD	AB	4	7	10	7	1
CD	AC	6	8	12	**8.33**	1

Summary

Several examples have been provided of scheduling algorithms designed to take the guess-work out of the challenging task of scheduling resources to satisfy stringent schedule constraints. The job scheduling method focuses on finding routing sequences from origins (e.g., software development facilities) to destinations (e.g., software test facilities) that will produce the maximum transfer rate and minimum cost. The Critical-Path Method (CPM) and the Program Evaluation and Review Technique (PERT) are scheduling methods that identify the critical path in a scheduling network. The difference is that, in PERT, three estimates—minimum, average, and maximum—are used in estimating activity duration, whereas CPM uses only one estimate. Thus, PERT is used on projects where there is more uncertainty about activity duration.

19

Forecasting Models

Objectives

Understand the strengths, weaknesses, and applicability of various forecasting models, using forecasts of software reliability, such as *time to next failure* and *cumulative failures,* as examples.

What You Will Learn From This Chapter

In many situations it is necessary to make forecasts of future events, such as the *time to next failure* of a software system. In this chapter you will learn about the leading models for making such forecasts. These time-series models—exponential smoothing, geometric exponential smoothing, moving average, regression, and autoregressive integrated moving average—in effect "average" past observations to make a fit to the observed data. (Note that "observations" and "actual data" are used interchangeably.) There are no restrictions on the type of data that can be used in these models, but it is important to select the most accurate model for your forecasts by evaluated their accuracy using relative error and mean relative error metrics that are explained in this chapter.

Subjects

Exponential Smoothing Forecast Model (ESM)
Moving Average Model (MAM)
Simple ARIMA Model
Model Limitation
Regression Model
Failure Data Used in Examples
Relative Error
Forecast Results
NASA Space Shuttle Software Release OI5

Exponential Smoothing Forecasting Model (ESM)

The rationale for using ESM is that, according to [BRO63], significant changes are possible in the data (e.g., *time to next failure* of a software system). Therefore, we must be able to easily adjust the number of past observations that are included in the forecasts. Whenever there is a significant change in the pattern, forecasts should be made using only the most recent observations. We can apply ESM—a simple yet effective model for forecasting the occurrence of events at time T, based on the actual value at time $T-1$ and the forecast at time $T-1$ [TUR93, BRO63].

Now, general equations are developed for single exponential smoothing forecasts and for estimating α, the smoothing constant.

Single Exponential Smoothing [TUR93]

Forecasts are developed recursively by using past smoothed data and forecasts, as shown below.

Definitions and Model Development

Item: x

> α: smoothing constant
> Actual x at $T = x_T$
> Actual x at time $T - 1 = x_{T-1}$
> Actual x at time $T - 2 = x_{T-2}$
> Forecast at time $T - 2 = X(T - 2)$

Develop the forecast at $T - 1$ using the smooth data and forecast at time $T - 2$ in equation (19.1):

$$\text{Forecast of } x \text{ at time } T - 1 = X(T - 1) = \alpha x_{T-2} + (1 - \alpha)X(T - 2) \tag{19.1}$$

Then using equation (19.1) recursively, produce equation (19.2):

$$\text{Forecast of } x \text{ at time } T = X(T) = \alpha x_{T-1} + (1 - \alpha)X(T - 1) \tag{19.2}$$

An option is to use equation (19.2) as the forecasting equation. This option uses the immediate past actual data and forecast. An alternative is a model that uses only actual data to make forecasts. Neither alternative always provides greater forecast accuracy for all problems. Therefore, we continue the development to produce a model that uses only actual data, as an alternative to equation (19.2).

Substituting x_{T-2} for $X(T - 2)$ in equation (19.1), the forecast at $X(T - 1)$ is developed in equation (19.3):

$$X(T - 1) = \alpha x_{T-2} + (1 - \alpha)x_{T-2} \tag{19.3}$$

The substitution is necessary because, of course, the forecast $X(T - 2)$ is unknown!

Finally, substituting equation (19.3) in equation (19.2), we generate equation (19.4), which now contains no previous forecasts—only *actual* values are used to forecast $X(T)$. This is a crucial point because texts typically show exponential smoothing equations in terms of a prior forecast, but the user is left to wonder about how the prior forecast was obtained! Therefore, equation (19.4) is the practical way to make the forecast.

$$\text{Forecast of } x \text{ at time } T = X(T) = \alpha x_{T-1} + (1 - \alpha)\alpha x_{T-2} + (1 - \alpha)^2 x_{T-2} \tag{19.4}$$

In order to not guess at a *constant* value of α, which is the traditional approach, we develop the equations (19.5), (19.6), and (19.7) for estimating α_{T-1}, corresponding to the three possibilities for the relationship between x_{T-1} and x_{T-2} in equations (19.5), (19.6), and (19.7). We desire to use a variable value of α. However, α cannot be estimated at time T because it depends on the data x_T, which are not available. Therefore, from this point forward, we use α_{T-1} in the forecasting equations.

$$\text{If } x_{T-1} > x_{T-2}, \text{ then } \alpha_{T-1} = (x_{T-1} - x_{T-2})/x_{T-1} \text{ (for } x_{T-1} > 0) \tag{19.5}$$

$$\text{If } x_{T-1} < x_{T-2}, \text{ then } \alpha_{T-1} = (x_{T-2} - x_{T-1})/x_{T-2} \text{ (for } x_{T-2} > 0) \tag{19.6}$$

$$\text{If } x_{T-1} = x_{T-2}, \text{ then } \alpha_{T-1} = 0 \tag{19.7}$$

Then, setting the forecast at time $(T-2)$ = the actual value: $x(T-2) = x_{T-2}$, we generate equation (19.8). Note: This is necessary because, of course, we must use the starting value x_{T-2} for this recursive process.

$$\text{Forecast of } x \text{ at time } T = X(T) = \alpha_{T-1}x_{T-1} + (1 - \alpha_{T-1})\alpha_{T-1}x_{T-2} + (1 - \alpha_{T-1})^2 x_{T-2} \qquad (19.8)$$

Once the appropriate value of α_{T-1} is estimated, using equation (19.5), (19.6), or (19.7), and simplifying equation (19.8), the forecast of x at time T is made in equation (19.9):

$$X(T) = \alpha_{T-1}(x_{T-1} - x_{T-2}) + x_{T-2} \qquad (19.9)$$

Double Exponential Smoothing [BRO63]

Using the single exponential smoothing equation (19.2), the idea in double exponential smoothing is to give less weight to the data at time $T-1$ and more weight to the forecast at time $T-1$. A constant value of α in the range 0, 1 is used, resulting in equation (19.10).

$$\text{Forecast of } x \text{ at time } T = X(T) = \alpha^2 x_{T-1} + (1 - \alpha)(1 + \alpha)X(T-1) \qquad (19.10)$$

Now equation (19.10) is not practical because, as noted before, the forecast of $X(T-1)$ is not available! In order to use this equation, we must assume that the first forecast $X(T-1)$ = the actual data x_{T-1}. A better alternative is to use the following substitution for $X(T-1)$ from equation (19.3):

$$X(T-1) = \alpha x_{T-2} + (1 - \alpha)x_{T-2} \qquad (19.11)$$

Then substituting equation (19.11) in equation (19.10), we arrive at equation (19.12):

$$X(T) = \alpha^2 x_{T-1} + (1 - \alpha^2)x_{T-2} \qquad (19.12)$$

Moving Average Model (MAM)

The rationale for MAM is that since data are usually varying across time periods, it makes sense to capture the variation by computing a varying average, rather than a single average across all time periods. This idea is expressed in equation (19.13).

$$x(T) = \frac{\sum_{i=1}^{n} x_{T-i}}{n} \qquad (19.13)$$

where $x(T)$ is the forecast for time T of item x, x_{T-i} is *actual* value of item x for ith period preceding T, and n = number of time periods to include in the moving average.

Simple ARIMA Model

A simple version of the autoregressive integrated moving average (ARIMA) model uses the immediate past value x_{T-1} and the average of the *difference* of two immediate past values x_{T-1} and x_{T-2}, to forecast the current value $x(T)$ [ARI]:

$$x(T) = x_{T-1} + ((x_{T-1} - x_{T-2})/2) \qquad (19.14)$$

Model Limitation

While the foregoing models are useful, it is important to understand that they cannot forecast beyond the range of the available data, *if the model uses only the available data.* For example, if we have a set of observations at times $T = 1, 2, \ldots, n - 1, n$, and at $T = n + 1$ we make a forecast, a model would typically use the two previous observations at $n - 1$ and n. Thus, the forecast at $T = n + 1$ is the last we can make. A forecast at $T = n + 2$ is infeasible because there are no data available at $T = n + 1$. On the other hand, some models use the *forecast* for $T + 1$ and the observation at $T = 1$ to make the forecast at $T = n + 2$. Both types of models are used in the example problems.

Regression Model

Regression involves making the "best" fit of a dependent variable to an independent variable (e.g., fit cumulative failures to software test time), based on a fit criterion such as least squares. It does not suffer from the above limitation because all of the data can be used to make the model fit. Unfortunately, if major jumps occur in the *future* data that were not present in the fitted data, the regression equation could result in inaccurate forecasts in the future space, even though there was a good fit in the historical space.

Failure Data Used in Examples

The failure data used in the examples are shown in Table 19.1 for NASA Space Shuttle software release OI4. These data are used to evaluate model forecasting accuracy. Then the models are applied to the next Shuttle software release OI5 to see whether the original ranking of models holds up for OI5. The failure data for OI5 are tabulated in Table 19.3 (p. 411). The entry "30-day failure count intervals" is the method used in the Shuttle software for recording failure counts. It is equal to *time to next failure* in days divided by 30.

TABLE 19.1   NASA Space Shuttle Software Release OI4

30-Day Failure Count Intervals	Time to Next Failure (Days)	Failure Count	Cumulative Failures
0.67	20	1	1
4.33	130	0	1
4.90	147	0	1
5.27	158	1	2
6.00	180	2	4
7.00	210	1	5
7.43	223	2	7
13.63	409	1	8
16.93	508	1	9
27.07	812	1	10
43.80	1314	1	11
135.33	4060	1	12
178.43	5353	1	13

Relative Error

The error metrics used in evaluating forecast model accuracy are defined as follows [FEN97]:

Relative Error (RE) = (Actual Quantity – Forecast Quantity)/Actual Quantity
The average of RE, for several forecasts, is the Mean Relative Error (MRE).

Forecast Results

NASA Space Shuttle Software Release OI4

Figure 19.1 shows how the raw data, in this case the *time to next failure* data of the Shuttle, can be used to fit a regression equation using Excel. Once the regression equation has been obtained, its relative error and MRE can be computed and its MRE tabulated in Table 19.2 on page 410. Furthermore, the regression equation will be used to forecast *time to next failure* for OI5.

Figure 19.2 (page 410) shows that the ARIMA model scores the best among the models by virtue of having the minimum deviations from the actual data. It is also of interest that geometric exponential smoothing forecasts more accurately than single exponential smoothing.

Table 19.2 compiles the MRE values for the several models that were evaluated, with ARIMA registering the best accuracy. It remains to be seen whether these results would be consistent with results to be obtained when forecasts are made for OI5. It is important to note that while the regression model has the worst accuracy, an advantage is that its parameters are estimated over a wide range of the independent variable (i.e., *forecast number* in Figure 19.2). Therefore, the model could be used to forecast over a wide range (whether the forecasts would be accurate is another matter). In contrast, the other models

FIGURE 19.1   NASA Space Shuttle OI4: Time to Next Failure Function $f(n)$ vs. Software Test Number n

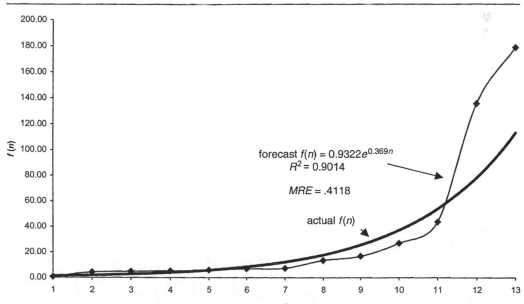

TABLE 19.2   Time to Next Failure Forecast Results: NASA Space Shuttle OI4

Model	Remarks	Alpha	*MRE*
Single ESM	uses combination actual and forecasted data	0.9	0.3291
Double ESM	uses actual data only	0.9	0.3015
Single ESM	uses actual data only	0.9	0.2806
Geometric ESM	uses actual data only	variable	0.2247
MAM	$n = 2$		0.3732
ARIMA			**0.1932**
Regression	$R^2 = 0.9014$		0.4118

FIGURE 19.2   NASA Space Shuttle OI4: Time to Next Failure *T* vs. Software Test Number *n*

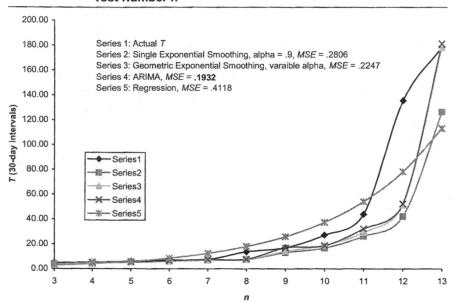

Series 1: Actual *T*
Series 2: Single Exponential Smoothing, alpha = .9, *MSE* = .2806
Series 3: Geometric Exponential Smoothing, varaible alpha, *MSE* = .2247
Series 4: ARIMA, *MSE* = **.1932**
Series 5: Regression, *MSE* = .4118

depend on observations immediately preceding the forecast time T in making their forecasts (e.g., ESM forecast at time T depends on observations in $T-1$ and $T-2$). Therefore these models cannot forecast beyond the range of the observations.

NASA Space Shuttle Software Release OI5

As predicted when analyzing the OI4 data, ARIMA is the most accurate forecasting model for the OI5 data and the regression model is the worst, as indicated in Figure 19.3. However, note that ARIMA has a forecast range limited to a single software test whereas the regression model covers the entire forecast range. Table 19.4 reinforces these results in that ARIMA has the lowest *MRE* for both OI4 and OI5. Based on these results, ARIMA would be the model to use when a forecast is needed for only a single software test; the regression model would be the choice when forecasts are required for many tests.

TABLE 19.3   NASA Space Shuttle Software Release OI5

30-Day Failure Count Intervals	Time to Next Failure (Days)	Failure Count	Cumulative Failures
7.43	223	1	1
9.77	293	1	2
12.73	382	1	3
17.50	525	1	4
23.70	711	1	5
45.17	1355	1	6
58.27	1748	1	7
65.03	1951	1	8
76.90	2307	1	9
181.27	5438	1	10

Problem

Using the data in Tables 19.1 and 19.3, determine which of the various models is the most accurate for forecasting cumulative failures. Your solution should provide plots and tables similar to the ones that have been illustrated. Plot one or two of the most accurate model forecasts, the regression model forecast, and the actual data. Include forecast results for all models in the tables.

Solution

1. First, the regression equation for cumulative failures $F(T)$ is fitted to the OI4 cumulative failure data in Table 19.1. Figure 19.4 is the result where $F(T)$ is plotted against T (30-day

FIGURE 19.3   NASA Space Shuttle OI5: Time to Next Failure T vs. Software Test Number n

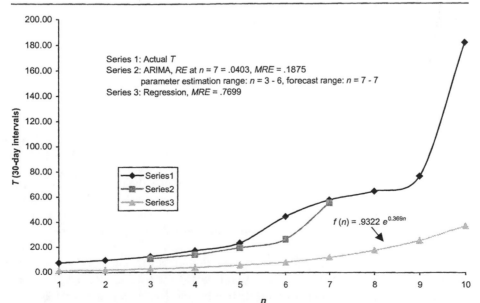

TABLE 19.4   Time to Next Failure Forecast Results: NASA Space Shuttle OI4 and OI5

Model	Remarks	Alpha	OI4 *MRE*	OI5 *MRE*
Single ESM	uses combination actual and forecasted data	0.9	0.3291	0.3028
Double ESM	uses actual data only	0.9	0.3015	0.3337
Single ESM	uses actual data only	0.9	0.2806	0.3146
Geometric ESM	uses actual data only	variable	0.2247	0.2456
MAM	$n = 2$		0.3732	0.3994
ARIMA			**0.1867**	**0.1875**
Regression	$R^2 = 0.9014$		0.4118	0.7699

FIGURE 19.4   NASA Space Shuttle OI4: Cumulative Failures F(T) vs. Test Time T

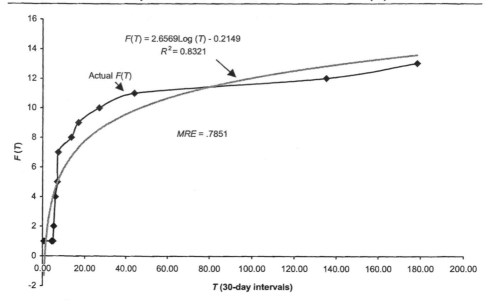

failure count intervals), using Excel, and a trend line is fitted in order to obtain the regression equation.

2. Second, provide Table 19.5 to obtain an overview of how the models did in forecasting cumulative failures. Again, ARIMA is the most accurate and regression the worst.
3. Third, we see from Table 19.5 that ARIMA and Geometric ESM are the most accurate. So to obtain a pictorial view of the results plot these models, the regression model, and the actual data in Figure 19.5.
4. Produce Table 19.6 (page 414) to obtain an OI4 versus OI5 comparison of forecasting accuracy for cumulative failures. Again, ARIMA is leading the pack. Thus far, the results for cumulative failures are consistent the results *for time to next failure*.

TABLE 19.5   Cumulative Failures Forecast Results: NASA Space Shuttle OI4

Model	Remarks	Alpha	*MRE*
Single ESM	uses combination actual and forecasted data	0.9	0.1864
Double ESM	uses actual data only	0.9	0.2145
Single ESM	uses actual data only	0.9	0.2021
Geometric ESM	uses actual data only	variable	0.1708
MAM	$n = 2$		0.2569
ARIMA			**0.1200**
Regression	$R^2 = 0.8321$		0.7851

FIGURE 19.5   NASA Space Shuttle OI4: Cumulative Failures $F(T)$ vs. Test Time T

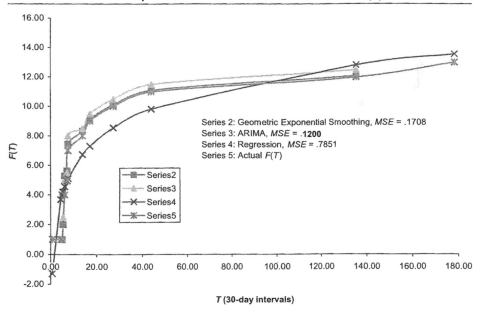

5. Plot Figure 19.6 (page 414) to show the large disparity in forecasting accuracy between ARIMA and regression models, bearing in mind that ARIMA is limited to a much smaller forecasting range compared with the regression model.

Summary

Various forecasting models were used to forecast software reliability metrics of the NASA Space Shuttle software. The ARIMA model consistently outperformed its competitors with respect to prediction accuracy. Given the simplicity of forecasting with this model, it is clear that it would be the first choice for forecasting software reliability metrics. However, it would be wise to use all the models on an application because ARIMA would not necessarily be the most accurate for all types of data.

TABLE 19.6   **Cumulative Failures Forecast Results: NASA Space Shuttle OI4 and OI5**

Model	Remarks	Alpha	OI4 *MRE*	OI5 *MRE*
Single ESM	uses combination actual and forecasted data	0.9	0.1864	0.2617
Double ESM	uses actual data only	0.9	0.2145	0.3273
Single ESM	uses actual data only	0.9	0.2021	0.3130
Geometric ESM	uses actual data only	variable	0.1708	0.3131
MAM	$n = 2$		0.2569	0.3764
ARIMA			**0.1200**	**0.2179**
Regression	$R^2 = 0.8321$		0.7851	2.0715

FIGURE 19.6   **NASA Space Shuttle Cumulative Failures $F(T)$ vs. Test Time T**

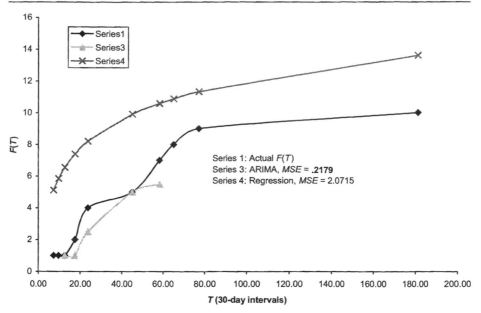

References

[ARI] Introduction to ARIMA: Non-seasonal Models, http://www.duke.edu/~rnau/411arim.htm.

[BRO63] Robert Goodell Brown, *Smoothing, Forecasting and Prediction of Discrete Time Series.* Prentice Hall, 1963.

[FEN97] Norman F. Fenton and Shari Lawrence Pfleeger, *Software Metrics: A Rigorous & Practical Approach,* second edition. PWS Publishing Company, 1997.

[TUR93] Wayne C. Turner, Joe H. Mize, and John W. Nazemetz, *Introduction to Industrial and Systems Engineering,* third edition. Prentice Hall, 1993.

Cost Analysis

Objectives

In this chapter you will be introduced to a variety of cost-analysis methods, with the objective of considering benefits and costs in making decisions on the deployment of technology. Too often benefits and costs are ignored in decisions concerning the development of technological products and services. The aim of this chapter is to provide the engineer with the tools to put cost-benefit analysis on an equal footing with technical considerations in making investment decisions.

What You Will Learn From This Chapter

You will learn how to construct and solve models directed to weighing alternatives, taking into account a stream of benefits and costs over the lives of the assets being evaluated. Solved problems enhance learning of the various subjects.

Subjects

Present Value Model: Exponential Growth
Finding the Rate of Return on an Investment
Identifying the Payback Period
Asset Comparison
Computing Annual Benefits
Maintenance and Salvage Costs Calculations
Activity-Based Costing (ABC)
Analysis of Costs
Standard Costs
Product and Standard Costing
Lagging and Leading Indicators
Performance Metrics
Break-Even Analysis

Introduction

The concept of net present value is to evaluate a sequence of benefits and costs over the lives of alternatives that are being considered for investment. Because benefits and costs occur at different points in time, future benefits and costs must be discounted by the interest rate i to make them equivalent to benefits and costs that could be realized at the present time (i.e., present value), if we make an alternative investment at interest rate i (sometimes referred to as the "rate of return"). "Net present value" refers to the fact that in most investment decisions, both benefits and costs are involved so that present value must be calculated on a net basis. It may also be necessary to deal with inflation in evaluating alternatives.

In these cases, future benefits and costs are discounted by the rate of inflation, in addition to discounting by interest rate.

In the problems that follow, hypothetical data are given for benefits and costs. The question arises: How would these data be obtained in practice? One way is to use historical data, if available, such as computer maintenance costs, assuming these data apply to the planned acquisition. Another way is to use the estimates of experts and attempt to achieve a consensus opinion.

Present Value Model: Exponential Growth

Notation

b_1:   benefit in year 1
R: benefit growth factor
c_i: cost in year 1
r: cost growth factor
b_n: benefit in year n
c_0:   cost in year 0

b_{11}:   benefit of alternative 1 in year 1
R_1:   benefit growth factor for alternative 1
c_{11}:   cost of alternative 1 in year 1
r_1:   cost growth factor of alternative 1
b_{1n}:   benefit in year n of alternative 1
c_{10}:   cost of alternative 1 in year 0

b_{21}:   benefit of alternative 2 in year 1
R_2:   benefit growth factor for alternative 2
c_{21}:   cost of alternative 2 in year 1
r_2:   cost growth factor of alternative 2
b_{2n}:   benefit in year n of alternative 2
c_{20}:   cost of alternative 2 in year 1

Net Present Value (NPV)

Benefits in year $n = 1$, b_1, grow at an exponential rate $(1 + R)^j$ in year j and costs in year 1, c_1, grow at an exponential rate $(1 + r)^j$ in year j, over n time periods (life of asset). Interest rate $= i$, salvage value b_n (benefit) in year n, and cost at time $n = 0 = c_0$ (purchase cost). Using these quantities, the present value at $n = 0$ is computed in equation (20.1).

$$\text{Net Present Value at time } n = 0 = P_0 = \sum_{j=1}^{n} \frac{((b_1(1+R)^j) - (c_1(1+r)^j) + b_n)}{(1+i)^n} - c_0 \qquad (20.1)$$

If it is desired to track total NPV of benefits, B, and costs, C, these values are computed in equations (20.2) and (20.3), respectively.

$$B = \sum_{j=1}^{n} \frac{((b_1(1+R)^j) + b_n)}{(1+i)^n} \qquad (20.2)$$

$$C = \sum_{j=1}^{n} \frac{(c_1(1+r)^j)}{(1+i)^n} + c_0 \qquad (20.3)$$

Comparing Alternatives

For comparing alternatives, there is the following question: Is the net present value P_{10} of alternative 1(equation (20.4)) smaller or larger that the net present value P_{20} of alternative 2 (equation (20.5)), when all benefits and costs over the life of the assets are considered? Equal lives n are assumed. If there are more than two alternatives, NPV is computed for all alternatives and the alternative with maximum NPV is selected.

$$P_{10} = \sum_{j=1}^{n} \frac{((b_{11}(1+R_1)^j) - (c_{11}(1+r_1)^j) + b_{1n})}{(1+i)^n} - c_{10} \tag{20.4}$$

$$P_{20} = \sum_{j=1}^{n} \frac{((b_{21}(1+R_2)^j) - (c_{21}(1+r_2)^j) + b_{2n})}{(1+i)^n} - c_{20} \tag{20.5}$$

Adapting equation (20.2) to the benefits provided by alternatives 1 and 2, produce equations (20.6) and (20.7), respectively.

$$B_1 = \sum_{j=1}^{n} \frac{((b_{11}(1+R_1)^j) + b_{1n})}{(1+i)^n} \tag{20.6}$$

$$B_2 = \sum_{j=1}^{n} \frac{((b_{21}(1+R_2)^j) + b_{2n})}{(1+i)^n} \tag{20.7}$$

Similarly, adapting equation (20.3) to compute the costs incurred by alternatives 1 and 2, produce equations (20.8) and (20.9), respectively.

$$C_1 = \sum_{j=1}^{n} \frac{(c_{11}(1+r_1)^j)}{(1+i)^n} + c_{10} \tag{20.8}$$

$$C_2 = \sum_{j=1}^{n} \frac{(c_{21}(1+r_2)^j)}{(1+i)^n} + c_{20}k \tag{20.9}$$

Problem 1

Given the specifications below, which computer alternative is better? Compare the benefits and costs of the alternatives to see how they differ over their lives.

Specifications

    Benefit b_{11}: of computer alternative 1 in year $1 = 5000$
    Benefit b_{1n}: of computer alternative 1 in year $n = 1000$
    Benefit b_{21}: of computer alternative 2 in year $1 = 8000$
    Benefit b_{2n}: of computer alternative 2 in year $n = 2000$
    Purchase cost of computer alternative 1, $c_{10} = 10000$
    Purchase cost of computer alternative 1, $c_{20} = 12000$
    Annual maintenance costs c_{11} of computer alternative 1 in year $1 = 2000$
    Annual maintenance costs c_{21} of computer alternative 2 in year $1 = 4000$
    Growth rate of annual maintenance costs of alternative 1: $r_1 = .0750$
    Growth rate of annual maintenance costs of alternative 2: $r_2 = .0250$

Growth rate of annual benefits of alternative 1: $R_1 = .050$
Growth rate of annual benefits of alternative 2: $R_2 = .080$
Interest rate $i = .10$
n: 5 years

Solution

Use equation (20.4) for computer alternative 1:

$$P_{10} = \sum_{j=1}^{n} \frac{((b_{1j}(1+R_1)) - (c_{1j}(1+r_1)) + b_{1n})}{(1+i)^n} - c_{10}$$

Use equation (20.5) for computer alternative 2:

$$P_{20} = \sum_{j=1}^{n} \frac{((b_{2j}(1+R_2)) - (c_{2j}(1+r_2)) + b_{2n})}{(1+i)^n} - c_{20}$$

Computer alternative 2 is superior due to higher present value for every year, as shown in Figure 20.1. Figure 20.2 shows that despite computer alternative 2 having higher costs for every year, this alternative has substantially higher benefits over the lives of the assets. Thus a lesson learned is that it is important to dig deeper into the benefit-cost analysis than NPV. It is important to analyze the components of NPV.

Finding the Rate of Return on an Investment

Variable Benefits and Costs

It may be necessary to find the value of i (i.e., rate of return) that will equate the stream of *variable* benefits and costs over the life of an asset to the original purchase cost. For example, we may want to find the rate of return of net benefits (benefits – costs), over the life of a computer, which will be equal to its purchase cost. When equation (20.1) is set to 0

FIGURE 20.1   **Present Value *PV* vs. Year *j***

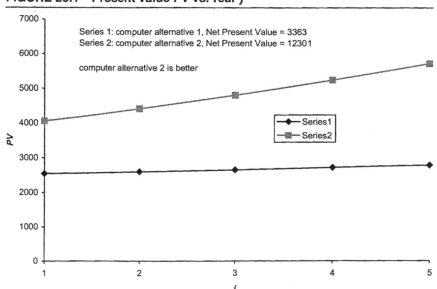

FIGURE 20.2   Benefits *B* and Costs *C* vs. Year *k*

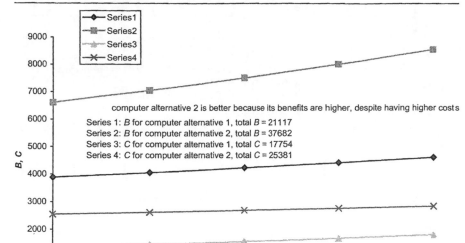

in equation (20.10), the interpretation is that the value of *i* will cause the stream of benefits and costs to equal c_0. Given the complexity of equation (20.10), we must solve for *i* by trial and error.

$$P_0 = 0 = \sum_{j=1}^{n} \frac{((b_1(1+R)^j) - (c_1(1+r)^j) + b_n)}{(1+i)^n} - c_0 \qquad (20.10)$$

In solving equation (20.10), when alternative investments are considered, the specific benefit and cost values must be used.

Problem 2

Using the data from Problem 1 and equation (20.10), compute the rate of return for the computer alternatives. Plot P_0 vs. *i* in order to identify the rate of return.

Solution

Figure 20.3 on page 420 shows that the rate of return is identified by where P_0 crosses the *x*-axis. Alternative 2 requires a higher rate of return due to its higher NPV, which was previously computed.

Constant Benefits and Costs

If the benefits b_j and costs c_j are constant in year *j*, then equation (20.10) can be more easily solved for rate of return *i*. Equation (20.11) is the result.

$$i = \left[\frac{n(b_j - c_j) + b_n}{c_0} \right]^{\frac{1}{n}} - 1 \qquad (20.11)$$

FIGURE 20.3   **Determination of Rate of Return: Net Present Value P_0 vs. Interest Rate i**

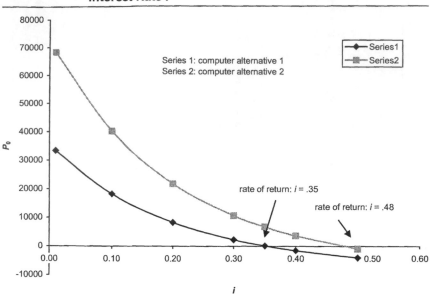

Also, it is of interest to attempt to find the value of n where i is a maximum so that we would know how long it would take to obtain the maximum rate of return on our investment. This value of n would be obtained by finding the rate of change of i with n and determining the value of n where the rate of change is zero. The rate of change is computed in equation (20.12). Unfortunately, this is a monotonically decreasing function in n, which would yield a value of zero at $n = \infty$. The only case where the function is zero is for $b_j = c_j$, which is unrealistic. Thus, it is infeasible to find the value of n where i is maximum analytically; we must do it by graphing i vs. n.

$$\frac{d(i)}{d(n)} = \frac{1}{n}\left[\frac{n(b_j - c_j) + b_n}{c_0}\right]^{\left(\frac{1}{n}-1\right)}(b_j - c_j) \tag{20.12}$$

Problem 3

Using the following specifications, find the rate of return for computer alternatives 1 and 2. Vary n, the life of the computers, over the values 5, 10, 15, 20, 25, and 30. Plot i as a function of n in Figure 20.4. Identify the value of n where i is maximum.

Specifications

  Benefit b_{1j}: of computer alternative 1 in year $j = 5000$
  Benefit b_{1n}: of computer alternative 1 in year $n = 1000$
  Benefit b_{2j}: of computer alternative 2 in year $j = 8000$
  Benefit b_{2n}: of computer alternative 2 in year $n = 2000$
  Purchase cost of computer alternative 1, $c_{10} = 10000$
  Purchase cost of computer alternative 1, $c_{20} = 12000$
  Annual maintenance costs c_{1j} of computer alternative 1 in year $j = 2000$
  Annual maintenance costs c_{2j} of computer alternative 2 in year $j = 4000$

FIGURE 20.4   Identifying Rate of Return *i* (Constant Benefits and Costs) vs. Life of Computer *n*

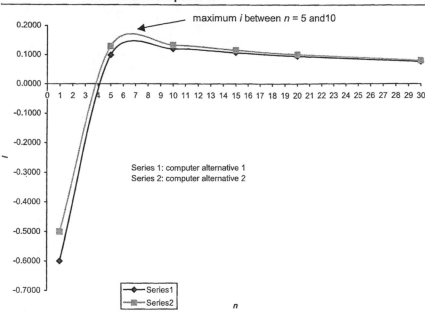

Solution

In Figure 20.4 both alternatives yield the maximum rate of return after operating the computers between 5 and 10 years.

Identifying the Payback Period

Variable Benefits and Costs

The payback period for *variable benefits and costs* is defined as the value of n that will cause P_0 in equation (20.10) to be zero. Again, the equation must be solved by trial and error.

Problem 4

Given the data from Problem 1, except for the value of n, solve for n in equation (20.10)—the payback period for the two computer alternatives. Plot P_0 vs. n in order to identify the payback period.

Solution

Figure 20.5 on page 422 shows the payback period as that value of n where P_0 crosses the x-axis. Since computer alternative 2 had a greater rate of return in Figure 20.3, we would expect this alternative to have a greater payback period in order to achieve a greater rate of return. Indeed that is the case in Figure 20.4.

Constant Benefits and Costs

When benefits and costs are constant, equation (20.13) is solved for n to produce the payback period. As seen in equation (20.13), this equation must be solved by trial and error because it is infeasible to solve explicitly for n.

FIGURE 20.5   Determination of Payback Period: Net Present Value P_0 vs. Life of Computer n

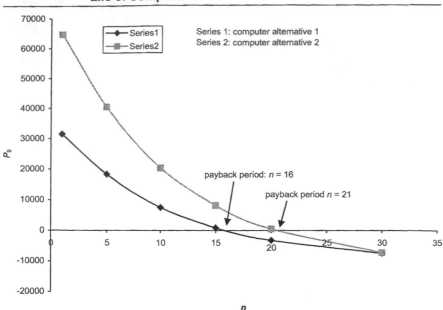

$$n = \frac{1}{\log(1+i)}\left[\frac{\log n(b_j - c_j) + b_n}{c_0}\right] \tag{20.13}$$

Problem 5

Using the data from Problem 1 and equation (20.13), solve for n by trial and error for both computer alternatives and plot the computed n vs. the given n. Secondly, compute the difference between given n and computed n in order to see where the difference is minimum.

Solution

Figure 20.6 shows that, as in the case of variable benefits and costs in Figure 20.5, computer alternative 2 has the longer payback period because it has the larger constant benefits and costs.

Asset Comparison

Definitions

j, k: asset identifications (e.g., j = computer hard disk, k = computer processor)
V_j: value of asset j (computer hard disk)
V_k: value of asset k (computer processor)
i: period
D_{ij}:   depreciation rate in period i (month) for asset j (computer hard disk)
D_{ik}:   depreciation rate in period i (month) for asset k (computer processor)

FIGURE 20.6   Determination of Payback Period (Constant Benefits and Costs): Computed *n* vs. Given *n*

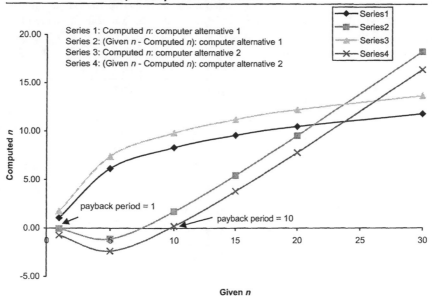

Series 1: Computed *n*: computer alternative 1
Series 2: (Given *n* - Computed *n*): computer alternative 1
Series 3: Computed *n*: computer alternative 2
Series 4: (Given *n* - Computed *n*): computer alternative 2

R: rate of return
I: rate of inflation
T: rate of income tax
N_j: life of asset j (computer hard disk)
N_k: life of asset k (computer processor)
NPV_j: net present value of asset j (computer hard disk)
NPV_k: net present value of asset k (computer processor)

The equations expressing the net present values of assets j and k are given in equations (20.14) and (20.15), respectively.

$$NPV_j = \left(\sum_{i=1}^{N_j} \frac{V_j(1-D_{ij})}{(1+I+R)^{N_j}} \right) * (1-T) \tag{20.14}$$

$$NPV_k = \left(\sum_{i=1}^{N_k} \frac{V_k(1-D_{ik})}{(1+I+R)^{N_k}} \right) * (1-T) \tag{20.15}$$

Problem 6

Using the specifications below, do the following:

1. Find value of V_k that would make asset k more attractive than asset j.
2. What are the values of net present value for assets j and k corresponding to the specifications that follow?

Specifications

The depreciation rates below were generated using uniformly distributed random numbers between 0 and 1.0, in order not to not bias the results. The random numbers can be generated with the Excel RAND function. You would not necessarily generate the same set of numbers as those shown below.

i	random D_{ij}	random D_{ik}
1	0.3702	0.9393
2	0.4256	0.2689
3	0.2040	0.7191
4	0.4638	0.4008
5	0.6350	0.6112
6	0.8184	0.9875
7	0.7722	0.7816
8	0.2006	0.2765
9	0.3008	0.4821
10	0.1180	0.1149
11	0.0253	0.6827
12	0.7559	0.4965
13	0.0693	0.9498
14	0.6327	0.0327
15	0.0046	0.6643
16	0.9426	0.9806
17	0.6239	0.9590
18	0.0346	0.2886
19	0.6680	0.0865
20	0.4548	0.5640

rate of return per month $R = 0.0125$
rate of inflation per month $I = 0.0025$
rate of income tax per month $T = 0.4$
$N_j = 20$ months
$N_k = 3$ months
$V_j = 5000 =$ value of asset j
$V_k = 1000 =$ value of asset k

Solution

1. Figure 20.7 shows that at $V_k = 6000$ the NPVs are equal. So, at $V_k > 6000$ asset k would be more attractive than asset j.
2. Based on the specifications, $V_j = 25570$ and $V_k = 4291$. Since, according to the specifications, $V_k = 1000$, it is clear, as part 1 indicates, that V_k must be increased significantly for asset k to be competitive with asset j.

FIGURE 20.7   Net Present Value NPV_j and NPV_k vs. Asset Value V_k

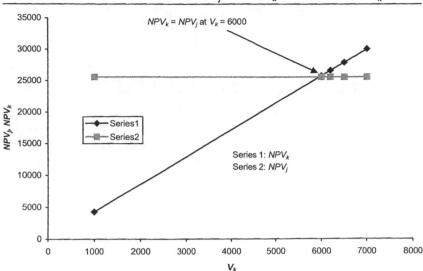

Computing Annual Benefits

Another issue in benefit-cost analysis is to compute the constant annual benefits b_j of an asset acquisition (e.g., computer), assuming a NPV_n in year n, and taking into account the purchase cost c_0, rate of inflation I, rate of return R, and rate of income tax T. The NPV_n is formulated in equation (20.16), where the tax rate T applies only to the purchase cost c_0.

$$NPV_N = \sum_{j=1}^{N} \frac{b_j}{(1+I+R)^N} - (c_0(1-T)) \qquad (20.16)$$

Since NPV_n is given based on assumed value of the asset in year n, and b_j is constant, b_j is computed in equation (20.17).

$$bj = \frac{NPV_N + (c_0(1-T))(1+I+R)^N}{N} \qquad (20.17)$$

Problem 7

Find the annual benefit b_j of installing a computer given the data that follow.

Specifications

    rate of return $R = 0.15$ per year
    rate of inflation $I = 0.03$ per year
    rate of income tax $T = 0.4$ per year
    computer installation cost $c_0 = 30000$
    life of project $N = 10$ years
    assumed NPV_N for year $N = 10$: 30,000, 40,000, 50,000, 60,000, 70, 000, 80,000, 90,000, 100,000

Solution

Figure 20.8 shows that there is a linear relationship between b_j and NPV_N. An organization that is contemplating the purchase of a computer could use this type of plot to forecast benefits required to obtain desired project NPV_N at the end of the life of the computer.

Maintenance and Salvage Costs Calculations

An organization planning a computer acquisition, with purchase cost c_0 in year 0, is confronted with estimating the cost of maintenance M_i in year i, over the life of the asset, and the salvage value S_i in year i that can be realized at the end of life. Therefore, equation (20.18) is needed for the NPV_N, with inflation rate I, that relates these quantities.

$$NPV_N = c_0 + \sum_{i=1}^{N} \frac{(M_i - S_i)}{(1+I)^i}$$ (20.18)

Problem 8

Using equation (20.18) and the data that follow in Table 20.1, 1) compute NPV_N for year 5, and 2) plot M_i, S_i, $PV_i = \dfrac{M_i - S_i}{(1+I)^i}$, and c_0 vs. i, and 3) find the value of i where PV_i goes positive ($M_i > S_i$).

Solution

The solution, in terms of the crossover between maintenance and salvage costs, is shown in Figure 20.9.

Activity-Based Costing (ABC)

Activity-based costing (ABC) is an accounting technique that allows an organization to determine the *actual cost associated with each product and service* produced by the organization *without regard to the organizational structure.*

FIGURE 20.8   Annual Benefits b_j vs. NPV in Year n, NPV_N

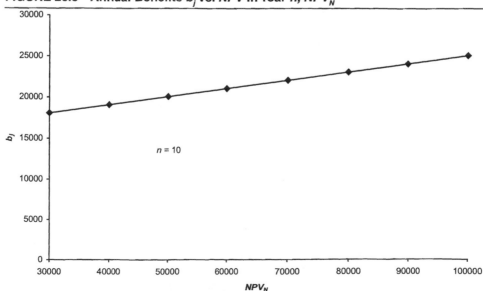

TABLE 20.1   Computer Maintenance and Salvage

Computer Purchase Cost c_0 = 120000, Inflation Rate I = .08

Year i	Computer Maintenance M_i	Computer Salvage S_i
1	35000	60000
2	38000	55000
3	43000	45000
4	50000	25000
5	65000	15000

Activities can be defined as *processes, functions, or tasks* that occur over time and have recognized results. Activities *use up assigned resources* to produce products and services. *Inputs are transformed into outputs* under the conditions set by controls performed by the organization. *Activities can be perceived as consumers of resources* in the production of materials, services, events, or information.

This costing method could be used, for example, in identifying and tracking the costs associated with the activities (e.g., design, coding, testing) required to produce software products in a software vendor organization.

Analysis of Costs

Direct Costs

A direct cost is directly attributable to the manufacturing of a product; it is the opposite of indirect cost. If a cost is directly linked to the service provided, it is a direct cost. Direct costs can be identified with a specific activity, product, or service. Direct materials, direct equipment, and direct labor are three main categories of direct costs.

FIGURE 20.9   Maintenance Cost M_i, Salvage Value S_i, Purchase Cost c_0, and Present Value PV_i vs. Year i

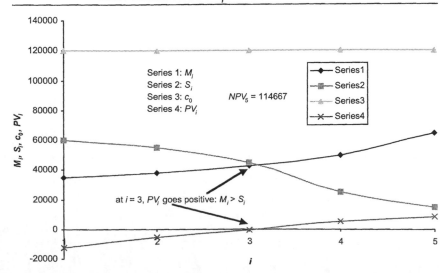

Indirect or Overhead Costs

If it is not possible to link a cost directly to a product or service, it qualifies as an indirect cost or overhead cost. An example is the cost of managerial personnel in a software production firm.

Overhead rate is defined as:

Overhead Costs/Direct Labor Costs

The purpose of this metric is to assess the indirect costs in relation to the direct labor required to produce a product or service.

Variable Costs

Variable costs change as the volume or level of activity changes. For example, the cost of producing software for various applications is a variable cost.

Fixed Costs

Fixed costs do not change as the level of activity changes. For example, the lease of office space does not vary with the number of software applications produced in that space.

Depreciation

Depreciation is an artificial expense that spreads the purchase cost of an asset over a specified time period. For example, depreciation taken on the purchase of a computer increases the after-tax present value of an asset [LIN01].

Problem 9

1. Given the data in Table 20.2 below, what are the direct costs?
2. What is the Assembly Center direct cost per hour?

Solution

1. In Table 20.2 tooling, depreciation, and direct labor are direct costs. The reason is that these costs can be associated with the activities in the centers.
2. Therefore the Assembly Center direct cost per hour = ($500 + $7200+ $24,200)/640 = **$49.84 per hour.**

Problem 10

Based on the data in Table 20.2, what is the *overhead rate* for the entire plant?

TABLE 20.2   Manufacturing Center Costs

Center	Machine Hours	Depreciation	Machine Tools	Administrative Labor	Direct Labor
Fabrication	600	$27,000	$5,000	$100,000	$72,000
Assembly	**640**	**$7,200**	**$500**	$50,000	**$24,200**
Finishing	1,320	$1,800	$7,000	$20,000	$62,800
Totals				$170,000	$159,000

Solution

In Table 20.2, administrative labor is the overhead cost. Therefore the overhead rate is:

$170,000/$159,000 = **$1.0692**

Standard Costs

Standard costs are the *expected costs* of *manufacturing the product.*
Standard Direct Labor Costs = Expected wage rate × Expected number of hours.
Standard Direct Materials Cost = Expected cost of raw materials × Expected number of units of raw material.
Standard overhead costs = (Expected Fixed Overhead) + (Expected Variable Over head × Expected number of units to be produced).
A standard cost system is a method of *setting cost targets and evaluating performance.*

Standard costs find more application in the manufacture of hardware than in the production of software because there is much less variation in the time and materials required to manufacture hardware than there is to produce a variety of software, with perhaps unique requirements.

Product and Standard Costing

In job order costing (*product costing*) costs are assigned to the product in *batches or lots—* for example, burning numerous compact discs, recording the same software.

In *process costing,* costs are *continuously* assigned to the product, since there are no discrete batches to assign costs—for example, the labor and computer time costs associated with producing the above software.

Lagging and Leading Indicators

Lagging indicator. A metric that changes value *after* the underlying conditions it measures have begun to *exhibit a trend.* Lagging indicators may confirm the *existence of a condition or trend,* but are *not used for prediction.* For example, the cost of software engineers is noted after the costs of software production have trended upward.

Leading indicator. A metric that changes *in advance* of a new trend or condition and *can be used in prediction.* For example, changes in technical stock price indices could be used to predict whether the introduction of new technology into the marketplace would be successful.

Performance Metrics

Process: The first step in developing performance metrics is to involve the people who are responsible for the work to be measured because they are the most knowledgeable about the work. Once these people are identified and involved, it is necessary to:

- Identify *work processes and customer requirements:* software testing and customer reliability requirements.
- Identify *results desired* and align them to customer requirements: software reliability obtained during testing and operation to meet customer specifications.

- Develop *measurements for the work processes and results:* measure and predict software reliability during testing and operation.

The establishment of performance goals can best be specified when they are defined within three levels, as follows:

- *Objectives:* These generally reflect goals based on the organization's mission. For example, the mission of NASA to use a Shuttle flight to deliver astronauts to the Space Station and return safely to earth.
- *Criteria:* Measurement values that evaluate the goals of a product or service. For example, a criterion of processing speed that must be achieved in a computer as a function of processor chip clock rate.
- *Measures:* Metrics designed to *drive improvement and characterize progress* made under each criterion. For example, processor chip metrics, like clock rates that a semiconductor company wishes to achieve.

Break-Even Analysis

Break-even analysis involves finding the quantity of a product where profit equals zero. At this quantity, sales revenue equals production cost.

Definitions

p: sales price per component
c_v: variable production cost per component
C_F: fixed production costs
D: break-even production quantity

Profit = {[(sales price per component – variable production cost per
        component)] * (production quantity)} – fixed production costs   (20.19)

Now, using the definitions in equation (20.19), and noting that profit = 0 at the break-even production quantity D, produce equation (20.20):

$$\text{Profit} = [(p - c_v) * D] - C_F = 0 \qquad (20.20)$$

Using equation (20.20), compute the break-even quantity in equation (20.21).

$$D = C_F / (p - c_v) \qquad (20.21)$$

Problem 11

A computer component company incurs fixed costs of $C_F = \$1,250,000$ per year. The variable cost of production is $c_v = \$10$ per component. Computer components are sold for $p = \$30$. Find the break-even production quantity D.

Using equation (20.21), the break-even quantity is computed as follows:

$D = C_F/(p - c_v) = \$1,250,000$ per year/($\$30$ per component – $\$10$ per component) = **62,500 components per year**

Summary

The reader has been provided with a number of cost and cost-benefit models that are applied to evaluating the economic aspects of installing and maintaining hardware and software systems. It is imperative that the engineer consider economic issues in evaluating technological alternatives, in addition to technical considerations. If this approach is not used, an organization could miss investing in projects that are moderately attractive from a technical standpoint but possess superior return on investment. On the other hand, if cost-benefit analysis is not employed, an organization could make disastrous investment decisions in projects that promise superior technical benefits but could drive an organization into bankruptcy.

Reference

[LIN01] Michael R Lindeburg, *Engineering Economic Analysis: An Introduction.* Professional Publications, Inc., 2001.

Index

Tables and figures are indicated by *t* and *f*, respectively.

Printed and bound by CPI Group (UK) Ltd, Croydon, CR0 4YY